TIKKUN

an anthology

TIKKUN

...to heal, repair and transform the world

an anthology edited by

MICHAEL LERNER

TIKKUN BOOKS • תיקון • Oakland, California • Jerusalem, Israel for Joseph H. Lerner & Akiba Jeremiah Lerner

Published by
         TIKKUN BOOKS
5100 Leona St.   P.O. Box 10528
Oakland, CA 94619-3002   Jerusalem, Israel 91103
(510) 482 0805

Printed in the United States of America

Library of Congress Cataloging in Publication Data

Lerner, Michael ed.
   Tikkun ...to heal, repair and transform the world

Library of Congress Catalogue Card Number: 91-076263

ISBN: 0-935933-03-4 (hard)   ISBN: 0-935933-04-2 (soft)

Contents

II. Culture and Philosophy

III. Feminism

IV. Israel

V. Being Jewish in the Contemporary World

VI. Judaism

VII. Fiction

Poetry

Drawings:

Anthony Dubovsky 53, 83, 116, 142, 167, 198, 338, 410, 414, 551; Noga Wizansky 149, 263, 271; Edina Sagert 57, 200; Barbara Levanthal-Stern 211; Leo Glueckselig 401; Susan Gross 123

Photographs:

Anne Flatté *xix;* Richard Bermack 4; Denise Poncher 19; A.M. Oliver & Paul Steinberg 297, 325, 345, 481, 501; Marke Darul Webb 309; Yehudit Elani 379

Acknowledgements

Tikkun was made possible by the generosity and leadership of its first publisher, Nan Fink. Over the years, *Tikkun* has particualary benefited from the intellectual clarity and depth of its associate editor, Peter Gabel, whose vision has shaped our approach to a meaning-centered politics. We've also benefited from the outstanding talents of a series of highly skilled editors, most notably Joshua Henkin in our early years and now Chris Lehmann, as well as our book editor, Michael Kazin, and his predecessor Alan Wolfe.

Special thanks to our dedicated and inspired poetry editor, Marge Piercy and her predecessor David Bromwich; to Fiction Editors Rosellen Brown, Marvin Hoffman, Marcie Hirschman, and Anne Roiphe, and for years of guidance from: Todd Gitlin, David Biale, Arthur Waskow, Sidra Ezrahi, Aaron Back, Beth Sandweiss, Adi Ophir, Gary Peller, Rachel Adler, Heather Booth, Gordon Fellman, Laura Geller, Arthur Green, Daniel Landes, Hillel Levine, Marshall Meyer, Jo Milgrom, Robert Pinsky, Letty Cottin Pogrebin, Aviezer Ravitsky, David Saperstein, Zalman Schachter-Shalomi, Chaim Seidler-Feller, Gerald Serotta, Stanley Sheinbaum, Milton Viorst, Albert Vorspan, Uri Simon, Martha Ackelsburg, Judith Plaskow, Milton Mankoff, Christopher Lasch, Phillip Lopate, Leonard Michaels, Francine Prose, Steve Wasserman, E. M. Broner, Gad Horowitz, John Felstiner, Colin Greer, Hal Jacobs, Reuven Kimelman, Tzvi Marx, Howard Schwartz, Ruth Messenger, Daniel Boyarin, Paul Berman, Arnold Eisen, Ilene Philipson, and Lisa Rubens.

Special thanks also to those who helped bring this anthology into the world; to David Fisher for managing the production, compilation, and design; to Joanne Nerenburg for proofreading; to David Stein for compiling the art and proofreading; to *Tikkun* Production Manager Anne Flatté for her guidance and support; to *Tikkun* Assistant Publisher Erika Henik for some much-needed last minute help; and to Rebecca Adams and Claude Cahn for their preparatory work. For their hours of careful reading, *Tikkun* thanks Molly Phinney, Ben Greenberg, David Jacowitz, Mark Rosen, Tony Frank, Rebecca Garron, Jacqueline Weiss, David Green, Heather Ashley, Alissa Blackman, and Douglas Belkin.

Introduction to the Anthology

When we started in 1986 we were surrounded by people who told us that our task was impossible, that "everyone knew" that in the heyday of Reaganism the Jewish world had moved "far to the right" and that those Jews who had not moved were so alienated from their Jewishness that they would not consider reading a magazine that called itself "A *Jewish* Critique of Politics, Culture and Society." Similarly, we were told that non-Jews would discount us also, and that our critique of the liberal and progressive world, our insistence that the Democratic party and the progressive social change movements would remain isolated until they had moved from a "politics of rights" to a "politics of meaning," would be totally ignored precisely because we had "isolated" ourselves by speaking as Jews.

Now that *Tikkun* has become one of the largest circulation independent Jewish magazines, and one of the most frequently quoted in the media and in the academy, our essays and fiction often anthologized by others (last year two out of the twenty essays selected for *Best American Essays* came from our pages), our success is seen as "inevitable" or the result of good timing, or "filling an obvious niche." Perhaps. But we think it may also have something to do with the quality of the ideas in *Tikkun*. Despite the "received wisdom" that all who once yearned for a more just and humane and fulfilling social order have now given up these "childhood fantasies," become "realistic," and are now focused exclusively on their own personal lives, we believe that there are millions of Americans who still yearn for a less alienated and more spiritually and ethically whole existence. These yearnings are sometimes expressed in ways seen as "apolitical" (through visual arts, dance, literature) or even "anti-progressive" (various right-wing religious communities), or as "merely" personal (the attempts to create a more humane environment for children, the attempts to beautify one's own neighborhood, home, or community), but they bespeak a desire for a world radically different from the one in which most people live their daily lives. *Tikkun*'s importance is that we are attempting to shape an approach to intellectual, cultural and political life that recognizes these desires as a central basis for healing, repairing and transforming the world.

The central struggle for us is the struggle against pessimism and cynicism—the dominant religions of our time. The typical stance of the alienated intellectual is that they "see through" all the hypocrisy and absurdity of contemporary life, place themselves "above the struggle," and take a cynical and detached position of superiority. As long as they haven't been fooled, or tricked into someone's dream, they can feel safe and powerful. Nothing is more threatening than the message of *Tikkun*—that the moral imperative to change the world remains as valid today as it ever was, that all is not OK, that change is still possible, and that one's individual choices make a difference (including how one chooses to *think* about the possibility of possibility). We are not a political movement—but we are interested in creating the intellectual preconditions for a movement of healing and repair and transformation. Toward that end, we seek to explain why the social movements of the sixties failed, why the way that liberals and progressives do politics ensures their continuing isolation in the periods ahead, and why many of the people who remain apolitical or skeptical have *good reasons* to be alienated from liberal or progressive movements, given the way they are currently constituted. Yet we are unequivocally committed to the reconstruction of a force for healing and transformation, even if it requires breaking with existing political parties and existing liberal and progressive movements and forging a very different direction.

We approach these issues from our specific perspective as Jews, even though our analyses are addressed to the larger intellectual and political worlds. Just as *Commentary*, a Jewish magazine, became the primary place in which new thinking on the American political Right was tested out, eventually forging the neoconservatism that shaped American politics in the 1980s, so *Tikkun*, speaking out of its Jewish commitments, is becoming the place in which one can read the new thinking to shape a different kind of progressive politics for the 1990s and beyond. Started as "the liberal alternative to *Commentary* and the voices of Jewish conservatism," *Tikkun* draws upon the wisdom of the Jewish experience as we seek to address the world. But the Jewish world and Jewish thought, too, are deeply in need of healing and repair. Born as a slave people who had witnessed the possibility of revolutionary transformation, we built a religion and a culture that were frequently radical in their challenges to the norms of surrounding societies. For that very reason, we were subject to persecution and oppression. Some of the results have been beneficial—a sense of humor, a wisdom, a sense of perspective about history, a determination to "keep at it," an outsider outlook that enables us to see what those enmeshed in a given reality often cannot see. But that oppression has also distorted us at times, made us paranoid and distrusting of others, and sometimes made us neurotically unsure of ourselves. So we speak from our tradition and our particular experience as Jews, but not with any sense that this tradition gives us superiority or makes us any better than others. It gives us a unique vantage point, but it also creates unique problems and unique distortions. And so any effort to change the world must also be an effort to change ourselves, both as individuals, and as part of the Jewish world. Our critique of current Israeli policy and of the organized Jewish community in the U.S., our struggles against sexism and heterosexism, are part of that project.

Yet the visionary project of *tikkun* (the Hebrew word for healing, repair and transformation) constitutes only a small part of the magazine *Tikkun*. Our vision is only one of many contending visions that appear in the magazine. We are involved in creating a community of dialogue, and to make that dialogue healthy I make sure that I disagree with at least 60 percent of the articles selected for publication in any given issue of the magazine (some even offend me). But that too is part of our notion of what will create a healthy world—one in which genuine intellectual struggle among diverse perspectives takes place. Too often the way people win their arguments is by ensuring that nobody but those with whom they agree is represented in the arenas in which they do their educational or political work. They thereby ensure that their views will always win—but they don't win very much, because they are preaching to the converted.

Not so in the *Tikkun* world. To take one central example, the editor and a minority of the editorial board are religiously observant Jews who believe that a religious perspective provides a better basis than secularism for healing and transformation. But the vast majority of writers we select for the magazine do not agree and do not particularly care to engage in conversation about that topic.

Some of those differences are represented in this collection, but not in anything like the magnitude that exists in the articles and letters we select for the magazine itself. Our reason is that in selecting the articles for this collection we had two concerns: to give some indication of the breadth and vitality of the intellectual life that takes place in the magazine; and to present some of the articles that we think best represent *Tikkun*'s perspective—so that we could use this book as a way to introduce people to the *Tikkun* community who had missed the first creative years. As a result, my own editorials are disproportionately represented in this collection, because they help provide a quick introduction to some of our central ideas. I feel uncomfortable with the outcome, in part because the magazine is *not* just an expression of my own perspectives, in part because in the magazine itself they rate about 5 percent of the space whereas here they rate 15 percent. I apologize for this. On the other hand, unlike many magazines in which each new edition stands on it own with no presumption that the reader has read articles from the past, *Tikkun* functions as an on-going dialogue between past and present, and so reprinting these editorials will make it easier for a new reader to enter the on-going discussions.

Moreover, trying to make the anthology not only an introduction to our thought but also represent the breadth of our writers and concerns was difficult. In order to present the literary, cultural, and Jewish-related sides of the magazine, we had to give less space to some of the most exciting debates that have taken place in *Tikkun*. To give a few examples of issues debated in the magazine but not represented in this collection: Has American Judaism has given too much attention to the Holocaust and is the conception of the Holocaust museum fundamentally misguided? Must a liberal be opposed to creationism and in support of evolution? In what ways can we still credit the feminist insight that "the personal is political" and what are the limits of that supposition? Does God play a role in history? What are the limits of liberalism and communitarianism? Is vegetarianism morally required? Why should traditional Judaism abandon its opposition to homosexuality? What are the limits of deconstruction? Was the Iraqi war worth fighting? Must liberals defend Robert Mapplethorpe? Why has the peace movement in Israel been so ineffectual? What's wrong with affirmative action? How do we assess the collapse of communism in Eastern Europe? How can we resolve the problem of Jerusalem in a peace settlement? Is Freudian psychoanalysis reformable or intrinsically repressive and sexist?

We don't claim that what we've put together in this book is "the best of *Tikkun*"—we had to leave out too many wonderful essays, poems, stories, book reviews, and even great letters to the editor. What we do hope is that you get a feel for the energy and excitement, that you take the ideas you find here and share them with others. Literally tens of thousands of other people have gotten excited by these ideas and have become part of a (still somewhat amorphous but nevertheless real) *Tikkun* community. Over seven thousand of them have attended *Tikkun* conferences in the U.S. and Israel. Many have become active in *Tikkun*'s education arm, the Committee for Judaism and Social Justice—a network of people who are dedicated to changing the Jewish world and changing the intellectual framework of the American liberal and progressive world, helping spread the ideas and perspective of *Tikkun*, or participating in local monthly *Tikkun* discussion groups, or creating intellectual and cultural *Tikkun* "salons" in which the ideas are discussed. Yet there are even more of our readers who do not involve themselves in any activity, disagree with various ideas they read here, and nevertheless love the magazine just because they find its ideas and energy more compelling than most of what passes for intellectual and cultural life in America in the 1990s. I hope you'll allow yourself to get involved in these discussions, allow yourself to get hopeful or angry or excited, and you will move from reading the book and sharing it with your friends to becoming a subscriber and possibly even an active participant in the dialogue in our community.

One last point we make to our readers in every issue and which we want to make to anyone who starts reading this anthology: *Don't feel guilty* if you don't read everything in this collection (unless you happen to be reviewing it for some newspaper or magazine!). Like the magazine itself, the collection is overstuffed with delicious morsels, and it's fine if you only taste some of them.

****

This is the first product of Tikkun Books, a progressive publishing house that will produce books that cover roughly the same range of topics that are covered within the magazine itself.

****

Tikkun has survived largely because of the generosity of its readers. We are, like National Public Radio, a reader-supported venture. Unlike *Commentary* or other major intellectual magazines, we do not have any major organization or financial "angel" financing our survival. We've come this far in part because we have a staff of people who are working at high energy jobs with low pay, in part because we have writers who are willing to write with only "honorary" compensations rather than serious pay, and in part because thousands of our readers have given generously to keep us afloat, and we have no reason to believe that their generosity will not continue. □

Michael Lerner, Editor
Tikkun Magazine
5100 Leona Street
Oakland, California 94619
(510) 482-0805

Note: Some of the pieces included in this anthology have been abridged from the versions originally printed in Tikkun. Major omissions have been indicated in the articles with elipses.

The Founding Editorial Statement

TIKKUN: to Heal, Repair and Transform the World

Michael Lerner

The notion that the world could and should be different than it is has deep roots within Judaism. But in the late 1980s it is an idea that seems strangely out of fashion—and those who still dare to hope often view themselves as isolated, if not irrelevant. In the context of Western societies too often intoxicated with their own material and technological success, in which the ethos of personal fulfillment has the status of "common sense," those who talk of fundamental transformation seem to be dreaming.

"Dreaming" has a different meaning for people rooted in Jewish history and culture. It is a phrase that was used to dismiss the Prophets and their message, and it was a phrase Jews applied to themselves when they first hoped for the return to Zion. For Jews who built a culture and religion out of the experience of slavery, it has always seemed possible to imagine that the dominant regimes of the moment might pass—that the seemingly invincible powers of Persia, Greece, and Rome would ultimately give way. To those who passed through a holocaust unique in history and then experienced a rebirth in the land of their ancestors after 1500 years of Exile, the current triumph of materialist values can seem unimpressive, unlikely to define the future of human history. As King Solomon's ring proclaimed, and as Jewish history has taught us, "This too will pass."

It is this refusal to accept the world as given, articulated in the Prophetic call for transformation, that has fueled the radical underpinnings of Jewish life. The great idol-smashers of the last 150 years, Karl Marx and Sigmund Freud, articulated a fundamentally Jewish sensibility—at the very moment that they developed a universalist perspective. The universalist dream of a transformation and healing of the world, the belief that peace and justice are not meant for heaven but are this-worldly necessities that must be fought for, *is* the particularistic cultural and religious tradition of Jews.

Tikkun Magazine hopes to provide a voice for those who still dare to hope, for those who are not embarrassed to dream, for those Jews and non-Jews alike who are still moved by the radical spirit of the Prophets and who insist on keeping their message alive.

Keeping the Prophetic tradition alive, as our spiritual mentor Abraham Joshua Heschel pointed out in his book *The Prophets,* means immersion in the details of daily life. The Greek philosophers spent much of their time talking about abstract concepts of goodness, virtue and justice. Eastern spirituality led its practitioners to the mountains, forests, and caves for meditation, and directed their energies away from ordinary, daily life—a life often dismissed as "illusory." But to the Prophets, God's message directed attention to daily life, to the marketplace, to the family and to the state. To the Prophets, each time the powerless were oppressed was a fresh outrage, each time

---

Tikkun's *founding statement appeared in its first issue, Fall 1986.*

religion was used as a cover for economic immorality was a new affront to God.

The commitment to change the world, to demand justice and love in a world that has given up on these ideals, is not some pious sentiment clouding one's eyes to a hard-nosed look at reality. On the contrary, the rejection of moral neutrality, the committed stance on behalf of the oppressed, makes possible a deeper understanding of the dynamics of culture and society. It is precisely in the process of acting to transform the world that the world reveals its deeper structures and meanings. Yet we shall insist that any social transformation requires a systematic and deep intellectual inquiry—we may get inspiration from the Torah, but we shall also engage in critical thinking that requires intellectual integrity, innovation and sustained analysis. *Tikkun* hopes to provide a forum for that kind of intellectual work.

The Liberal and Radical Traditions in Politics

Jewish religion is irrevocably committed to the side of the oppressed. Jewish history began with a slave rebellion and the success of that rebellion shapes our historical memory and our religious sensibility. Shabbat, our weekly celebration of the creation of the universe, is also a celebration of our liberation from Egypt. The message of our historical experience is a revolutionary message: The way the world *is* can be radically different—we know, because we were slaves who thought that we would always be in slavery, and then overcame our bondage.

There are many religions that celebrate the grandeur and splendor of the physical universe. Yet the message of the Sabbath is unique: that we not only must stand in radical amazement and awe in the face of creation, but we must remember that the world needs to be and *can* be transformed; that history is not meaningless but aimed at liberation; that the struggle of one people to move beyond slavery (retold each week in the Torah reading) is still a drama with universal meaning through which we can understand contemporary reality.

No wonder then, that Jews are deeply involved in politics, and strongly committed to both the radical and liberal traditions. Yet our historical memory and religious ideals also give us an independence from these traditions, and a vantage point from which to assess some of their limitations.

Jews have a deep commitment to the fundamental liberties. The insistence on respect for alternative views, the openness that the framers of Rabbinic Judaism encouraged in their endless debate and consideration of a wide range of possibilities, the spirit of dialectical inquiry, the notion that there will always be three opinions on any given matter where there are two Jews discussing it—all these express a Jewish approach that encourages tolerance and diversity. Through much of Jewish history, these attitudes guided the debate among the religious elite, although much of Jewish society did not partake in this pluralism and was closed, rigid and illiberal in its actual practices. In the past several hundred years, as Jews grappled with the modern world, we have become strong partisans of liberal values.

Liberal societies have historically been better for Jews—they have protected us from the imposition of the majority's religious and cultural traditions. Yet the commitment to these values has moved past a self-interested expediency—Jews have come to feel a deep commitment to democratic ideals, correctly seeing in them a modern expression of the fundamental dignity of human beings that the Torah originally proclaimed. We have a deep distaste for unjustified abridgements of individual freedoms. For that reason we have come to distrust dictators and oppressive regimes whether they justified themselves with right-wing or left-wing rhetoric. We would be critical of Soviet totalitarianism even if it did not specifically oppress Jews. Similarly, we reject the kind of apologia for unfreedom that is common among Jews of the Right—the attempt to distinguish between "authoritarian" policies of right-wing dictators, and the supposedly worse "totalitarian" policies of dictators identified with communism. This same commitment to liberal ideals makes us committed adversaries of Kahane, Sharon, and other anti-democratic forces in Israel, and foes also of the anti-democratic forces on the American Right (including those who have newly become supporters of Israel now that they see a potential for using Israel to advance an American military interest).

But we are not uncritically committed to liberalism. When liberal values are used as a cover for materialism and individualism, we say clearly that these are not our values. We stand for tolerance, but not for ethical relativism which is sometimes seen as either the primary justification for, or the logical consequence of a commitment to tolerance. We stand for freedom—but not for giving unlimited freedom to corporations so they can exploit the people and resources of the planet. Nor do we necessarily take at face value the claim of Western societies to be the living embodiments of the liberal ideals that they so proudly proclaim. If radically alternative policies to those held by the dominant parties are systematically excluded from serious public consideration, if anti-nuclear and anti-apartheid forces must use civil disobedience to have their views noticed (and even then not given a serious public airing), if U.S. military interventions can be financed despite the opposition of a majority of Americans, if freedom of the press actually amounts to freedom only for those with vast economic resources to buy media time or space, if economic power concentrated in the hands of the few pre-shapes the options so that the range of serious political choices becomes dramatically narrowed, then we can get a different kind of unfreedom—an unfreedom that celebrates itself as the paradigm of liberal ideals.

Jews are also drawn to the radical tradition in politics. Radical politics has often adopted the idealism and commitment to justice that are central to the Jewish tradition. The articulation of the needs of the oppressed, the unwillingness to compromise with unfair distributions of power and wealth, the historical link between the Left and the underdog, have brought many Jews into the world of radical politics. The utopian demand for transformation is something we proudly identify with—it remains a central ingredient in Jewish vision.

Yet we are also very critical of the Left. The Left has almost always tried to force Jews into a false universalism—denying the particularity of our historical experience, the validity of our religious insights, and the importance of our national survival. Jews have been forced to choose between loyalty to their own people and a loyalty to universal ideals. This has been particularly striking because the Left has often glorified "national liberation struggles," seeing in other people's insistence on their own customs and traditions a potential force for liberation. Yet it has often been demeaning and destructive toward Jews and Jewish culture. It is this attitude that explains the Left's ability to remain silent about oppression of Jews in the Soviet Union, just as it remains silent about the overt anti-Semitism that characterizes some of the social movements it supports.

The Relevance of Judaism to Liberal Politics

The greatest weakness in liberal politics lies in its limited view of human nature. Too often progressive politics projects the image of human beings as needing nothing more than material satisfaction and the right to participate in democratic processes. The image we get of human life is one of isolated individuals holding onto rights. This picture of reality unintentionally reinforces the conception of individuals as fundamentally, perhaps ontologically, independent of each other, and the main problem in the world as interference with that independence. The healthy society is one in which people would be able to stand alone, self-sufficient, and not dependent, weak or needy. The job of social movements is to win back those rights that have been unfairly denied or frustrated by present social arrangements.

It's only a short step to the pop psychology that articulates and seems to confirm the dominant individualism of the culture. In its right-wing form, the message is "Take care of yourself at all costs," "Win through intimidation," and "You are a fool if you haven't learned to make money and get power over others." In its liberal form, the message is, "Autonomy and freedom from the needs of others is the best way to live," and "Set limits, keep firm boundaries, and be sure no one is ever taking advantage of you." The common message from both sides: "You are fundamentally alone, you can't really trust other people, and all relationships start with the individual and work only when the individual has worked out a way to stand strong on her/his own."

Against this view of the world stands the biblical view, developed throughout Jewish history and incorporated into Jewish culture, folk wisdom, Halakha [Jewish law], and philosophy. By our account, human beings are most fundamentally *in relationship*. They are part of a family and part of a people and it is this rootedness in community that is ontologically prior and ethically fundamental. Important consequences follow from this Jewish conception:

• The healthy human being is not the one who has learned to stand alone, but the one who can acknowledge her/his need to be in a deep relationship with other human beings and with the community.

• If people are alone and not involved in a rich set of relationships, this is a result of some aberration in the society and should be rectified.

• Individual families get their strength and meaning through participation in a larger community, and the community at any given moment gets its strength and meaning from its relationship to the historical chain of generations that have preceded it and that will follow it.

Finally, it is in these relationships with others, and in community, that we gain access to God. Unlike the imagery of the lone individual saint or mystic who connects to God through isolated individual exploration or through a personal and lonely quest, the primary instance of Jewish revelation comes to and through a community, first the community at Sinai, and then the community of Israel seeking God through study, prayer, and social action. As Buber so eloquently taught, the primary word for Jews is not "me" but "I/Thou."

This provides us with our deepest critique of contemporary Western societies. The competitive culture, the philosophy of individualism, the economic structures that encourage war of all against all—these are unacceptable perversions of human possibility. No matter how much new technology and activity our society generates, it cannot, in the long run, be stable and satisfying. Nor can it be ethically acceptable—it contradicts our deepest understanding of what is good for human beings. The specific ways that our society rips us from connectedness with each other and from the organic cycle of life can never be acceptable to anyone rooted in the Jewish tradition. Instead, we are ethically and religiously bound to the healing, repair, and transformation of this social order (*tikkun*).

Why a Jewish Magazine

The pressure to be "universalist" and to reject a particularistic identity "in order to be taken seriously" is *the* major way that Jews were oppressed in the United States. In Europe and under absolute Islamic countries, Jews were oppressed overtly: legally, economically, and through physical violence. America offered a seductive deal: "Give up those elements in your identity that make you stand out and be different and we will let you fit into the society as one of the host of minority groups. Keep your religious ideas and divisions in your private life, and don't let them intrude into the public world of politics and economics."

What a relief that felt to a people whose physical survival was at issue in Europe! One could keep "Jewish identity" if it was done in quiet and "inoffensive" (that is, private) ways—e.g. by keeping

A section of the over 700 Israelis who attended Tikkun's *conference in Jerusalem, June 1991*

one's Jewishness restrained to weekend synagogue attendance, and involvement in the community center and social life. In experiential terms, this amounted to an intense pressure to abandon the part of one's religion that could not easily fit in (e.g. Shabbat observance when it conflicted with economic survival, or dressing differently, or speaking Yiddish) and reducing one's Jewishness to a neat, unobtrusive ethnicity. For a new generation of Jews, no longer traumatized by the threat of physical survival, it is no longer clear why we should accept this offer. No one in liberal or progressive communities would think that a Martin Luther King or a Jesse Jackson has marginalized himself because his politics is derived in part from the religious experience of the Black Church, even drawing upon its symbols, songs and language. Jews have a right to be treated similarly.

The greatest opposition to being "out as Jews" comes not from non-Jews, but from Jews who have internalized the anti-Semitic norms of the society. The intense sensitivity to "what they will think" is a survival mechanism that every minority group must develop while attempting to survive in a somewhat hostile majority culture. We tend to internalize the external oppression and to enforce upon ourselves the norms we suspect the majority to desire. So it was no surprise to hear women "putting down" those who insisted on raising the question of the status of women, or to hear Blacks who carefully try to remove from within their behavior and psyches any vestiges of Black culture. Similarly, it is no surprise to have Jews who will act uncomfortable in the presence of another Jew who is "too Jewish," and will try to reassure their friends or colleagues that they are "not that kind of Jew." It is these Jews who will be most vicious and unfair in their criticism of Israel, and most forthcoming when it comes to reassuring their friends in the progressive movements that Jews do not need to be counted among the long lists of oppressed groups. For these Jews, *Tikkun*'s Jewish articles will be a source of embarrassment—and we would not be surprised if they make a special point of letting their friends know that they don't read this kind of magazine.

We believe that the liberal and progressive forces, non-Jewish and Jewish alike, including the Democratic Party, the labor movement, the women's movement, the anti-nuclear and peace movement, the movements for equality and economic justice—all have something important to learn from Judaism and the experience of the Jewish people. Some of this was articulated in our discussion of "The Relevance of Judaism to Liberal Politics." More of it will become clear as the magazine develops.

For all of these reasons, we are willing to take the risk—and create a magazine that intends to be part of the public debate in the United States, that will print articles from a wide variety of liberal and progressive perspectives, and that still sees itself as an expression of Judaism.

It is reasonable to ask that we say something about the specific worldview we hold about Jewish issues that impact on secular politics. While we don't want to summarize all future editorials in this first one, there are two important issues we do want to address.

First, we believe that the most exciting and important development in contemporary Judaism has been the emergence of a movement for women's liberation. We strongly endorse the important attempts of women to reclaim Judaism as their own, and to take a leading role in shaping the future of the Jewish community. We hope to explore the different ways that this process has evolved, including the important work done by orthodox women as well as the contributions of Jewish feminists. We have only begun to see what these changes will ultimately mean for Jewish life. Our commitment to women's liberation means much more than a simple equality—it means reclaiming the parts of women's experiences that have been lost or repressed, learning from the insights of women as they develop new rituals and new ways of being Jewish and new forms of political and social action, and understanding that women's liberation is not just about women but about a transformation in what it means to be a human being.

Second, Israel. We are deeply committed to making Israel the "beginning of the flourishing of our redemption." That is, we believe that Israel has the potential to play an important messianic role in history. For that reason, we are often critical of specific government policies, and critical also of those in the religious world who mis-identify the actualities of contemporary Israel with the messianic goals that we need to strive for. It is not just Kahane or Sharon that upset us as we look at Israel, but the entire development of a militaristic mind-set that believes in physical strength rather than in moral righteousness as the key to building a Jewish state.

We are closely aligned with the worldview of the religious peace movement in Israel, articulated under the banner of Oz ve Shalom and Nitivot Shalom—an approach that is passionately committed to the survival of the Jewish state but is equally strongly committed to making Israel a society that embodies in its daily practice, including in its dealing with Palestinians, the moral imperatives of Torah. □

The Editor: A Personal Note

Michael Lerner

I
t's not always easy for me to strike the right balance between moral judgment and compassion.
I'd like to tell you a little about the way I can sometimes go astray. True, when it comes to
Israel, the objective situation sometimes makes one become judgmental. Yes, I have gone out of
my way to insist that we all understand the psychological impact of the Holocaust and the legitimate
anger that Israelis feel at Palestinians who rejected a state when it was offered in 1948 and who have
engaged in inhumane terrorist attacks on civilians for the past two decades. I've tried to acknowledge in *Tikkun* why it's hard for Israelis suddenly to trust the PLO or to be open to a PLO state
when for two decades the PLO has talked of eliminating "the Zionist entity."

But no matter how much I acknowledge our justified fears, it's hard not to fall into a very
judgmental tone toward my brothers and sisters in Israel, in light of the Israeli army's killings of
Palestinians. So many of the confrontations, after all, derive from the Israelis' desire to "show who is
boss" rather than from the need to keep a minimal security presence to protect Israel. And how can
we be less than harsh when we see thousands of Palestinians arrested and kept in inhumane prison
camps for months under "administrative detention;" hundreds of thousands confined to their
homes for days on end under arbitrarily imposed twenty-four-hour curfews; some in West Bank settlements required to wear badges saying "foreign workers" that even some right-wing Israelis recognize as parallel to the yellow star the Nazis required Jews to wear in public; the attacks by settlers on
random groups of Palestinians in a fashion much resembling the pogroms we Jews faced in Eastern
Europe; Shamir's refusal even to consider trading land for peace? It's very hard to keep an adequate
tone of compassion when the situation calls for moral judgments.

And yet I know how easy it is to fall into a misguided and alienating self-righteousness. If I insist
today that we give greater primacy to compassion it is only because I recall how destructive it was
for me personally and for all of us collectively when the liberal and progressive forces in the late
1960s were perceived as harshly critical of the lifestyles and values of American society.

I was reminded recently of how singularly judgmental and stupid I was in that period because an
article has been circulating recently to Jewish newspapers that selectively quotes some of the more
outrageous things I said and wrote in 1968 and 1969 at the height of my most self-righteous period.
In *Judaism* in 1969 I wrote that the Jewish community is "racist, internally corrupt, and an apologist
for the worst aspects of American capitalism and imperialism." Presumptuously adopting the
famous language of Isaiah who told the Israelites that God would prefer that they stop bringing
sacrifices to the Temple if they continued to live corrupt lives, I mused that the synagogues would
have to be shut down to give Judaism a chance to recapture its ethical roots. With all the bravado
and self-centeredness that so many of us mid-twenty-year-olds had in the late 1960s, I was aflame
with hyperbole and angry judgment.

I'd like to puzzle over how I could have gotten to this point in 1969. Outrageous as my statements

---

This editorial appeared in Tikkun, *July/August 1989.*

were, they emerged from a deep sense of painful personal disillusionment that I had while growing up in the American Jewish world. Only a few of my contemporaries seemed to share the pain—most had disengaged from the Jewish world by the time of their bar or bat mitzvah; they cared less about its internal dynamics, choosing instead to vote with their feet by walking away. To most of my generation I was an anomaly—someone who at the very height of the New Left experience was still claiming that there was something fundamentally important within Judaism that should not be abandoned, even though it should not be confused with the kind of Judaism being put forward in the organized Jewish community at that time.

So perhaps it won't surprise you to learn that I grew up in a family deeply involved in the Jewish world. Both my parents were committed and active leaders in the Zionist movement, and my own deep commitment to Israel was fostered by their wise education. What may surprise you is that to be a Zionist in the 1930s and 1940s was *not* to be part of the American Jewish establishment; rather it was to be part of a movement that had many similarities to the radical movements of the 1960s. Zionism was the national liberation struggle of the Jewish people; but until after the Second World War and the subsequent revelations about the Holocaust had sunk in, many American Jews were no more anxious to identify with a national liberation struggle than American Blacks were to identify with a Black liberation movement when it first emerged in the 1960s. Many American Jews still believed that the best strategy was to assimilate and not make waves.

The quintessential embodiment of this consciousness was the American Jewish Committee, dominated by the wealthiest of American Jews, who claimed that they could best represent Jewish interests by cuddling up to the American ruling class and quietly whispering into its ears a set of pro-Jewish messages. Only in the past decade are we getting a full understanding of how the reliance on this kind of strategy may have prevented American Jews from mobilizing their forces more effectively to save European Jewry from destruction. Historical records now suggest that the Jewish plutocrats may have been more interested in preserving their own credibility with their "friends" in the American ruling class than in aggressively pushing for American policies that might have saved thousands of Jewish lives.

The Zionist movement during this period was the genuine embodiment of the best interests of the Jewish people—and it tended to attract idealists, including many who had been (for good reason) disillusioned with the Communist party and with the anti-Semitism that was never fully purged from the international Left. (Zionists often perceived themselves as much in struggle with British colonialism and the American ruling elite as any lefty, and in conflict too, with the ruling elites in the American Jewish community.) The fundraisers and bureaucrats who set up endless testimonial dinners to commend their own generosity and wisdom may have already dominated other aspects of Jewish communal life, but they had not yet gained hegemony in Zionist circles. The Zionist movement was dramatically transformed in the early 1950s, once Israel's existence was secured. Those Zionists who did not actually move to Israel to build a Jewish society began to redefine their political tasks in America. The new goal was to seek power and respectability in America so that they could court political influence that would eventually be used to help Israel. Making money (part of which could be given to Israel) or getting political power was suddenly defined as the new way to be a good Zionist. From challenging assimilation in earlier decades, Zionists were now trying to "fit in" and join the great American self-celebration of the 1950s. A convenient deal: Jews could both "make it" in America and feel that they were doing so for the sake of the Jewish people. My parents did their bit. Active in the Democratic party, which was all too happy to exchange a few pious words about Israel for Jewish money and political energy, my parents were perceived by Democratic party leaders as among those Jewish leaders whose support they would have to seek, and they quickly moved up the political ladder. My home was frequented by congressmen, senators, governors, and former and future presidents. I listened intently to the flowery ideals, and then was shocked to discover in the *Congressional Record*, which I read every day, that these same men quickly abandoned the struggle for civil rights, health care, full employment—in fact, almost every liberal program, allegiance to which was supposed to differentiate them from the Republicans. In the name of fighting communism they could vote for military authorizations that then precluded serious funding for social programs. The political hypocrisy of many of these national leaders was matched only by their intellectual vacuity. My parents also saw that many of these people, who were being lauded by the press as the embodiment of liberal idealism and integrity, were empty and corrupt. Still, in my parents' eyes, the trade-off was worth it: after all, these people were supporting Israel. Maybe their commitment to liberal ideals turned out to be secondary to their anticommunism, but their commitment to Israel remained strong—and for my parents, that was the bottom line. So what if the cost of supporting these characters was that the Jewish community would become implicated in their compromises, involved in supporting their ideologies to the extent that it would begin to convince itself that Judaism and American liberalism were simply indistinguishable? At least it was good for the Jews.

Yet I wasn't convinced on that score either. I remember Adlai Stevenson, having been told he could rest before the political party that would soon begin downstairs, sitting in my bedroom in his underpants, arguing with me that America should put all its energy into trying to reunite Germany, because doing so would help the United States fight communism. I tried to talk to him about the failure of the American government to engage in a serious denazification of German society after the Second World War, but for him the issue of the Jews, our fate and our fears, was largely irrelevant: for the cold warrior everything, all values, were subordinate to the anti-Communist crusade. While viewed by millions of liberals as the idealistic champion of democratic values, in my bedroom Stevenson came across as a defender of America's corporate interests, an "enlightened" cold warrior whose primary concern was how best to preserve the world for American investment. If the Jews were helpful, fine; but if their interests needed to be sacrificed (as they had been a decade earlier during World War II), that too was fine. Years later, when others were disillusioned with Stevenson's defense of America's Vietnam policy, I remembered that moment as an early warning that when democratic values stood in conflict with American economic interests, Democratic party liberals of the 1950s chose the latter.

The more I learned from the inside about American politics, the more disgusted I became. I turned to Judaism to find a language to articulate my moral outrage. Why Judaism? Because within its prophetic tradition I discovered the voice of moral outrage at the corruptions of an established order. That voice was embodied for me both in the roaring articulateness of my own rabbi, Joachim Prinz, whose experience at the hands of the Nazis led him to identify with other oppressed groups whose causes he championed as president of the American Jewish Congress, and in the gentler tones of Abraham Joshua Heschel, whose works I began to study.

Yet the Judaism to which I was attracted flourished more at Camp Ramah, at some Orthodox synagogues, and in the sacred Jewish texts than it did in the triumphant institutions of American Jewish life. I began to understand why my grandfather, a Hasidic rabbi and disciple of Reb Nachman of Bratslav, buried himself in these sacred texts rather than deal with the daily realities of American life in general or American Jewish life in particular. So it was not long before I found myself part of the community of Jews who found within Judaism itself not only a language to critique American materialism, but also a basis for a critique of the existing Jewish world. Judaism, I learned, need not be an uncritical glorification of the Jewish people. In fact, the very chauvinism and self-intoxication that I found in the Jewish world, the materialism and anti-intellectualism that dominated many of America's Jewish institutions, were repudiated by the core of the Jewish tradition itself.

I had hoped to find this kind of Judaism flourishing at the Jewish Theological Seminary, where I enrolled in courses while pursuing my bachelor's degree at Columbia. Elected national president of Atid, the Conservative movement's college organization, I began to see the inner workings of the Seminary. I was saddened to find that the Seminary itself was far removed from the prophetic spirit of Judaism. Scientific study of Talmud and Bible, which often distanced students from the ethical imperatives of the prophetic message, a rigid attitude toward ritual, and a distancing from any sense of responsibility for changing the world permeated the Seminary.

My mentor, Abraham Joshua Heschel, felt the same distress. He repeatedly told me of his own isolation at the Seminary—touted in public as a *tzadik,* a prophet, the most original voice in Jewish theology, he was increasingly powerless to influence the Conservative movement itself or even to attract followers among Seminary students. Too many of these students found his passion for God and his commitment to social justice far from the skills they would need to function as "successful" pulpit rabbis. His involvement in the civil rights movement was seen as quaint; but his identification as a leader of Clergy and Laity Concerned About the War in Vietnam isolated him even further at the Seminary. He told me that even though by the late sixties some official Jewish organizations were willing to pass resolutions opposing the war, none of them seemed willing to put serious energy or resources into that struggle. He noted that the Jewish response compared unfavorably with that of the Catholic and Protestant Churches, which had backed their antiwar resolutions with money and considerable personal involvement.

In fact, a *larger* proportion of Jews was involved in the movement than Catholics or Protestants. But mostly we were not involved *as* Jews. So when I went to the University of California to pursue a doctorate in philosophy, I found a political movement made up of a disproportionate number of Jews; but they were Jews who had been alienated from the Jewish world for some of the same reasons that had led me into Judaism. They had been exposed to a Jewish life defined by gaudy bar mitzvah parties and fundraising, a world in which lofty ideals were rolled out on ceremonial occasions but rarely played a role in shaping daily decisions, a world in which those who had the most money seemed to have the most communal influence and respect. Most of these Jews in the movement had never had the privilege of being exposed to the revolutionary content of the sacred texts, had never known the intellectual seriousness and moral sensitivity that shaped our tradition, and had never met the kinds of righteous Jews whom I had been lucky to encounter. They had, quite naturally, identified Judaism itself with the materialism and anti-intellectualism and narrow-mindedness they had encountered in the organized Jewish community, and rejected the whole package.

But when I tried to argue that Judaism really stood for many of the moral values they supported, they asked me to show them living examples of this kind of Judaism. And that grew increasingly difficult in the mid- and late 1960s. I myself was fired from two jobs in the Jewish community, each time explicitly because the rabbi was embarrassed to have someone on his Hebrew School staff who was being quoted in the local newspapers making "unpatriotic" statements about the war in Vietnam.

In later years our opposition to racism, sexism, and American intervention in Vietnam would become standard liberal fare, but between 1964 and 1969, when our positions were "vanguard," the Jewish world seemed indifferent at best, and usually overtly hostile. It was no secret that some of the large donors to Jewish causes were slum landlords, that other Jews benefited from extensive investments in war-related industries, and that still others continued to insist that the best interests of Israel would be served if the Jews gave blind support to the U.S. administration (even while they privately knew that the Vietnam War was immoral and a tragic mistake).

I could tell my friends about Heschel's courageous example, but Heschel himself was telling me privately that he was finding it harder to function within the organized Jewish world. A group of us at Berkeley tried to keep alive a different vision of Judaism: We held a Chanukah service inside

Sproul Hall during the Free Speech Movement's sit-in, we organized freedom seders each year and brought hundreds of Jews together to reaffirm this aspect of their Judaism, we led High Holiday services and there rejoiced in the unequivocal statements from our prophets (the traditional Haftorah for Yom Kippur from Isaiah): "Is not this the fast I have chosen: to feed the hungry, to clothe the naked, to loosen the bonds of the oppressed?"

But it became increasingly difficult not to share some of the anger that my friends were feeling at a Jewish world that seemed more interested in achieving respectability than in embodying a moral vision. There were people around me who seemed to rejoice in "trashing" every icon of their past. Doing likewise held little joy for me. I still deeply respected my parents and their commitment, and I had met some very profound and wonderful people in the Jewish world. I had fought against assimilation and had insisted to my friends in the movement that there was a valuable vision within Judaism from which they could learn. So it was very painful for me to see the Jewish tradition being appropriated by apologists for the status quo—all the more so because by the late sixties many of us understood how oppressive and hurtful that status quo really was to American Blacks, to women, to the poor, and to many people still suffering from the impact of economic and political domination. Like so many others, I rejoiced at Israel's triumph in the Six Day War of 1967, but then grew deeply troubled when, instead of using the occupation of the West Bank as an opportunity to negotiate with the Palestinians—now finally free from Jordanian rule—the Labor party leaders denied the existence of a Palestinian people and began to set in place the mechanisms for a prolonged occupation. And I was dispirited to see significant numbers of American Jews, frightened by some anti-Semitic elements that had emerged within the Black liberation struggle, suddenly turn their backs on the struggle for Black equality now that it was moving from a focus on political rights in the South to a demand for economic equality in the North.

It was at this moment, in the late sixties, that the local B'nai B'rith chapter offered its "Man of the Year Award" to San Francisco State President S. I. Hayakawa, the man who had won national fame for his use of massive police force to break the back of a student-faculty strike. (He went on to become one of the most reactionary members of the U.S. Senate, though pro-Israel.) The strike centered on demands for increased enrollment of Blacks and the creation of a college of Third World studies. To the three hundred young Jews who demonstrated against the Hayakawa award, the B'nai B'rith presentation represented the worst elements in Jewish life. But in the eyes of most of our young Jewish friends, the award was not an aberration but the quintessence of Jewish life. Shortly after this event I wrote my diatribe against the Jewish world at the request of the editor of *Judaism*, the magazine of the American Jewish Congress. Despite the Congress' reputation for liberalism, the editor who published this article, Stephan Scharzschild, was promptly forced to resign—and told me that publishing my article had been the reason.

Looking back, I still believe that much of the fundamental criticism of the Jewish world was based on a correct reading of the distorting effects of the desire to "make it." The tone of that criticism reflected in part the radicalization of the late 1960s and the spirit of ruthless critique of all existing institutions and social arrangements that we in our mid-twenties felt empowered to make. At moments it seemed as though the antiwar and civil rights and women's movements were inspired by a prophetic sensibility—and the world is a better place because those movements existed. Those struggles were quite a bit more than a generational rebellion against parental authority; they addressed fundamental societal problems and proposed solutions that have made the world a better place. If only such a spirit once again emerged and became a social force in the 1990s. Twenty years later I still think that there was something fundamentally valuable and life-affirming in our willingness to speak truth to power—even if that meant raising very uncomfortable issues and pressing potential allies into facing issues they would have preferred to avoid.

But when I took that same tone into the Jewish world, my criticisms were too global and lacking in nuance. I did not adequately acknowledge the many principled and idealistic people working in the Jewish community who shared my values and my distress. Moreover, the principles I was enunciating came from the Jewish tradition and had been taught me by Jews active in the Jewish world. Even if the Jewish world wasn't living up to its own ideals, shouldn't it still be given considerable credit for articulating those ideals and teaching them to its young? I also had not acknowledged the incredible pain of the Holocaust and the role that event played in making survival so fundamental a concern of the Jewish people that other moral concerns might take a back seat. So what, I might have asked myself, if the organized Jewish world was somewhat obsessed with self-interest, defense, and survival? Twenty years after the Holocaust it would have taken a miracle for any group to be different! Good enough that this same community had produced a new generation of Jews who had captured enough of the spirit of the Jewish tradition to allow themselves to be led by its moral imperatives to fight for civil rights and against the war.

But worst of all, I had fallen into the same spirit of intolerant judgment that pervaded so much of the New Left of the 1960s. We articulated good moral ideals but then were furious when others did not immediately respond and become the perfect exemplars of those ideals. In our twenties, we believed that there was no obstacle other than selfishness to the moral lives we professed. So we harshly condemned everyone—first the conservatives, then the liberals, then the American people themselves. Finally, we turned on each other, finding in ourselves the unmistakable signs of egotism, racism, sexism, and all the other perversions that we had so ruthlessly critiqued in others. Despairing that we were similarly flawed, we began to treat each other with the same intolerance that made the inner life of the movement seem almost as inhumane (in its backbiting and sectarian squabbling and accusations about who was less sexist or racist or egotistical than whom) as the society we had come to critique. Our inability to accept our own weaknesses and limitations was of a piece with our inability to accept the limitations of the rest of American society, and with my own inability to accept some of the limitations in the existing Jewish world. Eventually, the spirit of self-destructive intolerance led most people to abandon the movements for social change.

Many who left the official organizations of the movement stayed committed to the movement's best ideals. As we tried to make sense of how we had defeated ourselves, I found myself looking to the Jewish tradition—and to the history of a people that, like the New Left, saw itself as a vanguard in the struggle for social transformation (*tikkun*). Throughout history the Jewish people had screwed up. Yet the Jewish tradition also teaches us that human beings are inevitably flawed, that the task is to serve God even with the *yetzer hara* (the evil inclination), the flawed and self-interested self. In other words, what I had forgotten or not yet adequately allowed myself to hear was the message in the Jewish tradition that would tell me, "Of course people are going to be screwed up, sexist, racist, egotistical, self-centered, needy; but that's who we are—flawed human beings—and that's who will have to change the world. Moreover, it's not only the people at large who are flawed, but also the leaders and organizers, the vanguard. And these leaders and organizers must be willing to accept their own inadequacies rather than ruthlessly trash themselves; otherwise they will never be able to accept anyone else."

I began to recognize that what was missing in our politics was a sense of compassion for ourselves. The problem wasn't that we were too egotistical or too sexist or too racist—though these aspects of ourselves must certainly be struggled against—but rather that we had somehow expected that human beings would magically transcend all these problems, that the very fact that we were part of the movement meant that we must immediately embody the ideals we sought for a future society. And it was this same utopian expectation that made it impossible for those of us who were Jews to accept the inevitable limitations and distortions in the Jewish world.

It might be a wonderful way to start to train ourselves to become effective in politics if we would counter our own tendencies to be unfairly judgmental of our own people, our own families, and ourselves. In this sense, the development of "Jewish consciousness-raising" groups by *Tikkun*'s Committee for Judaism and Social Justice (CJSJ)[*] might be understood not as leading anyone away from politics but as leading them toward a way to be deeper and more effective in mainstream American politics. It's only by learning how to replace self-blaming with compassion in our own lives that we will have the necessary skill to help others in American society do the same for themselves. And a liberal/progressive movement that does help people develop a sense of compassion for themselves will be a movement that finally gains the credibility it needs to heal and repair this society. If American liberals and progressives could learn how to develop a mass psychology of compassion, they would quickly become the major force shaping politics in the twenty-first century.

Nevertheless, compassion is not meant as a replacement for moral sensitivity, and there must still be a place for moral outrage. Certainly when we see Israel engaging in activities that are not only morally inappropriate but actually self-destructive, we must cry out in anguish. Taking strong stands against Shamir's policies, for example, is not inappropriate—though blaming the entire Jewish people or every Israeli or all of Zionism for what Shamir does is precisely the kind of globalizing that is destructive. Looking at my own mistakes in the 1960s, and knowing how easy it is to fall into these traps once again, I feel that I need to keep careful check on my judgmental tendencies. The task, I believe, is to mix that sense of outrage at injustice with an adequate dose of compassion so that we don't begin to turn on the Jewish people and judge ourselves too harshly. If I personally don't always achieve the right balance, at least it's worthwhile to articulate the goal. Writing editorials often pulls for an "all-knowing" tone that suggest that the author is somehow above the fray, managing to achieve an objectivity and wisdom superior to everyone else. So part of my reason in discussing these past mistakes is to publicly affirm how well I know that I am a limited and flawed human being, shaped by my own past and its battles, sometimes overly judgmental, inevitably seeing things from my own perspective, and not always right. So it's humbling and gratifying to know that despite my limitations, some of our readers have found some of my perspectives helpful and instructive. □

---

[*] The Committee for Judaism and Social Justice is *Tikkun*'s education arm. Over the years, it has organized *Tikkun* salons and discussion groups in dozens of cities around the U.S.; sponsored *Tikkun* conferences; organized public statements, petitions and newspaper advertisements articulating the *Tikkun* community's analyses and positions; and formed a nationwide association of progressive Jewish students (Students for Judaism and Social Justice). If you wish to be in a *Tikkun* discussion group in your area, or to join the CJSJ network, write to CJSJ, 5100 Leona St. Oakland, CA 94619.

I. Politics and Society

A New Paradigm for Liberals: The Primacy of Ethics and Emotions

Michael Lerner

The Spring of 1987 is a heady time for Democrats and for the liberal and progressive forces in America. Flush from a promising electoral victory in 1986, buoyed by Reagan's Iranian affair that left his supposedly "Teflon" presidency looking considerably less invulnerable, the Democrats have a unique opportunity to redefine their public image and put forward a vision of politics that will shape the debate well into the 1990s. The Democrats are at bat, and liberal and progressive social movements like those concerned with nuclear disarmament, anti-apartheid, women's rights, and social welfare will find their own prospects dramatically influenced by the degree to which the Democrats can foster a political climate supportive of innovation and social change.

But never underestimate the ability of Democrats to triumphantly snatch defeat from the jaws of victory. Centrists within the party, rightly understanding that Reagan and the Right have touched some critical nerve in the American psyche, yet not really understanding the nature of the Right's psychological appeal, are foolishly counseling a path of "me-too-ism" in which Democrats will show the nation that they are really just a more moderate version of Reaganite conservatism—complete with inflated military budgets and "tough talk" about Russia, scaled down expectations for solving domestic poverty, and pro-corporate economic policies based on "trickle down" economics.

Liberals in the party, meanwhile, seem to think that if they can articulate an overall plan to deal with economic decline and the threat of international economic competition, tempering calls for self-sacrifice and austerity with promises of expanding the "social safety net" for the poor, they will appear neatly balanced between pragmatism and idealism. Even if such a scheme works to get Democrats back into the White House, it will not provide a political mandate for liberal politics. Instead, as in the Carter years, we will have a Democrat articulating a fundamentally pro-corporate agenda and this would eventually lead to the recrediting of the conservative agenda. If supporting corporate interests and fighting communism are really the highest goals of politics, the conservatives are "the real thing," so why support the ersatz Democratic party version once the initial revulsion at "excesses" à la Contra-gate have been forgotten? Even in self-interest terms, then, the Democratic party has much to gain by encouraging its liberal wing to project a genuinely creative new vision for American politics.

Yet the new vision that is needed is not merely a rehashing of ideas that are popular on the liberal left. Of course we need full employment, health care, housing, disarmament, and equality in our society. But liberals will never have the political power to implement these ideas until they can speak to an even deeper level of human need. The liberals need a fuller understanding of the psychological and spiritual needs of the American people—and a vision of how these needs could be met within the framework of a new moral order. Putting together a list of "new ideas," trying to convince the

---

This editorial appeared in Tikkun, *January/February 1987.*

press that "we have the beef," will continue to be an inadequate strategy until the Democrats construct a vision which addresses the underlying philosophical, moral and psychological issues that motivate most people.

A new vision for Democrats will only be really new if it transcends two major weaknesses in contemporary liberal thinking: the myth of externality and the excessive focus on individual rights.

The Myth of Externality. This is the fallacy of conceptualizing people as being motivated by a narrow range of external economic and political self-interest issues. Operating from this fallacy, the task of the liberal Democrat becomes how to show that liberal policies will directly benefit people's material self-interest. So Democrats focus primarily on tinkering with the economy or providing funds to build highways and transportation, money for welfare, or better housing or health care, or higher social benefits for the elderly. This is supposed to be pragmatic, hard-nosed, and realistic.

It would be silly to deny that economic issues are important to many sectors of the population. The 1986 election showed that many economic populist themes had deep resonance within important sectors of the population. Democrats will be politically stronger if they have the courage to integrate these themes into their politics in the coming years. A smart plan to reindustrialize America, rebuild its scientific and technological infrastructure, and increase its ability to use its material and human resources in productive ways—if that plan includes increased democratic participation in the management of our corporations and in the investment of our resources—can only increase the Democrats' appeal.

It is equally important to note that these issues no longer enthuse as large a segment of the population as they seemed to in the days when the Depression (or in subsequent decades, its memory) shaped American political reality. In the 1980s we have had numerous instances in which the very workers whose economic well-being has been threatened by conservative policies nevertheless identify with the Right's social program and vote "against their economic interests." While acquiring a bigger share of the pie may influence many people's decisions in their private economic lives, it does not always determine their political choices.

It may even be a mistake to give an economic-reductionist account of the Democrats' original mass appeal during the New Deal. The New Deal, after all, did not solve the economic crisis of a faltering capitalism in the 1930s. Only vast military expenditures during World War II and the perpetuation of military spending through a post-WW II anti-Communist crusade managed to stabilize the economic picture for most Americans. It was not the economic miracle that tied most Americans to Roosevelt and the Democrats. Rather, the widespread feeling that these liberal Democrats could understand the inner experience of daily life encouraged identification with them. By articulating a social vision that helped people understand how the problems they were facing in their daily life were reflections of larger social problems and not of personal failures, the liberals helped to decrease the "self-blaming" endemic in a capitalist economy ("you get what you deserve") and to increase Americans' ability to have compassion for themselves. It was this compassion that was the basis for the Democrat's vast popularity, providing the foundation for a political mandate to carry out economic and political programs.

What has happened in the last few decades has been a shift in the locus of self-blame. Although America's economic expansion was eventually slowed by a rebuilt Europe and Japan, its initial economic hegemony in the post-WW II decades enabled American corporations to inherit many of the economic benefits of a faltering European colonialism and to use the wealth thereby accumulated to enlarge America's economic pie. While inequalities of wealth and power persisted, the growth in absolute terms of the standard of living for most Americans allowed American ideologists to proclaim a new age of affluence marred by only a few "pockets of poverty." Although never fully economically secure, and although now ridden with stressful work and intense competition, most Americans experienced their economic lives as considerably less problematic than in the past. Increasingly they came to believe that the "good life" was at hand; all they had to do was be "successful" and real human fulfillment would be theirs. Happiness was increasingly defined in terms of personal life, supposedly available to each person according to his/her own merit. And when people began to discover that their expanded material well-being had not brought an increase in satisfaction (indeed, the satisfactions of human community, friendship, and solidarity seemed less available after the Depression and WW II) a new and even more painful self-blaming came to dominate the social psychology of American life.

The new self-blaming is deeper and more intractable precisely because it draws upon the deepest wellsprings of our societal ideology. Inequalities of wealth and power have always been justified in America on the grounds of a supposedly meritocratic economic marketplace which allocates rewards according to ability and effort. This ideology seemed considerably less self-evidently true during the Depression when Democrats suggested everyone was suffering from a common economic problem. But with post-war prosperity, the ideology revived with an even deeper vigor and was extended to virtually every area of personal life. Everything was supposedly in the hands of the individual—s/he could shape a fate alone, based on his/her own decisions. "Take responsibility for your own life," "You've made your bed, now sleep in it," and "You can make it if you really try" are pop-psychology formulations of what became the deepest belief in America's religiously held ideology: the belief in meritocracy. If you merit happiness, you will get it; if you don't have it, you have only yourself to blame.

It is not hard to see how this way of thinking was functional for those with established power. Corporations could use the resulting psychology of self-blame and insecurity to sell their products: If you aren't yet achieving happiness in your personal life, it's probably because you haven't been using our product. But at a deeper level, the continued existence of fundamental inequalities of wealth and power could be portrayed as reflections of an inherently just society. As long as equality of opportunity was secured for all, the inequalities of outcome were merely reflections of different ability and merit. But the internalization of self-blame on the part of the masses of Americans produced a set of deep psychic scars, resulting in a growing crisis in personal life, increasing instability in family life, decreasing community ties and increasing difficulties in maintaining deep friendships, and the absence of larger ethical ties and commitments. In turn, all these social realities were interpreted by most people as personal deficiencies. The material well-being of post-WW II society has not produced a society full of happiness, but one full of pain and neurosis, a society in which people interpret socially generated problems like the increasing instability in family life as reflective primarily of their own personal inadequacies.

While the locus of self-blame has shifted, the locus of liberals' compassion has not. Liberals have rightly championed the poor and those facing overt racial and sexual discrimination. But for the most part liberal compassion has been restricted to the most overt economic and legal oppression. It's as if they remained frozen in 1930s consciousness, giving compassion only to people in the economic Depression, while ignoring the growing psychological depression. The result is that when they talk about compassion, they mean only compassion for the poor and those facing overt discrimination, leaving out nearly everyone else.

Given the externality fallacy, however, liberal Democrats are likely to hear a call for compassion as an appeal for more social welfare programs, only now addressed to the economic interests of middle-income voters. Certainly it is true that the Democratic party needs to develop programs that can link these voters with the economic interests of the poor, and that the development of programs for housing, health care, and full employment may provide such a link. But while such programs would follow from the compassion I am talking about, they do not constitute it. Rather, I am talking

Photo by Richard Bermack

about a new kind of compassion—a compassion that counteracts the self-blaming that dominates personal life today. It is by understanding and acknowledging the pain that people are experiencing in these not-strictly-economic arenas, the pain in families—the pain generated by the absence of community and an ethical frame to life—that the liberals can connect with the deeper needs that are central to contemporary American politics.

Ironically, it has been the conservatives who have been able to address these issues and thereby appeal to a large segment of Americans who might otherwise be resentful of the conservatives' defense of corporate interests. The pro-family politics the New Right has articulated has struck a chord precisely because it seems to address self-blame and despair. It is certainly true that right wing programs offer no plausible solution to the crisis of families. Many of the people who have been drawn to the Right have not been persuaded by the specifics of its program. But pro-family politics nevertheless has a powerful draw because it acknowledges the crisis in personal lives while pointing the finger at a set of social causes (feminism, gays, "liberal permissiveness") that are not the fault of individual Americans.

While strongly rejecting the conservatives' scapegoating, we can also see that by encouraging people to find a social cause for family crisis they decrease self-blame and increase self-compassion—and this is what makes the conservative pro-family package attractive to many Americans. Instead of denouncing the reactionary content, and implying that anyone drawn to pro-family politics is merely someone who wishes to oppress women and children (a line taken by, among others, feminist leader Barbara Ehrenreich), we would do well to see that the underlying needs to which these politics appeal are quite reasonable. It is perfectly understandable that people in pain would respond to those who seem to understand their pain and who articulate externalized social solutions.[1] The irony here, as I shall explore in greater detail below, is that it is precisely the economic order that the conservatives support which plays a central role in creating and sustaining the dynamics that undermine family life. But as long as the whole issue has been ignored by the liberals, or, as in the Democratic National Committee's latest attempts at "me-too-ism," simply dealt with by adding a few "pro-family programs" to a long list of other demands without any understanding of the deeper psychological and philosophical issues, conservatives will continue to appear as the pro-compassion force in society. No matter how often Democrats throw the word compassion around, as long as what they mean is compassion for somebody else (the poor, the oppressed) while ignoring the deep need for compassion of the average middle-income American grappling with the pains of daily life, they are likely to be greeted with distrust by most Americans (even those who on simple economic grounds have more reason to support the Democrats than their opponents).[2]

This analysis helps us understand the popularity of Reagan in the first six years of his presidency. Reagan's picture of an America in which people could find true community and pride in their lives offered a seductive alternative to self-blaming. We need not adopt or accept a similar patriotic chauvinism, but we do need to be able to understand the seductiveness of such an appeal. Instead of denouncing programs or ideologies as reactionary or fascistic, we must attempt to understand the underlying psychological needs that these ideologies gratify. We can then begin to ask how we might develop alternative programs and analyses that speak to what is legitimate in these needs. Who knows whether liberals in Germany, had they been able to think in these terms in the 1920s, might not have been able to develop a more relevant program in countering fascism, rather than just ineffectively denouncing it.

In our case, I have little hope of speaking to the hard-core twenty percent of the population enamored of racist, sexist and patriarchal notions. But there are many others, people who often represent the swing vote in an election, whose attraction to the Right has much more to do with the issues I am discussing than with a knee-jerk conservatism. These people will vote for candidates who

---

1. Throughout this essay I shall talk about the pain in daily life as a general and widespread social phenomenon, not confined to those who are in acute crisis, family breakdown, or seeking psychological help. The basis for this sweeping assumptions is defined more carefully in my book *Surplus Powerlessness* (Humanities Press, 1991) and is grounded in six years of empirical research that I conducted at the Institute for Labor and Mental Health in Oakland, California. In the course of analyzing several thousand interviews with working people from every sector of the work force, we discovered a deep pattern of pain, self-blaming, and internalized anger that is referred to in the analysis in this article. We should also note, of course, that alongside the pain there is also much joy and satisfaction in some aspects of family and personal life. Usually, it is this side that is accentuated, and used as a first level of cover or "defense" against dealing with the deep and pervasive pain that is also there. In this essay I focus primarily on the pain. In a more complete account, the elements of happiness and pride would also have to be acknowledged and addressed.

2. Liberal psychologists have only compounded the problem by popularizing the notion that the way to true emotional health is to learn to take responsibility for yourself and your own life. Of course, it is true that we should avoid the extreme of "victimization" that leads some people to feel passive and unable to act— conveniently blaming "the system" for their own failures to act in ways that could change their situation. But more often than not, the factors working to shape our reality are not created by one individual (or even one family) alone. Real empowerment, then, may require understanding the larger social forces that shape our individual situation, and then learning how to join with others in taking not individual but collective responsiblity for shaping our lives together. Our individual responsibility may often be to join with others—not to solve the problem on our own! To apply this to a current debate: It is true that seeing themselves as victims may not help inner-city Blacks—but neither has preaching to them about individual responsibility. What is most empowering is a vision of collective responsibility—that only by working together on an intolerable social reality can individual lives ultimately improve.

make them feel good about themselves or who at least can distract them from feeling bad. From this perspective, there is no magical mystique about Reagan as the "great communicator": his strength lies primarily in his ability to reduce self-blaming and provide a way for people to feel compassionate toward themselves. Similarly, the great candidates of the late 1980s and the 1990s will not be those who are most photogenic or have mysterious charisma, but those who are best able to make people feel affirmed, and who can help them deal with the real pain they experience because of the breakup of families, the decline in friendships, the breakdown of communities, and the absence of a morally coherent way of understanding their world.[*]

If one consequence of the fallacy of externality has been to keep Democrats from understanding ordinary Americans' central need for compassion, a second consequence has been to overlook the need for a moral framework for politics and daily life. The thirst for moral meaning is one of the deepest in American life. The latest rebirth of religion in America is partially a response to that thirst: within the religious community, one can find a moral vision to order events, locate oneself in history, and find one's own moral intuitions affirmed.

It is precisely this ability to speak to ethical norms, to call for a return to "traditional values," which has been engraved on the calling cards of the New Right. Yet it was the same commitment to ethical norms that also fueled the great social movements of the 1960s. Unfortunately, Marxist materialists and pro-capitalist cynics often join forces to reduce these struggles to seemingly narrow self-interest projects. For example, the anti-Vietnam War protests can be seen by these cynics as a self-interested struggle against the draft. But those who carefully chronicle the 1960s know that the militant demonstrations in which college students took serious risks to their lives and careers started before the draft reached into middle-class constituencies; that many of those who took part never were at risk of being drafted; and that the biggest anti-war demonstrations took place after the draft had stopped posing any serious threat to the majority of college students who participated in them. A deep moral outrage fueled the anti-war protests and the civil rights protests before them.

It was only when the New Leftists felt they had lost their internal sense of moral legitimacy (partially a result of the violence introduced into the movement by the Weathermen and other "super-militants," partly the result of the women's movement and its focus on the New Left's sexism) that activism gave way to a more internally focused approach to change. But even in the 1970s, when most 1960s activists had put some distance between politics and their pursuit of individual self-realization, they understood themselves not as having abandoned the moral quest for a good society, but as contributing to a social transformation—precisely by changing themselves. It was only with the triumph of selfishness in the 1980s that self-realization fully yielded to self-gratification, as many Yuppies left behind the larger moral vision (and even then, the moral claims were not renounced, but only put aside as "unrealistic for the 1980s"). Moral vision, far from being a "soft issue," is potentially the guts of American politics.

When moral concerns do sometimes play second-fiddle in politics, it's usually not because they yield to hard-boiled pragmatics and economics, but rather to personal pain that so grips our consciousness that we have trouble hearing our own inner moral voice. When people feel badly

---

[*] We do not want to substitute a politics of emotion for a politics of rationality. In the long run, the great strength of the liberal and progressive forces is their ability to provide a rational account of the world, and to increase the total rationality in the world. It is precisely because—and to the extent that—we speak the truth about the world that people have grounds to trust us. But we have been narrow in the focus of our rational thinking and have failed to address the rational foundations for people's emotional pain. Conversely, their pain has kept them from hearing the rational content of many of our ideas. To shift toward a focus on emotional life, then, is not a shift towards a primacy of feeling over intellect, but to a focus on using our intellectual strengths to give us guidance on how to repair the emotional damage created by our social order.

about themselves, when their lives seem to be confusing or meaningless, when they see themselves as "bad" or as "failures," it is hard for them to think in moral terms. This is why the term compassion as used by Democrats often has so little appeal. The people hearing this term feel that the Democrats are saying to them: "Don't worry about your own pain—there is someone else who is really in bad shape, and you are being selfish to worry about yourself." People resent that message. They don't intend to be selfish. Often, they feel that their own situation is not understood, and they resent that someone better off (a liberal Democrat who obviously doesn't know about the pains the rest of the people are experiencing) is telling them to pay attention to people who are worse off than themselves. When this resentment becomes strong, moral intuitions begin to cloud and childhood feelings of helplessness and need lead people to accept political views and follow political leaders they might otherwise dismiss, leaders who *seem* to affirm them and recognize their pain.

By ignoring these two central dimensions—the psychological pain of daily life and the deep need for a moral universe—liberal Democrats often put themselves in a strange kind of political isolation. They can sometimes win elections despite themselves—but they never perceive themselves as having a strong enough mandate to legislate adequately funded, comprehensive and coherent programs.

What they consistently fail to win is a deep level of trust. By staying away from the psychological and moral needs of their constituents they create a powerful barrier to ever getting the kind of support they need to make a lasting political contribution.

Nowhere is the centrality of these concerns more evident than in the fate of the Labor Movement and the women's movement. The labor movement is the purest embodiment of the externality fallacy. The economic reductionists who run the AFL-CIO have bet the future of the labor movement on the assumption that what all workers care about is bread-and-butter issues. The emotional detachment of union members from their own unions, the cynicism they express about their leaders, and the lack of interest in union meetings is largely a result of defining unions as a place to get benefits and due process when management acts against negotiated work rules. But the guts of the work process, the stress that people experience each day at the workplace, their lack of opportunity to use their intelligence and creativity, the lack of respect with which they are treated, the absence of workplace democracy—in short, everything that causes the daily experience of pain at work—these are all ignored as somehow "subjective" issues that supposedly the membership doesn't care about.

The women's movement burst onto the political scene in the late 1960s and early 1970s with a moral vision and psychological acuity that quickly commanded the attention of the American people. Based in consciousness raising groups, addressing the daily experience of people caught in the vice of sexist assumptions and practices, the feminists spoke with a moral authority and emotional depth that no one could ignore. Understandably, many women wanted to channel the incredible energy unleashed in this process into achieving concrete changes in political and economic realities.

Unfortunately, women too quickly traded "consciousness raising" for "hard-nosed" realistic politics. As their strategies became reduced to winning legislative victories, or convincing state legislators to vote for ERA, the connection to personal life began to seem more remote, and fewer and fewer women felt inflamed by the original passion. As legislative victories were won, it became increasingly difficult to pass the feminist torch to a younger generation of women for whom the right to legal equality seemed already given and who had never been challenged to understand the deeper meaning of feminism. By framing politics in narrow external terms, the realists managed to squash the moral fervor and emotional immediacy that had given the women's movement its main power.

"Individual Rights" Consciousness. This is the second element in the liberal paradigm that must be changed. Its core is this: the assumption that the individual exists outside of a complex set of human relationships, as a being apart. Others are seen primarily as potential threats to one's independence and autonomy. In this context, the liberals come forward as the champion of individual rights, protecting us from the external coercion of the state, the community or other individuals. Yet the emphasis on individual rights has important hidden costs.

The focus on the rights of individuals has given the liberals a tremendous credibility—and for good reason. Although the picture of the world painted by this focus is certainly distorted—human beings are fundamentally social and born into families and communities, they depend on each other for survival and cannot flourish without the loving affirmation of others—its original function was to provide a bulwark against a coercive form of communitarianism that was embodied in the feudal order. For thousands of years people lived in traditional or feudal societies in which every aspect of their lives and thinking was prescribed for them by the larger society. For those of us who are several generations removed from any community governed by traditional or feudal norms, it is hard to imagine the pain inflicted upon people who had no exit from arranged marriages, who were continually observed and judged by how much their behavior conformed with the behavioral standards of the community, and who were dominated by religious norms that made them feel guilty about their sexual drives and desires. The liberal rebellion against external compulsion was a breath of fresh air to people who felt themselves suffocating under the demands of family, religion and traditional values. The rights of the individual became the intellectual battle-rams used to smash through repressive legislation, customs, and traditions—and to create an ability to discern our own needs and wants from those induced through societal norms.

Yet the struggle for individual rights created a distorted tilt in liberal politics. First, it misidentified the real problem. Feudal societies were not really communities in any meaningful sense. They were hierarchies in which a small group of people (feudal lords and their allies in the Church or established religious and intellectual elites) used the language of community, family, religion and ethics to impose their private agenda on the rest of society. Liberals struggling against this coercion understandably overreacted, suspecting that every time someone talked about ethical obligation the underlying agenda was manipulation. They were unable to distinguish between the coercive use of institutions by ruling elites, and the appropriate use of notions like "obligation to community" when that community was democratically structured and provided respect and autonomy to its participants. This distinction would have seemed quite irrelevant to those who needed all the energy and moral righteousness they could amass to fight oppressive structures in the past—but it is critically important today when many of the battles against feudalism have actually been won.

Second, the struggle for individual rights, posed as a demand to keep society from making any claims on the individual, led in two different and sometimes contradictory directions. On the one hand, it allowed people to insist that they have the right to define for themselves the kind of life they want to live, with whom and under what conditions. On the other hand, it also was used as a justification for the newly emerging class of merchants, entrepreneurs, manufacturers, and bankers to insist on freedom of the marketplace. To them, individual rights meant their right to create an economic life not subject to interference by societal or ethical norms.

Over the past two hundred years much conflict has resulted from these two alternative manifestations of individual rights. Increasing numbers of individuals have come to realize that their ability to define lives for themselves is very limited if they have to spend most of their waking hours in a world of work that has been shaped by others. Yet, stuck with the commitment to an abstract concept of individual rights, fearing that any relegitimation of communal norms and ethical categories might give the society a mandate to once again dictate standards for personal life, the liberals have been unwilling to act on their correct instinctive belief that there must be some constraints on the power of capitalists to shape American economic life.

When the capitalist economy was in total crisis during the Depression, liberals created programs to alleviate the worst suffering generated by the system—but they did so not in the name of new values, but rather in the name of strengthening the system of individual freedoms, including the freedom of the marketplace. Ultimately, this has left the liberals unable to justify continued interference with the prerogatives of capital once the most serious elements of an economic crisis have abated. Unless they can develop a notion of ethical obligations to the community, liberals will always seem to be on the defensive when they advocate limitations on the rights of individual entrepreneurs while simultaneously proclaiming their highest value as the rights of the individual.

There are deeper problems caused by the view that the world is constituted of abstract entities called "citizens" who hold "rights." Once we begin to abstract from the concrete social and economic realities within which people really live, we fall easy prey to the mythology of meritocracy. The actual inequalities of wealth and power disappear, and once again we are faced with a picture of reality in which we have only ourselves to blame for not having fulfilling jobs and satisfying personal lives. If the individual is the core of reality, it is the individual we ultimately blame when satisfaction has not been achieved.

The deepest problem with individual rights consciousness is that this focus shapes human beings whose hallmark is their isolation from others. Liberals have fostered a world view in which individuals see themselves as isolated beings who enter into relationships with others on a contractual basis aimed at increasing individual satisfactions.

The picture itself is severely flawed. No human being is "self-made." Not only does everyone go through a long childhood nurtured by family or family-surrogates, but these families themselves stand in a rich web of social relationships which make it possible for them to provide the nurturance and support we need to develop. No matter how much of a "loner" any individual eventually becomes, s/he inevitably draws upon the linguistic, cultural and scientific legacies from previous generations. Even more important is this: Every human being has a fundamental desire to be recognized, desired and needed by others. It is an ontological necessity of being human that we be confirmed, seen, experienced, and loved. We are deeply rooted in a social history—yet the philosophy of individualism encourages us to think of ourselves as alone and separate from others, owing them nothing, and entitled to get what we can for ourselves even at the expense of others.

This focus on individual rights distorts human relationships. The logic of love is different from the logic of rights. Families are held together not by reciprocal exchange between independent contractors, but by cross-generational love. Parents' giving to their children is not and cannot be reciprocated by children who feel under some contractual obligation to repay what has been given them. Loving relationships between people are undermined to the extent that they become dominated by a bookkeeping of equal exchange. If relationships are seen primarily in terms of contracts between individuals out to maximize their own benefits, then very quickly we get to the current situation: a marketplace in relationships in which people are encouraged to discard the "old model" and find someone new the moment difficulties emerge. It is precisely this thinking which accelerates the contemporary crisis of the family.

In fact, what gets called the crisis in the family is actually a crisis in all human relationships. If everyone views relationships primarily from the standpoint of what s/he can get out of other people, then all relationships become much more problematic. This is why divorce statistics tend to underestimate the scope of the contemporary problem: even families which do stay together experience the growing sense of insecurity generated by a society in which everyone is taught to see affective ties as instrumental to achieving personal goals. Nor is the impact of this crisis confined to families: the growing sense that friendships "aren't what they used to be," that it is harder to establish and maintain deep loyalty and connectedness between friends, is not just a romanticizing of "good old days." These difficulties are, in part, generated by a society which encourages a level of selfishness and self-centeredness, parading under the banner of "individual rights," that makes deep friendship seem naive and foolish.

Is it any wonder, then, that many Americans, deeply aware of the emotional pains in their daily life, are unattracted to the liberals (even when they agree with many specifics of liberal programs)? On the one hand, the liberals seem unwilling to address the emotional and moral issues that are central to human needs. On the other hand, the liberals seem to advocate a way of looking at the world that reinforces self-blaming and undermines love and caring. For these fundamental reasons, anyone who is concerned about the political fate of the liberal forces in the U.S. has a deep stake in the liberals adopting a new political paradigm.

The irony in the plight of the liberals is that they have allowed themselves to become the fall guys for problems that they did not really create. The conservatives, positioning themselves as the champions of the family, traditional values, and obligation to community, have been able to hold the moral high ground only because the liberals have failed to take these issues seriously enough and have pursued instead a politics framed by a focus on the externals of politics. If liberals were to address the emotional crisis of self-blaming in daily life, the decline in moral vision, and the limitations of a philosophy of individualism, they could turn the tide in American politics.

The reason that liberals could change the picture is this: the basic problems we have been addressing are not the result of liberal ideas, but of social and economic realities that the conservatives are committed to defending. Let us consider, for example, the crisis in relationships that is often described as "the breakdown of the family."

Human relationships depend on trust, caring, and the ability to give to the other. These are not the personality traits fostered by our economic system. The "successful" American spends much of his/her day manipulating and controlling others. In a previous generation these were activities reserved primarily for the businessman and sales person. But today, being a successful manipulator of others is increasingly the ticket to success in all aspects of corporate life, in large government bureaucracies, even in academia. Moreover, in the past the goal was to sell a product. Today each person must increasingly view herself or himself as the product to be sold—and the task is to shape oneself to have the appropriate personality, appearance, education, even "psychological awareness" to make oneself an attractive commodity, the kind of person who will be rewarded with promotions, clients, or customers. People, then, must learn to manipulate others, and even to manipulate themselves—always with a view to how the abstract "other" will see them. But people who spend all day manipulating and controlling others eventually form personality structures that are narcissistic and removed from real feelings. They have no idea of who they are apart from what vision "will sell"—and so they are in no position to enter into intimate relationships. It's not so much that they are hiding themselves as that they increasingly have no contact with their inner core—so they have no way of opening it to others. On the surface they may be successful—but it is hard for them to keep in touch with anything deeper within themselves, much less to share that with others.

More than anything, it is the development of this kind of personality that undermines relationships, families, and friendships. Yet this is not a personal problem of a few "troubled" individuals—this is a major social reality that has increasingly dominated American life in the past several decades and threatens to grow worse. Precisely as we become a society less dependent on traditional manufacturing and more oriented towards information and service, these kinds of personality traits become generalized (in fact, even those who don't actually use them in their work see this way as being the strategy to success, and study various self-help books or take courses in self-improvement so that they can become more like the people who are actually "making it"). To the extent that this kind of personality takes root, friendship and loyalty, trust and commitment become harder to attain.

This is why no short-term "family programs" will ultimately work—because the problem is to create a society that fosters a different kind of personality, a personality that builds on trust, caring and the ability to give to others. That may take changes beyond the scope of any short-term program liberal Democrats are willing to propose at this point. But, nevertheless, simply articulating this analysis, helping people understand that the problems in their relationships are rooted in the way we are forced to succeed in the world of work can itself be an important contribution. Imagine if the Democratic party were to talk about the way that the world of work encourages people to act in ways that undermine our ability to love. Or imagine them addressing unmarried people about the problems of building lasting relationships with those who have to spend all day manipulating others. Imagine the Democrats talking about why it becomes hard, given the competitive thrust of economic life, for people to trust each other and build lasting commitments. Talking in these kinds of terms would help many understand the social context to their individual lives and families, would undermine self-blaming, and would provide a message of compassion that was at once true and nourishing.

Precisely because we need to foster personality structures that are open, loving and caring we must reject the philosophy of selfishness that guides conservatives in their dealings with the poor. A society that preaches miserly conduct to the disadvantaged, that makes the poor feel ashamed of their poverty and encourages its middle classes to feel ripped off to the extent that public funds are used to solve problems of the poor, is a society that will foster human beings who do not understand generosity of the heart. It is this way of thinking, encouraged by the political conservatives, that strengthens the character traits most destructive to friendships and family life. People begin to measure out every act of love and kindness—demanding an immediate return on their investment. Grown children no longer respond to the needs of their aging parents—after all, what's in it for them? The very essence of friendship—spontaneous giving to the other—begins to seem like naive foolishness. The way that we learn to treat others in the larger society, then, encourages a spirit of selfishness that fits well into the dynamics of a capitalist marketplace—but that simultaneously weakens our ability to have real friendships and commitments.

Apart from fostering a personality structure that is destructive to loving relationships, our economic and social arrangements, manifested in the world of work, play a more immediate role in undermining family life. The vast majority of Americans face work situations in which they are unable to use their intelligence, creativity and ability to cooperate with each other. Absent any significant control of this fundamental dimension of their life, they increasingly experience work as stressful—and this seemingly "merely subjective" valuation of their work has corresponded to a dramatic increase in stress-related physical health problems. Typically, stress is greatly intensified by self-blame. Rather than demand changes in their working conditions, most workers have bought into the ideology of the meritocracy. Although they know that their working conditions are fundamentally stressful, they believe it is their own fault for having this kind of stressful job. Most Americans nurture a story of self-blame that goes something like this: "If only I had been smarter, worked harder, made different choices or had been more attractive physically or more charming or had a better personality, or in some other way been different than I am, I wouldn't have this stressful job. So I have only myself to blame for my situation."

While inducing this way of thinking may be very useful for the conservatives—after all, their justification for the vast inequalities of wealth and power in the society rests on convincing everyone else that they only deserve what they have actually received—it is extremely destructive to family life. People return home from work not only stressed from their powerlessness, but also feeling terrible for having this kind of work. Instead of feeling angry at the situation and energized to change it, they feel angry at themselves (and discouraged about who they are as persons). The shame of not having "made it" into more fulfilling work—no matter what their actual level of achievement—

causes great pain; and many people spend their time at home frenetically seeking ways to drown that anger they feel towards themselves.

The methods vary. For some, the pain of internalized anger and self-blaming can best be attenuated by alcohol or drugs or watching television (particularly shows that are not real enough to remind one of these painful emotions). For others, frenetic participation in sports, aerobics, exercise, politics, religion, or social life (activities that may be valuable in themselves—but which get pursued in a frenetic manner when they are used as an escape from the pain of the world of work) may do the job. But whatever avenue is pursued, the person who feels the need to drown her/his pain is to that extent blocked from participating in the kind of openness and sharing that strong intimate relationships require. So family life becomes increasingly emotionally sterile. To share one's feelings in this case would be to share feelings of anger and shame and self-blame. Most people feel sure that sharing these kinds of feelings would only diminish them in the eyes of their family—the one place where they still have hopes of receiving the kind of respect that is so frequently absent in the world of work. So they do everything they can to "make things nice" by staying away from their real feelings and projecting a veneer of "everything is fine." Over time, they may become so efficient at this that they themselves have little direct contact with these underlying feelings. The emotional emptiness that many people report experiencing in family life is a predictable consequence.

In many families the underlying anger pushes its way through somehow—sometimes in an unexpected edge of coldness or hostility, sometimes in overt bursts of anger, usually inappropriately displaced onto spouse or children. Yet people rarely understand the coldness, the hostility, or the outbursts of anger as the legacy of the world of work. Instead, they see these feelings as coming from nowhere— "out of the blue"—and this makes them even more scary, leading the self-blamers to work harder to repress their feelings. But a person working hard to suppress her/his feelings is a very poor candidate for a lasting and loving relationship. So either the relationships blow up and dissolve, or people end up settling for family life that is superficial and devoid of real contact and feeling.

We may not expect an immediate transformation in the world of work that totally eliminates these dynamics. But if liberals begin to talk about the pain in family life in terms of the real underlying issues that make relationships so much harder to sustain they will both help in reducing the self-blaming and find that people begin to believe them when they say they are pro-family. Talking at this level will also quickly expose the shallowness and fundamental opportunism in the conservative's attempt to portray themselves as pro-family.

A similar kind of analysis could also show that the breakdown of communities and of moral values was more a product of the workings of the capitalist marketplace than conservatives have been willing to face. If people are spending all day long involved in economic relationships of exploitation, manipulation, and the subordination of ethics to profit, they will develop personality structures that have no place for ethical imperatives in their personal life. To strengthen America's moral fibre, we need to create an economic life that daily reinforces our desire to treat other people as ultimately valuable subjects—not as enemies with whom we must compete.

The liberal forces within the Democratic party should take the leadership in forging a new direction for the party: a direction that focuses on the central issue of creating a society that promotes rather than undermines love, friendship, community and moral values. It is precisely the liberals who should insist on reframing the political dialogue within the Democratic party, insisting on the priority of ethical vision and a commitment to dealing with the emotional needs of the American people.

The dominant paradigm for liberal politics should be the fostering of loving relationships within a morally strong community. The most important contribution they can make is to popularize an analysis of these problems that helps decrease self-blaming and increase compassion. Programs and legislation should be justified in these terms, public statements focused on these issues, and campaigns run on these themes.

Here are some of the concrete steps that must be taken:

1. Liberals should create a new national organization or coalition of existing organizations—perhaps we could call it Friends of the Family—that would articulate a pro-family agenda for the liberal world and would act as a public vehicle through which liberals in the Democratic party and outside it could work together to promote a pro-family politics.

2. Liberals in Congress in both parties should meet together and foster a pro-family legislative focus. Unlike Reagan and the right wing pro-family rhetoric, a liberal program would be based on the kind of analysis articulated above and giving particular focus to the way that the world of work and the psychodynamics of self-blaming undermined family life. Among the kinds of legislative issues to be considered would be: a.) mandating workplaces to allow the creation of workplace safety and health committees elected by the workers and empowered to force changes in the conditions of work, so as to promote greater opportunity for workers to cooperate with each other, use their own intelligence and creativity, and participate in decision-making both in their own shops and in the larger decisions of the enterprise in which they work; b.) supplemental parental financial supports during the first seven years of a child's life—both to relieve the burdens of families with incomes under $70,000 a year, and to communicate the message that even those who do not have children should bear some of the cost for those who take on the valued role of raising the next generation; c.) mandating that workplaces provide extra sick days for children's illnesses, and extra leniency for tardiness when family emergencies intrude into daily life; d.) requiring workplaces to provide fully paid paternity and maternity leaves for six months; e.) creating a well-funded nationwide network of community-controlled childcare centers based on a voucher system, so that parents could choose a model that fits their own ethical, emotional and religious beliefs, and funding communities to train childcare workers in programs shaped to meet the local communities' own needs; f.) a voucher system for supplemental support to the dependent elderly which they could use within either their own, their family's or well-financed community homes, hence giving many grown children the ability to afford to keep their parents in the home without fear of resulting financial destitution, while giving to the parents the financial security to be able to make the choice as to where to live their senior years.

Because these are practical, "external" programs it should be emphasized that these are only examples of steps that can be taken to build a pro-family reality. Congressional liberals must be careful to not reduce the focus to one of simple legislative remedies, but to talk to the underlying emotional realities. Liberals would do more to solve the problems in family life if they help people understand that these are shared and not just individual problems, problems that are rooted in the way we have built our competitive and self-interested society. If liberals dedicate time, money and energy to a serious campaign that attempts to undermine self-blaming and build compassion, to nurture ethical vision and promote real communities of caring—they will earn the respect and gratitude of the American people in a much deeper way than if all they do is to pass a few good pieces of legislation.

3. Together with liberals in state legislatures and city councils, Congressional liberals should promote the creation of local hearings in every neighborhood, where people can begin to discuss the real problems they are facing in daily life—with particular focus on the relationship between work and family life. Congressional hearings can highlight these activities, but liberals on the local level must be prepared to carry through and sustain on-going hearings aimed at helping people define for themselves what the shared problems are in family life, the world of work, and other aspects of daily life. The goal here is not simply to generate legislative remedies, though this can be one aspect;

the message must be one which emphasizes the activity of local communities as well, one that focuses on the ways people can provide support for each other, learn from each others' experiences, and together build family support systems in their own communities. Most importantly, these local activities should increase awareness of the commonality of family problems and of the ways that our shared pains are themselves in part a product of a social order that promotes selfishness instead of love.

4. No one will take seriously a pro-family shift by the liberals unless this move is done not as a momentary flurry to win an election but as part of a serious rethinking of liberal values. The Democrats should sponsor community forums and public discussions aimed at stimulating that discourse. They should challenge the popular notion, enshrined in pop psychology and liberal ideology, that the healthy person is the isolated person who has learned to be autonomous and not dependent on others, the person who can stand alone, facing the world as the courageous individual who, if s/he fancies, may connect with others.[*] We should instead insist that ontological priority goes to the human being in relationship to others, and that the very essence of being human is to be in relationship. The healthy human being is one who can allow him/herself to be vulnerable to others and who is not afraid of being in need and mutually interdependent with the human community, as long as that community is based on democracy and mutuality of respect. The liberals should create think-tanks and teach-ins, promote journals and magazines and use the media to help develop this kind of understanding.

It is easy to understand why Democrats and liberals will find this kind of advice somewhat difficult to accept in the Spring of 1987. The punctures in the Reagan balloon appear so critical that they may bring down any Republican candidate in 1988—and this thinking may lead Democrats to feel that they shouldn't rock the boat by pursuing new directions. But precisely because electoral victory may be more likely in 1988 it is important that Democrats attempt to use the opportunity to get a real mandate for a liberal program, and not just be forced into continuing Reaganism under a different name. It is particularly critical for liberals to seize this opportunity, because now they can speak to the American people with a moral authority that they had previously squandered under Carter. Yet if all that they offer is more of the same, they may only succeed in recrediting the politics that Reagan's moral blunders in Iran and Nicaragua have temporarily put into question with the majority of the American people. If ever there was a time for a new vision of politics, this is the moment. The liberals can succeed in creating a new agenda and a new balance in American politics. To do so now requires the kind of serious rethinking of fundamentals that has been described herein.   □

---

[*] Two caveats: First, liberals will rightly resist any attempt to define one "correct" model of family life, and insist that gay families and alternative families, insofar as they represent freely chosen alternatives and not simply accomodations to a bad reality, also deserve our respect. Second, we will resist any attempt to presure people to enter relationships to be socially acceptable, or to stay in bad relationships that cannot be improved. Love requires choice, and we must create support systems for singles and for people leaving relationships, so that when people do enter families they do so not through subtle societal manipulations, but as a reult of real loving choices. It is because we are pro-family that we must strongly resist any societal messages that put people down for being single or suggest that people are wrong to get divorced.

Yet we also reject any notion that being in a long-term loving relationship is just one possible choice among many equally valuable lifestyles. Huamn beings fundamentally need and are most fully realized within such relationships, and while we should avoid stigmatizing those who have not found them, we should see that the difficulty in finding and sustaining these relationships is one of the great indictments of our form of social organization.

The Legacy of the Sixties for the Politics of the Nineties

Michael Lerner

The specific way that the movements of the 1960s defeated themselves has much to teach us about the politics of the 1990s and beyond. These movements, particularly those dominated by the New Left, ate themselves alive! New Leftists were unable to accept their own or anyone else's limitations, and ultimately rejected their own accomplishments as useless or even destructive. In a frenzy of self-doubt and self-denigration, they were unable to see the value of what they already had accomplished. Instead, New Leftists immersed themselves in reckless attacks on each other for not being adequate manifestations of the ideals that they professed to share, thereby undermining the kind of trust and mutual confidence that is the cornerstone of any social movement.

Analyzing the collapse of the sixties has great contemporary political importance—it is not an exercise in historical nostalgia. Liberal Democrats, Presidential candidates, and social change movements of all stripes often face unconscious resistance by many Americans who, though they agree with specific political or economic programs of the Left, have a lingering distrust for those whom they associate with the movements of the sixties. To overcome this resistance, we must understand more fully how a social movement dedicated to bring "power to the people" could be seen as such a threat. Similarly, the hundreds of thousands of people who quit the social change movements in the period 1970–1974, often made that choice for good reasons, not because of narrow self-interest or lack of idealism, but because of their unsatisfying experiences within those movements. Though their current lives may be focused on securing career and family (and are therefore unfairly demeaned as "yuppies"), many of those "baby boomers" remain committed to the same values that inspired them in the sixties. Potentially, they remain a force that could play a major role in liberal and progressive politics in the 1990s. Though many maintain their own personal idealism, only political movements and leaders who understand the dynamics that turned them off to politics could ever succeed in mobilizing them.

Any analysis of the failures of left-wing activists of the 1960s must be pursued with great caution. It is true that the Left was unable to fulfill its dream of radically transforming humanity. Nevertheless, the movement played a tremendous role in ending the war in Vietnam and combatting the racism and sexism that pervade American society. The constraints on President Reagan's abilities to make war in Central America, the pressures that have pushed him to agree to a partial nuclear disarmament agreement, and the adoption by Congress of anti-apartheid legislation have all been the products of political movements whose current power derives from the changes in political awareness that the New Left generated in the sixties. It is fair to say that, despite the difficulties that still plague America, we live in a much better world thanks to the political activism of the New Left.

This editorial appeared in Tikkun, *January/February 1988.*

It is all the more important, therefore, to understand how the New Left self-destructed as a major force in American political life.

Yet an honest discussion of the way that the New Left self-destructed has been blocked by many who have a vested interest in obscuring the ways that New Leftists contributed to their own defeat. The tens of thousands who never quit find it difficult to acknowledge that they created a movement that turned off hundreds of thousands of others who were equally committed to social change. It's far easier to denigrate the commitment of those who quit, to suggest that they were in the movement only because it was popular or fun, or because of some narrow self-interest like avoiding the draft or to find support for their desire to experiment with alternatives to the dominant sexual and cultural mores of the society. Then there are the former-activist academics who may still be feeling some guilt at having put their primary energy into pursuing their careers at the point in the 1970s when their own intelligence and creativity might have been used to create organizational and intellectual alternatives. Conveniently, they hold on to various inevitability theories that purport to find some set of "objective conditions" that necessarily led to the collapse of the sixties—and all that any rational person could do, then, was to passively look on and observe as these objective conditions worked themselves out on the historical stage. Finally, there are many activists in today's movements, particularly the anti-intervention, anti-nuclear, and anti-apartheid movements, who show surprisingly little interest in learning from the experience of those who have gone before them— perhaps anticipating that they will experience a shock of recognition in the stories that they would likely hear about the debilitating impact on the New Left of the very "anti-leadership" and "anti-national organization" tendencies that are the hallmark of many left movements of the late 1980s. Ironically, the newer generations of activists purport to have "learned the lessons of the sixties" when they are actually completely copying the most self-destructive aspects of the New Left!

Of course, it would be unfair to think that the problems of the New Left were somehow unique to it. On the contrary, the most destructive elements in its thinking were direct products of the larger society in which leftists grew up—the New Left imaginatively appropriated and reshaped to its own historical circumstances individualist currents in American ideology that have played a decisive role in containing and subverting most of the important social change movements of this century. So let us start our enquiry by reminding ourselves of a myth that is taught over and over again by every institution in American life: that we live in a society in which anyone can become anything s/he wants if s/he really tries hard enough and has enough dedication and wholeness of heart. It is this "fact" which is supposed to make our society "fair." If anyone can be anything that she or he wants, given enough good intention and hard work, then what we actually do end up with is a product of our own actions. We have no one but ourselves to blame for what we have achieved in our lives. It is up to us as individuals to make our world in any way that we choose. This is thought to be the basic ground rule for America, its central self-justificatory fantasy. To some degree virtually everyone growing up in this society comes to believe some version of this idea—and to blame themselves, usually quite unfairly, for not having "made for themselves" a more fulfilling world.

New Leftists knew that there was something fundamentally unfair about the way rewards were allocated in American society. As successors to the liberal Democrats who had fashioned the New Deal, they understood that many people had been "left out" of the general prosperity, and that this was unfair. They went on to develop theories to explain the role of ruling elites of wealth and power. Yet it never occurred to them to question the deeper individualistic assumptions that pervaded American thought, particularly the notion that human beings could by acts of will make themselves into whoever they wanted to be. Having little or no appreciation of the ways that their own psychological and social conditioning might constrain the amount of change or transcendence that could reasonably be expected of any individual, the movement bought the assumption that it could shape a brand new human being in one generation through conscious acts of will. And when New Leftists failed to become the living embodiment of their own ideals, the movement became paralyzed with self-doubt and self-blame.

The possibility of radically reshaping themselves and the world through conscious acts of moral commitment was the central energizing fantasy of the New Left. New Leftists inherited a world that seemed populated by a wide variety of failed social transformers: Soviet Communists and their American supporters, who had seen the moral vision of socialist egalitarianism transformed into the Stalinist nightmare of political oppression and intellectual rigidity; American liberals, who had bought the benefits of a welfare state at the cost of an unprincipled alliance with militarists whose ultimate expression was the war in Vietnam; labor union activists, who had secured economic benefits for their membership by depoliticizing their members and emphasizing cooperation with multinational corporations that were systematically destroying the planet's environment; and university professors who had been radical in their youth but now taught that fundamental social change was either unnecessary or impossible. New Leftists were forced to confront the possibility of being corrupted in the same way that these earlier activists had been.

It was obvious to New Leftists that they could not rely on the Old Left's strategy of "We will change the society, and then the new society will create a new kind of human being." The failures of the Old Left made it all too clear that such a plan would fail because people who are flawed in the old ways will never create a new society. So the New Left took the opposite tack: "We will change ourselves, and then we ourselves will be the guarantors of the future society." But, having disregarded the ways a social order and past psychological conditioning restrain the level of change, New Leftists believed that the process of change would simply be a matter of will and moral seriousness. They insisted that their movement be, at that present moment, the living embodiment of the ideals they sought to bring into existence in the future. The guarantor of the future must be the present: the movement shall be now, in the daily lives and activities of its participants, the actualization of the society that eventually would be built. And if it must be now, there is no time to go through the process, no time for people to be supported as they gradually move through stages along the way. Rather, if it is all a question of will and commitment, then the defects will be remedied instantly—or not at all. Almost immediately, movement people began to judge themselves and each other in terms of how much they lived up to the ideals of the future, how worthy they really were. It was only a short step to an intense self-blaming, as they failed to live up to their own highest values.

It is true that the demands that New Leftists imposed on themselves produced moments of great heroism and remarkable personal transformations. Many people reached heights of courage and self-understanding that they had never dreamt possible. But all too quickly they began to burn out. Unlike previous generations of political organizers, many of whom had been involved in political movements for decades, New Leftists were unable to sustain the level of intensity that they demanded of themselves, and as a result, people began to drop out of active participation after a few years. They, in turn, were replaced with ever-expanding numbers of new recruits in the mid- and late sixties, who joined the fray by finding new and imaginative ways to raise the ante of acceptable demands on themselves and each other.

Little thought was given to how people with families or jobs might be able to participate in the movement. To ensure, for example, that the antidemocratic tendencies of the Old Left were avoided, New Leftists frequently insisted on achieving consensus on its decisions—a process that often lasted late into the night. Only those with neither job nor family could stick it through. The plausible alternative—having tightly structured agendas that restricted the number of speakers and granted time for deliberation on issues, deciding issues of principle and then empowering a democratically elected leadership to make important implementing decisions—this seemed less democratic than having endless meetings at which everything could be decided by some kind of consensus. So, in the name of being democratic, New Leftists effectively excluded from the movement those whose lives were filled with other real-world commitments, such as raising children or making livings. Is it any wonder that some people wondered exactly who the New Left had in mind when they talked about "power to the people"? And if this was living the values of the future in the present, those who imagined that life as a nonstop political meeting might not be so much fun began to question whether they really wanted to buy into a New Left future.

Living the values of the future in the present led to another distortion—a crude leveling that manifested itself in anti-intellectualism and antileadership. Intellectual activity was often seen as a form of elitism—after all, if everyone is to be treated equally, everyone's insights must be equally valid. As a result, New Leftists embraced the assumption that the only ideas worthy of serious consideration were those based on feelings. Since everyone's feelings were equally deserving of respect, and since truly vital ideas were based on deep feelings and passion, all ideas were equally worthy of attention. In such a climate, sustained intellectual activity was seen as, at best, an inauthentic way to spend time, and, at worst, dangerous. It followed, then, that anyone could become a leader, and that the main problem was to control the egos of some who thought that their previous experiences entitled them to a greater say in the current plan. A cult of antileadership emerged that effectively prevented New Leftists from learning from their own accumulated experiences. In the mid-1960s the main New Left organization, Students for a Democratic Society (SDS), adopted the policy of allowing its top leadership to remain in that position for only one year. By the late 1960s, in New Left organizations it was not unusual to hear people who had been in positions of local leadership for six months maligned as "the old leadership."

This very cult of antileadership forced those who wished to lead to seek other ways of achieving influence. Though some were undoubtedly driven by self-serving egotism, many were concerned that the movement needed someone to refute the lies being articulated by pro-war government spokesmen that were then broadcast as "truth" by the media. Hoping to influence events and seeing no alternative leadership that was officially sanctioned by the movement, some activists sought media attention to make their perspectives known. Yet most New Leftists interpreted their activities as motivated *solely* by a desire for ego-gratification and power.

The New Left assumed that ego needs are fundamentally illegitimate. By failing to acknowledge that ego motives are inevitable, and particularly acute in capitalist societies, the New Left wasted the opportunity to harness those needs to the goals of the movement (an insight they might have learned from the Jewish tradition of insistence that one serve God with all one's inclinations, including the *yetzer ha-ra* or "evil inclination."). Needless to say, it didn't take long for most New Leftists to discover that they themselves were "impure" (surprise of surprises: they too had ego motives). But instead of accepting this as inevitable and making room for the reality, New Leftists felt terrible about themselves and were determined to purge themselves of these imperfections.

Given these dynamics, New Leftists were easy targets for the crudest forms of manipulation. Whoever was willing to be the most militant in any situation seemed to be indicating that s/he was making a more serious commitment than others. The holier-than-thou dynamics that plague almost every political, religious, or moral movement were even more out of control in a movement that had no sense of external constraint. Considerable evidence now shows that the F.B.I. and state agencies manipulated this dynamic by sending undercover agents into New Left groups to encourage extreme actions designed to discredit the movement. The climate of mutual recrimination facilitated the success not only of agents provocateurs but of baiting by members of "oppressed groups"—the supposition being that because they were more oppressed, they were wiser, or that since the

Photo by Denise Poncher

dominant group had never allowed itself to be led by the oppressed, it was necessary to grant leadership to any member of an oppressed group regardless of their wisdom. After all, any judgment of the abilities of the oppressed was subject to prejudice. Here self-blame took one more decisive step forward: Not only were people to blame for not having changed themselves enough, they were to blame for being white or male or born into middle-class families. If their very essence was deserving of blame, nothing would ever be enough.

These destructive dynamics were held at bay as long as movement activists believed that their actions were effective in building public opposition to the Vietnam War. The decisive change came after the election of Nixon in 1968. Starting with a small group in SDS, (the Weathermen) and extending to larger and larger groups of New Left activists, a new perception began to spread: nothing had been accomplished through years of peaceful protest—the movement had been a failure. Though the Weathermen pushed this idea with the hope of generating a higher level of militancy and commitment, the U.S. government pursued the same idea with the hope of discouraging further radical activity. Nixon and his entourage firmly believed that the war had to be ended, but they were deeply committed to ending the war on terms that would give neither credit to the antiwar movement nor encouragement to political activists. The Nixon White House consciously set about a double-pronged strategy: on the one hand, massive disruptions of left organizations and overt repression of the leadership, and, on the other hand, a carefully crafted public denial that any attention was being given to the antiwar movement or its demands. Since the war seemed to be continuing and the level of repression increasing, many New Leftists began to doubt that their activity was accomplishing very much. Once that perception became widespread, there no longer existed an external constraint on the tendency towards self-doubt and self-blame.

In the absence of a belief that their activity was stopping the war, claiming adequacy as a movement would have required claiming that New Leftists were making essential and dramatic changes in their own lives, changes that could achieve the goal of actualizing the future in the present; and such claims required more chutzpah than anyone had. And, if the very legitimacy of the movement depended on its ability to embody a different kind of consciousness and spirit than mainstream culture, how could one justify continuing that movement—if it could be shown to be riddled with racism, elitism, sexism, and so forth?

The emerging women's movement of the late 1960s and early 1970s was decisive in this process. The analysis of sexism was so patently correct and important that it raised serious doubts about the legitimacy of many of the then-current political struggles. If the New Left itself was infused with sexist practices and sexist men, how could it possibly hope to be an embodiment of the future society? And if the movement was sexist, why should one risk going to jail on its behalf?

A rational response would have been to acknowledge the women's movement's critique of sexism in the New Left and to understand that people in any political movement, socialized in the larger sexist society, would inevitably have deep sexist distortions. Such an approach would have encouraged women to articulate their anger about sexism and would have recognized that the small-group discussions by which women were coming to link the pain in their personal lives with the larger social reality were a prototype for a new and far more revolutionary politics. It also might have encouraged men to engage in a profound reevaluation of their sexism without making them feel so defensive and worthless that they would run for cover (at times using the intensity of women's attacks as an excuse to avoid really confronting the truths of the feminist perspective). Instead, there was a new frenzy of people bashing each other and themselves. Many people simply quit New Left politics altogether in the early 1970s, using the critique of their own sexism as an excuse to "work on their own heads." And, although many women moved into feminist activity and carried on the social activism of the New Left, a great number of others retreated from politics, overwhelmed with disappointment when they saw their male comrades as sexist and untrustworthy.

There have been some attempts by neo-conservatives and former lefties having "second thoughts" to blame New Left failures on its alleged softness on communism. There were, to be sure, thousands of activists at the end of the sixties who became born-again worshippers of Third World revolutionaries. They tended to be the people who were most adept at grabbing publicity (it was "good TV" for the evening news to show demonstrators carrying NLF flags), and those who were best at intimidating others about their "lack of commitment." Yet these antics were just one of the many ways that New Leftists flailed about trying to find identities that would heal the pain of their growing conviction that they had failed to live up to their own ideals. That there was a propensity to overlook the faults of Third Worlders, and hence to glorify some of America's "enemies," was more a product of guilt that the U.S. was murdering hundreds of thousands of Vietnamese than a statement of attraction to Vietnamese communism, more a statement of shame about the U.S. role in the Third World than a political ideology for America. The fact is that most New Leftists, to the extent that they allowed themselves to think about ideological issues at all, were largely anti-Marxist, overwhelmingly anti-Soviet, and hostile to the legacy of the Communist party. Their early refusal to go along with demands to exclude communists was partly a healthy sign of the very kind of openness that eventually allowed police agents to infiltrate, and partly a refusal to let the debates of the thirties and fifties set the agenda for the sixties. In fact, the resolute anticommunism of the New Left was consistently attacked by leftist sectarians, who were always scandalized by it. The picture changed only in the late sixties when, overwhelmed by their perception of their own failure, some New Leftists were drawn to the notion that they must learn from the lessons of more successful revolutionaries elsewhere—Ho Chi Minh, Mao, and Fidel. But the strong democratic commitment of the vast majority of New Leftists led them to view those who joined communist sect groups with a mixture of suspicion and derision.

The attempt to attribute the problems of the New Left to "wrong ideas" without understanding the social and psychological dynamics that might lead people to adopt those ideas misses the point: any movement dominated by self-blaming, guilt, and surplus powerlessness may quickly adopt ideas that are far from its original intentions.

There is no doubt that repression, co-optation, and the changing economic situation of the early 1970s accelerated the process of disempowerment, but these factors would have never by themselves have been sufficient to defeat a vibrant movement. The economic crisis of the 1970s may have forced many to take jobs and to have less time for politics, but it also presented what could have been a golden opportunity to extend New Left consciousness into sectors of the society that a student-based movement had been unable to address. In the early 1970s, for instance, I used my position as a national leader in the antiwar movement to advocate that the New Left take up the issue of tax reform long before the Right in California used that as its mechanism to win popular support with the Jarvis-Gann Proposition 13. A tax initiative in California could have been developed that both relieved the pressure on middle-income people and simultaneously insured protection and even expansion of social benefits for the poor. A coherent and confident New Left could have addressed the economic issues created by the contraction of the economy, dramatically expanding its base in the process. In short, there was no inevitability in the New Left's decline. Objective conditions presented opportunities as well as constraints.

Similarly, the ending of the war in Vietnam was not the decisive factor. The New Left emerged as a coherent and powerful political force before the war became a major issue, and its internal collapse occurred before the bombings of Vietnam ended. Even though the ending of the war might explain why the movement no longer mobilized millions of people in mass marches, it cannot explain why hundreds of thousands of activists who focused on changing other aspects of American society dropped out of the movement in the next few years. Even the draft was not decisive for them: the biggest and most militant demonstrations occurred after the draft no longer directly affected the lives of the students and middle-class youth—the bulk of those who continued to protest from 1969 to 1972.

Repression, too, though an important factor, could never have been decisive. The indictments and jailings of leaders coupled with random shooting of demonstrators at Kent State and Jackson State certainly created deep fear. The frequency with which police used excessive force gives the lie to those who now rewrite history to pretend that New Leftists really were on a self-indulgent joyride or living in narcissistic bliss in the sixties. Even though many millions of peace activists only participated in the mass mobilizations in which there was very little personal risk, hundreds of thousands participated in other more militant demonstrations in which they believed (often correctly) that they were at risk of arrest and physical assault. Nevertheless, at an earlier stage, repression had actually enhanced the growth of the movement. It would have continued to do so, had the people inside the movement believed that the risks were worth it. But once they began to question the moral legitimacy of the movement, to doubt whether they were morally acceptable, repression became much more decisive. Why risk jail or permanent physical injury if the movement itself was somehow corrupt, racist, sexist, and elitist?

Some argue that an important reason why people lost faith in the movement was that the inhuman dynamics that I have discussed were themselves produced by police agents who infiltrated the movement. Congressional hearings of the mid–1970s revealed the extensive COINTELPRO program of the FBI, which often effectively disrupted New Left activities. These police and FBI agents helped instigate a climate of violence, both by committing outrageous acts that were attributed to the movement, and by denouncing other movement members for being too wimpy. Similarly, they frequently attacked the most effective leaders, spreading stories about them that reenforced pre-existing beliefs that these people were self-serving, sexist, and elitist. Yet none of this could have succeeded had there not already existed in the movement a basis for the provocateurs' appeal: a deep sense of inadequacy about who people were and what they had done.

The overall impact of these dynamics was to create a war of all against all in the movement. Everyone was suspect. Most people felt under siege; potentially at any moment they would be revealed as inadequate exemplifiers of the values everyone held. From the warmth and solidarity that prevailed in the early 1960s the movement quickly had turned into an arena of ugliness and mutual recrimination. No matter how attracted one might be to its values, the actual experience of being made to feel inadequate and guilty drove people away.

Yet, given the individualist ideology that pervaded the society, those who left the movement often misinterpreted their experience. Instead of realizing that any social movement will necessarily be filled with very imperfect people, and that the very experience of mutual self-blaming and intolerance were manifestations of the way that people had been hurt and weakened by this system, people who quit frequently thought that their experience had taught them about the fundamental bankruptcy of radical politics itself. It was not unusual to hear people declare that they had tried politics and discovered, much to their shock and amazement, that the people in radical politics were just as screwed up as everyone else! Or, as a frequently quoted Pogo comic strip of the time proclaimed, "We have met the enemy—and it is *us!*" Those who quit were still holding on deeply to the same fantasy of total individual transformation that had led the New Leftists to assume that by individual acts of will they could become living exemplars of their vision of the future. Given this interpretation of their experience, it is no surprise that so many of these former activists became involved in various other quests for personal transformation and individual salvation. To the extent that they believed that it was individual inadequacies that produced political distortions, it became a political priority to seek personal change. Some sought to become "perfect, enlightened beings" through various forms of Eastern spirituality; others to become "open and honest" through human potential movement offsprings; others to become "healthy" through psychotherapies, traditional or alternative. As Reichian ideas helped popularize the notion that neurosis might be an ingredient in the body as well, self-transformation led to a new attention to physical health, aerobics, diet, exercise and massage. It may seem only a few short steps from the self-involvement of the 1970s to the rise of "yuppie" self-indulgence in the 1980s, but it is important to recognize that the initial impulse that eventually led many people into self-absorption was often understood by the participants to be an extension of the same quest to make the world a better place that had led them into the New Left.

Many Americans sensed that the New Left held them and their lifestyles in considerable contempt. Although some Marxists within the movement continued to preach the centrality of "reaching the working class," most New Leftists appropriated the class prejudices of the American upper middle class. For example, Weathermen and their followers declared that the war and racism were products not just of a ruling elite, but of the "white skin privilege" of American workers. Counterculturists berated mainstream Americans for participating in the worlds of work and family life, since these were manifestations of the deadness of the larger culture. Some people in the women's movement derided all women who remained in relationships with men as being "male-identified" and selling out their sisters. Virtually everyone who retained a commitment to religion was treated with suspicion. Those of us who were in the movement precisely *because* of our religious commitment to peace and justice and to the sanctity of human life usually kept our metaphysical frameworks in the closet—or else faced marginalization at the hands of most hard-core activists.

The disdain for Americans was based on some real experiences that could strain anyone's compassion—the widespread racism shown by southerners against blacks who sought to achieve civil rights, and the continued willingness of Americans to vote for political candidates who supported appropriations for the war in Vietnam. Yet instead of asking what kinds of social conditioning might have led to this behavior, instead of reminding themselves that only a few years before they themselves had been prisoners of the same conditioning, they dismissed all the not-yet-converted to anti-racist and peace politics as stupid or evil. They would not allow themselves to overlook the areas of political disagreement so that they might hear the pain and frustration in people's lives.

This same lack of compassion reached even more explicit formulation in the folk wisdom of the 1960s "counterculture." If you worked for a living, you were accused of having bought into the system and thus probably an enemy! With deep contempt, Bay Area hippies would revile people driving home from work with shouts of "Work addicts! Shame on you!" Those who sought to build monogamous relationships were seen as possessive and sexually dead. Not only were people who lived traditional lifestyles attacked as "unhip," they were also accused of being the cause of all that was wrong in the world. For many in the counterculture, the problem was not an economic or political system, but the American people themselves. Although at first political New Leftists tended to distance themselves from the counterculturists, by the end of the sixties these countercultural values were increasingly articulated within the heart of New Left political movements, and the popular perception that these two tendencies represented one unified phenomenon increasingly approximated the reality.

Given this disdain for the lives of most people, New Leftists felt they had little to learn from Americans outside the movement. Had they listened with a compassionate ear, New Leftists would have heard that many Americans were raising the same kinds of questions about the ultimate worth of American materialism and the competitive marketplace that motivated many leftists. These Americans used a different language to articulate their concerns: they spoke about the decline of traditional values, the crisis in family life, and the need for a new and more vital spirituality (born-again religion). Rightists saw a golden opportunity here and helped provide people with a conservative vocabulary in which these concerns could be further articulated and linked to a politics that, ironically, supported the very institutions that generated the problems in the first place. Right-wingers succeeded, in part, because no leftists thought it important to enter this terrain with an alternative analysis, and, in part, because the virulent attack on their lifestyle and values from the Left predisposed many Americans to distrust anyone associated with the Left.

It was all too easy, given these attitudes, for a hostile press to portray the New Left as representing a repudiation and denigration of the values and attitudes of the majority of the population, not simply of the ruling elites. It was precisely this theme that enabled Nixon and Agnew to position themselves as battling against left-wing elitists and in favor of "the ordinary American" whose values were under siege. In adopting this stance, the Right took the first steps towards the creation of a populism that would eventually bring them to power in the 1980s. They no longer represented themselves as the champions of the elites of wealth and power, but rather as anti- elitists defending the majority against a vicious and contemptuous assault by a minority. Even in the late 1980s, the continued accusation that the Democrats are controlled by "special interests" derives its power from the legacy of the 1960s, the suspicion that these special interest groups have contempt for the lives of the American majority. Although the women's movement and Black spokespeople can rightfully point out that no one today is making those kinds of contemptuous statements, the popular perception was formed in the early 1970s as a result of real antagonism toward ordinary Americans. Until that image is systematically changed, by the conscious efforts of social change movements to convey a sense of respect for the problems and issues of the majority, any left movement is likely to find itself relatively isolated. Although Americans on the rebound from the Iran/Contra scandal and from the economic failures of the Reagan Administration may elect liberal Democrats in 1988, we may see in the 1990s the persistence of the phenomenon that governed this decade—majorities disagreeing with the Right on the substance of many specific programs, yet trusting these conservative forces because they seem to understand and care for them.

There is only one way that liberals and progressives can change the popular perception of the Left: they must begin to address the real pain that people experience in everyday life, show that they care about those pains, and present ideas about how to deal with the underlying causes. This need not mean the slightest abandoning of the progressive agenda: the fight for equal rights, for an end to militarism and nuclear weapons, for the democratization of the economy and rational economic planning, for a bill of economic rights that ensures employment and health care and housing, for a pro-ecology perspective, and for an end to apartheid cannot be abandoned even temporarily. But in order to be effective in these struggles, the liberal and progressive forces are going to have to overcome the feelings of so many Americans that those on the Left cannot be trusted. And the way to do that is to show that the Left deeply understands and cares about the daily life experiences and concerns of most Americans. Those concerns include the stress people experience at work, the pain in their family lives, the dissolution of ethical values that they see reflected in the behavior of their children, the rampant materialism, the lack of respect for the physical environment, the triumph of individualist values.

The irony is that once we begin to talk about these kinds of issues, it is precisely the Left that is in the best position to understand them and to show how these problems are rooted in the values of a competitive market society. It is the Left that should represent itself as the pro-family movement, because it is the values and operations of a capitalist society, decisively shaping narcissistic personalities ill-suited for loving commitments, that plays a major role in undermining family life. Similarly, it is the materialism and competitive individualism of the capitalist market that are decisive in creating a culture that values money and power over all other goods. Spiritual sensitivity that is so hard to find in this society, sought by many who are attracted to right-wing churches, is systematically undermined by the very institutions that right-wing politicians and ideologies work so hard to sustain! In short, once we take up the pains that people are feeling in daily life, we are in an excellent position to address their concerns in a far more compelling way than the Right can do— and in so doing we are immediately led to raise some of the most radical questions about the structures of our society. So, although a focus on issues like family, spirituality, and ethical values seems to be a step away from the list of traditional liberal/progressive issues, it may actually lead us more quickly to the underlying structural problems than some of the current reformist programs of the Left.

A central focus of the approach I am advocating is to foster a mass psychology of compassion. Liberals and progressives can help people understand that those pains are not their own fault, but the product of a psychological and social legacy that they cannot, at least as lone individuals, hope to change. Stripped of the self-blaming, however, they can be empowered to work with others to actually change at least some of the conditions that prevent them from having more fulfilling lives.

To build a movement that aims to transform the world must necessarily involve the other meanings of the word *tikkun:* to heal and repair. Any movement for social change must have as a central task the healing of those wounds that have made us unable to trust each other. And mutual confidence building, an ability to stay in touch with each other's humanity even as we disagree about specific ideas, strategies, or analyses of the situation, is the key to overcoming surplus powerlessness and building a transformative movement. In that process we will continually face moments in which we disappoint each other. Building compassion may prepare us for those inevitably painful moments. Imagine a movement that not only trained people to do canvassing for a political candidate or a cause, not only prepared people for non-violent action or public speaking, but also insisted that its activists do training around issues like: how to rebuild confidence in a meeting after someone has started to put down others; how to face moments when people act with greater cowardice or self-interest than you would wish; how to uncover the ways that people are unfairly blaming themselves—and how to help them see that more clearly; how to create celebrations of the little victories, so that people give themselves adequate credit for what they have accomplished; how to help sustain commitment through periods when there have been no immediate victories; how to show people in a social movement that they are really being cared for by each other even at moments when the focus is more outward on winning political victories.

Finally, a word more of compassion for the New Left. Given the psychodynamics of American society, it is all too understandable why movement activists would have been imbued with the same kind of individualism and consequent self-blaming as everyone else. Having compassion must, then, include having compassion for ourselves, including compassion for the ways that we are not as compassionate as we ought to be. It is all to easy to imagine a political movement that uses the ideas propounded here and proceeds to recreate a process of people trashing each other—for not being adequately compassionate! Indeed, to the extent that a movement can be seen to embody compassion for its own members and their limitations, to that extent it will be more effective in communicating a similar compassion to those outside it. While my analysis leads me to understand that there will be real constraints on how much we can embody this kind of ideal, it does not prevent me from seeing this as the necessary direction for our collective efforts.

If a spirit of compassion for all those who labor in the vineyards of social change is fundamental, then our reflection on the sixties should also express our deep appreciation for all those who gave part of their lives to the pursuit of moral ideals that remain worthy of our respect. Whatever your faults and weaknesses, we, together, showed that the desire for a morally ordered world continues to be a great hunger of humankind. The task of politics today, then, is to reaffirm our sense of trust in each other, to develop our ability to see through the inevitable defects and disappointments, and to build confidence once again in the possibility of possibility. □

Psychodynamics of the Election: Media Consciousness

Peter Gabel

I t's a mistake to think of the media as some impersonal entity, because it is really a form of consciousness, a way of looking at reality, embodied in tens of thousands of media practitioners and millions of readers or viewers—"the audience." The Democratic National Convention in Atlanta in 1988 helped me see through some of the media mystery.

The physical setup of the convention was a graphic representation of a deeper reality. There was the Omni, the building in which the convention actually took place. Almost surrounding the Omni was a huge complex, the Georgia World Congress Center (WCC) in which ten to fifteen thousand media people, many times the number who were actual political actors in the Omni, assembled to observe and report on the events in the Omni.

The consciousness in the WCC was one of constant observation. There were no visible discussions among the thousands of media people about their own relationship to the outcome of anything happening at the convention. Such discussions would have seemed to be "inappropriate": Members of the media were there as observers.

This observer mentality is the central characteristic of media consciousness. It enables people in the media to experience, in a voyeuristic way, being part of a political community and yet, at the same time, to insulate themselves from the risk that normally comes with being part of such a community.

Underlying media consciousness, then, is a destructive compromise between two conflicting impulses: both the desire to be and the fear of being connected to a community. The compromise is to watch it—with all the excitement that "watching it" implies—in a voyeuristic way.

This inner struggle leads to the negative tone that we hear from many members of the media, as well as the posturing and grandiose speech-making characteristic of politicians. Journalists are profoundly affected by the excitement that they experience safely outside of themselves. They are both attracted to the political actors, seeing in them the locus of meaning that they want, and contemptuous of them because of their own pain and anger at being isolated from a community of meaning. Their "role" as journalists makes this split legitimate because it "officially" tells them that it is appropriate for them to insulate themselves from their own desires, and it legitimates their unwillingness to take the risks that being part of the political community would require.

As a result, journalists inevitably are hostile toward the very things that they adore. For me, this point was clearest in much of the press' reaction to Jesse Jackson's speech. Several commentators distanced themselves from their feelings, suggesting that Jackson's speech would alienate a lot of whites. The degree of passion and emotional pull that Jackson actually communicated threatened

---

Peter Gabel is president of New College of California and associate editor of Tikkun. *This article appeared in* Tikkun, *September/October 1988.*

and almost contradicted the smooth defensive neutrality of the official commentators, leading them angrily to reject their own longing which was elicited by the speech.

At the same time, the insistence on distance, the denial that something that could have personal meaning is happening, makes members of the press most responsive to the politician who acts as a "public figure" rather than as a human being. This message, subtly but constantly conveyed to political actors, encourages the dominant form of political speech: a bombastic and silly exercise in words that emphasizes the distance between the speaker and the listener.

The absurdity of such speech-making was vivid in Atlanta. The speakers gave talks to audience members who might have wanted to hear the bombast, were they actually listening to the speeches. In reality, however, many of the speeches were not televised and most of the people in the Omni coliseum were not listening anyway—engaging instead in endless conversations and interviews with the media. The content of the speeches was defined by the "public" or media-oriented nature of the reality: No one would have dared say something like, "Look, folks, we are faced with the problem of Bentsen not really being what most of us wanted or liked, but on the other hand he might bring in Texas, so it's probably worth [or, someone else might have said, not worth] taking this move." Nobody could talk *to* anyone else because everyone was directing their speeches toward a media that required a level of bombast and distance—which, in turn, made almost all the speeches incredibly boring and irrelevant.

The distancing function of the media reflects a type of social consciousness that most of us share—ambivalence about genuine committed action. The way that the media presents reality is relieving to us because it allows us to remain cynically detached, protected from our deeper desires for connectedness as well as from our fears of being disappointed were we to let those desires guide our conduct.

Ironically, though, we resent the media for precisely the same reason that we appreciate it. The media breaks down community and discourages passionate involvement. On some level of consciousness, most of us know that the media helps to create a world that we really don't want. This hostility toward the media is what Spiro Agnew, in the early seventies, and Ronald Reagan, in the eighties, were able to appeal to when they engaged in media-bashing. Yet the American people, though attracted by this attack, would not let it go too far, knowing simultaneously that precisely what angers them about the media also protects them from their own all-too-scary desires.

The split described here helps to account for the schizoid nature of the convention and the election campaign. There exist two versions of reality—the media version, on the one hand, and the real convention or real election with politically significant meetings, exchanges of ideas, even changes in emotions undetectable by polls, on the other. If members of the media ever hope to capture this other reality, they can do so only by overcoming media consciousness and recognizing that they are real people with a great deal at stake in the outcome of political affairs. Journalists must be morally alive and emotionally connected human beings; otherwise their neutrality mirrors and reinforces the isolation of the reader or viewer.

But you, the reader of this article, can help in the process of undermining the media consciousness I describe. You can talk with your friends and coworkers about the issues and about how they are being "framed" by the media. You can invite people over to watch the debates and news coverage and you can become actively involved in supporting positions, candidates, and political movements that seem to articulate your own views. Most important, you (we) can overcome the tendency to be observers, resisting the inner voices that push for caution, self-protection, and cynicism.... □

After the Cold War:
Possibilities for Human Liberation

Michael Lerner

The Historical Framework

As we enter the last decade of the current millennium, the celebration of the status quo in the Western world has reached a new level of delirious self-deception. The self-satisfaction of the well-to-do burgher may indeed be shared by enough middle- and upper-middle-income people in the Western world to allow court intellectuals to declare that they have reached the best of all possible worlds, but anyone with a sense of history recognizes that this delusion has recurred often enough in the past two hundred years to require more than a little skepticism. A State Department operative writes an article about the recent advances for democratic regimes and hails the period as "the end of history." Nathan Gardels's *New Perspective Quarterly* dedicates an entire issue of his magazine to celebrating "the triumph of capitalism." The illusions nurtured on a well-stuffed stomach are endless and frighteningly naive.

The celebration of the status quo may turn to mourning quickly enough if the freedom of the marketplace, currently being toasted in the corporate and media boardrooms, continues to prevent the development of a worldwide system of rational allocation of the world's resources and productive capacities. I'm not talking, for the moment, about the fact that every year thirty million children die of hunger as a consequence of our current system of resource allocation. Such "merely" moral outrage is not likely to divert the ideologues from their festivities. Rather, I make reference to the fact that the much touted marketplace has encouraged, some would say required, a pillaging of the world's resources and a wildly irresponsible destruction of the physical environment. Just as people in a twentieth century dominated by world wars and unparalleled human destructiveness looked back on the "gay nineties" with a sense of incredulity that nineteenth-century intellectuals could have been so unaware of the tragedy they were helping to set up in the last decade of that century, so in the next century our half-hearted belief that we might save the environment without interfering with the freedom of the marketplace will be looked back on as the ultimate in stupidity. Indeed, one might write a history of the human race and its relationship to the planet that would point to an escalating destructiveness which reached its apex in the past several decades. Framing history in terms of threats to the survival of the human race might find us defining this period as one of history's worst.

There is a danger, however, in relying on this kind of formulation—the danger of falling back into an external account of reality that misses what we learned from the experience of the thousands of normally functioning Americans whom we at the Institute for Labor and Mental Health interviewed in the 1970s and 1980s. "Ecological catastrophe" may simply take the place of "economic collapse"

This editorial appeared in Tikkun, *January/February 1990.*

in the lexicon of the Left, while the more subjective and experiential issues may once again be ignored. If people are able to hear over and over again the "facts" about the way we are destroying our natural environment, and find themselves still unable to respond, that may well be because they are in so much pain in other parts of their lives that they don't have the emotional energy to give to this larger problem.

In this sense, solving the ecological crisis may require solving another crisis first: the sense of powerlessness and alienation that make people so despairing of themselves that they are unable to engage in politics. This crisis in personal life may be the distinctive feature of the contemporary historical period, brought into even sharper relief when contrasted with the collective action of millions of people in Eastern Europe. Given how powerless we feel to join together with others to change our situation, we may recognize the beginning of the 1990s as a particularly sad moment in the collective history of the West.

Even these preliminary remarks force us to understand that there is no way to take an "objective" look at our historical situation, because there is no such thing as "objective" history: How we situate ourselves historically depends on what our values and goals are as we approach the task. So where are we from the perspective of those who have "*tikkun*" as their goal?

First, the good news: the disintegration of Eastern European totalitarianism. Certainly one of the great tragedies of the twentieth century was the defeat of the liberatory forces within the communist movement and their replacement by antidemocratic and inhumane elites whose primary goals were the perpetuation of their own power. The willful murder of millions of the most dedicated socialists and communists by Stalin, in the name of socialism and communism, was for decades alternately denied or justified by many decent and idealistic people in the industrialized West as "necessary costs for the building of socialism." But it was not socialism that was being built so much as a totalitarian system of state control serving the interests of a well-entrenched bureaucratic elite that manipulated the language of Marxism to serve its own narrow interests. Eventually the truth seeped out, and there ensued throughout the West for most of the second half of the twentieth century a profound cynicism about the possibility of any humane reconstruction of society. The cynical misuse of the liberatory thrust of socialist and communist ideology by East European totalitarians fit perfectly into the needs of Western apologists for capitalism's excesses. "Yes," insisted the Western ideologues, "What you see in the Soviet Union, China, Poland, Rumania is communism. This is what happens when you try to overthrow a capitalist system in the name of humane ideals. So aren't you better off with capitalism?"

Never mind that Marx himself would never have described the Soviet Union as socialist or communist; for him the character of any society was determined by who actually controlled the means of production, and it would be impossible to argue that the working class actually had control in the Soviet Union or China or Eastern Europe. Never mind that New Leftists around the world for the past thirty years had rejected the apologists for these regimes and articulated a vision of liberation that was as critical of the East as it was of the West. Sufficient numbers of leftists in this country *were* willing to talk about the Soviet Union, China, and Eastern Europe as "actually existing socialism" to give credence to Western ideologues' charge that "You have seen communism and it does not work."

Don't misunderstand the intention of my argument. Although I *am* arguing that communism or socialism in the sense articulated by the classic communist and socialist thinkers has never been tried, and therefore cannot reasonably be said to have failed, I am *not* arguing that what we really need now is to push for a return to that classic conception. On the contrary, the fundamental conception of virtually all the liberatory forces, including those who were never seduced by the vision of Eastern European communism, is badly misguided at a much deeper level. What I am saying, is this, one of the major obstacles to any advance for a liberatory Left—the role played in the twentieth century by the international communist movement—is beginning to disappear, and this is good news. It will be harder in the twenty-first century to use fear of this kind of totalitarianism as a club against the liberatory desires of the world's peoples.

The bad news, however, is that the social change movements "waiting in the wings" have lost their way, have little following, and demonstrate little self-understanding as to what has gone wrong or how they might change their own directions. Yet the world is as badly in need of repair and transformation as ever.

One might have thought that the serious economic and environmental problems facing us would be sufficient to generate large-scale social movements in the West capable of reaching power and transforming social reality. Far from this being the case, the movements for social change, whether of the center (the Democratic party) or what might loosely be called the Left (the various social change movements), are deeply isolated and confused. The reason for this isolation is that life in capitalist society has generated a form of oppression that is not primarily a matter of economic or physical survival: namely, the destruction of the moral and spiritual environment within which human life must flourish.

This form of oppression appears and is experienced in our lives as merely "personal problems" which are supposedly rooted in our own individual failures as human beings. If we have work that is fundamentally alienating, this is supposedly because we have personally failed to advance ourselves adequately in a world that provides equal opportunity; hence, we can only blame ourselves. If it is hard to sustain loving and committed relationships, if families feel unstable and explosive, if friendships are hard to sustain and people seem to use each other more than nourish each other, this must be because we are individually inadequate and need some form of individual repair work (exercise, diet, psychotherapy, twelve-step programs, and the like are currently most in vogue). If drugs or crime flourish, this must reflect individual pathologies that can be dealt with through escalated forms of repression against the criminals.

Once the problems are understood to be personal, the solutions are necessarily privatized. The social change movements of the earlier part of the twentieth century, including the labor movement, socialist movement, and civil rights movement, often embodied and articulated a moral vision of community even while their explicit focus was more narrowly aimed at the level of "rights" or "economic goodies." It was not atypical for these movements to build strong internal communities by paying attention to the daily problems of its participants. They attended to the needs of family life; they celebrated births and marriages; they visited the sick; they helped bury the dead; and they created ritual and music for communal celebrations.

Yet these movements never understood the importance of this dimension of their own activity, never had an intellectual framework that emphasized the centrality of these psychological and spiritual needs. Attention to the needs of individuals, support for families, building communities—these were dismissed as expendable side concerns, not the economic heart of the matter. The movements could focus on the more "bottom-line" concerns of rights and money and leave all these "softer" concerns to personal life—exactly where the larger society said they belonged. No wonder, then, that these movements could provide no bulwark against the increasingly self-interested ethos generated by the capitalist marketplace. And the more nonideological and businesslike the Democrats and the unions became, the less they could inspire any deep devotion or sense of purpose. People might feel happy that unions or the Democrats could deliver some useful economic goodies—much as a good insurance company could provide good "coverage." But if the real locus of fulfillment or pain was in personal life, and liberal politics had nothing to do with that, then understandably people's energy would be withdrawn from politics.

So this very privatization of life becomes part of the problem. Families and friendships have traditionally been embedded in larger communities of meaning. The absence of those larger frameworks put an impossible burden on every particular relationship to provide "the meaning of life," which was supposedly developed out of the "fun" or "satisfaction" that each individual family or relationship or friendship could provide. Is it any wonder that relationships feel more fragile when they are constantly being scrutinized in terms of their adequacy in providing these kinds of satisfactions? When private life fails to provide the necessary satisfactions, most people blame themselves or their partners or their friends—incorrectly assuming that everyone else has managed to create these personal satisfactions, and simultaneously feeling that their own failure to do so is a direct reflection of their own lack of worth as a human being.

Ideally, the Left would help people understand the social determinants of these problems. By helping people see the ways in which capitalism as a system undermines ethically and spiritually grounded communities, the Left would help generate a sense of compassion for ourselves and each other that would uproot self-blaming and ultimately empower.

The Left is unable to make this move because it has directly contributed to the problem by championing the removal of ethical and spiritual concerns from the public arena and moving them into private life. Fearful that ethical and spiritual concerns might legitimate a new imposition of a particular religion on the entire society, and used to seeing religion itself as counterposed to the needs of human liberation, the Left is in no position to generate the politics of compassion that is key to a liberatory politics in the current period.

How Did the Liberal Left Get Into its Conceptual Muddle?

Whatever the liberatory potential inherent in the Exodus and prophetic traditions of the Bible, the actually existing religious communities of late antiquity were severely flawed, often so completely enmeshed with existing systems of class domination as to be indistinguishable from them. While some may argue today that Christianity checked the excesses of what might have otherwise been an even more brutal dark age, most of those who lived through it experienced Christianity as the essential element of feudalism. This element provided the fundamental justification for class hierarchy and oppression. Not only was the Church the largest landowner, it was the sanctifier of an entire social order in which the language of "community" and "morality" was manipulated to justify a hierarchical and oppressive community based on inequality of power. The Church also fostered a morality that taught people to stay in their place, learn their "station and its duties," and subordinate their own needs and desires to those of the wealthy and powerful. I am willing to imagine that the feudal order had its moments of sublime beauty, enriching human community, spiritual depth, and moral sensitivity, and that there were wondrous dimensions of human experience realized then that might be harder to realize today. Yet I give deeper credence to the collective memory of the human race which saw the medieval period as one so dominated by pain and oppression that any force that could deliver humanity from it would be hailed as a liberator, and that ideas used by the feudal order would be permanently tainted by association.

It is no wonder, then, that the struggle for human liberation that emerged in Western Europe took the form of a struggle against the imposed communities with which religion had been identified, and against an objective ethics that had been used to restrict human freedoms. The newly emerging class of shopkeepers, merchants, and bankers were particularly hemmed in by the Church's economic restrictions that limited their ability to charge however much they wished for the goods they produced, or to lend money for interest, or to engage in commerce on the large number of religious holidays that covered almost one-third of the medieval calendar.

Although at first the challenge to this order was very limited, the bourgeoisie over the next several hundred years increasingly began to formulate its own self-justification in ways that opposed the spiritual foundation of feudalism. If the Church was the guarantor of salvation in another world, the bourgeoisie could provide concrete results in this world. It could provide material goods that were verifiable by one's own immediate experience. If the Church claimed as its domain all that was unique, all that was "beyond" the scientific method, the bourgeoisie could not compete on spiritual terrain with the feudal order. What it could do was to deny the importance of the spiritual altogether. While the old feudal order talked of the realm of the spirit, of good and evil, of the higher responsibilities and refinements, the bourgeoisie talked of the material needs of the body, of immediate gratification, of making the evidence for its success visible where it could be seen, rather than in the sky or in some future life that the Church promised to the oppressed.

It was this insistence on material gratification of the body in the "here and now" that spurred the growth of the bourgeoisie and won for it growing support from other sectors of the population. The Church had a lofty set of ideas about community and morality—but the actual experience most people had in feudal "communities" involved oppression and injustice that the Church appeared to justify and from which it benefitted. Had there actually been a spiritually centered and moral community, the appeal of the bourgeoisie's materialism and the call for individual rights as a counter to the claims of community responsibility might have fallen on deaf ears. But since the actual experience tied to the Church's rhetoric was an experience of oppression, since all the Church could really offer was a promise of salvation in some future world (given that the actual world it had helped to create and sustain was so painful and unjust), its appeal increasingly declined when faced with the challenge of a bourgeoisie who could promise rewards in this world. If, as the bourgeoisie contended, those who sang the praises of the spiritual were really only concerned with their own material well-being anyway, then why not give power to the emerging class of traders, manufacturers, and bankers who could make the material realm flourish for greater numbers of people once they were allowed to follow their own unbridled self-interests?

The ideas that became central to the struggle for human liberation, then, were themselves a product of the particular distortions of feudalism and the specific way that the bourgeoisie framed its alternative to the old order. If the old order touted community and responsibility, the new class would proclaim the centrality of the individual and (usually *his*) freedom of choice. If the old order talked of spiritual reality, the new class promoted a conception of reality in which all that was real could be subject to empirical verification through the senses. Other forms of experience—aesthetic, ethical, and religious—were increasingly seen as problematic because they were nonverifiable in terms of the new criterion of reality. While many bourgeois theorists tried to maintain a place for these other ways of experiencing the world—postulating a fundamentally "private" or "nominal" world in which these other realities might be allowed—our collective and communal realities were to be emptied of these concerns and focus exclusively on that which we could intersubjectively verify as real through public observation under controlled and repeatable conditions. A form of science emerged that based itself on these narrowly empiricist assumptions. And as that science developed immense prestige through its ability to provide increasing mastery over some aspects of nature, its paradigm of reality increasingly came to be viewed as "common sense." Those who thought that human reality demanded something "more" increasingly seemed to be metaphysicians hanging on to an outdated conceptual framework, or well-intentioned religious nut cases who did best to keep their schemes to themselves.

Let me hasten to add that the struggle for human rights and individual freedom, emerging in the context of feudal oppression, was a necessary and important struggle—and not one that has yet been fully won. Once the bourgeoisie was able to overthrow the feudal aristocrats and build a new capitalist economic and social order, new problems emerged which seemed to indicate the limits of bourgeois ideology. The bourgeoisie had promised liberty, equality, and fraternity. But the liberty was only the freedom of each person to pursue his or her own individual interests—and in a context in which previous inequalities could be passed on to the next generations through inherited property, thereby generating a class system as thoroughly unequal as any that had supposedly been overthrown. Equality meant only equality before the law—and the laws were written in the interests of the industrialists and bankers. Fraternity seemed to be little more than the camaraderie of men who could rejoice in still being allowed to perpetuate a personal feudalism in their own families by reigning over wives and children whose rights were severely curtailed in law and in fact.

From this standpoint, the basic struggle of liberals and progressives in the past two centuries became the struggle to give more substantive meaning to the original struggle fought by the bourgeoisie. "The Left," as we came to be known (because of where we sat in the original Assembly formed after the French Revolution), insisted that the bourgeoisie take its original promise seriously. The promise of equality and freedom must be realized—and this meant pushing up against the new economic and political order established by the capitalist elites.

The division in the twentieth century between radical or revolutionary elements and those that became known as "liberals" was a division about how best to achieve that freedom. Liberals argued that the capitalist order itself was reformable in ways that could increase freedom and equality. The socialists and communists argued that concentration of power and wealth in the hands of the few substantially undermined the possibilities for freedom. As the media intensified its ability to manipulate mass consciousness in accordance with the needs of the ruling elites, individual freedom would increasingly be an illusion of choice within a reality of compulsion. This illusion of choice was only an extension of the dynamics people already experienced in the economic marketplace, where they got to sell their labor power to any owner of capital that they chose but meanwhile had no choice regarding the necessity of selling that labor power. Moreover, socialists pointed out, inequalities based on a history of racism and sexism severely limited the choices available to many, and made it easier for the ruling elites to set one sector of the population against another. Real freedom could only be achieved in a system that eliminated inequalities based on race, sex, or class.

For us at *Tikkun* to say that we are "progressive" means that we are part of the Left in this struggle to eliminate sexual, racial, and class inequalities and to promote the fullest flowering of human freedom and satisfaction. To call ourselves "liberal" is to identify with those in the liberal tradition who have demanded that in the course of building a more egalitarian society we must simultaneously insist on fundamental human freedoms of speech, assembly, dissent, and the right to resist attempts by the state or other coercive bodies (including the movement for social change itself) to interfere with our personal lives and require that we conform to some externally imposed standard of joint activity or thought. Nothing I am about to say about the limits of the liberal and progressive cause should be misunderstood to endorse those who use criticisms of the Left as a cover for hoping to reestablish a society in which the progressive and liberal programs are undermined or eliminated. The struggle for economic and political "rights" is, I believe, a righteous struggle. So we stand *with* the struggles of all those who resist the coercive power of communities that impose their values on the individual; *with* the struggle of workers against oppressive bosses or the manipulative and undemocratic structures of corporate and government bureaucracies; *with* the struggles of women against sexist practices; *with* women and children against oppressive family structures that require subordination of intellect, emotion, and will to a family power structure; and most generally *with* the struggle against any unjustly constituted authority that uses power in unfair and oppressive ways.

And yet all these struggles have not gathered the support they should have over the more than two hundred years since the American and French revolutions put these concerns on our common agenda. And the reason is that these struggles—fundamental and critical as they are—have been framed within a conceptual context that ignores other dimensions of human reality and have thus been unable to address the fullest levels of human need and dissatisfaction with the contemporary world.

The solution, we must stress, is not to adopt some tired form of communitarianism that glorifies past communities as an alternative to present individualism and alienation. People want community, but they also quite legitimately want freedom from coercive norms and are rightly wary of any attempts to lead them back into social forms that are externally manipulative. We do not need a resurrection of superego-based communities which tell people they must follow precepts X and Y, and that create a new load of externally defined "shoulds" to govern their lives.

The moral vision of the communities we hope for, then, cannot be embodied in a set of authoritative rules imposed on a mass of people conceptualized as "difficult human beings" who need external guidance. Rather, we have to imagine a democratic community in which the nature of the social practice of daily life is inherently ethical, since ethical concerns permeate the way people conceptualize their individual and collective situation. When ethical concerns become central to daily life, the medium of relationship becomes ethically shared commitments, commitments not imposed but freely embraced and continually re-embraced within the recognition of our human freedom. An ethical attitude toward existence becomes the medium of solidarity with other people, as we share a forward-looking perspective rather than suffering our individual existence as alienated beings who are powerless and resigned.

To have this attitude toward each other and toward our possibilities is not to submit to some authoritative order, but rather both to overcome the debilitating depression that shapes the consciousness of daily life in a privatized society and to recognize our common interest in playfully and lovingly shaping a world together. This common goal can be called "becoming a partner with God in creating the world," if one wishes a religious language, but one need not adopt any specific religious tradition in order to engage in this kind of thinking. Or, to the extent that I am talking about a religious perception of the world, it need not be based on Judaism or any other particular historical religious tradition, though there is much to be learned from such traditions.

In short, the vision of an ethically shaped community of meaning is a vision that can emerge from our own activity together as people committed to healing and repairing the world. Without this kind of vision, I'm afraid, social change movements quickly devolve into the logic of the established order wherein we remain condemned to a frantic search for our own personal solutions. The understandable discomfort so many of us feel when someone starts to talk in terms of ethics or religious vision, the sense that somebody is about to trick us back into a world without freedom and choice, can become an obstacle which prevents us from acknowledging the kind of ethical community that is democratically created and that generates freedom, spontaneity, and playfulness rather than a repressive order.

With all its problems, the liberatory movement of the 1960s gave some of us a taste of this possibility—precisely at the moments when it was most utopian and most willing to transcend not only the logic of capitalist society but also the logic of its own more narrowly framed political demands.

Prospects for the Twenty-First Century

Given this analysis, I find it hard to be optimistic about the chances for human liberation in the foreseeable future. As long as liberal and progressive forces remain tied to a conception of human reality derived from a metaphysics that has little place in it for love, ethics, and spirituality, they will continue to foster a politics that leaves fundamental aspects of reality unaddressed. Hence they will fail to ignite our passions in a sustainable way.

What is accomplishable within this framework is the transition from feudalism to capitalism—a repeat on a global scale of what has already happened to a significant extent in the U.S. Wherever we have overt forms of authoritarian control or extremes of economic and political domination, there the already existing framework of liberal and progressive politics will be relevant and useful. Missing will be the ability to transform capitalist societies to what needs to come next: societies in which our human capacities are actualized and in which loving relationships and meaningful work are sustained rather than undermined by the social structure.

Of course, the transition from feudalism, broadly understood, is nothing to be sniffed at! The potential of a triumph of civil liberties and human rights in the twenty-first century is a wonderful prospect, and one that will take the best efforts of many of us. I imagine that such a transition will involve at least the following: a worldwide struggle to equalize the economic differences between the Northern and Southern hemispheres of the planet, or roughly what we call the differences between the Third World and advanced industrial societies; a struggle to undermine racist practices in the advanced industrial societies; a struggle to eliminate the inequalities of power and respect between men and women; a struggle to replace authoritarian and totalitarian regimes with Western-style democratic regimes, replicating worldwide what is currently being achieved in Eastern Europe.

Won't this be a wonderful advance if this kind of defeudalization of the world is achieved in the twenty-first century? Yes. I enthusiastically embrace it and will happily join the relevant struggles. Yet I can also envision a world emerging from these developments that resembles in its totality the current reality of the United States. And while that will be a welcome advance, a march away from worldwide poverty and overt political oppression, it will be far from the kind of human liberation that we seek. For those who think in terms of historical stages, it may be absolutely necessary to go through that stage on a global level in order to be ready to put the question of human liberation on our collective agenda. But if so, then the levels of pain and unhappiness that currently drive so many people in the U.S. to alcohol, drugs, television, violence, and irrational acting out may become the common lot of humanity until we are ready to address a restructuring of our society in different terms from those that are put forward by the struggle against feudalism.

Moreover, to the extent that the model of progressive politics continues to ignore or downplay the psychological, spiritual, and ethical issues I've raised, we on the Left will continue to flounder. Consider how this might play in some critical areas of concern:

1. *The Awakening in Eastern Europe.* Framed as a liberation from communist totalitarianism, this awakening will perceive its central task as providing political freedom and economic growth to a population long starved for both. The Left will warn against the capitalist marketplace and score points by showing how the freedoms of the West may lead to unemployment and a new class system as oppressive in its way as the oppression of the older communist system. Yet, if the Left is arguing about the best way to achieve economic strength and political freedom, it would not be irrational for many Eastern Europeans to believe that the capitalist road is the quickest way to such strength and freedom—after all, they can see for themselves the successes of Western Europe and the U.S. If these are the primary terms of the debate, if the Left is unable to speak to the spiritual and psychological needs of the people, confining these needs to the realm of religion and ceding that realm to the Catholic Church, then there will be little chance of moving the discussion beyond a level on which the successes of the West may well trump every other argument.

2. *South Versus North.* One of the major developments in the next hundred years will be the industrialization of the Third World and the concomitant weakening of the power of the Northern hemisphere's imperialist powers (likely to be Japan, a Germany-dominated Europe, the U.S., and possibly a reindustrialized Soviet Union). Because this struggle will most probably be fought out in terms of equality and fairness, and because the liberal and progressive forces within the advanced

industrial societies will quite rightly dedicate some of their energies to supporting attempts to redistribute wealth and power to those who have been historical victims of imperialism, the dominant paradigms of the Left are likely to be reinforced. Those who talk in terms of spiritual, ethical, psychological, and aesthetic concerns will continue to be marginalized within the Left or dismissed as self-indulgent in the face of these larger issues.

3. *The Ecological Crisis.* We need a fundamental reconsideration of our relationship to nature. This should include a sense of awe and wonder at the universe that would preclude us from seeing our environment simply as a resource to be disposed of in more or less rational ways. Yet to think in these terms would require precisely the paradigm shift that the Left will not allow itself as long as it remains committed to the worldview it developed to fight feudalism. So, instead, the struggle will be fought out in more narrowly technocratic and scientific language that will make it extremely difficult for most people to understand or participate. In addition, because the Left will be unable to address the spiritual, psychological, and ethical crisis facing people in the advanced industrial societies, most of these people will continue to feel only a peripheral interest in politics—watching it more as a spectator sport and hoping that the good guys will win, but totally unable to mobilize themselves into political action.

4. *The Women's Movement.* Potentially the most fundamental of all the political struggles when it is conceived of as the struggle for "women's liberation" and not simply for "women's rights," the women's movement could be a vehicle for bridging the gap between the politics of rights and the politics that incorporate a deeper understanding of the spiritual, psychological, and ethical dimensions of human experience. Much of the strategic focus that we've developed at *Tikkun* in terms of articulating a politics based on the actual subjective experience and needs of human beings is learned from the liberatory tendency within the women's movement and is an attempt to extend its lessons to the population as a whole.

Yet the sad reality is that the liberatory movement in women's struggles has often been subordinated to a more narrowly conceived struggle for rights. While backing those struggles as absolutely necessary and justified, we can also see how a women's movement that focuses merely on equal rights for women can lose sight of a transformative vision that would challenge the entire picture of what it means to be human in the contemporary world. I do not advocate giving up the struggle for rights, but I also see how that struggle may subvert the women's movement its transformative potential just as it has already done so for the larger liberal and progressive forces in the past hundreds of years.

5. *The Struggle Against Interimperial Rivalries and Domination by the Multinationals.* On the one hand, the multinationals may appear to be a restraining force against the reemergence of the kind of virulent nationalism that led to World War I and which might be on the international agenda once again in the aftermath of the breakdown of the cold war. On the other hand, the multinationals may themselves become more powerful than many countries and dictate conditions of life that are as oppressive in their way as any dictatorial system of the past might have been. In this situation, nations may stand in the same relation to the multinationals that cities today stand in relationship to national capital—the more the people in cities gain local democratic power, the more they feel themselves powerless to influence corporate power that is able to shift resources and investment at will, shutting down plants and disabling local economies.

Given this kind of development, the Left will quite reasonably press for international democracy and international institutions capable of placing some constraints on the multinationals; internationalism will be on the agenda not just as a pretty moral ideal but as a practical necessity for those who wish to have any power over their own lives. And yet the Left will once again find itself unable to mobilize as much support as it should get on the issue—facing the same surplus powerlessness in the population as a whole that we have already discussed. The most frequently repeated comment about politics I heard in my interviews with American workers was some variant of the following: "Who am I to try to change the big picture when I've made such a mess of my own personal life? I need to spend my energy getting my own life together, and leave politics to someone else!" To the extent that people feel alone and overwhelmed by their personal lives, and blame themselves for the ways that their lives are not working, and to the extent that they feel that the ethical and spiritual void in their lives is not addressed by progressive politics, they are unlikely to feel that they have the time or energy to become involved in the huge efforts it would take to democratize a world economy. By failing to adequately concern itself with the inner life of their potential constituents, liberal and progressive movements will be unable to adequately mobilize people for the external struggles.

I've told this story in a relatively pessimistic way. Of course, there is hope that all of these struggles can go in a very different direction. We have developed *Tikkun* in the hope that a new politics may emerge in the next century that would begin to shake off the assumptions and constraints that have governed the forces of human liberation in the past several hundreds of years. That new politics would be based not primarily on human rights but on human needs. It would start from the assumption that we have a need to actualize our capacities to be intellectually and aesthetically creative human beings enmeshed in work and families and communities that provide a framework of ethical meaning and spiritual sensitivity—and it would then critique existing social relationships to the extent that they block our ability to actualize these capacities. It would demand the transformation of our society in ways that would encourage loving relationships and fulfilling work—but it would understand that our ability to be creative or loving is not a product of one narrow aspect of our world—not, for example, just a function of whether we have adequate pay or adequate child care—but rather a product of the entire way our lives are organized. Hence it would seek to transform those aspects of contemporary arrangements that encourage narcissism, cynicism, materialism, and me-firstism, and that encourage us to accept a less creative and loving life than we need and want.

Fundamental to that new way of doing politics would be the recognition of our need for loving relationships embedded in communities of meaning and purpose guided by a shared ethical vision. I have proposed that the Left form a "progressive profamily movement" to articulate the ways that loving relationships are stifled or undermined by the dynamics of a competitive marketplace and by the materialist and self-centered ethos of the capitalist system. Such a progressive profamily approach would champion not just the traditional family form, but all the other forms in which we are attempting to build long-term committed loving relationships, including gay families and single-parent families. It would insist on the importance of equality between the sexes and the rights of children within families, just as it would require restructuring the world of work to provide meaningful and nonalienating labor and opportunities for democratic participation.

That new way of politics would include the development of a political sphere that allows for and promotes a sense of awe and wonder at the ways of the universe, the grandeur of all that is, and a reverence for life in all its forms. This does not mean institutionalizing any particular form of religion or adopting a secularized and empty civic religiosity, but rather encouraging all of us to approach the world through a broadened conception of the real, a conception that reclaims much that was abandoned in the metaphysics of liberation adopted by progressive forces since the Enlightenment. A public sphere, free of its fear of religious violence, governed by a deep commitment to tolerance and mutuality of respect, could promote a new and significant discussion about alternative religious and spiritual conceptions. Encouraging this kind of discussion would give the liberatory movements a dimension of wisdom that cannot be found in narrowly framed debates about economic systems. □

The Transformative Possibilities of Legal Culture

Peter Gabel

The Impoverished Political Meaning of Existing Legal Culture

The need for progressive people to develop a new approach to politics does not apply only or even primarily to national elections like the most recent one. Presidential elections are an important element in the development of such a politics because they define—with special force because of the finality of the collective act of voting—what "we" regard to be the legitimate scope of national debate over ideas and social vision. On the one hand, it is often said quite rightly that presidential elections are too abstract and removed from the concreteness of people's everyday existence to expect them to have much of an impact on the reality of people's lives. On the other, it is much easier to get people to believe in the possibility of social change or in the possible realization of a new social vision if the people as a whole express themselves as taking such ideas seriously. There is a reciprocal relationship between the ways of being and the kinds of ideas legitimated in national elections and more local and concrete forms of social-political involvement (including everything from actual participation in specific political activities to the things that we talk to our friends about and the degree of passion with which we feel able to talk about them); each arena—national and local—helps to define the other's horizon, and each works to enable or limit the content and spirit of what can be expressed in the other. To give a simple example from a situation I was recently involved in, it is much easier for a health care advocate in Madison, Wisconsin, to say to a local legislative subcommittee that our ethical obligation to care for one another as we face death or infirmity together requires Wisconsin to provide statewide health care to all its citizens if the same compassionate vision is being expressed by a recognized national leader. If there is little or no indication that there is a larger "we" giving legitimacy to this kind of "soft" ethical discourse, the subcommittee is likely to respond cynically or with boredom to what they will think of as touchy-feely, unrealistic arguments and rely heavily on the "hard" data in the staff's cost-benefit analysis to make their decision.

The legal arena plays a particularly important role in shaping people's sense of the legitimate and the possible, because it is the democratically validated, public context for mediating the relationship between every specific local case or conflict and the agreed-upon universal values and vision that gives these values meaning. Lawyers, judges, law students, professors, media commentators on the law and the legal process, high school civics teachers, and legal secretaries are but some of the people who shape this culture, not to mention the long-dead architects who designed the hierarchical-majestic courtrooms in the local Hall of Justice or the producers, directors and actors of TV law

Peter Gabel is president of New College of California and associate editor of Tikkun. *This paper was originally presented at the Yale Legal Theory Workshop. It appeared in* Tikkun, *March/April 1989.*

shows like "People's Court" and "L.A. Law." Taken together, these people and many more convey the culture of law, expressed through such phenomena as the evocative qualities and substantive content of legal doctrine and reasoning, the symbolic meaning of the architecture of legal settings and the uniforms lawyers wear, and the way lawyers manifest themselves through their physical presence.

Here I will focus on only two aspects of existing legal culture—what I will call the "disembodiment" of lawyers and judges, and the technical-rational character of legal reasoning. Although each of these aspects of our legal culture at one time may have manifested a certain resistance to the religious moralism of pre-liberal society, they have now become part of the spiritual and moral emptiness of liberal political life.

To understand what I mean by the "disembodiment" of judges and lawyers, think of the physical bearing of a soccer goalie in the midst of game. S/he bends her knees and moves with quickness and suppleness from side to side, anticipating the next shot on goal, the feint that she must sense to avoid losing her balance, the fully extended leap to one side or the other that might suddenly be required. In this play this goalie is present in her body, and her mind and body are relatively unified in the sense that she lives her project as a goaltender through the coordinated "praxis" of her movements. In light of the weight and poise of her presence, it would be difficult to casually push her backwards.

Contrast the physical presence of a judge. She sits on an elevated platform, her body almost entirely concealed by a black robe. Her movements are usually minimal and narrowly functional, involving mainly the head and hands. We could say that her being is in her head and withdrawn from her body, so that we experience her presence mainly through a disembodied and slightly elevated style of speaking or writing, as if the law were above and outside of us and she were bringing it to us with her mind. This separation of mind and body corresponds to a separation of thought and feeling revealed in both the content and manner of her self-expression. In light of this absence of bodily presence, if she were standing, it would be very easy to push her off balance with a slight push.

The same disembodiment is characteristic of lawyers also. I have taught contracts for fifteen years and never fail to notice the change that comes over law students during October and November of the first year when they first being to learn how to "make arguments." The tentativeness, the intuitive orientation and the feeling for justice that characterizes the first few weeks gradually gives way to a glassy-eyed stare and a rigidification of musculature as the student learns to say in a monotone, "Well, it seems to me that you could argue there was no consideration at all here since the paper was entirely worthless." Full-blown lawyers tend to become quite addicted to this kind of glassy-eyed, disembodied power discourse in spite of the strain required to keep it up because the esteem and recognition that is attributed to it within the circle of collective denial makes it seem to be worth the repression required to keep it up.

My claim is that the effect of this separation of mind and body and thought and feeling is to reinforce the isolation of both the judge and lawyer and those who experience them by blocking the empathic channel required to link the person to the community of meaning that a good legal culture should constantly be in the process of constituting. The disembodied lawyer or judge withdraws his being from his public self in order to manifest a detached neutrality that mirrors and confirms the felt detachment of the client or citizen from the political community that the lawyer or judge is supposed to represent. To the degree that this way of being pervades legal culture as a whole, it serves to replicate the alienating structure-producing process I described earlier, because the law is made to appear as an authoritative system of thought outside of and above everyone and something to be "obeyed" as a condition of group membership, rather than as a contingent and developing expression of social and political meaning that we actively create and interpret.

Complementing this disembodied way of being is legal reasoning itself, which for the most part aspires to be a kind of disembodied thought. The training that lawyers undergo draws them toward becoming primarily technical analysts who learn how to "make arguments" as if their thought-process were simply a function of the law as an external and authoritative discourse. If I am right that the desire for mutual confirmation is as fundamental an element of our existence as any biological need and is central to understanding the meaning of any cultural phenomenon, then legal reasoning should not aspire to the kind of analytical rationality that places the reasoner at a distance from the world and that relies upon the "logical application of the law to the facts" to resolve human problems. It should aspire to an empathic comprehension which requires the thinker to immerse his or her soul in the so-called "facts" and to interpret their meaning in accordance with the moral and social end to which he or she believes the law should be directed. Yet the existing methods of legal education and law practice actually tend to invalidate and suppress this kind of comprehensive understanding, valorizing instead an unempathic and objectified way of looking at "fact" situations and "analytical rigor" in applying rules as well as in doing policy analysis. If the legal world were concerned about empathic rigor, the entire nature of law practice and legal education would have to be changed.

The reason for this misemphasis is not that people haven't thought the whole thing through properly, but that the processes that generate the collective denial of social desire also generate forms of social thinking which reinforce and justify this denial. The predominance of technical-rational over ethical-emotional thought within legal culture succeeds in draining legal reasoning of the qualitative dimension of human situations. By attributing a privileged authority to legal thought as the carrier of our political values and by excluding this qualitative dimension from it, we privatize and define as non-political what is probably the most important distinctively social aspect of our existence—the desire for social confirmation and meaning—even though the absence of this confirmation and meaning can be overcome only through a politics that produces public social change. This split in the law is paralleled by a split in the lawyer, who has a "personal" life in which she seeks qualitative satisfactions and is guided by comprehensive or intuitive knowledge and a professional life in which she converts herself into a kind of observer-analyst, funneling her client's goals into the essentially anti-intuitive conceptual knowledge of legal argumentation. As I will discuss in a moment, this division has had very bad consequences for both social change movements and public interest lawyers themselves, but it has bad consequences for all of us to the degree that it requires collusion with the social dynamics that inhibit the realization of our own deepest social need. For the insulation of legal reasoning and of the lawyer's self from the qualitative pull of social desire just fragmentizes or serializes this desire, pooling it up within each of us as individuals, instead of allowing it to have a public voice seeking qualitative public remedies.

A second aspect of the way that existing legal discourse reinforces what I've been calling collective denial is through the reification of legal categories. In the previous section I described the way that the internalized mistrust of the other's desire gives rise to de-centered or underconfirmed subjects who collectively project (through a kind of conspiracy of rotating doubt) an externalized source of social authority or agency which is then experienced, defensively, as fixed or "real." This dynamic is embodied in existing legal discourse, first in the sense that people believe the law to be something outside and above us that acts upon us when "it" is "applied" to our situations, but second in the sense that the categories of legal discourse form a perceptual grid that is experienced by most people as "the way things are."

To most non-lawyers as well as lawyers, the categories of "landlord" and "tenant," of "management" and "labor," of "employer" and "employee," are experienced not as contingent descriptive concepts subject to change, but as more or less fixed and immutable characteristics of the people enveloped by them. The *rights* of the landlord or tenant may be subject to change, but the categories of landlord and tenant themselves tend to be experienced as simply "part of the law of property that governs us." As I will argue in a moment, this might not have to be the case if legal interpretation were animated by a disalienating vision because the vitality of such a vision might have the effect of allowing us to remember the contingency of these categories as we use them. But so long as these categories are flattened out and hardened through the objectification that envelops phenomena when seen with a detached, analytical eye, they help to give a thing-like appearance to the very forms of blocked connection—to the "housing hierarchy," for example—that ought eventually to be opened up.

It is, of course, not the case that the existing legal culture is based upon no moral vision at all. The disembodiment of lawyers and the conceptual rationalism of legal reasoning are expressions of the aspect of liberal political theory that wants to use neutrality to secure the boundary between the individual and the group (to put it conceptually) or between self and others (to put it experientially). The ostensible goal of this view is to prevent totalitarianism whether feudal, fascist, or communist and to protect individual freedom. Without denying the importance of this idea to the development of human culture, it has always been based on a mistaken notion of social existence because its individualist ontology has failed to grasp the a priori reality of intersubjectivity and the absolute need of each person for the empowering confirmation of the other. Seen from this intersubjective perspective, the political morality of liberalism can tend to strengthen fascist movements as much as to prevent them, because it fails to recognize the nature of the social inclusion and meaning that people have no choice but to seek out. If liberal legal and political culture fails to speak to and validate this intersubjective need as a central constituent of political meaning, that culture will tend to create pathological forms of community (fundamentalism, for example) which do speak to this need in a distorted and dangerous way.

Transformative Possibilities for Progressive Lawyers

Whether they are Democratic party liberals or political radicals who continue to believe in the possibility of a humane, non-bureaucratic socialism, lawyers who want to work for social change must transform the way they think about law practice in much the same way that the Democratic party must transform its approach to politics. The failure to have engaged in this rethinking has played an important role in the spiritual enervation of the entire generation of public interest lawyers who were produced by the sixties. The splitting of desire and reason within existing legal culture that I described in the last section has had its worst effects on these lawyers because they have for the most part accepted its inevitability, defining their legal work as the endless "making of arguments" within the confines and assumptions of existing legal discourse and roles, while relegating the expression of their true political selves to meetings or demonstrations or participation in volunteer organizations in their private lives. Many of these lawyers are now in their forties and are burned out because of this schizophrenia and because their often exhausting work within their official legal persona has produced so much less than they had originally hoped for. It seems to me that as a group they feel both demoralized and confused about what went wrong.

Although "what went wrong" is a very complex story that certainly should not be blamed on these often courageous and self-sacrificing attorneys, it is nonetheless true that the public interest law movement of the late sixties and early seventies tended to undermine itself through its own very limited self-definition. From the beginnings of this movement until the present day, it has been difficult to tell most public interest lawyers from their corporate counterparts; they look, act, and speak alike, using the same legal language and sharing the same underlying assumptions, the difference being that the public interest lawyers represent relatively oppressed people and try to help them get their rights and entitlements, while the corporate lawyers represent relatively rich people and do more or less the same thing (if a tax shelter is an entitlement). In public interest law schools like New College where I work, we use "skills-training" classes and an apprenticeship program to teach our students the same things that corporate firms teach their young associates in their first years of practice—essentially a collection of specialized technical skills coupled with role training in how to act like a lawyer.

This approach to practice has allowed the lawyers' political and moral aspirations to be assimilated to a set of cultural meanings that contradicts these aspirations. Whether they were drawn into politics by the civil rights movement or the antiwar movement or more recently by the environmental or feminist movements, most of these lawyers originally conceived of social change in something like the qualitative terms that I have been using—they would not have used the theoretical vocabulary of desire, mutual confirmation, denial, etc., but they would certainly have said they wanted to help create a more humane world where people related to one another with more respect, affection, and solidarity. Yet the course that they chose, to the degree that it meant giving over their being to the existing legal culture, served to help reproduce in their own political arena the very social dynamics they wanted to change. However they expressed themselves and acted in their personal lives, in their public roles they felt they had to translate their socially transformative aspirations into a disembodied way of being and a technical-rational way of thinking, talking, and writing that suppressed precisely these aspirations.

In addition, the narrow outcome-oriented focus of the typical public interest practice, coupled with a theory of social change strategies that was limited to reform litigation vs. service cases, meant that they were accepting *a priori* the moral and political assumptions of liberal legalism as the framework for articulating the meaning of their own and their clients' goals. It is difficult to expect to generate movement toward the realization of greater social connection and mutual respect when the moral and political assumptions of your own legal discourse conceive of people essentially as discrete, competitive individuals who want to relate to each other at arm's length and who lack any common emotional-ethical desire except the desire to be free from governmental tyranny. Although most lawyers have not fully realized the nature of this ideological contradiction (in part because they were trained as legal technicians who simply used liberal legal doctrine rather than reflecting on its meaning), many of them have been demoralized and confused by it and now really have no clear notion of how their work can have a social impact.

The alternative to this older public interest law model is for progressive lawyers to build a legal culture that rejects the strategy of trying to win cases on the other's terms and that asserts in all of its manifestations the political legitimacy of its own moral and social vision. I use the term "culture" here to make it clear that I am referring to more than the substantive content of legal arguments— actually the idea that the law "is" nothing more than a conceptual-interpretive schema to which lawyers are more or less appended is itself part of the problem to be overcome, because it derives from the disembodied character of the existing legal culture that I discussed in the previous section. If the aim of social change lawyers is to give a new political legitimacy to people's psychological and ethical need to be part of a meaning-giving community, then they must actively try to reconstruct the political culture within which they work and which they partially constitute so as to overcome the existing separations between mind and body, thought and feeling, and analysis and comprehension as these separations manifest themselves in the public space of legal settings. This is to say that in the way they organize their offices, in the qualities of being they manifest with their clients, and in the way they relate to judges, jurors and other legal workers, they should seek to recover the relatively spontaneous and supple embodiment of the soccer goalie (obviously in a form appropriate to being a lawyer). The aim here is to reunify legal practice with the world by grounding it in being and to pull the law back from its imaginary location "above" and "outside" of the concrete settings where it is actually created and acquires its social meaning.

I don't mean by this that lawyers must wear blue jeans to the office or get deeply involved in personal conversations with their clients, but rather that they should systematically challenge, with a keen awareness of the customary constraints that limit the scope of their freedom, the modes of role-based, disembodied interaction that reproduce on an everyday level the divisions between private and public and desire and reason that I have been talking about in this essay. "Skills-training" is required for this because the legal arena is suffused with so much authoritarian symbolism (think of the portraits alone that one finds in the average courtroom) that one must develop a highly disciplined sense of how to retain the expressive forms of the existing legal culture enough to be recognized as a legitimate member of the legal community and yet infuse these forms with a new, morally autonomous cultural meaning. I doubt that one can do this effectively, for example, without understanding the psychoanalytic idea of "transference" as it applies to both the fearfulness and idealization that tends to characterize the way clients see lawyers, the way lawyers see judges, the way judges see the Founding Fathers, and so on. The idea is not to strike out against the existing system of roles in a self-marginalizing and self-defeating way, but to manifest in a disciplined way, in the totality of the manifestation of one's being as it appears in the pre-verbal but intuitively accessible expression of meaning revealed through the lawyer and her surroundings, her affirmation of the social desire that others have formed a "system" to deny.

The same kind of transformative possibility and constraint exists in the area of legal doctrine and reasoning. The analogue to the laundry list of redistributive entitlement programs in other recent Democratic campaigns is the endless demand on the Left for more rights for oppressed groups. The problem with defining political aims in terms of entitlements or rights is not the appeal for entitlements or rights themselves, but the failure to frame these appeals within an expressive or evocative moral vision that could give them a potentially universal, desire-realizing social meaning. At best, the pursuit of more rights within the presupposed liberal framework of conventional legal reasoning simply extends the post New Deal, liberal welfare state—that is, the ideological meaning of a conventional Fourteenth Amendment argument justifying the expansion of political rights serves to justify rather than transform an individualistic, competitive model of human nature and a pluralistic, interest group model of social and political life. At worst, this translation of transformative political aims into existing legal consciousness serves to actually destroy the transformative hope contained in a legal claim—as when an affirmative action argument based on past governmental discrimination that has impeded "equality of opportunity" to compete on the Law School Admission Test exam affirms both the legitimacy of competitive exams as ciphers of social value and the legitimacy of the narrow and anti-empathic analytical rationality tested on these exams as the kind of "skill" needed for mastering legal reasoning (while also tending to intensify societal racial conflict between relatively powerless white and minority groups, since the ethical message embodied in the interpretive schema tends to reconfirm that the whites really merit success on the competitive ladder and are being punished for sins which they themselves had nothing to do with).

The way to surpass this contradiction which has plagued progressive lawyers for at least my adult lifetime is to start telling the truth about the vision of social life that we are trying to make real and to treat the American people as a whole as if they also can and should believe in it. I have already stated the philosophical/ontological basis for the possibility of this occurring—the desire for mutual confirmation and the felt need of everyone to overcome the blockage of this social desire means that people will want to respond to (and in some cases, to defensively resist the pull of) evocative moral appeals which convey a sense of transcendant social purpose. Claims of right, when they are formulated with clients in law offices and whether they are made in court or through the media, should be justified legally in a way that is continuous with the qualitative political meaning that inspires them. As for the possible objection that this kind of thinking is "idealist" in the sense of not being grounded in the real socio-economic and cultural conditions that shape people's responses to such appeals (a view shared by both Marxists and conservative economic rationalists), let me say simply that any claim must be contextualized so that it expresses some particular tendency, already alive and moving within the culture, that carries a disalienating, potentially transformative meaning which can legitimately support the political expression of this meaning in public legal discourse. If the Constitution is an "evolving document," then its meaning should always be subject to a contested debate over who "we" are as social beings and how we are or should be "constituted" as a political community.

Here is one contemporary example of what I mean. The doctrine of comparable worth has emerged from the spread of mutual confirmation that gave rise to the women's movement, but the social meaning of both the movement and the doctrine at the moment are in doubt. In its early phases, the women's movement sought to fundamentally challenge the qualities of social interaction that have been valued in male-dominated society and are reflected in everything from the market economy to positivist epistemologies in the social sciences. Today, this transformative dimension of the women's movement is being contested by a more conservative notion, which defines success and failure primarily in terms of the number of women who occupy positions formerly held only by men and by the amount of money women earn relative to men. Certainly these two meanings of feminism are potentially compatible in the sense that the struggle for sexual equality within the existing society does not imply an abandonment of the more transformative goal—but I believe that the two visions are often in tension and that the latter threatens to co-opt the former or to neutralize it enough so that it no longer carries the sharp critique of prevailing forms of social alienation that it once did.

The choice of how to articulate a comparable worth claim reflects this tension. As far as I know, the principal way that comparable worth claims are currently formulated is to claim a right to equal pay for jobs traditionally occupied by women which are comparable, in terms of educational and skill requirements and other measurable factors, to higher paid jobs held primarily by men. The remedy sought is money damages. In one sense, this formulation does express the transformative dimension of feminism because it seeks to value—in the manner currently recognized as the measure of value—the compassion and intuitive wisdom that have long characterized many forms of so-called "women's work." But on the whole, those who have made these claims have tended to accept the division of desire and reason that feminism originally sought to oppose, emphasizing instead a quantitative meaning of equality defined by such factors as number of years of training and amount of monetary compensation which are assimilable to the prevailing liberal models of both market-based social relations and rights-based redistributive political intervention. Like labor-law jurisprudence in the decades following the rise of the labor movement, which to some degree redefined that movement's goals so as to emphasize higher wages and safer working conditions while de-emphasizing the qualitative and more transformative goal of workplace democracy, this approach to feminist jurisprudence may in the long run contribute to the dissolution of the transformative vision of human reciprocity that is at the heart of the women's movement's power to create social change. The law always has this potential power of dissolution because legal interpretation constantly reflects back to those inside and outside a social movement what society as a whole considers to be the legitimate aims of the movement; the law therefore offers its own promise of social recognition and inclusion, however alienated, that may subtly erode the movement's own self-understanding and original conception of its aims.

My claim is that it would be better, for the women's movement and for society, for feminist lawyers developing their legal theory to have as their goal a redefinition of human worth that challenges the market-based definition more directly than a pay equity theory does, and to seek a remedy that calls for some plausible modification in the organization of a workplace aimed at realizing a more nurturant and socially confirming conception of the nature of socially valuable labor. I cannot say at the moment exactly how such a claim would be formulated using the existing legal materials (there is certainly support in American legal history for a qualitative ideal of equality), but the great virtue of this approach is that it would allow the legal claim to be expressed in a way continuous with the moral passion and sense of social purpose that originally animated the women's movement itself. Not only would this fusion of desire and reason within an openly political discourse challenge the apparent inevitability of people's sense of underconfirmation by challenging the prevailing system of measuring social worth that produces it; such a fusion would also challenge the technical-rational character of existing legal reasoning and the reification of legal categories that results from it by calling for an interpretation of social equality that relies upon the "softness" of heartfelt thought and the kind of empathic comprehension of social qualities that dissolves the detachment of the anti-intuitive and hyperanalytical "legal mind." The moral power of such a claim, in other words, would not only be in its assertion of the possibility of a transformed workplace sensitive to the realization of a common social desire that women are speaking for, but in its assertion that political and legal reasoning must reform itself so as to be able to recognize this kind of desire if it means to really express the will of the people in the truth of their social being.

It may be that this way of framing a comparable worth claim is not currently feasible because the constraints within the social context or the available legal materials are too great. But even if the precise right asserted is more narrowly framed and the remedy sought is more conventional, the meaning of what is being asked for can be stated so as to express the deeper political goal, perhaps emphasizing primarily the intrinsic worth of the qualities immanent in the work to be valued rather than equivalence in educational qualifications. There is virtually no case to be litigated or bill to be lobbied for that does not offer progressive lawyers some opportunity to infuse their practical objective with a larger meaning that exerts a pull on the desire and longing of those who hear them, including their own supporters who face the same conflict between confidence and doubt that everyone else does. It would have mattered a great deal if Michael Dukakis had presented his student loan program within a framework of meaning that emphasized how the pay back provision would have enabled college graduates to devote themselves to public service instead of forcing them to become yuppies, and to have made it clear how this program was linked to the social vision behind his health care program and his child care program and his opposition to the war in Nicaragua and his determination to end the Cold War. In the same sense, it would matter a great deal if progressive lawyers formed themselves into a self-conscious community (through a series of national and regional meetings, for example) and began to give even their most modest legal claims a sense of social meaning and purpose that could make their work an affirmation of the desire for mutual connection that secretly animates each of us. Conservative forces began this kind of self-conscious organizing in support of their moral vision after the defeat of Barry Goldwater in 1964. It seems like the right time for us to do it now.

Letters

Thomas Kleven, Howard Levi; Peter Gabel responds

To the Editor:

Peter Gabel brilliantly and passionately exposes the alienation of modern social life. I thoroughly agree that people have a basic need for mutual recognition and confirmation that is un-

realized in social existence, that we collectively deny alienation by reifying the alienating aspects of social life as objective structures seemingly beyond human control, and that progressive social change demands an evocative and disalienating moral vision of a community whose transcendent social purpose is to make mutual confirmation an achievable reality.

It is important, though, not to be overly reductionist in our analysis of social life.

But to privilege the subjective and intersubjective aspects of life over the objective and individualistic is also reductionist. Life is neither objective nor subjective, neither atomized nor communal, but all at the same time. There is a physical world out there that conditions our subjective interpretations and circumscribes our ability to create the world in accordance with our moral vision of it. There is exploitation and oppression which must be overcome if the possibility of intersubjective connection and mutual confirmation is to be realized. And it is necessary to analyze the ways in which exploitation and oppression work, and therefore to some extent to reify its forms, in order to develop a moral vision of a reformed social order. Analysis necessarily reifies because objectification is to some degree endemic to language and to the very process of conceptualizing. But like Gabel, we can and must also use language to dereify our reifications, lest we delude ourselves into thinking that they are fixed and immutable and that we lack the power to change them.

I agree, as Gabel implies, that all too often Marxism has been reduced to a crude determinism which loses sight of human agency and intersubjectivity. But we must also guard against the countertendency to make everything a matter of subjective interpretation. For to do so tends to create the fantasy that alienation is simply a figment of our imagination which we can overcome by willing it away. What we must do, rather, is to actively change the social conditions which produce alienation as both an objective aspect of material life and a subjective aspect of mental life. In short, while we must not overly objectify the world, we must not overly subjectify it either.

Professor Thomas Kleven
Thurgood Marshall School of Law
Houston, Texas

To the Editor:

Peter Gabel's article "The Transformative Possibilities of Legal Culture" was a brilliant statement of what is new in *Tikkun*'s approach—and also reveals what is weak about your approach.

Tikkun avoids the old-fashioned reductionism that sees human beings as motivated by nothing more than economic necessity. Gabel is eloquent when he talks about the way that human beings seek mutual recognition and confirmation that is unrealized in their daily social existence.

But from this correct insight Gabel and *Tikkun* proceed to suggest that the Democratic party and liberal politics should be built around this insight and that this should be the center of their political program. In effect, this means replacing a focus on concrete programs with a focus on building a political party that resembles a church or a therapy community. To my way of thinking, the Democrats are failing not because they are too different from the right wing but because they are too much like it. They really present no program alternatives. If the Democrats were to build on the openings created by Gorbachev—offering dramatic reductions in arms spending and diverting those funds to badly needed social programs—they would recapture the old flame. Dukakis' suggestions for student loans, health care, and child care were moving in the right direction—but they were too timid, they didn't go far enough. But I see no need to raise issues about social connectedness and meaning—they are too abstract and would appeal only to the kinds of intellectuals who already support progressive causes.

And this leads to my second point. There's much to change in the law. As a progressive lawyer myself, I am constantly fighting to change the laws to make them reflect the liberal values that many of us hold. And I defend clients who are fighting for social change, or clients whose cases allow me to challenge oppressive laws. But Gabel wants something more—he wants us to contest who we are as social beings and how we are constituted as a political community. He wants us to tell the truth about the vision of social life that we are trying to make real as progressive lawyers. Now, this is an admirable goal—but it makes sense only in a law school classroom, not in the actual practice of the law—which is exactly why so many of the people attracted to Gabel's organization, Critical Legal Studies, are law professors and not practicing lawyers.

So get real, *Tikkun*. Get your theory out of the sky and into the reality of daily life in America, where things are far more right-wing than you folks seem to realize. But keep up the good work—I love reading the magazine, and in some funny way it gives me hope that everything I stand for is still possible. There's something to be said for keeping the vision alive.

Howard Levi
New York, New York

Peter Gabel responds:

Thomas Kleven and Howard Levi are right to emphasize the objective causes of the pain that people face in American society, and it would certainly be a mistake for *Tikkun* to be calling for an approach to politics that valued social connection and meaning at the expense of concrete programs addressing people's need for health care, child care, jobs, and housing. The last thing we need is to replace the technocratic and narrow policy-oriented thinking of today's liberals and radicals with New-Age fantasies about creating community that ignore the real conditions of people's lives.

The point of my article was not to downplay the importance of economic suffering and injustice, but to emphasize that people's social and psychological needs are just as real and "objective" as the need for food, shelter, and medical care. Contrary to the implication in Howard Levi's letter, it is not primarily intellectuals and professors who are in a frenzy about the sanctity of the flag, but working-class people who see it as a symbol of passionate

social connection that is otherwise largely lacking in their lives. My claim is that concrete proposals like the call for universal health care, for example, must be framed within a moral vision that embodies the same desire for social connection that the flag embodies—but in a way that could really generate this sense of connection between self and others instead of relegating people to the fantasized community symbolized by the flag.

I do strongly disagree with Levi's defense of conventional nuts-and-bolts law practice. The legal arena should be an important public context in which lawyers and clients argue with passion and moral vision for the creation of a more humane society. As long as progressive lawyers see themselves as technical rule-manipulators fighting for good causes, without understanding how they recreate the very thing they want to change by deferring to existing assumptions about how to act, think, and speak in their role as lawyers, they will never be a real threat to the system of existing power relations. There is real value in the work that Levi and other liberal lawyers perform on behalf of the oppressed, but to make that work socially transformative they must also challenge the ways that the existing legal system narrows (really flattens) meaning of important social debates and blocks the expression of the desire for mutual confirmation that is at the heart of every vital movement for social change. □

Marx Meets Muir: Toward a Synthesis of the Progressive Political and Ecological Visions

Frances Moore Lappé and J. Baird Callicott

Growing up in the South during the fifties, we both found a refuge from the pervasive racism and fundamentalism of the Bible Belt in the Unitarian "Liberal Religious Youth." When we reconnected romantically after twenty-five years, our friends' reactions came as a surprise: "Frankie, he's an environmental ethicist? What does he believe—that *trees* have rights?" And "Baird, she's the co-author of *Food First*? What does she want—us to end up with standing room only on her too-small planet?"

Reflecting on these reactions, we realized that from common social, regional, and intellectual roots, we had come to inhabit two distinct communities of thought—the progressive political and the ecological—often in opposition. Yet we sensed, intuitively, that these two seemingly disparate worldviews share certain underlying values that suggest the possibility of mutual enrichment.

But before exploring the possible convergences, let us sketch some of the more obvious conflicts.

The knee-jerk response of some progressive political types to the ecological vision is that environmental amenities—pure air and water, landscaped green belts, plenty of park land and wilderness—are luxury items for well-heeled yuppies. State and federal tax revenues spent for unproductive real estate means less money for entitlements and social programs. If you're Black, jobless, and hungry, the self-righteous concern of the comfortable white middle and upper classes for environmental quality seems to be one more statement of their insensitivity and selfishness in the face of others' suffering.

The excessive concern for nonhuman life—save the whales, the wolf, the eagle, the rain forests—is seen as a case of misplaced morality. If so-called civilized, democratic societies are engaged in the systematic exploitation and brutalization of people abroad while turning a blind eye to gnawing poverty, un- and underemployment, illiteracy, homelessness, and hunger within their own borders, isn't moral concern for nonhuman life just a little premature?

On the other hand, the environmentalists and deep ecologists are equally critical of the progressive political vision. Although we already are dangerously near the physical and biological limits to growth, the environmentalists point out, few political progressives advocate substantially reducing the material well-being of people living at the economic median in Western-style industrial countries. The progressives lack biological literacy: They see nature not as a living, functioning system, sensitive at many points to disruption, but as an inexhaustible emporium and as a mere

Frances Moore Lappé is founder of the Institute for the Arts of Democracy. Her most recent book is Rediscovering America's Values *(Ballantine, 1991). J. Baird Callicott, professor of philosophy at the University of Wisconsin, Stevens Point, is the author of numerous articles in environmental philosophy and ethics and editor of* Companion to a Sand County Almanac *(University of Wisconsin Press, 1987). This article appeared in* Tikkun, *September/October 1987.*

stage upon which political struggles are acted out. Nature enters the debate of political visionaries only as a source of wealth-producing raw material—as contested terrain between the peasants or workers deprived of its potential fruits and the wealthy elite now in control. Similarly, human beings are often reduced by progressives to narrow economic profiles, represented as producers or consumers of goods and services. Indeed, political progressives feel queasy about ascribing to people anything other than material needs, fearing that doing so might entail religious or metaphysical assumptions—dismissed as intellectually "fuzzy" and/or divisive.

From the ecological point of view, human happiness is stunted and incomplete if defined in purely economic terms— whether in the more radical terms of class consciousness and struggle or in "value neutral" economic terms of autonomous wants and preference satisfaction. Moreover, nature is not something to be exploited: It is the wider community to which human society is related as part to whole and as the living matrix which nurtures as well as supports human existence.

Yet beneath the very real differences of philosophy, temperament, and outlook in the progressive political and ecological visions lie several basic, shared attitudes and values.

The intellectual sources of both visions are deeply ethical. The lasting appeal of Marx, from a contemporary left-of-center political point of view, rests upon his moral outrage at the human misery and gross social injustice produced by the Industrial Revolution. John Muir, Aldo Leopold, Rachel Carson, and others who helped shape a radical ecological perspective were outraged by the heart-rending destruction of nature brought about by the same historical phenomenon.

The movements that were thus precipitated coalesced in the acute political climate of the 1960s. The same capitalist-military-industrial machine that was bombing Hanoi and the Ho Chi Minh trail, searching and destroying South Vietnam—with Black and white lower-class American youth as the cannon fodder—was also defoliating Southeast Asian rain forests, building nuclear power plants and nuclear weapons at home, and mining and polluting North American soils and waters. The broad popular environmental movement was really born at that intensely political moment in American history.

The concepts and rhetoric of resistance on behalf of the environment were appropriated from the political Left and its resistance on behalf of oppressed peoples. Thus, the contemporary, post-sixties ecological vision began as an extension of the progressive political vision. In fact, ecologists extended the concept of justice beyond the human species, using the same impetus of moral outrage and the rhetoric of resistance to defend the rights of other animal species. Peter Singer's animal liberationist vision was built in part upon a sense of moral outrage at the exploitation and oppression by a powerful minority of a powerless majority—thus extending the social ideal of justice to the wider sphere of the biotic community.

Beyond these shared roots in an ethical vision, both progressive and ecological movements tend to locate individual meaning within a larger whole—human society for progressives, the "biotic community" for ecologists. In this emphasis, both conflict with the dominant liberal tradition— which has so thoroughly shaped Western political thought—and the ontological priority it assigns to individuals. Indeed, it is precisely here that liberals tend to be most outspoken in their criticism of progressives on the Left—arguing that lefties tend to subordinate the interests and autonomy of individuals to the interests and authority of the social whole—a spectral menace, threatening the inherent worth, rights, and "freedom" of individuals. In parallel fashion, critics of ecological holism aver that it involves a mistaken subordination of the individual to the biota.

The progressive political and ecological understandings of freedom also contrast dramatically with the defensive liberal notion. Classically expressed by Isaiah Berlin, liberty is "the holding off of something or someone—of others, who trespass on my field or assert their authority over me— intruders or despots of one kind or another." In the liberal's world, where we social atoms bounce about in limited space, freedom is merely what's left over after others have established their turf—"my freedom ends where your nose begins." Freedom is elbow room.

The progressive political and ecological visions share a more positive and systemic understanding of freedom—with responsibility—because they see the manifold ways in which an economic and political structure can indirectly limit or enhance freedom. How many choices, for example, do the jobless have when unemployment rates are high? Freedom cannot flourish, says the political progressive, unless it is understood to include active responsibility for developing social structures which ensure opportunity to all. Similarly, the ecological visionary who links us systemically to the entire natural world understands our responsibility not just to refrain from directly harming nature ourselves but to strive to be active "stewards," responsibly safeguarding the well-being of the biosphere.

These central shared values present the possibility that the ecological and progressive political movements can both learn from each other's insights.

The ecological vision may offer a reinterpretation of the fundamental concepts of individuality and society which could give new life, meaning, and appeal to the progressive political tradition. Ecological science focuses attention on relationships. It reveals that organisms are not only mutually related and interdependent; they are also mutually defining. In general, species adapt to a "niche" in the biotic community, a role or profession in the "economy of nature." The fluctuations of temperature, rainfall, hours of daylight and darkness, the peculiarities of predators and prey, and hundreds of other variables all sculpt the outward and inward forms and structures of Earth's myriad of species. A species is thus "internally related" to its habitat. Its completely unique and identifying characteristics are determined by its network of relationships. It is what it is because of where and how it lives. From an ecological point of view, a species is the intersection of a multiplicity of strands in the web of life. It is not only located in its context, or related to its context; it is literally constituted by its context.

Viewing the human microcosm through the lens of ecology, a new picture of the relationship of individuals to society emerges. Rather than thinking of individuals as ontologically fundamental and society as either an emergent or an artificial abstraction, the social whole appears as the organic and enduring matrix which gives form and substance to human lives. From this point of view, the modern classical picture of a "state of nature" drawn by Thomas Hobbes, in which fully formed human beings once lived as solitaries in a "war of each against all," is patently absurd. Not only is it impossible to imagine human beings to have evolved in the absence of an intensely social environment, it is impossible to conceive of a fully formed human "person" apart from a social milieu. A person's individuality is literally constituted by the peculiar concatenation of relationships s/he bears to family, friends, neighbors, colleagues, and coworkers. Even in the eighteenth century, the heyday of Liberalism, our social nature was recognized by, of all people, Adam Smith: "It is thus that man, who can subsist only in society, was fitted by nature to that situation for which he was made."

Since we are ultimately interdependent, it is silly to pit individual welfare against individual welfare. And it becomes equally ridiculous to think in terms of trade-offs between social integrity and the individual's unfettered pursuit of happiness. The health and integrity of the social whole is literally essential to a socially constituted individual's well-being. Such a vision of individuality, drawn from ecology, would free the progressive political vision from both the destructive social atomism of classic liberalism and the equally chilling reification of class interests long associated with the Left.

Within the liberal tradition, freedom is a zero-sum equation—the larger is my freedom the smaller is yours, since there's only so much social space and goods to go around. But freedom is only finite when defined to mean freedom to possess that which is finite. If the concept of freedom is expanded to include our freedom to develop our unique human capacities, it becomes infinite. The ecological concept of synergy helps us understand why: If individuality is realized in large part through relationships, then how can freedom be conceived independently of these connections? It cannot.

Viewed in this way, what previously appeared to be burdensome social and environmental obligations may be seen as opportunities for personal expansion and enhancement. The "responsibility," for example, not to pollute or otherwise degrade the environment—a limitation on the negative concept of freedom in the liberal tradition—becomes something more like the opportunity to brush one's teeth or put on fresh clothes. Similarly, the "responsibility" to restructure social rules so as to end poverty—a seemingly impossible burden—becomes, on the contrary, an incredible weight lifted from our shoulders. Imagine walking through any neighborhood of any city in our country basking in the vibrant street life, with no fear of assault—either psychic or physical—by human misery and deprivation. Or, from the opposite approach, imagine the total deflection of your own energy were you to be handed a pink slip tomorrow with no hope for reemployment. Such positive and negative images might help us grasp the magnitude of human potential stolen from us by endemic poverty—and thus the incredible potential to be released by its eradication. Seeing freedom as the mutual expansion of horizons belies the whole notion of zero-sum.

While political progressives may fear that the focus on nonhuman forms of life in the ecological vision might divert energy from pursuit of universal human rights, in fact the opposite may be true. The more expansive notion of the "biotic community" lying at the heart of the ecological vision might serve to minimize the divisive differences among peoples, rather than deflecting concern away from human suffering. Human cultural, ethnic, religious, and racial differences may pale when moral horizons are extended to include sympathy and protection for whales, wolves, and redwoods. The essentially integrative, symbiotic vision of ecology could be used to further advance the progressive political agenda. If human life can survive only through mutually beneficial cooperation with other species, is it not more evidently true that the peoples of the Earth can only survive by recognizing and fostering analogous symbioses? The debilitating poverty in Third World countries, for example, starves people but feeds the military—because it takes force to keep people from alleviating their hunger. We all are made less secure in the ensuing militarization of national and international life. From a purely economic point of view, where elite-dominated social structures keep people abroad too poor to be customers for our goods, we are denied needed trading partners. And poverty wages paid halfway around the world now take the jobs and undercut the standards of living in Pennsylvania or Ohio. Hence, if it is clear that escalating the chemical warfare on insects, excelerating deforestation of the moist tropics, and the monocultural erosion of arable land pose a direct threat to the human population, how much more obvious it becomes that Western neo-colonial oppression and exploitation of the Third World leads to an economically and spiritually exhausting social dialectical as well.

So far we have emphasized some ways that political progressives might learn from the insights and methods of conceptualization that have flourished within the ecology movement. But there are also important insights that political progressives have to offer the ecology movement.

Consider the issue of population control. Ecologists hope for a zero rate of growth in the human population or even a negative rate of growth, to be followed by population stabilization and, later, a gradual and orderly retrenchment. Pressures on other forms of life would thus be reduced and strains on the ecosystem gradually relaxed, permitting nature to recover and human beings to reestablish a stable coexistence or even mutually beneficial symbiosis with fellow members of our biotic community.

Few political progressives would attack such a felicitous vision. But they worry that ecologists, schooled in population biology, might suggest that starvation—as in the case of deer and ducks—is simply a natural limiting device on a population which has outstripped its ecological niche. The progressives point out that a simplistic biological analysis of the human population explosion neglects what is unique about human culture and society. Sociologists and health workers teach us that when parents see their children dying from malnutrition and diseases exacerbated by it—that is, when infant death rates are high—their response is to have *more* children, not fewer. Even the relatively more enlightened approach to preventing births—wider distribution of contraceptives and the increasing use of coerced sterilization and long-term injectable contraceptives—cannot achieve the environmentalists' goal of population stabilization. Several comprehensive studies have shown that family planning programs in themselves contribute only marginally to reducing birth rates. A politically sensitive perspective is thus essential for ecologically motivated activists if they wish to realize their own agenda. For what the ecologists too often miss is that human reproductive decisions, in dramatic contrast to almost all other species, are not purely biological but are complicated by psychological, cultural, and social forces. Where society denies people (especially women) security, status, and opportunity, the family—and often the bigger the better—provides the only possibility for all three.

Seen from this perspective, the "population explosion" is not the unfortunate side effect of a basically beneficent transference of modern medicine to the Third World. Rather, high birth rates in the Third World today often reflect the destruction by colonialism of traditional security systems, while denying the majority of citizens any modern substitute. Increasingly robbed of their land, with few jobs in sight, having virtually no access to health care, education, or old age security, and with many of the traditional religious and communal forms no longer working to provide a framework of meaning, many Third World parents see in their children's labor and later incomes the only security they can hope for, and in their family life a compensation for the growing alienation they experience in the public sphere.

Ecological types would do well to let go of simplistic biological models and look at real-world human population growth patterns. Most of the handful of Third World societies which have been dramatically successful in lowering birth rates have also greatly extended economic security and opportunity, especially for women. Most provide state-aided access to food, either by guaranteeing a basic ration or by heavily subsidizing prices for basic foods or both.

There are important intersections, as well, when we consider issues concerning land use and agriculture. Both ecologists and political progressives challenge the model of industrial agriculture, characterized by monoculture, the intensive use of energy and chemical inputs, large scale, and wage labor. Gone are the days when political progressives were enamored of the large state-owned/collective model of agricultural organization, efficiently employing the latest technology to free peasants from the land. The ecologically sensitized now focus on how industrial agriculture necessarily exploits soil and water resources. The politically sensitized focus on how industrial agriculture exploits people. The politically motivated see in large landholdings in the Third World a most grotesque example of such exploitation—peasants starving while good land grows luxury export crops, enriching a few. Thus, both the ecological and political agree on the need for reform, distributing control of the land among the majority.

And what is to take the place of the deposed agricultural oligarchies?

The ecologically concerned stress the need for a sustainable agriculture, today often termed agroecology, in which the use of synthetic fertilizers and pesticides is minimal and sustainable production is achieved through reliance on the synergistic interaction of a variety of plants and animals. Political visionaries stress the need for those who work the land to have direct control over it. Minimal use of synthetic inputs appeals to them primarily because farmers are more independent the less they have to buy.

Yet here, too, there are important lessons for ecologists to learn from a deeper political analysis.

To be sure, those experimenting with the best crop mix for reducing erosion or working on an improved design for homemade solar corn dryers recognize that misinformed government policies are an obstacle to the realization of their alternative. Certainly, wrong-headed tax, credit, or price-support policies favor capital over labor and reward growth over efficiency. But political progressives can teach ecologists that even if enlightened government policies were enacted, an agriculture benign to both people and the land would still be thwarted—until fundamental principles of capitalism itself are questioned. Let's see why.

Three essentials of capitalism undermine a benign agricultural ecology.

First is the market/commodity system's glaring omission: It simply cannot provide the information needed to protect the land and the people who farm it. The only information the market offers is price. Yet prices—to which all producers in a capitalist market must respond to stay in busi-

Drawing by Anthony Dubovsky

ness—do not incorporate the true resource or human cost of production. Prices of farm commodities do not inform us, for example, that their production entails the erosion of topsoil, that now, on one-third of U.S. farmland, topsoil is being eroded faster than nature can rebuild it. Neither is drawing down of groundwater reserves registered in the market price. Because the market omits such critical information, it deludes us. The market price cannot incorporate the price to be paid by later generations for whom providing food will be more difficult on land with impoverished topsoil and depleted groundwater.

Like the prices of farm commodities, prices of farm inputs—fertilizers, pesticides, machinery—also send farmers false signals. Neither can they incorporate long-term costs or consequences. Following the market's cues, farmers will purchase manufactured inputs as long as they can estimate (hope) that market prices for their crops will be high enough to cover the input costs, plus turn a profit *this year*. The market cannot warn the farmer that his choice may be generating a dependency that will threaten his economic survival when his neighbor buys the same machine, pushing production up and commodity prices down. Neither can the market inform a farmer that his choice of certain inputs may heighten his risk of contracting our most deadly forms of cancer.

Most simply put, farming choices guided exclusively, or even centrally, by the market will be ecologically destructive because the market is blind to costs that can't be quantified. It assumes *no* cost to nature's supplies—topsoil, natural fertility, and groundwater. It assumes less than the real cost of inputs— pesticides, herbicides, fossil fuels, and fertilizers. And it "externalizes" such costs as environmental pollution and ecological degradation.

Second, within the market system, farmland is—like washing machines or waffle irons—in one sense merely another commodity to be bought and sold in the marketplace. But because the supply of land—especially good farmland—is limited, it is also a speculative commodity. People buy it as an investment. As a speculative commodity, farmland is treated as having a value of its own dissociated from the body of knowledge and skills which are a product of generations on the land. Wealth, not land wisdom, becomes the criterion for ownership. Farmland ownership becomes disconnected from the culture of agriculture.

Third, in the market economy, labor is a commodity as well. And as farmland becomes increasingly the domain of the wealthy—as today many absentee investors buy up land—more and more farm work is done by workers selling their labor to landowners. In the Third World, this process is far advanced. And now, for the first time in American history, most of the work on American farms is done by hired labor. But agriculture dependent upon hired labor belies the vision of agroecology just as much as does heavy use of petrochemical inputs. Agroecology is necessarily knowledge-intensive, depending upon all the faculties of the farmer. As agroecology replaces simple monocropping with a mix of crops and animals, farmers must understand the many subtle interrelations of their chosen mix in order to enrich the soil and minimize pest damage.

Thus, agroecology depends upon a specific type of relationship of the farmer to the land. It must be enduring, for only over time can the necessary information be acquired. And the farmer must feel a personal stake in the welfare of the land, in order to call forth not just the physical exertion required but also the mental alertness needed to observe and record subtle changes and interactions over decades. Where land and labor remain mere commodities, such a relationship of the farmer to the land will be the rare exception.

It follows that agroecology and capitalist economic rules are in direct conflict. The market is an insufficient—and often misleading—guide to land use. And land and labor treated as commodities dissociate agriculture from its sustaining culture. Agroecology represents an alternative to the machine in the garden. It can, perhaps, only be realized if at the same time we banish the machine from the marketplace as well. Integrating the principles of genuine democracy and economic justice into our economic decision making, political progressives emphasize, will allow us effectively to tame the market—without throwing it out altogether.

We have suggested here some of the ways that a creative dialogue might proceed between people committed to progressive politics and people moved by the ecological vision. The ecological vision could bring to the somewhat older political vision the exciting, integrative new paradigm now enlivening the contemporary sciences. It thus could free the progressive political vision from the well-worn structural assumptions of the liberal paradigm. By the same token, the political vision gives to the ecological vision badly needed analyses of distinctly human layers of complexity beyond human ecology—the economic and political rules that block the realization of the ecologists' own vision.

We are convinced that an allied progressive political/ecological vision could help to free both from their respective limitations. Listening to each other, both movements could become more convincing to the majority who now listen to neither. □

Listening to the Earth

Anthony Weston

According to James Lovelock of Gaia Hypothesis fame, Gaia—Earth as living organism—can't be doing so badly when, looking down from an airplane or from a height, we see mostly green, even in populated areas. There's something to this. From the knob where I am standing I can see the Hudson River Valley from Storm King to the lower Catskills, east to Connecticut and west across the river to the Shawangunks. In the barrenness of winter when nothing is hidden, I scan the dwelling place of maybe 200,000 people and still see mainly trees. Hills and trees. And here too, having come out to celebrate the rhythm of the seasons, I begin to sense what it might mean to regard the Earth itself as a living thing. The birds shuttle about as I climb to greet the sun on its first day north of the equator this year, the day of equal night and light, "equi-nocte"; pagan "Eostar," the return of light; Easter, the resurrection of life; Passover, deliverance. Already the buds are swelling and the red flowers of the maple wave in the still-wintry wind. An old, old rhythm. The sun will return, the flowers will yield to leaves, small birds now darting all around in the predawn light will consume and be consumed. Life goes on.

There are three power plants down the river opposite New Hamburg. I can see their white plumes rise straight into the air four or five thousand feet, then at some thermal boundary bend at a right angle and meander off along the horizon. Curiously, one drifts vaguely to the west, the other stretches out eastward along the whole southern quarter of my panorama. As I climbed, I thought they were the trace clouds of sunrise, pink-purple with the residue of night. The feeling is more sinister, now that I know the source. It reminds me of how the Angel of Death arrives in de Mille's *The Ten Commandments*: as a long, thin, green cloud, hovering below the moon. Not like a hurricane, not a banshee roar, but crystalline and silent.

Curling above my sleeping world floats the morning's contribution to global warming. Yesterday's *New York Times* spoke of unprecedented drought and dust storms in Kansas. This morning's local paper, which I collect on my way back, reports that Poughkeepsie is now for the first time in violation of federal air-quality standards. Last summer's record heat has caused excessive ground-level ozone and a steady wind from the south brings Gotham's carbon monoxide up the river.

Even this site may soon be gone. Its days as an orchard are apparently numbered: our neighbor, fighting one of those endless rear-guard battles with sundry developers, tells us that it has already been sold and is slated for housing of some sort. In a few years the suburbs will have risen even to these heights. Little brush birds may return, since the usual suburban vegetation tends to be more brushy than working orchards, and whatever of these fruit trees remain will no doubt be left untended. Wilder birds, not so easily bought off by the largesse of bird feeder and berry bush, and adamantly opposed to the permanent presence of humans, will not return. Another and more disquieting suggestion for judging the health of an ecosystem: Look for the presence, or absence, of the wildest animals....

Anthony Weston teaches philosophy at SUNY Stony Brook. This article appeared in Tikkun, *March/April 1990.*

By evening it is snowing—oddly, just about the first snow we've had this year. At midnight, this first midnight of spring, there is enough snow, barely, to cross-country ski through the woods and along the abandoned railroad bed across the road. Now the woods are silent, wet, almost sighing. For a moment it seems to be November, early December, the first and not the last snow of the winter. But in fact this is winter's last gasp, it is already spring, I have seen the buds. This year they come forth to the prospect of regional drought by midsummer; this year also the old railroad bed may become a new county road. So the reawakening is as if from an unsettled sleep. Bad dreams. A reflection of our own nervousness—or vice versa?

My Ph.D. seminar in the philosophy of nature is sitting on the ground in a wigwam in Hauppauge, New York, half a mile and four centuries or so from the Northern State Parkway. Perhaps the latter distance explains why we do not hear the cars. This is Long Island, or "Paumanok," which the Indians knew took the shape of a great whale, though they never saw the island from the air. It is drizzling, foggy, and cold. Wisps of fog and smoke, indistinguishable, cling to the outside of the wigwam, and inside, the mists from our voices rise to join the smoke seeking the small smoke-hole.

We are here because I believe that we cannot even begin to understand a Native American experience of the earth in any other way. Of course we have also done what all appropriate seminars do: read books and talked about them around tables in small rooms. In *The Reenchantment of the World* Morris Berman argues that from the medieval to the modern age, consciousness was turned from what he calls a "participating" mode, a sense of identification or "psychic wholeness" with one's surroundings, to the opposite, "disenchanted" mode all too familiar to us now. For Descartes, sitting on his stone in the midst of the Thirty Years War, the very justification of knowledge requires that we abstract ourselves from the world of the senses and of the body. Consciousness sets itself up *against* our surroundings, against the world. Thus, a certain world-alienation is virtually the essence of thought itself. "Painful incompleteness is the true mature experience," as Paul Shepard puts it in *Nature and Madness*, "and the meaninglessness of the natural world is its meaning."

Berman wants to recover "participation," a world that is once again "enchanted." So we read about Jung's use of alchemical texts to interpret dream images, about Reich's conception of the unconsciousness of the body, about reinterpreting the Indian rain dance not as a technology for producing rain but as, at bottom, an invitation to *relationship*: The Indians, Berman argues, were "asking in effect to make love to [the clouds], and like any normal lover they may or may not be in the mood."

We are struggling. Of course the ideas are strange and unsettling, but the struggle is more than that. Partly it is that too much in Berman's writing makes it sound as though "participating consciousness" is primarily a state of mind—and on some level, I think, that is what we implicitly believe. Berman speaks of participation as a form of *consciousness*, a word we inevitably hear with Cartesian overtones. His text itself invokes participation in a triply intellectualized form: citing a Jungian reading of the symbols in alchemical texts. Perhaps, scandalously, we ought to drop this talk of consciousness entirely, and stick with the adjective: participating. We need to recover a directly experienced closeness and also vulnerability. It is, Berman says, something that we can now glimpse or recover only under special circumstances. Sex and panic are his examples. The general suggestion is that we can recover participation only at the extremes, not as a normal mode of being but only when we are thoroughly and perhaps unexpectedly overpowered.

But there are other ways too. And so here we are, sitting on the earth in a wigwam on a cold morning, watching the rising smoke and the mists from our breaths, passing a cup, hearing the calls of the geese and wild turkeys—penned, to be sure, but still calling excitedly in the fog. We are talking about Abenaki creation stories. We are speaking slowly, for once, not covering all other sounds with our voices. And maybe that small matter of tempo in the end points to the very essence of participation: the sense of being simply *part of* a larger, living world. There is something to hear besides ourselves: the calls of the birds and the slow rustle of the winds; our fire echoing the hiss of the rain; and our voices, when we speak, interweaving among the animals'. This is what it means to truly feel that "the Earth is alive." For Lovelock it is supposed to be a scientific discovery at the very forefront of modern speculation. For the Indians it was an everyday experience that hardly needed to be thematized at all, until they encountered another people who, incredibly, had somehow missed it.

As we prepare to leave, I speak of a kind of "culture shock" in going back to campus. Many of the students return to an afternoon seminar on Hegel. I return to a balky xerox collator. Late in the day many of us find ourselves on the fourth floor of the university library, listening to a famous American philosopher hold forth on the question of

SAGERT

Drawing by Edina Sagert

whether a certain famous French philosopher did or did not draw normative conclusions from his exhaustive and penetrating cultural critiques, or whether his systematic avoidance of normative explicitness could really save him from the apparently dreaded problem of normative foundations. The suggestion seemed to be that the problem of "justifying" values is so central yet so insoluble that a philosopher might well structure his or her entire corpus so as to avoid ever having to face it. Yet no such "problem" would have occurred to us six hours earlier in the wigwam. And once again it is not merely a question of thinking ourselves into the necessary position. Perhaps what the morning showed us is that the divide between value and "fact" may be rooted in something as simple and pervasive as our architecture. It is not merely the preoccupation with texts or argument that subtly or not so subtly reinscribes the very nonparticipation we are trying to escape. We would do better to notice that the very settings in which texts or arguments present themselves already exclude the possibility of real participation. What happened on the fourth floor of the library would have been utterly impossible in the wigwam; and the reverse is also true. Nonparticipation is enforced by the concrete blocks and steel of the library walls, and by the windows that don't open, looking over asphalt plazas and a few disconsolately wheeling gulls. All of this is of course no more than the familiar landscape of human inhabitation, here not even particularly urban. Here the earth does not emerge as "alive": it barely even seems to have a presence.

We return to private cogitation, or more mundane tasks, in our own building. Here the windows open—it is an older structure—but otherwise everything is the same. We "do" philosophy, we try to comprehend the world, we are wholly surrounded by our artifacts; there are no animals, not even any children, not even, so to speak, ourselves. No new discovery, this, but the enormity of it is still astonishing. Our tradition tells us that to be able to think we must disconnect the senses, and to be able to do *that* we have had to disconnect and deaden the entire natural world in turn. Thus and only thus have we managed to persuade ourselves that it is dead.

How can we speak for the Earth? Can it be done at all on the fourth floor of the university library, in our disconnected mood generally? Should we try? We don't "speak for" our lovers, after all; we love them, as the Indians loved this earth. The spruce muskegs off James Bay, so-called barren land periodically proposed for flooding by Hydro Quebec partly in order to generate electricity for export to Long Island, are known to the Cree as "Kistikani" gardens. Of the primeval evergreen forests of the Pacific Northwest, rain-washed, fogbound, and now being clear-cut for timber, a Duwamish chief said:

> Every part of this earth is sacred to my people. Every shining pine needle, every sandy shore, every mist in the dark woods, every clearing and humming insect is holy in the memory and experience of my people.

Perhaps *he* is speaking for the land—though even that would not give anyone else the right. Even so, he speaks out of desperation and to an audience that hears mostly sentimentality. Can we actually understand those words—we whites, I mean, who in the Indians' view brought the idea of wilderness with us? *They* never saw this land as wild, threatening, needing to be tamed and controlled. "By seeking to dominate [nature]," writes Peter Matthiessen, "the white men set themselves in opposition to a vital healing force of which they were a part, and thereby mislaid a whole dimension of existence." Turn that phrase over in your mind: mislaid a whole dimension of existence. It is not a matter of having missed one or two connections. But then why should we expect to be able to recover that lost dimension at all, let alone in the old familiar rooms and with the old familiar words?

There is a deep and perverse logic at work here, actually a logic that works itself out not only with respect to nature but across the domain of ethics. This is the perversity: Violation can turn the violated into something that in the end "by nature" invites or allows violation. Thus one effect of "factory farming" cattle or chickens is to terrorize, cripple, and debase the animals to the point that the pitiful creature that results seems to be an utterly implausible candidate for anything but human "use" and consumption. People who work with those animals may find it impossible to feel any serious concern for them. People who speak up for them will inevitably seem to speak out of mere sentimentality. To this, I believe, we are now only able to say: so be it. What we are speaking up against is the very debasement itself, the deliberately undertaken process of turning the animals *into* creatures who can have no serious claim on us; creatures such as commercially produced chickens—debeaked, drugged, virtually blind, unable to fly or even walk. By now that kind of horror story can be repeated for many species of animals including ourselves. We are left to speak for what might have been, and maybe not so much against the suffering and violation of this particular animal as for a vision of what a more natural life for this *kind* of animal would be like. Of course this is a matter of some speculation. Of course it requires a leap of faith. The horror is that faith is all that is left to us.

To pursue the analogy one more step, recovery too must start from a posture other than *argument,* strictly or even loosely speaking. Argument takes seriously the demand to *show* that other animals can be companions, when precisely that demand already represents a way of closing ourselves off from the creatures in question (that's it: in question). Thus the last thing we need is the usual laboratory studies of other animals from a posture of studied neutrality about whether or not, as one dolphin researcher put it, "there's somebody in there." Human beings trip over their own feet when treated with such distance and skepticism, and there is no reason to expect other animals to do any better, especially when they are exquisitely more sensitive to the affective environment than we are. Not to mention that being "in there" is exactly what fully-sensed creatures are *not*: we are "out here," alive in a rich and responsive world. Participation, again, is not in the head.

I am suggesting that the very insistence on speaking personally and nostalgically in fact can be profoundly insightful and reconstitutive. Relatedness or the failure of relatedness depends as much upon our openness as upon any justification of values that philosophers might devise. So the task is to open up the possibility of relatedness, and for this we must speak in a different way, reflecting a different way of being. About other animals, then, what we really need to ask is not whether they are fit companions for us, but whether we are fit companions for *them*, and the answer, again, lies more in our willingness to invite and recognize reciprocity than in the usual issues about *their* ability to use language or to solve problems or the like.

"Relatedness" can also emerge in the experience of natural places, rock formations or rivers or pine-covered dunes. But there are very few natural places whose integrity remains intact, not reconstructed to human advantage or in accord with our notions or momentary needs, or simply destroyed. On suburban Long Island the mere fact that a piece of land is not built upon qualifies it as "barren" in the minds of planners and developers. Indeed the very notion of a "piece" of land does violence to an ecosystem point of view; this is why, as has often been noted, the Indians could not understand the idea of dividing and selling it.

In general, we have turned natural places into mere things even more thoroughly than we have turned other animals into things, sometimes even while seeming to acknowledge them. So "Old Faithful" scintillates under colored lights and the Park Service adds oil to the water to make sure the eruptions come off on schedule. So mountaineering becomes the new sport of choice, the new form of *exercise*. How would we know, having so thoroughly remade and re-rubricized the natural world itself, whether these places, ancient geysers or the jagged backbones of the world, might not have their own integrity and spontaneity? ... Here too, then, the first moment of an ethical relation is not the raising of questions about just what sort of thing nature or a natural place is, or just what, a priori, its possibilities are, as if we had enough "evidence" to answer such questions. The task is not to derive the value of nature from some more general criterion. Instead the first moment must be a reaching out, a willingness to be touched, an openness to the unexpected—and, correspondingly, an approach that at least struggles against the technologically remade environments that ordinarily close us off from the natural world. So "Old Faithful"—presumably renamed to acknowledge that she/he/it too has moods, like the skies that may or may not open themselves to us—might have to be approached in the manner of the Plains Indians: after elaborate fasts and ceremonies, perhaps first daring to come near the geyser only in dreams; then in person, purified and alone, after days of hiking through the bubbling earth and nights sleepless for the scent of grizzly bear. So someday such a pilgrimage might be necessary for anyone who claims to know something about what my graduate students are supposed to be learning: philosophy and ecology. Someday, like the Celts, we may set aside places that we all may climb to greet the equinoctial sun, each of these places a holy place, a center of the world, not a mere margin temporarily unsubdivided for more ranch houses.... ☐

Critical Support for Earth Day

Michael Lerner

W hy only critical support? When everyone from Barry Commoner to George Bush is on board, why shouldn't we be equally enthusiastic? After all, how can it hurt to raise environmental consciousness? It can't hurt, which is why we support it. Yet the attempt to legitimize this event by creating the largest possible coalition around it also subverts its potential impact. In the twenty years since Earth Day 1970, environmental consciousness has often been misdirected into programs and attitudes that did more to co-opt our indignation at the destruction of the earth than to fundamentally change things. Band-aids on a cancer are counterproductive—they divert energies that need to be mobilized more effectively.

Experts in ecology are increasingly convinced that the survival of the human race, perhaps of all life on the planet, hangs in the balance. If we do not immediately and decisively alter our entire relationship to nature, there is good reason to believe that within twenty years we will have done irrevocable damage to the life-support systems of the planet.

Hard as it might be to accept, some forms of ecological consciousness actually work in the wrong direction. For example, the notion that we are all polluters, and that what we really need to do is to be aware of our own responsibility for polluting the earth, is fundamentally misleading. Yes, it is true that many of us could make environmentally more conscious decisions in our personal lives—recycle, not litter, and so on. But the real and pressing danger to the planet comes from corporations and governments that decide to use resources and develop products in environmentally destructive or irresponsible ways. By focusing attention on the smaller issues in our personal lives, we get to feel good about ourselves and close our eyes to the larger structural issues which we sometimes feel powerless to change.

"But surely if people did not choose to purchase environmentally destructive products the corporations wouldn't produce them," runs one typical argument. "Similarly, if the people did not choose to spend hundreds of billions of dollars on wasteful weapons systems and other environmentally hazardous governmental projects, they could elect different representatives who would choose different priorities. So it's really people's attitudes that have to be changed." True enough, as far as it goes, but it doesn't go very far. The argument misses the economic and political realities that help shape our choices, and hence unfairly blames the people for choices that are at least understandable given the options they face.

Take, for example, one of the heaviest polluters—the automobile. The immense power of the auto and oil industries around the world has been mobilized to block the development of a rational system of mass transportation. In Los Angeles, for example, a rail transit system was bought up and dismantled by an automobile manufacturer—so that people would become more dependent on cars. Other powerful corporations, using their resources to encourage the election of sympathetic legislators, managed to prevent the introduction of serious auto-emission restraints, thus polluting

This editorial appeared in Tikkun, *March/April 1990.*

major industrial areas and threatening the population with the cancer emissions cause. In circumstances such as these, it makes sense for people to choose to live far away from the areas in which they work, and to rely on automobiles to get there. It misses the point to blame the individual consumers for making this choice or to ask them to raise their environmental consciousness.

Similarly, we will hear increasing talk about the danger being done to our environment by Third World polluters, those who are cutting down the rain forests, for example. Here, again, we miss the larger economic realities that have caused the problem. For hundreds of years Western colonialists, and for decades American corporate interests, have helped shape a world economy that has prevented Third World countries from developing economic independence. The massive poverty of the Third World has often been an outcome of economic arrangements imposed on them by the developed world—and in the process Western corporations and publics have benefited from cheap raw materials, cheap labor, and markets for goods. It is in this context that Third World countries hear the moralizing words of environmentalists. The environmentalists talk about the future of the planet; many people in the Third World worry about their own physical survival today. So the pleas of environmentalists fall on deaf ears.

Nor will corporations change their behavior as long as it is profitable for them to produce goods that may have long-term destructive consequences. After all, as a corporate manager your "responsibility to shareholders" is to maximize profits in the short run. You get no career benefits from maximizing the future of the planet. You may take a few minimal steps to project an image of corporate sensitivity to environmental issues, because that may help enhance corporate profits, but you certainly are not going to engage in a fundamental restructuring of what and how you produce. It's as wrong to stigmatize individual corporate managers as it is to attack individual workers in environmentally destructive ventures. All are caught in a web of entanglements in which it will be self-destructive to their own short-term interests to act in ways that would be environmentally rational.

We need an international system for rational planning of industrial production, farming, fishing, mining, energy resources, and the like. The human race could pull together, decide to prohibit all forms of interference with the natural environment that are destructive to the long-term survival of the human race, and enforce its decisions. But for this plan to work, we would need a moral revolution: a rejection of the self-interested ethics of capitalism. We would also need a powerfully decentralized democratic process so that we could all participate in the discussions and the decision making, plus a democratically elected and accountable body that could coordinate the various local decisions.

But rationally planned economies are precisely what have just failed in Eastern Europe, no? *Tikkun* had little sympathy for the Eastern European systems of government that appropriated the language of socialist visionaries to mask the reality of ruling elites who governed in their own selfish interests and ignored the will of the people. The idea behind those societies was that people were supposed to forego selfish interests and work for nonmaterial incentives—namely, the common good. But because these societies were not democratic, the common good was defined by ruling elites who used the language of community to advance their own private interests. No wonder, then, that many Eastern Europeans lost interest in working hard and sacrificing material well-being, once they realized that the language of the common good was a mere cover for the private good of a particular elite.

The same logic will hold whenever we ask any specific group within our society to sacrifice its own short-term interests for the common good. People will make major readjustments in the way they produce and consume only if they see that everyone is making fundamental changes, and that these changes do not leave them more economically vulnerable than others. In short, saving the planet puts the question of redistribution of the world's wealth and rational planning of the world's economy at the center of the human agenda. And the changes will require substantively democratic procedures so that people can participate as part of the community that debates and decides how to use the world's resources.

Short of this kind of thinking, we get the nearsighted strategies of major environmental groups and "environmentally sensitive" politicians. Afraid to challenge existing methods of production and consumption, government regulators and "environmentally sensitive" politicians delay for years the target dates for addressing the problems, set unconscionably high "acceptable" levels of environmental damage (such as poisons in the air and on our food), and make exceptions which guarantee that even when a specific problem is addressed it will not be solved. But even with the best of intentions, the piecemeal solutions are wildly inadequate—they serve more to soothe our frayed nerves than to seriously confront the magnitude of the problem. So the media select one of the innumerable ways that we destroy our natural environment (the destruction of the ozone layer, for example) and eventually government leaders acknowledge that there is a problem and make lame attempts to limit the damage. Meanwhile, dozens of other areas remain unattended and get worse, while we delude ourselves into feeling good that we've been paying attention to a few areas.

Once we understand the scope of the problem, many of us despair. Transforming the world economy? Creating a worldwide system of rational planning of the world's resources? "It's too big for me to handle" is a typical response. "I have enough trouble keeping my own life together. Let me do what I can do—recycle my garbage or vote for a candidate who says he or she will deal with a few of the worst environmental hazards."

Yet if this larger transformation is necessary to save the planet, then the feeling of powerlessness expressed in the above response becomes a major environmental issue. Environmentalists cannot afford to simply address environmental issues—they need to look at the issues that have led to this sense of powerlessness.

For this reason, anyone who wishes to save the environment must empower people so that they can overcome their "surplus powerlessness." Dealing with the pain in people's lives, the collapse of their spiritual and ethical environment, may be a necessary prerequisite for engaging them in the struggle to save the physical environment on any level except that of limited and inadequate reforms. Environmentalists may have to join with others in creating a liberal or progressive movement that would pay attention to the pain in people's lives

You may not think we have time to create such a movement. In fact, nothing else will succeed without it. Until people feel empowered to address the big picture, they may commiserate about the terrible destruction of the environment, turn out at Earth Day events and participate in narrow environmental struggles, but they will still vote for candidates who advocate the most minimal and piecemeal changes, and they will still watch the demise of the planet with the same detachment, passivity, and cynical despair that characterizes the rest of their lives. Therefore, building a new kind of political community—far different from anything being discussed at Earth Day 1990 and far different from the politics that dominates in the American political arena—is a major priority for anyone who wishes to save the planet.

Our task in the years ahead is to shift the level of the discussion, to understand how very much is at stake, and then adopt strategies aimed at changing the political climate so that what is necessary becomes what is possible. □

A Dialogue with Jesse Jackson

An Interview by Michael Lerner

A s liberals and progressives, people in the Tikkun *community rightly resist the tendency within the Jewish world to reduce all political issues to "Is it good for the Jews?" Indeed, we maintain that what is best for the Jews is a larger social transformation that would create a more just, peaceful, and loving world. For that very reason, many of our readers have been attracted to the political ideals articulated by Jesse Jackson. Whether or not they end up supporting the Jackson candidacy in the Democratic Party primaries—a decision that is for some based not just on political affinity but also on political assessments like "can he win"—many of our readers have appreciated in the past the willingness of Jackson to identify with the various social change movements, forces which could eventually help to make healing, repair, and transformation possible.*

Yet rumors of Jackson's anti-Semitism have persisted. So it seemed important to us to begin a dialogue with Jackson that explored some of the issues in his relationship to the Jewish community. In the dialogue that ensued, we pressed hard for clarity on points where we suspected there might be some ambiguity in the interpretation of his remarks. Rather than focus on the areas of common agreement around progressive politics, it seemed important here to explore areas of potential conflict—and to push (not always successfully) for the kind of clarity that would satisfy those who have been concerned about Jackson's position on "Jewish issues".

This dialogue was conducted in two interviews: on August 10 and on September 2, 1987. Afterward, we asked a variety of distinguished people in our community to respond to the dialogue or, if they so chose, to comment on the question "How should we think about Jackson and/or the Jackson campaign for the Presidency?"

Michael Lerner: It is the perception of many in the Jewish world that before the 1984 elections you spent a lot of time criticizing Israel and supporting the causes of various Arab nations. More recently you appear to be more even-handed. Some people in the Jewish world see this switch as based purely on political opportunism. What exactly has changed in your thinking, and what made it change?

Jesse Jackson: Nothing has changed. My positions are consistent; perhaps communication has changed. My position to support Israel's right to exist with security within secure boundaries is a consistent position. My position to support a homeland or a state for Palestinian people, that they might be liberated from a nomad status, is a key to peace in the Middle East and to the stability of other Arab nations as well as the security of Israel. I support the revival of Lebanon and its territorial integrity. It is to our distinct national interest to have normalized trade ties with the Arab world.

Jesse Jackson was a Democratic presidential candidate in 1988. This interview appeared in Tikkun, *November/December 1987.*

If in the Middle East we cannot protect America's interest (and now we're less able to do so), we cannot protect the interests of our allies. I supported Camp David, and I support Camp David accords being revived now. Although there were missing elements from that accord, Camp David was a step in the right direction, and it was a mistake for Reagan to let the Camp David accords collapse and not expand upon them.

Lerner: How do you mean to expand upon them?

Jackson: To expand to include the elements that were left out—to include other Arab nations, to include the representative of the Palestinians, because the accords would be incomplete until all the Arab nations, or as many as possible, are in it and a permanent place for Palestinians is resolved.

Lerner: Is it your sense that the Arab nations—Syria, Saudi Arabia, Iraq, Iran, Libya—would accept the existence of a state of Israel now?

Jackson: They already accept the State of Israel as a fact. They negotiate now in relation to that fact. There is no evidence of them using, for example, their collective might in a contrary way, because they know that their relationship to America is in some measure conditional upon their acceptance of Israel's right to exist. They also know that in some measure Israel has the right to defend itself militarily, and so what you have there is a de facto acceptance of Israel's right to exist.

Lerner: So you think that de facto acceptance could be made de jure?

Jackson: Yes, if we were aggressive in our diplomatic efforts. The present diplomatic efforts have failed. They have offered false security to Israel, but each day things are becoming less secure for everybody. Under Reagan, we've increased our military investment in the Middle East. But we've also increased our insecurity in the Middle East. In seven years of Reagan there are more Americans dead, more Americans held hostage, more Israelis dead, more Arabs dead, more chaos, and now we are on the brink of war, or really in a state of undeclared war, in the region. In the process of pursuing that policy, our government apparently pushed Israel into some positions that are now a source of vulnerability.

We are less able to protect our own interests in the Middle East, and therefore less able to protect Israel's interests. The American flag is not a badge of honor or security in that region. The American flag flew above the dormitory in Lebanon, but the Marines were killed. The American flag flew above American University in Lebanon, and some of its staff were taken hostage. It flew above the U.S.S. Stark, and it was blown up. And so now we find ourselves in the region with too few friends, too much exposure, and the inability to protect our interests and that of our allies.

Lerner: One thing that we've questioned in *Tikkun* is whether the interests of the people of the United States are the same as the interests of some of the oil companies of the United States in the Middle East. I wonder if you could tell me what you think are "our interests" in the Middle East, exactly?

Jackson: Well, our interests are, first, human interest. Approximately one hundred and twenty-two million human beings live in the Middle East. There are twenty-two nations in the Middle East. And we have geopolitical interests in the Middle East.

Lerner: By that you mean ...?

Jackson: The geography, the politics, where it is located are of interest to us. The Persian Gulf as a transportation artery to which oil is transported is of interest to us. So our interests are moral, they're human, they are geopolitical, they are national security interests. Right now we are becoming less able to protect those interests. We are becoming isolated in the region, so much so that now we're having to try to protect the Persian Gulf unilaterally in a situation that is very delicate.

Lerner: Well, I'm not a hundred percent sure I understand one part of this, about our geopolitical interests. In your conception do those geopolitical interests you cite involve an international struggle with the Soviet Union to prevent them from expanding their influence?

Jackson: That's one feature. Certainly we would be in a substantially weaker position in the world if the Soviets were occupying the Middle East. If the Soviets were, in fact, occupying the oil reserves, and occupying the Persian Gulf and the strait of Hormuz as an artery of transportation, we would be much weaker as a nation. On the positive side, we are much stronger if we have a Middle East in which we have substantial influence. We can engage in communication, various forms of commercial trade. Where America has bilateral relations it will help protect our interests in the region.

Lerner: It is the perception of many Jews that this is not a time in which Syria or Iraq or Libya are willing to make peace with Israel. They would read your words to mean that in order to have more influence, the United States should tilt away from a special relationship with Israel and be more evenhanded, where even-handed means, to some extent, abandoning the special protection that the United States has offered Israel.

Jackson: America has a special interest with Israel. That relationship must continue. America helped to found Israel. America helps to sustain it with outright annual grants. America's interest and will to protect Israel is substantial and seems unequivocal. America has an interest, a special interest with Saudi Arabia, that likewise must be protected, and you can see as the relationships have become more exposed now, just how fragile those interests are. America has a special interest with the Gulf states, and keeping the Strait of Hormuz open, so much so it is willing to flag Kuwaiti tankers in order to keep it open. So America has several interests in the region. Supporting Israel is an interest that is to our distinct national interest to protect and to preserve, but it would be fair to say that we have other interests as well. If we cannot protect our other interests, and cannot protect our own interests, we cannot protect Israel's interests.

Lerner: If that means strengthening forces that in the meantime see themselves as wanting to struggle against Israel, doesn't what you're saying amount to a tilt away from Israel and towards giving more military support to the enemies of Israel, possibly more economic support as well?

Jackson: No. That would not be my perspective. American interests must be first defined: Our needs can be reconciled with Israel's needs, its need to exist with security within international recognized boundaries. America would be hard put to do without the Saudi Arabian relationship. America needs Saudi Arabia. America needs bilateral relations and multilateral relations with the Gulf states. All of America needs the Strait of Hormuz open and free, and so we have needs in the region, and we must protect all of our needs. Our interests are reconcilable.

Lerner: Doesn't what you're saying lead in the short run to giving more military and/or economic support to forces that may be willing to accommodate to some of America's economic needs for oil, but that simultaneously want to destroy the State of Israel?

Jackson: I think that you use the word "oil" as a buzzword there, which is not what I'm saying. It's what you're saying. That's not what I'm saying.

Lerner: Yes, that's what I'm asking, because, we don't need the Strait of Hormuz for the sake of showcasing Kuwaiti democracy. We don't need the alliance with Saudi Arabia because of the good example they set on human rights. We need them, presumably, because of their economic strength, not because of their moral or political strength.

Jackson: We need them because of their geopolitical position relative to the Soviet Union. We need them because of the role they occupy in the Middle East. We need them because in many instances they have proven to be dependable to us. We need them to stabilize oil prices in the crunch, and their helping to stabilize oil prices has been an immense asset to American security and the American economy. So our relationship with them, and our needs for a mutual relationship are substantial. But there's also an understanding between this country and the Saudis. They will not abuse our relationship to attack the State of Israel, and they have not.

Lerner: And you think that same kind of understanding could be made with Syria, for example?

Jackson: I think we should try. It's a challenge, and it's necessary, and even possible if we work at it. We have not in the last seven years worked diligently on developing more favorable relations with Syria. My point of view is simply this: The more that our country can neutralize adversaries or win friends, the more it is capable of protecting our allies' interests. The less able we are to communicate with our adversaries, the less able we are to protect ourselves or our allies against them. So it is wholly irrational to have a country as militarily powerful as Syria is with contiguous borders with Israel, feeling no constraints if it chose to attack. That's just basic and simple military strategy.

Lerner: And what kinds of constraints could they be convinced to have by the United States?

Jackson: Well, the constraints could be economic considerations, trade, and mutual development. The constraints could be military, because we are committed to supporting Israel and its borders. The constraints could be diplomatic in terms of the free movement of their people, and so if we have enough of a relationship to have diplomatic constraints that make a difference, and economic and trade constraints that make a difference, then we are able to improve relations.

A classic case would be Egypt. If we had maintained the same attitude toward Egypt that we had in 1967, if we had not gone through a transformation and some redemption, then the Camp David accords would not have been possible. Just as we, through aggressive diplomacy, were able to improve relationships with Egypt, it can apply to other nations as well.

Now, let's go a step further. The most significant act to protect Israel's right to exist in the Middle East was not a military act. It was a diplomatic act. It was Camp David. To get the largest nation in the Middle East to agree not to take up arms against Israel, that diplomatic agreement was the biggest military agreement in the history of the region. That's why I stress aggressive diplomacy and economic, cultural, and trade ties, because the more people trade with each other, the more they culturally exchange, the more they pull barriers down, they reduce reasons to fight.

Lerner: Is there anything in your experience in Syria, or subsequent to your visit to Syria, that leads you to believe that the Syrian dictatorship, which is perceived by many Jews as ruthless and irrational, would actually be rational and suspend its desires for the destruction of Israel, and/or respond to the kinds of initiatives you're talking about?

Jackson: Frankly, we do not know what's possible diplomatically with Syria in the last seven years, because we have not worked on trying to improve relations diplomatically in the last seven years. When I went to Syria to bring Goodman back, clearly Assad was making an overture to Reagan, and a small window opened. Reagan sent a letter thanking Assad for releasing Goodman, but then the window closed back again. Now President Carter has been to Syria subsequently several times, continuously asking for more dialogue. If we employ more dialogue, and more diplomacy, and more trade, perhaps we will increase our influence.

Lerner: Let me turn to the Palestinians. Let's start from some of the history. What right do you think the Jews had to return to Palestine at the end of the nineteenth and beginning of the twentieth century? Was that return, in accord with the Zionist vision, a righteous act, or was it, as the Palestinians claim, either an extension of European colonialism, or at the very least, an unjustified usurpation? In other words, was the Zionist vision legitimate from the start, or is it only justified now because it succeeded and it's an existing fact?

Jackson: Let me answer it in this way. The Jews had a need for a homeland, and the political settlement was reached. I accept the political settlement as reality without getting into the religion of the matter. The incomplete work at that time was the failure to finally work out an accord on getting a homeland for Palestinians as well. It is precisely that crisis that lingers.

Lerner: *Tikkun* Magazine has argued that Zionism can be justified on the same grounds that today justify affirmative action programs, namely that there was a group facing historical oppression, that it had a right to have the historic picture rectified—even if in so doing other groups were temporarily disadvantaged, and even if some of the people so disadvantaged were not themselves personally responsible for the original oppression that is being rectified. This is the same kind of argument with which *Tikkun* supports affirmative action for Blacks.

Jackson: That's an interesting argument, but I don't think it's a good analogy. Many of the same Jews who support affirmative action—applied, in that instance, at all costs—do not support affirmative action being applied at substantially less cost in this society. Affirmative action here may have to do with setting some seats aside in a university or law school. Affirmative action for Zionism had to do with uprooting people from lands. The rectification there was a very painful uprooting: a series of wars took place. Affirmative action has not been a bloody series of wars in this country.

Lerner: There could have been bloody wars here had the American whites responded in the same way to Blacks that the Palestinians responded to Jews.

Jackson: Now the difference is that American whites accepted the guilt and the burden of slavery. They accepted the guilt and the burden of segregation. The American whites knew that they were morally wrong in conducting slavery. They knew they were morally wrong in conducting legal segregation, and an American white court of nine white males said separate but equal was illegal, and subsequently the majority population conceded the illegality of the historical behavior toward

Black people. It was determined by the courts of this country that slavery and segregation were wrong, illegal, and immoral, and that affirmative action would offset historical negative action—the negative action was documented fact—and there is no evidence that affirmative action hurt the majority white population. In fact, it improved everybody because it broadened the base of opportunity, and affirmative action has not applied specifically to the Blacks. It has affected women, who are 53% of our population, and Jewish women have been beneficiaries of that. It affected Hispanics. It affected Blacks as well. So it's a very different situation.

Lerner: But for those of us Jews who have supported affirmative action—which is a large number of American Jews—our situation is not that our great-grandparents owned slaves. We came to the United States after slavery had been abolished, and nevertheless recognize that the historic oppression of Blacks in the society was something that had to be rectified, even if that meant that some people who were not directly involved in being oppressors were going to, in some way or other, lose positions, or suffer in some way.

Jackson: Slavery's not a Black-Jewish issue. It is a White-Black issue. There are Jews who were slaveholders, just as other whites were slave owners, and they were not distinguished by their religion, but their privilege came from their race. They were not denied privilege because of their religion. Blacks were denied citizenship because of race. Many white American families came to this country after slavery was abolished; but affirmative action applies to everyone. The other point is that Jewish activists were among the leaders in supporting Bakke. They argued that opening up doors for Blacks and Hispanics represents a source of denial and pain for Jewish people.

I understand the concern with the use of quotas as a ceiling to deny upward mobility according to one's own abilities. Here, quotas were recommended by the courts as a remedy to establish a floor if those timetables and affirmative action fail. It was always a last resort if voluntary goals, timetables, and affirmative action failed. So it was unfortunate that some of our former Jewish allies seized the quota issue, which was a last resort, as if it were a first resort. The result of losing the Bakke decision has been a generation of Blacks and Hispanics who have been irreparably damaged.

Lerner: Many of our readers are people who support the demands for affirmative action and publicly opposed those people in the Jewish world who backed away from it. What I'm asking you conversely is whether you see any merit in the claim that the world as a whole has some responsibility on the same principle of affirmative action to deal with several thousand years of oppression of Jews. Do Christians in particular, who generated the ideology of anti-Semitism and created the context within which there was widespread genocide of Jews, have a corresponding responsibility on a worldwide level to rectify what happened to the Jews in the past?

Jackson: Well, what you're suggesting is that Israel at one level is an expression of international affirmative action and, given the historic negative action, the international affirmative action was corrective surgery. However, surgery half-done jeopardizes the patient. In this instance, not spending the same effort working out the Palestinian solution has left surgery half done. That's why we now have hostility forty years later, as opposed to the peace that was the original vision.

Lerner: I'm going to switch for a second to another topic. Do you think it was reasonable or wise for the Pope to meet with Waldheim?

Jackson: That was a decision that the sovereign head of the Catholic Church and head of a sovereign state had to make. He had some moral obligation because Waldheim was a Catholic, and his obligation to give private counsel. His obligation to reduce hostility, and try to increase communication was a part of his responsibility. You could not very well demand of the Pope who he should meet and not meet with.

Lerner: If there had been a worldwide movement to isolate the head of South Africa and the international head of the church was to meet with that person after the United States and other countries had decided not to meet with him as a symbol of opposition to what he stood for, certainly you would see that there was something wrong in breaking that boycott.

Jackson: The Pope has ties to Catholics in South Africa. So he maintains his relationship to his church and tries to use his Church as an agent to change the system. Israel has ties with South Africa diplomatically, the sale of arms to South Africa in substantial quantity, though the whole world is trying to isolate South Africa.

Lerner: Speaking again from the standpoint of liberal Jews in the United States, we're against that tie with South Africa and are pressuring Israel to break that tie. So the same moral right with which we criticize Israel on that might lead us to criticize the Pope for his ties to a former Nazi, regardless of the fact that he's Catholic.

Jackson: You have the right to that point of view. You ask me my point of view. I suggest the Pope made his decision as the head of his church and head of a sovereign state. If you challenge his right to use his judgment, then you open yourself to his challenging your religious obligations or your state obligations.

Lerner: I agree. I think that I would want to use one law, one moral law for all...

Jackson: Right.

Lerner: ... and the same criteria that we apply to Israel, we'd want to apply to others as well.

Jackson: So that's why if you apply that one moral law, you have to urge Israel to be very aggressive in trying to get freed of the moral law that's been broken with the West Bank occupation.

Lerner: We often hear people making moral demands on Jews. And because we take our history and our moral tradition seriously many Jews respond to these appeals. Some Jews feel, however, that when it is Jews on the receiving end, Jews who are being oppressed, there is a curious silence from all those who seek us as allies. So when it comes to Nazis or Soviet Jewry, there isn't the same kind of commitment from other oppressed groups that we try to give to oppressed groups when they're being oppressed. Do you understand why Jews might feel that at all?

Jackson: Well, Black American soldiers died fighting Nazism. We have Ralph Bunche, a Black American who helped to found the State of Israel. Yet Israel is selling arms to the people who are oppressing their allies of forty years ago. I take the position that we should not hold Israel to any higher or lower moral standard. It would be fair to say that Israel has gained from the high moral expectations the world has for them. It is never to one's disadvantage for other folk to have high moral expectations of you.

Lerner: Some Jews respond by saying "all of the moral concern of the world didn't lead to very much in the way of material support when the Jews were being wiped out in Europe." When you mention the Blacks fighting in the Second World War in the United States Army, there's very little reason to believe that most of those people thought that the reason that they were involved in that war was to save Jews, or to deal with the special oppression of Jews.

Jackson: It's hard to think of who the Blacks were at that time who were making policy decisions, but certainly Black soldiers fought strongly and courageously. There are two other dimensions of that as well, I would think. One is that Black Americans were the first to get to Dachau and Buchenwald concentration camps. Paul Parks, former secretary of education of Boston, got to Dachau first, with a unit—a segregated unit—of Black soldiers. Dr. Jones, I think his name is, in Philadelphia, got to Buchenwald first. And there's very little acknowledgment of those roles. Fifty to fifty-six million people were killed. The Holocaust crimes were the most heinous, but fifty-odd million people were killed. That's why the world must say, on the one hand, never again to a Holocaust, but also never again to unbridled fascism, because it was unbridled fascism, fanatical racism and classism that precipitated such a human scourge. And that is why people who were the victims of that and those who were the survivors of that situation should staunchly resist the Fourth Reich, which is South Africa. I mean every moral and ethical imperative that made us say no to Hitler and the Third Reich should make us say no to Botha in the Fourth Reich. One difference in the Third Reich is that so much of Hitler's dirt was in the dark. Many people found out very late just what was happening. In the case of Botha, he is bold, public, has nuclear power, an open relationship with America, an open relationship with Israel, is receiving arms from Israel, and even some of the Jews in South Africa who were victims of Nazi camps are operating within the context of that system. It is that entanglement that makes a very complicated and yet a morally challenging situation.

Lerner: The same kind of call for the extermination of a people exists today in an overt way in some of the Arab countries toward Israel. It may seem fanciful to an American when they hear the PLO covenant calling for the elimination of the State of Israel and the sending back of the Jews to "the countries where they came from," just as it may seem fanciful when they hear Syrians talking about pushing the Jews into the sea, but from the historical experience of the Jewish people, this is again a call for genocide that is at least as serious in its possibilities as any other genocide.

Jackson: Any call for genocide against any people is wrong. However, there's a difference between what's remotely possible and what's actual and real. The Palestinians cannot drive the Jews into the sea. The South Africans are driving Blacks into the sea. The South Africans are occupying militarily a majority population and, unfortunately, the Israeli government has been in complicity with the South African regime.

Lerner: Let's get back to the double standard question. It turns out, if you study the actual realities of South Africa and military and economic aid, that, number one, a great deal of that military aid comes from Germany and France. But when you listen to most Black Americans, the focus is exclusively on Israel. Similarly, Saudi Arabia plays a major role in economically providing South Africa with oil and with other needed economic benefits, but there's rarely any public outcry from Black Americans indicating and publicizing an upset with Arab countries for providing help to South Africa. Isn't there a double standard applied to Jews and to Israel?

Jackson: Here you have a situation where Israel gets about three billion dollars a year from the U.S.

for three million people. All of Africa, a half billion people, gets one hundred and seventy-nine million dollars. There is a double standard where Israel is the substantial beneficiary and is not resisting that double standard. Right?

Lerner: Yes. The U.S. should provide more aid to Africa.

Jackson: Yes. And that's the first fact. Secondly, when the congressional report came out about selling arms to South Africa, I contacted the embassies of France and Germany and Britain as well, and when I went to Japan, I challenged Japan's expanding role in South Africa. So a significant number of leaders have challenged other nations as well. The relationship between American Blacks and Jews is different, however, than American Blacks and Germany, or France, or Britain. The context of the relationship is different, and there are different expectations for Israel than for Germany and Britain and France. Our domestic relationships are different. Our religious relationship is different. Our historical relationship is different. We've not been in contention with the British or the French over the course of affirmative action, as a case in point. We've not been in contention with the British or the French in the struggles over quotas that we've gone through together in the last twenty years. Whoever is doing business with South Africa is wrong, but Israel is such a substantial beneficiary, Israel is subsidized by America, which includes Black Americans' tax money, and then it subsidizes South Africa. Some of what America cannot do in South Africa directly because of the laws, it is doing through Israel as a conduit.

Lerner: I want to deal with Farrakhan. Farrakhan, described as your former ally, called Judaism a gutter religion and praised Hitler. Do you think Jews were being reasonable to demand that you dissociate from him and renounce that kind of thinking?

Jackson: On one level there's been an overreaction to Farrakhan, as if Farrakhan has state power. He does not. So there is a certain exaggeration in the reaction. You, being the intelligent person you are with your background, should also deal with what has been Farrakhan's public explanation about Hitler: that he was saying that he was great to his people. That was not an adjective I would use; Hitler was wicked to the world, wicked, immoral, sinful.

If I were in Germany at the time of Hitler, I would have been with Bonhoeffer and that group of theologians who sought to overthrow Hitler, because he was consummate evil in the world at the time and was a threat to the whole human family. That's my position on that. Calling Judaism a gutter religion is wrong.

You know every text has a context. Newspapers tend to report that anti-Semitic dimension, but not the racist dimension. I remember that the Anti-Defamation League sent out a stack of papers to every publisher in America to discredit my campaign, which was a blow to the number of Black Americans who supported that campaign. We were threatened. Kahane announced he was going to picket my home.

Lerner: Most *Tikkun* readers have no sympathy for Kahane.

Jackson: But he made the threat against my home; that was the context.

Lerner: But our fascists, we denounce. Liberals in the Jewish world publicly denounce Kahane and say this guy has no right to speak for us. The question is whether you will denounce fascists in the Black world.

Jackson: Kahane threatened to march on the home of a presidential candidate who was Black in the United States of America. It was a very visible challenge. It is in that context that this whole Farrakhan thing got started. It was unfortunate, and we would do well to move on. I have given major public statements about it, and I will not continue to prolong it.

Lerner: Well, Jesse, this is not to embarrass you or to catch you up...

Jackson: I know you're not.

Lerner: ...but to try to open your thinking to people who want to support you but can't understand why you wouldn't dissociate more clearly from Farrakhan.

Jackson: Let me tell you this. When the Nazis were going to march on Skokie, I was there in the pulpit of the temple with my family, and when Gorbachev was talking disarmament I confronted him about Soviet Jewry. I was there, and before sixty million people at the Democratic convention I restated my position. I am not going to wallow in that. I have no need for it, and no one else who wants to go forward should have a need to go back into that.

Lerner: I'm not talking about back then, but subsequently. There have been rallies in which Farrakhan has been a spokesman for very explicit anti-Semitic statements...

Jackson: Do not give me the assignment or the responsibility to address your relationship with Farrakhan. That is not fair. You don't give yourself the burden to check all white people in this country.

Lerner: I would certainly think it would be fair for you to ask Jews running for office to dissociate themselves from Kahane, and to say that Kahane is not the kind of Jew they want to have anything to do with.

Jackson: If you want to start comparing how we approach problems, some of us approach problems differently. You called it process. You have to exercise judgment in resolving problems. You can't give me the assignment of how to solve a problem, as I will not you.

Lerner: Well, let me ask you another question. Farrakhan's rallies...

Jackson: For example: You would not want me to draw a line on support or non-support for Israel on its trade with South Africa. You would not. Am I right?

Lerner: Right.

Jackson: Well, that's enough. That says it all. Here's another matter where it can be resolved with process. It cannot be resolved using your method.

Lerner: Okay, let me ask you about anti-Semitism in the Black world apart from Farrakhan. Do you have any sense of, any strategy for how to reduce anti-Semitism in the Black world, and do you feel yourself having any special responsibility in relation to that issue?

Jackson: Every chance I get, I appeal to people to be non-racial, to not be anti-Semitic, to not be racist, not be fascist, and I'm consistent with that position. You see there's a difference between European anti-Semitism where many Europeans took the position that theologically related to Jews and Jesus. That was peculiar to the character of European theology. Hitler built upon that disposition, did he not? Now, my only experience from a Black point of view is that Black churches, strong institutions, do not take this same theological position on Jews and Jesus. We see Jesus as a Jew, and we see good guys fought for him and bad guys killed him. We see that as a human predicament as opposed to a Jewish trait. Do you see what I'm saying?

A lot of Blacks and Jews are in contention, not over things theological and philosophical, but over day-to-day relationships, which is something that's infinitely more reparable, if it's worked at. But for example, right now the Black South African kinship is stronger, very visible, and many people make judgments about allies and adversaries based on that. Many Blacks, for example, see in my campaign a ray of hope and so, the more that it is attacked and in ways that people feel unwarranted and unjustifiable, then it simply rubs them wrong. I would hope that calmer heads prevail and we would press forward.

Lerner: Why should Jews who are committed as Jews support your candidacy?

Jackson: Well, many Jews have, with whom I shared a domestic vision. Those who want to join in the struggle to wipe out malnutrition, establish affordable health care, housing, who want to stop the importation of drugs, who want to stop the exportation of workers, and the exportation of jobs, those who want to improve the quality of life in our country, those who want to end the arms race, those who want to shift from corporations merging to get them to plan to reinvest in America, retain our workers, reindustrialize our nation, we have a lot in common. My track record in social justice and economic justice is more substantial than any of my competitors. For those with whom I've worked over a twenty-five year period, with whom I've labored in the trenches, with whom we've shared civil rights demonstrations, and peace demonstrations, and environmental demonstrations, and with whom I've been at the plant gate when they closed on workers without notice, those with whom I've been at the shipyard, with those with whom I've worked on the domestic vision, my credentials from that struggle are more substantial than anybody else's has been.

And I can be trusted to fight for social justice. April 25th, when I was at the peace march against intervention in Central America, against South Africa, I was the only candidate there. When Ben Linder was killed, I called his mother and his brother. Mrs. Linder was our guest of honor at PUSH in Chicago. When the Nazis were going to march on Skokie I was there. Somebody was needed to confront Gorbachev, I was there. So I've been there for a long time. In foreign policy, if those progressive Jews want somebody with the courage and the intelligence to fight for a comprehensive Middle East peace plan, rather than a series of war plans, I will engage in that process, and in my experience I have met with enough of our allies and adversaries to be able to make a real difference. People who have only met your allies can't help you very much, because it is our adversaries we must be protected from. The very nature of defense is to defend you not from your allies, but to defend you from your enemies. I take the imperative that Jesus put forth, love your enemies, as a very strong imperative, not a romantic one that's empty. By that I mean this, if you love your enemy, which is a big challenge, you will not turn your back on your enemy, because you will not expose yourself. If you love your enemy you will talk with your enemy, even if you don't want to talk. That's what diplomacy obligates you to do sometimes. If you love your enemy, you may work hard enough to neutralize your enemy, and that's a victory of sorts. If you love your enemy, you may be successful enough to convert your enemy. It happens sometimes. By the way, when I was in seminary, the theologian that drove me the most was Rabbi Abraham Heschel. I have an autographed copy of every book he ever wrote.

It is not right for either us or our adversaries to over-study, to over-examine the Black-Jewish relationship apart from other relationships. It's like taking a flower out of a pot to see if it's still growing. It's the way to kill it. When a Black was killed at Howard Beach, there were no studies on Black-Italian relationships or whoever the ethnic group was that did it. When the Blacks were robbed in Forsythe County, Georgia, there was no rush to study Blacks and Southern Baptists. So sometimes the continuous investigation of how Blacks and Jews are doing is a way of isolating both. I want to move beyond investigation to cooperation.

Lerner: I want to ask one thing, finally, about Christianity, because it's something that is another level of concern that's sometimes raised about your candidacy coming from deep Christian roots. Do you think that there is any validity to Judaism as a religion after Jesus? Has Judaism's intrinsic value been supplanted by Christianity and, if not, what is the validity of Judaism?

Jackson: I think there is intrinsic worth to the Jewish religion, to the Pentateuch, the Torah, God's relationship with the Jewish people. Christianity draws its roots from Judaism, and Christians believe that Jesus was the fulfillment of Isaiah's prophecy and that he has brought a message in the world beyond justice, the message of redemption and love. I happen to think that redemption and love are critical to at-one-ment or atonement. So Jesus brought a special dimension, because he himself, of course, was of the Jewish religion. No one can deny the validity and the intrinsic theological worth of Judaism.

Lerner: You've made several visits to campuses in which you've spoken about the importance of a Black-Jewish dialogue. Could you talk more about that?

Jackson: As a moral imperative and as a matter of survival Blacks have had to choose dialogue. And even though sometimes we've faced violence from others, we haven't had the option to retreat or the luxury to not talk to them. The key to progress is dialogue, whether it is with Jewish groups or with the Irish, or Italians, or other groups.

Lerner: I've been told that you've actually challenged anti-Semitism on campuses when you've found it among Black students and stood up against it. Could you tell us about that?

Jackson: I have not found any anti-Semitism among Black students that needed to be stood up against. I have encouraged dialogue, particularly in light of tensions that have emerged because of tensions around the Bakke decision which had a direct effect in limiting Black opportunities, and in light of the Israeli-South African military relationship. In light of these it is important that we talk *to* each other and not *at* each other.

Lerner: I am told that you've had a history of caring about Soviet Jewry. Could you tell me more about your thinking on that topic including what led you to confront Gorbachev on this issue?

Jackson: I believe we must fight for human rights everywhere. And I've fought for these rights everywhere. The key to world peace is justice. So I told Gorbachev that although I support all the efforts to reduce nuclear weapons, and that was my primary reason for talking to him, that if he wanted to make a contribution toward creating an atmosphere of trust, he should change the situation of Soviet Jewry. He said that there was no problem. So I challenged him and said that there was a problem and that he had to deal with it if he really wanted to use this historical moment to achieve international peace.

Lerner: Governor Mario Cuomo has said in a speech in late August, 1987, that this was a good time to move toward ending the cold war. What do you think of this idea?

Jackson: We must thaw the ice between the superpowers. Both countries are behind the ice, and opportunities for peace and development are frozen. We should push for mutually verifiable arms reductions, for cultural and trade exchanges. Most Americans have never seen a Russian, and so there is fear. Pepsi Cola has 18 plants in the Soviet Union and they are expanding. Trade ties and cultural exchanges open up the possibilities for reducing tensions. If we didn't have diplomatic relations, if we didn't have trade ties, it would be more difficult to get Soviet Jewry free. It is because of these ties that we can negotiate to improve human rights.

Lerner: I want to switch now to discuss some of what the New Right calls "the social issues." Could you say something about your views on abortion?

Jackson: That women should have the right to make choices about their own bodies is a constitutional right. Abortion is not the right moral choice, I believe, except under very special circumstances—e.g. where it is medically indicated or where the pregnancy is a product of rape or incest. But women have those rights to make their own decision under the Constitution. I believe that sex education should begin earlier in the educational process. The other thing I want to note is that a lot of people who talk about the sanctity of the fetus don't seem to care much once the child is born. They don't fight for child care, they don't fight for health care, they don't fight for Head Start programs—and this, I think, is terribly inconsistent.

Lerner: Could you talk about gay rights?

Jackson: I believe that gays have a constitutional right to not be discriminated against. One doesn't have to endorse or participate in a particular lifestyle to fight for their rights. You don't have to be a female to fight for the ERA, you just have to be a civilized human being. You can endorse the rights without embracing the lifestyle.

Lerner: Is there anything you want to say to the readership of *Tikkun* that I should have asked you about but didn't?

Jackson: I think it is important for Blacks and Jews to build a coalition together. We share common struggles. When the Nazis went to Skokie and the ACLU defended their right to march, I thought that this was going beyond reason and causing much pain to the Jews there, and I brought my family and I went to the synagogue where the Jews were assembled and shared their risks. I think that we must learn to stress our commonalities and not just our differences. I think that we must stress dialogue. I think that the Jewish leadership is setting a very good example here in their relationship with the pope. It is a difficult situation for them, given the Pope's position on recognition of Israel, and that was complicated further by the meeting with Waldheim. The Jews were hurt by this—but I'm glad that the Jewish leadership engaged in active public and private diplomacy with the Vatican rather than just withdrawing into pain and hostility. I use that approach myself in all situations. With this kind of dialogue we can reduce tensions and create understanding. I happen to think that the Jewish leadership's approach here was a very good example of how to go about solving our problems and creating a dialogue between Blacks and Jews.

Reflections on the Dialogue with Jackson

David Saperstein, Fred Siegel, Abbie Hoffman

David Saperstein

Who is strong? He who conquers his inclinations.
Who is a hero? One who makes an enemy a friend.
—The Talmud

T he conversation between Rev. Jesse Jackson and Michael Lerner was what Martin Buber has termed a "mis-meeting." Two people who have so much to say to each other talked past one another and missed the opportunity to meaningfully address common issues. Lerner and Jackson did not meet each other as individuals, but as strange and rather distant symbols. An opportunity was lost.

Jesse Jackson has long had a Jewish problem. He knows it and we know it. It is not just a political problem, but a human one as well.

For the past three years, Rev. Jackson has been working rigorously to confront this problem, to sensitize himself to Jewish pain and to Jewish history, to overcome estrangement and suspicions and to wrestle with the political and personal issues that kept him at a distance from the Jewish community. In this one interview, he may have set back three years of intensive and disciplined work, reverting to expressions of insensitivity and misunderstanding which have been the foundation of his past tensions with the Jewish community. This interview is so replete with misunderstandings about the Middle East situation, about Jewish views on affirmative action, about the Holocaust, about Jewish fears and hopes as to make it almost irreconcilable with his statements and activities of the past few years.

Similarly, for the past year, Michael Lerner and *Tikkun* have been struggling to create a new type of Jewish consciousness, progressive in orientation, willing to think innovatively, to ask questions that the Jewish establishment has been unwilling to ask, and to raise issues that others would prefer to avoid. He, too, has set back this effort with an interview that failed to illuminate most of Jesse Jackson's activities since 1984, an interview which (perhaps because Lerner was playing the "devil's advocate") is as narrowly focused an interview as any a neo-conservative magazine would have done.

The "mis-meeting" was sad, perhaps, in some ways even tragic. My primary concern, however, is

Rabbi David Saperstein, a member of Tikkun's *editorial board, directs the Religious Action Center of the Union of American Hebrew Congregations in Washington, D.C. Fred Siegel is a professor of humanities at the Cooper Union, an editor of* Dissent *and* Telos. *Abbie Hoffman was a political activist for more than a quarter of a century and author of nine books, including* Steal this Urine Test: Fighting Drug Hysteria in America *(Penguin-Viking, 1987). These responses appeared in* Tikkun, *November/December 1987.*

less with the interview itself than with its context and its political and personal ramifications. What few Jews know, is that for three years, Jackson with scarcely a misstep, sought, through word and deed, to carve out a political position that is open to Jewish concerns without sacrificing the integrity of his positions or ignoring issues where the Jewish community and he differ. Among these actions which should have laid the groundwork for a vastly improved relationship with the Jewish community:

• He has begun speaking of "secure borders" for Israel (code words for changes in the pre-1967 border configuration to ensure Israel's security) as opposed only to "internationally recognized" borders (code words for return to the pre-'67 borders);

• He has openly supported the Camp David accords and the approach embodied in it, often to the chagrin of his Arab-American supporters;

• In front of the entire world, he confronted Gorbachev in Geneva on the issue of Soviet Jewry;

• In press interviews on South Africa, he has taken the position that while Israel should be criticized for its relations with South Africa, it was a distortion to single it out. Rather all nations dealing with South Africa should be criticized including our allies and the Arab countries which traded oil with South Africa. When the State Department report came out on April 1, 1987, detailing the involvement with South Africa of Israel and other U.S. friends, Jackson again resisted singling out Israel, and protested to the ambassadors of all the nations involved;

• He has given positive public speeches on Black-Jewish relations with some nationally prominent American Jewish figures (ironically reported far more extensively in the Black and general media than in the Jewish media) calling for significant improvements in relations; affirming the need for compromise and understanding; detailing the common agenda of the two communities; and most importantly, standing his ground against hostile Black youths who accused him of selling out;

• He has entirely disassociated Farrakhan from his 1988 campaign;

• In the wake of the Bitburg controversy, he visited a concentration camp and issued an eloquent statement about the unique meaning of the Holocaust.

Tragically, this interview fails to grapple with most of these developments.

To be sure, from the Jewish community's perspective, Jackson's "transformation" was by no means complete. He still refused to criticize Farrakhan directly. His statements on the Middle East reflected an unnuanced analysis that, if implemented into political programs, would have been alarmingly dangerous to Israel's security. He still manifested a disturbing discomfort with Jews whenever confronted with these lingering divisive issues—a discomfort which Lerner's interview exemplifies, focusing as it did on issues where change in Jackson's position has come most slowly.

But, on the whole, Jackson's positions were a vast, vast improvement over those espoused in the 1984 campaign, and they must be recognized as such. Any political candidate who reaches out to the Jewish community over a period of time should receive tangible and meaningful expressions of appreciation and encouragement. Yet, we failed to respond to Jackson's initiatives.

For three years, Jackson's efforts have been received by the Jewish community with apathy and silence. While the Jewish right wing has celebrated the "conversion" of Jesse Helms, the latest Senate *baal teshuvah* (based on a few token actions on Israel), liberal Jews and their leaders have been indifferent to Jackson's growth and to his many efforts to reach out. The result was a candidate who was increasingly disappointed and frustrated that positions taken so publicly and consistently, positions which earned him significant criticism from long-time allies, were accomplishing nothing positive with the community to whom they were addressed. It was almost as though the community was waiting for Jackson to slip up so as to validate their worst fears. Now faced with an interview which legitimizes renewed Jewish criticism of Jackson, the real question is how the Jewish community should respond.

We can merely ignore the contradictions and complexities of Jackson and pick up where we left off three years ago, launching a campaign of confrontation and castigation that will make Jackson the lightning rod in another Black-Jewish confrontation. The result will poison the atmosphere of the 1988 campaign, perhaps fatally weaken the Democratic party in the election and lead to the further deterioration of Black-Jewish relations.

Alternatively, we can focus on the contradictions in Jackson's record, on the complexities of the man, and continue to work with him and speak to him rather than at him and about him. The result would be to focus attention on the merits of our criticism of specific positions with which we disagree without turning our response into anti-Jackson hysteria and another Black-Jewish confrontation. We can educate the Jewish community and the American public on both the positive evolution of Jackson's views as well as on the lingering problems the interview delineated.

The most important reality the Jewish community must keep in mind during the 1988 election is that for the vast majority of the Black community, Jackson's views on the Middle East and Farrakhan are irrelevant to their support. To the extent that these issues are of concern at all, polls indicate that the substantial majority of Blacks disagree with Rev. Jackson. They support Rev. Jackson because he has become a symbol of Black aspirations to be accepted as a legitimate force in American political life; because he articulates the pain on the streets and speaks for the still restrained rights of minorities in America; because he is a powerfully effective political presence in America who raises moral issues other candidates fail to address. Indeed, even for Jackson himself, the Middle East and Farrakan are issues of only limited importance.

We can work with Jackson, publicly critiquing our differences even while encouraging the steps he has taken to reach out to our community. We can do so encouraging the steps he has taken to reach out to our community without sacrificing the integrity of our positions, the views we espouse, the values that we hold and without asking Jackson to sacrifice his.

I have known Jesse Jackson over many years. I have seen him grow and wrestle with difficult issues and personal hang-ups. We have not always seen eye to eye on specific issues. But he has been as willing to listen and to learn as he has been to try to convince me of his views. And, in keeping with the Talmudic insight with which I began, Rev. Jackson has shown real personal strength in seeking to overcome his own estrangement from the Jewish community. It will take similar strength from the Jewish community to work with Jackson to make him a friend.

I'm certain it is worth the effort.

Fred Siegel

There have been at least as many Jesse Jacksons as there have been Richard Nixons. In one guise there has been the earnest minister preaching temperance, hard work, and restraint; then there has been the global ambulance-chaser, the media hound whose actions have belied the words of his sermons. Jackson, the spokesman of "home truths," the moral tribune of the poor, has also been the pinky-ringed shakedown artist, the fruits of whose efforts for the poor have often produced contracts for his friends and retainers. Then there is the apostle of Christian nonviolence who has allied himself with political gangsters and Third World dictators. Recently Jackson was, first for the cameras, the spokesman for an interracial response to the tragedy at Howard Beach and then, off camera, the supporter of a Black nationalist-led boycott of all white-owned businesses.

Chronologically, Jackson, who was an integrationist when the going was good during the mid-1960s, became a proponent of a Booker T. Washington-like emphasis on Black self-reliance in the early 1970s. This was the Jackson who not only served for a while as the neoconservative's ideal Black leader because of his emphasis on self-reliance, but also the Jackson who in 1978 proposed a

Black-Republican political alliance. The next new Jackson carried his emphasis on Black self-reliance toward a hard-edged Third Worldism, the anti-Zionism of which, greased by Arab oil money, blended easily with his down-home distaste for Jews. The irony of the Reverend's Third Worldism, its message aside, is that Jackson is so classically American in his relentless self-promotion and vaulting ambition.

In February 1985 Jackson was pushed into what has become his latest incarnation as the spokesman for all the losers in the global transformation of the economy. If I'm precise about the timing, it's because it was in February 1985, in the wake of the Democrats' landslide 1984 defeat, that leading liberal columnists who had already noticed the monochromatic character of the Rainbow Coalition began to speak derisively of Jackson as a "hot dog" and "The mouth that roars."

To make matters worse for Jackson, it had become more and more difficult to peddle Third World panaceas. In fact, with the rise of Colonel Qadaffi, who allegedly had earlier supplied Jackson with money, the Third World had become downright unpopular. The trajectory of American opinion, from the Libyan attacks on the Rome airport to the murder of Leon Klinghoffer at the hands of Arafat's associates, left Jackson in an awkward position. When Qadaffi, speaking to Farrakhan's Nation of Islam, called upon Blacks to form their own army and rise against white America, Jackson was forced to repudiate him or forfeit any last pretense of filling Dr. King's non-violent role. Not surprisingly, like any shrewd politician, he began to repackage himself by emphasizing the very real social problems at home that had been exacerbated by the Reagan administration.

The newest Jackson reached out to farmers terribly hard hit by the recession of the early 1980s and to factory workers devastated by plant closings. As he told some reporters, he was following the advice George Wallace had given him: A politician has "got to lay down the grass where the goats are."

He also moved, after a fashion, to mend his fences with Jews. The man never too busy to stand in front of a camera publicly refused to repudiate Muslim minister Louis Farrakhan; but under great pressure, he did produce a grudging written criticism issued *sotto voce* by his Washington office. For his supporters and associates, the form of Jackson's perfunctory comments spoke against their substance. In fact, as the *Tikkun* interview with Jackson makes abundantly clear, far from repudiating Farrakhan, the good Reverend has sought to justify his friend's words as a response to Jewish hostility. And while Jackson has of necessity kept his distance, Jackson's political entourage is still in close contact with Farrakhan. According to a report in the *New York Times*, Jackson's retainers took pains at a recent Farrakhan rally to emphasize that the differences between the two men had been grossly exaggerated.

If the *Tikkun* interview suggests that Jackson is very reluctant to separate himself from Farrakhan's version of Black nationalism, it also show the "newest" Jackson, one who seeks to minimize his political liabilities through a "dialogue" with Jews. This détente of sorts has been highlighted by Jackson's somewhat incoherent thirty-second question to Gorbachev on the plight of Soviet Jews, a passing gesture which cost him nothing. If I'm grudging in my account of this very brief event, it's because so much else of what Jackson did indicated that his outreach to Jews was little more than a tactical ploy.

In January 1985, when the lives of the Falashas stranded in the Sudan were in peril, the widely respected mayor of Jerusalem, Teddy Kollek, called upon Jackson to ride to the rescue, but this time Jackson, afraid of angering his Arab patrons, refused to mount his steed. Instead, brandishing his selective nonviolence, he sniffed something about the 2,000 Falashas representing a military asset to Israel. In June 1985, when the TWA highjackers demanded that Israel free 700 Shiite gunmen, the always even-handed Jackson described the gunmen as hostages and instructed Israel on its moral duty to carry out the swap. The following month, Jackson presented in a television interview two examples of the doublespeak which embodies his double standard. Giving Arafat more than the benefit of the doubt, he asserted that the PLO leader wanted a free and secure Israel as much as anyone else. Jackson also explained that the problem with Castro, like himself a much misunderstood figure, was not that the Cuban dictator's jails were overflowing with political prisoners, but that the always articulate Castro did not know how to express himself in "clear language." Not surprising from a man who once explained that "Apartheid was worse than Hitler. Hitler was a man for a season. Once he was exposed he was rejected."

Finally, an example of Jackson's subconscious boiling up to the surface: In an article for *USA Today* calling for interracial cooperation in the face of economic dislocation, a worthy ideal, Jackson explained: "The 80 percent who are worse off economically than six years ago *must find a scapegoat—* thus a rise in anti-Semitism" (Emphasis mine.) Once again, Jesse will no doubt explain that he has been "misunderstood." The man's embraces are as intimidating as his punches.

The ugly reality is that, barring any startling new revelation, Jackson's media tactics have for the moment defused the Jewish issue for the general public. But given Jackson's opportunism, there is little reason to assume that, should conditions change—with, say, a new Arab oil boycott as we head toward oil shortages in the 1990s—Jackson's deeply felt hostility to Jews would not reappear. Jackson, grateful to the Saudis, as his answers to Michael Lerner suggest, for oil at $18 a barrel, no doubt could justify abandoning Israel as an act of American gratitude. In such a context, Jackson's anti-Semitism could be cloaked in the language of American national interests.

Part of what makes Jackson so dangerous is that the opportunism he shares with many other politicians is coupled with a grant of nonaccountability from both his Black supporters and the press. Jackson can withstand indiscretions and failures that quickly would have sunk a white politician. He has, for instance, lied repeatedly about his relationship to Martin Luther King, made blatantly sexist comments, massively mishandled as the *New York Times* has reported recently, the federal funds received by Operation Push, and frequently lapsed into bouts of rhetorical incoherence, all to no effect. Jackson, like Washington's "mayor for life" Marion Barry, need never pay for his wrongdoing: he has only to reach for his civil rights credit card. This has led Atlanta's Mayor Andrew Young to comment bitingly; "Only in America can someone who could not be elected mayor, governor, or Congressman run for president."

If anything, white criticisms, no matter how justified, seem only to intensify his supporters' loyalty as in the case of an earlier roguish preacher, Adam Clayton Powell. Jackson himself is skilled at playing on these sentiments, as when he remarks in the present interview that criticism of his 1984 campaign was tantamount to racism. At another point in the interview, Jackson, playing on the reality of the vast and often justified reservoir of Black anger, implied intimidatingly that opposition to his campaign was bound to engender hostility in his flock.

Leaving aside those all too eager to be taken in as they were in the 1960 by the likes of Huey Newton, most Jewish leftists and liberals seem genuinely troubled as to how to relate to Jackson. They are embarrassed when Jackson's record is laid out before them, and they readily admit that, like Ronald Reagan, Jackson not only speaks but actually thinks in terms of bumper sticker slogans. A substantial number are willing to strike a devil's bargain, much like the one which the neoconservatives have struck with the fundamentalist preachers. That is, just as the neoconservatives minimize the unsavory qualities of their allies in the name of achieving their long-term political objectives, many liberals think that they can use Jackson to advance social justice.

Those who think that working with Jackson, the moral questions aside, is a low-risk and potentially high-gain venture may think otherwise after the Democratic National Convention next August. While liberals and leftists are pleased by the prospect of a Jackson sufficiently strong to dictate the direction of the Democratic Party, the Republicans are pleased as well. Jackson, along with the Reverend Falwell, is one of the two or three most unpopular men in America in survey after survey. There is nothing that could please a weakened Republican Party more than to salvage the election by campaigning not on their economic record but against Jackson.

The great majority of Jewish liberals and leftists are, I suspect, deeply divided. They are drawn to Jackson's current rhetoric of economic populism but repelled at the idea that they might be voting for a Black version of George Wallace. Many will probably end up supporting the candidacy of Illinois Senator Paul Simon. Simon, a very liberal Democrat, who as a Congressman was repeatedly reelected from a conservative rural district and has long made economic justice the center of his concerns, is a candidate of great integrity. When Simon, a Lincoln scholar, entered the race in Iowa, he quickly shot past Jackson, his growth proportionate to Jackson's decline.

I'm personally partial to Simon, but even if Simon were not in the race, I'd be unable to support Jackson. In refusing to repudiate Farrakhan, Jackson has insisted on distinguishing between the sinner and the sin. In turn, Jews ought to trust the tale and not the teller. It's the tale of a deep-seated double-standard which ought to trouble not only American Jews but Democrats everywhere.

Abbie Hoffman

I worked on Jackson's campaign in 1984, even after the Hymie remark. I gave dozens of speeches on his behalf. On foreign and domestic policy issues we see eye to eye, but he won't get my support this year.

I believe in separation of church and state. If you are close to his campaign it seems more like a religious revival than an American campaign. If you go to the office there aren't a lot of political analysts there—it's more like a prayer meeting.

Jackson's cultural positions aren't acceptable to me. I'll take one that is particularly important to me, because I've just written a book about it: the issue of required urine testing to determine who takes drugs. This is the new loyalty test of the 1980s, part of the hysteria from having the drug menace blown way out of proportion. His staff people totally ignore my criticisms on this point. And Jesse has supported mandatory testing. He attacks casual sex and calls for cleaning up rock music in ways that sound no different to me than the conservative cultural Right.

I can't raise this with the Rainbow Coalition, because Jesse Jackson *is* the Rainbow Coalition—it only exists where he is at the time. The staff and the directors have no control over him. They all call him "Reverend" with bowed heads. There is no attempt to spread the charisma. He could do a lot to spread the Rainbow Coalition and make it more than just him. He could go around the country and pick key people who would be in his cabinet if elected, and they could then function with some real authority in his campaign. By using personalities that were known in all the critical areas of government—people who could articulate progressive ideas—he could make this Rainbow Coalition more than a one-man issue. Instead, what Jesse is doing is using 70 to 80 percent of his time to help elect local Black politicians in southern elections. This, of course, is a good thing, but it doesn't build a Rainbow Coalition that is a real political party.

Jesse didn't support Mark Green, for example, when he ran for the U.S. Senate in New York. Green is as progressive as you are going to find in America. It was a clear-cut race. Many people believed that he didn't get involved because Green was white. In that same election Jackson supported a Black running against Pete Rodino, who has a good history on civil rights and progressive legislation. The feeling was that he supported the Black simply because of color.

There is a second political criticism I have. Jesse Jackson is first and foremost a Democrat. So if his ideas are rejected by the Democrats he has absolutely no intention of bolting from the party. In some ways one could sympathize with Blacks who are willing to bolt towards the Republicans, because they see that they are being held captive by a political party that takes them for granted. But Jesse doesn't have real independence. When you look inside the machinations in the Democratic Party since 1984, at its changes in structures, you see that almost all of it was aimed at attempting to isolate, control, and manipulate Jesse Jackson and his constituency. The Rainbow Coalition isn't preparing to be a potential third party. To be a captive of the Democratic Party renders you power-less—I don't care what color you are.

Of course, if he were the Democratic Party candidate, I would be overjoyed. But I think that is impossible. Since it isn't, he has an extremely large public exposure which he should use to raise issues. But there's no point if he just raises issues to speak as part of the seven dwarves seeking the presidential nomination. He should raise the issues in a way that makes clear that we could have a third party in America that speaks to the needs of Blacks, poor whites, people who got screwed by the steel industry, farmers, and the small homeowners. Jesse is the perfect person to build a real movement of this sort—but it would have to have the built-in threat of the possibility of going somewhere outside the Democratic Party. It must say, "You Democrats, if you want to look like Reagan, if you want to talk like Reagan about the Red Menace, about people cheating on their welfare states—if you don't address the basic problems, we will go out and build another party." When he's ready to say that, he will have my support....

Cuomo gave a speech calling for an end to the Cold War that was equal to or possibly more progressive than anything Jesse Jackson is saying. So Jackson is tending to move towards the middle— and we have to pull him back. But the structure of the Rainbow Coalition doesn't allow us to do that. And if this continues to be true, perhaps we should just work on local campaigns and local struggles, because we won't get our money's worth out of a national campaign, and we will just come out of it exhausted and depressed....

I'm surprised that in this interview Jesse doesn't say something stronger about Farrakhan, because I have heard him say elsewhere that he dissociates himself and that Farrakhan will play no role in his campaign. Of course, if I thought that Jesse were anti-Semitic, that would be adequate grounds to dismiss him or any other candidate. Organized Jewry often defines anti-Semitism to mean anyone who opposes any of Israel's policies. For them, Peace Now (Shalom Achshav) does not exist, *Tikkun* does not exist. I see the larger Jewish community, as a whole, as hawkish, moving dangerously towards Republicanism, forgetting its roots in the ghetto, becoming class-oriented. Given this context, I think there is a bit of scapegoating happening towards Jackson on this question of anti-Semitism....

When I was a little kid, no matter what the issue, whether it was Sputnik or influenza or whatever, they always wanted to know, "is this good or bad for the Jews." I think we have to have a much broader framework. Being Jewish for me is a way of life—it's championing the underdog, it's the kids on the corner saying "The emperor has no clothes on," being the constant critic, the constant heretic, being the outsider, being the one who can look at society with eyes connected to one's brain and not being distorted by a blind faith in religion. I think that what's good for the Jews is what's good for the whole world, not just for the Jews. It's not good for the Jews that a small oligarchy owns most of the world's natural resources. In this sense Marx, Freud, Spinoza, Emma Goldman, and Gompers were all Jewish heroes. They were people who didn't assimilate in the fundamental sense that they chose not to go for the money, not to adopt the values and mores imposed by the particular power structure in whose land they were passing through at that time. They were the outsiders, the troublemakers, the dissidents: God bless them in Russia, in South Africa, all over the world, but they and we are a minority in the Jewish world. So the main problem for me is not the Jewish issues in connection with Jackson.

In 1984 supporting Jackson was a different matter than it is today. In 1984 the Democrats didn't have a chance, so why not have someone up there who could make some good points. But in 1988 the teflon has peeled off, the election is up for grabs, there's a chance to make some important political points and what we see is spineless, gutless Democrats versus self-centered Republicans. All we are seeing is a broadening of the middle.

Unless the structure of the Rainbow Coalition is changed so that people can actually influence it directly—and not just by trying to get Jackson's ear—then there is nothing to support. If it changes, I'd work for it full time. ☐

Drawing by Anthony Dubovsky

To Blacks and Jews: Hab Rachmones

James McPherson

About 1971, Bernard Malamud sent me a manuscript of a novel called *The Tenants*. Malamud had some reservations about the book. Specifically, he was anxious over how the antagonism between Harry Lesser, a Jewish writer, and Willie Spear, a Black writer, would be read. We communicated about the issue. On the surface, Malamud was worried over whether he had done justice to Willie Spear's Black idiom; but beneath the surface, during our exchange of letters, he was deeply concerned about the tensions that were then developing between Black intellectuals and Jewish intellectuals. I was living in Berkeley at the time, three thousand miles away from the fragmentation of the old civil rights coalition, the mounting battle over affirmative action, and most of the other incidents that would contribute to the present division between the Jewish and Black communities.

I was trying very hard to become a writer. As a favor to Malamud, I rewrote certain sections of the novel, distinguished Willie Spear's idiom from Harry Lesser's, and suggested several new scenes. I believed then that the individual human heart was of paramount importance, and I could not understand why Malamud had chosen to end his novel with Levenspiel, the Jewish slumlord who owned the condemned building in which the two antagonists lived, pleading with them *"Hab rachmones"* (have mercy). Or why Levenspiel begs for mercy 115 times. Like Isaac Babel, I felt that a well-placed period was much more effective than an extravagance of emotion. Malamud sent me an autographed copy of the book as soon as it was printed. Rereading the book eighteen years later, I now see that, even after the 115th plea for mercy by Levenspiel, there is no period and there is no peace.

Well-publicized events over the past two decades have made it obvious that Blacks and Jews have never been the fast friends we were alleged to be. The best that can be said is that, at least since the earliest decades of this century, certain spiritual elites in the Jewish community and certain spiritual elites in the Black community have found it mutually advantageous to join forces to fight specific obstacles that block the advancement of both groups: lynchings, restrictive housing covenants, segregation in schools, and corporate expressions of European racism that target both groups. During the best of times, the masses of each group were influenced by the moral leadership of the elites. From my reading of the writers of the extreme right wing, in whose works one can always find the truest possible expression of white racist sentiment, I know that the Black and Jewish peoples have historically been treated as "special cases." The most sophisticated of these writers tend to examine the two groups as "problems" in Western culture. Both share incomplete status. Both are legally included in Western society, but for two quite different reasons each has not been fused into the "race."

Until fairly recently, Jews were considered a "sect-nation," a group of people living within Western territorial states and committed to a specific religious identity. This extraterritorial status

---

James McPherson teaches in the Writers Workshop at the University of Iowa. His book Elbow Room *(Fawcett) won a Pulitzer Prize for fiction in 1978. This article appeared in* Tikkun, *September/October 1989.*

allowed Jews to convert and become members of a confessional community, as was often the case in Europe, or to drop any specific religious identification and "become" white, as has often been the case in the United States.

This second Jewish option is related, in very complex ways, to the special status of Black Americans and thus to the core of the present Black-Jewish problem. The romantic illusions of Black Nationalism aside, Black Americans have not been Africans since the eighteenth century. Systematic efforts were made to strip Black slaves of all vestiges of the African cultures from which they came. The incorporation of European bloodlines, from the first generations onward, gave the slaves immunities to the same diseases, brought by Europeans to the Americas, that nearly decimated America's indigenous peoples. The slave ancestors of today's thirty or so million Black Americans took their ideals from the sacred documents of American life, their secular values from whatever was current, and their deepest mythologies from the Jews of the Old Testament. They were a self-created people, having very little to look back on. The one thing they could not acquire was the institutional protection, or status, that comes in this country from being classified as "white." And since from its very foundation the United States has employed color as a negative factor in matters of social mobility, we Black Americans have always experienced tremendous difficulties in our attempts to achieve the full rewards of American life. The structure of white supremacy is very subtle and complex, but the most obvious thing that can be said about it is that it "enlists" psychologically those whites who view their status as dependent on it. It has the effect of encouraging otherwise decent people to adopt the psychological habits of policemen or prison guards.

Given this complex historical and cultural reality, most Black Americans, no matter how wealthy, refined, or "integrated," have never been able to achieve the mobility and security available to whites. Jewish Americans, by contrast, have this option, whether or not they choose to exercise it. Blacks recognize this fact, and this recognition is the basis of some of the extreme tension that now exists between the two groups. While Jews insist that they be addressed and treated as part of a religious community, most Black Americans tend to view them as white. When Jews insist that Jewish sensitivities and concerns be recognized, Black Americans have great difficulty separating these concerns from the concerns of the corporate white community.

And yet, despite the radically different positions of the two groups, there has been a history of alliances. Perhaps it is best to say that mutual self-interest has defined the interaction between Blacks and Jews for most of this century. In her little-known study, *In the Almost Promised Land*, Hasia R. Diner has traced the meeting and mutual assessment of the two peoples as presented in the Yiddish press to the two million Jewish immigrants from Eastern Europe and Russia who came to the United States during the first four decades of this century. Community papers like the *Tageblatt* and the *Forward* forged a socialistic language that brought together Jewish immigrants from different backgrounds, that helped them acculturate, and that advised them about the obstacles and opportunities they would find in America. These papers gave more attention to Black American life than to any other non-Jewish concern. They focused on Black marriage and family, on Black crime, on Black "trickery and deception," and on Black education, entertainment, and achievement. They linked Black suffering to Jewish suffering. Diner writes:

> The Yiddish papers sensed that a special relationship existed between blacks and Jews and because of this the press believed that the two groups were captivated by each other.... Jews believed that a history of suffering had predisposed Jews toward understanding the problems of blacks. ("Because we have suffered we treat kindly and sympathetically and humanly all the oppressed of every nation.")

The central theme was that Black people were America's Jews. Historical parallels were emphasized: the Black Exodus from the South was compared to the Jewish Exodus from Egypt and to the Jewish migration from Russia and Germany.

But there were much more practical reasons why the two groups—one called "white," the other defined by caste; one geared to scholarship and study, the other barely literate; one upwardly mobile, the other in constant struggle merely to survive—managed to find common ground during the first four decades of this century. There was the desperate Black need for financial, legal, and moral support in the fight against racism, lynchings, and exclusion from the institutions of American life. There was the Jewish perception that many of the problems of exclusion faced by Black people were also faced by Jews. Diner writes:

> Black Americans needed champions in a hostile society. Jewish Americans, on the other hand, wanted a meaningful role so as to prove themselves to an inhospitable [society].... Thus, American Jewish leaders involved in a quest for a meaningful identity and comfortable role in American society found that one way to fulfill that search was to serve as the intermediaries between blacks and whites. The Jewish magazines defined a mission for Jews to interpret the black world to white Americans and to speak for blacks and champion their cause.

Diner is describing the "interstitial" role, traditionally assumed by Jewish shopkeepers and landlords in Black communities, being extended into the moral sphere. Given the radical imbalance of potential power that existed between the two groups, however, such a coalition was fated to fail once American Jews had achieved their own goals.

For mutually self-interested reasons, I believe, the two groups began a parting of the ways just after the Six Day War of 1967. The rush of rationalizations on both sides—Jewish accusations of Black anti-Semitism, Black Nationalist accusations of Jewish paternalism and subversion of Black American goals—helped to obscure very painful realities that had much more to do with the broader political concerns of both groups, as they were beginning to be dramatized in the international arena, than with the domestic issues so widely publicized. Within the Black American community, even before the killing of Martin Luther King Jr., there arose a nationalistic identification with the emerging societies of newly liberated Africa. In the rush to identify with small pieces of evidence of Black freedom *anywhere* in the world, many Black Americans began to embrace ideologies and traditions that were alien to the traditions that had been developed, through painful struggle, by their earliest ancestors on American soil.

A large part of this romantic identification with Africa resulted from simple frustration: the realization that the moral appeal advocated by Martin King had authority only within those Southern white communities where the remnants of Christian tradition were still respected. The limitations of the old civil rights appeal became apparent when King was stoned while attempting to march in Cicero, Illinois, in 1966. We Black Americans discovered that many ethnic Americans, not just Southern whites, did not care for us. The retrenchment that resulted, promoted by the media as Black Nationalism, provided convenient excuses for many groups to begin severing ties with Black Americans. Expressions of nationalism not only alienated many well-meaning whites; they had the effect of discounting the Black American tradition of principled struggle that had produced the great leaders in the Black American community. To any perceptive listener, most of the Nationalistic rhetoric had the shrillness of despair.

For the Jewish community, victory in the Six Day War of 1967 caused the beginning of a much more complex reassessment of the Jewish situation, one based on some of the same spiritual motivations as were the defeats suffered by Black Americans toward the end of the 1960s. The Israeli victory in 1967 was a *reassertion* of the nationhood of the Jewish people. But, like the founding of Israel in 1948, this reassertion raised unresolved contradictions. My reading teaches me that, until the twentieth century, Zion to most Jews was not a tangible, earthly hope, but a mystical symbol of the divine deliverance of the Jewish nation. Zion was a heavenly city that did not yet exist. It was to be planted on earth by the Messiah on the Day of Judgment, when historical time would come to an end. But the Jewish experience in Europe seems to have transformed the dream of a heavenly city into an institution in the practical world. This tension has turned the idea of the Jews as a nation existing as the community of the faithful into the idea of Israel as a Western territorial sovereign. Concerned for its survival, Israel has turned expansionist; but the price it has paid has been the erosion of its ethical identity. It is said that the world expects more from the Jews than from any other people. This deeply frustrating misconception, I believe, results from the dual premise (religious and political) of the State of Israel. I also believe that American Jews are extraordinarily frustrated when they are unable to make non-Jews understand how sensitive Jews are to uninformed criticism after six thousand years of relentless persecution.

The majority of Black Americans are unaware of the complexity of the meaning of Israel to American Jews. But, ironically, Afro-Zionists have as intense an emotional identification with Africa and with the Third World as American Jews have with Israel. Doubly ironic, this same intensity of identification with a "Motherland" seems rooted in the mythologies common to both groups. In this special sense—in the spiritual sense implied by "Zion" and "Diaspora" and "Promised Land"—Black Americans *are* America's Jews. But given the isolation of Black Americans from any meaningful association with Africa, extensions of the mythology would be futile. We have no distant homeland preparing an ingathering. For better or worse, Black Americans are *Americans*. Our special problems must be confronted and solved here, where they began. They cannot be solved in the international arena, in competition with Jews.

Related to the problem of competing mythologies is a recent international trend that, if not understood in terms of its domestic implications, will deepen the already complex crisis between Blacks and Jews. The period of European hegemony, mounted in the fifteenth century and consolidated in the nineteenth, imposed on millions of non-European people values and institutions not indigenous to their cultural traditions. One of these institutions was the nation-state. Since the end of World War II, the various wars of independence in India, Asia, Africa, and elsewhere have exposed the fact that a European invention does not always meet the mythological, linguistic, and cultural needs of different ethnic groups competing within artificial "territorial states." We sometimes forget that it took many centuries for Europeans to evolve political forms suited to their own habits. Since the 1950s, colonized people have begun to assert their own cultural needs. The new word coined to define this process is "devolutionism." While devolutionism is currently a Third World phenomenon, two of the most prominent groups within the territorial United States, because of their unique origins, can be easily drawn into this struggle: Black Americans, because of our African origins and our sympathy for the liberation struggle currently taking place in South Africa; and Jews, because of their intense identification with Israel. Given the extent of Israeli involvement in South Africa, and given the sympathy many Black Americans feel for Black South Africans and Palestinians, it is only predictable that some Black Americans would link the two struggles. My deepest fear is that the dynamics of American racism will force Black Americans into a deeper identification with the Palestinians, thus incorporating into an already tense domestic situation an additional international dimension we just do not need. The resulting polarization may well cause chaos for a great many people, Blacks and Jews included.

I have no solutions to offer beyond my feeling that we should begin talking with each other again. I remember walking the streets of Chicago back in 1972 and 1973, gathering information for an article on Jewish slumlords who had "turned" white neighborhoods and then sold these homes at inflated prices to poor Black people, recent migrants from the South, on installment purchase contracts. I remember talking with Rabbi Robert Marx, who sided with the buyers against the Jewish sellers; with Gordon Sherman, a businessman who was deeply disturbed by the problem; with Marshall Patner, a lawyer in Hyde Park; and with other Jewish lawyers who had volunteered to work with the buyers in an attempt to correct the injustice. I spent most of a Guggenheim Fellowship financing my trips to Chicago. I gave the money I earned from the article to the organization created by the buyers. And although the legal case that was brought against the sellers was eventually lost in Federal District Court, I think that all the people involved in the effort to achieve some kind of justice found the experience very rewarding. I remember interviewing poor Black people, the victims, who did not see the sellers as Jews but as whites. I remember interviewing Mrs. Lucille Johnson, an elderly Black woman who seemed to be the spiritual center of the entire effort. Her influence could get smart Jewish and Irish lawyers to do the right thing as opposed to the legal thing. I asked her about the source of her strength. I still remember her reply:

> [T]he bad part of the thing is that we just don't have what we need in our lives to go out and do something, white or black. We just don't have love.... But this ain't no situation to get hung up on color; getting hung up on some of God's love will bail us out. I think of "Love one another" and the Commandments. If we love the Lord our God with all our hearts and minds, and love our neighbors as ourselves, we done covered them Commandments. And "Let not your heart be troubled; he that believes in God believes also in me...."

I think there was, a generation or two ago, a group of stronger and wiser Black and Jewish people. I think they were more firmly grounded in the lived mythology of the Hebrew Bible. I think that, because of this grounding, they were, in certain spiritual dimensions, almost one people. They were spiritual elites. Later generations have opted for more mundane values and the rewards these values offer. Arthur Hertzburg told me, "Anti-Semitism is the way Blacks join the majority. Racism is the way Jews join the majority. Individuals in both groups have the capacity to package themselves in order to make it in terms the white majority can understand."

Certain consequences of the Black-Jewish alliance cannot be overlooked. The spiritual elites within both groups recognized, out of common memories of oppression and suffering, that the only true refuge a person in pain has is within another person's heart. These spiritual elites had the moral courage to allow their hearts to become swinging doors. For at least six decades these elites contributed to the soul of American democracy. Their influence animated the country, gave it a sense of moral purpose it had not known since the Civil War. The coalition they called into being helped to redefine the direction of the American experience and kept it moving toward transcendent goals. With the fragmentation of that coalition, and with the current divisions among its principles, we have fallen into stasis, if not into decadence. Bernard Malamud's Levenspiel the landlord would like to be rid of his two troublesome tenants. I have no solutions to offer. But, eighteen years later, I want to say with Malamud: Mercy, Mercy, Mercy, Mercy, Mercy, Mercy, Mercy, Mercy, Mercy, Mercy

I want to keep saying it to all my friends, and to all my students, until we are strong enough to put a period to this thing. □

Black-Jewish Dialogue: Beyond Rootless Universalism and Ethnic Chauvinism

Cornel West

W hat is most striking to me both about *Tikkun* and about this conference is that they focus on the failure of empty internationalism and rootless universalism, that is, on the refusal to think seriously and critically about one's tradition and identity. In the period in which there was a stronger alliance between Blacks and Jews, some of that alliance depended on both sides' identifying with a form of universalism that did not highlight questions of identity. There is no going back to such a period. If there is going to be a renewed connection between these two communities, or even a sensible dialogue, it depends on our ability to remain sensitive to the positive quests for identity among Jewish Americans and African-Americans.

We need to be aware of the complex interplay between universalism and particularism so that we can avoid the traps of tribalism and ethnic chauvinism. We can no longer raise the banner of internationalism—a banner that should and must be raised—unless that internationalism is filtered through our particular experiences.

We live in a society that is characterized by increasing racial polarization and rising anti-Semitism. Blacks and Jews still remain the two peoples that are most loyal to progressive politics in this country. Both peoples have long histories of exploitation and oppression, degradation and devaluation. For us today the central question is, "What is going to be the *moral content* of our identity and the *political consequences* of it?"

When we look back, we have to acknowledge that there has always been anti–Semitism in the Black community and anti-Black racism in the Jewish community. But there was also, particularly in the period from 1945 to 1965, some serious attempts to build bridges and forge alliances that would run counter to these destructive tendencies. The turning point away from this alliance was in the period from 1965 to 1968, with the emergence of the Black Power movement, which perceived Jews simply as whites and began to push white activists out of the civil rights movement. Supporters of Black Power increasingly began to see the world in terms of the American empire pitted against Third World liberation movements—a profoundly Manichaean perspective, a simplistic dualistic perspective. There is a sophisticated way of looking at the U.S. as an empire as well as a sophisticated way of understanding Third World liberation movements, but the sophisticated version was not always what we heard in those early days when Blacks were seeking to assert their identity.

In 1967 Harold Cruse published *The Crisis of the Negro Intellectual*, which remains highly influential to this very day. The book contained a scathing attack on the role of Jewish particularism, with special focus on the Jews' role in the Communist Party, U.S.A. This was another sign of the

---

Cornel West, a professor of religion and Afro-American studies at Princeton University, is the author of Prophetic Fragments *(Eerdmans, 1988) and* The American Evasion of Philosophy *(Wisconsin, 1989). This paper was presented to the December 1988* Tikkun *Conference in New York and was published in* Tikkun, *July/August 1989.*

growth of particularistic consciousness within the Black Left. The loss in April 1968 of Martin Luther King, Jr., was significant in this respect because King promoted the legitimacy of Zionism to the Black community. King spoke explicitly about the importance of Blacks' learning from and promoting the progressive version of Zionism. With that loss we saw a crescendo of Black critiques of Zionism—most vulgar, though some sophisticated. I'm sure that a *Tikkun* audience understands that many critiques of Zionism are tinged with anti-Semitism. *But some critiques do transcend it.*

After 1968 we saw three major arenas of Black–Jewish tension. First, there was the issue of community control. In the sphere of education, this struggle was perceived as an attack on Jewish educators, but the community control issue extended also to an attack on Jewish entrepreneurs in the Black ghetto (particularly since a developing Black business class had an interest in freeing up space so that it could progress).

The second issue was affirmative action, which pitted many conservative Jews against Blacks *and* liberal Jews. It is too often ignored that many liberal Jews support affirmative action. For example, Thomas Nagel, a professor of philosophy, has put forward some of the most powerful critiques of the opponents of affirmative action, in the name of Kantian morality. This doesn't mean that we should forget about the neoconservative Jewish figures who argue against affirmative action. But we also need to understand their opposition as reflective of the boomtown character of Jewish ascendancy to the middle classes in a short thirty-year period. Many Jews expressed a deep anxiety about the reintroduction of quotas when those same quotas had been previously used against Jews in the anti-Semitic structures of higher learning. Yet when the previous anti-Semitic structures began to fall, Blacks perceived Jews as securing middle-class status in an astonishing manner. Blacks who were entering the mainstream found a disproportionate Jewish presence in the upper middle class of American society—in law, in medicine—in part because Jews worked hard to take advantage of the opportunities that had recently been opened to them.

Many first-generation Black middle-class persons began to wonder, "When are Black folks going to move into these institutions, given that there are a finite number of places?" Since they knew that they could not count on the "rationality" of white employers or administrators to overcome the history of past discrimination, they had to rely on affirmative action—and the attack on affirmative action, no matter how principled, was an attack on Black progress.

The third issue was the Black critique of American foreign policy. This critique coincided with the emergence of conservative forces in Israel after the 1967 and 1973 wars—first as a conservatizing influence in the Labor party, then as the triumph of Menachem Begin's right-wing coalition—and the increasing identification of Israel with an American foreign policy that was dominated by cold war preoccupations and a refusal to see anything good in Third World liberation struggles. This connection to American foreign policy made it easier for many Blacks to identify Israel as a tool of American imperial interests.

These were issues that tended to weaken the Black-Jewish alliance, but we should also note that there has persisted in America a very real alliance in the political arena. In fact, many Black elected officials would not be in office today if it were not for the Jewish voters who, in alliance with Black voters, helped put them in office. The grand example of the late Harold Washington looms large here.

Black anti-Semitism and Jewish anti-Black racism are real, and both are as profoundly American as cherry pie. All of us who are Americans must struggle against the devaluation of the Jewish people, which persists in the myths and symbols of what it is to be a citizen of this country. Blacks have a deep moral obligation to fight against anti-Semitism. And Jews have the same duty to combat Jewish anti-Black racism.

Black anti-Semitism is also a degraded people's resentment of a downtrodden people that is moving quickly up the social ladder. One sees this resentment in Louis Farrakhan, who evokes the image of alleged Jewish unity and homogeneity (certainly a myth!) in the process of asserting that if Blacks could be like Jews and create a sense of achievement and dignity among themselves, then they could succeed in similar fashion.

The state of siege now raging in Black America, the sense of frustration and hopelessness, pushes people to look toward a leader who speaks in bold and defiant terms. The Black elected officials tend not speak to these deep needs. Farrakhan tries to fill the vacuum—and this obsession with Jewish achievement and Jewish accomplishment is one of the means by which he tries to do this. I've argued with Farrakhan's people—first, insisting that they understand that Jews are human beings, but, second, trying to point out to them that Jews are not as important as Black Muslims think when it comes to the actual operation of economic or political power in this world. If you want to talk about power, start with multinational corporate America.

Farrakhan is a radical anti-Semite, but he is not a Nazi. It's important to make this distinction, because if every anti-Semite were a Nazi, we'd have to reconstitute the Allied Forces. Farrakhan says terrible things about the Jews, but he does not advocate that people physically attack Jews. He is different from the neo-Nazi skinheads who advocate the actual physical injury of Jewish human beings.

Jesse Jackson must, in turn, be understood as part of a Southern Black American Protestant tradition. Blacks in the South had very infrequent contact with Jewish people. Struggles in the South were primarily between Blacks and whites, with both sides being Protestant (there were not even that many Catholics in the South). Jesse's own perceptions of American Jews are shaped mostly by his encounters with the Jews after 1965, and the experience of American Jews in the period since 1965 is very difficult to square with the larger context of Jewish experience in the modern world. When Jesse sees Jews he doesn't think about the expulsion of Jews from Spain in 1492, the expulsion of Jews from England in 1290, or the expulsion of Jews from France in 1306. He sees Jews on the move in the middle classes. He doesn't seem to grasp the legitimate fears or the paranoia of American Jews, nor does he seem to understand the psychological impact of the Holocaust on Jews during the past forty years.

I do not believe Jesse Jackson is an anti-Semite; but there are shadows of anti-Semitic sensibilities shot through his language. In principle, he would struggle against anti-Semitism, demonstrate against it. But it's very problematic to have a leader of liberal left forces in America who has this kind of baggage. It's in some ways a tragedy.

In Jesse Jackson we have someone who highlights the unprecedented business attack on working and poor people in this country, one of the few people who emphasizes this issue and speaks with power and passion about it. How do we evaluate and assess such a figure who uses as his social base the most loyal group in America to progressive politics—Black Americans? Do we support him, hoping that he will continue to grow and move beyond the shadows of anti-Semitic sensibilities, or do we oppose him and then align ourselves with figures who won't talk about the business assault on the poor? Or do we try to tease out some of the Black elected officials who are much more sensitive but who have as encompassing visions as Jesse Jackson—the Bill Grays of this world? That's another option. Or do we wait for a third, extraparliamentary figure who boldly and defiantly challenges corporate power, racism, anti-Semitism, homophobia, and sexism? At the moment, I remain a critical supporter of Jackson's efforts to change America.

The future dialogue between progressive African-Americans and Jewish Americans will be difficult. On the international front, the conservative form of Zionism that regulates Israeli policies on the West Bank and Gaza Strip warrants wholesale rejection and fundamental reorientation. Palestinian national self-determination must be confronted and accommodated by all who take seriously Jewish national self-determination—on moral and political grounds. Similarly, Blacks must criticize the atrocities in Kenya, Uganda, and Ethiopia—not simply the ugly realities in South Africa—with the same moral outrage with which they criticize those atrocities committed against Palestinians as a result of the Israeli government's policies. On the domestic front, the Black-Jewish alliance must be rejuvenated and reconstituted—especially in the labor movement, among Black womanists and Jewish feminists, among Black Christians and Orthodox Muslims and religious Jews, and in the new emerging group of American liberal left activists now led by Jesse Jackson.

The first step is to break the ice with engaged dialogue, openness to change, and constructive attempts at collective thought and action. This is the road to substantive internationalism and rooted universalism. □

Porno Drive-In, Knoxville, TN

Willa Schneberg

As we watch a tanned tight-bodied man and woman make it in a
hot tub, we try to ignore the young red-necks in the '74 Ford
pick-up also parked away from the screen who cut moonshine
with beer and go one by one into the brush with a roll of toilet
paper, except when they press their faces against the window
on his side and yell, Black boy, got some white pussy for us?
Although we drive to the section of the lot farthest from them
we no longer feel safe. Your penis remains limp in my hand, my
vagina dry, no matter how much you rub my clitoris. We
straighten our clothes. You pick your afro. I switch on the car
light to put on lipstick and catch my face in the compact, my
white face, not the pink of the white boys, but the color inside
your palms. We squash ourselves into opposite sides of the car.

But soon we are sitting close. I nuzzle against your neck. We laugh about
the zebra-striped babies we would bring into the world if we weren't
careful and I retell the story of the Russian peasant who murdered my
great-grandmother, Rivka, hung her over the family clothesline and how I
wished we could have made it as if it never happened that you could have
carried her on your back, helping me to lower her gently in the narrow
bed and handed me gauze, until her wound was freckle-small and she
returned from the dead asking for a glass tea and a bissel challah. Then
you pull me again into the story of the house-slave, your
great-great-great-grandmother Adelaide forced to lie with the master and how you
wish we could have broken into her master's bedchamber, your hand over
mine, as we cut the bastard's throat, freeing her forever.

Demagoguery in America: Wrong Turns in the Politics of Race

Jim Sleeper

Research for this piece was supported by a grant from the Nathan Cummings Foundation.

I n the late 1930s, Irving Howe and his generation of democratic socialists concluded, to their dismay, that they would have to spend some of their best energies not on building a more decent, socialist world, but on defeating Stalinism—on trying, that is, to rescue the very hope of socialism from those who, starting from wholly legitimate grievances and rage, had bloodied its vision virtually beyond recognition.

Inevitably, this decision put democratic socialists on the same "side" as right-wing anti-communists in certain disputes. They were all too easily condemned as apologists for economic royalism and even fascism. The condemnation came not only from Stalinists but also from seemingly more moderate, honorable Americans who had chosen, out of elite guilt, naive idealism, or stubborn loyalty to the original vision, to excuse or even celebrate the Communists' brutality. Now that the peoples of the Soviet Union have spoken for themselves, we know that Howe and his colleagues had no morally or politically defensible choice but to risk the contempt of the parlor Left and the condescension of the Right. Democratic socialists may feel exhausted, but, in large measure, they have been vindicated.

The time has come for Black activists and all who support civil-rights struggles to face up to a more modest, yet in some respects equally dismaying, mission: that of isolating and defeating much of what now passes for Black protest leadership in New York City and some other parts of America. Now more than at any time in recent memory, progressive politics must dedicate itself to building an electoral coalition strong enough to reverse the federal abdication of responsibility for cities and the poor; destructive economic practices hypocritically justified as part of the workings of free markets; and, amid the devastation caused by these forces, a deepening of racial and ethnic hostilities that blights lives and forecloses coalition politics.

Instead of helping to build such coalitions, Black demagogues have embraced a series of disastrous misjudgments and destructive tactics, which I want to describe with reference to the events of August and September 1991 in Brooklyn's Crown Heights. Exploiting deep fault lines in what is now called "identity politics," these pretenders to serious leadership have conned other Black leaders who should know better into systematically burning their community's bridges to feminists, Asians, liberal Jews, Hispanics, and, more importantly, to everyone who aspires to share the obligations and rewards of a just, pluralist society.

The Reverend Al Sharpton, the Reverend Herbert Daughtry, and street activist Sonny Carson, the

---

Jim Sleeper, an editorial writer for New York Newsday, *is the author of* The Closest of Strangers: Liberalism and the Politics of Race in New York *(W.W. Norton & Co., 1990). This article appeared in* Tikkun, *November/December 1991.*

attorneys Alton Maddox, Jr., C. Vernon Mason, and Colin Moore, and other highly visible demagogues, are not the only ones responsible. So are a host of apparently more moderate leaders, white as well as Black, who have indulged them. Together, these groups have overshadowed and often intimidated a third group of Black leaders: those who have been working in neighborhood organizations, churches, labor unions, and electoral politics to reweave the Black community's devastated civic and political fabric, amid deepening economic depression and white contempt. The eclipse of these constructive activists has dimmed the prospects for the reemergence of the kind of Black leadership provided by A. Philip Randolph or E. Franklin Frazier—leaders who, faced with the much more intractable poverty and white racism of fifty years ago, managed to forge true movements for justice. Because such leaders are not emerging in New York and some other areas, the period of Black moral dominance within the liberal and civil-rights communities in those places is ending. We can argue about the reasons, but we cannot turn back the clock. Others must take up the initiative, much as Dennis Rivera, a Puerto Rican socialist, saved New York's Local 1199 of the Hospital and Health Care Employees Union from extensive damage by Doris Turner's pseudo-Black-nationalist demagoguery a few years ago.

Drawing the line against a Black misleadership that trades in lies, vilifies innocent parties, silences dissenters, and dehumanizes real and putative opponents will require soul-searching and courage on the part of Black progressives and those of us who would join them. We will have to endure being miscast as accomplices of such racists as New York's Republican Senator Alfonse D'Amato, who seldom misses a chance to bait Black demagogues. As we try to hammer out a new progressive consensus capable of touching mainstream America, we will sometimes be vilified as Uncle Toms or racists. And just as democratic socialists had to struggle not only against Stalinists but also against Stalinism's fashionable, sometimes eloquent apologists, so we will find ourselves challenging many Blacks and whites whose naive deference to the misplaced agendas of identity politics empowers the demagogues.

But it is precisely because racism, economic injustice, and conservative politics are such formidable enemies that leaders groping for an alternative politics cannot afford to indulge fantasies of ethnic or racial destiny that fracture potential coalitions for social change. They must learn to distinguish between group psychodramas, which have their place in communal theaters or churches, and the more farsighted interracial organizing and discourse, based on transracial truths, that are so desperately needed in pluralist arenas—in workplaces and courts, at the polls and in the streets.

Progressive politics simply can't make headway in a pluralist society without keeping certain commitments. One is to rational analysis—that is, to the primacy of admittedly provisional, evolving public truths over the mythic, communal ones enshrouded in racial narratives. Another is to the defense of individual over group rights in a context of civic and moral obligation to people across race lines— the right, for example, to dissent from one's own community, without fear of material harm, in order to protest a clear injustice. Yet, even on college campuses, where it is at its most benign, identity politics too often mystifies and divides. It too often mischaracterizes rational analysis and individual dissent from group norms as "Eurocentric" impositions simply because, by accidents of history, they come to us most directly from the European Enlightenment. Intending to mount liberating Afrocentric and other narratives against "hegemonic" racist ideas, practitioners of identity politics often draw their targets too broadly, attacking the very underpinnings of their own freedom in what is, after all—as they themselves insist—a diverse society. In so doing, they play into the hands of those who have been huckstering separate racial scenarios of truth to consolidate an illusory and destructive power.

"Who controls the past, controls the future," Orwell wrote in *1984.* We all know that history written by its "winners" works in this way. What this bloody century ought to have taught us is that the narratives of "losers" have a similarly destructive potential, that the oppressed can fight as blindly and as brutally as the oppressor. Serious history always struggles to escape this dilemma by resisting the service of ideological or ethnic ends. Its truths are written from the vantage of both "winners" and "losers" in communities of scholars who have the courage and the wisdom to balance tragedy and desire through an evolving discourse among peers. Even as we struggle to enrich and correct that never-completed consensus, we need the courage to defend it, in all its imperfection, against any self-proclaimed purity that masks brutality, whether it comes wrapped in a "great white male" theory of history or in a mythos of noble Black and brown insurgency against domination. Counter-intuitive though it may seem, we must sometimes speak truth to powerlessness, which can become as blind as power itself.

The public debate about slavery that was ratcheted up recently by City College professor Leonard Jeffries's allusions to Jewish control of the trade made this point well. International slavery turns out to have been an ecumenical business, the commodity market of its day. It was invented largely by Arab Muslims; instituted legally and financially in the West by Christians; enthusiastically adopted by Africans who sold their brethren; and bankrolled in part by Sephardic Jews who cornered much of the capital behind the sugar processing industry, which brought Black slaves to the West Indies. Jeffries exaggerates the role of the Jews in slave trading for purposes closer to home and to his own personal experience (which, in keeping with the premises of identity politics, he conflates with racial truth). His identity-driven version of history is about as truthful as that of a white racist or Black nationalist historian of the future looking back on the New York of the 1990s, seeing a Black mayor, a Black Ford Foundation president, a few Black CEOs, and scores of Black vice presidents for community affairs—and concluding that Blacks had shaped the urban capitalist agenda.

This is just the kind of distortion identity politics flirts with all the time. And it is in the streets and hard-pressed institutions of urban America that such distortions have taken truly ominous—I would say tribal—turns. There, as on campus, champions of identity politics claim to counterpose racial memories and truths to liberal society's insidious lies. But in the hands of a demagogic leadership, the intended social reform degenerates into a tit-for-tat recapitulation of the very wrongs it seeks to undo.

What protections do those who would carry their personal and racial narratives, unsullied by rational criticism, into academic and legal discourse offer against such a disaster? What do they say to Jeffries, and to the Reverend Al Sharpton and to Sonny Carson when they carry Jeffries's theories into shakedowns of Korean stores or riots in Crown Heights? How do they counter George Bush's cynical use of the Voting Rights Act in order to create legislative-district apartheid—and to increase the number of all-white, potentially GOP seats—by packing minorities into racially gerrymandered districts in the name of Black or Latino empowerment? How, indeed, when civil-rights groups driven by identity politics are already jumping at the bait? (In New York, some Hispanic activists are willing to contemplate a bizarrely shaped, nominally Latino district, which would throw Democratic representatives Stephen Solarz and Charles Schumer into the same electoral arena, thereby costing New York City one of these men's legislative clout.)

Some of identity politics' most serious assaults have been against the criminal courts, which the demagogues, with some justice, say are permeated with racism. But it is one thing to uncover and denounce racism in the criminal-justice system. It is quite another to concoct perversely comforting racial case narratives that falsify evidence, twist testimony, and intimidate witnesses, all in order to "prove" to Blacks that the system will never work for them. That is precisely what Black protest leaders have done in the cases of Howard Beach, Tawana Brawley, Bensonhurst, Central Park, the Korean boycott, and Crown Heights. But once they've stymied justice in order to dramatize racism, what next? Having whipped their followers into a frenzy, they have no answer. And they offer no alliances, for they have alienated people of other colors—and, indeed, many Blacks—who desperately seek a criminal-justice system free of lies and intimidation.

There is, of course, a signal and profound difference between Stalinists and the Black misleader-ship I am describing: Far from controlling the state and its means of imposing terror, as the Bolshe-viks eventually did, Black demagogues will never win such power in America. Like Stalinists, they have managed to silence Black dissenters and ruin the lives of innocent whites against whom they bear false witness. But they have not been able to prevent Black voters from repudiating their strate-gies, again and again, in the privacy of the polls. Aren't they really too marginal and powerless, then, to worry about? Anyway, aren't they just the media creations of racists who seek a foil for their own depredations?

At best, these rhetorical questions embody half-truths, unsatisfying not only to those Jews who have abandoned such speculations since the killing of Yankel Rosenbaum in Crown Heights, but to all decent people. The demagogues' tactics have so completely foreclosed any possibility of interra-cial coalitions in New York that Sharpton and his cohorts may as well have been working for D'Amato and Bush. And since New York City's two Black weeklies and the talk shows on its premier Black radio station, WLIB, relentlessly indoctrinate tens of thousands of readers and listeners in special racial truths, this brand of identity politics substantially chills debate within the Black community iself.

When, for example, state Assemblyman Roger Green denounced Sharpton during the Brawley af-fair for likening New York's attorney general to Hitler, Green's chairmanship of the Black and Puerto Rican Legislative Caucus was immediately contested by a Black state senator whose district over-lapped his. (She withdrew her candidacy after a few days, not wanting, she said, to project to the public an impression of Black division.) Ordinary Blacks who challenged the veracity of Brawley's story were vilified by talk-show hosts and newspaper polemicists. It took a Black reporter widely respected in his community, *Newsday*'s Les Payne, to expose the hoax in terms that made Black dissent possible.

After a brave Black civil-rights attorney, Michael Meyers, warned publicly during the Jeffries af-fair that Black leaders were failing to speak out because they wrongly, obsessively fear being cast as tools of the white establishment, he was deluged with hate mail. In the rest of the country, Black po-litical discourse has become greatly diversified through the work of such disparate figures as Cornel West, Shelby Steele, *Washington Post* columnist William Raspberry, law professors Randall Kennedy and Stephen Carter, and many others; but there has been no such flowering in New York. Too many people are afraid. Similarly, Blacks whose politics are at odds with that of the demagogues have learned to "work around" them, not confront them, when their carnivals are running at fever pitch.

For all these reasons, we must fight a two-front battle, against Black demagogues (and those who indulge them), as well as against racists (and those who indulge them). Nowhere was the case for do-ing so clearer than in the Crown Heights story.

"Here we go again," groaned a late-August front-page *New York Post* headline when Sharpton announced that Yosef Lifsh was driving while intoxicated. Lifsh, a chasidic Jew, had run a red light; his car bounced off another car, and then crushed to death Gavin Cato, a seven-year-old Black boy in Brooklyn's Crown Heights neighborhood. The *Post*'s sense of déjà vu was prompted, of course, by memories of the wildly false charges circulated by Sharpton and some other Black protest leaders in the criminal-justice cases I have mentioned.

Sharpton's intoxication charge and Carson's claim that Lifsh didn't have a driver's license were de-signed to justify Black demands for the arrest and indictment of Lifsh under New York's remarkably lax laws governing criminal liability in traffic accidents. But the accusations immediately blew up in the activists' faces—and only partly because Lifsh did have a driver's license and had been tested neg-atively for intoxication immediately after the crash. The activists' scenario collapsed when the press found that the same lax traffic laws that protected Lifsh had also protected errant Black motorists who had killed Chasidim, one a young boy, in the same neighborhood in the preceding five years. Besides, as the *Post*'s headline suggested, most of the city had by now caught on to the demagogues' tactics.

Then, too, in the minds of most decent New Yorkers, the accident, while tragic, had already been eclipsed by the fatal, apparently retaliatory stabbing of Yankel Rosenbaum, who was surrounded just hours after Cato's death by a crowd of Black youths as he walked home from the subway. His killing was indistinguishable from that of Yusuf Hawkins by a white mob in Bensonhurst in 1989—though one wouldn't have known it at first from the press coverage of the event, which doted eerily on the demagogues' every word about the auto accident and about the grievances of young Blacks hurling bottles, rocks, and anti-Semitic epithets at cops and at the supposedly privileged Chasidim. Allegedly, Lifsh's bad driving had compounded Blacks' long-standing grievances because he was bringing up the rear of Lubavitcher Grand Rebbe Menachem Schneerson's police-escorted motorcade at the time.

The media soon recovered their balance; an exhaustive investigation by *Newsday* reporters Jennifer Preston and Michael Powell showed that Chasidim had not received disproportionate city aid for some years. Mayor David Dinkins, who had muted his criticisms of Sharpton and Carson in order to sit down and negotiate with them as the rocks and epithets flew, finally declared that Rosenbaum had been "lynched" as surely as Hawkins had been.

None of this stopped Sharpton, Carson, the Reverend Herbert Daughtry, and attorneys Moore, Maddox, and Mason, all veterans of past scams, from succoring the rioters. It didn't stop Black *Amsterdam News* editor Wilbert Tatum, who had flamboyantly printed the name of the Central Park rape victim and characterized her assailants' trial as a lynching, from running headlines on the Crown Heights story such as "Many Blacks, No Jews Arrested." Nor did it stop the demagogues from turning Cato's August 26 funeral into a carnival of hatred so obscene that his bewildered, grieving parents were all but forgotten. "Rather than be scorned," wrote veteran activist Sam Pinn, the rock-throwing youths "should be recognized as freedom fighters.... The young people who are alleged to have murdered the rabbinical student Yankel Rosenbaum were striking a blow—not only a blow of revenge, but, in their view, a blow for justice." Cato family attorney and city-council candidate Colin Moore said the rock-throwing mob was "justifiably angry because Lifsh left the children to die." But, according to Police Commissioner Lee Brown, cops ordered a Jewish ambulance service to spirit Lifsh away because the crowd, instead of helping Lifsh lift the car off Gavin Cato and his injured sister Angela, stole Lifsh's watch, wallet, and car phone, and beat him (he received eighteen stitches at the hospital).

And yet, on Labor Day, the rioting and invective temporarily spent, decent opinion began to assert itself within the Black community. Crown Heights hosted more than a million Caribbean Blacks in the annual West Indian Day Parade without incident; a chasidic spokesman even marched with Dinkins as a grand marshal in a gesture of reconciliation. Carson pronounced himself so disgusted that peace had broken out on the site of young Cato's demise that he was thinking of leaving town forever; "white" talk shows and newspapers were deluged with offers to pay his one-way fare to anywhere on the globe. Sharpton flew to Israel, where he stayed just long enough to leave a civil summons for the driver Lifsh, who had fled there after giving the grand jury his testimony. Senator D'Amato, meanwhile, came to Crown Heights to condemn Sharpton and declare that Dinkins, who was planning a trip to Africa for November, shouldn't bother to come back. Yet less than two weeks after the rioting stopped, Colin Moore and C. Vernon Mason were defeated in their own race for City Council seats by white incumbents who garnered more Black votes than they did (albeit in contests where more than one Black candidate was running).

Returns in another council election proved equally revealing. Crown Heights's own long-time councilwoman Mary Pinkett, a lackluster, union-friendly Black politician of the sort that progressives find useful but uninspiring, spoke out for reconciliation and against demagoguery. She was overwhelmingly reelected, in an overwhelmingly Black district, against a strong challenger, Pete Williams, a young Black activist more congenial to practitioners of today's putatively progressive "identity politics." Williams, a staff member of the Medgar Evers College Center for Law and Social Justice, had assisted a council redistricting commission in drawing districts along racial lines, under cover of the Voting Rights Act. He proved sympathetic to the Crown Heights rioters and insensitive to a more pluralist understanding of the tragedy, which would never have rationalized Rosenbaum's killing as an acceptable expression of grievance. It is precisely people like Williams about whom progressives need to think twice; their confusion about the uses and abuses of racial identity widens the rifts we need to close.

Notwithstanding these electoral reversals for the demagogues, many Jews are enraged and appalled that virtually no "responsible" Black leaders, except Dinkins, Councilwoman Pinkett, and the New York Civil Rights Coalition's Michael Meyers, publicly deplored the Crown Heights spectacle, let alone faced down the demagogues. Equally appalling was the silence or barely audible response of such liberal Jewish politicians as City Comptroller Elizabeth Holtzman, State Attorney General Robert Abrams, Manhattan Borough President Ruth Messinger, and most mainstream Jewish organizations. Angered by this default, even some liberal Jews are succumbing to the stirrings of a tribal militancy. Yet for all their anguish and rage, Jews have emerged from the crisis not more isolated but closer to other communities: feminists already embittered by the Black activists' treatment of the Central Park jogger; Asians infuriated by their anti-Asian rhetoric and lies in the Korean boycott; and Hispanics angered over city-council redistricting that, they feel, was a power grab by Blacks to facilitate the candidacies of Mason and Moore. If there is any coalition aborning in New York today, it is one against Blacks.

If such a new coalition could transcend its members' parochial grievances and take itself seriously enough to hammer out a public, civic consensus that condemns demagoguery from any source, it would deserve to win some victories. Black leaders who have accommodated the demagogues would have no one to blame but themselves—not white racist conspirators, not economic royalists, not George Bush's abdication of federal responsibility for cities and the poor. To repeat, it is precisely because racism, economic injustice, and Republican irresponsibility are so virulent that Black protest leaders, backs to the wall, cannot afford to alienate potential allies with the self-indulgent, bunkerlike, conspiratorial mentality they have displayed in Crown Heights and earlier cases. And it is precisely because they chose that course that they must be fought, not on behalf of a countervailing Jewish or Korean nationalism but on behalf of progressive values and civic justice. Either that, or we will descend into Beirut.

Why have so many Black leaders taken their followers over a precipice—or stood by, watching the disaster unfold without finding heart and voice to warn of it? Why hasn't the cynical strategy of manipulating the criminal-justice system with false charges exhausted itself? Time after time, multiracial juries have rebuffed the scenarios of race hatred. Time after time, ordinary Blacks, working in neighborhood organizations and churches, cooperating with whites in schools, political groups, and workplaces, quietly put such scenarios aside. The demagogues never do well in the polls, though there is some troubling evidence that belief in conspiracy theories is rising. What, then, drives these self-destructive beliefs and tactics forward?

One obvious answer is that the Black community has a long, undeniable, often irresistible tradition of rhetoric divorced from responsibility. It's not hard to understand why. Under slavery and Jim Crow, and, indeed, until the 1950s, when Adam Clayton Powell, Jr., James Baldwin, and Martin Luther King, Jr., began to write and speak politically in ways that truly got under the skins of whites, Black political rhetoric tended (with some notable exceptions, such as W.E.B. DuBois, Booker T. Washington, and Frederick Douglass) to be flamboyant precisely because the words were weightless, of no consequence, unable to move the walls of white ignorance and indifference. For all the difference Powell, Baldwin, King, and their successors have made, the older tradition echoes even in Jesse Jackson's claim to be a "tree shaker, not a jelly maker."

It echoes, too, in a recent statement by the Reverend Calvin Butts, senior pastor of Powell's old Abyssinian Baptist Church in Harlem, that he "can understand" Leonard Jeffries's claim that Jews and the Mafia conspired against Blacks in Hollywood. "Can understand"? No one expects Butts to be a historian; still, a leader owes his listeners something better than a sly, polemical appropriation of wild charges. It is as if Butts (who campaigned in the streets for C. Vernon Mason in the council races) and Jackson were saying: It is our duty to evoke and provoke; it is somebody else's duty—the real grown-ups?—to determine the truth and set matters to rights. We will spin our pain into webs of narrative and metaphor. Someone else, always someone else, will turn them into politics and policy.

Economic desperation, ignorance, and profound marginalization may also explain why some people do not assume responsibility. But Blacks in the Jim Crow South showed the world that even poor, uneducated, and marginalized people can shoulder great burdens, and some of this country's greatest Black leaders have arisen amid conditions far more dire than those that obtain today. These explanations are inexcusable, in any case, in those who call themselves leaders. Calvin Butts is not desperate; nor are City College president Bernard Harleston and New York NAACP chief Hazel Dukes; nor is Percy Sutton, multimillionaire owner of WLIB; nor are Wilbert Tatum of the *Amsterdam News* and Andrew Cooper, publisher of the city's other Black weekly newspaper, *The City Sun,* which also parrots the demagogues' lies. Even Sharpton, Daughtry, and Jeffries are not under siege, except by conscious choice; these three leave New York City's ghettos every evening for their homes across the Hudson in suburban Teaneck, New Jersey. They have the room and hence the responsibility to rethink their strategies.

A deeper answer to the question of why they don't was offered in September in a compelling *New York* magazine article about events in Crown Heights. Joe Klein described the use of Gavin Cato—like Brawley before him—as a figure in "Black martyrology," a system that misappropriates current events to dramatize historic truths about racism. That may mean, as we have seen again and again, altering the facts and slandering innocent whites: Howard Beach motorist Dominick Blum became in the rhetoric of Black protest a racist accomplice of Michael Griffiths's assailants, even though he was a young amateur actor who'd played in Lorraine Hansberry's *A Raisin in the Sun;* and Dutchess County Assistant District Attorney Steven Pagones was publicly accused by Sharpton and Mason of raping Tawana Brawley.

This is a theme I explore at some length in *The Closest of Strangers*. Brawley's account of her violation by white authorities, for example, brought to the surface an archetype, seared into Black memory, of the most intimate, passional sort of exploitation—the illicit, coerced master-slave liaisons of the Old South. Even the discovery that Brawley's own story was a hoax became a justification, in the minds of Sharpton and company, for another ancient script: For centuries, whites had falsely accused Blacks of raping white women. Now, the tables would be turned; whites, too, would taste victimization by lie, and this seemed to give any number of otherwise intelligent people a certain satisfaction. Recall, too, the Black and Latino youths who, having raped and bludgeoned the Central Park jogger, became, in the minds of editor Tatum and other Black leaders, the victims of a "lynching," like the Scottsboro Boys.

It should not surprise Jews that the historic hurts of racial and ethnic groups are released periodically from communal amnesia by the grindings and proddings of current events. These traumas rise to the surface of group consciousness, demanding to be interpreted and reworked—much as the hurts individuals carry within them from childhood surface, sometimes unpredictably, for renegotiation. The 1963 trial of Adolf Eichmann, for example, unleashed a torrent of emotions that many Jews had repressed immediately after the Holocaust and kept down for nearly twenty years.

But because Eichmann was actually guilty, because he was tried by institutions that Jews had constructed in the real world according to essential and universal principles of justice, his trial did not pervert and dehumanize his accusers. Black interpretations of the Brawley, Central Park, and other cases, too, reflect a community's intense need to renegotiate historic hurts of monstrous proportions. But, in the hands of Sharpton and his ilk, they have come to resemble a neurotic individual's reenactments of old grievances using the wrong targets. Such behavior brings only fitful, temporary release; one is condemned to repeat it, again and again.

There are, of course, mythically unsatisfying but practical ways to reduce racism in the criminal-justice system and in society at large. One is to apply a community's electoral muscle, in concert with other communities that share at least some common goals, to elect judges and district attorneys who feel a political as well as moral obligation to racism's victims. This strategy has already elected people such as Brooklyn D.A. Charles J. Hynes, who won in 1989 with a strong Black vote due to his success as a special state prosecutor in Queens in convicting the Howard Beach assailants in 1986. And there are ways other than Sharpton's to organize public protests; there can be demonstrations that embarrass whites into decency by embracing them in the process of confronting them, as the civil-rights movement did so brilliantly in the South in the 1960s.

Doing that means assuming a public responsibility that transcends tribal memories and myth-making agendas. It means rising above a neurotic attachment to victimhood in order to display a disarming magnanimity and to affirm universal principles of human dignity. It means, in short, having a larger vision. Just as some Jews, whose goodwill has been curdled and deformed by the horror of the Holocaust, are incapable of sustaining that vision, preferring instead to find genocidal anti-Semitism in every untoward encounter, Black demagogues and the writers and politicians who indulge them are incapable of practicing a serious, healing politics of justice. Their intimations of a common human enterprise are blocked by their pain, which they embroider endlessly, almost lovingly. Every trial that they cast in Black and white against all the evidence becomes a psychodramatic reenactment of that pain, not a constructive reworking of it tied to real-world consequences and rewards. In Crown Heights, Black protest leaders turned on D.A. Hynes, even after he took the unusual, propitiatory step of impaneling a grand jury to investigate whether there were any grounds for indicting driver Lifsh. After the grand jury concluded there were no grounds, Hynes was vilified for his trouble.

As long as protest leaders lie about evidence while prosecutors and juries stick to the truth, demagoguery will continue to be rebuffed. But in the minds of these charlatan leaders and their followers, the rebuffs only confirm the existence of a racist cover-up. Perversely, that warms them and gratifies them because they find it more satisfying to hurt than to hope. They anticipate pain, savor it, eroticize it, historicize it, and project it onto situations where it is inappropriate. This confirms the old, familiar inner coordinates of the demagogues and their adherents. It gives them marching orders, the sheen of embattled heroism. It spares them disorientation, risk, and the fear of the unknown, which come with hoping and with reaching out. People trapped this way cannot lead movements for racial justice, only movements for revenge.

Jews, too, have had demagogues, such as Meir Kahane, who elaborate and embellish visions of endless embattlement and pain. But, seductive though their appeals can be in moments of genuine communal peril, we have, in America, at least, found the security and psychic freedom to hold them at arm's length. The Jewish community made City College professor Michael Levin a pariah after his ideas about Black inferiority were publicized; unlike his colleague Jeffries, with whom he is often compared, Levin was not followed around by adoring throngs of Jewish students or deluged with speaking invitations. Only journalists seeking to "balance" their stories about Jeffries call him. Otherwise, his phone never rings.

For reasons at once obvious and profound, the Black community in America is far less secure, its psychic margin of freedom much narrower. America is, historically and even now, the locus of Blacks' violation, the land of their enslavement and humiliation. Without question, our society's endemic racism continues to subject countless Blacks to relentless psychic assault. What is appalling and tragic about the New York Black community's need for martyrological narratives and fantasies of revenge is that it has become so intense, so unrelieved, that it silences even those Blacks who clearly see the political and cultural costs. If identity politics offers a way out of this trap, let its defenders show us the way.

The genocidal brutalities that went into the building of the United States are roughly on a par with those of every other civilization in human history. What is unusual and potentially redemptive about America is that, as a self-conscious and deliberate human creation, it is the first truly multi-racial civilization since ancient Rome to nourish the seeds of its own transcendence. People of all colors, believing this, have watered those seeds with their blood, sweat, and tears to make them grow, again and again. When the otherwise disappointing Mario Cuomo says, "We are the sons and daughters of giants," that is what he is talking about.

Identity politics is a fantasy for smaller people. It fears the cold truth that humans and their institutions emerge only slowly from the primordial slime. It prattles on about the fact that Thomas Jefferson held slaves and never gave the rights of women a thought when he wrote the Declaration of Independence, instead of taking what he wrote as a uniquely precious text awaiting interpretation and fulfillment, as many ordinary women and people of color have done with great courage. We can recite the inanities and inhumanities of white, patriarchal oppression, or we can be brave enough to examine the paradox that only in the constitutional framework inherited from dead white men do women and minorities—and multiculturalism itself—find breathing room and footholds. Feminism and minority rights do not fare well in the Islamic world, Africa, or most of Asia.

Dinesh D'Souza is not wrong to observe that the classic texts and traditional cultures of the Third World are politically incorrect—often monstrously so. Nor was Arthur Schlesinger, Jr., wrong to respond to a New York state social-studies curriculum committee's complaint that European colonization had eradicated "many varieties of traditional culture and knowledge" by asking: "Like infanticide? slavery? polygamy? subjection of women? suttee? veil-wearing? foot-binding? clitordectomies? Nothing is said about the influence of European ideas of democracy, human rights, self-government, rule of law." One might pose similar challenges to Jewish tradition; those who are changing it do so as children of the European Enlightenment and of America.

Racial, ethnic, and religious groups tap mythic wellsprings that go back to the dawn of humanity, but they have done so only while existing across thousands of years in relative isolation and mutual suspicion—or within relations of domination and subordination. These conditions have warped them profoundly, equipping them poorly for life in the global village. New wells will have to be sunk. Americans—and, at least partly under our cultural and technological influence, all citizens of the world—now fitfully acknowledge an overlay of common claims and bonds, an emerging, universal culture linking us across the old communal boundaries on terms of increasing equality, if not mutual respect. That prospect is problematic and exhilarating. There may be much to mourn in what we have lost, but there is also much new ground to gain.

In any case, there is no turning back. Whether through intermarriage or assimilation, tens of millions of Americans are by now generations removed from any easily recoverable ethnic, religious, or even racial identity. These new Americans may wind up drawing the lines of their communities without reference to religious inheritance, skin color, or surname. The nation has no choice but to keep faith with them. They, not the demagogues of race, are our future.

What will they affirm? That you cannot build a movement for social justice on lies and intimidation, and that people need training in these truths if they are to learn to detect and reject demagoguery from any source. That, in a diverse society, which no one of our groups can dominate and from which none of us can really secede, anyone who would lead protest politics must demonstrate the ability to build alliances across racial and ethnic lines. That we must honor individual rights and rational analysis as something more than Eurocentric ruses or impositions. That a viable progressive movement cannot be built on demands for reparation for past suffering, much less on revenge. That class is, after all, as important as race.

The more the theatrics of a debased identity politics like Sharpton's and Carson's chill internal debate among Blacks and alienate other groups, the more isolated the Black community will become from this larger national and global project. The more isolated it becomes, the more fertile ground it will offer for theories of conspiracy and fantasies of redemption through vengeance. As the Black community becomes what the historian Fred Siegel terms "an exotic appendage to the polity," playing by special rules of evidence and entitlement, it will become also the object of increasingly awkward liberal condescension and rising mainstream ridicule.

Blacks who can see where this vicious cycle is leading have a historic obligation to break it, for the sake of their own people and on behalf of all humanity. It is our obligation to join and to prod these potential leaders, the people we share platforms and microphones with, the people we too often accommodate with a racist double standard when they rationalize the demagogues' depredations. Those who have made careers out of trading on special racial exemptions from the principles I have just listed must be read out of the progressive movement. The time for squirming and temporizing has ended. In demonstrations and elections, at panel discussions, in the pages of newspapers, and on talk shows, we must find the strength in ourselves to tell such leaders that, henceforth, among the oppressed as well as the oppressors, silence equals death. It certainly did in Crown Heights. □

I Went to the Movie of Life

Allen Ginsberg

In the mud, in the night, in Mississippi Delta roads
outside Clarksdale I slogged along,
Lights flashed under trees, my black companion motioned "Here they are,
your company."—Like giant rhinoceri with painted faces
splashed all over side and snout, headlights glaring in rain,
one after another buses rolled past us toward Book Hotel
Boarding House, up the hill, town ahead.
                                  Accompanying me, two girls
pitched in the dark slush garbaged road, slipping in deep ruts
wheels'd left behind sucking at their high heels, staining granny
dresses sequined magic marked with astral signs, Head groupies
who knew the way to this Grateful Dead half-century heroes'
caravan pit stop for the night. I climbed mid-road, a toad
hopped before my foot, I shrank aside, unthinking'd kicked it off
with leather shoe, animal feet scurried back at my sight—
a little monster on his back bled red, nearby this prey a lizard
with large eyes retreated, and a rat curled tail and slithered
in mud wet to the dirt gutter, repelled. A long climb ahead, the girls'd
make it or not, I moved ahead, eager to rejoin old company,
Merry Pranksters with aged pride in peacock feathered beds,
shining mylar mirror-paper walls, acid mothers with strobe lit radios,
long haired men, gaunt 60's Diggers emerged from the night
to rest, bathe, cook spaghetti, nurse their kids,
smoke pipes and squat with Indian sages round charcoal
braziers in their cars; profound American dreamers,
I was in their company again after long years, byways
alone looking for lovers in bar street country towns
and sunlit cities, rain & shine, snow & spring-bud backyard
brick walls, ominous adventures behind the Iron Curtain.
Were we all grown old? I looked for my late boyfriends,
dancing to Electric Blues with their guns and smoke round jukebox walls
the smell of hash and country ham, old newspaper media stars
wandering room after room: pentagon refugee Ellsberg, old dove Dellinger
bathing in an iron tub with a patch in his stomach wall
Abbie Hoffman explaining the natural strategy of city political saint
works, Quicksilver Messenger musicians, Berkeley orators
with half-grown children in their sox, dirty faces, alcohol
Uncles who played chess & strummed banjos frayed by broken fingernails,

where's Ken Kesey, away tonite in another megalopolis hosting
hypnosis parties for Hell's Angels, maybe nail them down on stage
or radio, Neal must be tending his daughters in Los Gatos,
pacifying his wife, coming down amphetamines in his bedroom,
or downers to sleep this night away & wake for work
in the great Bay Carnival tented among smokestacks, railroad
tracks and freeways under box house urban hills.
Young movie stars with grizzled beards passed thru bus corridors
looking for Dylan in the movie office, re-swaggering old roles,
recorded words now sung in Leningrad and Shanghai,
their wives in tortoise shell glasses & paisley shawls & towels tending
cauldrons bubbling with spaghetti sauce, & racks of venison,
squirrel or lamb; ovens open with hot rhubarb pies—
Who should I love? Here one with leather hat, blond hair
strong body middle age, face frowned in awful thought,
beer in hand by the bathroom wall? That Digger boy I knew
with giant phallos, bald head studying medicine walked by,
preoccupied with anatomy homework, rolling a joint, his
think fingers at his chest, eyes downcast on paper & tobacco.
One by one I checked out love companions, none
whose beauty stayed my heart, this place was tired
of my adoration, they knew my eyes too well. No one I could find
to give me bed tonite and wake me grinning naked, with eggs
scrambled for breakfast ready, oatmeal, grits, or hot spicy sausages
at noon assembly when I opened my eyelids out of dream. I
wandered, walking room to room thru psychedelic buses
wanting to meet someone new, younger than this crowd of wily
wrinkled wanderers with their booze and families, Electronic
Arts & Crafts, woe line brows of chemical genius music
producers, adventurous politicians, singing ladies & earthy paramours
playing rare parts in the final movie of a generation.
The cameras rolled and followed me, was I the central figure
in this film? We'd passed dark starred crossroads & risen over bridges,
the ghost-lit caravan party of gypsy intellects had passed thru USA in
front of an eye recording visual tape better'n celluloid—
I'd known most faces and guided the inevitable cameras room to room,
pausing at candle lit bus windows on flooded cotton fields
we'd seen by daylight, familiar stars whispering by coal stoves,
public headline artists known from Rolling Stone & NY Times,
actors & actresses from Living Theater, gaunt faced and eloquent
with lifted hands & bony fingers greeting me on my way
to the bus driver's wheel, tattered dirty gloves on Neal's seat
waiting his return from working the National Railroad, young kids
I'd taught saluting me wearily from worn couches as I passed
bus to bus, cameras moving behind me. What was my role?
I hardly knew these faded heroes, friendly strangers
so long on the road, I'd been out teaching in Boulder, Manhattan,

Budapest, London, Brooklyn so long, why follow me thru
these amazing Further bus party reunion corridors tonite?
or is this movie, or real, if I turn to face the camera I'd break
the scene, dissolve the plot illusion, or is't illusion
art, or just my life? Were cameras ever there, the picture
flowed so evenly before my eyes, how could a crew follow
me invisible still and smoothly noiseless bus to bus
from room to room along the caravan's
painted labyrinth. This wasn't cinema, and I no hero
spokesman documenting friendship scenes,
only myself alone lost in the cabin with familiar strangers still looking
for some sexual angel for mortal delights
no different from haunting St. Mark's Boys Bar again solitary in a tie
jacket and grey beard, wallet in my pocket full of
cash and cards, useless.
                              A glimmer of lights
in the curtained doorway before me! my heart leapt
forward to the Orgy Room, all youths! Lithe and
hairless, smooth skinned, white buttocks ankles, young men's
nippled chests lit behind the curtain, thighs entwined
in the male area, place I was looking for behind
my closed eyelids all this night—I pushed my hand
into the room, moving aside the curtain that shimmered
within bright with naked knees and shoulders pale
in candlelight—entered the pleasure chamber's empty door
glimmering silver shadows reflected on the silver curtained veil,
eyelids still dazzling as their adolescent limbs
intangible dissolved where I put by hand into a vacant room,
lay down on its dark floor to watch the lights of phantom arms
pulsing across closed eyelids conscious as I woke in bed
returned at dawn to New York wood slatted Venetian blinds over the
windows on E. 12th St. in my white painted room

AIDS Activism:
A Conversation with Larry Kramer

An Interview by Marcia Pally

Marcia Pally: AIDS pushes so many buttons in us—sexual, moral, fear of contagion and death. What is most important to understand about it now?

Larry Kramer: We have now entered the age of treatment; before we had the age of death. Just as many people live with potentially fatal illnesses such as heart disease or diabetes, we can now establish a holding pattern for AIDS patients while research continues to look for better treatments.

Pally: Though more people die from heart disease or cancer than from AIDS, the government has appropriated more funds for AIDS than for any other...

Kramer: Don't go any further. AIDS warrants the funding becuase it's transmissible. However tragic these other illnesses, they don't spread like AIDS. The Centers for Disease Control estimate that there will be 100,000 new cases in the next fifteen months; just for comparison's sake, it has taken the last ten years to get the first 100,000 cases. That's 222 cases a day, one death every half hour. That's why I formed ACT UP. We have no time to waste.

We're a very large organization—we get 400-600 people at our weekly meetings in New York—and we work on women and AIDS, prisoners and AIDS, pediatric AIDS, AIDS among the homeless. But for me, the most important committee is Treatment and Data, fighting for the faster release of experimental AIDS drugs.

We fought so hard to get Congress to appropriate money for AIDS and around 1985 or 1986 the money started being appropriated in sufficient quantity.

Pally: Are you satisfied with government appropriations today?

Kramer: One will never be satisfied because there will never be enough money. I'm more concerned that the money be well spent. The delays are bureaucratic, not financial or scientific.

President Bush's commission on AIDS issued a report saying that we must appoint someone to spearhead and organize AIDS efforts. This is the third commission to tell that to a president (the National Academy of Sciences around 1986, Reagan's commission in 1988, and now this). How many times does a president have to hear that you must put someone in charge of a mess that now involves nearly every government agency, most of which don't get along with one another? You

Larry Kramer is the founder of the AIDS Coalition to Unleash Power (ACT UP). Marcia Pally writes film criticism for Penthouse and other journals. She is a member of the Communications and Media Committee of the American Civil Liberties Union. This article appeared in Tikkun, *July/August 1990.*

don't have a D-day without an Eisenhower; you don't reorganize Chrysler without an Iacocca.

While Bush's rhetoric is good, in actuality we now have the second do-nothing, uncompassionate president. John Sununu, Bush's chief of staff, is as unfeeling and uninterested as Gary Bauer was under Reagan. So we have a high-ranking official carrying out the president's orders—covertly or otherwise—to do nothing.

The head of the National Cancer Institute has said that there is a cure for AIDS, but we're not getting one because there's no one in charge of finding it. When the government wanted to make the A-bomb, it set up a Manhattan Project at Los Alamos with the resources, privacy, and organization to do it. We need a Manhattan Project for AIDS.

Pally: How much AIDS funding has been appropriated?

Kramer: A quarter of a billion dollars for 1986-87 and another quarter billion for 1988-89, and here's what the government did with it:

AIDS research falls under the National Institute of Allergy and Infectious Diseases (NIAID) headed by Dr. Anthony Fauci. Fauci decided the best way to spend all this money was to set up a system of local hospital-based centers for testing new AIDS medicines. Hospitals around the country were invited to put in grant applications, and it took them two years to get the system up and dispense the funding. Then, they set up committees to decide which drugs were going to be studied. They had only one doctor at NIAID designing these guidelines. Then the Food and Drug Administration (FDA) got into the act, and in the meantime more and more people are getting sick.

Most of the studies were confined to various dosages of AZT (azidothymidine)—no other drugs that attack the AIDS virus and no drugs that treat the secondary infections. Meanwhile, the patient-activist community found out there was a treatment for Pneumocystis pneumonia called aerosolized pentamidine which, if taken prophylactically, would prevent the illness.

Pally: How did you find that out?

Kramer: Dr. Don Abrams, who runs a community research program in San Francisco, and Dr. John Armstrong and his associate Edward Bernard at Sloan-Kettering Memorial Hospital in New York knew pentamidine was effective in treating Pneymocystis, and they got the idea to try it prophylactically.

We are approaching the tenth year of the epidemic and the enormous community of sick people by now knows more than most doctors because doctors have chosen not to educate themselves fully, and beacuse most of the treatments they could have given their patients have not been approved by the FDA's overlong procedures. Patients have been trying new drugs themselves.

We have an exceedingly well-organized drug underground—I'm talking AIDS medicines, not cocaine. We have treatment newsletters that go out to tens of thousands of people; John James' *AIDS Treatment News* from San Francisco is by far the best. A lot of the information is anecdotal, but if have enough anecotal evidence on a drug it becomes sustaining enough to try.

In 1987 I was invited to the Institute for Immunological Disorders in Houston. It was a beautiful hospital, brand new, with a committed staff and room for over a hundred patients. But it's a private for-profit hospital, and Texas is the only state in the union that doesn't reimburse health care providers for the medical expenses of people who are uninsured. There were perhaps six patients there. it was heartbreaking. The hospital went broke and is now closed.

The leading physician there, Peter Mansell, said, "I have all these sick people and I've got drugs that I think—that I *know*—are useful and I can't legally prescribe them because they aren't OK'd by the FDA." He told me that Dr. Fauci's two-year was a farce; people with AIDS weren't even enrolling in the government experimental drug trials.

In government tests, half the patients get placebos. Nobody who's dying wants a placebo, so when a patient got his first dosage he'd have it analyzed and if it was a placebo he'd drop out of the experiment, so government researchers weren't getting any results. The government also required that patients in government tests give up any other medicines they were using, and you can't expect people who are dying to give up any other medicines that may be working. AIDS activists told the government all this, we told Fauci to his face, and he wouldn't listen. Mansell showed me his requests to the FDA to test new drugs. The FDA would send the application back objecting to three or five words. "Changing those five words," he said, "will take nine months for me to send it to them and for them to send it back to me."

After the first $250 million was wasted, the NIAID set up another system that was in essence exactly like the old one: the same hospitals, the same grants, the same doctors. And now two years after that's been running it has exactly the same problems. People are not enrolling in the trials; they're testing only AZT. So there goes another quarter billion.

After my trip to Houston, I wanted to scream. I made a speech at New York's Gay and Lesbian Community Center and that was the beginning of ACT UP.

Pally: Who's in the drug underground? How does it work?

Kramer: It started around 1985 with medicines (isoprinosine and ribavirin) that were available in Mexico but not in the U.S., and with AL721, a drug developed in Israel that was thought to be promising but which couldn't be exported because of some patent problem. People in California started smuggling the Mexican drugs across the border and People with Aids (PWA) Coalition formed a buyers' group for AL721. We have so many sick people it's not surprising they've found ways to get medicine. They're desperate....

Pally: Who in government has been helpful in getting medicines to AIDS patients?

Kramer: Everyone is government is the enemy and has been, at the city, state, and federal levels, across the board. The AIDS epidemic is here today because of three people: Ronald Reagan for ignoring a fatal epidemic, New York City's former Mayor Ed Koch for ignoring it in his city, and A.M. Rosenthal, the former editor of the *New York Times*, who systematically kept AIDS coverage out of his paper wihen the public needed to know it was transmissible....

Bush did one good thing for AIDS: when ACT UP was trying to get DDI (dideoxyinosine)—a new drug that works like AZT—on parallel track, he helped. Parallel track is where a drug is administered to patients through community groups and physicians while the government is still running final tests on it. It allows us to get more quickly to drugs that may save lives. ACT UP had to get the NIAID and the FDA to OK the idea, and then persuade the manufacturer, Bristol-Meyers, to provide the drug free of charge as a "compassionate use" medicine—otherwise, no go.

What the world doesn't know is that Bush and Bristol-Myers CEO Richard Gelb both went to Yale, and Bush called Gelb about DDI. Everything is the old boys network. I don't know if the call was between Gelb and Bush or between Gelb and Bush's personal physician, but I know calls were made.

If an AIDS patient is rich, he can get many drugs that will save his life. Unfortunately, most aren't, and the costs of AIDS treatments—of any health care—are mammoth. Doctors and pharmaceutical companies are so greedy. Burroughs Wellcome, the manufacturer of AZT, is charging exorbitant prices for a drug that didn't even bear the cost of developing. The National Cancer Institute developed AZT, the government sold the patent outright, and Burroughs Wellcome has been profiteering ever since.

AIDS is going to force a change in the health care system, and that means national health insurance. Hundreds of thousands of people will be sick; shall we let them die? When you read that the government spent $159 billion to bail out the Savings & Loan banks, you wonder where our priorities are. ACT UP has started researching national health plans, looking at Sweden's, Germany's, and the Kaiser Permanente plan in California. We want to come up with one that will work.

Pally: Do you think the AIDS epidemic has made gay people seem more sympathetic to the non-gay public?

Kramer: In part. There has been an increase in anti-gay violence, but I think there's been a lot less than I expected. Even though people say terrible things about us, when it comes right down to it everybody realizes we're their sons and daughters. One out of every four families has been touched by AIDS. Gay people are frequently seen on TV; we're not so frightening perhaps as the word "homosexual" is when you actually see us and we look just like people you know. I don't want to overstate this because we're ten years into an epidemic and if sympathy had been there from the beginning we wouldn't be in this state.

Pally: In your work with ACT UP you've wasted no words about Cardinal John O'Connor and the Catholic response to AIDS. What about the Jewish response?

Kramer: Do you mean, would I tear up a Torah the way that Catholic man destroyed the host at St. Patrick's Cathedral [during an ACT UP protest] last December? If the Jewish religion was doing to me what Catholicism was doing to my Catholic gay friends, I can't say I'd be upset if someone went in and tore up a Torah. I can't say I'd do it, but I understand the rage.

Because of the way Judaism is structured, there's no one official resonse to AIDS as there is from the Vatican. And there certainly have been some very compassionate rabbis, like Rabbi Balfour Brickner in New York. Manistream Judaism isn't advocating that homosexuals be annihilated or that sex education not be taught or that people not use condoms, as the Catholic Church does. I don't hear much that's pro-gay from Jewish organizations, but I don't hear much that's anti-gay either. So as long as things are relatively quiescent, the Jewish response to AIDS isn't first on my list of wrongs to right. All this, of course, is excepting the ultra-Orthodox.

You know, one day gay people will be allowed to marry legally, and I hope Judaism allows these rites in a religious framework if people want them. And if a gay couple adopts a baby boy, they sould be able to have a *bris*; it's the same for all rituals. A lot of intelligent Jews realize that homophobia doesn't rebound well to those who practice it.

Having said that, I must also say I feel abandoned by my religion. I have little desire to practice it again and I question gay religious organizations that are so determined to find acceptance by religions that don't want them. I understand the desire to fight for religions that they feel are as much theirs as anyone else's, but I wonder what they find in religions that are so annihilating. It's doubly true for lesbians, who suffer second-class status and rejection as women and again as gay people.

I no longer believe in God or organized religion. Organized religions have so much blood on their hands over the centuries, they're not for me.

Pally: Jews, if only because of a history of persecution, have less blood....

Kramer: You'd think that a people who had been underdog for so long would have sympathy for others. It's not something Jews have done so well lately. Where are their ears, where are their memories?

Pally: You use "holocaust" to describe the AIDS epidemic; the word is also in the title of your latest book. Do you think there's a distinction between government neglect in the AIDS crisis and Hitler's intentional genocide?

Kramer: I always use a small "h," not the big "H," but we must remember that Jews don't own the word. I'm not talking about inadvertant neglect in the case of AIDS but intentionality as sure as if a Hitler were at the helm. With AIDS, there are a number of Hitlers at the helm. We'll never know if AIDS was introduced intentionally, but it has intentionally been allowed to get out of hand. I refer readers to my book, *Reports from the Holocaust: the Making of an AIDS Activist*, and *Modernity and the Holocaust* by Zygmunt Bauman, a professor at Leeds University, published in the U.S. by Cornell University Press.

I'd like my last words on the subject to be these: the war against AIDS has been lost. By the time it's over, millions of people will have died needlessly. A disease has been allowed to develop into an epidemic, then into a pandemic, and finally a plague. If that is not a holocaust, what is?

Pally: Many people feel compulsory AIDS testing would help control the epidemic: if we knew who was infected with the AIDS virus, they wouldn't unwittingly infect others. But you're against compulsory testing.

Kramer: It would be wonderful if we knew how many people were infected, but compulsory testing won't achieve that—education will. People must be convinced that it's to their advantage to come in and be tested now that there are treatments, like AZT, that can help them stay alive. Compulsory testing will terrify people away because there are no guarantees against discrimiation if you test positive. We need anti-discrimination policies so people won't lose their jobs, health or life insurance, or their passports.

Pally: Let me ask one more question about politics: many people, gay as well as straight, object to the civil disobedience and other disruptive tactics that ACT UP employs...

Kramer: Many people also support us completely. Actually, it doesn't bother me what people think. One of the lessons I learned as a writer is that some people will like what I say, others won't, so I might as well say what I want. ACT UP does civil disobedience, we lie down in the street and block bridges, but we also do a great deal behind the scenes, like the DDI-FDA-Bristol-Myers negotiations.

There has to be room for civil disobedience or even more extreme forms of activism. When you have an extreme group of activists it makes it easier for the center to negoatiate. With us out there asking for the moon, the moderates can get a few stars, to be poetic.

I'll give you a case in point. There was severe criticism of ACT UP at the 1989 International AIDS conference in Montreal. We took over the opening session, we heckled endlessly, we make ouselves pains in the asses. My own doctor wouldn't talk to me she was so furious that we disrupted what was supposedly a scientific session. On the other hand, we were the big story. We made every paper and network news in the world. We were asked to join three major committees in Washington, we were asked for input on the 1990 AIDS conference and we negotiated with Bristol-Myers for DDI.

I said to my doctor, "You can yell at us and disapprove, but when you get DDI for your patients just remember it was because of us that you got it." She took me out to dinner last week. If you want to know the truth, I wish ACT UP were ten times more radical than it is.   □

Autobiography

Don Pagis; translated by Stephan Mitchell

I died with the first blow and was buried
among the rocks of the field.
The Raven taught my parents
what to do with me.

If my family is famous,
not a little of the credit goes to me.
My brother invented murder,
my parents invented grief,
I invented silence.

Afterwards the well-known events took place.
Our inventions were perfected. One thing led to another,
orders were given. There were those who murdered in their own
way,
grieved in their own way.

I won't mention names
out of consideration for the reader,
since at first the details horrify
though finally they're a bore:

you can die once, twice, even seven times,
but you can't die a thousand times.
I can.
My underground cells reach everywhere.

When Cain began to multiply on the face of the earth,
I began to multiply in the belly of the earth,
and my strength has long been greater than his.
His legions desert him and go over to me,
and even this is only half a revenge.

All Quiet on the Western Front?

Peter Gabel

very morning, every one of us wakes up with the desire to overcome our isolation and
connect with others in a meaningful, life-giving, passionate way. We long for the sense of
confirmation and validation that can only come from participation in real community. As we
peer out at the day in front of us, however, we feel compelled to suppress this desire, to actually
forget about it as best we can, because we have become resigned to the fact that no one else seems
to want what each of us wants.

Having grown accustomed to a life deadened by bureaucratic work and family routines, to
passing people on the street whose blank gazes seem to indicate an inner absence, we each internalize the sense that in order to feel part of what little community there is in the world we must deny
our deepest needs and adjust to things as they are. And so we don our various social masks and become "one of the others," in part by keeping others at the same distance we believe they are keeping
us. In this way, social reality takes the form of a "circle of collective denial" through which each of
us becomes both agent and victim of an infinitely rotating system of social alienation. Trapped in
this alienation, people in the West are often unable to imagine themselves acting to change things,
no matter how deeply they may desire a different kind of world.

Social movements are in significant part attempts to overcome this circle of denial, to replace
alienation and distance with connection and solidarity. The very idea of "movement" suggests this,
since no one physically moves anywhere. What "moves" is social desire itself, as it partially breaks
free of the denial that has enveloped it. People "take to the streets" with a new feeling of mutual
empowerment and possibility, instead of consigning each other to the sidewalk where they (we) feel
weighed down by a world that seems to be going on outside of us—a hallucination that results from
our collective feeling of powerlessness and passivity.

To understand why there is no true social movement in the United States today, we must
understand both the elaborate social mechanisms we have set up to prevent us from fully recognizing and confirming each other, and the psychological scars—dating from our earliest childhood—
that undermine our ability and even our motivation to do so.

Human beings have many sophisticated methods of containing social desire in order to maintain
the status quo. One of these is to shape the world into hierarchies. We are shaped by hierarchical
pictures of the world to the extent that we believe that our self-worth depends on the approval of a
"higher authority" and to the extent that we come to feel that our sense of social well-being and inclusion is satisfied in being obedient to that authority. The prevalence of hierarchies in our workplaces, schools, and families leads us to develop a virtually erotic attachment to all cultural images of
authority beginning in childhood.

A second such social mechanism is the media. One result of the isolation engendered by the circle

Peter Gabel is president of New College of California and associate editor of Tikkun. *This article appeared in*
Tikkun, *July/August 1990.*

of collective denial is an overwhelming longing to be seen for who we really are—and, concomitantly, an immense rage at rarely, if ever, being able to achieve this recognition. Television, VCRs, and even multiple editions of afternoon papers like the *New York Post* help people to tolerate these emotions by satisfying their volatile repressed feelings in an imaginary way. In watching TV, we can remain withdrawn (as "watchers") and at the same time experience some emotional relief through fantasy by identifying with the images of both social connection and violence that pervade the soaps, real-life crime shows, and even the news. The mass media become an aspect of social reality that we have created in order not to feel the threatening need to act on our desire for change.

It is remarkable to see the lengths to which we have gone to ward off the connection with reality that might come from true contact with one another. Everything from the majestic symbolisms of The Law and "organized religion" to the micro-messages transmitted by billboards and cereal boxes ("TOTAL brings you these words from the Founding Fathers") works to protect us from the contact we both desire and fear.

If these dynamics were simply imposed upon us from the outside—it was all something that "they" were doing to "us"—we could rightly expect to find many more ways in which people would be consciously engaged in resisting the isolating effects of these dynamics. But the truth is that we all bear psychological scars from our very first encounters with other people that interfere with our motivation to emerge from the dreamy pain of our isolating routines.

Families are rarely pockets of social movement, and parents—themselves conditioned within the circle of collective denial—are rarely capable of fully reciprocating the desire for empowering confirmation which emanates from the soul of every newborn child. So they inevitably transmit to us a sense of self that has a small hole in it, a hole that exerts a drag upon our capacity for building a more meaningful social world.

Before we speak our first words, we come to sense that in order to remain "with" these others who are the first to hold us and shape us by their sight, we must accept the boundaries of what is possible. This notion of the "possible" is communicated to us through the sense of loss and compromise that others have come to feel. And as we grow up, we become partly addicted to the poignancy and depression that accompanies this memory of loss, because these painful emotions allow us continually to relive our initial bond with our parents in the face of a world that seems to offer us little possibility of a deeper and more fulfilling form of community. The paradox is that these early attachments tend to reinforce the circle of collective denial and thus make it difficult for such a community to come into being.

There are, of course, many specific historical and cultural factors that account for the present quiet on the Western Front, but mere historical analysis will not get us far.

Unless new social movements find a way of addressing the psychological and social dynamics that inhibit us from developing a confidence in each other more powerful than our dependency on the status quo, any political activity is likely to fail, even if in the process they are successful in bringing about important economic or political reforms. We need to stop thinking of social change simply in terms of fighting for more economic benefits or more legal rights, and focus instead on developing new forms of activism that can overcome the doubt in our own hearts. □

How Many Lefts Are Left?

Todd Gitlin

Why is the whole of the Left no greater than the sum of its single-issue, single-constituency parts? My sketch of an answer starts with the observation that for the better part of two centuries after the French Revolution, "Left" referred to a universalist politics—a belief in rights that flow from membership in the universal category of humanity. Men and women of the Left opposed slavery in the name of the rights of the person. So did they oppose war, the exploitation of labor, the forced labor of children, the subordination of women and racial minorities. Marxism followed in this tradition. A purely deductive scheme, it dissolved differences into the universal category of labor. Capitalism, it argued, was the grand solvent of difference. Marxism took it upon itself to spin necessity into virtue. Was the bourgeoisie dissolving all social bonds? Not to worry! Under hypothetical communism, *everyone* would hunt in the morning, fish in the afternoon, criticize at night. What could be more universalist than the closing line of the "Internationale": "The international working class shall be the human race"?

Nationalism was, of course, a belief in the particular. It valued the tribe against the empire. The cause of the small nation pitted the weak against the strong and so could appeal to the Left. The universalist spin that the Left preferred was the idea that once the small nations were freed from imperial grasp, they would coexist happily in a league of equal nations.

Meanwhile, the postrevolutionary tradition of the Western Right started out by holding the line against the revolutionary promise of universal rights and evolved into two conflicting traditions. On the one hand, the Right defended the privileges of elites (who are, by definition, minorities) or of particular nations or communities and their distinct traditions. In this spirit, the Right stood for the virtues of difference—the heroic individual versus the faceless herd, the superior nation versus the lowly. Not even Milton Friedman could imagine an international congress of conservative parties ending with a chorus of "The international capitalist class shall be the human race."

But grant the Right its ingenuity. In tension with its exaltation of the few, the Right developed its own universalism—the universalism of the market. Capital, penetrating everywhere, would bring universal freedom in its wake. Indeed, in this utopian mood, the Right has *equated* the universal penetration of capital with freedom. (Indeed, it was against the spurious universality of capital that the Marxist Left propounded the universality of labor.) Since the equation was most advanced in the United States, the Right could logically claim that America was already the embodiment of universal values. Americanism could compete with Marxism on the playing field of universalisms. It followed that the extension of American power served universal ends. It followed that significant difference amounted to "un-American" subversion. However unstable the ideological mélange, the Right held together. The cement consisted, above all, of anticommunism, along with three correlative values—trust the market (and suspect the state, with exceptions below); trust the police; father

Todd Gitlin, professor of sociology at the University of California, Berkeley, is the author of several books, including The Sixties: Years of Hope, Days of Rage *(Bantam, 1987). This article appeared in* Tikkun, *July/August 1990.*

(a.k.a. canon, a.k.a. church, a.k.a. science) knows best. As the cold war melts down, the Right still tries to hold together by sanctifying the other authorities.

The curious thing is that over the centuries Left and Right have exchanged positions. The Right speaks of unity, the Left of difference. The Left, such as it is, is content to lack cement. There is no coherent whole, not even a vivid aspiration toward one. We see, rather, an assortment of particulars. Its rhetoric may carry a lingering appeal to universals (democracy and justice), but the practical activity is specialized—in the domestic sphere as pro-choice, pro-AIDS spending, pro-affirmative action, pro-homeless aid, anti-censorship, anti-development; and in the international arena as pro-rain forest, anti-Salvadoran military aid, pro-statehood for Palestine, pro-Sandinista.... On campuses and in common culture, the rallying cry is "diversity"—of faculty, students, cultures. Apart from sectarian groups awaiting the latest incarnation of The Revolution, politics on the Left shows a tendency to devolve into lists.

Why? The scatter of specialized movements is one legacy of the sixties. Many of the upwellings of that decade were generalizations of an impulse toward the protection and sanctification of difference. This fact was disguised by the exigencies of the Vietnam War. If there seemed in the late sixties to be one big movement, it was largely because there was one big war. The Marxist fantasy of The Revolution was a move to finesse actual differences into a reconstituted universalism—one fine day, The Revolution/Party/Class would dissolve all difference.

That fantasy had a pathos that derived from its nostalgic attempt to square the circle. What was happening instead was that the liberation impulse, ignited by Blacks, was becoming generalized. Millions, then tens of millions of Americans were looking for some self-definition close to home. They wanted to find roots, not nondescript Americanness. They preferred color to bleach, whole wheat and rye to white bread. They lost their desire to speak with one voice. They aspired to become not Americans, but women, Puerto Ricans, Jews, Italians, Poles, Chicanos, gays, lesbians. Ethnicity and gender became badges of pride. The idea of a common past was excoriated by New Left, feminist, Black, and other historians as a silencing that worked to the advantage of white males. Claims of universality were seen as the mask of privilege. Even establishment institutions lost confidence in their ability to speak in the name of universal needs. Markets fragmented. Where there had been *Life* and *Look*, there emerged *Runner's World* and *Savvy*.

The balkanization of American society, as of the Left, has its affirmative side, just as nineteenth-century nationalism did. The freedom to slip out of the melting pot is basic. Single authority that descends automatically from on high is oppression. So the emergence of difference and the proliferation of identities—of ethnic caucuses and hyphenations—was and remains defensible. The question is: Does the Left want to stand for something other than an aggregation of interest groups? And if not, are we willing to cede national power to a Right that has no ambivalence about authority? For how many more decades?

America today, along with its Left, suffers from an exaltation of difference—as if commonality were not also a value. While the Left brandishes the rainbow or the quilt, the Right wraps itself in the flag of "common culture." That is what it has instead of a largeness of vision. It can happily sit in the box seats and amuse itself at the spectacle of Jews and African-Americans, African-Americans and Korean-Americans, Chinese-Americans and Latin-Americans knocking each other around.

Meanwhile, instead of federating to take advantage of the cold-war thaw by organizing for drastic cuts in the military budget *to the benefit of all minorities as well as the working poor*, the various Lefts have been preoccupied with their distinctive and sometimes competing—dare I say parochial?—concerns. Instead of thinking together about limits to the market as a principle of economic organization, we have in effect ceded economic thinking to the Right. As a result, a marvelous political opportunity has been squandered. Functionally, the Left has limited itself to those who think of themselves as members of one or another tribe.

I hasten to add that the idea of multiculturalism has value as well as tremendous appeal, but is undeveloped, incomplete. Where does the symmetry of the rainbow come from? Or the stitches of the quilt? Just what do we mean when we speak of living multiculturally? On what common ground do we meet to cooperate? I do not know what a Left—or America—would look like if it sought to transcend or honor the differences of its constituencies. I am saying that we—from all our preoccupations—ought to be asking these questions. After twenty years of caucusing, we know where the gulfs are; we ought to be looking for bridges. □

Drawing by Anthony Dubovsky

Being "Only Human" versus Being a Mensch

Marian Neudal

The Problem

Ever since I first started working with conscientious objectors during the Vietnam War, I have been made acutely aware of the fact that we live in a culture that is fundamentally hostile to the efforts of ordinary people to formulate and live by a standard of morality. The people I was working with were the most decent young men imaginable, but they were frequently unable to express their most basic and crucial beliefs without liberal helpings of the raunchiest profanity. Crippled by doubt and embarrassment, they lacked the vocabulary and concepts necessary to make the most important decisions of their lives. They had been raised believing there was something wrong—not only unmasculine but actually unsavory—about trying to formulate a moral code and live by it.

We worry a lot these days about religion and the Right; some of us are doing some hopeful thinking about religion and the Left. But it is the ideology of the "extreme center"—what ordinary decent Americans operate on most of the time—that cripples us and burns us out, individually and collectively, by making us embarrassed and ashamed of our best impulses and efforts, as well as hypercritical of ourselves and others for our respective shortcomings. ("Us" in this context means, among others, people in movements for social change, people in the "helping professions"—nursing, social work, legal aid, elementary school teaching, community organizing—and people who spend their time taking care of other people—small children, aging parents, or disabled spouses.) The theological underpinnings of the ideology of the "extreme center" constitute a kind of pop-Protestantism. They are not, in their entirety, the received doctrine of any existing church that I know of, but probably the majority of churchgoing Americans think these ideas are their church's official beliefs. They pervade our culture and affect all of us, regardless of our political and religious orientations.

I. Original Sinfulness: People can't be good, and usually can't do much good; "I'm only human" is not a boast.

Corollary 1: Anybody who aspires to a moral code loftier than that of Al Capone is a phony and a hypocrite, and not to be trusted.

Corollary 2: If one does have an insuperable urge to do good, one should at least have the decency to do it in secret, while being as open as possible about one's vices, since confession is good for the soul.

Marian Henriquez Neudal is a practicing attorney, teacher, and writer. This article appeared in Tikkun, *November/December 1988.*

Corollary 3: A whole vocabulary of opprobrious terms has arisen to describe the aspirant to virtue—more about that later.

II. Individualism: To the extent that people can accomplish anything worthwhile, they can do it only as individuals.

Corollary 1: Collectivities can be very powerful forces for evil but can never be forces for good—even when that is their avowed purpose.

Corollary 2: In fact, a collectivity organized for the purpose of doing something good can be the most dangerous kind of tool for evil.

Corollary 3: On a world-historical scale we are doomed to do evil collectively, wholesale, and good individually, retail.

III. Intentionality: The moral value of an action is determined not by its effects, but by the state of mind of the individual who is performing it.

Corollary 1: It is worse to do the right thing for the wrong reason than not to do it at all.

Corollary 2: Doing the wrong thing for the right reason may even be highly praiseworthy.

Corollary 3: The only way to protect people from the temptation to do virtuous acts for the sake of extrinsic rewards is to remove from the social system all extrinsic rewards—material, social, psychological, whatever—for virtue, and perhaps even to build in some punishments for virtue and some rewards for viciousness.

IV. The Double Bind

A. Anybody who does socially beneficial acts for external rewards is a whore and a mercenary.

B. On the other hand, anybody who does anything, good or evil, for inadequate or no compensation is incompetent or a fool.

V. The Double Standard

A. Anybody who opposes one evil but not all evils is less trustworthy than an outright exponent of one or more evils.

B. There is more joy in heaven over a single George Wallace to whom the power of prayer belatedly reveals the power of the Black vote, than over ninety-nine Albert Schweitzers who spend their lives caring for the sick in Africa but have occasional racist thoughts.

C. A schmuck who occasionally acts like a mensch will get better publicity than a mensch who occasionally acts like a schmuck.

D. Which explains how Republicans keep winning elections.

A Proposed Solution—A Jewish Ethic of Liberation

Following are some philosophical principles for building and maintaining a community in which moral behavior is not only possible but encouraged; they work equally well in the communities in which we carry out our daily business and in the communities of movements for social change.

I. People are capable of doing good, both individually and collectively.

II. Effects matter more than intentions.

Corollary: It is easier to change consciousness by changing behavior than to change behavior by changing consciousness.

III. Therefore we should rig our social system with external rewards for socially beneficial acts. "Thou shalt not muzzle the ox that treads the grain."

IV. It is better to do something decent, however inadequate, than nothing at all. People who do something should be praised and rewarded more than people who do nothing, and if at all possible they should not be picked on, at least not until the people who do nothing have been properly admonished. As a practical matter, if one tells somebody who is doing something decent that what s/he is doing is inadequate, s/he won't do more—s/he'll say "to hell with it" and stop doing anything at all.

(Example: Many years ago I spent a lot of time studying the life and writings of Gandhi. After a while I became thoroughly turned off by the way he treated his wife, and I essentially wrote him off as a sexist pig. Somewhat later, it occurred to me that, pig or not, Gandhi had formulated some remarkable ideas and had done some remarkable things. Instead of dismissing him as inadequate, I chose to admire him for the good that he did. Eventually I decided to try, the next time I met a sexist man, to ask myself, "Could this guy be a closet Gandhi?")

V. Don't wipe out hypocrisy—improve the quality of it.

(Example: If my boss refrains from calling me "honey" and patting me on the fanny, if he pays me adequately and treats me fairly, but only because he doesn't want me to find out what a sexist he really is—that's *fine* with me. The more praiseworthy the mask he feels obliged to wear, the better my working life will be.)

Furthermore, an environment in which we do good only in secret, while arsonists, adulterers, and ax murderers are encouraged to "let it all hang out," makes it all too easy for us to justify following in their footsteps because "everybody does it." Instead, we ought to encourage those who do evil not to be proud of their conduct—to hide it, to be hypocritical. Even if the total number of arsons, ax murders, and so on cannot be significantly reduced, some well-applied hypocrisy may at least alleviate their influence on the social environment.

VI. Practicalities

A. We have made impressive strides in cleaning up the sexist and racist locutions in our everyday language. Now it's time to work on the words and phrases that are oppressive to do-gooders—

beginning, of course, with "do-gooder" itself. Once more it is time to challenge people who use oppressive words and to weed out our own vocabularies.

Watch for:	*Especially when used to mean:*
Do-gooder	
Bleeding Heart	Anyone who aspires to be good
Hypocrite/Phony	but is not yet perfect
Righteous	Self-righteous
Well-intentioned	Ineffectual
Ideals	That which cannot be made real
Liberal Establishment	Any two or more people to the left of Louis XIV who have ever been introduced to each other
Rhetoric	Any political locution whose subjects and verbs come out even (see also: glib)

B. Important exercise for strengthening your vocabulary: Try to use the words "sin," "vice," or "virtue" at least once a day *in some other context than diet or exercise.*

We need to stop trashing ourselves and apologizing for the best things we have ever done or tried to do. Instead, we must accept ourselves as imperfect but nonetheless worthy and potentially effective people who have the right to be judged and—if we choose—rewarded by the same standards as anybody else. We have to stop denigrating ourselves and one another for imperfections we would never even notice in a sinner or a Republican. That way lies burnout. Above all, we need to recognize the lesson of Shabbat: that we—all of us struggling human beings who are trying in one way or another to bring the messianic age to our homes, our families, our communities, our nations, our planet—have the right to a regularly experienced foretaste, in our ordinary lives, of what we are ultimately struggling for. □

The Pro-Flag and Anti-Abortion Pathology

Michael Lerner and Peter Gabel

In recent months, the right wing has managed to galvanize large numbers of people around pro-flag and anti-abortion campaigns. What accounts for the popular attraction of these causes? Israeli philosopher Yishayahu Leibowitz says that from the standpoint of Jewish law (Halakha), a flag is simply a *shmate* (a rag) on a pole. So why all the passion? And why the seeming deeper commitment to the fate of the unborn than to the fate of the millions of children living in severe poverty and conditions of oppression?

Of course, some of the people involved in these movements are motivated by the surface arguments and have reasonable things to say. The abortion issue, for example, is complex, and many of those who have been most committed, as we are, to the pro-choice position, nevertheless insist that abortion is often troubling, and that it is reasonable to make complex moral judgments about when abortion is appropriate. Still, it appears to us that pro-choicers have a more consistent pro-life attitude than many of those in the anti-abortion movement, who care little about the fate of the fetus once it becomes a baby. While many individuals have legitimate moral concerns about abortion (and we all need to struggle with these concerns), the anti-abortion movement exhibits distinctly pathological features. We also understand the legitimate desires of Americans to hold cultural symbols of their shared values, but when they are whipped into such a frenzy that they would amend the Constitution to defend the flag from a mere handful of people who wish to burn that flag in order to signify their anger at various aspects of American society, we are dealing with a phenomenon that goes far beyond rational concerns.

To understand the pathology fully, we need to look at the pervasive pain and frustration, the feelings of worthlessness and lack of connection to others, and the alienation and desperate search for communities of meaning and purpose that underlie so much of contemporary American politics. In a society that offers people few opportunities to achieve the mutual recognition and affirmation that are fundamental human needs, the longing for connection with others is frequently coupled with a melancholy resignation that such longing is utopian and cannot be fulfilled in this world. Yet the desire for this connection—a desire normally denied by human beings so alienated by the dynamics of contemporary capitalist society that most people have given up all conscious hope for its realization—remains a driving force in the unconscious lives of most Americans.

Part of the energy of the anti-abortion movement comes from its ability to symbolically address this desire. The fetus is a symbol of an idealized, innocent being—actually the little child within us, who is not being adequately loved and accepted in our daily experience. The desire to be loved and accepted as human beings—a completely rational desire—is split off and projected onto the fetus. This object of fantasy is idealized and made pure—an innocent and perfect unborn creature (and because unborn, not yet sullied by the world).

Peter Gabel is president of New College of California and associate editor of Tikkun. *This editorial appeared in* Tikkun, *September/October 1989.*

But because this projection and process of idealization in fact involves an evasion and denial of actual pain, it is accompanied by another split off part of their consciousness: the rage and hatred that people feel when they are not confirmed in their fundamental humanity. That anger is directed at a demonized "other" whose humanity is ignored or denied, transformed by imagination into the "murderers" killing little babies; the communists who are to be nuked out of existence; the criminals who must be executed; the drug addicts upon whom we must wage war; the Jews, Blacks, or Arabs who are routinely deemed responsible for the world's or a given society's problems. This is why it makes sense for so many supposed "pro-lifers" to fanatically oppose abortion and yet support the death penalty and American militarism. At the rational level, these views may seem inconsistent, but at the deeper psychological level, they are expressive of the same distorted dynamic. Both the unborn fetus and the evil "other" are imaginary constructs that carry an unconscious meaning reflecting repression of people's most fundamental social need.

A similar loss of connectedness underlies the frantic attempts to amend the Constitution to "protect the flag." The commotion isn't really about a *shmate* on a pole, but rather is about the loss of the idealized community that the flag symbolizes. In the past, part of what gave coherence to individual and family life was its embeddedness in larger communities of meaning and shared purpose. Religious, ethnic, and political communities, even unions and social change organizations such as the socialist and communist parties, provided a context within which people could feel connected to a larger purpose and historical meaning that transcended their individual lives.

With the erosion of genuine community within which people can feel recognized and confirmed for who they are, people in their isolation feel driven to seek out the imaginary communities provided them through an identification with "the nation." Yet the very lack of substance in these fantasies makes people's connection to these pseudo-communities feel unstable, and hence generates a frenzy and hysteria that is used to sustain a sense of a reality that might otherwise fade. In this context, the flag, the symbol of a perfect community that exists only in the imagination, becomes the vulnerable embodiment of all that people fear they are losing.

Ironically, though, there is one element in the fantasies people have about America that actually is real—and it is precisely that one real element that is threatened by the controversies over the flag and abortion. That element is the real way that America *has* preserved individual freedom. While preserving individual freedoms is not a sufficient basis for the creation of a community of meaning that can replace those that have eroded, the absence of this value is one reason why some of the previous communities lost their popular support. Individual freedom would certainly be a central value in any new community of meaning we would try to create. From a tactical standpoint, civil libertarians might have wished that the Supreme Court had not agreed to hear the case and involve itself in the flag issue at this historical moment. Yet, it is precisely in the willingness to say that even the symbol of the society, the American flag, can be attacked, that the Supreme Court embodies what is very best in American society. We do not advocate that people burn the flag, but we applaud the Supreme Court for confirming that flag-burning is constitutional. That the Supreme Court in effect allows us to look at America's most holy symbol as though it were a *shmate* on a pole, gives us immense reason to be proud of the United States of America. It was this fierce commitment to individual liberties and to the right of people to make up their own minds about what to call holy that made it possible for our foremothers and forefathers to find haven on these shores. Shame on those pathetic political misleaders in the Congress, Administration and the media who now seek a way to overturn that decision.

Ironically, the best way to defend these important freedoms of choice is *not* to insist on the sanctity of choice. Freedom of choice is just another candidate for what should be holy—and it has to contend on the same level as the various right-wing candidates for holiness. Rather, the task is to understand the unmet needs that lead people to an irrational and pathological politics. Then we must charge the liberal and progressive forces with finding more healthy and rational ways to address those needs by showing a better way for people to secure the recognition and connectedness they rightfully desire. Only then will we reconstitute communities of meaning that have been undermined by the individualist ethos.

If all this sounds a bit too psychological for you, just look at how unsuccessful the liberal and progressive forces have been in waging a defensive war against a right wing that is willing to talk about these issues. It's time to deepen the level of analysis and insist that political strategies address this fundamental dimension of human reality. ☐

Drawing by Susan Gross

Jews and the Gulf: Fallout from the Six-Week War

John B. Judis

Research for this piece was supported by a grant from the Nathan Cummings Foundation.

The Six Day War in 1967 not only changed borders in the Middle East, it also permanently altered the contours of American Jewish politics. By creating new respect and enthusiasm for Israel, it laid the basis for what would become known as the "pro-Israel lobby." Marginal before 1967, the American Israel Public Affairs Committee (AIPAC) would become a major player in American politics after the war.

The Left's radical hostility to Israel's gains in the war alienated Jewish intellectuals such as *Commentary* editor Norman Podhoretz and Harvard professor Martin Peretz and contributed, among other things, to their eventually cutting their ties with the Left. In 1972, many of these Jewish intellectuals would oppose Democratic presidential candidate George McGovern. By 1980, some of them, such as Podhoretz, would support Ronald Reagan against Jimmy Carter and help Reagan win legitimacy as a middle-of-the-road rather than as a far-right candidate.

The six-week war to dislodge Iraq from Kuwait may have had an equally profound impact on the politics of American Jews and Jewish organizations. In the war's aftermath, American Jewish organizations found their own power and prestige enhanced. They benefited from their support for the war and from Israel's newfound status as an innocent victim of Saddam's missiles. The war not only nurtured the alliance between major Jewish organizations and the Bush administration; it also gave birth to growing ties with the leaders of Saudi Arabia and Kuwait.

The new thrust of mainstream Jewish politics was symbolized by the Committee for Peace and Security in the Gulf, the main group that promoted the use of force in the Gulf. The committee was organized by an unlikely trio: left-wing Democrat and Jesse Jackson-backer Ann Lewis, former Reagan administration official Richard Perle, and moderate Democrat Representative Stephen Solarz (D-N.Y.). It relied for its funds on the blessing of the Saudi ambassador to the U.S., Prince Bandar bin Sultan Al-Saud, and the largesse of American defense contractors. And for its efforts it won the praise and gratitude of the Bush administration.

Over the next year, this new thrust in Jewish politics could prove successful if the Bush administration is able to create a rapprochement between Israel and the Gulf states. In that case, the alliances formed during the war will be seen as foreshadowing the future realignment in the Middle East. But if the administration fails—either because of its own ineptitude or because of Saudi or

John B. Judis is the Washington correspondent for In These Times, *a contributing editor of the* New Republic, *and the author of* William F. Buckley Jr.: Patron Saint of the Conservatives *(Simon & Schuster 1988) and* Grand Illusion: Critics and Champions of the American Century, *(Farrar, Strauss & Giroux 1992). This article appeared in* Tikkun, *May/June 1991.*

Israeli intransigence—then the Jewish organizations could find themselves isolated, with the fundamental premises of their political strategy compromised. The euphoria of victory could give way to the disillusionment of stalemate.

For Jews active in the peace movement and in Jewish organizations, the war led to sharp differences with the opponents of U.S. intervention. The rift was very similar to that created two decades ago by the radical response to the Six Day War. Jews on the Left—who had identified anti-Semitism largely with ultraconservatism and with Black nationalism—now found it within the antiwar movement. Moreover, they discovered that they disagreed with their erstwhile comrades not only about Israel, but about how to understand America's role in the world.

This process of change and recognition—on the part of both the Jewish Left and mainstream Jewish organizations—unfolded over seven months: from Iraq's invasion of Kuwait on August 2 to the cease-fire declared at the end of February. It took place fitfully and painfully. In the first phase, lasting from the Iraqi invasion to November 29, when the U.S. secured United Nations agreement for the use of force against Iraq, Jews were virtually paralyzed by decades-old charges of "dual loyalty." Only in the second phase of debate, from November 29 to January 16, when the U.S. went to war, did Jewish organizations, prodded by Solarz's committee, close ranks behind the administration's threat to go to war.

I. Buchananizing the Jews

In the first three months after Iraq's invasion of Kuwait, an eerie silence emanated from America's major Jewish organizations such as AIPAC and the American Jewish Congress. Leading Jewish Democrats in Congress such as Los Angeles Congressmen Howard Berman and Mel Levine also scrupulously kept their own counsel. Like cautious bathers, prominent Jewish leaders were willing to wade in the shallows of agreement with the most general objectives of the Bush administration, but they wanted no part of the stormy debate over means and ends that was taking place in deeper water. Those organizations whose members identified with the peace movement—such as the Organization of American Hebrew Congregations and the American Jewish Congress—couldn't agree on what position to take. The leaders of the largest and most powerful of the Jewish organizations—such as AIPAC and the Conference of Presidents of Major American Jewish Organizations—knew that they wanted the U.S. to take military action against Saddam Hussein, but were reluctant to say so aloud. They were afraid that their advocacy of military action against Iraq would be construed as an attempt to get America into a war on Israel's behalf.

Unfortunately, such fears were well founded. In this first phase of debate, both right-wing and left-wing opponents of administration policy accused Jewish columnists and foreign policy experts who openly favored force of placing Israel's interests above America's. On an August 24 appearance on the television talk show "The McLaughlin Group," former Reagan and Nixon aide Pat Buchanan charged that the only people who supported a war in the Middle East were "the Israeli Defense Ministry and its amen corner in the United States." In a widely syndicated column opposing military intervention, Buchanan singled out for criticism *New York Times* columnist A. M. Rosenthal, former Secretary of State Henry Kissinger, columnist Charles Krauthammer, and Richard Perle, all of whom are Jewish—ignoring such prominent non-Jewish advocates of force as William F. Buckley, Jr. and Senator Richard Lugar (R-Ind.). On television, Buchanan also referred to the "Israeli-occupied Congress."

Buchanan's attacks were double-edged: He was exploiting popular anti-Semitism, identifying as exclusively Jewish a political position that Christians and Muslims shared with Jews; and he was attempting to discredit the opinions of Jewish intellectuals such as Kissinger—who was clearly more concerned about Gulf oil than about Israel—by claiming that they wanted the interests of Israel to dictate the terms of U.S. foreign policy. Whether or not Buchanan himself is an anti-Semite, this way of attacking opposing views is rooted in the history of American anti-Semitism. Before World War II, for instance, right-wing isolationists such as Charles Lindbergh and Albert Jay Nock had tried to discredit American support for intervention in Europe by identifying it with Jews.

When Rosenthal, the *New York Post* editorial page, and the *New Republic* counterattacked against Buchanan, some conservative pundits leapt to his defense. *National Review* editor Joseph Sobran, who had in the past tried to dismiss the *New York Times* as a Jewish newspaper, accused Jews of attempting to "repress candor." Jews, Sobran wrote in a September 24 syndicated column, "have become in a way psychically segregated from other Americans, separated by the nervousness that also gave them status and power. And when that separateness is broken down, as by Buchanan's mockery, some of them ... can only understand it as a threat."

Buchanan's charges of dual loyalty were also echoed on the Left. The *Nation* magazine, edited by prominent Jewish writer Victor Navasky, had skirted the shores of anti-Semitism before, publishing a bitter screed by Gore Vidal that painted *Commentary*'s Podhoretz as an Israeli agent. Now the magazine made similar charges against Jewish proponents of war. In a September 17 editorial, the editors rejected what they called "the Israeli scenario" of "preemptive air strikes on Iraqi targets ... recommended by Henry Kissinger in the *Washington Post* and tummeled by Israel's personal messengers to the *New York Times* op-ed page, William Safire and A. M. Rosenthal." Neither the editor's religion nor the idiomatic use of Yiddish could disguise the editorial's anti-Semitic thrust.

In the wake of the furor over Buchanan's remarks, a new expression was born: Jewish politicians and organizations who favored military intervention had been "Buchananized"—that is, intimidated into silence. AIPAC, whose top officers favored the strategy put forth by Kissinger and Safire, did not participate in the debate over the war until January 10, when Congress began debating whether to authorize the use of force. Likewise, the Conference of Presidents did not take a position until January 8. The reason, as one Washington Jewish official acknowledged, was a "perverse fear that a resolution might be viewed as coming from Israel rather than the United States."

Jews and Jewish organizations who identified with the peace movement were no less stymied and confused during the first phase of debate over the war, but for different reasons. As might be expected, Jews were active on all sides of the peace movement: as editors of the three major left-wing publications, the *Progressive, In These Times,* and the *Nation*; and as sponsors and organizers of the two major anti-intervention coalitions, the National Coalition to Stop U.S. Intervention and the National Campaign for Peace in the Middle East. Nonetheless, important differences began to emerge between the leaders of the anti-intervention movement and Jews who had been active as Jews *and* as members of the peace movement.

The leaders of the anti-intervention coalitions and the editors of *In These Times,* the *Progressive, Mother Jones,* and the *Nation* focused on opposing the Bush administration's strategy in the Gulf—regardless of whether that would entail the loss of Kuwait. They viewed American intervention through the prism of the 1960s—"Not Again!" Daniel Ellsberg's anti-intervention essay in *Mother Jones* was headlined. Invoking the "anti-imperialist" politics of the New Left, they described the administration's actions, in the words of the *Progressive,* as "the war of the affluent and industrial North against the South." Neither antiwar coalition backed sanctions against the Iraqis. One coalition, led by Ramsey Clark and the neo-Stalinist Workers' World Party, tilted toward the Iraqis; hard-line Workers' World ideologues portrayed Saddam as a crusader against Western imperialism. The other coalition, led by survivors of the various anti-intervention movements of the 1980s, nominally condemned Saddam, but was not prepared to support any measures against him for fear of identifying itself with administration efforts.

Some of these leftists were actively hostile to Israel. Jack O'Dell, director of Jesse Jackson's

Rainbow Coalition, applauded Saddam's attempt to link Israel's Occupation of the West Bank with Iraq's occupation of Kuwait. The Ramsey Clark-Workers' World coalition called for ending all U.S. aid to Israel and endorsed Saddam's proposal for an international conference. For them, the crisis created by Saddam's invasion created a useful pretext to roll back what they, with Saddam, branded American and Israeli imperialism.

In contrast, most Jewish intellectuals who were active as Jews and in the peace movement believed that Saddam Hussein was a genuine menace who sought hegemony over the Middle East and had to be stopped. While continuing to criticize the Israeli government, they rejected Saddam's call for linkage as sheer opportunism intended to obscure his brutal annexation of a smaller, militarily weaker, but wealthy country. The question was whether he could be stopped without war; and if not, whether he was a sufficient menace to justify the extensive loss of life that such a war might demand.

Mitchell Cohen, an expert on the Middle East, expressed the view of many of these intellectuals in an editorial he wrote for *Dissent* that fall. Cohen rejected the anti-interventionist view of Iraq as part of the embattled "South": Cold warriors reduced every regional conflict to an apocalypse of Communists versus anti-Communists, regardless of local realities. The Left should not think like neoconservatives, only substituting "imperialism versus anti-imperialism" for "communism versus anticommunism." In any event, Saddam's anti-imperialist rhetoric is simply a cover for his own regional imperialism. However, Cohen also brushed aside Bush's stated objectives in the region:

George Bush says he is protecting the American way of life in the Gulf. I don't believe that. Neither, I suspect, does he. But I don't care. I care about the long range impact of an expansionist Iraqi regime pursuing mastery in a volatile region; and, yes, I fear its dominion over a resource vital to the world.

Cohen favored the use of force to expel Iraq from Kuwait and to destroy Saddam's "lethal resources." Other Jewish intellectuals—for instance, the leadership of American Friends of Peace Now—opted for using sanctions. Jerome Segal, the president of the Jewish Peace Lobby, argued for this position in *Tikkun* (November/December 1990), endorsing a "long-term embargo of Iraqi and Kuwaiti oil as the primary vehicle for putting pressure on Iraq."

During the fall, these differences among left-wing Jewish intellectuals loomed large and led to confusion and stalemate within organizations such as American Friends of Peace Now and the Union of American Hebrew Congregations (UAHC). The UAHC was typical. In September, it produced a tepid analysis that focused on the "implications" of policy without recommending any, complaining that the "rationale for American intervention remains ambiguous." In November, the UAHC board produced a resolution that, in staff member Rabbi David Saperstein's words, "said nothing. We said to avoid force as much as possible but leave force as an option." As a result, these organizations had as little influence on the public and congressional debates as the mainstream organizations did over U.S. policy in the Gulf.

But the differences within the Jewish Left were really over means rather than ends and would largely disappear once war began, while the difference between these Jewish intellectuals and the leaders of the antiwar coalitions would endure and grow far more serious. These two groups were looking at the same conflict from entirely different perspectives. If the Jewish Left tended to focus more on the specifics of the Middle East, the antiwar activists continued to view the region through the prism of 1960s antiwar rhetoric. "I think so many of these people have invested in a sense of America as a center of evil," historian Fred Siegel, a member of the *Dissent* editorial board, explained. "To give up that separate reality is to give up part of their identity."

II. Field Marshall Solarz

After the November election, the Bush administration transformed the debate—first by announcing on November 8 that it would double the number of troops in Saudi Arabia, and second by winning UN endorsement of the use of force if Iraq were not to leave Kuwait by January 15. The question now became whether to go to war after January 15—and the very urgency of this question forced both Jewish organizations and Congress to enter the debate.

By the time Congress began deliberating about whether to authorize force, the major mainstream organizations had all approved its use. Nine-term Brooklyn Congressman Stephen J. Solarz played the key role in shaping this public consensus. Solarz was to be attacked later by Congressmen Pete Stark (D-Cal.) for fronting for Israel—Stark referred to Solarz derisively as "Field Marshall Solarz"—but in fact Solarz was acting on his own. Unlike Levine, Berman, or Congressman Larry Smith (D-Fla.), Solarz had never been a dependable ally of AIPAC or the Israeli government—for instance, he had rejected their demands to move the U.S. embassy from Tel Aviv to Jerusalem. While his district is predominantly Jewish, he has not had to rely on funds from pro-Israel political action committees. As a member of the House Foreign Affairs Committee's East Asian Subcommittee, Solarz has developed a solid financial basis among Asian Americans. If Solarz had been known for anything prior to the debate over the Gulf, it was his longstanding opposition to Philippine dictator Ferdinand Marcos. Like other Jews who advocated the use of force against Saddam Hussein, Solarz was undoubtedly moved by Saddam's threat to incinerate Israel and by the danger that Saddam would pose to Israel if he acquired nuclear weapons and hegemony over Arab oil. Chiefly, however, Solarz responded to the analogy between Saddam's brutal drive for expansion in the Middle East and Hitler's conquest of Central Europe in the 1930s. Hitler, of course, had been in a position to do considerably more damage than Saddam—but as Solarz wrote in the *New Republic,* Saddam, like Hitler, showed "an unappeasable will to power combined with a ruthless willingness to employ whatever means are necessary to achieve it." Solarz's friends and congressional colleagues confirm that this was his principal concern. As one close friend put it, "To Steve, Israel was part of the calculation, but the most important thing was that this was a rerun of World War II."

Solarz first began trying to win support for a military response to Iraq in September. At a breakfast meeting in Washington attended by Jewish congressional leaders, Saudi ambassador Prince Bandar, and several other interested parties, Solarz broached the idea of forming a committee to win support for the use of force against Iraq. Bandar gave his blessing to the idea—and Solarz recruited Perle, now a fellow at the American Enterprise Institute (AEI) in Washington, and Lewis, former political director of the Democratic National Committee, as the committee's codirectors. Perle had credibility with conservative Republicans; Lewis, with liberal Democrats. Solarz called the group the Committee for Peace and Security in the Gulf.

According to a source present at early planning meetings, Perle was responsible for most of the fundraising. He raised most of the committee's money from defense contractors and from the conservative Bradley Foundation. Joel Johnson, the international vice president of the Aerospace Industries Association of America, a key industry lobby and link to the Saudis, confirmed that Perle solicited and won contributions from defense companies. Johnson claims that the companies did not contribute out of hope of future sales in the Middle East, but rather "to encourage general support for the president." But other sources familiar with the committee and the defense companies say that the companies contributed because they were led to believe that the Saudis and the Kuwaitis, prime customers for their weapons, would look kindly on their doing so. "There were personal calls from Perle and guarded messages that this was what the Saudis and Kuwaitis wanted," said one knowledgeable source.

The committee itself would not reveal who its funders were. "One potential corporate donor did not want their name publicized, and we made a general decision not to publicize our donors' names," Lewis explained later. But the committee's decision undoubtedly reflected more than a desire to spare one company embarrassment. Public knowledge that it was funded by defense contractors would have substantially undermined its credibility. As it is, the committee's defense-heavy funding raises serious doubt about the ethical and political judgment of Solarz, Perle, and Lewis, quite apart from their position on the Gulf War.

Solarz announced the committee's formation in a press conference on December 8—but he and Perle had already begun airing their views the month before. Solarz wrote a long article for the *New Republic* that had been solicited by its literary editor Leon Wieseltier, who, along with editor-in-chief Martin Peretz, later joined the committee. Perle testified before the House Armed Services Committee on November 29. On December 20, Lewis took the field with an op-ed piece in the *New York Times*. The three also became staple guests on television and radio talk shows.

Solarz, Perle, and Lewis gathered names for an ad campaign that would eventually appear the week of the congressional debate. They failed to get such heavy hitters as former Middle East troubleshooter Robert Strauss and former vice president Walter Mondale, but they were able to recruit former UN ambassador Jeane Kirkpatrick (who had initially equivocated about the use of force) and former White House chief of staff Howard Baker.

While the three were forthright in arguing that force would be necessary, their arguments still reflected fear of Buchanan's charges. Both Solarz and Lewis went so far out of their way to avoid mention of Israel that their arguments seemed disingenuous. Lewis rested her entire case for military intervention on the threat to Saddam's Arab neighbors, while Solarz did not mention Israel once in his sixty-two-hundred-word *New Republic* manifesto. In their ad, Solarz, Perle, and Lewis, all of whom are Jewish, were careful to balance Jewish signatories with gentiles, but they also went considerably beyond this, identifying retired American Jewish Committee lobbyist Hyman Bookbinder as "Former Staffer, Office of Economic Opportunity," a position he had held twenty-five years ago in the Johnson administration. Bookbinder says he was "astonished" when he saw how he was listed. "They were fearful of giving our adversaries something to point to so they could say it was a Jewish war," Bookbinder says.

Solarz and Lewis were very effective in winning support within the liberal Jewish community. On December 2, Solarz attended a meeting of the Board of Trustees of the Union of American Hebrew Congregations in New York to debate a resolution on the Gulf crisis. "He gave a strong speech that swept up our board," David Saperstein recalled. In its resolution, the board declared that the "use of military force to accomplish the restoration of Kuwaiti independence, the freeing of all hostages, and an effective deterrent, or end to, Iraq's capacity to threaten other nations" was "an acceptable response by the United States and other nations." Solarz had carried the day.

Lewis and Solarz also played an important part in winning the American Jewish Congress's support for the use of force. Through December and early January, the Congress members debated whether to support the use of force, with a significant minority of local members favoring the continuation of sanctions. At the climactic meeting of the Congress's Governing Council in early January, Lewis, an active Council member, spoke persuasively for the Council's final resolution—approving "whatever steps necessary" to oust Iraq from Kuwait.

Solarz and his committee certainly didn't have to convince AIPAC and the Conference of Presidents to back the use of force, but at a December meeting with their representatives, he did try to get the groups to take a more public role in the debate. Where Solarz failed, the Bush administration's pleas—delivered in White House meetings with both groups—finally succeeded, winning their endorsement of the president's position on the eve of the congressional debate. As Congress met, the only significant Washington Jewish organization not on record in favor of the administration's position was American Friends of Peace Now, which favored the continuation of sanctions.

Neither the Jewish organizations nor Solarz's committee had significant influence over the congressional debate that took place in January. With Buchanan's specter still hovering over its operations, AIPAC kept a low profile. The organization's Washington staff was in Israel as the debate began, and its president and regional leaders were left to lobby still-undecided senators such as Richard Shelby (D-Ala.) and Charles Grassley (R-Iowa). In the House, neither AIPAC nor Solarz significantly swayed the debate. Solarz's main contribution was in winning Bush administration support for a resolution that acknowledged Congress's war-making powers. But according to sources in the House, the two most effective supporters of the Solarz-Michel resolution authorizing force were Les Aspin (D-Wis.), the chair of the Armed Services Committee, and Representative Robert Torricelli (D-N.J.). Aspin provided the military rationale for backing force—arguing (correctly, as it turned out) that the war could be won without a large number of American casualties. Torricelli, meanwhile, provided the diplomatic rationale, framing an argument for war in terms of collective security.

Jewish Democrats were split during the debate, but their divisions—like those between Jewish-oriented leftists—were tactical rather than strategic. Everyone acknowledged that Saddam had to be stopped; the question was whether sanctions should be given more of a chance. Moreover, the final votes did not clearly reflect constituency pressure. Mel Levine backed the Solarz resolution in spite of widespread and very vocal opposition in his district, dramatized by a sit-in at his district offices. Congressman Charles Schumer (D-N.Y.) voted for sanctions in spite of considerable support in his heavily Jewish district for the use of force. In the end, Jewish House members of what Buchanan had called the "Israeli-occupied Congress" voted seventeen to sixteen against the use of force, while Jewish Senators voted five to three against the administration. And despite AIPAC's lobbying, several senators heavily dependent on Jewish PACs, including Grassley, Tom Harkin (D-Iowa), and Daniel Inouye (D-Hawaii), voted against the use of force.

III. Breaking the Ranks

When the war began, Congress, including those Democrats who had voted against authorizing force, closed ranks behind the administration. As the Scud missiles hit Israel on January 18, those Jewish intellectuals and members of Jewish organizations who had backed sanctions also came around to backing war rather than unilateral withdrawal. For some, the Scud attack had brought home Israel's stake in the conflict. But for most, it had simply dramatized what *Dissent* editor Irving Howe called Saddam's "active evil."

Typical was Jo-Ann Mort, communications director of the Amalgamated Clothing and Textile Workers Union and a board member of Americans for Peace Now. Mort had favored sanctions, but once the war began, she reasoned that withdrawal would only strengthen Saddam. She described her new position as "critical support of the air war." Gail Pressberg, the codirector of the Center for Israeli Peace and Security, also decided to back the war effort. "I decided one had to support the war and hope that it was over as soon as possible," Pressberg explained.

As these Jewish intellectuals abandoned the movement against intervention, they found themselves "Buchananized" as well. Jewish leftists critical of Saddam Hussein were quickly reduced to crude caricatures of their Jewishness, and their support for Israel was translated into endorsement of the Israeli status quo. When Paul Berman, Paul Starr, and Irving Howe came out in favor of the war, left-wing columnists and peace movement activists issued snide ad hominem attacks. In a *Newsday* column, John Leonard identified "pro-warriors" as "Jewish males" and cited with approval the remark of a friend, "for the Irving Howes and Paul Starrs, there is a new definition of a just war—a war with Israel in it." *Village Voice* columnist Douglas Ireland repeated the quip. Indeed, I experienced the same anti-Semitic calumny in the letters column of *In These Times* after I expressed qualified support for a "limited war with limited aims." I had mentioned Israel only once in the article, had not written about Israel for seven years, and even then, had harshly criticized the Occupation of the West Bank and Gaza. Nevertheless, readers who responded to the piece reduced my views to knee-jerk Zionism. One letter called me a "Jaundiced Jew" and "covert Zionist." Another described me as a "Jewish neo-liberal."

At the same time, Jewish intellectuals who favored continuation of the war encountered within the anti-intervention movement a deep hostility toward Israel that verged on anti-Semitism. Peace activists did not merely criticize Israel's government or policies; they blamed the Jewish state (as a previous generation had blamed Jewish bankers) for the ills of the world, including millennial conflicts between Arab peoples. Jewel Bellush, a political scientist at Barnard, had led the fight in the American Jewish Congress against the use of force, but once the war began, she argued, like others, that it was better to see it to its conclusion. Now she found herself assailed for supporting Israel. "I am a friend of Israel, but I also believe in a Palestinian state," Bellush explained. "But the peaceniks I met—I am not sure whether they cared what happened to Israel."

Fred Siegel was more emphatic about the anti-Semitism he encountered in the anti-intervention movement. "It's essentially the notion that the Arabs are peace-loving people, and if Israel hadn't roiled the waters, the region would be a land of milk and honey," Siegel explained. "It's a kind of demonology. When you ask people about Scuds, they write them off as Western media hype." Surprisingly, the Scud attacks further widened the distance between many Jewish intellectuals and the anti-intervention movement, heightening both Jewish concerns about Israel and radical left-wing hostility toward the Jewish state. When the movement leaders who organized the first major antiwar demonstrations in Washington were asked to comment on the possibility that if the U.S. withdrew, Israel would get into a bloody war with Iraq, they displayed their enmity for Israel. Their response, explained *In These Times* correspondent John Canham-Clyne, who covered the demonstrations, was "Fuck Israel."

Yet the conflict between the Jewish intellectuals who now supported the war and the anti-intervention movement was not just about Israel. Like the conflict between the radical Left of the late sixties and the Jewish liberals who would later form the cold-war liberal anti-McGovern wing of the Democratic party, it was about competing visions of America's role and place in the world. Jewish intellectuals like Mort, Pressberg, and Siegel held to a complex view of American intentions and world conflict, which allowed for the possibility that the U.S. could be on the side of God as well as the devil. The remnants of the 1960s Left still adhered to a bipolar view of the world divided between imperialism and the anti-imperialist forces, in which Israel's only significant role was to serve as an ally of American imperialism.

Meanwhile, mainstream Jewish organizations were also closing ranks with the advent of war. Almost every one of the major organizations sent groups to Israel who offered moral support by donning gas masks. These groups also abandoned their Buchananized silence to cheer the Bush administration's prosecution of the war. After the war was over, participants at a Conference of Presidents meeting in Washington on March 5 and at AIPAC's annual policy conference March 17–20 were euphoric in contemplating U.S. success. Shoshona Cardin, the new president of the Conference of Presidents, captured the new mood by describing President Bush as "our brave, bold, and fearless leader."

There was also a feeling of newfound unity within the liberal and conservative, Democratic and Republican branches of organized Jewry. If liberal David Saperstein had risen a year ago to ask a question of Richard Perle, he would have been expected to be highly critical of the hawkish Perle, but when Saperstein addressed Perle and policy expert Martin Indyk at the Conference of Presidents meeting, he said, "I want to give my expression of appreciation to the two speakers. I don't think anyone has done more than the two of you to understand the threats that Israel faces." Yet behind the postwar euphoria and bonhomie lurked dangers for organized Jewry. The war had transformed the terrain on which mainstream Jewish organizations worked, reinforcing certain trends over others, and introducing a new alliance linking the mainstream Jewish organizations with the Bush administration and the Arab emirates. Such an alliance could lead to a new stage in the Middle East peace process, in which Saudi Arabia and Kuwait would join Egypt in recognizing Israel, but it could also lead to profound disillusionment and isolation for American Jewish organizations and for Israel.

The administration's success in the war—and the congressional Democrats' initial opposition—reinforced a growing tilt in both the Conference of Presidents and AIPAC away from the Democrats and Congress and toward Republicans and the executive branch. AIPAC had begun to shift its focus in 1985, when Steve Rosen, the lobby's research director, wrote a memorandum calling for AIPAC to concentrate on lobbying the executive branch. Such a strategy required AIPAC to elevate in its leadership Jewish Republicans with ties to the Reagan and Bush administrations. After the 1988 election, AIPAC's chief congressional lobbyist, stalwart Democrat Douglas Bloomfield, quit over AIPAC's new strategy, leaving the organization's political direction largely to Rosen.

Critics of the new strategy charged that it reduced the organization's clout, since executive branch officials did not have to fear punishment from pro-Israel PACs if they failed to heed AIPAC's advice; worse still, lobbying the executive branch would necessarily require trade-offs and deals that would undermine the organization's message and defeat the aim of forthrightly defending Israel in Washington. In the first two years of the Bush administration, the critics appeared to have been proven right. AIPAC was unable to prevent the administration from developing an acrimonious relationship with the Shamir government, while pro-Israel Democrats on Capitol Hill no longer trusted it to act in Israel's behalf.

Nothing better illustrated the pitfalls of AIPAC's new approach than the battle over the $21 billion Saudi arms deal that was announced last September. Ten years before, under Bloomfield's leadership, AIPAC had fought a no-holds-barred struggle against the sale of AWACS reconnaissance planes to the Saudis; but when this new larger sale was announced, the organization confined itself to a tepid declaration that it would "oppose" rather than "fight" it—a crucial terminological difference in the world of lobbying. Believing that AIPAC's lack of opposition reflected its attempt to win favor with the Bush administration, congressional opponents of the arms deal deliberately kept AIPAC out of its strategy sessions for fear that it would leak their plans to the administration. After pro-Israel Democrats had forced the administration to postpone $14 billion of the $21 billion sale, one congressional staff member involved in the fight described AIPAC's lobbying as "minimal."

The results of the war seemed, however, to vindicate Rosen and AIPAC's Republicans. Not only did the administration succeed in destroying Israel's most dangerous enemy; Bush's success, combined with initial Democratic opposition to the use of force, virtually assured the president's reelection in 1992 and perhaps laid the groundwork for the Republicans to capture the Senate. At AIPAC's policy conference on March 17–20, the organization's representatives once again paraded their close ties to the administration.

But AIPAC and organized Jewry could eventually suffer from their dependence on the administration's good will. As Iraq disintegrates after the war, pro-Israel organizations are already under pressure to acquiesce in the survival of Iraq's Baathist party, and perhaps of Saddam himself—a possibility that deeply concerns war supporters like Ann Lewis, who now says she is "disappointed, but not surprised" by the administration's tilt toward the Iraqi leadership.

The real crunch will come, however, in negotiations with the Israelis. If the Bush administration and Israel once again find themselves with swords drawn—as seems very possible, given the Shamir government's determination to avoid any territorial concessions—then AIPAC and other Jewish organizations will once again be caught in the middle.

The ties between the Jewish leadership and Saudi and Kuwaiti representatives in Washington that were created during the war could also prove as perilous as they now appear promising. These ties were largely initiated by Saudi Prince Bandar. From August to the war's end, Bandar held meetings with representatives from the Simon Wiesenthal Center in Los Angeles, the American Jewish Congress, and AIPAC. He consulted regularly with Jewish Democrats on Capitol Hill, including Solarz and Levine.

In January, he invited three well-known Jewish policy experts—Indyk from the AIPAC-linked Washington Institute for Near East Policy, Michael Mandelbaum from the Council on Foreign Relations, and Elliot Cohen from the Johns Hopkins School of Advanced International Studies—to inspect the Saudi military. "It was a remarkable departure," Cohen said. "The Saudis had never looked favorably on Jewish intellectuals."

The Saudis wanted something from these overtures; and the Jewish organizations and policy experts expected something in return. The Saudis were immediately interested in Jewish backing for war against Iraq but, according to Arab sources, they also wanted to neutralize opposition to future arms sales from the U.S. The Jews who met with the Saudis expected that after the war, the Saudis and Kuwaitis would make significant gestures toward normalizing relations with Israel—dropping the secondary boycott of firms that do business with Israel and perhaps also exchanging military information. "What we were told by Prince Bandar was that as long as Saddam Hussein effected hegemony over the Middle East, no movement on the Palestinian issue was possible," American Jewish Congress Director Henry Siegman explained. By Siegman's account, Prince Bandar implied that "if Saddam Hussein is no longer, most countries would then approach the issue on pragmatic terms."

In the first weeks after the war, Jewish activists and intellectuals waxed eloquent on Bandar's role and on the prospects of peace between Israel and the Gulf states. Indyk told the Presidents Conference meeting in Washington that the Saudis "are now in a position to lend support to an American-led [peace] process, and I believe they are prepared to do so. They talk in realistic terms about Israel." Perle praised the "wise" and "remarkable" Bandar as one of the four people most responsible for the war's success.

But Jewish intellectuals and organizations could come out on the short end of this Saudi relationship. The Saudis got major Jewish backing for the war effort, but when Secretary of State James Baker met with the Saudis after the war, he was not able to extract any concessions from them on improved relations with Israel. Afterwards, the American Jewish Congress took out a full-page ad in the *New York Times* urging the Arab members of the coalition to "seize the moment," but implicitly, as Siegman admitted, expressing its disappointment with the Saudi response to Baker. Afterwards, Doug Bloomfield, now a columnist for *Washington Jewish Week,* was skeptical about the Saudi relationship. "If there is a sea change, it is still low tide," he said.

In the months to come, pro-Israeli organizations will be watching for signs of a public thaw in the Saudi attitude toward Israel. The Saudis will be looking to see whether the pro-Israel organizations will merely "oppose" or will "fight" the remaining $14 billion Saudi arms deal that the administration is putting before Congress. Such a sale could once again accelerate the arms race in the region, making it necessary for Israel, already weighted down by enormous arms expenditures, to increase its spending. And of course a new infusion of arms into the region could make possible the rise of a new Saddam. Yet pro-Israel organizations that now depend on their links to the Bush administration and hope for a breakthrough from the Saudis will be sorely tempted to give the Saudis what they want.

In the wake of Operation Desert Storm's success, Jewish Democrats who backed the use of force were vindicated, while those legislators who had opted for sanctions rather than force felt threatened by reprisals both from voters and from political action committees. In the weeks following the vote, two House members from New York, Chuck Schumer and Nita Lowey, faced serious revolts in their district from Jewish constituents. And there were hints of retribution from pro-Israel PACs. In March, the largest pro-Israel PAC, NATPAC (National Political Action Committee), run by former AIPAC director Morris Amitay, sent out a newsletter to contributors listing those House and Senate members who had voted for the use of force. In response to these political threats, some legislators have recanted. Schumer—whose tenth district in Brooklyn may be redistricted into Solarz's thirteenth in the next election—held a meeting in his district with Jewish activists who were threatening to demonstrate at a March awards dinner where Schumer was going to be honored. Schumer told them that he had made a mistake in voting against the Solarz–Michel resolution.

Jewish Democrats who voted against the use of force also have rushed to sponsor legislation that would endear them to the PACs. Lowey cosponsored a nonbinding "sense of Congress" resolution opposing U.S. pressure to get Israel to give up ground on the Palestinian issue. Schumer sent a letter to Bush urging him to "place official recognition of Israel by the members of the Arab League at the top of your agenda for peace in the Middle East." Such efforts could undermine the Bush administration's attempt to create "two-track" negotiations between Arabs and Israelis and between Palestinians and Israelis, by giving priority, as the Shamir government does, to the Arab-Israeli negotiating track.

Out of these conflicting efforts could come three very different kinds of results. The most unlikely is that the administration's two-track effort could bear fruit in agreements between both the Arab coalition states and Israel and the Palestinians and Israel. In that case, AIPAC, Bush, and Bandar will have earned the world's gratitude, and Jewish Democrats can stop looking over their shoulder at the PACs. But more likely are two messier scenarios.

In the first, Israel would gain recognition from the Gulf states without making any significant concessions to the Palestinians. In that case, Israel would become another emirate, albeit one with an unusually large ruling class, presiding over an alien majority. Such a result would deeply trouble mainstream Jewish organizations, most of whose members bear little affection for Likud's revanchist aims. In addition, this scenario would probably unravel within a few years as the Palestinians regroup and leadership changes occur in the Gulf. Most likely, perhaps, is that this administration initiative will prove no more successful in gaining peace than the 1989 Baker plan. If that happens, whatever sense of triumph Jewish organizations felt after the war will become a dim memory. With Congress pushing solidly in one direction, the Bush administration in another, and AIPAC torn between the two, Washington's Jewish community will be as anguished and disarrayed as it was prior to the war.

Jews who were active in both the Left and in Jewish organizations have even more reason to fear for the future. In the war's aftermath, they find themselves as alienated from the American Left as they are from Israel's right-wing government. They don't suffer from dual loyalty but dual alienation. At the Friends of Peace Now conference in Washington on February 28, these left-wing Jews consoled themselves with the argument that the Shamir government is out of touch with the real inclinations of the Israeli people—an argument that American leftists, with equal lack of merit, used to make about the Reagan administration's relationship to the American people.

But besides worrying about the revitalization and growth of the Israeli Left, these Jewish intellectuals and activists also have to fret about the American Left. Indeed, they have to decide whether they are still part of it. Will they, like the neoconservative refugees of the Six Day War, abandon the Left entirely to the avatars of 1960s-style anti-imperialism, or will they seek to rebuild it into a movement that can speak to the promise as well as perfidy that Americans see in their country? □

Our Problems with the Antiwar Movement

Michael Lerner

Though any antiwar movement would have had an extremely difficult time successfully opposing this war, the actual antiwar movement that emerged managed to cripple itself far more than it needed to. Suffused with what I call "surplus powerlessness," this movement managed to marginalize itself and alienate many of those who wanted to be part of it.

The most obvious difficulty was that the antiwar movement tried to fit the complex realities of the 1990s into the categories of the 1960s. Saddam Hussein is no Ho Chi Minh nor even a Daniel Ortega. We were dealing with a cynical dictator and mass murderer—and the task of the antiwar movement was to find a way to convince Americans that containment and blockade would be preferable to bombings and ground war.

The 1960s-style demand to "Bring the Troops Home Now"—like the music of "We Shall Overcome" or "Give Peace a Chance"—does not fit for the 1990s. Saddam Hussein and the Iraqi military that he symbolizes are an evil force that deserve to be stopped. The majority of those who opposed this war opposed it because it was the wrong means to achieve the end of stopping him. U.S. troops should have been gradually phased out, and replaced by a UN army—the U.S. should not have been the primary policeman of the world. But there does need to be a policeman.

We in the *Tikkun* community are not in the habit of crying "anti-Semitism" at the drop of a hat. All too frequently it is we who are being accused of being self-hating Jews because we are critical of Israel's occupation of the West Bank. Our support for the creation of a demilitarized Palestinian state and for the convening of an international conference to resolve all the conflicts of the Middle East, including the Israeli-Palestinian issue, puts us in opposition to many Jewish organizations. We are very wary of those who see an anti-Semite behind every criticism of Israel. But it is precisely *Tikkun* readers who are reporting the unmistakable presence of anti-Semitism. Among the reports:

• Speakers at peace rallies who have nothing bad to say about Saddam Hussein but who spend all their time excoriating the Israeli occupation of the West Bank. We oppose the Occupation too—and we single it out from among all the unjust policies in all the world's countries to criticize, because this is a Jewish issue. But when we go to a rally in the larger world and hear Israel being singled out, we want to know why. It's no defense for those who single out Israel to say, "Israel really is doing something wrong in the West Bank." To see why this is no defense, consider how you would react if at each rally some speakers were to talk about Black crimes and Black murders in the ghetto, and how destructive this is for American society. Now, the truth is that there are plenty of Black crimes and Black murders—but there are also plenty of white crimes and white murderers. So if you selectively focus on one group, you can be doing so in a racist manner even if what you say is true. Thus, when Jews attend antiwar demonstrations in which speakers list the "crimes" of Israel but fail to list the crimes of Syria, Iraq, Jordan, Turkey, Iran or Saudi Arabia, we begin to suspect that we are being scapegoated.

This editorial appeared in Tikkun, *March/April 1991.*

• Demonstrators at protests with posters that say "Israel is the real problem" or "Zionism kills" or "Stop Jewish power" or "Israel is worse than Iraq."

• Speakers at teach-ins who talk about the "crimes of Zionism" and who then move on to talk about "Jewish reporters" who distort the news and "Jewish power in Congress."

• Distribution of literature from classic anti-Semitic texts—reappearing at literature tables of "anti-imperialist" and Black nationalist and groups.

• Speakers who unfairly argue that Saddam's power-grab in Kuwait is analogous to Israel's occupation of the West Bank. Though the Occupation is unjust, it is motivated by a fear of surrounding Arab states who wish to destroy Israel; while Saddam's invasion of Kuwait was not motivated by security considerations.

• Listing of Palestinians as "people of color" while excluding their Semitic Jewish brethren from this category.

• Listing oppressed groups but never mentioning Jews, thereby obliterating from collective memory the fact that one of every three Jews alive in the twentieth century was murdered because of anti-Jewish racism.

Many leftists don't notice the problem, because they think that all they are doing is voicing legitimate criticism of Israel. Yet the left-wing analysis of Israel tries to force it into the category of "colonial oppressor"—a category that is ahistorical and misses the inner political reality of the Occupation: the majority of those who vote for the Right in Israel are Sephardic Jews who fled from Arab states where they were a persecuted minority. The Left likes to pretend that Israelis are merely taking their paranoid fears from the Holocaust and unfairly applying them to the Palestinian people. In fact, the Palestinians have always insisted that they are part of the Arab people—and it is precisely this Arab people who have a long history of racism toward Blacks and anti-Semitism toward Jews. This history meant that for more than a thousand years Jews lived in oppressive conditions; and when they finally fled the Arab states and moved to Israel they brought with them a deep-seated antagonism toward Arabs that has made them vote against the peace movement and for the Occupation. Over and over again they will tell you, "I lived with the Arabs, and I know that they only respect force. If you show them any weakness, they will walk all over you."

I disagree with the Sephardic Jews on the Israeli Right, and I don't think that the conclusions that some draw from their own experience ought to be legitimated. But this is also why I oppose Farrakhan and Black Nationalists of his stripe—because even though Blacks have been oppressed in this country by whites, I don't think it appropriate to generalize that experience to a distrust of all whites. But neither would I turn around and say something like, "These Blacks who support Farrakhan are nothing but racists." The fact is that their feelings derive from a long history of oppression. I think that most people on the Left can understand this about Blacks—but they refuse to see how it may also be true of the majority of those who support the Israeli Right—the refugees and children of refugees from Arab lands.

The failure to tell the truth about reality is deep in the soul of the Left. This is in part because the anti-Semitism in this society and throughout the world is so deep that the Left has been willing to recognize the national liberation struggles of every other people, but has refused to recognize Zionism—the national liberation struggle of the Jews.

And one of the reasons for this refusal has been Jews within the Left, many of whom have internalized the society's anti-Semitism and who desperately try to show their non-Jewish friends how un-Jewish they really are. This internalized anti-Semitism is widespread among all Jews. We've tried to look like non-Jews, shaved our beards or had nose jobs or straightened our hair or adopted the right clothes or tried to endlessly exercise so that our bodies fit the models of the WASPs who are the standards of beauty. Over and over again Jews have tried to show that we really aren't too

Jewish—that we can be polite and not talk loud and not be pushy and not be too much into our heads or too intellectual: "Now, will you love us please; now will you please not push us into concentration camps?" And this is what happened to many Jews who are on the Left—they know nothing about the details of Jewish history, they know nothing of the classics of their own tradition, they know nothing of the great languages and literatures of their people—instead they are doing their best to convince everyone that they can be more tough on the Jews and on Israel than anyone else can. What perfect cover these Jews provide for the anti-Semitism in the Left—so no one on the Left has ever to ask about the specific form of oppression against Jews. They can say to themselves, as people on the Left frequently do, "The Jews are all right—after all, they have financial security." Of course, if you took that argument and said to women, "Those of you who have relative economic security, those of you who have been born into middle-class families and will get middle class jobs—stop complaining," everyone would understand what was wrong with that, because sexism doesn't just work through economic oppression: it's a whole cultural system. But so is anti-Semitism. The economic security of Jews in Germany in the 1930s did nothing to protect them. The fact is that the way Jews are oppressed is not primarily economic—though there are hundreds of thousands of poor Jews and most Jews are neither rich nor powerful.

Jews have been betrayed by the Left throughout most of the twentieth century. This issue seemed less pressing to us in the 1960s when Israel seemed secure and there was a need for a unified struggle against the outrages of the U.S. in Vietnam. But it can no longer be ignored in the 1990s when some people on the Left are blaming Israel and the Jews for the war, or suggesting that it was Jewish power that influenced the U.S. to enter the war, or that it was love for Israel that shaped U.S. policy. The truth is, as I've argued above, that this war is a disaster for Israel and for the Jews. And a majority of Jews in the Congress voted against taking the military path.

But though the war may be a disaster for Jews, the antiwar movement may also be a disaster if it does not consciously, publicly, and unequivocally engage in a struggle against the anti-Semitism that has recently emerged in its ranks. No wonder, then, that Jews are feeling deeply ambivalent, both about the war and about the antiwar movement.

There may be one very salutary development that emerges out of this: a recognition of the need for a new and deeper exploration of our Jewishness on the part of many liberal and progressive Jews who have thought that this side of our being could have a lower priority. Jewishness is once again in question. We need a new consciousness-raising movement for Jewish liberals similar to that which accompanied the second wave of the women's movement of the late 1960s. Liberal Jews need to join small groups that meet each week to explore the problems we face in a society where anti-Semitism comes at us from both the Right and the Left. And in those groups, we need to begin to rethink our own lives, and come to a deeper understanding of how the particulars of our lives have been shaped by the fact that we are Jews living in a world where forces hostile to Jews still exercise considerable power. It is just such a process that might provide us with the internal clarity and strength to help deepen the perspective of the current antiwar movement and make it more credible to Jews and non-Jews alike. □

The Dynamics of Anti-Semitism on the Left

Cherie Brown

The oppression of Jews manifests itself in two ways. The first is more widely understood: specific acts of scapegoating Jews. We all know about the overt acts, the bombing and burning of synagogues, the acts of violence against Jews, the discrimination against Jews. But there is another way that we are oppressed that is more subtle, but nevertheless equally vicious. Jews occupy some highly visible positions in public life that make them appear to be economically or politically powerful, though in fact by and large we are not. We are in positions where, by the nature of the jobs, we exert daily control over the lives of more visibly oppressed groups. We are not the owners of the corporations, but we are the managers, the lawyers, the doctors, the teachers, the social workers who staff large corporate and governmental bureaucracies. And we are the shopkeepers of small- and medium-sized businesses. The particular jobs that Jews hold are ones that give us the appearance of power or control over more visibly oppressed groups—and they resent us instead of the people who hold the real power. Jews are sometimes the ones who stick out, and this provides a focus for antagonism that might otherwise be directed at the real oppressors. When groups who are hurting, particularly economically, look for someone to oppose, they often turn against Jews.

Jews really have an invisible "loose noose" around their necks: Jews have more economic and political mobility than many other oppressed groups, so it doesn't look like we are oppressed. But the invisibility of our oppression is central to keeping us in this place. Every Jewish person fears that when times get tight it is possible that Jews will become scapegoats again. So most Jews carry inside feelings of terror and insecurity, and fears of imminent betrayal.

We Jews often push ourselves to function on top of the layer of terror. When some groups get scared, they become paralyzed. But when Jews are scared, we build five new organizations. Fear propels us into constant new activity and busyness—this is our particular survival strategy. Unfortunately it's very difficult to maintain fresh, creative thinking and responses when there is still so much fear propelling our thinking.

This survival strategy differs from that which others adopt when facing internalized oppression and fear. I saw this once when working with two Dutch women, one a working-class Catholic raised on a farm, the other a Jewish survivor of the Holocaust. Both decided they wanted to learn how to dive. The Jewish woman immediately went to the diving board and dove off; the Catholic woman required two weeks at the pool before she was willing to go to the diving board. Then one day, long after the Catholic woman was secure enough to dive, the Jewish woman got to the edge of the board and froze in terror. She hadn't overcome her terror just by acting as though she weren't scared. It was only after the Catholic woman felt more secure that the Jewish woman could risk feeling her own fears.

Cherie Brown is the executive director of the National Coalition-Building Institute in Arlington, Massachusetts. This article appeared in Tikkun, *March/April 1991.*

This is what happens to Jews. Our fears are still there. They show up in insomnia, in asthma, in overeating, in a failure to take good care of ourselves, in a drivenness to constant activity—all rooted in a deep terror. And living with that fear—and the crippling impact it sometimes has on our lives—is part of the way that Jews are oppressed. The worst part of it for many Jews, particularly progressive Jews active in social change movements, is that there is so much denial of any real anti-Semitism that we end up believing these difficulties are just individual problems—we don't know to connect these difficulties to less visible forms of institutionalized anti-Semitism being directed at us.

These dynamics have a big impact on how Jews act in the political arena. Many Jews find themselves having to choose between two different ways to live. They either choose a life built primarily on the theme that, "I'm for everybody else, I'm a humanitarian"—and embedded in this form of self-presentation is a great deal of shame about being Jewish, which leads people to take on everybody else's struggles and *not* Jewish struggles. Or they choose a life of being visibly Jewish, proud of being Jewish, and living a life predominantly with Jews, though all too often isolated from deep relationships with other groups. Most Jews are on a continuum somewhere between these two poles. These choices have dramatic consequences for how Jews function in the public arena.

There are plenty of Jews active in the leadership of progressive movements, but they are not there *as* Jews. As a result, the Jewish commitment to those struggles becomes invisible to other people in those movements. Internalized anti-Semitism often limits our ability to be effective in political work. I have yet to meet a Jewish person (even those who lead actively Jewish lives) who does not carry somewhere inside an internal recording of self-disgust, deriving from hundreds of years in which the world has said to us: "There's something so wrong with you that you don't deserve to exist," and now, "You don't deserve a homeland." Those messages *do* get internalized, even in those who are proudly Jewish. One way that this disgust gets manifested is in not taking care of ourselves and our bodies, because at some deep level we don't see ourselves as precious beings. And we don't always have the courage to take care of each other or of the Jewish people.

Every oppressed group internalizes the record of its oppression and turns against members of its own group, particularly those who in any way behave according to stereotype. Some Jews will turn against Jews because they aren't "good enough Jews"; others will turn against Jews who act "too pushy" or "too assertive." Jews who more visibly show their fears tend to generate a lot more disgust or withdrawal from other Jews. I've listened to some Israelis, for example, who pride themselves on being strong Israelis who express contempt for Jews who look or act "like Holocaust survivors." It seems to be too painful for many of us to stay close to each other when we see the scars of the oppression etched in each other's behaviors. We can be highly critical of one another, holding each other to the same perfectionist standard that the world holds us to.

Rarely do Jews get praised by each other for the work that they do. We are good at pointing out the negative and forgetting to express the appreciations. Instead, we abandon each other or viciously attack one another—particularly when a Jew or small group of Jews tries to do something new or courageous. Our fears about security are enormous—so we attack those who try new directions or those who take courageous stands for fear that they will endanger all of us. However, none of these responses are our fault; they stem from a long history of anti-Semitism. We need to get rid of all these manifestations of internalized anti-Semitism, but we also need to be gentle with each other—even when we are acting out the internalized oppression.

Complicating all this, making it all the harder for us to build alliances is this: It's difficult for many Jews to relax enough to allow deep closeness to develop. Jews have historically been kept separate from the world, and have become used to feeling isolated from others. Even though the initial experience of isolation may have been with non-Jews, this isolation also gets internalized and will keep us from building close, trusting bonds with each other. And this sense of isolation often affects family relationships and our ability to have genuine closeness. We love each other, but we don't trust each other. A fear of being abandoned always keeps even the closest relationships from having a deep sense of trust.

Some non-Jews have accused us of being pushy, manipulative, controlling. What they don't understand is that they are seeing our terror and our isolation, not our power. In social change movements and the antiwar movement to date, the whole nature of anti-Semitism and internalized anti-Semitism remains unknown and unchallenged. Anti-Semitism involves *two forces*. Most people understand one or the other, but rarely both. Jews will sometimes participate in the oppression of another group (in Israel, it's the Palestinians) because we have been convinced by outside forces that it is our only path to safety. Then, when we participate in this role of "surrogate oppressor," we get isolated, targeted, attacked, and betrayed. It is not the fault of Jews that this dynamic happens. Throughout history, ruling class interests have set up individual Jews over and over again to be visible oppressors. The only reason Jews have ever agreed to this role was the slim hope of survival—and the oppressors' offer to protect Jews. In this dynamic, the leaders representing the ruling class (Saddam Hussein, for example) are able to use Jews as a convenient scapegoat when they need one. Many leaders within the Jewish community will actively and correctly speak out about Jewish vulnerability and scapegoating but fail to understand and speak against the collusive role that Jews or Jewish leaders have been forced into playing, which contributes to this scapegoating. Many members and leaders of progressive social change movements will actively and correctly identify the collusive role that some Jews (or the Israeli government) play but will fail to understand or speak against the very *real* vulnerability and lack of security for Jews. This isolation pushes Jews further toward the Right. The antiwar movement then sees this alignment with the Right and incorrectly blames Jews even more. And so the cycle continues. The very policies the antiwar movement is striving to achieve will not happen without an active and vigorous policy against anti-Semitism.

The Left likes simple forms of oppression—"good guys" and "bad guys"—so they miss anti-Semitism, which requires a more complex analysis. It is this double dynamic—real, very systematic vulnerability followed by an effort to overcome vulnerability by accommodating to oppressive forces, who are only too willing to let Jews become the more visible oppressors of others. One of the major ways that progressive movements could effectively respond to the Gulf conflict would be for them to make a major commitment to dealing with anti-Semitism in all of its manifestations—because it is precisely this anti-Semitism that Saddam Hussein is seeking to exploit in the war.

Because of our internalized fears, Jews on the Left have had a difficult time requiring the peace movement to deal with anti-Semitism. Since the real dynamics of anti-Semitism are not understood, many Jews do not realize that combating anti-Semitism is not just good for Jews but absolutely necessary for the success of *every* social change movement. Anti-Semitism is not in the interests of Blacks, not in the interests of the labor movement, not in the interests of anyone who really wants to see a transformed world. The way anti-Semitism functions is that these groups come to believe that Jews are the impediment to their own progress—so that they never get to take on the real source of their oppression. Fighting anti-Semitism is really in the interests of all social change movements. None of these social change movements will succeed until they also deal with anti-Semitism.

There can also be enormous despair and discouragement and a fear that we will never have real allies in progressive movements. One way to break that cycle is to act from the assumption that there are allies out there waiting to be reached. They need the information about anti-Semitism just as much as we need them to have it. We need to heal enough of our fear so that when we are at peace events or other social change events we speak out about anti-Semitism. And we need to require that the issue of anti-Semitism be included in the central agendas of all progressive movements.

Jews need to have consciousness-raising sessions just as people did in the women's movement.

We need to identify and heal the internalized messages that keep us scared and then functioning on top of fear (which leaves us open and vulnerable to being targeted). We also need to practice and coach each other to speak up against anti-Jewish policies and statements. We need to coach each other to reach out for allies with confident, powerful voices. And ultimately, we must expect that our allies in social-change movements will themselves speak out against anti-Semitism so that this does *not* fall entirely on Jews. We can do this by making one-to-one friendships in these movements and then by asking our friends to speak out.

The struggle against anti-Semitism in the Left and in the peace movement is a high priority—and should be seen as such by anyone who wishes to build an effective opposition to Bush and his policies. ☐

Drawing by Anthony Dubovsky

II. Culture and Philosophy

תיקון

Looking for Addictions in All the Wrong Places

Michael J. Bader

I am indebted to Ilene Philipson, Ph.D. who carefully reviewed and edited this article.

opular psychology is becoming increasingly addicted to addictions. Robin Norwood's *Women Who Love Too Much* (WWL2M), which has sold over three million copies and spawned numerous imitators (e.g., *Men Who Hate Women and the Women Who Love Them* and *How to Stop Looking For Someone Perfect and Find Someone to Love*), is an important example of this trend. Women who choose unhealthy partners and then can't seem to leave them are "relationship addicts,"according to Norwood, and should be understood and treated according to the same theories used to understand and treat any other addict. Similarly, the increasing public focus on the so-called Adult Child of Alcoholics (ACA) is another attempt to relocate certain psychological problems within the addiction model. In this case, the difficulties of the ACA are said to result from an adaptation to the addictions of a family member. According to Janet Woititz, author of *Adult Children of Alcoholics*, growing up with an alcoholic creates a unique constellation of personality traits and problems that must be treated in a special way—through a program similar to one recommended for an alcoholic.

The model of behavior and treatment that both of these books articulate has clearly struck a chord among large numbers of American laypeople and among many professionals. The National Association of Children of Alcoholics has grown over the last five years from a formal membership of twenty-one to seven thousand. Since the early 1980s, the number of groups of Al-Anon-affiliated children of alcoholics meeting regularly has increased from fourteen to eleven hundred. From Donahue to Oprah, *Newsweek* to the *New York Times*, the media have picked up on the ideas of "co-dependency"and "relationship addiction"and have helped to make them household terms. Suzanne Somers wrote a bestseller about her experiences as an ACA, and Glenn Close became a nightmarish icon of the eighties as a woman "addicted" to Michael Douglas in 1987's top-grossing film, *Fatal Attraction*.

I do not intend to question the claim that the therapeutic approaches advocated by this model—particularly the self-help "recovery" groups—have helped many people. Nevertheless, I wish to examine the psychological and social sources of the popularity of this approach, as well as its limitations. In truth, the addiction model, when applied to psychological and interpersonal problems and traits, contains unexamined assumptions and meanings that block attempts to understand these problems from both social *and* psychological perspectives. At the same time that the model strikes a

---

Michael J. Bader, a candidate and affiliate member of the San Francisco Psychoanalytic Institute and faculty member of the Graduate Psychology Program of New College of California, is in private practice. He is also a member of Tikkun's *editorial board. This article appeared in* Tikkun, *November/December 1988.*

chord in people, it renders attempts at deeper self-knowledge or critical analysis impossible.

The family system that generates the pathological behavior, the relationship addiction, and the masochism of the WWL2M or the ACA is depicted by this literature in a surprisingly uniform fashion. Its salient features may be summarized as follows:

1. Dysfunctional families are those in which the parents don't provide the child with love, nurturance, and respect. These parents are not healthy enough to be good role models for the child, nor can they fulfill their roles as caregivers or as happy marital partners. They are psychologically disabled, usually by addictions of some kind or by other forms of mental illness, and they make unpredictable and narcissistic use of the child, who consequently feels neglected or abused. The parents deny various aspects of reality: Most important, they deny their own addiction, and they invalidate the child's accurate perceptions about that addiction.

2. The child becomes the caregiver in the family, either because s/he is identified as such by the parents or because the parents are just too disabled to be able to care for themselves or others. The child mothers the mother and/or the father and comes to accept guilt and responsibility for the family's problems.

3. The child mistakes being needed for being loved. Moreover, since s/he can never quite solve the family's problems, her or his underlying feeling of being unloved and worthless only intensify. The child then redoubles the efforts to secure love by giving "until it hurts," which escalates the entire process.

4. The child's attempts to "cure" the parents through self-sacrifice, though never successful, are continually elicited by the parents' inappropriate dependence on the child and by the child's underlying need for affirmation. The child gets "hooked" into a no-win situation.

5. These patterns continue into adulthood. People repeat what they experienced as children because it is "familiar," or because, now that they are adults, they want to make it come out right. In other words, repetition is often an attempt at mastery.

6. Specifically, this repetition means that people raised in this kind of family system choose partners and relationships in which their own needs are subordinated to the needs of others, in which they again play the role of the overly responsible caretaker or parent.

7. In repeating their childhood dramas, people once again mistake being needed for being loved and desperately try to change their defective partners into the men or women of their childhood dreams. These attempts, of course, are of no avail and only deepen these people's depression and self-hatred. Their adult relationships, therefore, are exactly like addictions—they use them to escape from depression, but these relationships simply aggravate the original symptoms.

8. These adults are inordinately hard on themselves, self-punitive, and often driven, because they believe that their misery and self-sacrifice will be rewarded with love and approval and will make up for the faults and deficiencies of their loved ones.

9. Many of these adults become alcoholics or substance abusers because of a combination of heredity, imitation, and/or an intense need for relief from anxiety and depression. They then begin this process anew when they start their own families.

These are the portraits of family life and the resulting psychological conflicts that fill the pages of this literature. Readers repeatedly identify with various parts of these characterizations and consequently adopt the underlying explanatory addiction/disease model as well.

Their conclusion is not warranted, however. The process by which a child responds to a depressed or addicted parent—by becoming a caretaker, for instance—is complex and multidimensional. One outcome might be the kind of masochism that Norwood and Woititz focus on, but other adaptations are equally frequent. The child might defensively retreat from any kind of dependency at all, thereby making future relationships difficult. For example, a woman might develop a disdain for men that masks her underlying disappointment and choose men who justify her low opinion of the opposite sex. She might become depressed like her parent(s) and withdraw from the romantic arena altogether. If the family environment is disturbed enough, she might even become psychotic.

Furthermore, since the dysfunctional family is described in these books in such general terms, it is likely that even people with relatively healthy, nonaddictive relationships could relate to some of this picture. Who hasn't felt constrained by loyalty to or guilt about one's family? And yet many of us *don't* have romantic lives dominated by pathological addictions. How are we to account for this fact?

The point is that a number of different interpretations of, and "solutions" to, the problems presented by this dysfunctional family portrait are completely ignored. The literature's narrow approach leads the reader to conclude falsely that s/he has an "addiction," which therefore should be treated as recommended. Rather than engaging in further analysis, the reader has a kind of "aha!" experience that involves locating him- or herself within this formal addiction framework. Yet shouldn't one attempt to understand and treat a psychotic Glenn Close differently from a neurotic, guilt-ridden woman who masochistically hangs on to men who are using her?

The treatment process referred to in this literature is often called "recovery" in order to keep it within the addiction framework. The goal is "abstinence,"and the backbone of any treatment program is some kind of support group, the purpose of which is to allow the addict to share common problems, decrease isolation, increase insight about different aspects of the disease, and begin to stop the compulsive behavior "one day at a time." The addict attempts to correct each compulsive trait, using the group or a therapist as support, until the new, healthier behavior or thought patterns take hold and become firmly implanted. So, for instance, Norwood's relationship addicts are advised to put their own well-being, desires, and needs *first* and not last in a relationship; to recognize their intrinsic self-worth; and to "learn" to tolerate other people's anger and disapproval. Woititz suggests that her ACA readers correct their inability to have fun by changing their behavior, by planning "fun" time in their daily schedule, and by getting in touch with the child in themselves.

Furthermore, both authors emphasize the importance of group support for these changes and minimize the role of individual insight. The group provides a completely accepting atmosphere in which to share experiences with others who (one assumes) have lived in similar family systems and have similar problems. The assumption is that insofar as individual or depth psychotherapy may be helpful, the therapist must be specially trained in working with addicts and their co-dependents and must work in conjunction with some kind of group program. In any case, the parallel to physical addictions is explicit: The goal is to stop addictive behavior, and the method is to break through the denial, identify the problem, and abstain from the behavior.

I have found from my experience as a psychotherapist that the idea that children in dysfunctional families parented their parents and *continue* to do so as adults with their defective partners—at the cost of their own gratification—is what resonates most clearly with the average reader. The experience of being self-destructively attached to an unsatisfying partner is apparently a common problem in our culture, and this literature purports to explain and provide a way to correct it. The permission or even injunction to "take care of yourself first" can feel liberating to someone crippled by guilt and by the need to deny one's needs in order to protect or take care of others. To be supported in one's self-assertion by a group can be even more freeing. And the disease model itself is liberating, since it is based on the premise that the ACA or relationship addict is not at fault. The reader or client is a victim of a dysfunctional family over which s/he has no control. After all, the parents have a disease, so the children naturally and automatically pick "it" up.

Many people report that their lives improve greatly as a result of being part of these groups. Unfortunately, however, the fact that a treatment can relieve suffering is no guarantee that the analysis of the disorder is correct or that the method of treatment is even the "best" approach to that suffering. Astrology might relieve Nancy Reagan's anxiety about her husband's safety, but that doesn't imply that world events are influenced by the heavens or that a better solution might not lie in the real world of politics.

Since the addiction model places the blame on the "dysfunctional family"—an abstraction, really, without actual human culprits—or on parents crippled by a disease over which they have no control, it is unable make sense of the deeper social or psychological causes of familial dysfunction. Moreover, this model is only partially accurate—correct in some of its descriptions, but lacking in any analysis of the complex social, historical, and psychological influences that shape the families in question and that account for their "dysfunction." It fails to address questions of deeper social cause or meaning because addiction is a self-contained concept that requires no further analysis. One has a disease, and the goal is to cure it. One is considered to be addicted to a sadistic person because one's family was dysfunctional, or one's mother was depressed or an alcoholic. No further explanation of a mother's depression or alcoholism is required. The social theorist is blocked from examining society, the psychotherapist from examining the intrapsychic life of the patient, and the patient from doing both.

But the social theorist knows, for instance, that parents'—particularly mothers'—narcissistic use of their children has complex social and historical roots. Psychoanalytically oriented social theorists have suggested, for example, that changes in post-World War II America—changes that isolated women in nuclear families, cut them off from kinship networks and productive work roles, and celebrated their primary responsibility as child-rearers—framed and facilitated maternal over-investment in children. Lives that were emptied of *social* meaning became filled with a preoccupation with mothering. As kinship networks and household size shrank, the importance of the primary mother-child bond was increasingly sanctified in professional journals as well as in popular culture. The exclusion of women from the work force and their isolation in insulated nuclear families were justified on the grounds that such exclusion and isolation were the fulfillment of women's true nature and of their roles as the sole guarantors of their babies' proper development. The quiet lives of desperation described by Betty Friedan in *The Feminine Mystique* were in part the consequence of the fifties' celebration of female domesticity. The undercurrents of dissatisfaction, frustration, and self-blaming are eloquently described by one woman whom Friedan interviewed:

> I ask myself why I'm so dissatisfied. I've got my health, fine children, a lovely new home, enough money. My husband has a real future as an electronics engineer. He doesn't have any of these feelings.... I can't sit down and read a book alone. If the children are napping and I have one hour to myself I just walk through the house waiting for them to wake up.

This woman is a prototype for the mothers of women who love too much and the alcoholic mothers of the ACA. Similar changes in social life, including the rise of bureaucratic forms of the modern corporation, deeply affected the lives of fathers and the gender asymmetries and antagonisms in these men's marital relationships. The fifties' "organization man's" anxieties concerning bureaucratic work, his declining authority in the family, and the social and media images of threatened masculinity were stimulated and reinforced by these historical changes. The idealized vision of male authority, captured by Robert Young in "Father Knows Best," was undermined by and in tension with images of the anxious and emasculated male, as seen in such figures as Dagwood Bumstead and Ralph Kramden. Anxieties about being judged on the basis of one's personality rather than skill on the job—a vulnerability captured then by Phillip Riesman in *The Lonely Crowd* and more recently by Richard Sennett in *The Fall of Public Man*—were reinforced by a subtle undermining of paternal authority in the home and in child rearing. Many different social and psychological responses to these anxieties have been described (see, for example, Barbara Ehrenreich's analysis of the Playboy Philosophy in *The Hearts of Men*). The fathers of WWL2M and ACAs often retreated into depression, work, or alcoholism, and some of them became abusive in a variety of ways. While the particular form of response depended primarily on the idiosyncratic psychology of the father, the underlying pressures were often the same.

I am not attempting to propose a social or historical theory that accounts completely for relationship addictions. Rather, I am sketching the kinds of social and historical pressures that have shaped the dysfunctional family. This complex interaction cannot

Drawing by Noga Wizansky

be analyzed under the addiction model, since under the addiction model the social world is ignored, much as a doctor may ignore the pathogenic primacy of the environment when s/he is trying to heal a patient. Ignoring these factors, is not only narrow-minded clinically, but also scientifically incorrect—as research into the relationships between stress, the immune system, and transmission of disease demonstrates. And, even more than viruses, psychological traits are intrinsically psychosocial. A child who represses her or his own needs for nurturance in order to care narcissistically for an alcoholic parent is attempting to heal a social and psychological injury. That child does not acquire a disease. S/he participates in a relationship designed to restore the illusion of parental care and love, and s/he attempts to cope with the parent's disability—a disability that has broad social and economic, as well as psychological, dimensions. In order to understand fully how so many children have become "parentified," one has to examine the social conditions that facilitate this perversion of the parent-child relationship. The children described by Woititz and Norwood, by attempting to "fix" their "addicted" parents, are actually attempting to "fix" people who have deformed themselves and been deformed in relation to a sick social world.

A *psychological* theory about the deforming effects of society is not obligated, of course, to account also for the underlying social factors themselves. Nevertheless, a psychological theory should not be *incompatible* with such a broader analysis. Modern medicine can valuably study the effects of a virus on a particular cell, but its theories of how and why the cell is changed shouldn't be incompatible with what we know about the immune system. Similarly, one's psychological explanatory concepts should elucidate the subjective dimension of a problem in a way that complements and enriches the social dimension—and vice versa. The addiction model fails to play this role, since a disease model is intrinsically ahistorical and asocial. The dialectical tension between one's inner desires and needs and the social world is lost in a theory that views problems such as masochism and dependency simply as symptoms of an illness.

The explanatory account of addictive relationships is superficial and flawed not only in its social dimension, but also in its psychological understanding. A deeper analysis of the so-called ACA or WWL2M profile reveals a more complex picture than the one presented by Norwood and Woititz. It has become clear to me from my clinical experience with patients who fit the profile of relationship addicts that the kind of self-sacrifice that the ACA and relationship-addict literature highlights can and usually does have numerous etiologies. The child may mother her mother in order not to experience her hatred for her mother, her wish to separate from her mother, or her profound disappointment in her mother's weakness. She may feel guilty about a secret and selfish wish that her mother die so that she, the daughter, can get on with her life; and she may deal with this wish through an overcompensating solicitousness or self-denial. She may, as Norwood herself admits, "parent" the mother in order to defend against uncomfortable sexual feelings. She may settle for being needed because being loved represents a triumph of symbolic parricide (about which she feels guilty), or a threatening separation. The point is that there are many layers of desire and fantasy, many sentiments that the traits described are designed to deny, repress, or otherwise ward off. We have darker sides for which we feel deeply culpable, ways of being or desiring that we unconsciously associate with danger—to ourselves and/or our loved ones—and for which we feel profound responsibility.

The ACA and WWL2M literature has a way of flattening out childhood experience, of referring to vague "needs" for love, nurturance, and respect that then somehow get perverted. It doesn't address childhood passions, primitive aggressions, grandiosity, exhibitionism, contempt, and the urge to separate—feelings that the ACA and WWL2M may feel guilty about and that often lie at the heart of the self-destructive behavior that we as clinicians see. For instance, at some point in early development, the child confronts the limits of her or his own power and influence. S/he becomes aware of the fact that others have lives of their own that s/he cannot completely control. Such a discovery, though it marks a developmental achievement, can be traumatic for the child, constituting what in psychoanalytic theory is called a narcissistic injury. Commonly, the child reacts with rage, among other emotions. Eventually the child comes to confront the imperfection of the parents as well, which can also be traumatic. The child may react to this disappointment with contempt, and s/he may devalue the parents. These feelings—rage, disappointment, contempt, and devaluation— are frequently so extreme that the child worries that they might damage or disrupt the relationship with the parents.

When the feelings and danger are great enough, symptoms result. So, for example, the patient might become self-abnegating in order to protect the loved one from her or his own disappointment and contempt. The child—and later the adult—*knows* that s/he has secret wishes to enslave the other, to get revenge for feeling helpless, to devalue others so as not to be disappointed in them. Patients unconsciously "know" what they feel, even though they don't always know why they feel it; and being told that they *really* desire quite reasonable and valid things can offer only a temporary respite from guilt and anxiety. The addiction-model literature too quickly and superficially exonerates the child within us without appreciating the deeper ways that we feel like criminals. It is simply not enough to tell people that feeling responsible and guilty is unnecessary or destructive. The childhood theories of cause and effect, the early experiences of guilt for powerful passions and fantasies, and the absolute dependence of the child on the parent cannot be corrected by cognitive rehearsal, injunctions to take care of oneself, or group permission and encouragement to be autonomous. Instead, these interventions often run up against the wall of deeply unconscious guilt, which is frequently exacerbated by a demonstration of support and kindness. Every clinician knows that simply telling a masochist that s/he is good and not bad often only heightens the masochist's inner feelings of unworthiness. Such encouragement misses the boat because it doesn't connect with the person's actual subjective experience. After all, the principal sentiment underlying unconscious guilt is that one doesn't *deserve* to be loved or told that one is essentially normal and good. The addiction models are not able to comprehend this resistance because their analysis of the cause of the problem is at the level of behavior, habit, and conscious thought patterns.

Just as the addiction model inappropriately exonerates the child, thereby offering short-term relief from guilt while leaving untouched deeper feelings of badness, it also, ironically, exonerates the parents and again offers its devotees a superficial and easy way out of an intolerable psychological dilemma. The parents, after all, are victims of a disease themselves; and, although the WWL2M and the ACA are taught on the one hand to put the blame back on the parents, they are told on the other hand that no one in the family can be blamed since the entire system is in the grips of a pathological process that nobody can control. It is easiest for the child to believe that the parents were ultimately helpless in their sadism, neglect, or extreme narcissism, since the most frightening reality the child may be frantically trying to deny is that the parental hatred, neglect, or narcissism were real and intentional. Saying "of course your father beat you; he was an alcoholic,"or "of course your mother seemed to barely know you were alive; she was drunk half the time and during the other half was denying it," has the subtle effect of suggesting that somehow the child's parents couldn't "help" it and therefore, in their heart of hearts, couldn't have really meant it. Such a claim is extremely relieving to "the child within" for whom the reality of the parental hatred or egocentrism is intolerable. The addiction literature thus supports our defensive need to distort certain realities.

But the relief that this literature provides is not the same as really curing us. It rarely does the trick because we unconsciously know better. We unconsciously "know" that our injuries as children were often intended by parents who *really* used or abused us, however much we might labor to deny it.

A more subtle version of the same maneuver runs something like this: "Your parents hated you, not because you were really bad or because they were intrinsically evil, but because they were victims of a destructive social order." I would argue that this message also reinforces denial. At the hypothetical moment when one would have to face the terror and pain of remembering and experiencing one's parents' real hatred, one conveniently "understands" the parent as a cipher expressing a social and thus more anonymous form of attack or neglect. The switch to a social analysis, much like the switch to a view of parent-as-addict, might be factually or theoretically correct, but it is still *used* as a way to get someone off the hook. Placing responsibility on the social order can at certain moments be as pathological as falsely blaming oneself for what is really a social problem. After all, our parents were no more imprisoned by their social world or their addictions than we are. They had at least some small area of choice and freedom within which they could have resisted their conditioning. And we as children intuitively understand this fact, and therefore we secretly resist, even while manifestly welcoming, any theory that makes our families—or ourselves—completely innocent.

Only a theory that views people as simultaneously responsible agents and socially powerless, as intentional yet conditioned, as making their own history but not under conditions of their own choosing—only such a theory can adequately analyze the causes of problems that the addiction literature addresses. The disease model eventually exonerates everyone, but the cost is theoretical and therapeutic superficiality.

Given this broader and more complex understanding of how and why we feel responsible for our disabled parents, we can see that we repeat this behavior in adult life not simply in order to master it, as Norwood suggests, or merely because it's "learned behavior," as Woititz argues. Rather, ACAs pick alcoholic mates and WWL2M find men with whom they can repeat their childhood "parenting" roles in order to continue to avoid experiencing dangerous childhood feelings and coming to terms with traumatic truths about their loved ones. They feel guilty and responsible in order *not* to feel rage, contempt, disappointment, loss, and separation—all of which are imagined to be (because they once were) overwhelming and intolerable. They sometimes even feel guilty about superficial inadequacies in order *not* to feel *really* guilty about deeper crimes.

One can see, then, how the messages of these books can both facilitate and retard psychological growth. On the one hand, the reader is exonerated from any wrongdoing; permission is given for the emergence of "some" of the warded-off feelings and desires ("It's OK to put yourself number one and to be selfish"). Group support for these changes further dilutes the burdensome sense of individual responsibility. On the other hand, many feelings and wishes for which we feel pathologically responsible either are *not* addressed or are glossed over by this literature. Sadistic wishes to turn the tables on our addicted parents and the realization that our parents might have hated us regardless of their alcoholism are examples of feelings and perceptions that are *not* addressed but that can have powerful psychological impact. People who are dimly aware of such feelings might be temporarily relieved by the focus on the child's and parents' helplessness as well as by the attack on self-blaming contained in this paradigm, but they also often feel misunderstood—or else they eventually reject this approach altogether. The message of this model has to be continually reinforced because often it is secretly not believed.

Finally, the message often can't be fully internalized because it doesn't and can't address the deep *attachment* that people have to their guilt and self-destructiveness. Masochism always involves an attachment to a frustrating or destructive figure and a corresponding compulsion to deny real feelings and perceptions. The explanatory power of psychoanalytic theory comes from its recognition that the child's unique prolonged period of one-sided dependence and attachment to the parent means that all of the child's passions, drives, and fantasies must be shaped in such a way as to maintain this relationship. The danger of losing the other is catastrophic, and all the psychological symptoms that are described by the addiction literature—including masochism, guilt, and distortions of responsibility—must ultimately be understood as compromised ways of maintaining a psychological relationship with the other. For this reason, "giving up" one's addiction is like giving up a friend or a loved one, with the exact same danger—of being alone—looming ominously. The fact that relationship "addicts" feel that they are in the grips of compulsion is often taken at face value by the addiction theorists and not recognized as disguised desire and attachment.

In terms of providing therapy, the effect of this literature and of increased consciousness about addiction has been to create the illusion that a therapist must somehow have special training in treating addicts in order to treat someone with a relationship addiction. Since, according to this model, almost everyone seems to suffer from a "relationship addiction," the implication is that this "specialized" knowledge base should be standard fare in the training of all psychotherapists. Thus, we have an explosion of training seminars, conferences, and workshops that purport to teach the "special" skills needed to work with someone with these kinds of symptoms. Further, since the ACA and WWL2M models encourage the group approach and shorter-term focused therapy, this movement dovetails nicely with the current emphasis in mental health—created primarily by fiscal constraints and by requirements of third-party payers, insurance companies, and the like—on treatment that requires less time and money.

The costs of such an approach are profound, even if they are not instantly obvious. Therapists lose confidence in their ability to treat people they used to think they knew how to treat since they become convinced that these more focused problems require a "specialist." As a result, we see an increase in specialization where the patient is steered to this "expert" on ACAs or that "expert" on relationship addictions.

This therapeutic approach splits off parts of the self as if these parts were curable without treating the whole person, and it invites the person seeking help to have magical expectations of the therapy. In the process, various forms of collusion develop that enable the patient and therapist to avoid really investigating the patient's unique inner experience. Finally, since many clients feel confused about their "identities," being labeled can prove comforting.

As this new language of addictions becomes part of our daily discourse, including the discourse of psychotherapy, labels and catchphrases substitute for real understanding and analysis. A patient will say, "That's my ACA stuff," and invite the therapist to collude under the reassuring pretense that this phrase explains something important, when in actuality it reflects the patient's desire *not* to analyze what s/he is really feeling. Once again, short-term relief is purchased at the cost of long-term cure and insight. Granted, many people have felt understood and helped by the addiction-model books and by the educational and therapeutic interventions that these books have spawned. As a result of this literature and this new awareness, many people have come out of the closet of personal suffering and self-destructive relationships—which should be seen as a positive step.

My purpose here has not been to argue that individual depth psychotherapy is the "correct" alternative to the addiction model, but simply to articulate the latter's limitations. While psychoanalytic theory has a great deal to say about the intrapsychic and interpersonal causes of self-destructive behavior and compulsions, I am not advocating undergoing psychoanalysis as the ultimate or only "real" cure. Nevertheless, we must recognize that even if self-help groups and therapies based on addiction models sometimes work to help people feel better, it does not necessarily follow that their understanding of the cause of the problem or of the treatment process is correct. My purpose has been to use both psychoanalytic and critical social theory to explore the limited psychological and social *meanings* of the addiction model. Sometimes the consequences of this model may be therapeutic change that is superficial or deadlocked, but this is not the crux of my concern. More important, this model mystifies the client, the therapist, and the psychological and social theorist, ignoring the depth and complexity of the real problem. The broader social world is made opaque, the family becomes one-dimensional, and intrapsychic conflict is flattened out.

Psychological traits, neurotic suffering, and relationship conflicts reflect the influence of social and historical processes. At the same time, the changes in family and social structure and in relations between the sexes—changes that have shaped Norwood's and Woititz's dysfunctional families— have to be described in conjunction with a parallel exploration of the internal and subjective dimension of people's lives. This process involves asking questions about the relationship between subjective experience and broader social change. Why, for example, do we respond to changes in the social, economic, and psychological status of men and women, of mothers and fathers, by developing so-called relationship addictions? Psychoanalytic theory is best equipped to answer such questions, since it is a theory of the subject—of a desiring, wishing, feeling individual—and as such it is able to sketch this internal landscape richly and in depth. We need to have a model for understanding behavior that can expand in both directions, inside and outside. The addiction model blocks both movements. □

Progress: The Last Superstition

Christopher Lasch

Neither liberalism nor Marxism, its principal competitor, seems to hold out much hope for solutions to the mounting problems that threaten to overwhelm us. Hence the search for some third position, as evidenced by recent interest in civic humanism, communitarianism, and other submerged traditions of social criticism that have been overshadowed by the dominant traditions deriving from the Enlightenment. The search for a third way, neither Marxist nor liberal, reflects a growing fear, that people are no longer in control of their lives.

Whether it is possible to imagine a convincing alternative to the ideologies that have shaped the modern world and what such an alternative would look like depend on our understanding of just where the old ideologies went wrong. My own view is that the roots of the difficulty lay in their common commitment to the idea of progress—which is why I am so deeply opposed to an attempt to stake out a new position that continues to define itself as "progressive." That way, nothing but confusion lies.

The first thing we need to understand is that hope does not demand a belief in progress. It demands a belief in justice: the conviction that the wicked will suffer, that wrongs will be made right, that the underlying order of things is not flouted with impunity. Hope implies a deep-seated trust in life, which appears absurd to those who lack it. But hope serves us better, in steering troubled waters ahead, than a belief in progress. Not that it prevents us from expecting the worst. On the contrary, the worst is always what the hopeful are prepared for. Their trust in life would not be worth much if it had not survived disappointments in the past, while their knowledge that the future holds further disappointments demonstrates the continuing need for hope. Believers in progress, on the other hand, though they like to think of themselves as the party of hope, actually have little need for it, since they have history on their side. Still, their lack of hope incapacitates them for intelligent action. Improvidence, a blind faith that things will somehow work out for the best, serves as a poor substitute for the disposition to see things through even when they don't.

This fatalistic optimism, this confident assumption that history works on the side of enlightenment, equality, and individual freedom, was the source of Marxism's notorious indifference to the morality of means and ends—the issue that troubled those who believed that progress was a mixed blessing at best. For Marxists, the choice of means was simple: whatever hastened the proletarian revolution. The "natural laws of capitalism," Marx said, worked "with iron necessity towards inevitable results." This did not mean that every nation had to go through a bourgeois phase on the way to socialism. When the Bolsheviks seized power in Russia, they could cite Marx's statement that Russia might be able to "obtain the fruits with which capitalist production has enriched humanity without passing through the capitalist regime." Without a bourgeois revolution, however, the social-

---

Christopher Lasch is Don Alonzo Watson Professor of History at the University of Rochester and a contributing editor of Tikkun. *His most recent book is* The True and Only Heaven: Progress and Its Critics *(W.W. Norton, 1991). This article appeared in* Tikkun, *May/June 1989.*

ist regime would itself have to do the work of capitalism, beginning with the expropriation of the peasantry; eventually this logic became the rationale for Stalinism in the Soviet Union. The upshot of the Marxian scheme of history was that certain things had to happen in sequence, whether they happened under bourgeois or "proletarian" auspices: the destruction of the old landed aristocracy; the rise of a new ruling class in its place; the "annihilation" of small-scale production; the transformation of peasants and artisans into wage workers; the replacement of communal, patriarchal, and "idyllic" arrangements by contractual arrangements; the rise of a new individualism in personal life; the collapse of religion and the spread of scientific habits of thought; the demystification of authority. Some such series of developments had to take place whether anyone wanted them or not and no matter what groups happened to be in charge of the state at any given time. Marx's theory of history, political philosopher Jon Elster writes, was "strangely disembodied." By "working backward from the end result to preconditions," it "could dispense with actors and their intentions." Because it dispensed with actors, we should add, it could also dispense with questions of politics and morality.

According to Marx, socialism would reconcile the individual and society. It represented a "higher synthesis" between individualism and "organic unity." Elster, a sympathetic critic, finds the "indiscriminate solidarity" envisioned by Marx and Engels both unconvincing and a little ominous. People need a "narrower focus of loyalty and solidarity than the international community of workers," Elster argues. Altruism flourishes in "small, stable groups" and "declines as the circle of individuals expands." "Free-floating benevolence" is incompatible with "personal integrity and strength of character." But Marx could not have acknowledged the value of small, stable groups without sacrificing his unilinear theory of progress, according to which history moves inexorably in the direction of more and more inclusive forms of solidarity.

The liberal theory of progress, on the other hand, is less rigid and therefore more easily reconciled, it seems, with evidence that history does not always move in a single direction. It was not the secularization of the Christian belief in Providence that gave rise to the eighteenth-century idea of progress, as is so often alleged, but the more specific assumption that people's appetites, formerly condemned as a source of social instability and personal unhappiness, could drive the economic machine—just as people's insatiable curiosity drove the scientific project—and thus insure a never-ending expansion of productive forces. The moral rehabilitation of desire generated a new sense of possibility, which announced itself most characteristically not in the vague utopianism of the French Enlightenment but in the hardheaded new science of political economy. For Adam Smith, it was the self-generating character of rising expectations, newly acquired needs and tastes, and new standards of personal comfort that broke the old cycle of social growth and decay and gave rise to a form of society capable of indefinite expansion.

The decisive break with older ways of thinking came when human needs began to be seen not as natural but as historical and constantly changing, hence insatiable. As the supply of material comforts increased, standards of comfort increased as well, and the category of necessities came to include many goods formerly regarded as luxuries. For Smith, the "uniform, constant, and uninterrupted effort of every man to better his condition" became the "principle from which public and national, as well as private opulence is originally derived." Smith's defense of high wages, unusual for its time, rested on the premise that "a person who can acquire no property can have no other interest but to eat as much, and to labor as little as possible." The hope of improving his condition, on the other hand, would encourage Smith's working man to spend his income on "things more durable" than the "hospitality" and "festivals" preferred by the wealthy; and the accumulated effects of this kind of expenditure, even though they might reflect a "base and selfish disposition," would maintain a whole nation of industrious workers.

The history of liberalism, for our present purposes, can be seen as the periodic attenuation and abandonment of these ideas, on the one hand, and the periodic rediscovery of them, on the other, by a long line of thinkers, culminating with the proponents of Keynesian economics, who made the most refined attempts to link social progress to the indefinite expansion of consumer demand. The concept of progress, as the most astute liberal theorists have understood, can be defended against intelligent criticism only by postulating a never-ending expansion of desires, a steady rise in the general standard of comfort, and (most important of all) the continual incorporation of new groups into the culture of consumption. It is only in this form that the idea of progress has survived the calamities of the twentieth century. More extravagant versions of the progressive faith, premised on the perfectibility of human nature—on the unrealized power of reason or love—collapsed a long time ago, but the liberal version has proved surprisingly resistant to the shocks to easy optimism administered in rapid succession by twentieth-century events.

Liberalism was never utopian, unless the democratization of consumption is itself a utopian ideal. It made no difficult demands on human nature. It presupposed nothing more strenuous in the way of motivation than intelligent self-interest. It assumed that almost everyone had a stake in increased productivity, higher wages, shorter hours of work, and a more creative use of leisure. Capitalism, said Horace Kallen, the political philosopher of consumption, had "... raised the general standard of living, ... transformed scarcity into abundance, awakening wants where none had been before, multiplying few into many, bringing more and more varied goods to more people at lower prices, so that what had been formerly, if at all, available only to a few ... was now in reach of many of those who had produced much and consumed little." It remained only to complete the capitalist revolution by making the "blessings of leisure" available to all. No improvement in mental capacity was required in order for the desirability of this goal to be generally recognized; nor did the realization of the goal require altruism and self-sacrifice—only a willingness to subordinate short-term pleasure to long-term peace and prosperity.

Even this modest level of discipline, however, has proved difficult to sustain in societies propelled by the imperatives of mass consumption. In American politics, the kind of intelligent conservatism that reconciled the business classes to the need for social justice is clearly on the wane, perhaps because demands for reform voiced from below have grown increasingly faint. During the age of reform, imaginative statesmen like Theodore Roosevelt, Woodrow Wilson, and Franklin D. Roosevelt could cite the radical pressures mounted by Populists, socialists, and militant labor unions as an incentive to implement more modest reforms. For a variety of reasons, however, it has become more and more difficult for popular demands to get a hearing. Third parties are weaker than they used to be; the consolidation of the press into a handful of giant chains eliminates small papers and narrows the range of political debate; the dominance of television further encourages this homogenization of opinion; the growth of the executive branch of government at the expense of the legislature makes officials less directly responsible to a popular constituency, while the courts, the least accountable branch of government, have assumed an increasingly important role in policy-making; and the system of direct primaries, instituted in the hope of bringing government closer to the people, has had the opposite effect, increasing the financial resources necessary to mount a successful campaign and transferring the selection of candidates from party managers to the mass media more than to the voters. The effect of these changes in making government appear remote and inaccessible to ordinary people is evident in the decline of voting, in widespread political apathy, and in the distrust of Washington on which the New Right has played so effectively.

From the beginning, liberalism placed less emphasis on the duties of citizenship than on the right to enjoy the good things of life. The function of the state was to guarantee those rights, not to provide citizens with a political education or to interfere in any way with the pursuit of private advantage.

Democracy (insofar as it was identified with liberalism at all) thus came to be identified with an equitable distribution of goods rather than with the widest possible participation in public life. A general improvement in the standard of living seemed to justify the choice of distributive democracy over participatory democracy. Recent experience, however, suggests that it may be impossible, in the long run, to achieve one without the other. The favored few cannot be trusted to consult the needs of the many, even when, as Keynes and Kallen pointed out, it is manifestly in their long-term interest to raise the general level of consumption. If the many now enjoy comforts formerly restricted to the few, it is because they have won them through their own political initiative, not because the wealthy have voluntarily surrendered some of their privileges or because the market automatically assures abundance for all. The decline of popular initiative in politics, together with the decline of intelligent conservatism, therefore wears a menacing look; a steady progress toward equality, to put it mildly, can no longer be taken for granted.

Liberalism ultimately presupposes the creation of a global market that embraces populations formerly excluded from any reasonable expectation of affluence. But the prediction that "sooner or later we will all be affluent," uttered so confidently only a few years ago, no longer carries much conviction. The global circulation of commodities, information, and populations, far from making everyone affluent, has widened the gap between rich and poor nations and has generated a massive migration to the West, where the newcomers swell the vast army of the homeless, unemployed, illiterate, drug-ridden, derelict, and effectively disenfranchised. Their presence strains existing resources to the breaking point. Medical and educational facilities, law-enforcement agencies, and the job supply—not to mention the supply of racial tolerance and goodwill, never abundant to begin with—all appear inadequate to the enormous task of assimilating what is essentially a surplus or "redundant" population, in the cruelly expressive British phrase. The poisonous effects of poverty and racial discrimination cannot be ghettoized; they too circulate on a global scale. "Like the effects of industrial pollution and the new system of global financial markets," Susan Sontag writes, "the AIDS crisis is evidence of a world ... in which everything that can circulate does"—goods, images, garbage, disease. It is not surprising that "the look into the future, which was once tied to a vision of linear progress," has turned into a "vision of disaster," in Sontag's words, and that "anything ... that can be described as changing steadily can be seen as heading toward catastrophe."

The gist of my argument up to this point is that the consumerist program cannot succeed without popular participation in government and without a heightened sense of civic commitment, both of which, however, tend to be eroded by the consumerist emphasis on private satisfactions (and by many other features of consumerist culture as well). To this we can add a second point: that consumerism requires a global market and a continuation of the trend toward political centralization, whereas civic participation is far more effective in small communities where people feel directly responsible for their actions. I see no way out of this dilemma except to choose one of its two horns, either equality or economic growth, either citizenship or consumerism. We can't have both, and there is no point in pretending that we can somehow combine "community" with large-scale organization or civic revival with a continuing commitment to a more and more affluent standard of living.

My conviction that our progressive society is approaching the end of the road and that we will have to face hard choices in the near future is strengthened by another consideration, namely, the mounting evidence that the earth's finite resources will not support an indefinite expansion of industrial civilization along its present lines. While the attempt to maintain the existing standard of living enjoyed by industrial nations without sharing it with the rest of the world would be unconscionable, the attempt to export Western standards would eventually mean the exhaustion of nonrenewable resources, the irreversible pollution of the earth's atmosphere, the drastic alteration of its climate, and the destruction, in short, of the ecological system on which human life depends.

Rudolph Bahro, a leading spokesman for the West German Greens, writes:

> Let us imagine what it would mean if the raw material and energy consumption of our
> society were extended to the four and a half billion people living today, or to the ten to
> fifteen billion there will probably be tomorrow. It is readily apparent that the planet can
> only support such volumes of production ... for a short time to come.

If Bahro is right, we have only two choices: to make the West more than ever an island of prosperity
in a poverty-stricken world, barricading ourselves against our neighbors; or to accept a general
reduction of our own standard of living. Neither alternative, it hardly needs to be pointed out, is
consistent with the ideology of progress.

If there is any merit in the sketchy arguments outlined here, they suggest a final point: the need to
clarify the communitarian critique of liberalism and to face its social, political, and cultural implications without flinching. Communitarianism, if that is what we want to call it, does not imply a return
to the New Deal, the revival of the progressive tradition in American politics. It implies a repudiation of that tradition. It implies small-scale production, workers' control of industry, and community
control of education. It also implies, I think, a willingness to undergo the risks of public controversy
about morality and religion. The exclusion of moral and religious issues from politics has been one
of the hallmarks of liberalism and one of the preconditions, in all likelihood, of economic progress.
It was only when the separation of church and state put an end to the wars of religion that the West
was able to devote itself wholeheartedly to the all-engaging task of increasing productivity. Once the
state ceased to be the guardian of religious orthodoxy, it could assume what has since come to be
recognized as its primary function—that of keeping the economy in good working order.

The price of this policy, however, has been a certain trivialization of public debate. One of the
reasons people take so little interest in politics today, aside from the inaccessibility of the bureaucratic structures that dominate political life, is that politics fails to address issues of overriding moral
importance. It won't do, therefore, for communitarians to call for a revival of civic spirit while
deploring the Right's attempt to put divisive moral and religious issues on the political agenda. Liberals can consistently argue that such issues are matters of private choice and therefore do not
belong in public, but communitarians don't enjoy that luxury. If they are serious, they will have to
engage the religious Right on its own terms, recognizing that a community is constituted by vigorous
public debate about the issues that really matter, not by universal agreement about those issues.
Orestes Brownson once said, "I always hold that to be important truth, wherein I differ from
others." One of the more farsighted of nineteenth-century social critics, Brownson pointed out that
the separation of politics and religion actually led not so much to the exclusion of religion from
public life but to a bland, nondenominational civil religion that helped to enforce the socioecono-
mic status quo. When he criticized the separation of religion and politics, he meant that questions
concerning the "destiny of man" ought to become questions for public debate, not that a new
religious establishment should provide authoritative answers. "Peace is a good thing, but justice is
better.... Give us the noise and contention of life, rather than the peace and silence of the charnel-
house." Communitarians would be well advised to take these words to heart. □

The Nostalgia Disease

Sven Birkerts

O ur culture is awash like never before in repackaged bits of the past. We find them on screen and radio, in books and magazines, even in the posturing about patriotism and "family values" that so recently confused our electoral process. Our appetite for the stuff is bottomless. We have just emerged from eight years of a nostalgia presidency—a grand, collective bathing in the images and pieties of an earlier, less cynical and compromised era (what an irony: here was the most ruthless cynicism, here were the gravest compromises!)—and there is no sign that the impulse is slackening. Indeed, nostalgia now threatens to become a permanent feature of our cultural life, a kind of ground bass against which we play our changing ideals and aspirations.

Consider just a few of its recent manifestations. On television, the closest thing we have to a national psyche, we not only have shows like "thirtysomething," "Wonder Years," "China Beach," and "Almost Grown," but every second commercial comes wrapped in the musical and visual tissue of the past. The radio dial lands on oldies and rock "classics" with each turn of the wrist. Or else it gets stuck on yet another repeat broadcast of one of Garrison Keillor's down-home Lake Wobegon monologues. Recent movies that have more or less successfully mined the vein include *1969*, *Eight Men Out*, *Bull Durham* (an odd instance of nostalgia filtered through the present), *Tucker*, *Stand By Me*, *Everybody's All-American*, and *Imagine: John Lennon*, just to name a few. And wherever we look we see headlines beaming the return of Elvis, or yet another anniversary special on JFK, Marilyn, or 1968.... The barons of mid-cult have grasped the formula for success. Processions of what we've somehow lost—once we've been tipped off that that's what they are—are as irresistible as sex and scandal. It appears that our desire for the clarity and certainty of the imagined past will batten repeatedly on certain surefire images. Country roads, weathered barns, city scenes with fedoras and oldfangled cars, beaded hippies flashing peace signs: all that matters is that these emblems tell us how we were before self-consciousness and fragmentation afflicted us. Before everything changed.

Some might argue that nostalgia has always been with us, that we find the longing for a better past in Sappho and Homer as well as in Norman Rockwell and Currier & Ives. And to be sure, all of us, as individuals, experience nostalgia sharply at times—more sharply, I think, as we grow older. This was as true of our great-grandparents as it is now of us. But something is different. The impulse has deepened and strengthened; it has become commodified. Where once it may have waxed and waned in the self and the culture, it is now a constant—we live by looking over our shoulders. The reasons for this are many. But chief among them is the fact that we now have a technology for collective cultural experience that did not exist even fifty years ago. Pulsations did not then move through the whole of the body politic, certainly not at such a rate or intensity. We were not joined, as we are now, by a finely meshed electronic net. We were not then alerted at every instant to the

Sven Birkerts recently published The Electric Life: Essays on Modern Poetry *(William Morrow and Co., 1989). This article appeared in* Tikkun, *March/April 1989.*

universalized state of things. We brooded over the disappearing past privately, more fitfully.

Technology and media are part of the equation; changing historical circumstances are another. Nostalgia could not have thrived so vigorously in an earlier day because people were not so mesmerized by the past. Present and future held too strong a claim on the attention—there was too much to be done just to survive, to inch forward into the future. No longer. In the past few decades everything about the way life is lived has altered. At some point in the post-World War II period, technological and societal changes attained critical mass. Suddenly (at least from a historical vantage point) the bedrock certainties about our experience of reality shifted and assumed new configurations. We are now squarely—and perhaps irrevocably—stuck in a fragmented and self-conscious condition that some have labeled "postmodernism" (I will take this up shortly). And nostalgia is now no longer an occasional fibrillation in the psyche—it is more akin to the persistent sensation felt by the amputee in his or her "phantom" limb.

The reasons for this change are fairly obvious, at least on the surface. We are, psychologically, all creatures of habit, programmed to desire constancy and security. But it happens that we now find ourselves in a world that is locked into an ever-intensifying spiral of change. One could argue that our fundamental modes and rhythms have been altered more since the 1940s than during all the millenia that came before. Until then—and I must generalize—we lived in relation to an ancient and familiar paradigm of country and city. True, we had mass-production industries and air travel. But most individuals could, if pressed, have found the continuity between their way of life and the age-old human pattern.

Things are radically different now. For most of our hundreds of millions of citizens, the city-country distinction has been exploded into the anonymous surround of the megasuburb. We can no longer just look around to see where we fit into the scheme. Analogously, the physical ties of family and community have come unraveled, only partly replaced by the psuedoimmediacy of telephone communications. And how we do what we do—not to mention the *what* itself—has been revolutionized past recognition. Information crisscrosses the country on screens and via fax machines; business gets conducted from terminal to terminal. We look up from the panel just long enough to see whether we need our galoshes or sunglasses. And at the end of the day we cushion our spent selves with vivid washes of music and the numbing flicker of televised images....

Our longing for what we perceive as the certainties of the past is, of course, only partly conscious. We carry it around as a need, as something akin to a biological drive. Or a defense, a place to run to. Or a mode of orientation. Our picture of the past, preserved, amplified by the incessant images that envelop us, becomes an internal compass; the more lost we feel, the more often we need to refer to it. A fact, as I have suggested, that is hardly lost on our politicians and imagebrokers. Their instincts zero in on the true condition of the populace more quickly and accurately than any market survey could hope to. As our need intensifies—it does so daily—so does the purveying of packaged offerings. More and more every day, the past is being offered to us as a commodity for consumption. We learn to react to our sense of loss by taking out our pocketbooks.

Nostalgia is the easy response of the individual who feels cut off from the past, from the secure continuity of tradition. It is a compensatory reflex before the anxiety of disconnectedness. The psyche avoids the hard work of mourning and tries to fill its void with a set of images. Here I should clarify one thing: that these are almost never images of the real thing. For the real thing, truly recalled, places one in danger of grief. Nostalgia is the response elicited by the simplified and stylized image—the general store, the old porch swing, grandma handing out lemonade. The more stylized it gets, the closer we are to kitsch. Nostalgia is a look at the past, an attempted emotional connection, that comes *after* desire has falsified and colorized it. There is little or no true relation to the event as we might have experienced it while embedded in the then-uncertain present.

This brings us, in not all that roundabout fashion, to a consideration of the so-called postmodern condition.... Briefly, postmodernism espouses the view that a permanent change has taken place in Western culture in the past few decades. The time line, which was the indicator of progress, of directional movement into the future, has shattered. The great eras of growth and innovation are ended. We are postindustrialist, posteverything; there are no more terrestrial frontiers. What's more, cultural energies (like our natural resources) are depleted. The kinds of transformations that now lie in store for us are mainly organizational—they involve new distribution of information and refined modes of processing (computerization), as well as a more thorough saturation of every societal sphere by the electronic media. In the arts, the subject of so much postmodernist theorizing, we no longer look to an avant-garde pushing its vector into the unknown; we no longer think of art as discovery. Instead, we have an aesthetics of combination, the presentation of old materials.

Todd Gitlin summed up this aesthetic quite concisely in his essay, "Hip Deep in Post-Modernism," (*New York Times Book Review*, Nov. 6, 1988):

> Post-modernism ... is indifferent to consistency and continuity altogether. It self-consciously splices genres, attitudes, styles. It relishes the blurring or juxtaposition of forms (fiction-nonfiction), stances (straight-ironic), cultural levels (high-low). It disdains originality and fancies copies, repetition, the recombination of hand-me-down scraps. It neither embraces nor criticizes, but beholds the world blankly, with a knowingness that dissolves feeling and commitment into irony. It pulls the rug out from under itself, displaying an acute self-consciousness about the work's constructed nature. It takes pleasure in the play of surfaces and derides the search for depth as mere nostalgia for an unmoved mover.

Among the proponents of this aesthetic, Gitlin cites artists like David Byrne, Robert Wilson, John Ashbery, Laurie Anderson, Spalding Gray, David Hockney, Italo Calvino, and Don DeLillo. Of the "vision" itself he writes:

> In effect, post-modernism expresses the spiritless spirit of a global class linked via borderless mass media with mass culture, omnivorous consumption and easy travel. Their experience denies the continuity of history; they live in a perpetual present garnished by nostalgia binges.

The whole point of the postmodern project is to affirm that our connection to history has been ruptured. We have left the old perspective—which saw styles and expressions as naturally bound to their times—and have embraced a perspective of hyperconscious pluralism. Overrun with information and stimulus, we have lost a distinct sense of what our time means or how it differs from (and grows out from) former times. We respond to our confusion by browsing freely and indiscriminately among the relics and styles of the past. Everything flows together, unsutured by any sense of causal connection or sequence. And when there are no laws about how things fit together, irony—bemused detachment—is the inevitable consequence.

"Nostalgia," the word, comes from the Greek *nostos*, which means to return home and survive. *Webster's Third New International Dictionary* gives the archaic definition as "a severe melancholia caused by a protracted absence from home." The more current meaning given is "a wistful or excessively sentimental ... yearning for return to or return of some real or romanticized period or irrecoverable condition or setting in the past." This nostalgia, this longing for connection that is projected upon falsified images, increasingly replaces what were once natural linkages emerging from an understanding of the progression of experience. The more that the objects of our nostalgia become calculated media commodities, the further we get from being able to grasp our condition.

The yearning itself is authentic, I have no doubt, but as the object and the indulgence are generally false, the process can only be debilitating. Nostalgia, fostered by the products of our popular culture, sets us ever more deeply into a schizophrenic relation to ourselves. When we discharge our pain and sadness at the loss of meaningful parts of the past by consuming manufactured images, we break contact with ourselves and with the truth of that past. Such nostalgia short-circuits the mourning process. And where mourning lets us lay the past to rest and get on with things, the bathos of nostalgia keeps us floating in a perpetual illusion about an attainable or renewable past. By immersing ourselves in the afterglow of our own history—the seductive, doctored afterglow—we lose the initiative to keep making history. That is, to perform freely and unself-consciously in the face of the present.*

The self-consciousness, which goes hand in hand with the distanced perception of irony, is the most insidious aspect of the nostalgia transaction. Heightening and sentimentalizing the images allows for safe consumption; it shields us from the pain of the genuine. Irony, incorporating the attitude of knowing, of being "wised-up," anticipates and preempts true response. We are rendered passive. When Garrison Keillor delivers his Lake Wobegon stories, his tone and arch pauses do the work of distancing. His every vocal gesture is telling us that, hey, this is cute and folksy, that we ought to be comfortably amused by the doings of these dear, benighted small-town folks. What was once in earnest exists now to be chuckled over. The truth has not come closer—it has receded. And when one of the characters on "thirtysomething" launches into yet another paean to the lost ideals of the sixties, it is always with a grimace that derides the very clichés that are being vented. Again, the matter of the past is hedged around with the quotation marks of our supposed superiority. The net effect is the divestiture of the past: We can't find our way back to it because its soul has been leached away.

Prepackaged nostalgia builds easy bridges to what is finally a dream about how things were. The more that such bridges are built, and the more that we use them in our daily traffic, the more likely it is that the truth about the past will slip away. That truth is complex and difficult. It reflects to us images of the present that are not always pleasing. It posits the ongoing work of culture as a massive task. Postmodernism, by contrast, offers simple, even inviting, views. We can venture into a bazaar of images and attitudes that lay no claim on us; its ironies feel cool, fashionable. But until we can break out of the cage we have made for ourselves, those ironies and the self-consciousness that attends them will be our fate.

And here is the demonic irony at the root of all others: that the quality we most prize in all of these trumped-up images of the past is the *lack* of irony and self-consciousness. We long for nothing so much as a time when people did things out of simple necessity and desire, when everything was not tainted by self-awareness, when the guy running to meet his girl under the Biltmore clock was not simultaneously watching himself running to meet his girl under the Biltmore clock. □

---

* One might, of course, uphold the opposite case: that we take our bearings for the future from the fond ideals—and idealizations—of the past; and indeed, that to uphold a sense of purpose a nation must look back upon something brighter and nobler than the history that revisionists would offer us. What could have been more nostalgic, in this sense, than Ronald Reagan's farewell address to the nation, his invocation of John Winthrop's "city upon a hill"? I would not want to argue that we should do away with the heightenings and distortions that must attend such a vision. But I would point out that even the president—the prince of nostalgia—warned in the same speech against "an eradication of the American memory that could result, ultimately, in an erosion of the American spirit." Though his exhortation was for all Americans to learn the patriotic facts, he too was aware of the dangers of memory gone awry. The drive to nostalgia must be recognized for what it is, and it must be tempered consistently with the complicated truth. Otherwise we are condemned to keep dreaming.

Reason and the Mob:
The Politics of Representation

Gary Peller

you might be sitting in a history class/listening to the analysis of "what was going on" in the thirties in new york, say/and you hear nothing of shtetls where grandma's generation came from/and the descriptions of sweatshops sound oddly abstract and disembodied, that is, emphatically unsweaty-scientific-full-of-clear-light—spared of the dust of ripped cloth—and quiet so you can hear yourself (someone else) think and the machines' screaming bobbing has stopped, all put in terms of an analysis of the labor structure of the immigrant population, complete with statistics/and politics sounds like this or that labor policy adopted by this or that administration/not at all what grandma described going to work as/but you came to school to learn/and it feels like an interesting addition to what you already know from family history and hot tea mornings in kitchens in brooklyn apartments/but it still seems like the viewpoint of the other, of the officials giving the official line on what was happening—the politics at the pinochle games just can't be reduced to "labor unrest"/but we're going too fast

then it's years later and you wonder again about the shtetls and what you might have lost in the history class/and you focus on some imaginary moment when it happened—when the statistics and the analysis of the labor structure were no longer just interesting additions to the lived experience in new york of grandma and her friends but instead became the reality itself; and grandma's description about why her boss acted like he did was just shtetl superstition, or worse, silly. because at some point the feeling of learning new things was replaced by the idea of learning things the way they really are, free from superstition and prejudice, and stuff might be left out for the sake of time but what was there, presented as knowledge, was knowledge, in a particular form and in a particular language that you recognize as not the way you started out looking at things. but we're for education, after all

and then you start wondering, what if the language of true knowledge that you learned, the way of talking about things intelligently and dispassionately, was itself a mythology that contained prejudice and superstition; and then that it's not just new york in the thirties, it's the way the whole picture is organized, a whole hierarchy of what counts and what doesn't that might present itself as neutral knowledge but is really just an ideology of power/and the imaginary moment that you crystallized, the moment when the statistics and the analysis began to represent the true and the real against the superstitious, was the moment of self-denial and treachery as you implicitly agreed to a test of truth that would count out most of what you know most deeply. even if you can't prove it.

The moment that I have tried to evoke here, the point at which we begin to believe the dominant Enlightenment teaching about the differences between truth and myth, between reason and sentiment, and simultaneously begin to suppress our particularity, our history

Gary Peller is a professor of Law at the University of Virginia School of Law. This article appeared in Tikkun, *July/August 1987.*

and our place in the social world, is incredibly important in the creation of social power in society. Even after the philosophers have abandoned the epistemological project, the attempt to find some firm ground to distinguish truth from myth, and even after the notion that the world can be neatly divided in the Cartesian way between the mind and the body has been rejected intellectually, these categories for perceiving and talking about the world continue to play powerful roles in our day-to-day lives, in the way that we understand ourselves and each other.

And the reason is simple. The construction of a realm of knowledge separate from superstition and the identification of a faculty of reason separate from passion was not, after all, simply some mind game played by philosophers and professional intellectuals. These categories have always served political roles in differentiating groups as worthy or unworthy and in justifying particular social hierarchies. They were not mere abstract musings about the ultimate nature of things, but rather part of the everyday texture of the way we construct our world and its possibilities. And a continuing thread of that construction of the world has been the notion that there is a radical distinction between truth, the representation of the way the world really is, and myth, an interpretation of the world that cannot be proven and thus is merely sentimental or poetic. It is this sense, of some grand distinction between truth and myth, that is supposed to distinguish the rational from the emotive, the legal from the political, the scientific from the aesthetic, the civilized from the primitive, the objective from the subjective, the neutral from the interested, and fact from opinion.

Which brings us to the topic of this essay: the current intellectual controversy about new critical attitudes toward interpretation. For the past decade or so in the United States, and a little longer in France, traditional interpretive assumptions have been directly and fundamentally challenged by the rise of "deconstruction" and other "post-structuralist" approaches to interpretation. Here the notion of "interpretation" is broadly conceived to include issues about the meaning of such things as literary works, newspapers, philosophical texts, and legal documents, as well as the meaning of social events such as the relations between doctors and patients, teachers and students, or workers and managers. The general idea, characterized by the term "critical theory," is that similar issues are confronted whenever one is involved in thinking about the meaning of social products, whether those social products are the traditional "texts" of literary interpretation or, in the newer forms of critical practice, the "texts" of our social institutions and interactions.

The labels "deconstruction" and "post-structuralist" have been used fairly loosely to describe what are actually widely diverse critical practices. The new critical modes do, however, share the commitment that there is no possibility of a neutral or objective interpretative practice or of merely representing (as opposed to interpreting) the world. When we attempt simply to represent, free from bias or distortion, we must always do so through language, broadly conceived as a socially-created way to categorize perception of and communication about the world.

But language necessarily mediates perception and communication by shaping ways of thinking about the world that are themselves not necessary and natural, but social and contingent. When we try to move beyond language and rhetoric, beyond the means of representation, to what is being represented, we find only more language, more metaphor, more interpretation. According to the new critical approaches, there is no objective reference point, separate from culture and politics, a-vailable to distinguish truth from ideology, fact from opinion, or representation from interpretation. And thus philosophy, science, economics, literary criticism, and the other intellectual "disciplines" can be interpreted according to the same process that has been traditionally reserved for literature and art—they, too, can be read merely as "texts" organizing the thick texture of the world according to their own metaphors. They enjoy no privileged status vis-à-vis the "merely" aesthetic or subjective because they, too, are simply languages, simply ways of carving up what seems similar and what seems different in the world. Moreover, these approaches are "post-structuralist" precisely because they reject the notion that there is some deeper logic that governs the production of meaning, and thus they include within their critique the grand theories of Freud, Levi-Strauss, Marx, and other structuralists who purport to have found a unified, underlying scheme of social life that itself stands outside the play of rhetoric and metaphor.

This is not, of course, to say that the new critical approaches deny that we can, and do, make decisions about the world—about what is important and what is bullshit, about what makes sense to us and what doesn't. The point is that there is no grand organizing theory or principle with which to justify our social choices as neutral and apolitical, as the products of reason and truth rather than of passion or ideology.

These new critical approaches, in short, deny the central Enlightenment notions that we have described above, that is, that there is a difference between rational, objective representation and interested, biased interpretation. This new attitude toward interpretation emerged first in literary criticism and philosophy and now has at least some practitioners in virtually all the fields of the humanities, including sociology, anthropology, history, economics, and law.

The controversy about the deconstructive stance is in many ways played out in professional journals as a typically dry, intellectual competition between philosophical positions. (My theory is bigger than yours.) But the issues that have emerged in the controversy seem to me to present important political questions about the way that power works in social life—questions that revolve around what I have described above as the struggle over truth and reality presented as one confronts official knowledge and compares it with one's own experience of and feeling for the world.

As I see it, the deconstructive approach puts at issue what have been the traditional mainstays of our liberal and progressive commitment to Enlightenment culture. Indeed the whole way that we conceive of liberal progress (overcoming prejudice in the name of truth, seeing through the distortions of ideology to get at reality, surmounting ignorance and superstition with the acquisition of knowledge) is called into question. The new critical approaches suggest that what has been presented in our social-political and our intellectual traditions as knowledge, truth, objectivity, and reason are actually merely the effects of a particular form of social power, the victory of a particular way of representing the world that then presents itself as beyond mere interpretation, as truth itself. The deconstructive attitude is oriented toward uncovering the ways in which, say, the rational sociology of New York in the 1930s is a cultural and political construct, built on exclusions of other, "less worthy" knowledge, like my grandmother's knowledge of her social situation.

The deconstructive approach is controversial to traditionalists because it challenges what they believe their whole task is about. If what separates the rational from the irrational is the claim that the rational approach is able to purify itself of ideology and mere social conventionality, the deconstructionist wants to challenge reason on its own ground and demonstrate that what gets called reason and knowledge is simply a particular way of organizing perception and communication, a way of organizing and categorizing experience that is social and contingent but whose socially constructed nature and contingency have been suppressed. When the particular way that knowledge and legitimacy have been organized is rejected, the traditionalists see an abyss of meaning and therefore charge that the deconstructive stance is "nihilist."

On the other hand, to those who have already rejected the traditionalist vision of knowledge and truth as ideological and biased, the deconstructive approach seems abstract and apolitical, a kind of super-skeptical discourse that is of no help in getting past the ideology of official knowledge to the embedded reality of our lives. Moreover, to many committed leftists, the deconstructive stance appears disengaged, as a kind of radical chic that stands outside the existential questions we face in social life.

I believe that the rise of the new interpretative approaches marks an important movement toward unmasking the politics of intellectual life, and opens up new possibilities for understanding the politics of social life more generally. Accordingly, I want to discuss deconstruction with a particular focus on the social and political issues that I believe are embedded in the current intellectual controversy. And rather than attempt some kind of summary of the "premises" of deconstruction or post-structuralism (a slightly absurd task for an intellectual movement that poses itself against totalizing theories or methods), I will first provide an example of a deconstructive reading of a text.

I have chosen parts of an article from the *Virginia Quarterly Review* written by Nathan Scott, Professor of Religious Studies at the University of Virginia. Since Scott is writing about deconstruction, which he believes has engendered a "crisis in humanistic studies," his article provides a convenient starting point from which we can get an idea of what a deconstructive approach might do with a particular text and at the same time consider the political and social implications of the deconstructive stance through the issues that are raised in interpreting Scott.

Today, of course, the enterprising anti-humanism of the post-Structuralist movement is in full tide, and it presents us with the great example in contemporary intellectual life of the new trahison des clercs. This phrase forms the title of a once famous book by the French critic Julien Benda which was first published in 1927, and in English the phrase is best rendered as the "betrayal of the intellectuals." [Benda] was moved to advance the rather extravagant charge that the typical intellectuals of the modern period, identifying themselves with class rancor and nationalist sentiment, have abdicated their true calling in the interests of political passion: instead of quelling the mob and beckoning it toward true community, they have joined the mob, concurring in its lust for quick results and adopting its devotion to the pragmatic and the expedient.... And it is his fiercely reproachful term that appears now to be the appropriate epithet for the intellectual insurgency that is currently sowing a profound disorder in the ... humanities.

This paragraph is supposed to form the general context for Scott's warning about the threat of post-structuralism to modern intellectual life. As Scott sees it, the humanist approaches he defends depend for their "cultural authority ... on what can be claimed for them as disciplines aimed at *knowledge* and *truth*." The problem with the new critical approach is that it is a form of "nihilism"—as such, it "radically impugns any truly cognitive dimension of the human endeavor, it strikes at its most vital nerve—more threateningly than anything else in our period, since it strikes from within."

Scott identifies the humanist approach with the "intellectuals" and the "post-Structuralist" approaches with the "mob." But in order for these associations to constitute an argument against the new approaches, the reader must first understand what is bad about the mob and what is good about the intellectuals. Thus, a useful place to begin unpacking the text would be to determine what the contrast between the intellectual and the mob means and what conceptions allow us to make sense of the elevation of the intellectual over the mob.

Scott's rhetoric helps in this analysis because it contains a group of associations with the intellectuals and with the mob that can assist us in determining its meaning. The distinction between the mob and the intellectuals and the justification for the superiority of the intellectuals are suggested by the fact that the mob is characterized by social desire—it is associated with "class rancor," "nationalist sentiment," "political passion," "lust," "disorder," and "insurgency."

The intellectual, on the other hand, stands in contrast to these features: the intellectual is supposed to represent order and dispassion rather than "rancor" and "sentiment," neutrality as opposed to politics, the "disciplined" search for "knowledge and truth" rather than the lustful satisfaction of

Drawing by Anthony Dubovsky

passion and desire, the ideal and the long-term as opposed to the "pragmatic and the expedient."

In short, Scott's argument seems animated by a structure of meaning where reason and passion are distinguished from each other. Reason is associated with the intellect, knowledge, truth, neutrality, and objectivity; passion is associated with disorder, politics, sentiment, class rancor and unthinking nationalism. Finally, reason is elevated to a superior position vis-à-vis emotion.

Next we must consider why reason should presumptively enjoy this privileged status, what it is about the two categories that makes it seem beyond question that right-thinking and progressive minded people would "naturally" understand from the text both the contrast between the two categories and the superiority of the rational over the emotive.

To understand the way that Scott succeeds in communicating, to uncover the manner in which his language resonates with what a reader might already understand about the world, we might at this point imagine the contrast between the rationality of the intellectuals and the passion of the mob in terms of individual, rather than social, issues. Here we recognize the relationship between the mob and the intellectual in the relationship between reason and desire, the mind and the body. Just as the text associates being civilized at the social level with subordinating the mob—social desire—to the intellectual, so we have reference to a cultural language in which being civilized and mature as an individual means subordinating the passions to reason, making the mind the ruler of the body rather than the other way around. In addition, the sense of the temporal relation between the short-sightedness of the mob and the long-view of the intellectuals is repeated in the notion that the mind must delay the satisfaction of desire in the civilized individual—the regulative function of reason is temporal, to keep emotion and desire in their proper places at their proper times, to resist the animal urge for immediate satisfaction.

And at this level of the individual, the full force of the superiority of the intellectual and the mob is exposed, for the body represents our natural, animal side, and the mind our human side. Just as the intellectual must "quell" the mob's passion and lust in order for the humanist position to survive, so the mind must quell the urges of the body if we are to be civilized and escape our animal selves. Our animal passions represent the continuing hold of nature over us, just as the possibility of mob action represents the need for the continuing vigilance of the intellectual, lest social life degenerate to an animal state. To transfer the issues back to the social level, then, Scott's appeal is to a general language of social progress and development—the intellectual is favored over the mob because the mob is, in a sense, less human, closer to nature, primitive.

We have in our cultural knowledge concrete historical images that support the reasonableness of the hierarchy of reason over passion. Probably the most powerful single image in the American experience is the image of the Southern lynch mob—there, in the common understanding, the mob, ruled by irrational racism against Blacks, bypassed the orderly, rational, and judicial means of dispensing justice in favor of the "pragmatic and the expedient," simply acting on the basis of their passionate emotions. In this image, reason can play a heroic role and justify its privileged status vis-à-vis passion, by standing against the forces of the mob and speaking from principles, objectivity, and dispassion.

At this point, it seems that we have a good hold on the meaning of the text. We are asked to reject the mob in favor of the intellect just as we must reject our passions in favor of our reason. In either sphere, the failure to regulate the emotional with the rational would in a sense be giving in to our animal urges, opening up the possibility of regression and the end of civilization.

But just as soon as we begin to feel that we have gotten a hold on this determinate meaning of Scott's argument, we also feel it begin to slip away. If the "reason" for subordinating the mob to the intellectuals is the threat of the mob to coerce with its passion, then it strikes us as initially dissonant that the intellectuals are asked to "quell" the mob. The very ability of the intellect to "quell" suggests that in some way the intellectuals are like the mob, possessing coercive power. Yet it was the potential for the mob to coerce that justified its regulation by the intellectuals.

This power of the intellect to "quell" introduces the possibility that reason is actually a means of discipline, a coercive technology, for the social regulation of passion and emotion. Both at the individual and the social levels, reason plays the role of standing in the place of desire and deferring it to another time or place. Accordingly, we imagine reason at the individual level deferring desire until the "right" place, e.g., in our social mores, reason defers passion to the privacy of the home, or perhaps to the marital relation. At the social level, the intellectuals defer the passion of the mob into the courtroom or other "appropriate" places.

But once we see reason as the regulator of passion, as a technology, we also realize that reason is constructed out of social power. The notion of reason regulating desire to "appropriate" times and places exposes the ways that reason embodies social choices about what is appropriate or inappropriate. With respect to sexuality, for example, regulation might occur according to the Victorian notions of propriety or according to "our" modern permissiveness. Reason itself yields no determinate basis that would allow us to choose between the alternatives. Reason does not tell us whether to prefer the nuclear family over the alternatives, nor whether the present segregation of reason and desire according to public or private realms is reasonable. Any choice of this or that mode of regulation seems to reflect merely a preference, a desire. Short of some "natural" embodiment of the relationship between reason and desire, any choice looks political, willed, a reflection of desire itself.

By this strange twist, reason can only "quell" desire on an individual level by the means of desire itself, by becoming the desire to defer desire, and reason can only control desire on a social scale by becoming social desire—the mob. Thus reason is only desire that has become institutionalized as good sense, that has achieved social conventionality, that is no longer recognizable as a mob because it no longer bears the signs of its emotion, the rage that marked the historic efforts to repress the passion of the other, the infidel and the heretic. Reason appears as desire that has been frozen in its "appropriate" place, and, having achieved its goal, reason can appear free of the violence that is its history. Like the mob, reason promises a coerced social order based on a particular social desire. In contrast to the sharp, qualitative distinction we began with, here reason and passion appear simply as different points on a spectrum; neither concept refers to anything positive and substantial.

Reason appears as a social choice about how to regulate passion, but as such it only has meaning as the flipside of passion, as a deferment of passion that is ruled by passion itself. Reason is simply what is not passion, but only social choices tell us in any particular instance which is which.

Moreover, this indeterminacy with respect to the relation between reason and passion, the intellectuals and the mob, extends to what we think of as the "mob." Our earlier model of the irrational, threatening mob was a lynch mob. But when we look again at the ways that social history has been constructed, we find a multitude of contexts where there was an attempt to identify a lustful, emotional mob unworthy of power and in need of discipline. The mob of immigrants through Ellis Island, the mob at the Bastille, the mob at wildcat factory strikes, the mob at the sweatshop sewing machines, the mob in the housing projects and the Polish ghettos, the mob in the March on Washington.

What seems to connect the meanings of "the mob" in these contexts is a consistent pattern of dominant groups justifying their privileged status by associating the "other" with base, animal urges—a pattern extending from Nazi caricatures of Jews, to white racist caricatures of Blacks, to the middle-class vision of the poor, to male visions of femininity, to factory owners' visions of workers, to skyscraper office images of the people on subways. In each class relation, the dominant group projects the other as emotional and primitive, ruled by irrational passion. In this interpretation, the language of the distinction between reason and passion seems to be simply the language by which the powerful and dominant justify their own power on the basis that they are more civilized and human—and as such, the very categories of reason and passion, far from giving us a vantage point from which to distinguish politics from truth, seem to be merely one form of the rhetoric of social power. The text's reference to the "mob" is indeterminate. The choice between which group to call "the mob" is a political choice, one which "reason" can't decide.

Moreover, this indeterminacy about the text's meaning is not even limited by what we earlier assumed was the paradigm of bad group action, the lynch mob. We initially understood the text by identifying the lynch mob with the coercive threat of civilization disintegrating to an animal state. The lynch mob acts irrationally, in a prejudiced fashion against the Black person being lynched, out of passion rather than reason.

But when we look inside the language of the lynch mob itself, we find the same terms used to justify the lynching. What made Blacks threatening and "other," in need of the discipline of the lynch mob, was, from the lynch mob's point of view, the passionate, lustful, sexual nature of Blacks. It was precisely the white group's view of Black lust that made Blacks represent for the lynch mob the threat of the insurgency of a primitive, animalistic nature that threatened the civilized social order.

Here the interpretation seems to be at a crossroads with no sure way to determine how we are to understand Scott's argument. If it is lust and passion, the animal side, that must be regulated and quelled, then the lynch mob's self understanding of what it was doing is consistent with Scott's claims. Surely Scott doesn't mean that—that's not the point here. Rather, what is called into question is the notion that something called "reason" can neutrally and dispassionately dictate how we are to distinguish the bad mobs from the good. What started out as the paradigm of the mob threat to overcome reason with emotion can, from a different point in history and a different place in social life, become the identification of the mob with reason.

Reason and passion can both be associated with the mob; the association of passion with particular groups, and the association of reason with other groups are political acts that can't be determined by reason itself. In this interpretation, reason can't be the *source of* the intellectual's legitimacy in Scott's text since the content of reason is simply an *effect* of a particular group being in power and therefore able to categorize others as irrational. Accordingly, in Scott's own terms, reason is actually nothing more than some mob having the social power to define its coercive force as what is necessary to quell the passion of the other.

At this point, Scott's text seems to be at war with itself. Scott seems to suggest that the intellectual is to be favored over the mob because the intellectual would be rational, objective, and neutral, while the mob is passionate, biased, and coercive. But the language of the distinction between reason and passion is indeterminate. Nothing in the concepts or the words determines what is being referred to; determinacy is achieved through a contingent social choice, that is, through politics. Rather than point away from politics and toward reason, the text simply advocates a particular politics, a particular disciplinary discourse of social order; the text's invocation of a place outside of politics and passion, a social space outside the mob, seems to be simply one form that the social struggle between groups takes.

This interpretation of Scott's text is an example of one of the many ways that a deconstructive reading might proceed. At the risk of reductionism, we can at this point articulate some aspects of the approach to Scott's argument that are often present in deconstructive readings. First, we were able to show that Scott's text yielded no stable, authoritative meaning; to the contrary, Scott's argument could be read in one way as advocating the elevation of reason over passion; yet, we were also able to use the text's own terms of analysis to reverse this meaning, to find that there is no qualitative distinction between reason and passion and that reason is simply a particular form of passion. Second, the reading also demonstrated the active participation of the interpreter in constructing meaning; the interpretation was not neutral and passive, but rather depended on the sense that the reader brought to the text, on the conceptual language that the reader already possessed. Finally, we identified a critical opposition in the text, the contrast between the intellectual and the mob, and showed how the text itself could be read to subvert the good sense of the contrast upon which the argument is built. By reversing the relationship between reason and passion, and thereby showing how reason might be seen as simply the effect of passion rather than its regulator, this critical interpretation showed how the rational, determinate sense of the argument actually depended on an initial, arational association between reason and particular cultural and political visions of social life.

The point of this kind of reading is not that Scott was somehow insufficiently rigorous in constructing his argument, that, had he been more careful, he could have articulated his position in a way that would have made it immune to the kind of interpretation I have pursued. Any text can be read in this manner. Meaning does not somehow reside in a text, to be discovered by an innocent, unbiased reader; and language is not a self-executing, static reference to objects in the world. Meaning is always constructed, and always subject to being constructed differently. The attribution of meaning to texts and events is a political process that cannot be determined by the authority of reason. So it is not that something is bad about Scott's argument because it can be shown to depend on a particular ideology, on a particular language for attributing likeness and difference in the world. The point, rather, is that there is no way to flee from the politics of interpretation to the purity of reason.

I believe that Scott has correctly identified the political nature of the challenge that deconstruction represents to the traditions and institutions he defends. Deconstruction, in Scott's view, poses the threat of the mob coming to power, because deconstruction subverts the legitimacy of the discourse with which authority commonly justifies social hierarchies such as the superiority of the "intellectuals" over the "mob." The position and prestige of the intellectual depends, in Scott's view, on laying claim to being rational and apolitical. Reason is not itself supposed to be power, but the way that power is tamed to ensure that it is legitimate and appropriate. But if the category of reason is itself a social construct, and if the mantle of social legitimacy depends on being called reason, then the question of what to call reason is a political question about a contingent exercise of the social power of marginalization and exclusion.

The deconstructive approach works to politicize the boundaries between knowledge and superstition, truth and myth, reason and passion, fact and opinion. In doing so, it helps to expose the ways that these distinctions are not simply natural and necessary ways to divide up the world, but rather form the language for a particular discourse of authority and power. As such, the point of demonstrating that, say, Scott's commitment to reason against the mob actually rests on a particular ideology about the world is not to fault his analysis for being partial or political. The goal is not simply to reverse the hierarchies and thus to favor passion over reason, the mob over the intellectuals, superstition over knowledge, but to see that these very ways of thinking and talking about social life already embody a particular discourse of power that seeks to legitimize social hierarchy by claiming to have escaped politics, superstition, and the mere conventionality of language.

And that is why, I think, so much controversy has arisen over the deconstructive project. By exposing the dependence of supposedly rational or scientific interpretations of the world on language and textuality, on the contingent ways that the thick texture of the world might be carved up, the deconstructive practice subverts the claim of the Enlightenment tradition to have transcended time and space, to have found through reason or science a place outside of historical struggle and beyond the partiality of a particular place in the terrain of social geography. Thus, we can recognize in Scott's argument about reason a particular language for interpreting the world—a language within which it seems natural rather than controversial to divide up the world according to the categories of reason and desire, the elite intellectual and the popular mob, knowledge and superstition, principles, and politics. But these categories are not, in fact, natural or necessary. They are, rather, social constructions that can be deconstructed to reveal their history, to reveal the excluded voices that have been diminished as "primitive" or "passionate" or "emotional" in the march of "enlightenment" and "progress." And this language can be deconstructed to reveal its place in the current social geography—in the claims of the powerful that their power is justified by their superior reason or education, or by their civilized nature in sublimating their passion and desire according to middle-class notions of propriety. Or in the more general cultural tradition marked by fear of passion and sexuality, fear of emotion, keeping proper public appearances.

We can also see in the analysis of Scott's text a particular way that such a language or ideology works to, in a sense, cover its tracks, to suppress the constructed nature of its categories. For the coherence of Scott's approach depends on believing not only that his categories for interpreting the social world are natural and necessary, but also that they can be applied apolitically because they are not merely words or ideas but refer to something real in the world, something out there somewhere prior to the mere convention of language which the distinction between reason and desire reflects. The point of showing that reason is simply what is not desire and vice versa is to demonstrate that there is no escape from the contigencies of language. There is nothing in the words or concepts of "reason" and "desire" that dictates that they be associated with particular experiences; the two concepts exist only as they are socially constructed within language.

The notion that there is no escape from language and politics, no way to represent the social world free of ideology, is not meant simply to correct some intellectual mistake that academics have made in the process of interpreting the world. Rather, it is to oppose the authority of official knowledge on its own terms, to demonstrate that if the justification for certain people being marginalized and excluded from social power is that they view the world through the lenses of myth and superstition, so, too, do the so-called rational and civilized. The significance of the deconstructive practice is not simply to reveal the constructed nature of what gets taken as fact, knowledge and truth as opposed to opinion, superstition and myth. It is an important practice because, in our social world, these claims to truth have played powerful political roles in the construction of our social relations—in the ways that those in power have justified their power and those out of power have been made to feel that their powerlessness is their own fault and inadequacy.

Moreover, the deconstructive practice is significant to the extent that it works to demystify the ideology of necessity and naturalness not only in intellectual life, but also in social experience. The notion that we are always perceiving and communicating about the world through language, through socially created and contingent ways of articulating the social space, is relevant not only to "texts" in the sense of written documents, but also to the "text" of our social relations themselves. One aspect of the textuality of experience is reflected in the language of social roles. We approach each other in large part through a social matrix for distributing meaning that influences how the other will be perceived and how we perceive ourselves. Accordingly, social power, represented in the language of social roles, influences every social relation. For example, the relations between men and women proceed largely on the basis of what it means to be a man or a woman within the particular language of social roles. As recent feminist work has powerfully articulated, there is no basis outside social power for the way that these roles have been constructed. The language of gender roles does not reflect some objective, natural reality. It is a construct with a particular history and place in the social field.

But so long as this language of social roles is taken to reflect something positive and substantial, something that pre-exists language and is merely reflected by language, so long as it appears that gender relations are conducted in a certain way because that's the way men and women "are," the social construction of gender rules is suppressed and gender rules assume a place outside of politics, outside of history, and beyond the possibilities of social change.

The Enlightenment tradition of opposing knowledge to ignorance, truth to mythology, and reason to passion beckoned us toward a place of universality where we would meet outside the play of politics and passion, free from the hold of mythology and the particularities of our history. But the most successful form of social power is one that presents itself not as power, but as reason, truth and objectivity. Rather than continue the quest to find a place that is outside politics and independent of social struggle, it is time to look at all the ways that social power is at stake across the social space, in what gets called "politics" as well as what gets called "reason," in what gets called "private" choice as well as what is recognized as public power. Rather than compulsively search for a vantage point of neutrality, we should recognize as acts of political power the exclusions of those who are marginalized as merely ideological or superstitious in the Enlightenment mythology of truth.

The deconstruction of the dominant forms of knowledge is only the first step of a committed critical practice. We then are faced with the task of taking a stand, or asserting what the world means, of constructing new meanings and new understandings of what is happening in our social lives. Having debunked the dominant form of knowledge because it suppresses its socially created character, we are thrown into the task of creating meaning socially, the task of politics itself.

To some, like Scott, the assertion that there is no neutral, authoritative, and apolitical interpretation of social life available sounds like a message of hopelessness and nihilism. I think this reaction is rooted in a conviction that the only kind of knowledge worth having is a kind of knowledge that can be elevated above social life and social history, that can be immunized from bias or change. For me, the message of social construction and social contingency is one of hope. It is hopeful because it also suggests that there is no objective necessity or rational principle to justify the way things are, to legitimate the hierarchies and status quo distribution of wealth, power, prestige, and freedom. Because our social relations are social products, there is no "reason" why they cannot be remade by us, working and struggling and dreaming together. □

On Passionate Reason: Transcending Marxism and Deconstructionism

Peter Gabel

I n the current historical period, progressive forces in the United States and actually throughout the world find themselves without any coherent vision that could articulate either what is wrong with the way things are or what kind of world we want to bring into being. We are caught between two points of view, both of which are inadequate to grasp the true problems of social existence. One point of view I will simply call Marxism, which is the most developed form of progressive thought to emerge from the "objectivity"—the separation of passion and reason, and the separation of subject and object—characteristic of the Enlightenment. The problem with Marxism is not simply that it "hasn't worked," but that it was always based on a mistaken and overly objectified view of the nature of human desire and need itself. Its tendency to explain social phenomena by reference to economic dynamics, however plausible in light of the brute facts of nineteenth-century life and the mystifications that justified the economic oppression characteristic of feudalism and earlier forms of society, reflected a positivism that eclipsed the most distinctively social aspect of existence itself—namely, the desire of every living being to be recognized and confirmed by others and the attendant desire to create a vital world of social meaning and purpose based upon this social connection. Marxism was "smart" in the sense that it could plausibly correlate actual social and historical processes with apparently "objective" processes beyond the will or conscious control of any human being or group of human beings. It nevertheless misunderstood this very correlation, failing to see that it was social alienation, an alienation and distortion of social desire, that underlay the very "objective" and involuntary character of economic dynamics or of the so-called economic system itself.

There has as yet been no theoretical account of this social alienation that has gone beyond the psychoanalytic theory of the family and enabled us to understand the social-psychological dynamics that actually constitute and reproduce large-scale social processes and institutions. The legacy of Marxism still dominates progressive thought. People on the Left still talk primarily in economic terms about the nature of and solution to fundamental social problems because they do not yet have any other way to talk. As a result, conservative forces, which have a better instinctive understanding of the centrality of social connection and meaning to people's lives, have gained ascendancy in the West through their affirmation of religion, the "free" world and market, traditional family values; and through appeals to the imaginary or "substitute" social connection symbolized by, for example, the flag. This conservative ascendancy cannot be effectively challenged by the Left's prevailing economistic worldview, because that worldview simply fails to address the desire for a community of meaning that is the very heart of the Right's message. As we have been arguing in *Tikkun,* you

---

Peter Gabel is president of New College of California and associate editor of Tikkun. *This article appeared in* Tikkun, *November/December 1989.*

can't fight the passionate appeal of the conservative vision with a laundry list of economic programs.

The failure of progressive forces to develop a social theory based on an understanding of alienation can be traced in part to the effects of the second point of view currently enveloping the Left—the one associated with post-structuralism and deconstructionism, with the work of Derrida and Foucault and their followers. This point of view has reacted against the horrors associated with Marxism and other totalizing social theories by rejecting the project of social theory altogether. Post-structuralists find in such theories an intrinsic tendency toward domination (Foucault's famous link between power and knowledge), which makes social theory itself part of the problem rather than part of the solution.

The post-structuralist line of criticism has many virtues, including its modesty, its emphasis on pluralism and "different voices," its emphasis on the importance of particularity and context in interpreting the meaning of social phenomena, and its capacity to disarm the sort of Big Theorizing that has been used for centuries to oppress and to justify the oppression of women and minorities. Yet, ironically, post-structuralist criticism remains as dependent upon the limitations of the Enlightenment as the type of social theory it criticizes. The specific error of post-structuralism is that it unjustly equates social theory with the explanatory conceptual schemes that have followed upon the rationalistic project of the Enlightenment; then it declares these grand conceptual schemes to be false on their own terms as well as socially repressive (Derrida's attack on "*phallologocentrism*"); and, finally, it rejects *any* universalist theory of social interpretation that could tie disparate social phenomena together and help make the problems of the world intelligible as a whole to people. The post-structuralists do not allow for the possibility that there is a kind of reason and general knowledge that can emerge from passionate understanding, and that this kind of reason is precisely what is needed for the illumination of the meaning of social phenomena expressive of the movement of social desire.

The post-structuralist "ban" on social theory has weakened the Left's ability to develop a moral critique of the existing society and to articulate a compelling vision of the kind of society we want to create. The goal of both philosophy and social theory traditionally has been to establish a true link between being and knowledge, or to make what is as yet unrevealed to consciousness about the meaning of its own existence accessible to critical reflection. For those who have sought to transform the world in a more emancipatory and humane direction, this intellectual activity was meant to provide people with a common reflective knowledge that could, through the experience of shared insight, inspire people to act to change things. The current left-wing academic and intellectual climate in the United States, increasingly influenced by post-structuralism and deconstruction, is impeding the continuation of this project by making a fetish of the notion of "different voices," by failing to tie the particularistic knowledge it values so highly to any common, general insight into the truth of social life *as a whole*. The goal of wrenching away the distinctive experience of women and minorities from the oppressive, universalizing categories of the dominant culture has certainly been a laudable one. But the denial, in the name of cultural uniqueness, that there is any way to reunite and illuminate the meaning of these diverse experiences through the development of a more supple and experiential social theory grounded in our common humanity makes it difficult for us to challenge the Allan Blooms and William Bennetts of our society. The effect of essentializing our differences and, therefore, of relativizing social knowledge has been to leave progressive forces open to conservative and neoconservative charges of "nihilism." It deprives us of any common intellectual language with which we might criticize the existing society as a whole, or discover our common social objectives.

The methodology that would take us beyond Marxism and deconstruction must involve an explicit attempt to overcome the separation of passion and reason characteristic of Enlightenment "objectivity" as well as what might be called "irrationalism" implicit in the post-structuralist rejection of the possibility of social theory altogether. It must be a method based on what I earlier called "passionate understanding;" and its epistemology has its roots in the phenomenological tradition of philosophy—in the work of Husserl, Heidegger, Merleau-Ponty, and Sartre and is implicit in much feminist writing. Such a methodology proceeds on the assumption that all human reality shares a common ground and is expressive of a common social being, even though this common reality is manifested in a potentially infinite number of distinct and unique social forms; that every person has the capacity (under supportive social circumstances) to transcend the particularity of cultural conditioning so as to understand, on the basis of one's own being, the meaning of the experience of others; and, finally, that the validity of this understanding is based not on any logical "proof" characteristic of detached scientific analysis, but on the persuasiveness of one's evocative and critical "comprehension" of the phenomena that one is describing.

This way of linking being and knowledge has really always been at the heart of the true elements in psychoanalytic thought, although in Freud's day it was dressed up in a sort of metaphorical scientific vocabulary. Today, there are few psychoanalytic writers who do not, at least implicitly, acknowledge the centrality of engaged, intuitive comprehension to the construction of psychoanalytic knowledge. But this point of view has yet really to make its way into critical social theory, in part because the tradition of philosophical phenomenology (with the exception of Sartre) consists largely of individualistic introspection by abstruse German and French thinkers whom almost no one understands. The kind of critical social thought that I'm talking about here demands that people passionately throw themselves forward into the lived experience of the social phenomena that surround them and attempt to illuminate through evocative description, rather than detached analysis or "explanation," the universal realizations and distortions of social desire that these diverse phenomena share across the cultural richness of their differences.

To some extent, we have been trying to develop this kind of thinking in *Tikkun,* and we will do so more forcefully in issues to come. But one central point about the link between this new social theory and politics can be stated directly: transcendent social knowledge can emerge only from transcendent social experience. True social change can only occur through the building of social movements that allow us to recover our awareness of the desire for mutual confirmation and to gain the confidence that this desire also exists in the heart of the other. This implies a rejection of the simplistic notion of "revolution," although not of the radicalism that the notion of revolution has traditionally symbolized. Instead, we should think of social movements as more or less spontaneous outbreaks of social desire which must become vehicles for the gradual building of a true historical confidence in the possibility of genuine reciprocity. The success of any such effort requires an awareness that this process of confidence-building will be continually undermined by the history of our alienation and mutual distrust. True social change requires a kind of collective strength and compassion that progressive forces have yet to demonstrate in the social movements that have arisen thus far, and it requires the building of forms of culture that enable us to internalize the conviction that the kind of change I am speaking of really can occur beyond exhilarating outbursts like the sixties. Not to knock such exhilarating outbursts—in the face of the media's "nostalgia" idiocy and the many other anxious public attempts to suppress our memory of what we can still become, it is important to affirm the silent knowledge shared by millions of us that the sixties were among the most wonderful times that have blessed our existence together on this earth. It is only by retaining our memory of that experience, as well as other perhaps more partial ones like it, that the kind of expressive theory I am speaking for can come into being and allow us to communicate about how to move forward. □

The Bank Teller

Peter Gabel

I. Ontological Passivity and the Constitution of Otherness Within Large-Scale Social Networks

Imagine a row of bank tellers serving customers in a typical American bank. Although each of them appears to be performing competently, taking and giving paper, opening and closing drawers, showing for the most part efficient politeness and a good mood to each person who approaches the window, we know that each of them is under a great deal of stress. We know this not primarily because we know the objective conditions that define their respective situations—that they must perform a repetitive series of manual operations very rapidly in order to keep their jobs, earn a subsistence wage, and so forth—but because we detect in each of them, simply from the vantage-point of an onlooker, a continual artificiality. Each reveals in every word and gesture what we might call the attitude of being a bank teller. Each of them feels compelled to *enact* an "efficient politeness" and a "good mood." They feel this politeness and good mood not as spontaneous expression, but as a kind of role that is somehow superimposed on their being from an experiential "outside."

Thus we can detect that they feel somehow "outside" themselves and "inside" the enacted role of being-a-bank-teller. And we can detect that this is stressful to each of them precisely to the degree that it is artificial, that through being compelled to feel artificial in this way they feel at the same time unable to express themselves spontaneously. Neither we nor they can know what this spontaneous expression would "look like" exactly because both we and they feel it only as an absence.

A good way of measuring this absence is to notice that each gesture is a moment "behind" or "too late," and it is this fraction of delay-time that reveals to us the gesture's enacted quality. We can see that they are perpetually acting *as if* they were bank tellers, and one way of measuring the gap between these as-if performances and the absent spontaneity that is somehow buried inside of them is in the felt sense that if spontaneity were to somehow "break through" (as sometimes happens), the delay-time would vanish, absorbed in the plenitude of total presence. A whole person would have momentarily erupted through the split being of the "bank teller"; through the split "between" the as-if performance and the absence that is immanently bound within it. In a milieu of as-if performances like those of the row of bank tellers, the absent spontaneity cannot be described positively, but only negatively as something "not there," although we would immediately recognize its positive incarnation if it were to suddenly appear—we would feel that *that* is what was missing or "not there" a moment before.

This feeling of being perpetually trapped within an as-if performance that seems to come from the outside is an experience of ontological passivity. By this I mean that in their very being these bank

---

Peter Gabel is president of New College of California and associate editor of Tikkun. *This article appeared in* Tikkun, *January/February 1987.*

tellers feel a loss of agency in relation to their own movements. They feel compelled to enact a "self" that is somehow not *their* self but another self that seems to move through them in the form of a role and that leaves them feeling "other" to themselves, and "other" to each of the others with whom they interact. Yet this feeling of "otherness" is not a feeling that descends on each of the tellers individually; it is rather a collective phenomenon that unites the tellers to one another in a perverse way. Thus a new teller, when she first arrives at the bank, will proceed to indoctrinate herself into her own passivity by taking cues from all of the others in discovering how to act (or how to enact herself), and in so doing she will gradually come to feel "with" the others in an as-if way, in the sense that she will come to feel, as do each of the others, that they are all undergoing the same passive experience which establishes among them a social bond. But since this social bond is constituted as a feeling of being-other-than-themselves-together, of being collectively trapped within the same role, it is simultaneously pervaded by a collective sense of universal isolation, since no one is capable of really making contact with any of the others spontaneously without violating the norms of "being-a-bank-teller."

Ontological passivity is, therefore, a collective experience that simultaneously divides a group of people by an infinite distance and unites them in the false communion of being-other-than-themselves-together. The source of this collective passivity and impotence is to be found in the relation of the tellers to the bank as an institution. This "bank" has a double reality, or rather its singular reality must be understood simultaneously from two points of view. On the one hand, the bank is a functional organization of human labor that has a determinate relation to economic production, in that it serves to reproduce finance capital in what economists call an "efficient" way. There is a certain division of labor that corresponds to a certain level of technological development, and the functional organization of work that derives from this correspondence bears a definite relationship to a system of economic pressures (this bank must compete with other banks, and so forth). But this approach to defining what the bank is can tell us nothing about why the tellers behave and feel as they do, because it is an approach that turns the bank into a thing.

To understand the bank as a living milieu, we must attempt to grasp "the bank" from the inside, as it is experienced by the people who dwell "within it" and who thereby create it as a collective gestalt. In this subjective sense, the institution of "the bank" is, as we shall see, an imaginary entity to which the tellers (as well as the other bank personnel, the customers, and so forth) have given over their being by believing in "its" existence as a determining power. Precisely to the degree that the tellers feel a loss of agency in relation to themselves, they feel themselves to be agents of "the bank" as an imaginary entity, and they feel themselves to be united with one another or socially bonded in relation to this imaginary entity. It is not an economic method of explanation but rather a socio-phenomenological method of description that can make "the bank" intelligible as a lived experience for the people who create and then inhabit it.

The first step in gaining access to this lived experience is to detach ourselves in a radical way from the social milieu that is generated through the communication of signs (spoken language, tone of voice, gestures, and so forth) within the bank. If we can manage to attain this hyper-objective viewpoint, we can observe something that is at once perfectly obvious and normally very difficult to see or "remember"— namely, that "the bank," for all of its pretense and style, consists of nothing more than a group of people in a room. From this position of hyper-objectivity through which the social interactions before us are stripped of their symbolic and signifying content, we do not experience "the bank" at all except perhaps as a kind of random fact about what they call this type of social gathering ("this is what they call 'a bank'"). Yet to the people immersed within the socially communicated reality within the room, "the bank" has a ubiquitous presence—in fact, they cannot, except in very private and quasi-unconscious moments of distraction, escape from their absorption in "the bank" and see before them simply a room full of people. This person who approaches the window is first of all a "customer," that person on the left is first of all a "teller like me," those velvet ropes are first of all not merely ropes but signs that "the bank" uses to "line up the customers," just as the adjacent machine with the green lights is first of all a "computer" that "the bank" uses to retrieve information about "customer accounts." Every object and person within the room, in other words, is always already layered over with a relatively impenetrable symbolic coating that seems to derive from this "bank," this entity that appears to allocate to each person a role and to each object a signifying power.

Yet from this subjective point of view, "the bank" *is* nowhere. It does not reside in the Board of Directors or in the President's office, or anywhere else except in the minds of those who believe in its existence as a kind of phantom presence that has vampirized their being and made them agents of its imaginary power. How does this collective internalization of "the bank" take place?

The answer to this question is to be found in a complex reciprocal relationship between the role of collective anxiety and the role of the bank hierarchy in shaping the internal experience of each of the bank's members. At a very deep and basic level, every person in the room feels that she is subject to both the physical and psychological power of other people, that if she fails to conform to the norms of expected behavior within the bank, she will be thrown out of the bank by force or be subject to psychological humiliation. If a "customer" fails to act like a "customer," he will be thrown out by a man with a gun; if a "teller" fails to act like a "teller," she will be fired or at least risk being socially ostracized; the same or similar sanctions are available for the "president" and even the "chairman of the board." This fear of dismissal in both the physical and psychological sense is ever present at what we might call "the base" of everyone's experience, and it establishes the experiential ground for the transmutation of people's being that occurs through the internalization of the "bank," in the sense that if these conditions were not present, people might refuse to conform to what was expected of them and recover their spontaneity.

What is the source of this shared anxiety among the banks' members that each of them is endanger of being "dismissed" or humiliated by a dominant other? In part, this fear is a rational response to real inequalities of power in the bank, to the fact that many of the banks' workers must depend for their survival upon owners who maybe indifferent to them except as factors of production and who have the power to deprive them of both their income and their sense of social identity. But a deeper reason for the anxiety, and one which may even account for the persistence of the inequalities of economic power, is a contradiction that exists at the heart of every one's experience. On the one hand, each person wants to connect with the others in a life-giving way, to make contact in a way that would produce a feeling of genuine recognition and mutual confirmation. This desire is fundamental to being a social person, and it animates all of us in every moment of our existence. Yet at the same time, everyone has learned to fear this very desire because its realization implies an openness to the other that leaves the self essentially vulnerable and risks a kind of total humiliation should the other respond with "disconfirmation," domination, or rejection. Since the experience of genuine connection and confirmation has been very rare for all of the banks' members owing to the alienation and mistrust that pervades our social world, and since their desire for it is therefore associated with the anticipation of pain and loss, the very existence of others has become a source of ontological anxiety for them. Each person has learned to expect to be "dismissed," and so each seeks to avoid being fully present to the other by mediating their presence through a distancing persona and by making themselves unconscious that this mediation has occurred.

The transmutation of each person's authentic being into a false or as-if self, therefore, occurs through a process of collective and reciprocal flight on the part of everyone from experiencing their own desire for real contact and the vulnerability that this implies. By absorbing themselves in their role-performances and implicitly asserting (to themselves and others) that these performances constitute who they really are, the banks' members try to withdraw the immediacy of their social presence from their outward appearance, becoming anonymous "bank tellers," "customers," "vice-presidents," and so on, whose artificiality makes them inaccessible to the threat of the other's gaze. The lack of agency that we earlier observed in the tellers' relationship to their own movements can now be understood as the outcome of an intentional effort to "empty" their role performances of any signs of authorship or personal identity, and the delay-time we observed in their gestures can now be seen as reflective of a chronic self-consciousness through which their outward expression is repeatedly uncoupled from its generative foundation. Yet we must ask ourselves why, if the desire for genuine connection is really a basic aspect of our being, do these tellers not find a way of resisting this perpetual flight which can only leave them continually threatened and isolated? The answer is that while they all feel the same unrealized desire, no one can ordinarily gain the confidence that the desire she feels within herself is also felt by those around her. From the point of view of her isolated position, each person always already experiences all of the others as other-than-themselves, as participants in collective flight. And since the possibility of recovering one's authentic being can come only through being recognized as fully human by another, no one can normally find the strength to resist in a milieu where the possibility of such a recovery is reciprocally denied. Instead, each person feels compelled to become "one of the others" and participate in the collective flight that holds everyone's alienation in place.

The medium through which this collective flight is carried out is commonly called a hierarchy. The bank-hierarchy, as I am using the term here, is a purely imaginary entity that is generated by the felt need of everyone to "identify" with "the bank," to establish the ontological basis for one's passivity as a false self by constituting an "other" before whom one can be recognized as false. This hierarchy bears no relation to the direct interpersonal relations through which real power is exercised in the bank, since real power is exercised not "from above" (there is no "above") but by one person acting directly upon another, by the subordination of one to another's will. The hierarchy is rather conjured up imaginatively as a way of escaping the universal sense of danger that I have described: It provides what we might call the imaginary vehicle through which everyone becomes able to find an imaginary and passive station in relation to everyone else. The hierarchy allows each person to substitute a legitimate authority, which is "the bank" itself as a subjectively constituted institution and which can serve as the relational agent for each person's self-falsification, for the illegitimate sense of humiliation that haunts each person's true being and true sense of what is going on in the room.

To see how the hierarchy comes into being, we need only look carefully at the reciprocal interaction that commonly takes place among two tellers and their so-called "supervisor." Let us suppose that the two tellers are called Jane and John, and that the supervisor is called Harold. Jane and John work side by side at their windows. Harold, who is otherwise engaged in a variety of lower-management clerical tasks, walks back and forth behind Jane and John and occasionally looks at them to see not only what they are doing, but who they are being. Jane discovers the contours of her as-if performance through watching John, as John does through watching Jane, and in this sense Jane and John "recognize" one another as "bank tellers." Both, in other words, take the position of "other" to the other and in so doing discover the way of becoming other to themselves. Yet because this relation of reciprocal otherness involves a loss of agency in relation to themselves and a sinking into ontological passivity that is measured by this loss of agency, both of them require an agent to ground their impoverished "identities." They must project onto a third-party the active power to establish the ontological basis for the series of performances which they experience as passive and lacking in any self-generated agency. Without such a third-party, they could not "exist" as "bank tellers" because there would be no source for their being. This role is allocated to Harold, whom they perceive to be their authority (author-ity). And in together perceiving Harold as the source of their being, they also discover their own unification as "tellers-together," which is to say that they discover a social bond through their perception of how they believe Harold perceives them, and this bond reassures them to the degree that it compensates for the feeling of actual isolation that dwells within each of them. Harold allows them to feel the illusion of being "with" one another to the degree that each, in being "other" to each other and "other" to themselves, are "other-together" before Harold, as they perceive him. And because Harold must always remain with them as their relational "authority figure" in order for them to exist as tellers-together, they internalize him and "identify" with him as the one to whom they owe their own identities. Even in his absence, they know how to act because they have internalized his authoritative image and made it part of themselves.

Harold knows how to play his part through his empathic understanding of how tellers are supposed to be, and in fact he enacts his authority in all of his relations with them, in his way of approaching them, advising them, and in criticizing their performances. Yet it is evident that this "Harold" that we are describing is no more an actual person than are Jane and John. Harold merely plays the part of "supervisor," in that however "active" and "authoritative," he appears for John and Jane, he remains passive in relation to himself. He discovers his being-as-a-supervisor only through the reciprocal internalization of themselves-as-supervisors that characterizes the relations among the supervisors at his level in "the bank," relations which are pervaded by the same passivization that pervades the inter-relations among the tellers. The supervisors, in enacting their authority in relation to the tellers, are also "other" to each other and "other" to themselves, and as a result they also require an agency outside of themselves to activate and ground their own passivity. Harold finds this agency through his own supervisor, who is perhaps a "vice-president" and who performs for all of the supervisors at Harold's level the same ontological function that Harold performs for the tellers. Thus Harold discovers how to become a supervisor through watching and internalizing how the others at his level enact themselves as as-if authorities, while their actual experience of collective passivity is grounded for them by a superior whom they project and then internalize as the agent of their as-if selves. Thus, in the relation teller-supervisor-vice-president we discover the ontological foundation of the hierarchy as a form of collective being, a form that I am calling imaginary because it creates the appearance, among people who are in fact simply people, of a top-down ordering that serves to establish each person's sense of his or her imaginary social place.

The paradox of the hierarchy, however, is that no one actually feels in command because the authority that the hierarchy distributes throughout itself is never more than the active role-complement of the universal passivity out of which the hierarchy is born as a projected-internalized, imaginary entity. If, for example, we reach the "top" of the hierarchy, we find a "president" who does not feel himself to be his own "author," because his authority is merely the as-if authority of a "president" in a "bank." He receives his authority, in other words, from the subjects who constitute him, and this requires of him that he find the basis of his own being outside of himself in precisely the same fashion as the others. Yet there is no *one* "above" him; his ontological recourse is to the board of directors, who are constituted as the "fiduciaries" of "the bank." In the realm of the imaginary, the board of directors is comparable to the modern "State," in that just as the State serves as the imaginary basis for the political unification of the "United States" and so establishes for each of us our imaginary identity as "Americans," so the board of directors is the incarnate representation of "the bank's" existence as a political organization (and this board is itself enfranchised by the State, which establishes the political legitimacy of "the bank" as an entity that derives its existence ultimately from the democratic constitution of "the nation"). Thus the "president," like all of the other bank personnel, finds his agency outside of himself and shapes his being to the set of performances required of him by "the bank" as it is embodied for him through the board to which he is "accountable" in an imaginary way. And since the board members experience themselves as fiduciaries in the service of "the bank," we find that the ultimate source of authority within the hierarchy is "the bank" itself, as a phantom "other" to whom everyone "within the bank" owes their as-if existence. In this milieu of universal otherness, "the bank" is believed in as a kind of "God," as an object of belief which is invested with authorship or authority for the group as a whole.

The relationship of "the bank" as an imaginary entity to the hierarchy as an imaginary ordering is, therefore, that the hierarchy is the vehicle that the group uses to bring "the bank" to themselves through a series of embodied human gazes. The underlying fear of domination and humiliation from which everyone flees is transmuted, through the constitution of "the bank" and the hierarchy through which it is concretely and intersubjectively mediated, into the shared submission of being-"other"- together before an imaginary object with whom everyone identifies as the active foundation of their passive and false selves. In and through this process, they recover an imaginary sense of being "with" one another as "of the bank," even as they are utterly lost and isolated from one another as real people who would know themselves as agents of their own collective activity.

The self that is produced within this hierarchical environment is, to borrow R.D. Laing's phrase, an ontologically divided one that has a rather complex organization. Each person experiences his or her authentic being as a privatized non-self that is denied recognition and that is therefore "invisible" or unconscious: It is known or comprehended only through the experienced bodily tension that derives from not being-oneself and through a continual obsessive and pre-conscious fantasy life that reaches a dim awareness in moments of distraction (as in being vaguely aware of wanting to sleep with a customer, or in vaguely noticing that a shape on a wall resembles a wild dog). The "visible" or conscious self that is enacted in behavior is experienced as a "public" or "outer" synthesis of as-if performances which is at once lived as passively undergone to the degree that it lacks any sense of its own agency and yet is "owned" to the degree that each person feels this self as "I." And corresponding to this ontologically passive public self is a projected-internalized active or authoritative "other" which serves as the passive self's agency and which generates within everyone the feeling that one's being is fashioned from the outside. This ontologically divided self-organization is the internalized residue of all forms of social organization within which people lack the actual power to express themselves freely in their practical activity together, which is to say virtually all forms of social life that have existed in human history and that exist today on earth.

Yet because each person's privatized and authentic being continually clamors for recognition in order to realize its desire and explode the false "outer" self which contains this desire, we must look more carefully at the interpersonal dynamic through which everyone's true needs are perpetually subdued in order to see how the clamoring of desire for genuine recognition by the other perpetually checks itself through being held in check by the other. The way to do this is to observe what happens in the event of a disturbance that reaches visibility, as when John begins to complain to the other tellers that he really hates his job, that it somehow makes him feel unreal and like an automaton. If John makes this complaint to Jane alone over a cup of coffee, there is no threat posed to the collective belief in "the bank" because coffee with a quasi-friend (they work at adjacent windows) is sanctioned as a private space appropriate for passive commiseration, or in other words the complaint remains sufficiently private to elicit a restorative concern.

But if John begins to "go public" with his dissatisfaction, he threatens to expose the imaginary nature of "the bank" as the vehicle of collective flight, producing within everyone an anxiety that the humiliation that which everyone is fleeing from will be drawn to the surface and will *occur* for each of them. As a result, to the degree that John reveals himself publicly as being in pain, everyone will adopt toward him the position of the authoritative other through which their passive selves are secured. They will see themselves in John, see their own alienation from themselves and one another *recognized* through his affirmation of its existence, and so they will secure their own "otherness"' to themselves and to one another by taking the position of the agent through whom their passivity is founded. They will act toward him, in other words, as if he is "crazy" and indicate to him that he ought not to be *being this way*. But in addressing him, they will actually be addressing themselves as they are revealed through him, simultaneously quelling their own anxiety and reestablishing their imaginary connection with one another as depersonalized "personnel," as "of the bank." In taking the position of the authoritative other, they secure a collective reassurance which is also a collective denial. And through this collective denial they perpetually supress their true desire to recognize one another as fully human beings.

The clamoring for authentic recognition of which I speak is therefore held in check by the perpetual anticipation of this "reversal of voice" whereby the others adopt the attitude of the Other toward each other and themselves. And it is the perpetual conflict between the clamoring for recognition and the anticipation of rejection (for each person knows that he, too, would join the others in rejecting another) that produces collective despair and adaptation. But in order to guarantee that this reciprocal holding-in-check will not unravel, the "lines of authority" through which "the bank" is sustained as a totemic source of unification are usually externalized and represented in a "flow-chart," which may appear in an office manual or may even be posted on a wall. This "flow chart" is nothing other than a "constitution" of the imaginary ordering in the hierarchy, and it is the institutional analogue to "the law" insofar as it attempts to legalize in an authoritative document, the alienated relations that comprise "the bank" as an imaginary entity. Its image resides within the consciousness of everyone as something that can be pointed to in the event of a disruption, and its effect is to reify these alienated relations, to represent the collective experience of passivization and otherness as a timeless "fact" of "bank life." To the degree that the flow-chart is internalized by everyone in this way, it establishes for everyone the basis of their abstract integration with all of the others, or in other words it generates an appearance of social unification that contradicts the felt sense of isolation and unconnectedness that pervades each person's private experience of being in the room. As such it is both reassuring and compensatory insofar as it signifies to each person that she is "of the group" (that she is "part of something"), and repressive insofar as its abstract image of social integration is a denial of each person's concrete sense of the truth.

As a sign that is "pointed to" in the event of a disruption, the flow-chart becomes an interpretive document that inscribes the necessity for both the passivization of the self, which is signified as an abstract "role" within each box, and the inevitability of reversal, which is represented in the lines linking the flow-chart boxes from top to bottom. The chart is therefore a spatial representation of the temporal experience (for everyone) of being-in-the-bank, and because the spatial inscription appears as something fixed (instead of being merely the drawing that it actually is) it functions, insofar as it is internalized, as a social defense mechanism. It becomes, in other words, a shared internalized representation of "the group" that simultaneously inhibits everyone's genuine impulses for connection and recognition and partially gratifies these impulses in an imaginary way.

This, then, is a "bank" as it appears to the people who "inhabit" it. As a social institution, or an institutionalization of a particular way of being social, it is obviously not unique, but rather typical of virtually every social formation in contemporary society. Changing such institutions requires overcoming the alienation and fear that give rise to them. And this will not happen until we find a way of collectively gaining confidence that the desire we each secretly feel within ourselves exists with equal intensity in those around us, no matter how remote, threatening, or unreal they feel compelled to make themselves appear. □

The Writing Life

Annie Dillard

What if man could see Beauty Itself, pure, unalloyed, stripped of mortality and all its pollution, stains, and vanities, unchanging, divine, ... the man becoming, in that communion, the friend of God, himself immortal; ... would that be a life to disregard?
—Plato

I have been looking into schedules. Even when we read physics, we inquire of each least particle, "What then shall I do this morning?" How we spend our days is, of course, how we spend our lives. What we do with this hour, and that one, is what we are doing. A schedule defends from chaos and whim. It is a net for catching days. It is a scaffolding on which a worker can stand and labor with both hands at sections of time. A schedule is a mock-up of reason and order—willed, faked, and so brought into being; it is a peace and a haven set into the wreck of time; it is a lifeboat on which you find yourself, decades later, still living. Each day is the same, so you remember the series afterward as a blurred idyll.

The most appealing daily schedule I know is that of a certain turn-of-the-century Swedish aristocrat. He got up at four and set out on foot to hunt black grouse, wood grouse, woodcock, and snipe. At eleven he met his friends who had also been out hunting alone all morning. They converged "at one of these babbling brooks," he wrote. He outlined the rest of his schedule: "Take a quick dip, relax with a schnapps and a sandwich, stretch out, have a smoke, take a nap or just rest, and then sit around and chat until three. Then I hunt some more until sundown, bathe again, put on white tie and tails to keep up appearances, eat a huge dinner, smoke a cigar and sleep like a log until the sun comes up again to redden the eastern sky. This is living.... Could it be more perfect?"

There is no shortage of good days. It is good lives that are hard to come by. A life of good days lived in the senses is not enough. The life of sensation is the life of greed; it requires more and more. The life of the spirit requires less and less; time is ample and its passage sweet. Who would call a day spent reading a good day? But a life spent reading—that is a good life. A day that closely resembles every other day for the past ten or twenty years does not suggest itself as a good one. But who would not call Pasteur's life a good one, or Thomas Mann's?

Wallace Stevens in his forties, living in Hartford, Connecticut, hewed to a productive routine. He rose at six, read for two hours, and walked another hour—three miles—to work. He dictated poems to his secretary. He ate no lunch; at noon he walked for another hour, often to an art gallery. He walked home from work—another hour. After dinner he retired to his study; he went to bed at nine. On Sundays, he walked in the park. I don't know what he did on Saturdays. Perhaps he exchanged a few words with his wife, who posed for the Liberty dime. (One would rather read these people, or

Annie Dillard is the author of seven books. Her most recent novel, The Living, *is about the pioneer generation on Puget Sound. She and her family live in Middletown, Connecticut and Cape Cod, Massachusetts. This article appeared in* Tikkun, *November/December 1988.*

lead their lives, than be their wives. When the Swedish aristocrat Wilhelm Blixen shot birds all day, drank schnapps, napped, and dressed for dinner, he and his wife had three children under three. The middle one was Karen, later known as Isak Dinesen.)

Like Stevens, Osip Mandelstam composed poetry on the hoof. So did Dante. Nietzsche, like Emerson, took two long walks a day. "When my creative energy flowed most freely, my muscular activity was always greatest.... I might often have been seen dancing; I used to walk through the hills for seven or eight hours on end without a hint of fatigue; I slept well, laughed a good deal—I was perfectly vigorous and patient" (Nietzsche). On the other hand, A. E. Housman, almost predictably, maintained, "I have seldom written poetry unless I was rather out of health." This makes sense, too, because in writing a book you can be too well for your own good.

Jack London claimed to write twenty hours a day. Before he undertook to write, he obtained the University of California course list and all the syllabi; he spent a year reading the textbooks in philosophy and literature. In subsequent years, once he had a book of his own under way, he set his alarm to wake him after four hours of sleep. Often he slept through the alarm, so, by his own account, he rigged it to drop a weight on his head. I cannot say I believe this, though a novel like *The Sea-Wolf* is strong evidence that some sort of weight fell on his head with some sort of frequency—though you wouldn't think a man would claim credit for it. London maintained that every writer needed experience, a technique, and a philosophical position. Perhaps the position need not be an airtight one; London himself felt comfortable with a weird amalgam of Karl Marx and Herbert Spencer (Marks & Sparks).

I write these words in my most recent of many studies—a pine shed on Cape Cod. The pine lumber is unfinished inside the study; the pines outside are finished trees. I see the pines from my two windows. Nuthatches spiral around their long, coarse trunks. Sometimes in June a feeding colony of mixed warblers flies through the pines; the warblers make a racket that draws me out the door. The warblers drift loosely through the stiff pine branches, and I follow through the thin long grass between the trunks.

The study—sold as a prefabricated toolshed—is eight feet by ten feet. Like a plane's cockpit, it is crammed with high-tech equipment. There is no quill pen in sight. There is a computer, a printer, and a photocopying machine. My backless chair, a prie-dieu on which I kneel, slides under the desk; I give it a little kick when I leave. There is an air conditioner, a heater, and an electric kettle. There is a low-tech bookshelf, a shelf of gull and whale bones, and a bed. Under the bed I stow paints—a one-pint can of yellow to touch up the window's trim, and five or six tubes of artists' oils. The study affords ample room for one. One who is supposed to be writing books. You can read in the space of a coffin, and you can write in the space of a toolshed meant for mowers and spades.

I walk up here from the house every morning. The study and its pines, and the old summer cottages nearby, and the new farm just north of me, rise from an old sand dune high over a creeky salt marsh. From the bright lip of the dune I can see oyster farmers working their beds on the tidal flats and sailboats under way in the saltwater bay. After I have warmed myself standing at the crest of the dune, I return under the pines, enter the study, slam the door so the latch catches—and then I cannot see. The green spot in front of my eyes outshines everything in the shade. I lie on the bed and play with a bird bone until I can see it.

Appealing workplaces are to be avoided. One wants a room with no view, so imagination can dance with memory in the dark. When I furnished this study seven years ago, I pushed the long desk against a blank wall, so I could not see from either window. Once, fifteen years ago, I wrote in a cinder-block cell over a parking lot. It overlooked a tar-and-gravel roof. This pine shed under trees is not quite so good as the cinder-block study was, but it will do.

"The beginning of wisdom," according to a West African proverb, "is to get you a roof."

It was on summer nights in Roanoke, Virginia, that I wrote the second half of a book, *Pilgrim at Tinker Creek*. (I wrote the first half in the spring, at home.) Ruefully I noted then that I would possibly look back on those times as an idyll. I vowed to remember the difficulties. I have forgotten them now, however, and I do, in fact, look back on those times as an idyll.

I slept until noon, as did my husband, who was also writing. I wrote once in the afternoon, and once again after our early dinner and a walk. During those months, I subsisted on that dinner, coffee, Coke, chocolate milk, and Vantage Cigarettes. I worked till midnight, one, or two. When I came home in the middle of the night I was tired; I longed for a tolerant giant, a person as big as a house, to hold me and rock me. In fact, an exhausted daydream—almost a hallucination—of being rocked and soothed sometimes forced itself upon me, and interrupted me even when I was talking or reading.

I had a room—a study carrel—in the Hollins College library, on the second floor. It was this room that overlooked a tar-and-gravel roof. A plate-glass window, beside me on the left, gave out on a number of objects: the roof, a parking lot, a distant portion of Carvin's Creek, some complicated Virginia sky, and a far hilltop where six cows grazed around a ruined foundation under red cedars.

From my desk I kept an eye out. Intriguing people, people I knew, pulled into the parking lot and climbed from their cars. The cows moved on the hilltop. (I drew the cows, for they were made interestingly; they hung in catenary curves from their skeletons, like two-man tents.) On the flat roof just outside the window, sparrows pecked gravel. One of the sparrows lacked a leg; one was missing a foot. If I stood and peered around, I could see a feeder creek running at the edge of a field. In the creek, even from that great distance, I could see muskrats and snapping turtles. If I saw a snapping turtle, I ran downstairs and out of the library to watch it or poke it.

One afternoon I made a pen drawing of the window and the landscape it framed. I drew the window's aluminum frame and steel hardware; I sketched in the clouds and the far hilltop with its ruined foundation and wandering cows. I outlined the parking lot and its tall row of mercury-vapor lights; I drew the cars, and the graveled rooftop foreground.

If I craned my head, I could see a grassy playing field below. One afternoon I peered around at that field and saw a softball game. Since I happened to have my fielder's glove with me in my study, I thought it would be the generous thing to join the game. On the field, I learned there was a music camp on campus for two weeks. The little boys playing softball were musical whizzes. They could not all play ball, but their patter was a treat. "All right, MacDonald," they jeered when one kid came to bat, "that pizzicato won't help you now." It was slightly better than no softball, so I played with them every day, second base, terrified that I would bust a prodigy's fingers on a throw to first or the plate.

I shut the blinds one day for good. I lowered the venetian blinds and flattened the slats. Then, by lamplight, I taped my drawing to the closed blind. There, on the drawing, was the window's view: cows, parking lot, hilltop, and sky. If I wanted a sense of the world, I could look at the stylized outline drawing. If I had possessed the skill, I would have painted, directly on the slats of the lowered blind, in meticulous colors, a *trompe l'oeil* mural view of all that the blinds hid. Instead, I wrote it.

On the Fourth of July, my husband and our friends drove into the city, Roanoke, to see the fireworks. I begged off; I wanted to keep working. I was working hard, although of course it did not seem hard enough at the time—a finished chapter every few weeks. I castigated myself daily for writing too slowly. Even when passages seemed to come easily, as though I were copying from a folio held open by smiling angels, the manuscript revealed the usual signs of struggle—bloodstains, teeth marks, gashes, and burns.

This night, as on most nights, I entered the library at dusk. The building was locked and dark. I had a key. Every night I let myself in, climbed the stairs, found my way between the tall stacks in the dark, located and unlocked my study's door, and turned on the light. I remembered how many stacks I had to hit with my hand in the dark before I turned down the row to my study. Even if I left only to get a drink of water, I felt and counted the stacks with my hand again to find my room. Once in daylight I glanced at a book on a stack's corner, a book I presumably touched every night with my hand. The book was *The World I Live In*, by Helen Keller. I read it at once: it surprised me by its strong and original prose.

When I flicked on my carrel light, there it all was: the bare room with yellow cinder-block walls; the big, flattened venetian blind and my drawing taped to it; two or three quotations taped up on index cards; and on a far table some books, the fielder's mitt, and a yellow bag of chocolate-covered peanuts. There was the long, blond desk and its chair, and on the desk a dozen different-colored pens, some big index cards in careful, splayed piles, and my messy yellow legal pads. As soon as I saw that desktop, I remembered the task: the chapter, its problems, its phrases, its points.

This night I was concentrating on the chapter. The horizon of my consciousness was the contracted circle of yellow light inside my study—the lone lamp in the enormous, dark library. I leaned over the desk. I worked by hand. I doodled deliriously in the legal-pad margins. I fiddled with the index cards. I reread a sentence maybe a hundred times, and if I kept it I changed it seven or eight times, often substantially.

Now a June bug was knocking at my window. I was wrestling inside a sentence. I must have heard it a dozen times before it registered—before I noticed that I had been hearing a bug knock for half an hour. It made a hollow, bonking sound. Some people call the same fumbling, heavy in-sects "May beetles." It must have been attracted to my light—what little came between the slats of the blind. I dislike June bugs. Back to work. Knock again, knock again, and finally, to learn what monster of a fat, brown June bug could fly up to a second story and thump so insistently at my win-dow as though it wanted admittance—at last, unthinkingly, I parted the venetian blind slats with my fingers, to look out.

And there were the fireworks, far away. It was the Fourth of July. I had forgotten. They were red and yellow, blue and green and white; they blossomed high in the black sky many miles away. The fireworks seemed as distant as the stars, but I could hear the late banging their bursting made. The sound, those bangs so muffled and out of synch, accompanied at random the silent, far sprays of color widening and raining down. It was the Fourth of July, and I had forgotten all of wide space and all of historical time. I opened the blinds a crack like eyelids, and it all came exploding in on me at once—oh yes, the world.

My working the graveyard shift in Virginia affected the book. It was a nature book full of sunsets; it wholly lacked dawns, and even mornings.

I was reading about Chasidism, among other things. If you stay awake one hundred nights, you get the vision of Elijah. I was not eager for it, although it seemed to be just around the corner. I preferred this: "Rebbe Shmelke of Nickolsburg, it was told, never really heard his teacher, the Maggid of Mezritch, finish a thought because as soon as the latter would say 'and the Lord spoke,' Shmelke would begin shouting in wonderment, 'The Lord spoke, the Lord spoke,' and continue shouting until he had to be carried from the room."

The second floor of the library, where I worked every night, housed the rare book room. It was a wide, carpeted, well-furnished room. On an end table, as if for decoration, stood a wooden chess set.

One night, stuck on an intractable problem in the writing, I wandered the dark library looking for distraction. I flicked on the lights in the rare book room and looked at some of the books. I saw the chess set and moved white's king's pawn. I turned off the light and wandered back to my carrel.

A few nights later, I glanced into the rare book room and walked in, for black's queen's pawn had moved. I moved out my knight.

We were off and running. Every day, my unseen opponent moved. I moved. I never saw anyone anywhere near the rare book room. The college was not in session; almost no one was around. Late at night I heard the night watchmen clank around downstairs in the dark. The watchmen never came upstairs. There was no one upstairs but me.

When the chess game was ten days old, I entered the rare book room to find black's pieces coming towards me on the carpet. They seemed to be marching, in rows of two. I put them back as they had been and made my move. The next day, the pieces were all piled on the board. I put them back as they had been. The next day, black had moved, rather brilliantly.

Late one night, while all this had been going on, and while the library was dark and locked as it had been all summer and I had accustomed myself to the eeriness of it, I left my carrel to cross the darkness and get a drink of water. I saw a strange chunk of light on the floor between stacks. Passing the stacks, I saw the light spread across the hall. I held my breath. The light was coming from the rare book room; the door was open.

I approached quietly and looked in the room from an angle. There, at the chess table, stood a baby. The baby had blond curls and was wearing only a diaper.

I paused, considering that I had been playing a reasonable game of chess for two weeks with a naked baby. After a while I could make out the sound of voices; I moved closer to the doorway and peered in. There was the young head librarian and his wife, sitting on chairs. I pieced together the rest of it. The librarian stopped by to pick something up. Naturally, he had a key. The couple happened to have the baby along. The baby, just learning to walk, had cruised from the chairs to the table. The baby was holding onto the table, not studying the chess pieces' positions. I greeted the family and played with the baby until they left.

I never did learn who or what was playing chess with me. The game went on until my lunatic opponent scrambled the board so violently the game was over.

During that time, I let all the houseplants die. After the book was finished I noticed them; the plants hung completely black dead in their pots in the bay window. For I had not only let them die, I had not moved them. During that time, I told all my out-of-town friends they could not visit for a while.

"I understand you're married," a man said to me at a formal lunch in New York that my publisher had arranged. "How do you have time to write a book?"

"Sir?"

"Well," he said, "You have to have a garden, for instance. You have to entertain." And I thought he was foolish, this man in his seventies, who had no idea what you must do. But the fanaticism of my twenties shocks me now. As I feared it would. □

Criticism and Restitution

Geoffrey Hartman

For most people literary criticism is something of a mystery. They hear of the latest turbulence in those skies: that deconstruction, for example, is shaking things up, and has been claimed by a faction in the law schools or by an eccentric group of architects. Or, a new battle of the books makes it into the *Sunday New York Times Magazine,* after conferences at Yale and Princeton on the "canon" and a big curriculum fight at Stanford. What it adds up to is not easy to explain.

Critics face, on the one hand, a simple, down-to-earth task: Books must be reviewed, courses must be taught. At a time when shelves are filling up, when a greater and greater number of subjects are competing for prestige and attention, decisions have to be made not only about what to study, but about what every educated person, irrespective of profession or specialization, should know. Can we prescribe a "core" list that might contain, at least talismanically, what should be read by all? Are there books that could be shared by everyone, when even the Bible, today, is no longer the passion or obligation of every person? On the other hand, the issues debated by literary critics are far from down-to-earth, because they involve not particular books but how to read them. The point is made that it was less the Bible as such, or the classics as such, that inspired or oppressed, than did a certain kind of reading, an enforced mode of interpretation sanctioned by a religious, cultural, or political elite. This elite not only chose the books to be read, but limited the way they could be understood. Once we shift the emphasis from books to the mode of their interpretation, however, we cross into an uncertain and disputatious country.

The distinction between a canon of books and modes of reading is not absolute. New books have the power to change habits of reading; they not only follow but create methods of study. Our ideas about artistic greatness, and certainly about the English language, are influenced by Shakespeare. And, obversely, a hermeneutic discovery like Freud's can stimulate a new type of representation: Psychoanalysis gradually changes the way we depict character, describe what goes on, and record what we dream. Hitchcock's *Psycho* can serve as a popular emblem of that change. That there is an interaction between reading and representation simply increases the difficulty of identifying the one reading list everyone should consult.

Not that literary criticism—the formal study of books *and* methods of interpretation—can bring order out of chaos. Criticism is often part of the problem rather than the solution. Indeed, skeptics say that whatever the pretension of critics who promote new readings or renew older ones, critics remain in the service of a dominant ideology, even if it is as uncomplicated as consumerism. From this perspective, literary criticism is not an independent science or field of study, but a by-product of the culture—surplus verbal and cerebral energy that leaks from the art of the period and has to be blotted like excess ink.

Geoffrey Hartman is a professor of English and comparative literature at Yale. He has recently edited Bitburg in Moral and Political Perspective *(Indiana University Press, 1986) and, with Sanford Budick,* Midrash and Literature *(Yale University Press, 1986). This article appeared in* Tikkun, January/Februaruy 1989.

A more flattering view is that literary study, as it reviews and sometimes creates methods of reading, enters the cultural scene as an authoritative voice rather than as a dubious by-product. Books, films, and paintings require an interpretive field to sustain themselves, and then to become traditionary: to survive beyond a "generation," "decade," or "movement." Art does not have its axis of influence only in itself; a certain type of reading may have contributed to its formation, and certain habits of interpretation facilitate its reception. Culture depends on this interaction of the "primary" text (scripture or artifact) with the "secondary" text (the work of reading that edits, interprets, mediates).

In the last hundred years there has been an accelerated historical shift from art to sophisticated theories of art, sometimes even abetted by the artists themselves. Mallarmé's poetics are couched in a prose as subtle as the diction of his poems: at once self-advertisements and adventures, his pronouncements have their own curious and in-wrought integrity. Authors begin to market their very nonconformity: They take back what they feel was alienated from them by theorists and critics. The aesthetic imperative of a Mallarmé, Proust, Rilke, or Stevens acknowledges that a prosaic world, a tide of opinion and theory, is threatening to overwhelm or dilute art; and these writers seek to preempt or transform that world with their own, highly self-conscious practice.

The astute critic does not automatically take the side of art against the tide of conversation, gossip, or commentary elevated into theory. The reason is twofold. First, the fetishized artwork may be as damaging to cultural life as overelaborated criticism. Second, for culture to be participatory, artworks must circulate, not only by passing from private houses to public museums, but also by being widely thought about, talked about. There may be a greatness *not* in being monumental but in disappearing into the stream of life, the stream of language. I don't quite believe that myself. The real harm, I think, is done not by monumentalism, or haunting ideas of greatness, but by a hierarchical prejudice that holds that creativeness can be achieved only in certain genres, to which other genres are subordinate. In theocracies or totalitarian regimes, both art and criticism serve; in the epoch often called modernism, criticism serves art. A dichotomy reestablishes itself in modernism, with great art idolized despite, or perhaps because of, the skepticism of the age.

I am often identified with a position that urges a "creative criticism," but that position does not entail a confusion of art and critical essay, or a reversal of values. Rather, I just don't think we can restrict the locus of creativity. A critical essay, a legal opinion, an interpretation of scripture, or a biography can be as inspiring and nurturing as a poem, story, or painting. The prejudice that separates the creative from the interpretive is a reaction to the fear that the creative impulse in culture is being swamped by institutional or commercial forces. The wildest paradox in this attitude is that criticism, though placed on the side of institutionalization, often allies itself with the new or the popular: both criticism and innovation are outsiders, and usually a wave of art, sophisticated or demotic, breaks in together with upstart critical ideas.

Yet can that anxiety about an atrophying creative genius be dispelled? Some such fear runs deep in every age. Today it fixes on criticism, because criticism really is a force to contend with. A culture of criticism is developing—one that inspires as well as depresses, one that breaks down media and genres in favor of "discourses." Yet our problem is not, I think, hypercriticism or commercialism, or even the burden of the past in the form of institutionalized Western classics. It is a strange inertia in our progressive thinking.

The heroes of a previous generation, modernists such as Flaubert, Proust, Mann, Henry James, Joyce, Wolfe, Yeats, and Lorca, fostered an art-ideology. They attacked bourgeois values rather than the concept of the Great Book or Masterpiece. The work of art became, if anything, more of a sacrificial idol. Have we really jettisoned the modernist art-ideology? Doesn't it keep sticking to us, even in this "postmodern" era?

The problem I discern is the spread of that diluted modernist ideology to every text used as a wedge to "open the canon." Though postmodernism seems to assert the opposite by deprivileging the acknowledged work of art, it may simply be privileging the yet-unacknowledged work. The very notion of criticism is threatened by a proliferation of "significant" or "representative" works, not just by a proliferation of theories. Critical judgment, which had been austere and exclusive—in theory, if not always in fact—is asked to be compensatory and restitutive. The vitality, but also the confusion, of literary studies reflects this double burden: multiplying theories of reading, multiplying works that claim a share of greatness.

To question, as I have done, the prejudice that keeps criticism out of the literary system does not help either the canonizers (the art-ideologists) or the decanonizers. It presents, rather, a conundrum, and it challenges an inside-outside or hierarchical way of thinking. Criticism has its own strength; even commentary, as French anthropologist Dan Sperber points out, does not disappear into the code or scripture it interprets, but must itself be interpreted. A salient example of this is the Jewish Oral Law, the Talmud, and adjacent compilations called midrash. They cannot be reduced to a purely exegetical function. They extend or reenvision the original, the "primary" text.

Midrash, in fact, has always been exemplary for me. I am intrigued by its liberty and autonomy as well as by its strict adherence to prooftexts. My interest did not start in the 1980s: I tried to develop a secular parallel in earlier essays. In *Beyond Formalism* I wrote:

> Great exegetes ... have always, at some point, swerved from the literal sense of the text. This text, like the world, was a prison for Rabbinic, Patristic, or Neoplatonic interpreters, yet by their hermeneutic act the prison opened into a palace and the extremes of man's dependence and of his capacity for vision came simultaneously into view. I feel the poverty of our textual imaginations compared to theirs. The very idea of interpretation seems to have shrunk.

Anthropologists, more skilled in the devious relation of code (which can be a corpus of stories) to interpretation, especially in oral cultures, may have some sympathy with what I am saying.

I do not argue that there has been no advance, but that with advance comes loss or disregard. We live among restitutions, yet the rabbinic mode of reading (or religious exegesis in general) is still disregarded by most secular critics. My plea is not for midrash as such, but for an enrichment or even a reconstitution of the literary-critical field. If there is a symbiosis between a discipline and what it seeks to recover, it might be said that criticism today is engaged in a project of *self-restitution*: that midrash is more important for literary criticism than the latter is for midrash. By including midrash, criticism would exercise its power to revalue an alienated practice, and it would enlarge itself at the same time.

When we look across the entire expanse of literary history, we find many moments of revaluation and recovery. The greatest of these may have been the Renaissance. Despite the fact that Europe remained Christian, it brought back a repressed heritage, the pagan classics. By an artistic amalgamation that we are still trying to fathom, religiously alien forms blossomed again, fusing with a Christian content. A Jewish medieval tradition, similarly, is only now being retrieved for the nonorthodox world. We have something to learn from a religious culture in which the creative energies went almost totally into commentary and the same basic method of reading was used for law (Halakha) and lore (Agada). But while a lost masterpiece, once recovered, is like an *objet trouvé*, a neglected tradition requires decades of research and absorption. In an era of restitution, midrash still needs finding: as a cultural achievement, as a work of the social imagination, and as a distinctive mode of reading.

What is all this talk about midrash? You're supposed to be a deconstructionist! Well, there was life before, and there is life after, Derrida. The foolishness of labeling aside (about which decon-struction has things to say), the problem facing us is that this age of restitution is also an age of resentment. There is no end to the demand for "identity," as something available to groups or individuals yet denied them by the social order. The new emphasis on identity is like a rash left by movements that have rigorously questioned it in philosophy, fiction, and social thought. We seem to be passing from exquisite scruples about the "question of the subject" to a creedal insistence on the "subject position." To confess "where one is coming from" is no longer a form of modesty but a required affirmation.

> Something about this flight *to* identity is visionary:
> All Human Forms identified, even Tree Metal Earth and Stone, all
> Human forms identified, living going forth and returning wearied,
> Into the Planetary lives of Years Months Days and Hours, reposing
> And then Awakening into his Bosom in the Life of Immortality
>   —William Blake, *Jerusalem*

Restitutive criticism has absorbed this type of liberation theology. Its secular career began with historicism's "resurrection of the past." The massive research inspired by historicism showed how little we knew of other cultures and how much in our own culture had been marginalized and suppressed. When J. G. Herder, a German philosopher only somewhat older than Blake, charac-terized the neglected poetry of ancient peoples as "voices," the metaphor was just: it indicated an oral source that was effaced by print culture, and it pointed to something that *cried out* to be heard.

Yet this Philomela project (the restoration of voice to mute classes of people) has had a strange result. Retrieval of the past has produced a conspicuous increase of guilt-feelings about culture as such. This guilt operates both at the level of intellectual consciousness, as we become aware of how much overhead (Nietzsche called it culture-debt) we must carry along, and at the level of moral consciousness, because history is no longer seen as the story of liberty, of progressive emancipation, but rather of denial, censorship, repression. What can be said for a civilization that exploits its poor, prosecutes bloody wars, and invents genocide? The philosophy of history—the attempt to find a meaningful, progressive pattern in the passing of time—is a dying discipline because a quickened sense of social justice does not allow us to forget realities discounted by previous generations. His-tory, it appears, was always written from the perspective of the conquerors. ("What were the con-querors but the great butchers of mankind?" Locke observed.) Contemporary historical research has become, especially in literary circles, a sort of protest against history: the use of the past to in-criminate both past and present.

Walter Benjamin saw that the Renaissance model of restitution was flawed: it merely joined Roman triumphalism to Christianity. Though we are moved by the sheer magnificence of the monu-ments this combination produced, Benjamin was right to charge that such achievements may be tainted by barbarity. Are they not built on the blood and sweat of anonymous masses, on victims whose history is ignored? The New Historicism wishes to recover that history (primarily the story of everyday life), and in the process to restore the "material base" of art. It too, however, faces the problem that the material base has largely vanished, and that the process of restitution (of righting wrongs) seems endless.

The task remains visionary insofar as a voice must be given to the anonymous, even if there is no voice. We can retrieve, for instance, only a portion of women's experience; the rest has disappeared, or lost its gender-specific aspect. The Black experience too can only be reanimated in part. The archives yield something, in the form of letters, unpublished efforts, legal depositions. Great novels or dramas also yield something, when imbued with the vernacular energy of a Rabelais, Cervantes, or Shakespeare—or their modern equivalents. Yet historians or critics must often construct a legal fiction—invent, that is, a persona for absent presences.

What, finally, of deconstruction in relation to this protest criticism with its visionary program? Though deconstruction seems negative rather than affirmative in its posture—compared to a curricular politics that *represents* minority interests against the canon—it did set in motion a close questioning of concepts of privilege. Nourished by sources in philosophy and semiotics, it dismantled such essentialist values as origin (genealogy), intent (original intent), and identity (nature) through a study of the temporal aspect of human existence (how our truths remain contingent, how we are never present or transparent to ourselves) and a method of reading that showed an irresolvable doubleness in language. There is the drive of language toward unmediated expression or sheer transparency of thought, which could make words superconductive. (Think of merging telepathy and telecommunications, or of a universal sign-system to overcome the babel of tongues.) But there is also the historical and analytic fact that every language is a system of differences, one that defers even while it anticipates meaning—"Success in circuit lies" (Emily Dickinson). In deconstruction the emphasis on difference rather than identity is not essentialized. The challenge becomes how to support Third World writing, say, or the "minor" literatures, without counteridentifying them so strongly that we reinstate once again the contested notion of privilege as well as essentialist—and at worst, racialist—slogans that have bedeviled an era of catastrophic nationalism.

Perhaps only one thing is certain after such movements as deconstruction or the Frankfurt School ("Critical Theory"). Essentialists are instrumentalists in disguise—that is, they present practical or culture-bound ends as universals—and instrumentalized reading has been the norm. Yes, we hunger to engage literature, morally and politically; we want to escape Georg Lúkacs's contempt for the Western intellectual's "permanent carnival of fetishized interiority." But this goal can't be achieved by turning up the volume of moralistic pronouncements through affirmations (denunciations) that act as the equivalent of loyalty tests. Today the entire landscape of moral philosophy is in motion, shaken by events that hardly seem related to questions of language, but that are not separable from an inveterate pattern of verbal abuse that has come to light.

Restitutive criticism is an important development and needs serious debate. It is something old rather than new, and it is still a sharp turn on society's path toward the recognition of collective as well as individual rights and talents. The classic analysis of recognition in a situation of social inequality is by Hegel: a famous section of his *Phenomenology of Mind* traces the arousal of consciousness between master and bondsman as they grow aware of their interdependence. Recognition is the key rather than restitution, though restitution is often the acknowledgment of an achieved recognition. The end is not righting wrongs as such (there may be several rights in conflict), nor is it a reversal (which serves a retributive rather than a restitutive end); it is a new sense of respect that is spiritually as well as politically effective.

Turning from political philosophy to literature, we ought to recall the recent emergence of oral history. Popular traditions challenge as well as inspire high culture; they question the confusion of art with ideas of order and unity by revealing the heterogeneous and often folkloric elements of canonized books such as Homer and the Bible. Literature grows from traditions rather than tradition, as the ballad collectors knew, and literary criticism is restitutive by helping to honor such sources. The Philomela project might even rediscover the Oral Law and bring it into the mainstream of our culture, because the Talmud, which comes out of the formative period of rabbinic Judaism, is a vernacular encyclopedia despite its legal and patriarchal orientation. It is imaginative, diversified, many-voiced, and totally unembarrassed about the everyday life it seeks to encompass. □

Who Killed High Culture?

Jackson Lears

Highbrow/Lowbrow: The Emergence of Cultural Hierarchy in America by Lawrence W. Levine.
Harvard University Press, 1988, 306 pp.

Nearly twenty years ago, in Jules Feiffer's *Little Murders*, Elliot Gould played a photographer who several times stared into space intensely and asked, "Where the hell are standards?" In an otherwise forgettable film, the question stood out. It implied that the quest for artistic novelty was dissolving into a puddle of nihilism. As things turned out, artists had barely begun to dip a toe in those murky waters. These days—when artistic values are so often reduced to surface glitter and flashy technique, when television advertising is celebrated as the hippest "postmodern" art form, and when cultural criticism from any perspective is dismissed as "elitist"— there are grey moments when I find myself asking questions similar to Gould's. Where the hell *are* standards?

To pose the question is to risk sounding like every right-thinking leftist's *bête noire*, Allan Bloom. And that is a serious risk, for Bloom has done more to cloud cultural debate than any public figure since Spiro Agnew. The charges against Bloom are familiar, and accurate—that he is a misogynist, a Eurocentric snob, a self-proclaimed defender of the past whose historical memory stops in 1968. The last is perhaps Bloom's most insidious failing. Instead of giving a genuine historical explanation for the cultural disintegration he sees all about him, Bloom can provide only a hysterical account of the caperings of campus radicals. For Bloom, as for so many contributors to contemporary public discourse, the diagnosis of current problems begins and ends with "the sixties." Yet for all his myopia and malice, Bloom is right to ask fundamental questions about cultural meaning and value, and how they can survive in a relativist atmosphere. The problem is that the controversy he has initiated is uninformed historically, and the shrill exchanges only confirm the combatants' caricatured views of each other.

That is one reason Lawrence Levine's fine book is so welcome: it provides depth and complexity to a debate that has degenerated into stale polemics. By unearthing a wealth of fascinating details about American culture in the middle and later nineteenth century, Levine shows us how much changed en route to the twentieth. In particular, he reveals how recently the categories of "high" and "low" culture came into being, and how thoroughly they were shaped by class prejudice and ethnocentric anxiety. My only complaint is that Levine is insufficiently attuned to the institutional changes that have shaped both the production and consumption of culture in the twentieth century. *Highbrow/Lowbrow* is absorbing and provocative, clearly a product of humane judgment and mature reflection, and a pleasure to read.

Once upon a time, Levine makes clear, Americans mingled in theaters and concert halls much as

---

Jackson Lears is a professor of history at Rutgers University. This review appeared in Tikkun, *January/February 1989.*

they do at sporting events today. The atmosphere in places of amusement was raucous and partici-patory. The audience felt no more compunction about hurling rotten fruit at the pretentious Shakespearean actor William Macready than the Baltimore Orioles' fans did about pelting Reggie Jackson with garbage after the varlet had fled their fair city in pursuit of George Steinbrenner's millions. Nor were the forms of entertainment uniformly uplifting. People expected to see *Macbeth* with an entr'acte of dancing bears, *La Traviata* followed by jugglers and hootchy-kootchy girls. Shakespeare's plays were not sacred texts in an unchanging canon but part of a genuinely popular culture—as vulnerable to parody as were minstrel shows or sentimental novels. Actors thought nothing of reciting Hamlet's lines in Irish brogue or Negro dialect, or of telling Ophelia: "Get thee to a brewery!" Even toward the end of the century, advertisers were claiming Libby's corned beef could fatten the lean and hungry Cassius, and Ivory soap could wash Duncan's blood from Lady Macbeth's hand. The assumption was that potential customers knew Shakespeare well enough to get the point. And what was true of Shakespeare held true for operatic music as well. The Swedish soprano Jenny Lind excited mass adulation on her visit to the United States; Italian libretti were frequently translated or travestied, to the amusement of multitudes; conductors felt free (or forced by the crowd) to precede *Il Trovatore* with *Yankee Doodle*. In music as in theater, what we now think of as "classic" works were not enshrined in a temple of taste but integrated into a rough-and-ready democracy.

By the early twentieth century, all that had changed. The now familiar boundaries between high and low culture had fallen into place. Theatrical producers began to think of Shakespeare as difficult and unpopular, a bad bet for big bookings. Opera was no longer translated but performed "correctly," before coteries rather than crowds. Theater and concert audiences, as well as museum visitors, were increasingly policed into polite passivity. The Great Tradition was effectively cordoned off from ordinary folk.

How had this happened? With respect to Shakespeare, Levine acknowledges a variety of possibilities: the decline of oratory, oral tradition, and "romantic idealism" in a more prosaic age with more naturalistic tastes; the influx of non-English-speaking immigrants; the rise of rival visual entertainments like baseball, boxing, vaudeville, and movies. But, in his view, none of these changes is adequate to explain the broader shift away from a heterogenous, democratic culture and toward a segmented, hierarchical one. Unfortunately, Levine's own argument about this transition is curiously narrow. He focuses on the whining WASP elites of the late nineteenth century, who fancied they had been jostled aside by immigrants and plutocrats—every would-be patrician from Henry Adams and Henry James to Henry Lee Higginson, the founder and virtual dictator of the Boston Symphony Orchestra. Desperate for order amid a chaotic new social universe, such men embraced a sacralized vision of culture as a sanctum of sanity undefiled by the vandals at the gates. They were assisted by the likes of Frederick Law Olmsted, who imposed rigorous rules for decorum on his own Central Park, and the conductor Theodore Thomas, who required audience passivity on a scale his predecessors could have only imagined. In general, these new standards meant that culture could become a more effective emblem of upper-class solidarity; conformity to these standards could become a precondition for admission to elite status, a way of screening out the unworthy among the nouveaux riches and unattached professionals as well as the vulgar hordes. As Levine writes, "The cloak of culture—approved, sanctified, conspicuous culture—promised to become a carapace impervious to assault from above or below."

This is an effective argument, up to a point—a deft demonstration that cultural standards presumed to be timeless have originated in the foul rag-and-bone shop of the upper-class heart. But, in the end, it is too easy and neat. It oversimplifies the motives of the elites: certainly the more thoughtful among them were sacralizing culture from religious as well as social motives, from a sense that their own liberal Protestant tradition was played out and that they needed a more compelling source of transcendence. Jewish and Catholic immigrants, not to mention more theologically conservative Protestants, may have had less need for a sacralized culture; they had synagogues and churches (or—sometimes—the utopian promise of radical politics).

A more serious problem with Levine's interpretation is that he rounds up the usual suspects: the twelfth-generation old-monied WASP-types that every good progressive loves to hate. His argument tells us what we want to hear. It makes us think that contemporary cultural problems can be traced to the machinations of a few snobs at the turn of the century. It overlooks the complexities of the relationships between cultural elites and the institutional forces for change.

Perhaps the most compelling of those forces was the intertwined power of corporate capital and technocratic expertise. Levine gestures toward these connections from time to time. He notes that during the years around the turn of the century, "American entertainment was shaped by many of the same forces of consolidation and centralization that molded other businesses." He mentions the rise of theatrical syndication, the growing need of symphony orchestras to seek corporate sponsorship, the tendency for audiences to become passive spectators at movie theaters and political campaigns as well as at concert halls, the spread of deference to experts "in a wide range of activities that had been relatively open during the nineteenth century and that were being professionalized and codified at its close." While hinting at a more ambitious interpretation of "the emergence of cultural hierarchy in America," Levine never fully integrates these faint suggestions into his own argument. Along the way, he misses a number of opportunities to connect cultural with institutional change.

Consider, for example, the history of avant-garde art. Certainly the avant-garde had been one of the key forces widening the gap between elite and popular culture in the twentieth century, yet it is mentioned nowhere in this book. What really set the twentieth century apart, José Ortega y Gasset wrote in 1925, was the "dehumanization of art"—the turn away from recognizable representations of everyday life. Clement Greenberg transformed this development into a positive virtue in his essay "Avant-Garde and Kitsch" (1939), arguing that modern artists rejected familiar subject matter (indeed rejected *any* subject matter) in order to paint paintings about painting and write poems about poetry. Whatever did not self-reflexively call attention to its own technique, Greenberg consigned to the dustbin of kitsch, the sentimental trash that Hitler had resurrected as the pure expression of the Nazi folk. (Hitler's war on the "decadent art" of Weimar preceded by twenty years the American Congress's opéra bouffe version of the same struggle: the House Un-American Activities Committee's investigation of Abstract Expressionism.) In counterposing avant-garde and kitsch, Greenberg raised a host of political questions (though he resolutely avoided them in his own formalist criticism). We know that modernism could ally itself with fascism, but it is also important to remember that popular art could be just as firmly rooted in sinister soil. It could define itself as the simple and familiar in opposition to the difficult and strange, the wholesome and patriotic in opposition to the subversive and un-American, or simply the manly in opposition to the effeminate. (The nineteenth-century audiences' assaults on the effeminacy of English actors reminded me of the American Scene painter Thomas Hart Benton's tirades against the "third sex," which he claimed had taken over the art world in the 1940s.) Popular art, in other words, could also be a bearer of virulent intolerance.

Yet the resentment behind popular art could also stem from an understandable provocation. What many ordinary people found so enraging about avant-garde art was its willful obscurity—the impression that its meaning could be decoded only by a priesthood of expert interpreters. By the middle of the twentieth century those experts had assembled in the humanities departments of major universities and had begun to assimilate the modernist "classics," creating a new canon even less accessible to the man and woman on the street than Shakespeare and Goethe had been. Upon completing *Finnegan's Wake*, James Joyce reportedly said, "That should keep the professors busy for a hundred years." He succinctly summed up the symbiotic relationship between avant-garde art and the cult of expertise in the university. Surely that connection is relevant to "the emergence of cultural hierarchy in America."

What is even more relevant is the consolidation of corporate power. Levine alludes to the subject but misses its significance. Rejecting hierarchy, he nevertheless stays inside the perceptual universe of people like Henry James, who viewed skyscrapers as emblems of "the huge democratic broom" that was sweeping away the traditions he cherished. James was a smart man, but he didn't know much about skyscrapers. They were citadels of the new power of finance capitalism; they embodied the eclipse of democracy, not its triumph. Far above the thronging sidewalks, they elevated the men who controlled much of the capital that lubricated the workings of organized cultural enterprises— publishing companies, film studios, theatrical syndicates, symphony orchestras. Culture, as Levine points out, was becoming increasingly organized during the early twentieth century. And the model for efficient organization was the hierarchical, bureaucratic corporation.

Levine neglects this powerful institutional thrust toward cultural hierarchy, I think, because he views class conflict as essentially a matter of taste and style. The audience's hostility to the hapless Macready throughout the 1840s is, for Levine, simply a case of American democracy *versus* English aristocracy. But a great deal of the criticism focused on Macready's effete mannerisms. He resembled innumerable Horatio Alger villains: scorned for his mincing effeminacy but not his wealth. The problem with this "democratic" fixation on foppishness is that a representative of elite interests can easily overcome the difficulty merely by demonstrating that he's not a "wimp"—Theodore Roosevelt, Ronald Reagan, and even (most recently) George Bush come to mind.

Levine's redefinition of class as cultural style and his inattention to consolidated power allow him conceptual space for an upbeat conclusion. Surveying the "cultural diet" proffered by the *New York Times* in 1985 ("American Ballet Theatre, Norman Mailer, Cannes Film Festival, Kiss, New York Shakespeare Festival, ... Santa Fe Light Opera, *The Big Chill*, Warren Beatty, ... Diane Arbus...."), Levine decides that "evidence of what appears to be a growing cultural eclecticism and flexibility is everywhere at hand." Having properly debunked Bloom's notion of a timeless Great Tradition, Levine slips into the characteristic liberal left response to neoconservative cultural criticism—a celebration of a countermyth of American pluralism. Somehow the centralization of financial power, the spread of bureaucratic hierarchies in education and the workplace, the growing deference to experts (which even Levine acknowledges) have all left our arts and letters untouched. Somehow Levine can see a revival of nineteenth-century egalitarianism in a symphony orchestra president's determination to "get to the Yuppies pretty fast" or in Andy Warhol's monotonous celebrations of mass-produced kitsch. I fear Levine has been taken in by the propaganda of postmodernism. This may be because, in the face of all the evidence, Levine believes in the democratizing impact of "the market." When high-culture forms were "subject to free exchange," he writes, they "remained shared culture," and "the manner of their presentation and reception was determined in part by the market, that is, by the demands of the heterogenous audience." That may have been true for some times and some places during the nineteenth century, but to carry the same assumption forward into our own time is absurd.

Market exchange is simply not a benign, unproblematic form of mediation between artist and audience. The most vital art forms often survive in *spite* of market forces, not because of them. The big-time cultural marketplace has become oligopolistic and bureaucratic; even the most resourceful and innovative filmmakers or museum curators require sizable grants from corporations or government agencies, the sort of funding sources that tend to promote a bland, safe product. The audience has next to nothing to say about the matter. The cultural marketplace is also segmented;

particular audiences and particular products are packaged for each other. And, within these segments, the processes of selection and dissemination are often grotesquely caste-bound. Thus, a minor novelist like John Updike can become a critical and commercial success, a Serious Writer, automatically featured on the front page of the *New York Times Book Review* every time he commits another nuisance in print. Why? Because his work resonates with the world of private school educations and summer homes on Martha's Vineyard; because it captures the *New Yorker* subscriber's condescending fantasies about the fatuities of life in all those boring suburban tract houses. This is democratic?

Finally, in some fundamental sense, market exchange has a destructive as well as an anti-democratic impact on culture—most obviously if we think of the built environment as part of our culture. How many times has any of us seen irreplaceable cultural artifacts sacrificed to commercial "development"? The familiar sight of bulldozers crashing through graceful nineteenth-century farmhouses causes me to question Levine's formulation of "the real debate": between those "who perceive culture to be something finite and fragile, which needs to be conserved and protected from the incessant Philistinism that threatens it, and those on the other side who, possessing no map and little liking for fixed and unmovable fences and boundaries ... conceive of culture as neither finite nor fixed but dynamic and expansive...." Does one really have to be an Allan Bloom to distrust the notion that cultural values (like real estate values?) can be infinitely "dynamic and expansive"? Does one have to turn in one's left credentials to believe that certain cultural traditions do need to be "conserved and protected" from the merciless inanities of the managerial ethos?

The university is one obvious place to carry on that conservationist struggle. A serious left critique of contemporary culture would recognize the reality of the educational disarray that Bloom describes—the aimlessness of many students as they bump from one requirement to another and the absence of any zeal for truth beyond the next midterm—without accepting his explanation for it. The problems of contemporary universities can be traced not to democracy but to technocracy: the triumph of a managerial ethos, an instrumentalist stress on technique rather than purpose. This technocratic emphasis drew strength from the Prussian model of a university imported during the late nineteenth century. The idea that the university would train civil servants to staff the bureaucratic nation-state was Americanized to include service to the modern corporation, but the preoccupation with hierarchy, efficiency, and expertise persisted. Only the liberal arts tradition retarded the full development of this utilitarian nightmare. But during the post-World War II era, when the university was fully assimilated to the needs of the national security state, many a campus began to approximate what Clark Kerr approvingly described as his "knowledge factory" at Berkeley.

What happened at Berkeley and countless other less-publicized campuses across the country in the 1960s was a rejection of the technocratic or managerial conception of the university, a resurgence of the traditional faith that universities constituted a site where students could question and formulate ultimate meanings and purposes. Forget the fulminations of Bloom and others: the 1960s were a great time to study (and probably also to teach) the humanities. The study of great literature, if not a religious surrogate, was nevertheless an exalted pursuit. Students—I was one of them—pored over the writers we all assumed were "major": Faulkner, Melville, Shakespeare. They helped us understand what we were up against: the proud man's contumely, the insolence of office. They helped us challenge that pride, that insolence. Poetry, contrary to Auden, made something happen. Tradition proved it had a radical edge.

Now that edge is considerably duller, worn away by the Big Lies of Bloom & Co. Humanities enrollments are down: who wants to study a collection of stodgy unchanging masterpieces preserved in amber? Granted, for those who trouble to investigate it, the humanities tradition is now broader, more capacious, more vital because of its inclusion of nonwhite, nonmale, and non-Western texts. But, on most campuses, the consumer demand is elsewhere. A couple of years ago, I was in the University of Missouri library on a lovely May afternoon when I spotted a young man reading a book labelled PASCAL. Ah, I thought, youth in the pursuit of truth, even on a Friday in spring. Then I moved a little closer and discovered he was studying a computer "language." So much for philosophy. This is what we are up against in the fight to preserve and vivify our culture: not a handful of old "elitists" but an army of young managers who don't know a bard from a bare bodkin. ☐

Drawing by Anthony Dubovsky

The Workshop and the Wasteland

Jonathan Wilson

I recently returned from the first Jerusalem poetry festival. It was early spring in the city, lemons on the lemon trees, almonds in blossom, that sort of thing. It was exhilarating.... Mishkenot Sha'ananim, which is a kind of Yaddo overlooking the Hinnom Valley, assembled more than sixty poets, thirty from Israel and the rest from abroad. Among the Israelis were three Israeli Arabs—among those from abroad, three Palestinians representing the "West Bank," which was listed as a "country." Soon after the festival began, the "West Bankers" withdrew. They claimed that a verbal agreement with the festival organizers to have them listed as coming from "Palestine" had been broken.

Each poet received approximately ten minutes' reading time. As they read, translations appeared in English on a large screen behind their backs, then the poems were read in Hebrew by Israeli Arab actors from the Haifa Theater Company. The Israeli Arab poets read explicit and slightly less explicit political stuff. They received ovations from the audience. The audience was largely left-leaning, composed of what the Gush Emunim character in Philip Roth's *The Counterlife* nastily calls "nicies and goodies"—academics, literati, media people....

The big question that a poetry festival might answer is "What's going on in world poetry?" In the long run this might even turn out to be a bigger question than "What's going on in Jerusalem?" In his blurb for the festival program Yehuda Amichai wrote, "In our world, in which ideologies break down and values collapse and words constantly change, poetry has stayed, as always, the great hope for peace and peace of mind for all human beings." Amichai's rhetoric has an old-fashioned ring; Auden's "poetry makes nothing happen" seems a more fitting credo for our deconstructed universe. And yet, Salman Rushdie proved that poetry can make things happen, and if they can happen for the bad then perhaps they can, after all, happen for the good—hence, Václav Havel....

Some people think that poetry has had it in the States (average sales of a well-established poet, 2,500; population of the United States of America, 250 million; average sales of a similarly well-established poet in Israel, 1,500; population, 4 million) not only because of the crassness of our pop culture—TV, airport novels, and so on—but because American poets aren't writing anything interesting. They may be getting this message from the poets themselves. In Jerusalem, the audience consisted of grown-ups who listened intently to poets who took themselves and their work seriously, and who read without a mediating spiel. They let the poems stand alone, like pictures in an exhibition. At home, as anyone who has been to a poetry reading recently knows, the audience is made up almost exclusively of creative writing students, and the reading is a striking performance.

The American poetry circuit looks more and more like a branch of the entertainment industry, its poets low-paid stand-ups, almost indistinguishable from their comedy club colleagues. Here's how it goes. Before you read, you make a few self-effacing, self-aggrandizing remarks in order to establish

Jonathan Wilson is associate professor of English at Tufts University. This article appeared in Tikkun, *July/August 1990.*

credentials: for a man, you have lived in a tough region, the Southwest or the Midwest, or somewhere very cold, Maine or Alaska; for a woman, you are from a region. You (men and women) have not had money for much of your life and you're not making much now. You may, at some point in your life, have stolen something; you have taken drugs but—a wink to the students—you don't anymore (the students laugh, they geddit). You have certainly had an intense relationship with one of your parents. Twenty years ago you had wild sex, you are still open to suggestions but they come less frequently. You have worked in many menial jobs (but we must not think "summer vacation") and so you know well the working men and women of this country. Eventually it's time for the poem, but not before you have "explained" and literalized it in various ways, and raised up and put down your book a dozen times. You must make a special "in crowd"

Drawing by Edina Sagert

joke for your buddies in the front row before you read the poem; this is to let the student audience know from what it is that they are excluded, and how much fun it would be to be included. It's these little jokes, in fact, that make them want to become poets.

What is communicated is a diminished sense of the poem's power to engage the listener and a heightened sense of the reader as celebrity. Think of those celebrity photos in the *American Poetry Review* dwarfing the poems that accompany them. Pynchon got all this down in *The Crying of Lot 49*, dull narcissism replacing the numinous power of The Word. The new texts, when we do get to hear them, are noticeably homogenous, while the lives that they reconstitute are generic. Everyone seems to recognize that boredom and a sense of sameness predominate; American poets themselves always complain about the "workshop-type poetry" of other poets and deplore the vanities of the college reading circuit. The real excitement, as I gauge it from my conversations with poets, is to be found in the gossip-and-intrigue department, especially where college jobs and high-profile grants are concerned.

It is worth noting, given that poetry career issues are sexy, a striking absence of the "campus poem" from the work of contemporary American poets. Novelists have never been ashamed to draw on their campus experiences as subject matter—and John Berryman certainly had a good go at it in *Love and Fame*—but today's poets, even more campus-bound than their predecessors, seem worried that acknowledgment of their quotidian reality would lead to the production of poems that are not oppositional enough, poems that would dull the outlaw image honed in the public readings.

I don't offer the "campus" poem as a prescription for vitalizing American baby-boomer poetry, but rather I note its absence as emblematic of the kind of dishonesty that everyone feels to be present in "workshop poetry." Such dishonesty, though, is primarily emotional. It manifests itself most clearly in the contemporary elegy, a popular form which has become a kind of self-serving lament in which the death of a loved one or well-known artist is exploited to highlight the characterological efficiencies of the poet.

There are alternative orders to "workshop" poetry: the highly allusive new formalism, which might be explained as a conservative reaction to fin-de-siècle worries about things falling apart (again), is one. However, the bloodless High Church writing of the new formalism is no more challenging than the controlled sentimentality of "workshop" poetry. Of course, and luckily for us, there are more than a few independent spirits out there too—those writing in an alternative tradition, largely outside the sour grip of the university. (And the strongest American poetry has come from the tradition of independence.) But most baby-boomer poetry gets written in the comfort zone.

What is strikingly absent from my generation's poetry is politics—not the politics of the poet as personality, which are always foregrounded (romantic, anarchistic, jokingly chauvinistic or feminist), but those of the poems, which generally eschew the relationship between political and personal worlds. The observable distinction between the outspokenness of a poet in the interstices of a reading and the timidity of the poems themselves may have something to do with poets' awareness of the ambiguities of their situation.

It is not easy to keep up the pretense of being on the wrong side of the stockade when you are tenured faculty at an American university. As a former poet-colleague of mine once said, "We must never tell anyone the truth about this job." More than this, however, we live in a country where, up until recently, it has been easy for writers thinking about their own lives to mistake the presence of democracy for the absence of politics. The autobiographical moments and stock characters that take up so much space in contemporary American poems—those tortured fathers, beautiful girls from high school, and wonderful story-telling, bread-baking grandmothers—all seem to emerge from some ahistorical universe where private and public worlds fail to impinge on one another.

In North America we are living, of course, in what Philip Roth has called the World of Total Entertainment—and everyone, poets included, is in danger of getting sucked in. The best efforts of individuals to purify the dialect of the tribe are as nothing next to the mawkish seductions of commerce and celebrity. The poetry ratings are down, and what can poets learn from the culture about raising them? Only that news-readers are more interesting than the news the papers bring and that contemporary viewer/listener/readers are, above all else, voyeurs.

The *desire* to hear people say something that matters in poetry was still in evidence in Jerusalem, however, which gives hope that it may be latent here.... □

Opening the Family Closet

Gad Horowitz

Many years from now when I look back on the history of my relationship with my daughter, three moments will stand out in sharp relief: the joyous moment of her Bat Mitzvah, the very sad moment of her father's death—my husband's death—and the moment just a few weeks ago when she said to me: "Ma, I'm a lesbian." My only child, only eighteen years old.

What shocks and upsets me most is not that she's a lesbian, but my own inability to simply accept this. Since I was a youngster I've been socially and politically progressive. I have had lesbian friends. I have challenged expressions of homophobia. If anyone had asked me: What would you say if your daughter turned out to be a lesbian?, I would have responded sincerely that it would make no difference to me.

But it does make a difference. I keep thinking: My only daughter will never have a boyfriend, she'll never get married, she'll never have children, I'll never have grandchildren, she'll be lost to our people. And I keep thinking: Maybe she's not a lesbian. Isn't it true that at her age homosexual impulses and even homosexual experiences don't necessarily mean she is a lesbian? Shouldn't she be encouraged not to come to any conclusions about her sexual orientation until she's older? And I keep thinking, would this have happened if her father were still living? Could this be a psychological manifestation of mourning, involving an unconscious fixation on her father, or an unconscious decision never to rely on the presence of a man?

So far I've put on a big act, pretending everything is OK. I try to ignore it, I try not to think about it. It really is OK, but I do keep thinking these things. Why can't I stop thinking these things?

You can't stop thinking these things because you are not perfect. "Homophobia" has been an essential feature of Jewish, Christian, and Muslim culture for hundreds of years. Only in the past few decades has it been possible for people who are sexually attracted to their own gender to come out and say proudly or matter-of-factly "I am a lesbian" or "I am a gay man." These new identities are emerging out of the struggle of every single homosexual person with his or her internalized homophobia. Why should the mother of one of those persons be exempt from the struggle?

These things you are thinking are not simply homophobic nonsense; they deserve to be thought through, to be treated respectfully, and to be put in perspective. It's true that at her age homosexual desires and actions don't necessarily mean fixed identity as a lesbian. However, it's even more true that at her age heterosexual desire and behavior wouldn't necessarily mean she's heterosexual. After all, she has been raised from babyhood in an exclusively heterosexual world, completely surrounded by heterosexual imagery, heterosexual language, and heterosexual models. Yet, if she had said to you: "Ma, I'm a heterosexual," you would have thought: maybe she's not heterosexual, maybe she's simply mirroring the behavior she sees all around her. The reason this would not have occurred to

---

Gad Horowitz teaches political science at the University of Toronto and is a practicing psychotherapist. This article appeared in Tikkun, *March/April 1991.*

you is that our culture is not simply homophobic; it is heterosexist. Only exclusive heterosexuality is assumed to be natural and normal. Homophobia—actual aversion to homosexuality—is just one extreme manifestation of heterosexism. There is no good reason why young homosexuals should be expected, any more than young heterosexuals should, to shun any conclusions about their sexual orientation until they are older. As a matter of fact, persons of all ages need not come to any final conclusions about their sexual orientation at any time.

The more we question heterosexist presuppositions, the more normal homosexuality becomes not only for identified homosexuals, members of the "gay nation," but for everyone. It's already clear that the "homosexual-heterosexual" polarity is a terrible simplification imposed on a complex and fluid reality. It fails to adequately describe not only homosexuals and heterosexuals, but also people who are simultaneously homosexual and heterosexual in various ways and various degrees ("concurrent bisexuals"), people who alternate between homosexuality and heterosexuality ("sequential bisexuals"), and people who have very little interest in sex (maybe that can be normal too!). And people can move from one of these positions to another several times or many times during their lifetimes.

Would your daughter be a lesbian if her father were still alive? Is her lesbianism merely a manifestation of something else, having to do with the loss of her father? I would suggest that issues relating to mourning may well call for your attention, and that these issues ought to be considered entirely separate from the matter of sexual orientation. Since Freud we have been taught to question every conscious motive, to treat all motives as disguises for something deeper, less conscious, often less praiseworthy. We have been taught to ruminate endlessly (Freud himself called it "analysis interminable") about why we want this and not that, why we behave thus and not otherwise. Maybe that's what Freud meant when he said to Jung, en route to New York to introduce psychoanalysis to the Americans, "Little do they know we bring them the plague." Psychoanalytic investigation and speculation, interesting and productive as they may sometimes be theoretically (and even clinically), have for almost a century raised cultural prejudices and taboos to the level of Scientific Truth. Homosexuality is an "arrest of development" or a "disorder." The clitoral orgasm is a sure sign of "immaturity." A baby is a "compensation" for the missing phallus. Young revolutionaries are "fixated" in the Oedipus complex. But the only truth in these matters is our ignorance. Nobody really knows why people are heterosexual or homosexual, have different kinds of orgasms, make babies, and try to change the world. We do know that people have an incredibly powerful tendency to stigmatize those who are different in any remarkable way.

Some analysts might find a connection between the death of the father in this case and lesbianism. Others might not. The former position would deny the validity of your daughter's revelation of her lesbianism: she's not really lesbian, she's really just reacting to the death of her father. Psychoanalytic thinking deserves to disappear unless it stops putting itself in the service of sexism and heterosexism. If your daughter had announced that she was going steady with a man, the question of a connection with the death of her father would not have come to mind—unless the man were too young, too old, belonged to the wrong religion or ethnic group, or were otherwise unacceptable. Sexual orientation is a mystery, one among many mysteries which require no explanation unless we are seeking to control or destroy them. We don't know and we don't need to know why someone is heterosexual or homosexual. It would be more helpful in many cases to ask why someone is afraid of homosexuality, or heterosexuality, or voluntary celibacy, or any perennial aspect of the human condition. If you feel that there is some message for you about your family history in your daughter's lesbianism, it's up to you to decide whether and how to clarify that message without invalidating her lesbian desire.

Even if your daughter never has a boyfriend and never gets married she may still choose to have children; and even if she becomes totally heterosexual at some point in her life she may choose not to have children. I think that this part of your question comes out of the sadness you feel when you see that your daughter's way of life may be very different from yours. For many thousands of years, parents have been pouring their lives into their children and in this way trying to attain a kind of immortality. If we are childless, or if our children do not replicate and perpetuate our own identities and ways of life, it is almost as if they have died, and with them essential parts of ourselves. Jewish parents, even in these times, might "sit *shiva*" if a child diverges too far from the paths acceptable to them. Whether she has children or not your daughter may not replicate your way of life, or that of your family, or that of the Jewish people, sexually speaking. But we should remember that it is not gay people who have separated themselves from the Jewish family and the Jewish community; it is the Jewish family that has excluded its gay sons and daughters.

It's time to realize that the exclusionary nature of many of our traditional identifications is narcissistic and idolatrous, confusing adherence to God's will and teachings of the Torah with self-perpetuation. Heterosexism need be no more necessary an aspect of Jewish identity than animal sacrifice and the subjugation of women. In these times the Jewish people are called to liberate the sense of self so that it is no longer captured by any rigid forms. We are called to expand our personal, family, and national-religious identities so that they include those which have hitherto been excluded. This is particularly difficult when it is a matter of sexual practice which is often so closely bound to our deepest images of ourselves. But you can't not think about it. If you try to ignore it, you exclude your daughter, and you perpetuate the conflict within yourself between your old identities and this new unintegrated identity: mother of a lesbian. Therefore, be brave: Do think about it, but more completely, and in a new way: Picture in your mind's eye two women whom you could admire or respect, making love. Then let one of them be your daughter. Dwell with these images until you feel comfortable with them. Then, again be brave: Imagine what it might have been like for you to have been in love with a woman, until you are comfortable with that. You will have extended your sense of self into those images. You will have expanded your identity, and resolved the conflict within yourself.

Nor should this process stop with your own inner conflict. A gay psychotherapist and community activist in Toronto, Jeff Kirby, has initiated a project called Letters from Home. The idea is to ask gay people all across Canada to get their families to write to the Canadian government to say: "This is my sister.... This is my brother.... This is my child.... This is my spouse.... This is my cousin ... and I demand that they be treated and seen as equal because they are part of my family." Kirby says: "I am asking gay people to take ownership of themselves as family and to offer the opportunity for their families to own them in a way that could be pivotal for the inclusion of gay people in family status." Conservative groups "only see family as they want to see it, not as it really is." Your sons and daughters are reaching out to you. The response must go beyond pretending it's OK and trying not to think about it. □

What's the Matter with Sex Today?

Jean Bethke Elshtain

Robin Williams is on stage at a comedy club in San Francisco, improvising on whatever the audience cries out. "Safe sex," one man shouts. Williams responds: "Safe sex? Are we interested in having sex in a safe? *No.* Can you masturbate and be safe? How do you know where your hand's been?" The laughter seems to be both hearty and nervous. New standard slogans like "safe sex" and new verbs like "to condomize" are meant to reassure but mostly they remind us that sex isn't what it used to be. I will make the case that sex was *never* what it "used to be" according to the claims of sexual revolutionaries in their most utopian, politically innocent, and morally insouciant expressions. The position I will take is not "antisex," but is, instead, a meditation on whether it is possible to construct an understanding of sexuality that is generous in its approach to diverse forms of sexual expression but that insists, simultaneously, on an ethic of limits.

My textual support does not come from the extremes of Andrea Dworkin's world in which the average bedroom is tagged a Dachau, with men cast as Nazi defilers and women as their hapless victims; or from morality-in-media fulminations in which nearly all of us become sexual suspects, given the collapse of male dominance; or from the sorry, self-exculpatory rhetoric of those who proclaim that children should be "free" to have sex at any age ("eight's too late"); or from the many writings of either rabidly homophobic or intemperately homophilic publicists. Instead I tap the thoughts of a few of those who have offered up interesting, controversial markers on the matter of sexuality today and I recall conversations I have had over the past fifteen years with my students, with my feminist friends, and my own children as they became sexually aware, moving through adolescence into early adulthood.

If we came of age in the 1960s, we were told that sexual revolution presaged the total transformation of society; and that all the evils in the world—from imperialism to racism, militarism to environmental decay—could be traced to repressed, patriarchal standards of sexuality. A pop version of Wilhelm Reich's theories of sexuality held that orgasmic sex (Reich limited it to heterosexuality, but later epigones did not) was the solution to the problems of civilization. Previously suppressed libidinal energy, once it flowed freely, would automatically result in an antiauthoritarian ethic of liberty and justice for all. Did not Reich promise that those who are "psychically ill"—read *everybody* in our repressed world—"need but one thing, complete and repeated genital gratification"? Sex became an individual and social anodyne and the cause of pleasure was at one with the cause of justice—every horny kid's wish and justification. Followers of Marcuse, streamlining his arguments down to a series of injunctions and promises, also located sex as the key factor in the creation of a nonrepressive society. By making love, one was striking a blow against making war.

But does not anonymous lovemaking, free from constraints, mimic rather than challenge the anonymous killing of war? There was a dark underside to all of this from the start. Since that time,

---

Jean Bethke Elshtain is the author of Women and War *(Basic Books, 1987). This article appeared in* Tikkun, *March/April 1988.*

many young women, including my daughters now in their twenties, have told me something like this: "The sexual revolution probably opened up some things. A positive aspect might have been fighting the double standard—so women could fool around the way men had and get away with it too. But it wasn't ever 'free.' We were pressured more than ever to be sexually liberated *by* men and then were accused of being uptight and puritanical if we didn't want sex or wanted more than sex." Recently, a twenty-six year old woman, an artist and a dedicated feminist, told me: "My whole peer group, men and women both, are confused about what relationships are supposed to be. All the women are working on, well, I guess I would call it the spiritual aspects of sexuality. They don't want sex for its own sake anymore and they think, and I agree, that a lot of the sexual revolution stuff set up a standard where women got to act like predatory men. I'm sick of it. Now, with AIDS, we're not having sex at all ... and still finding it hard to achieve a decent relationship."

That the generation of those now in their twenties finds having and sustaining a relationship a burden of nearly overwhelming scope speaks both to the turmoil and promise of our humanity. It also signifies a *particular* sign of these times: the inevitable, collective letdown from the false promises of sexual revolutionaries.

How did sex become so important to us in the late twentieth century that we created a culture of narcissism embracing sexuality as its definition of human essence? Our "sex" both defines us and separates us from one another as each sexualized self belongs to one of a rapidly expanding set of categories—not just heterosexual or homosexual, we are now sado-masochistic, or one of many brands of fetishists, or vanilla or butch lesbians or.... The privilege of our sexual identities extends to our utterances. Each of us speaks "the truth" about him or herself, the sexual truth—and since nobody can speak for anybody else, we cannot cross the great divide to understand anybody else. As for sexual morality, it, too, has been fashioned by the self alone, tailored to the individual's desire for pleasure. The loneliness of the long-distance sexualist. Whatever happened to dreams of community?

Slowly more and more folks have realized that it isn't so simple after all. What about violent pornography? What about people's responsibilities to one another? What about the dubious fruits of unbridled sexual predation? Is a language available to discuss these questions or are we doomed to fall back into the usual "Thou shalt nots?" Pro-sex or anti-sex: two sides of the same coin. But most of us are neither "pro" nor "anti" as these terms are usually construed. Instead, we are troubled—troubled by the moral vacuousness of an earlier vision of sexual liberation, troubled by the moral censoriousness of current demands to return to ancient *diktats.*

The AIDS crisis has crystallized ruminations that had already begun to take shape. It provides a most fearful and intemperate opportunity to celebrate God's righteous wrath in the suffering of other human beings; but it also gives all religious groups the chance to respond with compassion as exemplified, for example, in the recent statement from the National Conference of Catholic Bishops that calls AIDS a human illness, not God's judgment, and proclaims that "discrimination or violence directed against persons with AIDS is unjust and immoral;" it makes even more urgent the work of those in the homosexual community who promulgate an ethic of responsibility and care, instead of promiscuity; and it prompts heterosexuals to rethink whether or not the sexual liberation standard was from its inception the generalization of a norm of adolescent male sexuality writ large onto the wider social fabric.

We are moving toward a vision of sexuality that is both mysterious and powerful. For instance, feminists who are mothers are articulating what they previously *felt* in the interstices of their bodies and souls—that maternal sexuality coexists complicatedly with male/female sexuality. Sue Miller's *The Good Mother* unearths this conundrum with great sensitivity and power, highlighting, for example, the strangeness of the mother's breast simultaneously as an object of male desire and fantasy and a source of loving nourishment to an infant. Perhaps sexuality is the giving to another who can respond in an equal, intimate way. We cannot return to the good old days when men were men and women were women and homosexuals had the good taste to stay in closets. Nor do I and others, long skeptical of how sexual liberation got billed on the social marquee, want such a return. We have struggled too long to carve out more equitable relations between men and women. We have seen too much pain inflicted upon our homosexual brothers and sisters because they *are* who they are. A politics of limits, of which sexuality is one feature, respects a zone of privacy where what goes on between people is nobody's business but their own and those who love them.

But this is the beginning, not the end, of reflection. The fact is that *every way of life* is built upon notions of morality; that *every way of life* creates barriers to action in certain areas, most especially, in the words of the philosopher Stuart Hampshire, "the taking of human life, sexual functions, family duties and obligations, and the administration of justice." What ought those constraints to be in a world that can no longer rely upon, and reproduce automatically, traditional limits? Without a set of moral rules and prohibitions, basic notions and symbolic forms, no *human* society could exist. Viable representations of human sexuality for our time are those that recognize that all conflict between our sexual and social selves cannot be eliminated—an impossible task—but might grow more nuanced and less destructive; that our sexual identities are not the rock-bottom "truth" about ourselves but, instead, one feature of our complex selves; and that homosexuals and heterosexuals can come to accept one another as finite beings who for a brief time, are compelled to live out their mortal existences in one another's company. Unlike abstract plans of a society to come, all those wholly rhetorical pictures of the future that promise that one day we will become *real* persons and lead a good life, confronting sexuality *today* is a series of concrete imperatives, threaded through and through with ideas and deeds that link us to other human beings in the present and also weave together past and present.

In Woody Allen's *Manhattan,* Woody confronts his closest male friend and urges him to think seriously about his use and abuse of his wife, his lover, and Woody, his friend. Woody's soliloquy deploys wit in the service of serious intent. An upright human skeleton, the prop for biology classes, bears silent witness to his pleas. We human beings should pay more attention, he beseeches frantically, to just how we are going to be regarded by others and talked about once we've " ... thinned out like this fellow"—Woody's skeletal doppelgänger. Linking explicitly intimations of *mortality* to human *morality,* Allen highlights a mode of thought American society is in peril of losing, namely, those ethical realizations that take place in and through our bodies and the ways we use or abuse them in relation to the bodies of others. The body may no longer be the temple of God but it *is* a site of meaning and purpose. Sexuality today is the slow, uneven realization of this intractable and solemn fact. ☐

Dead, Dinner or Naked

Evan Zimroth

I. Adam and Eve in the Blue Ridge Mountains

Dinner first: some blue-plate special
buzz of Gallo
garden-variety plastic ferns, the weight
of his eyes on her
the snake out of his tree

later they will deflower each other
slightly potted
illegally locked
in a floral motel room
(ersatz colonial)
somewhere
in the Blue Ridge
the blue heaviness of the mountains
blue mists around the trees

though hardly great, or even good
she is book-perfect:
weeping a lot
blue-blooded, a little broken

II. Later, at a Bar in Gramercy Park

Beyond worn-out
they drank California
while she lay on him
all her ancestry
branched and heavy as a candelabra

and he so light
so, even now, without history

between trips to the ladies' room
she told him marvelous drivel
scandal
saying, each time,
don't listen
you shouldn't have to hear this

wide as a shot of valium
wide as an expressway

he listened, prelapsarian,
still thinking he would live forever

III. Much Later, Adam Dreams of Two Women

There is something about him
both twisted and lyrical:
quasi-alcoholic, insomniac, hearing music
in the scrapings of steel

there he is, in bed,
Eve on one hand, a beer in the other,
and _Blue Velvet_ on the VCR;
he would be thinking
of some other woman, if there were one,
wondering
what she would do, if

or he is dreaming
into the future of Abraham
having it both ways
with Sarah and Hagar

Adam's sin is now millenia-old:
he could make love
to one while imagining another—
he wants to be clear of the Garden
to fall and be tortured forever

IV. The Forevers

From the fall
of the 2nd Temple to the camps
from the Milvian Bridge
to the camps, from cuneiform
and cunnilingus, starfish
and star wars, from haiku
and terza rima, it is always
good-bye, good-bye, snaking out
of the garden, as if
there were an out, as if
there were anything but dead, dinner, or naked

Thinking About Sex

Judith Levine

I n the past decade we've witnessed sex, the question, transformed into sex, the problem. The problem of teenage pregnancy has become the problem of teenage sex, so we try to teach abstinence instead of contraception and convince ourselves that teenagers have sex only because of peer pressure. AIDS is perceived not as a horrible disease of the body, but as the wasting away of the morals of the body politic. The cure is to contain, not the virus, but nonconventional, nonmonogamous sex.

But you don't have to travel far rightward to discover such attitudes. The middle is rife with them, too. No presidential candidate is unqualifiedly pro-choice. No Congress member objects when Jesse Helms fulminates on the Senate floor about "safe sodomy." Bill Moyers speculates that promiscuity—too many undisciplined young cocks strutting around the inner city's roosts—is the cause of the black family's dissolution. Jesse Jackson, instead of refuting him, drops his economic analysis and preaches a return to the Church and its sexual morality. Recently, on NBC's "Scared Sexless," host Connie Chung reacts quizzically to Education Secretary William Bennett's remark that "AIDS may give us an opportunity to discourage [sex], and that might be a good thing." But she concludes that, plagues or no, less sex is better, especially for teenagers. She doesn't say why.

In response to all this, the Left says nothing. In fact, it consistently puts sex at the bottom of the agenda (my mother has been fighting with my father, both of them old leftists, for forty years about the political centrality of abortion) or demonstrates downright antisex and antipleasure biases. In the 1980s, ever more squeamish about appearing unserious, it distances itself from popular culture (which is all about fun) and from pro-sex feminists, gays, and other erotic minorities for whom sexual freedom is a fundamental struggle. This is more than an abstract problem: according to the Centers for Disease Control, in the 1990s, AIDS may kill more Americans annually than were lost during the entire Vietnam War, yet no left group makes the epidemic a forefront issue.

Meanwhile, progressives dismiss the Sexual Revolution as a childish flight of caprice, and though they don't see AIDS as the scourge of God, they use the disease as a justification for endorsing certain kinds of sex and relationships and censuring others. Not as coldhearted as Bennett, but equally insulting to the people dying, these "progressives" find in AIDS the silver lining of newly "meaningful," committed sex. Even from the gay community a pious monogamism emanates—_vis_ the mass marriage ceremony at the gay and lesbian march on Washington.

As for feminists, a small rowdy band of pro-sex guerrillas like No More Nice Girls carries the flame of women's sexual freedom, but all around them the flame dims to a flicker. Influential moderates like Betty Friedan eschew public discourses on lesbianism and sex as "exhibitionist," and steer activism elsewhere. In the early 1980s, abortion is suddenly a "family" issue, and a secondary

Judith Levine writes for many national publications about sex, gender, feminism, and family. She is the author of My Enemy, My Love: Man-Hating and Ambivalence in Women's Lives _(Doubleday, 1992) and a contributing editor at_ New York Woman Magazine. _This article appeared in_ Tikkun, March/April 1988.

one at that. If there were good daycare and socialized medicine, the argument runs, we'd all want children, and the demand for abortion would disappear. Lately, abortion finds itself nestling under the antiseptic rubric of "reproductive freedom," with forced caesareans, *in vitro* fertilization, surrogacy, and other politics of modern motherhood. It's as if sex—which, if I'm not mistaken, is the cause of pregnancy—had nothing to do with it. In fact, the feminists most consistently passionate about cocks and cunts are Women Against Pornography—and they would wash my mouth out with soap for saying it!

All this distresses me mightily, because, like Emma Goldman, who didn't want a revolution she couldn't dance to, I don't want one I can't fuck to. I consider pleasure a revolutionary goal. And I still endorse the commitment of the Sexual Revolution and the early women's movement to forging new personal alliances, new forms of love and friendship—including sexual ones. Though never a smash-monogamy zealot, I believe in destabilizing traditional sexual setups and struggling, as we did in the 1960s and 1970s, with the emotions that go with such a cultural upheaval.

At the risk of sounding "nostalgic," or, in the age of AIDS, either frivolous or mad, I contend that we can't change society if we don't challenge the sexual hegemony of the nuclear family and resist its enforcement of adult heterosexual monogamy and its policing of all other forms of sexuality within it and outside it. Supporting "alternative" families or giving lip service to gay rights isn't enough; we must militantly stand up for everybody whose sexuality falls outside "acceptable" bourgeois arrangements—even far outside of them.

But you can't do this without asking fundamental questions about sex. Questions like, is monogamy better? (My answer: not necessarily.) What's wrong with kids having sex? (Often, nothing.) Why is it worse to pay for sex than to pay for someone to listen to your intimate problems or care for your infant? (You tell me.) You can't ask those questions if you whisk sexuality to the bottom of the list of "serious issues" after peace, or childcare, or even AIDS.

Indeed, AIDS should have us thinking harder than ever about how to preserve pleasure in our lives. If the disease limits our options, at the very least we don't have to be sanctimonious about it! I may currently like having sex with only one person, but I don't like feeling I'd better sleep with him exclusively from now on, or death will us part. Fear of death is about as felicitous a motivation for monogamy as fear of impoverishment is for staying married.

We shouldn't be looking for meaning in sex at all, in fact, but rather trying to strip implicit meaning from sex. I don't mean pushing for casual sex, but allowing a separation of sex from commitment and then, by conscious decision only, rejoining the two. This would not only emancipate women to make the choices men have always made about what sex means in a given relationship, it would enhance the possibility for stronger alliances, both passionate and emotional.

In thinking about how that could be done, I recall a 1983 piece by Edmund White, "Paradise Found," about his circle of gay friends and lovers. Outside the rules and expectations of family, relationships were highly fluid. Unlike heterosexual couples, who date, become monogamous, marry, integrate into one another's families, have children, and adjust their sex lives accordingly, a gay lover could be anything from a trick to a husband, or over time, both. Though radical gayness singled out sexuality as an essence of identity, it also freed relationships from being defined by sex. In the novel *Dancing in the Dark*, Janet Hobhouse described "these loving friends, admitted into their Giotto heaven one by one as each 'came out' and professed the faith, free to touch and kiss like angels ..." If the meanings of sex were myriad, the use of sex was plain: pleasure.

Our task today is not to pine away in nostalgia, but neither is it to disavow the sexual liberation we fought for in the past decades. We need to keep pleasure as a vital part of the progressive vision at the same time as we confront AIDS, which vanquishes pleasure more powerfully than any repression the Right or the Left could ever dream up. We must help our children feel that sex is

Drawing by Barbara Leventhal-Stern

good in an era when sex can bring death, and learn how to relate sexually to each other when new relationships are shortcircuited, and old ones sustained, by fear.

The first priority (and it's sickening that this doesn't go without saying) must be a unified fight against AIDS. We must demand government funds for research, medical treatment, and education, and oppose repressive policies on testing, employment, housing, and schooling. And since AIDS is becoming a disease of the poor and drug-addicted, we must redouble our efforts to eradicate poverty.

We have no choice but to teach children safe sex, but we must avoid hysteria, too. If a boy is gay, he is at high risk, but politicized awareness of his identity is his best defense. Vigorous education in the gay community has stabilized the spread of AIDS there. A lesbian child is virtually risk-free. Only one case of "apparent" female-to-female transmission has been reported. Now the media are sounding the alarm about heterosexual transmission—and indeed it is rising. Still, by far the most likely heterosexual carriers are poor, Black, or Hispanic IV drug users and their partners; the most sensible AIDS-prevention technique, then, is to give kids real reasons and resources to stay away from serious drugs and away from sexual relations with people who use them. Excluding drug users, only four percent of people with AIDS are heterosexual. We are all fearful enough about sex; there's no point exaggerating the danger.

Nobody should make assumptions about what kids know about sex. Research shows that while they're highly aware of sex generally, they're often pretty ignorant about the details. Good sex education is safe sex education too. Helping kids to be aware of their bodies—of health and contraception, masturbation, sensual touching, and fantasy as well as intercourse—and of their feelings about sexuality can only make them better able to practice safe and egalitarian sex in what could be history's most honest chapter of sexual relations.

Sexual behavior, moreover, should never be governed by a separate category of morality. If we want our kids to balance their own desires with responsibility and consideration for others, to express their needs and objections freely but cooperate within a community, then we should practice and teach our kids these values in sex, too. Teaching abstinence as "right" is not only puritanical and ineffective in limiting sexual activity, but it fuels prejudice against people whose sexual expression may be more flagrant, and it implies that disease is a punishment for sin.

AIDS presents one of the biggest challenges in history to our survival as a loving community. Both safety and compassion require us to stop seeing those we've been taught to revile as the Other. When we are ruled by fear and alienation, it is easy for extreme attitudes and repressive policies to start sounding reasonable. On the day of the 1987 gay march in Washington, D.C., for instance, the *New York Post*'s lead story, headlined AIDS MONSTER, stereotyped the classic diseased and depraved homosexual, hunted by police for molesting what seemed like countless boys. It is easy to see through the *Post*'s bigotry, but the story plays on the same assumption that supports mandatory testing and disclosure: that people with AIDS lie, remain selfishly ignorant, and deliberately infect—murder—others, so desperate and devoid of social responsibility are they. When "they" are so unlike "us," Draconian measures like tattooing or quarantine seem necessary "for the greater good." In reality, the greater good demands reaching deep to find our human similarities and also respecting our sexual differences.

The anti-sex hysteria of the 1980s also presents a great challenge to us as lovers. Fear and malaise are counter-aphrodisiac (the number one complaint sex therapists hear is lack of desire). We need not exacerbate them with self-righteousness. Married people, who these days seem to have no sensual outlet besides stroking Baby's cheek and watching the VCR, go around gloating about their maturity and security. Single people are home watching their VCRs, too—and watching their backs. With movies like *Fatal Attraction*, it's no wonder. Once envied, singles are now blamed; once considered free, they're now portrayed as trapped.

Where can we look for pro-sex messages in the AIDS era? I found one in the most threatened quarter, the gay community, in the educational comic books distributed by the Gay Men's Health Crisis. These depict sexual types from leathermen to clones, gorgeously built and hung every one, having phone sex, masturbating, or role-playing, all with minimum risk and maximum heat. Explicitly, humorously sexual, indeed happily pornographic, these pamphlets are pragmatic: They meet their constituency where it lives and do not try to preach living differently. But they imply more—that it's unnecessary to foment aversion to sex through moralizing or hyperbolizing. Death is aversion enough. It's driven many back into the closet and made celibates of countless more.

Instead, the lascivious comic-book hunks are saying: affirm sex. While death is all around us, let us nurture pleasure—for pleasure is life. Even now, especially now, just say yes. □

Why Modernism Still Matters

Marshall Berman

In 1968, when the students at my alma mater, Columbia University, rebelled and occupied the campus, a senior professor, the critic Lionel Trilling, described their actions as "modernism in the streets." I believed then, and I still believe, that he was right: In the troubles of those days, which at the same time tore up the streets of our cities and gave them new life, modernism was alive and well. This was the modern movement that I set out to explore and to chart in the book that eventually became *All That Is Solid Melts into Air*. Modern society, according to that book, is racked with pain and misery, yet it is also a place where men and women can become freer and more creative than men and women have ever been.

Modernists, as I portray them, are simultaneously at home in this world and at odds with it. They celebrate and identify with the triumphs of modern science, art, technology, communications, economics, politics—in short, with all the activities, techniques, and sensibilities that enable mankind to do what the Bible said only God could do—to "make all things new." At the same time, however, they oppose modernization's betrayal of its human promise and potential. Modernists demand more profound and radical renewals: Modern men and women must become the subjects as well as the objects of modernization; they must learn to change the world that is changing them and to make it their own. The modernist knows this is possible: The fact that the world has changed so much is proof that it can change still more. The modernist can, in Hegel's phrase, "look the negative in the face and live with it." The fact that "all that is solid melts into air" is a source not of despair, but of strength and affirmation. If everything must go, then let it go: modern people have the power to create a better world than the world they have lost....

Many of the abiding modern themes are unveiled with great flair in the first part of the *Communist Manifesto*, which appeared at the beginning of 1848. The bourgeoisie, Marx says, "has been the first to show what man's activity can bring about." Their obsessive and insatiable activism, which they have enforced on their own workers, and then on the whole world, "has created more massive and more colossal productive forces than have all the preceding generations put together." Marx presents a short list:

> Subjection of nature's forces to man, machinery, application of chemistry to industry and agriculture, steam-navigation, railways, electric telegraphs, clearing of whole continents for cultivation, canalization of rivers, whole populations conjured out of the ground—what earlier century had even a presentiment that such productive forces slumbered in the womb of social labor?

A century later, we might lengthen the list to include the whole field of electronics (and an amaz-

---

Marshall Berman teaches at City University of New York. He is working on Living for the City *(Random House), a book about New York during the last twenty years. This article appeared in* Tikkun, *January/February 1989.*

ing array of electronic forms of communication), tremendous breakthroughs in public health, a more than doubling of the average human life span from Marx's time to our own, cybernetics and computerization of everyday life, the understanding and utilization of nuclear energy, knowledge of genetics and biotechnology, flight through the air and into outer space, and many more developments. What makes all of these changes distinctively modern is not the inventions themselves, but a process of incessant inquiry, discovery, and innovation, and a determination to transform theory into practice, to use all we know to change the world. Marx gives the bourgeoisie credit for starting this process; like every other modernist, however, he expects the process to go a lot farther than they would like, and indeed farther than they can even conceive.

Another great bourgeois achievement, which should also lead far beyond bourgeois horizons, is the internationalization of everyday life. "The need for a constantly expanding market for its products," Marx says, "chases the bourgeoisie over the whole surface of the globe. It must nestle everywhere, establish connections everywhere." Moreover, Marx notes, internationalization takes place not only with respect to economic matters, but also with respect to people's intimate inner lives:

> And as in material, so also in intellectual production. The spiritual creations of individual nations become common property. National one-sidedness and narrow-mindedness become more and more impossible, and from the numerous local and national literatures there arises a world literature.

Thus the modern bourgeoisie, interested only in increasing its private property, inadvertently creates a world culture whose creations are public property. This is the culture of modernism itself. Although it embraces the world horizons of modern capital, it ends up subverting capitalism, not necessarily because it sets out to subvert (though it frequently does) but simply because, as a network of "spiritual creations," it cannot help but express values radically opposed to the profit-and-loss calculus of the bourgeois bottom line.

One of the central themes in modernist culture, starting in the 1840s, is the drive for free development....

Under the pressure of the market, modern men and women are forced to grow in order to survive. But their growth is channeled and twisted into narrow—that is, marketable—directions. Still, Marx believes, the inner dynamism that capitalism creates in its subjects is bound to recoil against bourgeois rule. Sooner or later, modern men and women will inevitably feel that the boundaries of the capitalist bottom line are fencing them in; after a lifetime of forced and distorted development, they will begin to clamor for free development. This desire, more than any mere economic need, will propel the modern masses into movements for radical change. Indeed, when communism finally arrives, Marx says, its gift to humanity will be "an association in which the free development of each is the condition of the free development of all." ...

More than a century later, the drive for free development has spread all over the world and has energized a mass public, millions strong, to demand universal education, freedom of expression, and support for what Mill in *On Liberty* called "experiments in living." This public, remarkably open and responsive to any activity or creation that appears to be authentically new, has helped to keep many modes of modernism alive. It has encouraged generations of artists, scientists, and quite ordinary men and women to believe that, if they aren't constantly transcending themselves, they might as well be dead. (Ironically, this public has also become the audience for postmodernism, which it imagines as the newest modern movement in town.) The ideal of free development, elaborated in the 1840s, soon brought about a powerful undertow. From then till now, this undertow has been a primary source of trouble in modern life. I will call this undertow the problem of *nihilism.* Nihilism is often considered to spring from the overheated and drugged imaginations of some of the "bad boys" of modernism: Baudelaire, Nietzsche, Rimbaud. In fact, it can be found in the most sober nineteenth-century accounts of everyday life in the modern world. Tocqueville, for instance, on his visit to the ultramodern United States, saw a pattern of incessant movement everywhere, tremendous expenditures of human energy in the pursuit of happiness. But he could not help but ask where all these people were going. What was their perpetual motion *for*? What did all their activities *mean*? What frightened him, when he thought about the human prospect ahead, was the clear possibility that it didn't mean anything at all....

If free development for everyone is going to be the basic norm of the new society, won't this norm engender new modes of nihilism that are even broader and deeper than the mode they replace?

Modernists of the 1840s created a vocabulary that made it possible to raise such questions. They did not have answers then, but they had faith in the capacity of modern men and women, in the process of free development, to generate answers in the future. Hence they could accept modern nihilism, in Nietzsche's words, as a great clearing away, "a simplification for the sake of life," "a pathological transitional state," a preface to the creation of new and better values.

Meanwhile, however, modernism's undertow was gathering force fast. The ruin of the revolutions of 1848 and the new despotism of Napoleon III made it impossible not to see its force. "The struggle seems to be settled," Marx wrote after Louis Bonaparte's coup d'état of December 1851, "in such a way that all classes, equally impotent and equally mute, fall on their knees before the rifle butt.... France, therefore, seems to have escaped the despotism of a class only to fall beneath the despotism of an individual, and, what is more, beneath the authority of an individual without authority." In short, there was a very large modern public—no one knew quite how large—that, far from yearning for a future of free development, fought to flee from a present in which they felt already much too free.

For Marx, the collective desire to escape from freedom was a subject for comedy, though indeed a black comedy. (The genre of Marx's *Eighteenth Brumaire* is actually much more typical of our time than of his own. It belongs on the same shelf as Lenny Bruce and *Catch-22*.) Thirty years later, Dostoevsky, in his parable of the Grand Inquisitor (included in *The Brothers Karamazov*), brought out the tragic gravity of this theme. The parable is narrated and supposedly written by Ivan Karamazov, the one character in the book with a distinctively modernist sensibility. Ivan brings to life a modern and humanistic Jesus: the idea of freedom of conscience is central to his revelation. The Inquisitor's objection to this version of Jesus is that he is bestowing more freedom on human beings that they can handle. Thus, he visits Jesus in the cell in which he has imprisoned him and entreats him to fade away before the Inquisition burns him for heresy. Doesn't he understand that he is making life too hard? "I tell you," the Inquisitor says, "man is tormented by no greater anxiety than to find someone to whom he can hand over the gift of the freedom with which this ill-fated creature was born." Jesus lacks true charity and mercy: He fails to see "that man prefers peace, and even death, to freedom of choice in knowledge of good and evil. Nothing is more seductive for man than his freedom of conscience, but nothing is a greater cause of suffering."

The Inquisitor now steps out of his medieval setting and addresses Dostoevsky's modern audience: "Look," he says, "now, today, people are persuaded that they are freer than ever before, yet they have brought their freedom to us and laid it humbly at our feet." The masses rebel, but they "lack the courage to carry through their own rebellion." They are like schoolchildren who riot and drive the teacher out of the room, only to recoil in horror when they see that there is no one in charge but themselves. Then they will throw themselves on the mercy of "the three powers which alone are able to hold captive the conscience of these impotent rebels"—a modernist anti-Trinity of "miracle, mystery and authority"—rather than take responsibility for their own lives.

Dostoevsky's parable is frightfully prescient, a prophecy of twentieth-century fascist and totalitarian movements. He comes closest to home, not so much in his profile of the leadership of these movements (though his Inquisitor does uncannily prefigure the Ayatollah Khomeini), as in his vision of their followers: modern men and women who grow up in a state of partial freedom but who find this freedom so terrifying that they are willing to sacrifice everything, even their lives, to any leader or movement that will take this freedom away. The Grand Inquisitor can teach modernists that they are in a far more precarious and vulnerable position than they think. Marx and his whole generation canonized Prometheus as their primary culture hero. After the Grand Inquisitor, modernists may remember how many people out there are rooting for Zeus, how many would apologize to the gods and give back the fire if they could. From this point on, if modernism is to grow, it will have to learn to incorporate this potentially fatal undertow into its inner life and development....

In August 1914, immense crowds danced in the streets of every European capital, and masses of men jammed the recruiting offices. Modernists were among the dancers, and they marched off joyfully to the battlefront. This chauvinistic fervor—rare in the history of modernism, whose horizon has nearly always been international—needs some explanation. World War I broke out in the midst of one of the most creative periods, not merely in the history of modernism, but in the whole history of culture. Cubism, futurism, and the first great leaps into abstract art; the theories of relativity and indeterminacy in physics; psychoanalysis; poetry and literature that shattered all the old unities of space and time; automobiles and airplanes, skyscrapers and electrified cities; breakthroughs in cinema, radio, and sound recording; the emergence of a whole array of new mass media—it sounds like an understatement to call this a revolutionary age.

The modernists of 1914 were breathless in their admiration for these new breakthroughs; the critical perspective that had always marked modernist art and thought shattered like the planes in a cubist painting. The modernists identified with speed, bursts of light, and explosive firepower; they named their magazines *Bomb* and *Blast!*, and they looked forward to seeing modernism put into practice on a spectacular scale. French cubists and German expressionists used all their talents to create elaborate camouflage, proud to help their respective soldiers kill each other. Proust's Baron Charlus stood on Paris roofs during air raids, singing Wagner arias and saluting a spectacle that was at once high tech and primeval.

By early 1917, however, the modernists who were still alive (many of the most creative were dead) had come to see the horror of the war: far from being an expression of heightened creativity, the war had reduced humankind to the most helpless and alienated sort of passivity. "Neither race had won, nor could win, the War," said the poet Edmund Blunden after surviving the disastrous Battle of the Somme. "The War had won, and would go on winning."

Thus, if the Italian futurists of 1914 to 1916 typified the modernism of the war's start, the Central European dadaists of 1917 to 1920 best expressed the modernism of the war's end. Their outrages and provocations were meant to shock people into reflecting on what had been done to them and what they might do in return. Although this movement didn't last long, it still helped to expand people's minds—often against their will—to the point where the people pulled down several predatory empires and struggled, for awhile at least, to create modern society anew.

One of the great works of modernist self-education, written in the midst of the war, was Freud's 1915 essay, "Thoughts for the Times on War and Death." Freud tried to understand what forces had erupted within modern men and women that led them to press all their energy and creativity into the service of mutual assured destruction. He guessed that the scientific, artistic, and organizational triumphs of modern civilization had imposed unreasonably high ethical demands upon humanity, which eventually extracted devastating psychic costs. In the respectable world of the prewar middle class, men and women were forced to repress their strongest and deepest feelings—

not only sexual feelings, but, at least as important, feelings of terror and violent anger—and therefore "to live psychologically beyond their means." In August 1914 the respectable facades had finally cracked. The war made it clear, Freud said, that "the state forbids wrongdoing and violence, not, however, in order to abolish it, but in order to monopolize it." The modern state enlisted people who were seething with repressed rage—rage against parents, children, siblings, author-ities—and mobilized them to displace their unresolved private enmity onto socially sanctioned public enemies. Freud's clinical work had taught him how many people there were in modern society whose psyches were like bombs ready to explode; the war taught him how willing and able the mo-dern state was to supply detonators and targets. In uniform, normally peaceful and decent men could perpetrate unthinkable atrocities and not only avoid criminal arrest, but win medals and praise in the daytime—and, because the state assumed responsibility for their actions, sleep well at night.

Freud's insight into the dynamics of patriotic gore is developed and deepened in his most important late work, *Civilization and Its Discontents*. The book reaches a climax with what may be the definitive vision of the contradictions of modern life:

> Men have gained control of the forces of nature to such an extent that, by using their powers, they would have no difficulty in exterminating one another to the last man. They know this, and hence comes a large part of their current unrest, their unhappi-ness, and their mood of anxiety.

Modern men and women are in desperate need of self-knowledge if we are going to gain the power to protect ourselves from our own might.

But it is not enough merely to defuse ourselves; we moderns must find a way to live. After sum-marizing the profound destructive forces around and within us, Freud adds—and ends the book this way: "And now we may hope that the other of the two primal forces, eternal Eros, will put forth his strength so as to maintain himself alongside his immortal adversary." Thus, the drive for self-knowledge that forces us to see through our world and our place in it, and brings us face to face with our heart of darkness, will bind us together in a new and more viable life. The dreaded negative powers of modernism turn out to be driven by the power of love. Freud's lifelong critical quarrel with the modern world ends with a dialectical hope.

Having laid out the paradigms of modern society and modernist culture, I will now briefly charac-terize several attempts to establish "postmodern" culture over the last twenty years or so; then I will focus briefly on several roughly contemporary works, works that I think are doing what modernism has always done and that show how, in spite of many obituaries, modernism is alive and kicking.

The first postmodernism emerged in the bohemian enclaves of American cities about 1960. It sprang from the people who invented happenings, assemblages, environments, and the art that would later be called pop art—people who, without knowing it, were inventing the 1960s. For the most part, they were too busy to worry about labels. But they were at least intermittently willing to answer to a postmodern label because they all despised the cultural orthodoxy that seemed to preempt the label of modernism in the 1950s. This orthodoxy, hard to recapture today, was narrow, solemn, and hieratic. Its high priest was T. S. Eliot, not the revolutionary poet who wrote "The Love Song of J. Alfred Prufrock" and "The Wasteland," but the grey eminence "Mr. Eliot," a clerical personage who presided over culture as over a sepulcher and demanded that art be treated with the hushed reverence due to the dead.

The worldview of this orthodox culture is characterized aptly by Norman O. Brown (in *Life Against Death*, a book that helped to shatter it) as "the politics of sin, cynicism and despair." Its overseers were ever vigilant in warding off threats to "high art" from "mass culture," as if art were a delicate antique that could be shattered by any loud noise or strong vibration. Moreover, these over-seers demanded that practitioners of each art form should forsake all others and should concern themselves only with the essence of their particular discipline. Thus, the only legitimate subject of painting was the nature of painting, all poetry had to be about poetry, and so on.

Nothing would have appalled the 1950s trustees of culture more than the idea that serious art could be fun. The new wave of artists in the early 1960s, by contrast, struggled to make art fun. They mixed media, styles, and genres, incorporated in their work motifs from the mass media and from large chunks of the industrial world, and brought art out of the studios and into the streets. The critic, Leslie Fiedler's formula for this new wave was "Cross the border, close the gap." "I am for an art that tells you the time of day," said Claes Oldenburg, "an art that helps old ladies across the street." These artists opened culture to the immense variety and richness of materials, images, and ideas that the exploding "global village" of the great postwar boom was bringing forth. The new faces of the sixties were more active politically, and far more radical in their hopes, than were the modernists of the cold-war years. At the same time, they were in love with the world they wanted to change. The spirit of those times still lives in Allen Ginsberg's poem "America," in James Rosen-quists's mural "F-111," and in Bob Dylan's song "Desolation Row." It is all there in a wonderful phrase from Jean-Luc Godard: "the children of Marx and Coca-Cola." This generation often thought of itself as postmodern, and, compared with the modernist patriarchs of the 1950s, it was. But the children of Marx and Coca-Cola have a far better claim than do their predecessors to the spirit and honor of modernism: They engaged the contradictions of their times, struggling to make the teeming and boiling society of the sixties their own.

If the first wave of postmoderns was composed of the people who invented the 1960s, the second (and still current) wave is a strange combination of people who were born too early to participate actively in the sixties and people who were born too late and therefore missed the sixties. This postmodernism was created by Parisian academics who spent their whole lives as members of the enviably privileged French mandarin class. For two minutes in May 1968, their lives were transfig-ured—a terrible beauty was born; in two minutes more, all their hopes were dead. The postmodern-isms of the past twenty years grew out of this trauma, and also out of a refusal to confront it.

Instead, the Left Bank exploded with all the feverish rhetoric and sectarian fanaticism that typify radical politics at its worst, combined with a total abdication of concern for political issues in the grubby real world. (Indeed, it was typical of Parisian postmodernism to insist that there was no such thing as a real world: as Jacques Derrida said, there is "nothing outside the text.") Derrida, Roland Barthes, Jacques Lacan, Michel Foucault, Jean Baudrillard, and their legions of followers appropri-ated the whole modernist language of radical breakthrough, wrenched it out of its moral and political context, and transformed it into a purely aesthetic language game. Eroticism, revolution, terrorism, diabolical possession, and apocalypse were now simply ways of playing with words and signifiers and texts. As such, they could be experienced and enjoyed—*jouir* and *jouissance,* Roland Barthes's favorite words—without engaging in any action, taking any risks, or paying any human costs. If modernism found both fulfillment and defeat in the streets, postmodernism saved its believers the trouble of having to go out at all. One could be ultraradical without ever leaving one's desk. If this is nihilism (and these postmoderns are constantly invoking Nietzsche and Heidegger to show that it is), it is a radically new form of nihilism—nihilism without tears. The first time it was tragedy; the second time it's farce.

When this production crossed the Atlantic amidst great fanfare and played to full houses of people who bowed their heads in awe instead of laughing, I was mystified for awhile. Then I noticed that the most devoted followers of French postmodernism were rather younger than I was, and, in fact, were people who were too young for the 1960s. Coming of age in the 1970s, they inherited all the bitterness of the sixties left and the Vietnam War generation without any of our experience of protracted struggle leading to limited but significant changes in the world. This generation appropriated and deepened all our radical negations but ignored our radical hopes. The most impressive achievement of this 1970s generation, it seems to me, is punk rock: a medium that dramatizes, in the most compelling way, a state of radical negation without radical hope, and yet manages to create some sort of hope out of its overflow of energy and honesty and the communal solidarity it ignites in its audience.

I have recently been reading Jean Baudrillard, the most recent postmodern pretender and the object of cultic adulation in downtown art scenes all over America today. Here is a bit of Baudrillard, just enough to convey the flavor:

> The end of labor. The end of production. The end of political economy. The end of the dialectic signifier/signified, which permitted an accumulation of knowledge and meaning.... The end of ... capital accumulation and social production. The end of linear discourse. The end of the classic era of the sign. The end of the era of production.... Power is no longer present except to conceal the fact that there is none.... Illusion is no longer possible because reality is no longer possible....

Having read these words, I began thinking to myself, Where have I heard all this before? Then I remembered. I turned to my record collection. It was the Fugs' "January nothing, February nothing, March and April nothing.... Capital and labor, still more nothing, Agribusiness nothing." It was the Sex Pistols' "No Future" shouted all night till the band members dropped. It was Flipper's "Not to believe what you believe, Nothing. Nothing. Nothing. Nothing." It was the Minutemen's "No heart/soul, no working at that goal.... Not living/dying, life just means surviving.... No world/no fair, lost hope, I no longer care."

We can feel the metaphysical affinities here, yet they speak in such different voices! The punks put themselves on the line; the desolation of their world fills them with dread; they open up their inner wounds, in the vein of Rousseau and Baudelaire, Artaud and Billie Holiday, Jackson Pollock and Sylvia Plath; in their musical and emotional contortions they are trying (as Nietzsche urged us all to try) to break the windows and leap to freedom. Their spirit moves in the orbit of modernism, whether they know it or not.

The voice of the postmodern mandarins, by contrast, seems to emanate from a very different and distant space. They don't say "lost hope/I no longer care,"—maybe because the supposed death of the subject precludes it—but they manage to sound like they mean it. They announce The End of All Things in tones of serene aplomb, proclaim incoherence in elegant neoclassical antitheses, and assert with dogmatic self-assurance the impossibility of truth and the death of the self. It sounds as if, after the failure of their one great leap into actuality, back in 1968, they collectively decided never to go out again—to seal up the windows and convince themselves that there is nothing out there. Like the pharaohs, they have built themselves a grand, luxurious tomb; it's a splendid setting for a postlife, a fine place to stay cool. But is the post-sixties generation really ready to join this kingdom of shades, to collectively die without ever having lived? Let me appeal to them—no doubt, to some of you—with a 1960s slogan: Hell no, don't go!

Finally, I want to address some of the ways in which modernism is continuing to evolve. The artists I will mention—Laurie Anderson, Maya Lin, and Les Levine—are all concerned with creating some sort of public space or common wavelength in a radically privatized and fragmented world.

Laurie Anderson's world often seems to bear some of the hallmarks of the postmodern worldview: landscapes as cold and lifeless as outer space (often they are outer space, courtesy of NASA), with cold and darkness enveloping us all; people engaging in arguments with their shadows, mirror images, magnifications, or computer clones; hypnotic trance music, electronically made; photographs, shadows, drawings, simulations, and montages layered or blended with real things and people; communication that seems cryptic and erratic at best—the theater we're in feels like a high-tech version of Plato's cave. But Anderson's stance toward this weird world is radically different from the postmodern perspective. When she brings her *United States* to life, she is always there, at or near the center of the stage, gliding or rushing about from microphone to synclavier, from vocoder to electric violin: she is the subject of everything that is said or sung, played or portrayed—incestuous families, missile silos in farmers' barns, mothers who blend with oil wells and bombs, tigers breaking into family picnics (and becoming part of the family), amorous encounters with President Carter, flights from stranglers on the Hollywood Freeway, Indians confessing to anthropologists that they really never knew their tribal chants, travelers in search of towns that are purely hypothetical, and more.

So she goes, propelled by an amazingly rich imagination: *United States* is the sort of thing James Joyce might have created if he had had cybernetics to work with. The enormous world that rotates around her looks like an update of Chaplin's *Modern Times*—only this time the human controls the machines. "There are ten million stories in the Naked City," she says, as skyscrapers flash on the screen, "but no one can remember which is theirs." She is determined to find out, both for herself and for us all. *United States* ends with Anderson onstage alone in darkness, looking toward us, with fog lights shining from her eyes.

Maya Lin's Vietnam Veteran's Memorial in Washington, dedicated in 1982, shows how the idioms of the modernist movement in architecture, so often criticized for supposed indifference to the historical, may be uniquely qualified to tell the truth about contemporary history. The memorial's design is distinguished in its purity of form, its open and gently flowing space; it displays an austere honesty in its use of materials and in the directness and simplicity of its gestures. Furthermore, the memorial is as remarkable for what it leaves out as for what it says. It leaves out all the grandiloquence, pomposity, and vainglory that have poisoned so many monuments—and, indeed, so many wars—through the ages. This memorial's rejection of historic associations enables it to create a protected space—we might say, a fortress without walls—where everything is honest and clean. It brings us back to Hemingway's insight, in *A Farewell to Arms*, that, for the men who were under fire in the Great War, "abstract words such as glory, honor, courage or hallow were obscene beside the concrete names of villages, the numbers of roads, the names of rivers, the numbers of regiments and the date." The memorial gives us virtually nothing but the names, and it reminds us how, in design as in writing, the sparest and most reductive modes of modernism can be immensely liberating: they can set us free from lies and give us space to make a fresh start so that we can construct personal and public lives of which we won't have to be ashamed.

We move down a gentle slope in the landscape, drawn forward by the giant extended wings that form the memorial's walls. As we get closer to the thousands of names, we see ourselves reflected in the black granite with amazing vividness: we may never have seen ourselves so clearly till now. Everybody who goes through this experience cries. We all cry here, no matter how we felt, or what we did, about the war. The Vietnam Veteran's Memorial shows how modernism can help us look the negative in the face and live with it; it shows us how to open up our wounds together so that we can begin to heal them. It is not a bad way to start to be a community.

I've focused on modernism's capacity to heal. But this emphasis shouldn't lead us to think that it has lost its flair for making trouble. The New York conceptual artist Les Levine made plenty of that in 1985, when he was invited to create a series of giant billboards over all the streets of London. Levine, a Jew from Dublin, went up to Derry in Northern Ireland, where he took a series of photos of Catholics and Protestants threatening each other and flaunting their banners and guns. He turned the photos into enormous paintings, in strong industrial colors, with a tonality that is aggressively flat and crude. He made these people dreadful to look at, in ways that remind us of the post-World War I caricatures of George Grosz. But the captions, in huge block letters, are even more disturbing: All the words, in different but inescapable ways, accuse and implicate God. Thus, overlaid on a grim and worn old lady and an undernourished boy, Levine inscribed a command to STARVE GOD. Over a huddled squad of British soldiers in battle fatigues, ATTACK GOD. Over Loyalist patriots waving their flags (one has actually turned herself into a flag) and grimacing at the camera, PARADE GOD. Over a squad of border guards beaming lights at us through barbed wire, BLOCK GOD. Over a soldier prodding a blanketed corpse with his gun, while an old man in shock turns his face away from us and toward the ground, KILL GOD. Over an urban ruin, BOMB GOD. And so it goes.

Mounted together in an art gallery and displayed as paintings, these works are devastating, in the vein of Leon Golub's Mercenaries and Interrogations paintings. Displayed as billboards along the London streets (as they were in September 1985), incorporated into the mass media, sandwiched in between advertisements for tires, cigarettes, and *Rambo,* they had an even more explosive impact. The Institute of Contemporary Arts in London has reproduced some of the many letters and editorials that express unmediated hysterical panic. The posters seem to have forced a large assortment of people to think quickly and intensely, not only about their relationship to the troubles in Ireland, but about the meaning of history and human life itself. And thinking in this way seems to be too difficult for many people to bear. They have not been consoled by the hopes expressed in some of the posters—hopes that they, or people like them, might have (or could gain) the capacity to PROTECT GOD; and even to CREATE GOD. Les Levine seems to have spoken more truth than he thought he knew, just as he has penetrated deeper into people's inner lives than he meant to go. Works like these should make it clear to us what modernism is for: to force modern men and women to come to terms with themselves and their world, to pour the heaviest and deepest meanings in modern life out on the street.

Thus we have returned to where we began: modernism in the streets. It may be that the most exciting modernist work of the 1980s will turn out to be the people of Manila's collective creation. In January 1986 they spilled out into the streets and onto the boulevards, waved homemade signs proclaiming "People Power," looked into the eyes of the soldiers who were sent out to shoot them, placed flowers in the rifle barrels and around the bayonets, and somehow, amazingly, got the soldiers to lay down their arms. These crowds don't seem to have been very well-organized (and they are not much better organized today). They don't seem to have had a very clear idea of what they were fighting for—though they did know exactly what they were fighting against. Their "People Power" was both naive and ambiguous; yet, like so much innovative modernist art, it was open-ended, reaching toward a future in which its meaning could be worked out.

There was something absurd about their whole enterprise, and even they seem to have grasped the absurdity. Still, they showed us that modern men and women do not have to live out their lives as passive objects or martyred victims, that they can seize the day and make a real difference. I wouldn't be surprised if we were to see more days like those in Manila in the years to come. Indeed, people may today be learning to recognize each other, and recognize themselves, on city streets all over the world. So long as they do, I think we can say modernism is alive and well. □

University Truths

Arnold Eisen

This is not an easy time for American higher education. The university where I teach currently bears the brunt of an effort by the federal government to slash its contribution to the "indirect costs" associated with scientific research. Stanford's budget deficit for the next two years stands at $95 million; faculty and staff salaries have been frozen until March and morale is at an all-time low. State universities and community colleges throughout America are in even more serious trouble. The legislators whom they depend upon for their survival find higher education a safe target: its constituency is diffuse, its faculty is widely perceived to earn too much and teach too little, and its institutions can be tarred with labels that have a venerable history in America's anti-intellectual populist tradition: elitist, irrelevant, bastions of privilege. The quintessential liberal institution—the very symbol of open debate, free expression, and meritocratic advancement—may emerge from this time of trial as weak as liberalism itself in contemporary America.

Enter the debate over multiculturalism, featuring partisans of reform who make precisely the same charges against the university as do philistines on the Right. They claim that we are elitists, having for centuries excluded women and persons of color. We are irrelevant, having accorded pride of place to the books of "dead white males" while ignoring the contributions of America's ethnic minorities and the world's many victims of European imperialism. And we are decidedly bastions of privilege, to this day boasting few tenured women or minorities, and refusing to recognize, as Evan Carton puts it, that "knowledge and the organization of knowledge are products and instruments of power." The radical Left and the populist Right join in attacking the most fragile institution of the center, invoking precisely the same rhetoric to precisely opposite ends. I respond passionately to these attacks from Left and Right not only because I am impatient with their pious simplicity, but because they threaten me. The Left is no less dangerous to a life and career I hold dear than is the Right. I wonder—and not at all rhetorically, these days—if this particular center is strong enough to hold.

The debate over multiculturalism is at bottom a debate over definition and possession of that center. Like most liberal faculty, I have no problem agreeing with the charge that universities have for too long excluded women and persons of color. I am a Jew who taught at Columbia (where Lionel Trilling was the first Jew admitted by the English department) before becoming a professor of religious studies and Jewish studies at an institution reputed to have long excluded Jews. Shall I deny the need to have Jewish studies in the American university curriculum, or Asian-American studies, or Afro-American studies, or women's studies? Shall I cavil at the demand that a curriculum that long excluded my religious tradition from consideration be widened to admit the contributions of others deemed irrelevant to the march of civilization? Of course not.

Two things, however, profoundly disturb me about the advocacy of multiculturalism. First, its

---

Arnold Eisen is an associate professor of religious studies at Stanford University. This article appeared in Tikkun, July/August 1991.

case is too often put crudely by intelligent people who should, and do, know better. How easy, how cruel, and how utterly stupid to lump thousands of years of texts—Jewish, Christian, Islamic, and secular—in a rubble on which one scrawls the obscene label "dead white males." The image smacks to me of the crematorium. It shows no respect whatever for human dignity—of the individual or of the group. It holds up the finger to me, a one-day-to-be-dead white male, and announces that my irrelevance has already arrived. Please: I am not only an American who treasures the works of Herman Melville and Abraham Lincoln, I am a Jew obligated in my bones to three thousand years of my ancestors' reflection and behavior. And I am a professor who can bear witness to the fact (reported by participant after participant at a discussion this past December at the conference of the Association for Jewish Studies in Boston) that all across America multiculturalism and ethnic studies seem inclined to exclude the study of Jews—because we are after all "white," and all too often males. So much for the distinctiveness that has enlivened our souls for three millennia and, again recently, led to the destruction of our bodies. Multiculturalism, in the name of opposition to cultural imperialism, almost everywhere denies us the right to cultural self-definition.

My fears for the survival of classrooms relatively free from state interference should be no more surprising. We are not entirely free from outside influence; the people who fund us keep a close eye on what we do. They give us unusual time and space for maneuver in return for tangible contributions to individual growth and social well-being. We at the university generally pay this price gladly because we are convinced that we can and do make those contributions, while retaining a significant degree of freedom over the content of our teaching and the direction of our research. If we are perceived to exchange the search for truth and the promotion of common value—however difficult these may be to achieve—for the pursuit of PC, or the promotion of divisive social agendas, legislators wielding the budget axe will not be slow to react.

Radical critics would say: Bad faith, servants of the status quo, apologists for oppression. They seek purity—and power. I would reply: Knowledge is an instrument of power but not only that, just as you and I are more than our ideological commitments or our genders or ethnic loyalties. Universities are far from propagandists for their government and corporate sponsors. Can't we find a way for Chicano studies to exist alongside Jewish studies and, yes, Western Culture (which includes the others!), all the while believing, and convincing the public, that the outcome of the university's particular blend of criticism and commitment will be a stronger and wiser America? I believe we can—and now is the time when it must be done. □

Freedom of Hate Speech

Richard Perry and Patricia Williams

U ntil well after the Second World War, American institutions of higher education were bastions of a sort of cheery and thoughtlessly jingoistic nativism (isn't this some part of what we've always meant when we spoke of "that old college spirit"?). Except for the historically Black and women's colleges and a couple of schools serving immigrant populations (such as the City College of New York), the vast majority of the student bodies of America's hundreds of colleges were overwhelmingly U.S.-born, male, Christian, and of Northern European descent, and their faculties were even more so. The structure of the core liberal arts curriculum suggested that the university understood itself as an umpire of timeless values, high above the rough and tumble of mere politics, standing at the summit of Western civilization, which from this vantage point could be seen to have risen in an unbroken crescendo from Plato to NATO.

However, the assumptions that made the university an arbiter of "universal values" have been questioned, as multinational business and research institutions have evolved into ever more global and ethnically diverse enterprises. On the home front, meanwhile, the hard-won material gains of women and ethnic minorities have produced halting progress toward the goal of making American universities truly representative of the country's population as a whole. Responding to these historical developments, many have sought to make the core curriculum a more effective preparation for the diverse, multicultural environments of both the contemporary United States and the world. There have also been efforts to make the campus itself a more hospitable place for its newly heterogeneous population, most notably amendments to the campus conduct rules intended to discourage harassment on the basis of race, religion, ethnicity, gender, and sexual orientation.

These reform efforts have been met with a virulent reaction, a backlash recently fueled by a series of often scurrilous stories in the most visible national magazines, and by fervent denunciations from the Left, Right, and center of political debate.

This confusion stems largely from the dishonest manner in which the debates have been reported. Most accounts of this campus dispute have been characterized by repeated distortions of fact and a profound bad faith with history. First, it is preposterous to claim, as many opponents of multiculturalism have, that these debates are about some supposed new infringement of the First Amendment rights of American citizens. No position seriously advocated by multiculturalists would have the slightest effect upon our right as Americans to be nativist, racist, anti-Semitic, sexist, homophobic, or just as narrowly monocultural-as-we-wanna-be in our personal lives. So too it remains entirely possible to stand in the public arena and call one another any of the whole litany of terms with which we as Americans have learned throughout our history to abuse one another. One might

Richard Perry is a research fellow at the Center for Philosophy of Law at the University of Louvain, Belgium. Patricia Williams is an associate professor of law and women's studies at the University of Wisconsin at Madison. She is the author of The Alchemy of Race and Rights *(Harvard University Press, 1991). This article appeared in* Tikkun, *July/August 1991.*

instructively compare this situation with the new Canadian constitution, which specifically limits the protection of certain kinds of hate speech, without much evidence that this provision has started Canada down that slippery slope toward being a Stalinist police state.

Nor do the multiculturalist reforms pose any institutional threat to the many securely tenured professors on the most prestigious faculties who teach doctrines (such as sociobiology and kindred theories on the margins of intellectual respectability) that are patently demeaning to members of the most long-abused groups. And the debate over multiculturalism scarcely disturbs the work of eminent scholars who regularly contrive to put a revisionist happy face upon the history of slavery, the Czarist pogroms, the Nazi genocides, the colonial subjugation of indigenous peoples, or the oppression of women.

What has never been true is that one member of an institution has an unrestrained legal right to harass another member and remain in the good graces of the institution. Yet the recent barrage of media coverage would have us believe that some novel restriction is being imposed in multiculturalist speech and behavior codes. This misinformation has been conveyed by those who are apparently unable to distinguish between a liberty interest on the one hand and, on the other, a quite specific interest in being able to spout racist, sexist, and homophobic epithets completely unchallenged— without, in other words, the terrible inconvenience of feeling bad about it.

There is a sharp paradox at the heart of all this, a contradiction whose effective message is: "I have the right to express as much hatred as I want, so you shut up about it." It may be appropriate to defend the First Amendment rights of students who, for example, openly advocate Nazi policies. However, there has been a good deal of unacknowledged power-brokering that has informed the refusal even to think about the effect of relentless racist propagandizing on educational institutions in particular. Now those who even criticize this selective invocation of the First Amendment on the behalf of one social group over another are themselves called Nazis.

This fundamental paradox has bred a host of others. Conservatives such as George Will hurriedly discard their hallowed distinction between the public and private spheres when expediency beckons. Not long ago right-wingers were asserting that the evangelical Bob Jones University should be allowed to practice segregation and still be given a tax exemption—because it was a private institution. Where were these free-speech patriots in 1986 when Captain Goldman, a U.S. Air Force officer and an Orthodox Jew, was denied by the Reagan Supreme Court the right to wear a yarmulke at his desk job? And where are they now, when the new Supreme Court of our new world order has just asserted that the government can control speech between doctor and patient—heretofore one of the most sacred of privacy privileges—when the clinic receives federal funds and the topic of conversation is reproductive choice?

These ironies of free-speech opportunism have been accompanied by a breathtaking effort to rewrite our history. The multiculturalist reforms on campus have been characterized as being at odds with the two moral touchstones of recent political memory: the World War II-era fight against the Nazi theory of Aryan supremacy; and the American anti-slavery and civil rights movements. Both of these struggles were in fact fought over—among other things—the sort of contested social meanings that can be traced directly to the present university discussions. The new interpretation of these two contests, however, rewrites them as triumphs of the inevitable, forward-marching progress of modern liberal individualism. Commentators from George Will to Shelby Steele have consistently depicted Martin Luther King, Jr., for example, as having pursued the higher moral ground of individual achievement rather than the validation of African-American collective social identity—as though these notions were inherently in opposition to one another. We are to imagine, for example, that the brave people who faced fire hoses and police dogs and who sat-in at lunch counters in the 1950s and 1960s were after nothing more than, say, the market freedom of an individual Black

American to eat a grilled cheese sandwich in the company of raving bigots. Conservative opponents of multiculturalism would have us forget about the other part of that struggle: the fight to expand the social space of all Blacks, and to re-articulate the political semantics of the collective identity of the descendants of slaves.

Another striking paradox is the way that much of this backlash proceeds in the name of democratic values, while mounting a sustained assault precisely on the democratic process of academic self-governance. The academic Right devotes itself to attacks on changes in curricula and conduct codes that have been adopted only after lengthy deliberation and votes by the faculty senates (such as in the Stanford Western Civilization reforms or the Berkeley ethnic studies requirement), administrative committees, or student bodies. More curiously still, these assaults are typically said to be conducted in defense of something like "a free marketplace of ideas." Yet the recent multiculturalist changes might accurately be viewed as shifts in an intellectual marketplace where several positions have been rising in value, while another, older position, adamantly refusing to innovate, has been steadily losing its market share. There is a certain irony, therefore, in the spectacle of William Bennett and company engaged in a kind of status brokerage, trading on their appointed positions of authority for advantage they cannot gain via democratic votes in faculty senates or in the governing bodies of professional organizations.

Such distortions of the debate have worked to obscure what could be a genuine opportunity. The market idea, considered not simply as the nineteenth-century social-Darwinist mechanism whereby big fish eat little fish for the greater good, might serve as a multidimensional matrix for the representation of certain types of social information. If, for example, we could ever get to the point where we can honestly speak of having achieved a level playing-field in the marketplace of ideas (for this is precisely what is at stake in the present debates), then we might begin to understand the market as one means of representing multicentered networks of social interaction. Just as the American monetary system went off the gold standard in 1934, it is now time to get off the traditional rational man standard (the straight, white, male, Christian, English-speaking, middle-class individualist) as the universal measure of humanity. It is time to initiate a perestroika of personhood—to make a world in which all of us, in our multiple, overlapping, individual and collective identities can come to terms. ☐

Is Psychiatry Going Out of Its Mind?

Michael J. Bader

Psychiatrists and the general public increasingly understand mental illness in biological terms. Newspaper articles appear monthly touting the discovery of a neurobiological or genetic cause of emotional or behavioral problems ranging from schizophrenia and depression to stuttering, eating disorders, aggression, cynicism, addictions, and anxiety. Theories that explain the causes of mental suffering in psychological or social terms, such as psychoanalysis or family systems theory, are increasingly regarded as passé. Psychological and social models of mental illness are seen as unduly blaming families and children alike for problems that neither are ultimately responsible. In 1987, the *New York Times* ran a special four-part series on schizophrenia that concluded that "the old notion that families were to blame for causing the disease has given way to the notion that biological factors play a major causative role." A month later the *Times* reported on depression in similar terms: "It has become clear that severe depression can result from a shortage of certain natural chemicals in parts of the brain."

Families of the mentally ill have banded together in organizations such as the National Association of the Mentally Ill (NAMI) to educate the public about the biological basis of mental illness, seeking to take the family "off the hook." As one NAMI official recently wrote in a letter to the *Times*, "Recognition has been long overdue that this terrible brain disease [schizophrenia] is the fault neither of the victims nor their families, but is of neurobiological or genetic origins." NAMI has even gone so far as to join with others in attempting to have the license of a Maryland psychiatrist, Peter Breggin, revoked after Breggin appeared on the "Oprah Winfrey Show" arguing against the use of psychoactive medication and against the use of the medical model in treating the mentally ill.

As any mental health professional who has worked with schizophrenics or with profoundly depressed or manic patients knows, antipsychotic, antidepressant, and antimanic medication can be of great therapeutic value. But, in spite of the innumerable "discoveries" that the mass media report, we are no closer today than we were ten years ago to "curing" patients. In fact, the "scientific" claims are grossly overstated in the interest of promoting the competitive interests of one professional group—psychiatrists. This group's zeal in arguing for a biological model of mental illness has the effect of directly or indirectly devaluing attempts to understand the psychological and social meanings of patients' suffering.

Biological models for understanding the cause and treatment of mental illness, particularly the more severe disorders such as schizophrenia and depression, have gained hegemony in modern American psychiatry. This marks a dramatic change from the fifties and sixties when American psychiatry was dominated by the influence of psychoanalysis, a theory and practice that locates the source of psychopathology in a patient's family dynamics. Today, almost every psychiatry department

Michael J. Bader, a candidate and affiliate member of the San Francisco Psychoanalytic Institute and faculty member of the Graduate Psychology Program of New College of California, is in private practice. He is also a member of Tikkun's *editorial board. This article appeared in* Tikkun, *July/August 1989.*

in every major medical school in America is chaired by someone committed to biomedical research and treatment. In the fifties and sixties, these same positions were usually held by psychoanalysts. One major medical school in California saw its psychiatry chairman, an internationally renowned psychoanalyst and clinical researcher, replaced by a psychiatrist whose background was not in clinical work but in electrophysiologic studies of the nervous system of slime molds. In earlier years, the teaching of the psychodynamic techniques of psychotherapy was the core of the psychiatric residency. Today, by contrast, clinical techniques that emphasize psychopharmacology are considered prize assignments, and residents are often unable to discuss the psychological meaning of a patient's symptoms or family life. At recent meetings of an organization composed of the directors of psychiatric residencies in American medical schools, serious proposals were debated to make training in psychotherapy optional to psychiatry residents since it has been "established" that psychopharmacology, not psychotherapy, is the treatment of choice for so many patients. Articles are beginning to appear in professional journals arguing for the merger of psychiatry and neurology. The pendulum has swung from the total rejection of neurobiology in the 1940s and 1950s to its celebration in the 1980s.

Before analyzing further the repressive consequences of psychiatry's scientific orientation, I want to make clear that American psychoanalysis as an institution has also participated in self-serving practices under the guise of science. In direct opposition to Freud's own beliefs, psychoanalysis became the monopoly of physicians when it was imported to the United States. This medical emphasis, as Russell Jacoby notes in *Social Amnesia* and in *The Repression of Psychoanalysis*, has certainly had repressive consequences for psychoanalytic theory-building in the U.S. Nevertheless, psychoanalysis at its best—a theory of unconscious meaning and conflict, of the social construction of internal mental life—is radically different from and opposed to the biological reductionism sweeping psychiatry and our popular culture. Psychoanalysis and biological reductionism have to be analyzed on their own merits and not primarily on the basis of the political practices of the groups promoting them—except insofar as these political motives substantially shape the theoretical claims.

The move toward a biological understanding of mental illness is related though not reducible to a concerted effort by the psychiatric profession to strengthen its weakening hold on the field of mental health. For complex political and economic reasons, in the last ten years, insurers, government health care planners, and corporate underwriters have sought to cut medical costs, and psychiatric benefits have often been the first to go. When mental health coverage has been included in these newer, pared-down health plans, it has often been limited. In this context, conflicts have arisen as to which mental health professionals are to be covered. Psychiatrists have fought to restrict various forms of reimbursement and privilege to medical doctors, thereby excluding from coverage others who arguably have equally good or better abilities to deliver some form of care: providers such as psychologists, social workers, and counselors. With the shrinkage of the health care dollar and the disproportionate cutbacks in mental health benefits, battles over distribution have intensified and interprofessional rivalries have escalated. Payers and health planners have raised questions about the cost effectiveness of high-priced psychiatric services when compared to similar, less expensive services offered by non-M.D.s. Non-M.D.s themselves are increasingly better organized and are challenging psychiatry's monopolistic practices on a greater number of fronts than ever before. A recent example of this challenge is the attempt by psychologists to gain hospital-admitting privileges in California, a move opposed by psychiatrists and currently under judicial review.

With its economic base shrinking and its professional status under attack, psychiatry has reacted by attempting to redefine its boundaries and stake out a privileged territory that will ensure its safety and hegemony in the mental health marketplace. Psychiatry has needed to be accepted by organized medicine, from which it became estranged during the post-World War II years of psychoanalytic hegemony and during the tumultuous community-mental-health years of the 1960s, when forces within psychiatry itself attacked the medical model on behalf of a liberal vision of social change.

This objective has been achieved with the help of the ideology of biological reductionism. Psychiatrists have been able to argue that their reimbursements shouldn't be disproportionately reduced because mental illnesses have been shown to be as biologically based and as biologically treatable as any other reimbursable medical condition. Psychiatrists' fees should therefore continue to be greater than those of non-medically-trained therapists, they claim, because only their training provides access to and understanding of the latest revelations concerning the biological foundations of mental illness.

Psychiatrists and health-policy planners are constructing new models of service delivery consistent with the new fiscal constraints of insurers in which all patients with psychological problems must first be evaluated and, if necessary, treated by a psychiatrist in case a biological disorder is involved. This process will insure the centrality of the M.D. in all aspects of mental health services. Furthermore, as the media increasingly tout the biological basis for most mental disorders, support grows for greater funding of neurobiological and psychopharmacological research. As a result, psychiatry—the mental health profession most associated with this area of research—also grows in status.

I do not mean to imply that all or even most psychiatrists acquire a biological orientation for selfish reasons. I *am* arguing, however, that the leaders of organized psychiatry are quite conscious (as are other mental health professionals) of their declining status in the marketplace and are promoting and marketing the aspect of psychiatric practice—namely their medical background—that they believe privileges them over other practitioners. This approach coincides with a genuine technological explosion, which has helped buttress the psychiatrists' claims. Individual psychiatrists may make their treatment decisions based on good intentions and a firm belief that the patient's best interests are being served, but the philosophy and training informing these decisions are deeply influenced by complex political, economic, and ideological pressures that shape the psychiatric profession as a whole.

Correspondence Versus Causation

The proponents of biological psychiatry make two related claims. First, they argue that mental illness is caused by biological processes in the brain (genetically inherited, most likely) that interact with the environment to produce the symptoms of mental disorder. The weight assigned to the environment may vary, but the essence of the claim is that a biological process or state causes a psychological process or state. In other words, the biological state is assumed to be prior to the emotional one, both temporally and ontologically. Second, proponents of biological psychiatry claim that since the cause of certain mental illnesses is biological, the most appropriate and effective treatments are also biological—involving, in most cases, the use of psychoactive medications.

Studies of the neurobiology and pharmacology of schizophrenia, manic-depressive illness, depression, anxiety, phobias, obsessive-compulsive disorders, and so-called borderline conditions fill the pages of the major psychiatric journals and are routinely reported on by the print and television media. The brains of schizophrenics are found to have too much of the chemical dopamine, a substance that transmits signals between nerve cells; the brains of depressives have a deficiency of or an altered sensitivity to the neurotransmitters norepinephrine or serotonin. Specialized computerized imaging techniques have been developed to replace X-rays and are used to show that the brains of schizophrenics have a different size and shape than normal brains. The newest radiological tool, called the PET scan (Positron Emission Tomography) can actually depict which areas of depressed patients' brains are less metabolically active than the corresponding regions of normal brains.

As the chemistry and structure of the brains of disturbed patients are analyzed with increasing sophistication, the claims of those doing the analyzing get more bold. Ross Baldessarini, a leading psychopharmacologist, asserted as long ago as 1977 that "effective [medical] treatments now exist for most of the major psychiatric illnesses." The 1985 edition of the *Comprehensive Textbook of Psychiatry* informs us that the "necessary genetic component" of schizophrenia and affective disorders has been discovered and is widely accepted.

It is important to keep in mind that when researchers or reporters describe a biological *basis* for a psychological problem they are always implying that the biological is more "basic" than the psychological, that this more "fundamental" level of reality produces the behavioral or psychological reaction. This is biological reductionism, which suggests that the more we are able to explain psychological or social behavior on the basis of smaller and smaller levels of analysis—ultimately leading to the level of molecular biology and genetics—the closer we will get to the truth.

This, however, is not the only way of viewing the relationship between biology and psychology. Using a more cautious or critical perspective, we might say that it is possible to speak only of correspondence between these two radically different levels of experience, not causation. In the most general sense, human psychology is a function of the human brain. Consciousness, love, sadness, and conflict are all impossible without the brain. Further, it is probably the case that my brain is in a different state when I'm writing than when I'm sleeping or jogging. In other words, there should be some very *general* correspondence between brain and mental state if one takes seriously that we are biological as well as social beings. But this does *not* say anything whatsoever about causality or temporal sequence. It is not possible to prove that the brain state always precedes the mental state or vice versa.

It is always theoretically possible that the mental event in question precedes the brain state being described. Depression, for instance, might lower brain activity in certain areas of the brain and thereby account for the differences found by the PET scan or assays of brain chemical levels. Researchers like Marian Diamond have conclusively proven that enriched environments can increase brain size and complexity. Neuroanatomic studies of patients with multiple personalities—a syndrome widely accepted to be of psychogenic origin—demonstrate variations in such brain processes as blood flow, electrical activity, and neurotransmitter levels among the different personalities of the same patient. Even the best studies of the genetic transmission of schizophrenia and depression, which appear to suggest that these disorders may be partially hereditary, have been criticized on methodological grounds and have not even come close to demonstrating *what* is inherited that might later produce the mental illness in question.

Although the logic of the reductionist argument is faulty, its purpose is clear. Richard Lewontin, Leon Kamin, and Steven Rose use an interview from the February 1981 issue of *Psychology Today* with two leading psychiatric researchers to illustrate this purpose. Paul Wender and Donald Klein argue that "for each schizophrenic there may be ten times as many people who have a milder form of the disorder that is genetically ... related to the most severe form.... Eight percent of Americans have a lifelong form of personality disorder that is genetically produced" and that should concern the public, which "is largely unaware that different sorts of emotional illnesses are now responsive to medications." In other words, since schizophrenia has been proven to be genetic, and since genes affect biology, schizophrenia and related "personality disorders" should be treated with drugs. But as Lewontin, Kamen, and Rose point out, even if the first statement is true, it doesn't follow that biology is the primary cause of schizophrenia, that social or interpersonal conditions might not be the more important factor. Furthermore, even if the biological "derangements" are etiologically significant, we know that altered psychology and behavior can change brains, and so it in no way follows that drug treatments are the only effective form of treatment.

Drugs and the Reductionist Fallacy

Researchers often erroneously link theories of biological causation with the necessity for biological treatments. The logic is this: Drug X helps some symptoms of schizophrenia—say, agitation. Drug X is found to interact with metabolic pathway Y in the brain. Therefore, a disorder of metabolic pathway Y is deemed an important cause of schizophrenia. In reality, no such conclusion is logically warranted. Steven Rose, a radical neurobiologist, offers a good analogy: aspirin reduces the pain of a broken bone by inhibiting the synthesis of the chemical messenger prostaglandin, which is found all over the body. In what sense can it be said that the prostaglandin synthesis causes the broken bone? If aspirin also reduces the pain of a toothache, does it follow that the "cause" of a toothache and of a broken bone are similar? The discovery of how a drug acts in the brain says nothing clearly about the cause of the symptom it treats, particularly—as is true with psychiatric drugs—if the drug has such a diffuse effect throughout the brain.

The practitioner and the lay consumer need to put the actual efficacy of these drugs in some kind of perspective. The antipsychotic medications, for instance, are clearly effective in reducing the terror, agitation, and aggressiveness of an acutely psychotic or schizophrenic person, and are often the precondition for any successful psychotherapy to occur. Claims that these drugs ought to be the "treatment for schizophrenia" are problematic, however. For example, it is widely acknowledged that delusions—the core of schizophrenia—are often *not* eliminated by medication, nor are common symptoms such as apathy or withdrawal. Tranquilization, in other words, while often important, does not cure the symptoms of schizophrenia. In fact, it is increasingly the case that high doses of medication are used more because they hold someone together in the absence of adequate social and psychotherapy services than because they have an antischizophrenic effect. As mental health services become less available, psychotic patients are given medications in doses and for durations that would not otherwise be advisable. In other words, medications increasingly fill the gap left by therapists and other mental health providers; they are a kind of "better than nothing" solution—a necessity, not a virtue.

Studies that compare the effects of antidepressants with a placebo on depressed patients show that an *average* of 60–70 percent of those treated with medication improve as compared to 30–40 percent of those treated with a placebo. This is clearly a significant finding and suggests that these medications are useful. Little attention, though, is paid to the astonishingly high placebo rates of depressed patients who get better either spontaneously or by virtue of the purely psychological effects of taking a pill or being the object of research attention. Further, the possibility exists—but is never studied—that medication, by physiologically altering one's mental state, might be psychologically interpreted by the patient in a manner that then leads to improvement. It seems that to the extent that findings support a psychological theory of depression, they are not subjected to the same intense scrutiny.

The Social Consequences of Biological Reductionism

The biological reductionism sweeping psychiatry has important social and psychological consequences that social critics and professionals alike need to understand. Every form of medical technology used by psychiatry on the mentally ill in the last fifty years has been justified on scientific grounds. From insulin coma therapy to electroconvulsive therapy to psychosurgery, dangerous and dehumanizing treatments have been linked to various discoveries about the biological basis of mental illness. This model of the mind locates the problem within the individual, not within the family or society, and it does so in a way that suggests limits on the individual's capacity for self-transformation. Intended or not, this worldview tends to justify the difficulty of changing someone's behavior on the grounds that the innate behavior is a result of biological deficiencies.

This argument understandably falls on welcome ears. People who have worked with schizophrenic patients for any length of time confront the apparent intractability of the disorder and naturally look for explanations that account for the patient's profound resistance to change and for their own chronic feelings of professional failure. Sitting with a depressed person week after week, and watching one's empathy, insight, and advice fall on deaf ears, can lead a therapist to find explanations that mitigate his or her own feelings of guilt, responsibility, and ineffectiveness. Crisis clinic workers struggling to pull together vanishing community resources for their psychotic walk-in patients only to find these patients returning in identically bad shape two months later need a theory that accounts for this frustrating recidivism.

A theory that blames genetically transmitted biological deficiencies fits the bill perfectly. Such a theory implies that it is not the therapist's fault for failing to cure the patient and that the kind of intense emotional involvement that psychotherapy demands is misplaced from the outset. Instead, the psychiatrist can justify the more familiar and emotionally distanced role of diagnostician and pill dispenser, helping the patient and family understand and adapt to the "illness." Nonmedical psychotherapists, in turn, are given a justification for giving psychiatrists the responsibility of treating their depressed or schizophrenic patients. These psychotherapists are relieved of their own helplessness, their nonmedical role now being restricted to a focus on secondary psychological symptoms. Crisis clinic workers can also protect themselves by viewing their charges as permanently damaged people who would function better if they would only take their proper medication. At a time when the frequency and duration of psychotherapy is being drastically reduced by those who fiscally underwrite these services—which makes the work of people in the mental health professions increasingly difficult—the rationalizations that the ideology of biological reductionism has to offer are particularly helpful.

What is the effect on the patient of this view of suffering? Biological reductionism is, after all, conveyed to patients both explicitly and implicitly. In addition to the increasingly frequent practice of directly *teaching* patients about the biology and pharmacology of their illness, the process of giving a patient medication conveys multiple and subtle hints about how the therapist views the patient's problem. If, for instance, a psychiatrist fails to examine the *meaning* of medication to the patient, the patient may think the doctor believes that the main problem is a biological deficiency.

The problems with this attitude become apparent when one recognizes that patients who are profoundly depressed or schizophrenic often have powerful fantasies of being deficient, damaged, helpless, "bad," and incapable of changing their feelings. Biochemical theories about neurotransmitter "deficiencies," which locate the main problem in "things" over which one is helpless, such as brain chemistry, reinforce these pathogenic fantasies.

Granted, this biological approach can be relieving to a patient for several psychological reasons. First, it displaces a frightening sense of badness and responsibility onto the patient's brain. It's as if the patient's unconscious mind were able to say: "Since I need to punish myself for being such a horrible and destructive person, it's a relief to know that it's only my brain; and further, if these medications make me feel bad or unpleasantly sedate or numb, I'm being properly punished anyway." Second, a patient who doesn't feel fully human, perhaps because of a lifetime of being treated as such by narcissistic or psychotic caregivers, often is terrified of human intimacy and recognition. Being treated in an "objective" way by a doctor whose focus is only chemistry and not psychology can therefore be reassuring. Third, a patient who cannot tolerate his or her longing for love and caretaking may find in the medication not a chemical answer to a chemical deficiency but a symbolic unconscious answer to an intrapsychic or emotional emptiness—an answer that makes the patient feel better. After all, the patient may accept and rely on medication and the theories that support its use for psychological reasons that have little to do with the theories of the treating or research psychiatrist.

The problem is that the gratification that some patients get from biological approaches to their condition may ultimately point to their resistance to change. When one's sense of self is confirmed, one may easily feel partially understood and get some relief, while one's underlying distortions are left intact.

On a broader scale, biological psychiatry functions as an antidote to burdensome feelings of responsibility that affect people in our culture in various ways. On an obvious level, if the problem is biological then it is not social. People's families, work environments, and economic stress don't produce severe depression or psychosis; their brain physiology does. Further, society doesn't need to fault itself or its leaders for cutting funding for long-term treatment facilities since our current success with psychoactive drugs makes such treatment unnecessary anyway. Biological reductionism is a twist on blaming the victim: here the victim isn't even a person; it is someone's genes or biology. Consequently, the victim, as well as the victimizer, is exonerated.

These issues of responsibility are starkly revealed in the growing political and educational lobbies representing the mentally ill and their families. Groups such as NAMI and the National Depression and Manic-Depression Association wield increasing clout in political and funding circles. In addition to their laudable efforts to eliminate the social stigma of schizophrenia and manic-depression, these groups strongly lobby for increased research into the etiology and treatment of these disorders, *provided* that the etiology is biological and the treatment medical. Families are often understandably eager to get out from under terrible feelings of guilt and responsibility, and this movement offers an effective method. Any theory that contradicts this approach by saying that families are profound forces in psychological development, healthy or pathological, is treated as if it blames the parents.

Both approaches are distortions. The fact that parents and families can and regularly do pathologically affect the emotional development of children and are more than capable of making their children schizophrenic and depressed does not mean that parents are evil or that their children are weak failures. As much as psychoanalysis locates the etiology of psychopathology in the family, it also debunks the prevailing morality that sees people as good or evil, perpetrators or victims. Parents can also be victims of their own families, and children have psychological desires and conflicts not purely of their parents' making. But the movement today that exonerates everyone, and instead blames genes and neurotransmitters, views psychology as an enemy seeking to make families and patients feel like moral failures.

A theory that says that parents shouldn't take any responsibility for their children's emotional and mental problems prevents us from critically confronting the way that social institutions ravage our lives. It makes it difficult for us to recognize the most personal and "interior" forms of alienation in our culture, and the unconscious distorting and emotional violence within family life. Contrary to the protests of family groups and biological ideologues, saying that families hurt children can convey the greatest sympathy for all parties involved. Parents, after all, experience and raise their children in social contexts not always under their control, and under the influence of intrapsychic conflicts and damage suffered at the hands of their own families.

What we need is an approach to psychiatry that neither places the burden only on the family's shoulders nor dismisses the notion of family and societal responsibility altogether. Without such an approach the exonerating ideology of biological reductionism will continue to reign, representing another step in the progressive collapse of critical thinking that marks our culture today. □

The Existential Politics of Dr. Suess

Betty Mensch and Allen Freeman

Theodore Suess Greisel, also and usually known as Dr. Suess, has been one of the most succesful writers of children's literature in the history of the English language, ranking with such giants as Lewis Carroll and Beatrix Potter. He has sold more than one hundred million books. Some dismiss Dr. Seuss's incessant, bouncy anapestic rhythm and lively, memorable rhymes as doggerel. But in opposition to the conventional—indeed, hegemonic—iambic voice, his metric triplets offer the power of a more primal chant which quickly draws the reader in with its relentless repetition. Moreover, what seems to be the silly whimsy of his books—the made-up words, the outlandish creatures and machines—carries an empowering message. Seuss is a smasher of conventional boundaries. He invents his own words, defying the language/nonsense boundary; he invents his own creatures, defying the human/animal boundary; he is unceasingly sarcastic and satirical yet profoundly serious, ultimately defying the boundary between what is serious and what is absurd.

This form reaches the powerless, such as small children and old people, who are expected to be passive and are objectified through their nonconsensual submission to authority. For such readers (or, listeners, in the case of the children), the books offer a discourse of resistance; they are accessible, easily consumed, and utterly irreverent. Their suggestion that categories need not be taken for granted is empowering to those who are told they have no choice, that that's the way things are, that "life is like that."...

Empowerment is the core theme in Dr. Seuss, for with all of his irreverent nonsense he offers readers a space within which they can search for both identity and virtue, free from the oppressive force of authority and orthodoxy. Seuss develops this theme with surprising richness and complexity. Described thematically (rather than chronologically), he starts by exploring the child's struggle to achieve identity in the family, with its conventional norms of behavior and its demand for passive compliance with authority. Seuss moves from there to a description of the need for authentic, existential struggle in the world generally. He then explores quite specific forms of oppression in the modern world—hierarchy, racism, environmental devastation, and militarism—and all the suffocating ideological forms which are used to justify them. Finally, Seuss suggests the possibility of moral and political transformation. This transformation requires the creation of new selves, liberated from orthodox assumptions about scientific truth, gender, and the limited range of moral choice in the world. So transformed, we might even become open to the experience of forming an authentic community, in which virtue and authority are no longer at odds with each other, but reunited in new conditions of freedom.

In our world, especially in its public realm, we experience authority as disconnected from virtue. Virtue means the possibility of living a moral life; authority is what obliges us to conform to social

---

Alan Freeman and Betty Mensch are, collectively, parents of Jonathan, Jennifer, Joshua, James, and Jeremy. They are also both professors of law at the State University of New York at Buffalo. This article appeared in Tikkun, *March/April 1987.*

or, more exactly, legal norms. Virtue, for most of us, means personal morality that is subjective and privatized. Authority means the state or one of its disciplinary agents. There have been times in our history, however, when it was imagined that virtue and authority might reside in the same place. Such was the claim of medieval monarchy, which supposes itself divinely sanctioned. In contrast, the modern secular state merely enforces an aggregate of subjective political choices. There remains, however, one realm in our contemporary experience where the two still purport to be united: the role of the parent. To empower children in their own quest for virtue inevitably means subverting the role of the parent. Therefore, a description of Dr. Seuss's work properly starts with his lively family psychodrama, *The Cat in the Hat.*[*]

In *The Cat in the Hat*, with the simple elegance of a 220-word vocabulary, Seuss depicts in powerful symbolic form the core childhood dilemma of identity and authority within the family. The (nameless) narrator is a boy—the archetypal male child seeking to define himself in relation to his mother and also in relation to both conventional morality and his own chaotic, anarchic impulses. Thus the book is quite specifically about *boyhood,* and the male quest for self-definition in the nuclear family of the 1950s, when mother was the most powerful repressive presence in the family and the most immediate representative of convention. (It is a testament to the power of gender in that culture—and also in the traditional Freudian version of childhood—that *The Cat in the Hat* would be a very different book if written about a girl.)

At the start of the book the narrator and his sister, Sally, are alone and bored at home on a cold, rainy day, accompanied only by their fish in a bowl, when a loud bump suddenly announces the unexpected arrival of the slyly grinning Cat in the Hat. This cat promises "lots of good fun that is funny," and quickly dismisses the fish's strident objection that the children must not let the cat in when their mother is away:

> But our fish said, "No! No! Make that cat go away!
> Tell that Cat in the Hat you do NOT want to play.
> He should not be here. He should not be about.
> He should not be here when your mother is out!"

The cat insists that the children should "Have no fear!" and repeats his promise that "we can have lots of good fun...." This he then demonstrates with his first game, a complex juggling trick that begins with the fish being tossed high in the air. After this balancing act collapses, the fish once again scolds the cat and orders him out. The cat refuses to leave, instead summoning two nameless things from a red box, thing one and thing two, who are strange, soulless, golem-like creatures resplendent in their perfect amorality. Once released, the things enter into a chaotic frenzy of unrestrained play. Like demon spirits from an animalistic id, the things run wild, wreaking havoc and even violating the absent mother's most intimate realm:

> On the string of one kite
> We saw mother's new gown!
> her gown with the dots
> That are pink, white and red.
> Then we saw one kite bump
> On the head of her bed!

---

[*] For a similar reading of *The Cat in the Hat*, stressing its psychodramatic and anti-authoritarian qualities, see chapter six of *Down the Rabbit Hole* by Selma Lanes (1971).

Just as the children are becoming nervous at the extent of the destruction, the fish, quaking with fear, announces that mother is home. Finally frightened, the narrator seizes the things and orders the cat to take them away. As the fish laments the awesome mess left in the house, the cat returns with a magic machine and restores order. When mother does return, and asks what the children did, they are uncertain what to tell her. Then, in the last two lines of the book, another voice asks us all a dreadful question: "What would you do if your mother asked you?"

The children are thus confronted with powerful cultural images. The fish, with his incessant scolding, articulates all the socially constructed norms defining what good little children should do, norms which parents systematically and unreflectively instill in their children. Drawing on an old Christian symbol (the fish was an ancient sign of Christianity), Dr. Seuss portrays the fish as a kind of ever-nagging super-ego, the embodiment of utterly conventionalized morality. Thus, as if under seige by Nietzsche himself, the fish scolds, frets, chastises, and tries to induce anxious fear of authority, but unlike the cat, he can attract the children with no independent power of his own, and his demands are designed to make the children utterly passive. The fish would have them just, "sit, sit, sit, sit." Therefore, Dr. Seuss is merciless in his mockery of the fish and the conventionality the fish represents. In the hands of the cat (his natural predator) the fish is subjected to madcap, slapstick violence—he is balanced on the cat's umbrella, dropped into a teapot, and dangled from the lines of a kite.

With all of his elaborate (and not always successful) juggling tricks, the cat seems to act as a kind of mediator: However irreverent, he complies with social norms at least enough to avoid dreaded punishment (he *does* clean up his mess), while at the same time retaining his utter commitment to having fun. Unlike the accomodationalist ego of Freudian imagery, however, the cat is more liberator than integrator, too much a fierce deconstructor of norms to be content with mere balancing. With his magical, prescientific technology and his offer of unrestrained fun without accountability, he is the most destabilizing character in the story. The cat has long served in Western culture as an embodiment of magical, even satanic forces. Here the cat carries on that tradition by demonstrating to the boy narrator a possibility of powerful action in the world, action unconstrained by the fish's fearful anxiety and obsession with propriety....

Four of Dr. Seuss's books have dealt with familiar and quite specific social issues: illegitimate hierarchy, racism, ecology, and the arms race. In each, however, Dr. Seuss pushes beyond conventional liberal cliché to offer a more radical version of both the problems and the likelihood of their eventual solution.

One of Dr. Seuss's earliest and most obviously political stories was *Yertle the Turtle*, written in 1950. Its central theme is hierarchy, which is depicted with stark, corrosive simplicity. Yertle is the turtle king who constructs his throne by requiring his subjects to stack themselves in an ever-higher pile. The weight on the turtles below becomes heavier and heavier as Yertle feeds his arrogant, fantasy rulership of all he can see. Only Mack, the plainest and lowliest of the subjects, dares to voice his opposition:

"Your majesty, please ... I don't like to complain,
But down here below, we are feeling great pain.
I know, up on top you are seeing great sights,
But down at the bottom we, too, should have rights."

Finally becoming indignant when he sees the moon rising higher than himself, Yertle announces that he will stack his subjects all the way to heaven. At that point, when the pain becomes unbearable, Mack becomes "a little bit mad," and does a "plain little thing": He burps, and that burp tumbles the whole precarious pile of turtles. Yertle takes a nose dive and is returned to his proper station—resituated in the pond, he is mockingly called "king of the mud," while all the other turtles "are free/As turtles and, maybe, all creatures should be."

In *Yertle*, and in later stories as well, Seuss ruthlessly exposes the artificiality of hierarchy. Oppression is not just evil—it is petty and pointless as well, serving nothing except the self-important delusions of those who rule. As Yertle rises up and his field of vision expands, he proudly (and ludicrously) proclaims:

> "All mine! ... Oh, the things I now rule!
> I'm king of a cow! And I'm king of a mule!
> I'm king of a horse! And, what's more, beyond that
> I'm king of a blueberry bush and a cat!
> I'm Yertle the Turtle! Oh, marvelous me!
> For I am the ruler of all that I see!"

Since Yertle's authority is premised on deluded consciousness alone, submission to his oppression is therefore not an act of political necessity, but one of exaggerated fear, so that the oppressed are essentially complicit in their own oppression. The turtles trembled with fear when Yertle *"bellowed and brayed"* out his orders, and they obeyed. As it turns out, however, they are not nearly as powerless as they felt, for only one slight, whimsical act of opposition is enough to send Yertle's whole structure toppling. The scene at the end is one of joyful frolic, as the turtles happily cavort together in the pond. While Yertle scowls out from under his crown of mud, the others play in a state of anarchic but companionable pleasure.

Yertle the Turtle provides an important lesson about surplus powerlessness, but Mack's burp might have been *too* easy—a single, slight, contemptuous gesture is sufficient to topple oppression and transform the turtle world into utopia. Nevertheless, in dealing with specific social issues Dr. Seuss became increasingly unwilling to suggest that solutions were easy; as time went on there was a mounting pessimism in his work, combined, however, with a greater sense of urgency in the call for committed moral action.

The Sneetches, written in 1953, a year before *Brown v. Board of Education*, is an indictment of racism.[*] In the story Seuss mocks the way in which culturally constructed otherness becomes the basis for oppression. Despite his mocking tone, however, Seuss also recognizes how deeply embedded the construct of otherness is in our culture.

The Sneetches opens by describing a society whose central, organizing principle is domination and subordination based on a supposedly important and natural physical difference: some Sneetches have little stars on their bellies, while others do not. Those with stars maintain their social domination through a process of systematic exclusion:

> But, because they had stars, all the Star-Belly Sneetches
> Would brag, We're the best kind of Sneetch on the beaches
> With their snoots in the air, they would sniff and they'd snort
> We'll have nothing to do with the Plain-Belly sort! ...
> When the Star-Belly Sneetches had frankfurter roasts
> Or picnics or parties or marshmallow toasts,

---

[*] Which is not to suggest that Dr. Suess is perfect on the question of racism. In *If I Ran the Zoo* (1950), he failed to rise above his generation, depicting both Asians and Africans as racially stereotypical caricatures.

They never invited the Plain-Belly Sneetches
They left them out cold, in the dark of the beaches.
They kept them away. Never let them come near.
And that's how they treated them year after year.

By itself, this description ridicules the insidious social practices based on racism. Dr. Seuss's analysis goes one step further, however. Seuss is not only sensitive to the unjustified self-importance of the excluders, but sensitive as well to its effects on its victims. He understands that the experience of exclusion can push victims to the point of wanting to take on the norms and values of their oppressors, so that they try to deny their own identities in order to pass as dominators. It is that psychic reality of racism, and cultural domination in general, which provides Seuss with a point of departure for a critique that is far more radical than the conventional liberal denunciation of racism as simply not rational or nice.

In fact, Dr. Seuss introduces a third party who represents a class whose interests might well be served by the perpetuation of racism. In his story, the key character is Sylvester McMonkey McBean, a predatory and exploitative entrepreneur who plays skillfully on the fears and anxieties of the Sneetch victims who are caught up in the racist world view of their oppressors.

For three dollars each, McBean, with a very large machine, transforms the Sneetches without stars into creatures indistinguishable from their former oppressors. Confronted with the abolition of physical difference, the original Star-Belly Sneetches desperately proclaim,

"We're still the best Sneetches and they are the worst,
But now how in the world will we know ...
If which kind is what, or the other way round?"

McBean, looking as sleazy as can be, now charging $10 each and using a fancier machine, removes the stars from the bellies of the original oppressors. Next, of course, McBean offers to remove the stars he has sold to the original victims. As this selling process escalates, the scene turns into an orgy of capitalist exploitation, with constant streams of Sneetches paying to enter one machine to be starred and then to enter another to be unstarred, while McBean stands grinning in the center, in front of an ever-growing mountain of cash.

The chaos ends when the Sneetches all run out of money, and McBean, with capitalist complacency, laughs as he leaves, noting, *"They never will learn. No, you can't teach a Sneetch!"*

Nevertheless, the Sneetches ends on a note that is at least slightly hopeful. Having been so fully and relentlessly exploited, the Sneetches manage to achieve a consciousness breakthrough that obliterates the racism of their culture:

But McBean was quite wrong. I'm quite happy to say
That the Sneetches got really quite smart on that day,
The day they decided that Sneetches are Sneetches
And no kind of Sneetch is the best on the beaches.

That Sneetch recognition of shared victimization, however, came only after the complete economic destruction of Sneetch society. Having been reduced to common economic powerlessness, the Sneetches finally realize a unitary class consciousness.

Dr. Seuss's book about environmental destruction, *The Lorax*, is more dark and despairing in mood, with only the slightest glimmer of hope at the end. As in the Sneetches, a prevailing and destructive ideology takes hold and becomes utterly totalizing. In *The Lorax*, visual imagery intensifies the bleakness of mood, as even the once proud capitalist, now a miserable and guilty hermit, despairs at the wasteland produced by his own pursuit of gain. Colors are dark blues, grays, purples, and browns, and the only visible vegetation is an occasional thin strand of stiff Grickle-Grass.

The ideological mainstay demolished by *The Lorax* is a basic one: Market Freedom. According to conventional wisdom, in a free economy bright entrepreneurs discover novel techniques for fashioning from raw materials new products for the satisfaction of authentic human needs, which are expressed through choice and exchange on a free market. In Seuss's account the extraction of raw materials becomes the rape of the natural world, as an entire species of trees (the Truffula Trees) is destroyed, along with the fragile ecosystem of birds, animals, and fish that once depended on it. This destruction is accompanied by the pollution which is the inevitable by-product of manufacture.

Meanwhile, the product whose manufacture requires this wholesale devastation of the environment makes a mockery of the market ideologies of both need and utility. The Thneed, claiming to be everything useful, is in fact nothing but a representation of the artificiality of consumer demand as created and manipulated by the greedy producer. The capitalist at first defensively claims universal utility for his new product ("A Thneed's a Fine Something-That-All-People-Need/It's a shirt. It's a sock. It's a glove. It's a hat ... You can use it for carpets. For pillows! For sheets!/Or curtains! Or covers or bicycle seats!") Nevertheless, even he wryly observes after his first sale, "You never can tell what some people will buy."

Despite this early self-awareness, the capitalist is quickly captured by his own ideological role as acquisitive accumulator, to the point where production, which at least in theory should be a function of rational economic planning, becomes an obsessive and irrational felt necessity. Thus, he at first "felt sad" when the frolicsome, little bear-like creatures, the Bar-ba-loots, were forced to leave because they could not live without Truffula Fruit, although he quickly convinces himself:

"But ... business is business
And business must grow ... I meant no harm.
I most truly did not.
But I had to grow bigger. So bigger I got.
I biggered my factory. I biggered my roads. I biggered my wagons. I biggered the loads
Of the Thneeds I shipped out, I was shipping them forth
to the South! To the East! To the West! To the North!
I went right on biggering ... selling more Thneeds.
And I biggered my money, which everyone needs."

With capitalist and consumer alike caught up in the totalizing culture of greed, acquisition, and gratification, the possibility of critique from within is remote if not lost. The sole critical voice is that of the Lorax, a wizened elfish being who seems to antedate Judeo-Christian culture and take us back to a world where nature could speak for itself and be heard. Akin to a Druidic spirit, he emerges from a tree to scold the foolish capitalist and by extension any culture which in its self-importance thinks it can stand apart from its immersion in the interconnectedness of the natural world.

Unlike the capitalist, who uses the traditionally masculine mode of rational analysis to distance himself from his own feelings, the Lorax is unfailingly emotional, engaged and sympathetic. The discourse he uses, while fretful and even angry, is always one of empathy, not logic ("My poor swomee swans, why they can't sing a note./No one can sing who has smog in his throat."); and he consistently speaks not for himself, but for others, for those who are unheard ("I speak for the trees, for the trees have no tongues ... ") Similarly, the capitalist defines his responsibilities legalistically, in terms of individual *mens rea* ("I meant no harm. I most truly did not") and by reference to a protected sphere of private conduct ("Well, I have my rights, sir, and I'm telling you/I intend to go on doing just what I do.") By contrast, the Lorax defines responsibility by the consequences that acts have on others, on the whole interconnected community of nature, and he tries to force the capitalist to take personal responsibility for the harm he does when exercising his "rights."

Nevertheless, the Lorax is ignored, and the scene at the end is one of bleak despair. The Lorax departs, leaving nothing but desolation behind him. Even the capitalist retreats into isolation, in a bizarre, aerial, Dickensian hovel, to reflect on the Lorax's last word: "Unless."

That final word represents the core of Seuss's message: There is always choice. No matter how heavy the weight of the past, the possibility of existential, committed action remains. Thus, the final point is one of freedom, not necessity. Even conditions of seeming oppression can be transformed into empowering moral statements and become expressions of genuine commitment. Also, in *The Lorax*, as in most of Dr. Seuss's work, it is a child, with some link to a natural innocence which can never be completely regained, who is given the final opportunity to act. The capitalist tosses a small seed to a young boy, with the urgent instruction:

"You're in charge of the last of the Truffula Seeds.
And Truffula Trees are what everyone needs.
Plant a new Truffula. Treat it with care.
Give it clean water. And feed it fresh air.
Grow a forest. Protect it from axes that hack.
Then the Lorax and all of his friends may come back."

Dr. Seuss's most pessimistic story is the recent *Butter Battle Book*, in which Seuss once again uses his favorite political weapon (his "bat," to use the imagery of Solla Sollew), which is mockery. *The Butter Battle Book* is a bitterly sarcastic history of the arms race, which takes us to the present moment of uncertain dread caused by the threat of nuclear warfare. Dr. Seuss refuses to relieve the tension of that uncertainty: At the end of the story, a boy, afraid of the bomb, shouts out to his bomb-carrying warrior grandfather, "Be careful! Oh Gee! Who's going to drop it?/Will you ... ? Or will he ... ?" Grandfather's only answer is the terrible, "Be patient ... We'll see/We will see ..."

Equally terrifying is the extent to which the ideology that justifies the arms race—the ideology of hysterical national moral superiority and contempt for cultural difference—pervades society. With fierce, Swiftian satire Seuss describes that ideology as transparently foolish at its core. The great difference between the Yooks and the enemy Zooks is the way they spread their butter on their bread, yet this trivial difference forms the basis for a hatred which dominates national life. At the start of the story, the young narrator is carefully instructed by his grandfather:

"It's high time that you know of the terribly horrible thing that Zooks do
In every Zook house and in every Zook town
every Zook eats his bread with the butter side down! ... " Grandpa gritted his teeth.
"So you can't trust a Zook who spreads bread underneath!
Every Zook must be watched! He has kinks in his soul!"

As the Yooks and Zooks absurdly wage war with each other to the point of mutual extinction, the citizens uncritically participate in the patriotic frenzy. The Butter-up Band and the Right-Side-Up Song Girls, singing "Oh be faithful!/Believe in thy butter!" urge the soldiers on. Then, in an especially bleak scene, the Yook citizens are all ordered underground to prepare for war. They dutifully do as they are told, still deeply believing in their country's moral supremacy:

> I noticed that every last Yook in our land
> was obeying the Chief Yookeroo's grim command
> They were all bravely marching with banners aflutter,
> down a hole! For their country! And Right-Side-Up Butter!

Closely linked to the ideology of patriotism is the celebration of technological advance, which Seuss exposes as nothing but destructive absurdity. Each new Yook weapon is matched by an equally powerful Zook weapon, as military inventiveness becomes ever more elegantly ridiculous. Thus sling shots are rapidly replaced by elaborate weapons like the Eight-Nozzled, Elephant-Toted Boom Blitz, until finally the bomb—the Bitsy Big-Boy Boomeroo—renders all other weaponry obsolete.

While the Yook citizens cheer this process on, the pervasiveness of the nationalist ideology has rendered them essentially passive and unreflecting. The real architects of the arms race are the militarist Chief Yookeroo and his technocratic "Boys in the Back Room." In their dark closet labeled Top-est Secret-est Brain Nest they perform all the seemingly unquestionable, rational mathematic calculations that lead to the most irrational outcome of all—the threat of annihilation. Under the pressure of militarist ideology, political choice has become nothing but passive complicity in this cult of Scientific Expertise and National Superiority.

The terrifying uncertainty at the end of *The Butter Battle Book* can be interpreted as a call for *real* choice, a plea for self-willed human action taken to challenge a suffocating and absurdly destructive amoral technocratic society. As other Seuss books illustrate, however, choice is not just defiance and opposition. While Seuss's most obviously political books expose evil, others, ultimately no less political, also explore the meaning of virtue, especially in the form of lived choice in the world. Seuss's early and still popular stories, *Horton Hatches the Egg* and *Thidwick the Big-Hearted Moose,* provide well-known examples. In each, a routine request for a social favor is transformed into a powerful act of moral choice.

In *Horton Hatches the Egg* the lazy Mazie Bird asks Horton the elephant to take a turn sitting on her egg. Horton reluctantly agrees, and while Maggie flippantly sings out "Toodle-oo" and flies off to Palm Beach, Horton totally commits himself to the transformative task he has undertaken, as expressed in the familiar refrain "I meant what I said and I said what I meant,/An elephant's faithful one hundred per cent."

This commitment proves to be no idle one, as evidenced by the series of trials Horton endures. First is physical pain, as the rains and snows beat down on him; then comes the mockery of his friends, who jeer at the absurdity of an elephant sitting in a tree and trying to hatch an egg. After his friends desert him, Horton must even stare death in the face, when hunters aim their rifles at Horton and he still stays with the nest. Finally comes the harshest trial of all: Horton is turned into a commodity, sold to a circus that hauls him across the country so that crowds of people can pay ten cents apiece to laugh at him.

With Horton, Seuss thus takes the convention of promise-keeping and then explores what it would mean if it were taken seriously, as moral obligation. Promises are usually associated with social nicety or self-interested bargaining. Operating within either of those realms, Horton would never be expected to follow through on his promise. Mazie herself defies social norms by never returning, which should relieve Horton of all further obligation; nor could Horton ever be supposed to have foreseen the difficulties he would encounter. To use conventional contract vocabulary, if he were a rational self-maximizer on the market, he would never have assumed the risk that a simple promise to help out could become a mission that would inform every moment of his life.

Promising and contracting always play upon our genuine impulses of niceness and commitment, yet we are never obliged to stake ourselves to the ultimate follow-through. In the ideological realms of both politeness and contracting, there is always an excuse. Horton, however, in the purity of his vision, discovers and seizes the core niceness of promising, making it the basis for an ultimate act of self-realization.

Significantly, that act of self-realization also requires that Horton appropriate a role and identity which, by all conventional assumptions, is utterly female. He must be the nurturing mother. The ridicule of his friends is doubtless directed not just at his size in relation to the tiny nest but also at his womanish behavior. According to the norms of the 1940s and 1950s, only wimpish nerds would act like Horton.

Horton's seeming passivity is intensified by the fact that he must not leave the nest; therefore he stolidly remains in the tree, while others abuse him in the process of acting out their stereotypically masculine roles as hunters and successful entrepreneurs. Paradoxically, however, it is really Horton who has made the active choice, the choice to defy norms in the quest for a virtue rooted in freedom rather than convention.

That Horton has a happy ending is irrelevant, for that ending is wonderfully outside the scope of all rational expectation: As it turns out, the egg hatches and the child within has magically become Horton's own ("It had ears and a tail and a trunk just like his!") Children rejoice at the outcome, yet they and we know that the purity of Horton's commitment was such that results were never the issue.

In *Thidwick the Big-Hearted Moose* Dr. Seuss once again takes niceness beyond the hypocritical realm of politeness, to the point of a seemingly absurd and also burdensome—indeed, life- threatening—commitment. In *Thidwick the Big-hearted Moose* a variety of pesky, selfish creatures take up residence in Thidwick's antlers. Thidwick longs to be rid of the self-indulgent pests, but that would be wrong. The resident creatures, like yuppie real-estate developers in a gentrified neighborhood, make a mockery of communitarianism when they keep urging others to join them at Thidwick's expense. Then, when Thidwick must swim across the lake for the moose-moss on which his survival depends, his guests all foolishly vote to keep him on shore, thereby reducing participatory democracy to the mere expression of trivial, short-sighted, self-interest. Even in the face of this destructive pettiness, however, Thidwick feels bound to the obligation (here again a traditionally feminine virtue—hospitality) he has assumed and stays ashore.

As in *Horton Hatches the Egg*, the ending is utterly appropriate, yet wholly outside the scope of Thidwick's expectation. He sheds his antlers, a natural event he did not anticipate, and the oppressively selfish guests confront an equally petty, self-important selfishness, but one that is vastly more powerful: Still on Thidwick's discarded antlers, they end up stuffed and mounted on the Harvard Club wall.

Thus Thidwick, like Horton, makes a powerful statement about the revolutionary possibility of empowerment. Thidwick seizes the very tools of his oppression—i.e., the burden of conventional obligation—and transforms that burden into a self-willed act of moral choice. By the purity of their commitment, both Horton and Thidwick become active, living subjects, not mere playthings of their petty oppressors. The residents of Thidwick's antlers typify the alienated community of the selfish, atomistic, and self-important. An alternative, the possibility of true community, is offered to us by Dr. Seuss in *Horton Hears a Who*. Unfortunately, within orthodox society the voice of true community can barely be heard. When the ever attentive and protective Horton listens to a faint voice, coming from a mere speck of dust, the other animals start to ridicule him. Passing onto her child the received conventional wisdom, a mother kangaroo announces: "Why, that speck is as small as the head of a pin./A person on that ... Why, there never has been!"

Thus Horton, whose innocence of spirit gives him access to alternative possibilities, must once again confront the suffocating oppression of orthodoxy, in this case parading as scientific truth about Objective Reality. The orthodoxy is so pervasive that it rules out and denies any alternative discourses, or, as Foucault would call them, "subjugated knowledges." Thus Horton finds he must stake his epistemological ground against mockery, humiliation, and physical abuse in order to save what he has started to recognize as a voice of real community.

At the end, Horton must call upon the Whos to save themselves by making their collective voice heard. This requires that all the Whos call out together in one loud voice. Nevertheless, one "young twerp of a Who" is found self-indulgently bouncing a yo-yo and ignoring the collective effort. Seized by the angry mayor of Whoville, he is forced to give up his individualized pleasure and to join the others in shouting from the highest tower. That one extra shout is the margin of victory for Whoville ("Their voices were heard!/They rang out clear and clean"), and the authentic voice of the fully participating community captures and transforms even the mean-spirited mother kangaroo. Horton then cries out triumphantly ... "They've proved they ARE persons, no matter how small./ And their whole world was saved by the smallest of All!"

In his Christmas story, *The Grinch*, Seuss once again takes up the possibility of authentic community trying to realize itself in a setting of ideological contradiction. The Grinch, a cynical and bitter fifty-three-year-old (notably, Seuss was fifty-three when the book was published) is disgusted with Christmas in all of its crass and materialistic trappings. From the Grinch perspective this materialism is so pervasive as to constitute the whole social meaning of Christmas, and that perception might be said to validate the Grinch's terroristic approach, which is the critical negation of Christmas through theft: Pretending to be Santa Claus, the Grinch sweeps down into Whoville and carries away all the food, presents and decorations associated with Christmas. In this guise of critical negator, the Grinch is a revolutionary hero.

As it turns out, however, the Whos prove themselves to be something other than soulless bearers of social form, for they have fashioned for themselves a Christmas experience that accords with true community life, one that is ultimately indifferent to the commercialized version seized by the Grinch. Thus, even though the Grinch successfully carries away all the material goodies of Christmas and leaves Whoville quite bare, the Whos nevertheless come together to experience Christmas as genuine fellowship, something the Grinch's sneering thievery could not take away from them:

He HADN'T stopped Christmas from coming!
IT CAME!
It came without ribbons! It came without tags!
It came without packages, boxes or Bags! ...

From the Who perspective, the Grinch, in his mode of critical negation, has been neither hero nor villain, simply a sad and lonely creature cut off by his own cynicism from authentic social being. When the Grinch begins to witness the real fellowship which remains at the core of an otherwise conventionalized and commercialized cultural ceremony, a moment of transformation occurs: He becomes, like Thidwick, big-hearted rather than small-hearted (" ... the Grinch's small heart/Grew three sizes that day!") and can then join the Whos for their Christmas feast. Notably, this represents no change in the Grinch's rational, intellectual analysis (something the radical religious tradition has always understood to be ultimately irrelevant), but rather a transformation of spirit and feeling, a new way of perceiving the world which in turn leads to the possibility of community unmediated by social form and category.

With this goal of transformation in mind, it is appropriate to return to the question posed in the last two lines of the *Cat in the Hat* ("What would you do if your mother asked you?"), for that question poses once again the dilemma of virtue's relation to authority. This question is profoundly disturbing to children, for good reason. To choose conventional morality in alliance with authority is to surrender all possibility of existential realization. To be for no other reason than that they tell you to be is not to be at all. On the other hand, children rightly understand the reality of power in the world: Individualized, direct confrontation with authority will surely fail. The child who would defiantly celebrate the cat's visit is doomed to awesome punishment, yet the child who contritely tells the truth forestalls punishment at the price of self-respect. The other choice is to abandon the search for virtue altogether, making a pact with powerful satanic forces in an orgy of joyful self-gratification that will ultimately lead to empty despair.

As starkly presented, those choices are no choices at all. As children instinctively know, what is first needed is some distance, some space—to get authority off one's back long enough to begin to fashion oneself as moral actor in the world, without having to be either a clone of authority and conventional morality or its equally objectified negative mirror image. Books like *Yertle the Turtle*, *The Butter Battle Book*, and *The Lorax* are about the necessity of reclaiming some space in the world, of opening up the way for new possibilities.

But space alone is not enough. So long as that space is filled with selves as we now know them, oppressive hierarchy and orthodoxy will reassert themselves. Other Dr. Seuss books suggest a different kind of self—a self that without intellectual reflection is caring (Horton), sharing (Thidwick)—or, finally, open to spiritual transformation (Grinch). Children cannot articulate or intellectualize the choice for a different kind of self, but Seuss directs his question to them because, of all people, they alone in their accessibility may be most able to make it. As a writer, with his mocking spirit, Seuss has, in effect, aligned himself with the anti-authoritarian cat, in order to give children the space they need to make more morally affirmative choices. □

Hostage Philosophy: The Ethical Thought of Emmanuel Levinas

Martin Jay

The Levinas Reader, edited by Seán Hand. Basil Blackwell, 1989, 311 pp.

How does an octogenarian Jewish philosopher from France, little known outside of specialist circles until recently, come to merit that most honorific of publishing tributes, a "Reader"? How does he join the "Reader" elite, alongside such intellectual luminaries as Julia Kristeva, Jean-François Lyotard, and Jürgen Habermas? What, moreover, is the intended audience for these often demanding and esoteric texts; who is the Levinas reader likely to be?

Emmanuel Levinas has been known to serious students of European philosophy for sixty years, ever since the publication of his influential study of Edmund Husserl, the work Jean-Paul Sartre said had introduced him to phenomenology. Some of his other writings, such as the demanding *Totality and Infinity,* have been available in English since 1969, and there are several recent collections of scholarly essays devoted to his thought. Moreover, the 1978 translation of Jacques Derrida's warm if not entirely uncritical evaluation of Levinas meant he was cautiously assimilated into the discourse of post-structuralism as well as that of phenomenology.

And yet, because of the difficulty of his French prose and the indirect quality of his reception, Levinas has always remained a somewhat shadowy presence in the English-speaking world. But this situation is certain to change with the appearance of *The Levinas Reader*, masterfully edited and annotated by the Welsh scholar Seán Hand. Levinas is poised on the threshold of occupying the role that no one has really filled since the death of Martin Buber: that of the Jewish sage able to speak to the universal concerns of modern (or perhaps better, postmodern) men and women. Why, to repeat our opening question, has this apotheosis occurred?

Born in Lithuania in 1906, Levinas came to France after the First World War to study philosophy, particularly as it had been developed by Henri Bergson and his followers. In 1928 and 1929, however, he spent time in Freiburg, where he attended lectures by Husserl and Martin Heidegger. In the 1930s, when he assumed French citizenship and worked for the *Alliance Israélite Universelle*, Levinas served as a critical champion of the phenomenological ideas he had absorbed in Germany. During the Second World War he was a prisoner of war but avoided being deported to the death camps. After its end, he returned to Paris and the directorship of the *Ecole Normale Israélite Orientale*, as well as a series of academic posts culminating in a professorship at the Sorbonne in 1973. Diligently pursuing his scholarly and religious interests at once in the universalist camp of the university and the sectarian one of the talmudic seminary, he slowly emerged as a powerful and respected figure in French intellectual life, discussed admiringly by a range of commentators from Maurice Blanchot and Lyotard to Paul Ricoeur and Luce Irigaray.

Martin Jay is professor of history at UC Berkeley. His most recent book is Fin-de-Siècle Socialism and Other Essays *(Routledge, 1988). This review appeared in* Tikkun, November/December 1990.

His French audience found in Levinas an extraordinarily subtle thinker who provided an original and challenging reading of the legacy of phenomenology strongly inflected by his Jewish beliefs. From Husserl and Heidegger he derived an understanding of the importance of lived experience prior to the intellectual reflection of the Cartesian *cogito*. He had first studied temporality with the Bergsonians, but his thinking was vastly enriched by Heidegger's explanation of its role in the drama of human finitude. And from the phenomenologists Levinas came to appreciate the costs of a philosophy of essential form based on the distant contemplation of a disembodied subject.

But in his radical critique of Heidegger's and Husserl's obsession with the ontological issues of Being and totality—an obsession he traced back as far as the Greek origins of Western philosophy—Levinas's particular Jewish identity explicitly came to the fore. For Levinas, the ultimate questions are ethical rather than ontological. The dominant focus of his thought became humanity not as immanent in Being, but as Being's transcendence, its beyond, its fracture. Or more precisely, it is humanity as the recipient of ethical commands from elsewhere that has concerned him. Levinas's abiding preoccupation remains less knowledge in the guise of descriptive statements of what is, than injunctions in the form of prescriptive imperatives about what ought to be.

Although Levinas has been careful to abjure the role of preacher, he gives a strong account of what might be called the ethical *a priori* underlying all moralizing. The fundamental ground of ethics is not, he claims, the abstract formalism of Kant's categorical imperative or the reciprocal "I-Thou" relationship of Buber's theology of dialogue. It is instead the submission of the self to the other, the principled suppression of self-interest in order to honor alterity (otherness). Ethics is thus rooted in asymmetry and hierarchy, in which other is always superior to self. The responsibility for the other is generated by what Levinas calls the *encounter* with his or her face, an encounter which is less directly visual than aural. We do not "know" the other by reference to his or her image, but rather enter a relationship of communicative proximity with him or her. Manifest in the intersubjective act of saying and listening, rather than in obedience to the already said, ethics demands that we put ourselves unconditionally in the place of the other without expecting anything in return. "Under accusation by everyone," Levinas concludes, "the responsibility for everyone goes to the point of substitution. A subject is a hostage."

The goal of ethics is thus not fusion with the other, nor is it even egalitarian reciprocity. It is instead the assumption of our own heteronomy, the willing abandonment of our ego's sovereignty, without cravenly accepting abasement or servitude. It is a never-ending openness to alterity, which embraces infinity without yearning for the closure of totality or the harmonious resolution of dialectics. Ethical conduct thus involves a nonerotic love for our neighbors that looks for nothing in return. As such it is uncompromisingly disinterested, in the etymological sense of not being "among beings" (*inter esse*), but rather being open to what transcends them. Ultimately, ethics thus means openness to God, who is not so much the divine creator as the ethical lawgiver. Although we can have no direct encounter with God, no I-Thou interaction with the supreme Other, He is present in the Third, the other, who is always in our midst, yet signifies something beyond.

Not surprisingly, Levinas is critical of humanist self-aggrandizement. Freedom as the autonomy of the acting self, the self of projects and initiatives, is a pernicious mirage. Sartre's famous identification of the subject with the "for-itself" should be supplanted, he argues, by the "for-the-other," a state best exemplified by maternity. What he calls our "difficult freedom" paradoxically requires accepting our ultimate dependency on the other. Modern anti-humanism, Levinas approvingly writes, "clears the place for subjectivity positing itself in abnegation, in sacrifice, in a substitution which precedes the will. Its inspired intuition is to have abandoned the idea of person, goal and origin of itself, in which the ego is still a thing because it is still a being." Instead of the active, Faustian self so much a part of the Western tradition, Levinas calls for a more passive self, which is not the shepherd of Being, as Heidegger counseled, but rather the caretaker of the other.

The austere rigor of Levinas's ethical paradigm is exemplified by his suspicion of aesthetic pleasure, especially in the form of static visual images. Such images redirect our attention to the existing world of what is, rather than to what should be. Calling the Mosaic proscription of graven images "truly the supreme command of monotheism," he trusts only in the literary art of a Proust, Leiris, or Blanchot, whose work opens up questions of absence, temporal deferral, and the permanent exile from Being. He is likewise hostile to religious attempts to achieve ecstatic fulfillment in the here and now, preferring the formal law and ritual of Orthodoxy to the mystical communion of, say, Chasidism. Only the unbridge-ability of the gap between divine command and human obedience can preserve the fundamentally ethical transcendence that is the essence of Jewish revelation.

If one were to simplify Levinas' argument into a series of antithetical pairs, the following would readily appear: immanence/transcendence, presence/absence, totality/infinity, vision/hearing (or touch), interest/disinterest, ontology/ethics, truth/justice, reciprocity/asymmetry, distance/proximity, sub-stance/relation, active/passive, ego/alter, being/becoming, philosophy/religion, and said/saying. In all of these cases, the first term is deemed problematic and generally identified with Hellenism, the second is praised and seen as Hebraic. Although these dichotomies cannot always be automatically mapped onto each other—listening to God's word, for example, is called active when Levinas discusses the tradition of midrashic interpretation—they all tend to line up in the same direction. Even when he tries to over-come one of them, for example in his claim that there is a "passivity prior to the passivity-activity alternative, more passive than any inertia," Levinas still chooses the higher passivity over activity.

Not surprisingly Derrida, for all his admiration for Levinas, felt compelled to deconstruct his binary oppositions. Derrida followed Joyce in asserting that "Jewgreek is Greekjew. Extremes meet." However much one wants to, it is impossible to step outside the Hellenic metaphysical tradition entirely; even not-philosophizing, Derrida insisted, is still on some level philosophizing. Levinas's answer, contained in the essay entitled "God and Philosophy" in this collection, draws on what he calls a state of "insomnia"—in which the self is awake but not intentionally engaged with the world—as the way to get beyond philo-sophy. But it is not clear if this state is invulnerable to a further deconstruction, especially when we note how entangled in the web of philosophizing—with its truth claims and totalizing discourse—Levinas' own work is. Although he points to ethical commands outside of theoretical statements and gives them pride of place, his writing itself exemplifies how deeply imbricated the two are. Levinas's work is after all a kind of descriptive metalanguage which tries to prioritize prescription over description.

Whether or not Levinas's argument is damaged by criticism of this kind, criticism his later work struggles to take into account, it has not hindered the recent upsurge of interest in him. The reasons for his popularity may by now be a bit easier to discern. To the extent that the Enlightenment project of emancipating individuals from their state of heteronomy is now widely discredited, that humanist hubris toward the rest of creation is damned as "species imperialism," and that intellectual claims to know totality are denounced as inherently totalitarian, Levinas is very much a thinker of our time. Too rigor-ous to be confused with the sort of mystical New Age irrationalism we have wisely learned to distrust, his thought nonetheless provides a provocative challenge to many of the most fundamental assumptions of conventional "progressive" thought.

So too the current fascination with ethical questions, coupled with continued doubts about the possibility of rational justifications for moral systems, has fostered a climate favorable to considering Levinas's ideas. And at a time when the oculocentric bias of Western culture is on the defensive in many fields, Levinas's celebration of hearing and touch over sight strikes a responsive chord. Reading Levinas's challenge to the hegemonic biases of Western thought may cause us, as Derrida famously said, to tremble, but it seems we do so more and more in tune with the *zeitgeist*.

There may well be still another source of Levinas's appeal: the political implications of his work. In a 1984 interview with Richard Kearny not included in the *Reader,* Levinas ruefully acknowledged that "as soon as there are three, the ethical relationship with the other becomes political and enters into the totalizing discourse of ontology." Here he adds, "I think there's a direct contradiction between ethics and politics, if both these demands are taken to an extreme.... Unfortunately for ethics, politics has its own justification." At a time when the redemptive project of political emancipation, especially that of the Left, is shipwrecked, the escape from politics back into ethics has seemed very attractive to some. When the young Maoist enragé Pierre Victor, who was Sartre's constant companion in his last years, turned back to the religion of his fathers and reassumed the name Benny Lévy, his conversion was reported to have come through reading Levinas.

Levinas, to be sure, has not himself been entirely indifferent to political issues; *The Levinas Reader* contains several examples of his concern for Israel's fate. Arguing against the equation of Zionism with conventional nationalism, he claims that the existence of the state of Israel can only be justified if it becomes an unapologetically religious entity based on talmudic law. It is, in fact, legitimate only as a vehicle to realize the justice enjoined by that law. Zionism, Levinas argues, has a genuinely messianic role based not on securing a holy land, but on fulfilling a scriptural obligation.

And what of the nonobservant Jew who lives in Israel? Levinas's answer is consistent with his uncompromising stance: "Modern humanist man is a man in a State. Such a man is not merely vulgar; he is religion's true antagonist within the State of Israel itself." And what of the non-Jews who find themselves under Israeli rule? Here Levinas's position becomes even more intransigent and, alas, more troubling. He earnestly insists that the highest ethical imperative is responsibility for the other, and that "the traumatic experience of my slavery in Egypt constitutes my very humanity, a fact that immediately allies me to workers, the wretched, and the persecuted peoples of the world." But when he was asked in the wake of the Sabra and Shatila massacres, "for the Israeli, isn't the 'other' above all the Palestinian?," his reply was chillingly closed-minded: "My definition of the other is completely different. The other is the neighbor who is not necessarily kin, but who can be. And in that sense, if you're for the other, you're for the neighbor."

Here the infinity of alterity, the transcendence of mere being by ethical commands, the hostage-like substitution of self for other, are abruptly circumscribed by the cultural-cum-biological limits of permissible kinship alliances. Ontological considerations of who people are interfere with the ethical injunction that we ought to treat all others with responsibility. As Derrida rightly argued, the binary opposition between is and ought is harder to maintain than Levinas contends. And in this case, the trembling that results from being Levinas's reader is not quite so pleasant an experience.

Paradoxically, however, two criteria that Levinas ascribes to Greek thought, reciprocity and symmetry, are the only way to check the descriptive (Hellenic) tendency to place limitations on the Jewish subordination of self to other. For only when I look for reciprocity, when I can see the same in the other, the neighbor in the stranger (even the stranger outside my kinship circle), will the likelihood of future Sabras and Shatilas diminish. Only when the realm of the polis is understood as the site to adjudicate differences, and not unethically to suppress them in the name of totalizing sameness, can the dignity of the other be genuinely upheld.

Although Levinas' profoundly moving reading of the Hebraic tradition has revivified that tradition for an international audience of Jews and non-Jews alike, it may nonetheless be worth pausing before we plunge too eagerly down the path of his "difficult freedom." For along with the Hellenic concern for Being, truth, and universality, there are also ethical-cum-political injunctions in the Hellenic tradition worth taking seriously. The costs of forgetting the Jewish dimension of Western culture Levinas has brilliantly demonstrated; the no less dangerous costs of suppressing the Hellenic is a lesson we have to go elsewhere to learn.   □

Death of Popeye

Shana Penn

He doesn't go away. His movements make me dizzy. The circular rhythms grow hypnotic and weaken the grip of my muscles. They shake me loose, unanchor me. My will to be concealed unravels.

I am three-and-a-half years old. Trapped beneath hungry gyrations. Suddenly I am wise beyond my years, beyond my choice to kick. I am frightened. Should I forget?

I know this boy. A neighborhood teenager. Oily complexion. He never played with the other kids on the block. I hear my mother remind me, "Be nice to the baby-sitter."

Wet, mute lips lick my nape. Fog sweeps down my neck. His weight crushes my spine. I am pushed into the crisp, white sheets, forced through the springs and cotton fluff of the mattress, squashed between bed and floor. Nerve endings retreat from the interior walls of my skin to dodge his touch. I slither and slide across muscle, tissue, pumping blood. Where am I going? A crack or hole, I must escape.

Earlier that night he followed me around the house and watched me play my favorite game: Popeye Shipwrecked on a Desert Island. In the living room I find shelter from a storm under the glass coffee table. I crawl on hands and knees between green paisley chairs and floor lamps, and scour the island for spinach. Spinach will give me strength to rebuild my boat. Climbing a hillside covered with poppies and dandelions, up the steps from the foyer to the second floor, I spot leafy greens. Noisily I munch my fill, then stand erect, facing west, to await transformation from sailorman to Superman. My body begins to swell, veins pop out, thighs throb. Muscles of a weight lifter ripple through my blouse and shorts. I explode into superhuman dimensions and torpedo through the house, unleashing a whirlwind that magically repairs my boat. Seconds later, I set sail from the top of the staircase. The ocean waves are choppy. I bump down the steps on my behind. Home to Olive Oyl.

The entire evening I play and he watches. Occasionally I feel his eyes on my body. "Want to play?" I ask. He shakes his head no. My brother Andy would have raced me up the stairs to gobble down the spinach. He would have held me and reassured me, told me not to be afraid during the storm. This boy just watches. He hardly speaks at all. Eventually I exhaust myself, and he tells me it is time for bed. Later that night he wakes me to his own game.

He doesn't have a sister. He doesn't know how to play. I hide under a pillow and crawl into a clenched fist. A coward, feigning sleep. In the silence of his motions, I wait for him to leave my body, my bedroom, my space. Not once do I speak. Nor do I open my eyes. I am abandoned to a task I never asked for.

I wake up burdened. Bruised with memory, the weight of his body, the silence of my room. It is

---

Shana Penn is writing a book about women's lives under communism in Eastern and Central Europe, to be published by Valentine Books in 1993. She is an editor for the Elmwood Institute in Berkeley. This article appeared in Tikkun, *September/October 1989.*

Sunday morning. Everyone is home. I hear my brothers rolling around on the living room floor. Down the hallway, the television is playing in my parents' bedroom.

I could be watching Popeye.

Rising from my bed, I inch down the hallway to my parents' bedroom. Reaching through shadows, I gather my will into knuckles that tap at their door.

My parents are reading the Sunday paper. I shuffle about awkwardly. The gray-blue carpet swallows my knees. I am treading in gray-blue carpet. My voice is a scant flutter of light across shadows.

"Mommy, Daddy, I don't like the baby-sitter. He hurt me."

My father raises his eyebrows and for one brief moment looks at me. He clears his throat and continues to read the paper. My mother glances at him, then leans toward me. Her newspaper section collapses between us.

"What did he do to you?" she asks.

"He hugged me," I mumble from the foot of the bed.

Her eyes tug at me. My throat caves in. Why doesn't she hold me? Why doesn't he say something?

My father swallows his breath and flips through the pages. His legs press into the bedding. My mother looks at my father.

"Don't worry," she says. "We won't let him baby-sit again." I hear her tell me to run downstairs and play with my brothers.

I retreat to the doorway. My mother and father return to reading. Emptied ice cream bowls are stacked on the night table. Bathrobes are draped over a gray stuffed chair. My father yawns. My mother sighs. The bedroom starts to fade. Tears blur my vision, remain planted in my eyes. I am scared to hold myself.

I descend the hallway stairs one by one past last night's hill of spinach. I return, a castaway, to my desert island. My brothers are wrestling in the living room. Their heads bob up from the floor behind the sofa. Grinning monkeys. They taunt me to join them. I smile weakly. If I play with them, I'll wind up with a busted lip or bruised behind. Not today. I am Olive Oyl, stuck in an empty can of spinach. No one knows that I am lost.

I climb upstairs to my bedroom, stand tiptoe on the desk chair, and raise choice onto the highest shelf. Squeezed among the books, trolls, and trinkets. One day I'll huff and puff and blow the lid off this can of spinach. Choice will leap off the shelf and sink into my arms. □

III. Feminism

Wombs for Hire

Nancy Ehrenreich

Birth Power: The Case for Surrogacy by Carmel Shalev. Yale University Press, 1989, 201 pp.

Choice is the dominant trope through which liberal legal thought conceptualizes individual action and the relation of the state to society. Liberal theorists limit the role of government to the facilitation of private interactions between freely consenting individuals. Within this framework, governmental intervention into the "private" sphere of such personal transactions is justified only when necessary to protect one person's will from being wrongly subordinated to another's. Thus, sex without consent is rape, contracts produced by misrepresentation or duress are invalid agreements, "unwelcome" flirtation with an employee is sexual harassment—and government can interfere with "private" relations only when such coercive acts justify regulation.

The modern women's movement, of course, has sought to throw into doubt the liberal assumption that there really exists a separate private sphere of personal freedom. The slogan "the personal is political" captures much of the feminist challenge to liberal orthodoxy. Feminists contend that focusing on the private lives of individuals obscures the cultural dimensions of social problems, encouraging women to believe that their dissatisfactions are due to personal, psychological frailties. That focus, in turn, prevents women from seeing their grievances as arising from attitudinal and systemic barriers to their survival and fulfillment, such as their relegation to devalued and undercompensated work roles. A similar insight has informed radical critiques of law, which draw upon a similar slogan, "law is politics," to convey the idea that legal rules, like culture, are deeply implicated in the constitution of the private sphere of individual freedom that law is thought merely to regulate.

Despite the affinities between these two critiques of the ideology of private choice, feminist legal theory does not always connect up with the "law is politics" critique. Indeed, many feminist analyses of gender and the law implicitly accept the traditional liberal notions of individual choice and the public/private dichotomy. In doing so, they serve to reinforce and legitimate law's role in the subordination of women, rather than to challenge it.

In her book, *Birth Power: The Case for Surrogacy*, Carmel Shalev addresses the issue of choice in the context of contract parenthood, concluding that a refusal to enforce agreements to conceive and gestate children "denies the notion of female reproductive agency and reinforces the traditional perception of women as imprisoned in the subjectivity of their wombs." Although Shalev's analysis stands as a thorough and original treatment of the issue from a liberal perspective, it also reveals the limitations of that perspective as a vehicle for accomplishing fundamental social change.

In the basic structure of its argument, the book evokes the familiar debate in feminist legal theory—sometimes called the equal treatment/special treatment debate—about what kind of rules

Nancy Ehrenreich is an assistant professor at the University of Denver College of Law. This review appeared in Tikkun, *May/June 1991.*

are the best route to equality. Most of the major issues that have split feminist ranks over the last decade have devolved into debates over questions of choice versus coercion, equality of opportunity versus equality of results, sex-blind versus sex-specific treatment. Shalev's argument is consistent with the "equal treatment" prong of liberal feminist analysis, which asserts that equality for women can best be attained by attacking the negative stereotypes used to justify limiting their participation in political and economic life. Under this view, sex-blind legal rules are essential, not only because they directly increase women's autonomy, but also because they undercut the notion that women are different from men.

The "special treatment" position focuses instead on the extent to which existing inequalities constrain women's exercise of choice. Rather than seeking merely to remove formal barriers to equal opportunity, its proponents advocate affirmative governmental intervention into the private sphere—if only temporarily—to assure equality of results for women. The "special treatment" view underlies the position on surrogacy that Shalev explicitly rejects—that women's decisions to sign surrogacy agreements are sufficiently different from most other contractual promises to justify not enforcing such agreements.

What makes Shalev's book particularly interesting—despite the fact that it revisits some familiar terrain—is the way in which she constructs her argument that treating parenthood contracts as chosen rather than coerced will eradicate harmful stereotypes of women. Shalev sees contract parenthood as the last step in a progressive change in the definition of parenthood, from a "biological" one based on blood connection to a "social" or "legal" one based on individual intent. She argues that this change to a social definition of kinship will free women of the "double standard of sexual-reproductive conduct" that the biological definition produced. By rejecting the genetic element of fatherhood, she says, we can eliminate the male need to control female sexuality in order to assure the paternity of offspring. And by rejecting the genetic and gestational elements of motherhood, we can undermine the biology-is-destiny view that has justified relegating women to a child-rearing role for which they were thought to be instinctively suited.

While Shalev's analysis is provocative and original, it ultimately fails to account for the many ways in which contract parenthood arrangements reinforce, rather than undermine, traditional patriarchal categories of thought. For example, the "problem" supposedly addressed by surrogacy—infertility—is only a problem in a culture that values biological reproduction (and that devalues minority, disabled, and other "imperfect" babies). The primary reason that William Stern, the biological father in the Baby M case, preferred contract parenthood over adoption was to perpetuate his genetic heritage. Of course, the fact that Stern's parents were the only members of his family to survive the Holocaust—leaving him the sole person capable of continuing his line—makes such a desire particularly understandable. However, such special cases aside, it seems quite likely that the impulse to use surrogacy rather than adoption will usually reflect simply a more straightforward interest in biological connection. In surrogacy, the biological definition of motherhood is rejected, but the biological definition of fatherhood is left very much intact.

Moreover, as Barbara Katz Rothman has pointed out, what Shalev calls the "social" definition of parenthood results in a legal scheme in which it is the woman's relationship to the father of the child that determines whether she is the mother. Thus, if the ovum donor is a stranger to the father and the gestator is his wife—in whom the embryo has been implanted—then the gestator is the mother. But if the ovum donor is the wife and the gestator a stranger, as in a recent California case involving a white couple and a black "surrogate," then the ovum donor is the mother. To the extent, then, that the intent-based or "social" view does undermine the biological definition of motherhood, it replaces that definition with an alternative that reduces women to their marital status: whether a woman is a mother becomes a function of whom she is married to.

Focusing on intent also does not necessarily undercut the vision of a maternal instinct that Shalev seeks to eradicate. Rather, an insistence that contract parenthood arrangements be allowed, especially if accompanied by a sympathetic concern for the frustrated intent of the infertile couple, suggests not only that biological fatherhood is every man's right, but also that motherhood, biological or otherwise, is so important to women that some will go to any lengths to accomplish it, including getting someone else to provide the baby.

Besides, as Shalev perceptively points out, not all women are seen as instinctive mothers to begin with. She describes how, for example, the unmarried birth mother is not seen as having any maternal instinct at all, but instead is criticized as "selfish" if she decides to keep her child, rather than put it up for adoption. The unmarried woman who wants to obtain artificial insemination is likewise seen as selfish, rather than as acting out her instinctive drives. Thus, it should not be surprising that in the context of surrogacy there is also a "good girl" and a "bad girl": the "selfish" surrogate (even the term "surrogate" implies the illegitimacy of her claims) and the sympathetic wife of the biological father—the "true" mother whose dreams of a child have been shattered. Nor should it be surprising that here, too, the implicit scheme of female virtue should break down along class lines, with the poor or lower-middle-class woman given the bad girl role, and the upper-middle- or upper-class one the good.

Yet Shalev fails to recognize the repetition of these patterns in the contract-parenthood context. Instead, she erroneously concludes that enforcing parenthood contracts will undermine the biological definition of kinship upon which the notion of a maternal instinct is based, and thus will dismantle, rather than perpetuate, the dichotomy between "good" instinctive mothers and "bad" selfish mothers. Attributing women's oppressed status solely to their biologically defined role, she fails to appreciate the complex interrelation between class and gender. It will take more than redefining motherhood to dislodge patriarchy.

Shalev's complex (if ultimately unconvincing) argument that invalidating parenthood contracts will reinforce negative images of women does more justice to the "sex-blind" side of the liberal debate than does her less persuasive claim that invalidation also undermines women's autonomy. She begins this latter argument by distinguishing contract parenthood situations from adoptions, where a waiting period is usually required before the birth mother's promise will be enforced. Surrogacy is different, she asserts, "in view of the deliberate nature of [contractual] conception." Starting from the premise that "[i]n modern society ... a person may generally acquire social, economic, or political position as an independent agent by means of free agreement or contract with others," Shalev views any suggestion that women could be coerced by their circumstances as decidedly paternalistic. But in her efforts to avoid paternalism, she cleaves to a rigidly individualistic vision of the actual social setting of surrogacy arrangements, a vision that fails to capture the complex motivations—conscious or otherwise—that surely affect a woman's decision to bear a child for money.

As a consequence, Shalev's analysis ignores both the ideological and the material contexts in which such decisions get made. Rightly concerned with eliminating the ideological equation of womanhood with motherhood, she nevertheless overlooks the fact that many women themselves have internalized that conception of their role, and thus are particularly susceptible to sales pitches like the sort given to Mary Beth Whitehead, who became convinced that she wanted to "give the gift of life" to the Sterns. Shalev's vision of surrogacy relies on a model of the rational weighing of personal preferences that seems sorely inadequate, for example, when it comes to explaining why Whitehead would have signed a contract that paid her the equivalent of $1.57 per hour for nine months of life- and health-endangering, emotionally difficult work.

Nor does Shalev adequately address the material inequalities that constrain women's choices. Sex-based wage differentials, for example, make it inevitable that a married woman will be the one to stay home with the children, and thus be limited to piecework, fudge-making, or pregnancy-for-pay as about the only ways to add to the family's income. Worse still, the single mother struggling to support her children and faced with the opportunity to, in a sense, hold two jobs at the same time, might find that an offer to enter a parenthood contract is one that she virtually cannot refuse. Yet Shalev's response to such concerns about the potential for exploitation is disturbingly dismissive:

> [T]here is concern that a free market scheme would relegate underprivileged women to a new oppressed and undignified occupation, like prostitutes and wet nurses. But it should be obvious that the idea of a free market in reproduction does not attempt as such to rectify existing social inequities.

Yet, even though this rejection of the "coercion" position seems out of touch (if not unconcerned) with the lived reality of many women in our society, it also has some appeal. Shalev correctly emphasizes, for example, that it is paternalistic to suggest that women who sign these contracts really have no idea of what is good for them, but merely sign because they overidentify with the traditional image of selfless motherhood. To view them this way surely also reinforces the notion that all women are indecisive, irresponsible, and need protection in the competitive, "male" world of the marketplace. Moreover, the concern with economic coercion is equally paternalistic: Even if these women are faced with a choice between two evils (exploitative contracts versus material deprivation), why shouldn't they themselves be allowed to make it?

In addition, it is difficult to distinguish the economic pressures that might affect a decision to enter a contract-parenthood arrangement from those that affect a plethora of decisions that Americans make every day—such as the decision to work in a hazardous workplace, remain in a demeaning job, or join the military. In short, the argument that the coercion in these contracts stems from unequal bargaining power is either a utopian attack on the entire capitalist system or a troubling elevation of reproductive labor over other sorts. Moreover, the economic coercion argument is easily perceived as an illegitimate demand for more than one's fair share of social benefits. Why should women be allowed to escape contracts that their circumstances forced them to sign, when men cannot?

By now, the cat-chasing-its-tail quality of the debate between the two liberal positions should be apparent. While the equal treatment approach validates women's decision-making ability, it also perpetuates systemic inequalities and fails to address women's immediate needs. And while the special treatment approach addresses existing social and material inequities, it also essentializes women, denies their agency, and risks creating resentment against them among other groups. Indeed, the conflict between the two can seem to be quite intractable, a product of the complex, contradictory situation of women in American society.

Shalev frames the issue nicely, as the problem of how to "transcend socially defined sex-based constraints and to acknowledge the individual woman's right to self-definition, without denying the social parameters of women's oppression as a class." Unfortunately, however, she doesn't provide a satisfactory answer, and merely retreats into the terms of the liberal debate by concluding that "we women, as human beings, are capable of exercising reason with respect to reproduction and of sharing our birth power with those less fortunate than we." For Shalev, as for most liberal feminists, to demand that society change a woman's situation, we must be willing to characterize her as lacking either the capacity or the power to have created it herself, something Shalev is unwilling to do.

One could discuss, of course, whether she thereby strikes the right balance between the sets of pros and cons posed by the choice/coercion tension. But my point here is, rather, to suggest that the liberal formulation that she applies is itself the problem and will never provide a satisfactory way out of the dilemma. In addition, it is an ultimately apologetic position, legitimating the system that it seeks to reform. By assuming that the only way to justify not enforcing these contracts is to label them involuntary and/or irrational, both liberal positions accept the notion that there is a sphere of private decision-making unaffected by governmental power. Correspondingly, agreements that do not fall into the deviant category must be seen as the products of freely exercised individual autonomy. The liberal frame for the issue thus implicitly legitimates the choice/coercion dichotomy itself, and reaffirms the idea that it is an accurate description of reality to say that some choices are "free" and others are "coerced."

And what is wrong with that? one might ask. Certainly some decisions are the product of individual will, and others are not. But my point here is that although all of us surely perceive the world in such categories, the terms themselves have no inherent meaning. Rather, individuals—and perhaps groups—infuse the concept of choice with their own content, content that will be intimately tied to their own perceptions of the particular social contexts in which the term is raised. To some, silently pushing away a sexual overture suggests consent; to others it constitutes refusal. To some, remaining with a battering spouse is a freely made decision; to others it is not.

Thus, choice is not a determinant of results so much as a vehicle for justifying them. Moreover, contract doctrine, in drawing the line between "free" and regulable market transactions, will inevitably institutionalize a particular vision of what constitutes choice. In deciding when the protection of individual freedom requires enforcing a contract and when it requires instead refusing to do so, courts are defining, rather than merely facilitating, individual choice.

My point here is not that courts can avoid defining choice, or that refraining from doing so would purge contract law of its problems, returning it to a neutral facilitative role. Rather, my point is simply that government is inevitably implicated in contractual arrangements. A certain agreement is enforced not because it reflects the will of the parties but rather because it comports with the law's current vision of just and fair interpersonal or commercial relations and thus is *seen* as reflecting contractual choices. This means that when people agree to enter contracts as a result of emotional manipulation, or despite being inadequately paid, or without complete knowledge of flaws in the product being sold, we need not accept as a given that such agreements were the product of free and autonomous choice. Just as, under existing doctrine, courts will imply a promise of good-faith dealing into a contract, so they could also imply a promise of a fair wage, or full disclosure of information, or meaningful participation in the governing of the workplace. Since we already use contract law to structure interpersonal relations, nothing should prevent us from doing so in a progressive and humane way.

Finally, to the extent that liberal legal theorists treat choice as something that exists outside of and prior to law—as something that courts merely enforce after it occurs—they ignore the constitutive role that law plays in the production of choice. Shalev's book itself provides much data to support this point. For example, she convincingly documents how legal regulation of both adoption and artificial insemination has traditionally enforced a rigid role definition for women, for it emphasizes the importance of childbearing (and rearing) for married women while simultaneously refusing to recognize or protect any maternal interests or rights of unmarried women. While ap-plauding the trend toward open adoption on the grounds that it undermines this image, she neglects to consider the impact that the traditional adoption and artificial insemination rules must have had on how women themselves conceptualize their roles and thus, on the current choices they make.

But if there is no separate and distinct private realm of social relations unaffected by governmental power—if law both defines and constructs choice—then the role of contract rules is not to facilitate the making of private agreements but rather to establish a particular regulatory regime controlling such agreements. Because law decides what will be called freely chosen contract relations, and affects the choices people make to begin with, no realm of private contracting exists separate and apart from governmental influence. Thus, if there is no private sphere of interpersonal relations—if law is politics—then we should not be talking about preserving private freedom at all, but rather about how to structure humane and fulfilling contractual and reproductive relations in our society.

As far as contract parenthood agreements go, that question can be answered in a number of different ways. For example, in Great Britain, formal, compensated surrogacy arrangements are forbidden, as is the use of brokers or advertisements to procure them. In a similar vein, law professor Margaret Radin has suggested that the closeness of contract parenthood to baby selling and the harmful effect of commodifying women's reproductive capacity justify allowing only unpaid surrogacy arrangements. Reproductive capacity, like children and bodily organs, may just be something we don't think people should be allowed to sell. Moreover, by focusing on the nature of the thing being sold instead of the contractual capacity of the participants in the exchange, removing surrogacy from the market might actually elevate women's status, treating reproduction as an important social activity.

In contrast, merely regulating parenthood contracts might reinforce the negative stereotypes about women's decision-making capacities that worry Shalev. Even very stringent regulation—including, for example, generous minimum payment to "surrogates," visitation rights, independent review of the contracts, etc.—risks having this effect. A regulatory approach also replaces the woman's decision about her own interest with the state's. Better, it seems to me, to recognize the limitations on choice inherent in market exchanges in current society than to attempt to use existing patriarchal institutions to police such exchanges.

Anyone who wonders why the issue of surrogacy has "suddenly" arisen cannot help but be skeptical about the prospects for change. The problem of surrogacy is not, as Shalev sometimes suggests, a product of society's inability to keep up with technology: turkey basters have been around nearly as long as turkeys. Nor, as I have argued, does it stem from a wholesale rejection of the biological definition of kinship. Rather, it is the product of an increased willingness to see women's reproductive capacity in instrumental terms, as a means to the ends that individual men, and society as a whole, define for it. Unfortunately, however, this instrumental view of women is merely obscured and legitimated, not undermined, by a legal analysis that fails to challenge the dichotomies between choice and coercion, private and public, good girls and bad. □

Victimology

Jessica Benjamin

Michael Lerner criticizes the way that the New Left and the women's liberation movement attacked the family, on the grounds that such attacks alienated many people who would otherwise have been interested in our cause. And he notes that many of us who were once the attackers later felt terrorized by our own censure. One could, in fact, censure others for things that one (perhaps unconsciously) suspected as weaknesses in oneself. For many years now, as I have reflected on the history of the Left and the women's movement, I have been concerned with understanding this species of attack—the problem of the kind of absolutist, totalizing, and moralizing critique that has been generated by every radical movement since Jacobinism. Some of those movements even ended up murdering large numbers of people. In the United States, radical movements, while just as dogmatic and authoritarian, have been relatively nonlethal, owing to their lack of success: a mixed blessing. This historical fact has at times obfuscated, or made Americans indifferent to, the consequences of radical righteousness, as if our powerlessness exonerates us from thinking about the problem.

This problem is intertwined with another issue: the split between the values of liberalism, rationalism, and the Enlightenment and those of communitarianism, idealism, and the particularism of a specific group. Typically, the liberal stress on individual rights and liberties has been the standpoint from which to critique radical zealotry, while radicals' commitment to transcending the existing order has formed the basis for charges that the liberal side is half-hearted. This conflict between enlightenment and messianism is central to radical political experience, and I think to Jewish politics in particular. At different times I've found myself on different sides of this issue—but ultimately I've come to realize that one needs to be on both sides, to be critical of both sides, and to hold up a kind of tension between them. I suppose the reason I had not realized this sooner is because I had previously misconstrued that position as liberalism; and, in a Marxist way, I thought that contradictions had to be resolved rather than sustained.

What most affected me in formulating my critique of radicalism was a set of little stories, of which I'll mention two. I have a cousin who, growing up in the twenties with anarchist parents, made speeches in the park about Sacco and Vanzetti. She used to correspond with our Uncle Aaron, a prominent anarchist who was exiled to Siberia by the Bolsheviks. She once asked him, "What do you do for fun out there?" and he responded, "Dear Sophele, I have no time for fun; there are too many important things to be done." She probably would have gotten the same response thirty years earlier from Aaron's father, a very pious and scholarly Jew, and a Zionist. Although torn by differences in ideology—communism, anarchism, and Zionism—the members of our family had much in common when it came to righteousness, fervor, and asceticism.

Jessica Benjamin is a psychoanalyst practicing in New York City, and is the author of The Bonds of Love: Psychoanalysis, Feminism and the Problem of Domination *(Pantheon, 1988). This article appeared in* Tikkun, *March/April 1989.*

The second story is that some years ago there was an autobiographical account by Peggy Dennis in *Socialist Review* of her years in the Communist party (she was married to Eugene Dennis, who was chair of the party for some time). She related how she had left her small son in the Soviet Union, where they had spent some time being prepared for their work here, and she didn't see him again until he grew up. This story horrified me. It was frightening that people would be willing to sacrifice their children in this way. It was even more horrifying to think that behind the ostensible reason for leaving him—to prevent the American authorities from discovering that they had illegally visited the Soviet Union, as the child now spoke only Russian—probably lay the policy of keeping the children of prominent Comintern officials in the Soviet Union in order to control them politically. Such testimony recurs in the memoirs written by European ex-Communists who, unlike American Communists, had their eyes opened by the fate of those comrades who had fled fascism only to wind up in Stalin's camps.

These stories and others like them led me to a personal revulsion against a certain kind of left-wing idealism and asceticism, a style of righteousness and personal self-sacrifice which, it seemed, led directly into submission to the most ominous authority. It was sad to see that this kind of right-eousness—radical guilt, as it were—could be found in less virulent form right here, in our very own women's movement, which had been dedicated to personal as well as public liberation.

Of course, the danger of founding politics on the personal derives, at least in part, from the replication of that old trick: universalizing the particular—as in the socialist movement's universalization of the working class. In the name of the revolutionary subject, the movement makes world-historical claims: when the working class comes to power all human history will change; prehistory will come to an end. In the feminist movement there was a similar construction of a universal out of a particular group at its inception. We thought that as 51 percent we were a good candidate for being the universal liberator, the group that embodies the solution to the most universal contradiction, and thus the group with the maximum righteousness.

A certain transition in politics, which occurred in the sixties, was required to pave the way for such thinking: the construction of the idea of the oppressed group as liberator. The notion of a class uniquely situated to oppose the ruling class because its exploitation is the hidden source of power gave way to a more simple proposition that the oppressed would rise up politically. In the sixties we evolved a new kind of "scientific" radicalism, the pursuit of what we might call "victimology," the highest stage of what Lenin never called "left-wing moralism—a gerontological disorder." Victimology is the search in your group's present and past for sufficient amounts of suffering in order to absolutely legitimate and sanctify its righteous aspirations and demands. There has been a considerable contest during the past twenty years among groups engaged in this pursuit.

What we have learned is that there is a tremendous moral capital in suffering, even if you aren't suffering any more. It is like the old Jewish story of the man who was sleeping in a berth on a Russian train when he began to hear sounds from the man in the berth above him: "Oy, oy, oy." When this persisted so long that he despaired of ever getting any sleep, he asked the man what was wrong. The man responded, "Oy, oy, am I thirsty." Convinced that he would get no sleep until the man's thirst was quenched, he procured for him a glass of water. He had almost returned to sleep when he was again disturbed by the man moaning "Oy, oy, oy." "What's wrong now?" he demanded. "Oy," said the sufferer, "oy, was I thirsty!"

Philip Roth, commenting on the misuse of the past, wrote a section in *The Counterlife* in which he ironically proposed that we "remember to forget" the suffering of the Holocaust. The point, of course, is not that we should really forget it, but rather that we need to remember that remembering can be abused—that it is possible to lose all sense of other groups and to create a universal claim for your own particular group.

Women have a good case for focusing on their own suffering, for much abuse has been and continues to be inflicted on women directly by men. The question is: How to have a politics that recognizes injustice and recognizes abuse and suffering without degenerating into the victimological stance, without engendering the righteousness and sacrifice that has so long accompanied this position. For example, the more righteous a position feminists take about heterosexuality, the more self-scrutinizing they have to be about their own sexuality, regardless of what kind it is. In sexuality there is only a short step from censorship to proscription and inhibition. For most people it's not possible to continually mobilize resentment against women's sexual objectification and violation in pornography and then feel free to have a good time with their own sexuality. Of course, we might suspect that those who are inspired by this righteous position have taken the stance they do because they have suffered under the current organization of sexuality, not because they have enjoyed it. But, whatever the case, the liberation of sexuality in the interest of pleasure has lately been replaced as the goal of the movement; the goal now is to expose heterosexuality as fundamentally organized by the principle of domination.

Of course, this exposure of heterosexual dominance and submission is filled with its own passion. You can mobilize human passion in reaction formation just as much as you can mobilize it directly. The fantasy of transgressing norms and boundaries that is the turn-on in pornography is also mobilized in the campaign against pornography. In this sense, the antipornography movement inherits the side of zealous radicalism that is idealist and absolutist. The problem with the liberal, rational, Enlightenment position of universal liberties is that it tends not to mobilize any sort of passion. When people listen to the argument that censorship of pornography in any form will erode civil liberties, although many of them are persuaded, they often go to sleep listening. Most people are highly charged only by the evocation of an enemy (the Other), or by the possibility of transgression, or by the idea of putting an end to all transgression. So people are turned on by the issue of pornography, with its revulsion against transgression and violence and its offer of a position of righteousness, more than they are turned on by practical struggles for concrete things of direct interest to many women.

There is no easy solution to this dilemma. Everything that we can mobilize in the way of human passion has a dangerous or a repressive side. But without some form of vision and passion, we can go nowhere. We therefore recognize that there needs to be a constant tension between passion and self-awareness, between being "into" things and standing critically outside them. My personal solution to this dilemma is to add to these opposites a combination of irony, humor, and self-criticism. The kind of self-criticism I mean is not that which says, "Comrades, let us list all our errors and correct them immediately." It is based on life without historical teleology, in which we do not imagine that being right now can absolve us of responsibility for the past, or that right and wrong will be lifted above ambiguity by an objective historical process. It is my hope that the next phase of our movement may embody a very different kind of spirit, one which allows us to be committed while seeing the drawbacks of that commitment, to respect the reality of suffering without making it a brand of righteousness, to articulate a vision that does not demand human sacrifice, to play even with what is serious, and above all to accept—not resign ourselves to—living with contradiction. □

Judging Mothers

Carol Gilligan

Chris Menges' beautiful and disturbing film about South Africa, *A World Apart*, has been widely discussed as a story about the conflict between good politics and good mothering. The film recounts a true story, taken from the life of Ruth First, a white journalist who was involved with the African National Congress and who was arrested and held in prison twice in 1963 under the 90 Day Detention Act. Diana Roth, the character in the film who is based on First, is not a bad mother, critics say, but she is a distracted mother, which amounts to the same thing—one who has more time and emotional energy for suffering blacks than for her daughters. In the end, Pauline Kael writes, "she's willing to return to prison and shatter her family."

Roth's dilemma is the one Sartre posed in the context of the Nazi occupation: Should a young man join the Resistance or stay with his mother? Roth in essence abandons her daughters—at least once the South African government passes the Detention Act. A chorus of reviewers concludes with Kael that Roth is "a woman who loves humanity so much that she has only a small corner of her heart left for her children." A brave freedom fighter, perhaps, but at her daughter's expense.

And yet, the film itself—written by First's daughter, Shawn Slovo, and told through the eyes of thirteen-year-old Molly (a fictionalized representation of herself)—presents a more complicated story about motherhood. Molly's sadness is overwhelming when her mother is taken away to jail, and her anger is unquestionable at being shut out of the emotional center of her mother's life. But Molly's observations of other women undercut the reviewers' judgments about good versus bad mothering and instead raise the question: What does it mean to be a good mother in a corrupt society?

This point is made from the beginning. In the opening scene of the film, Molly and her friend Yvonne are driven home from their Spanish dancing lesson by Yvonne's mother, and they witness a black man knocked off his bicycle by a white hit-and-run driver. When Molly suggests that they take the bleeding man to the hospital, Yvonne's mother says that she does not want to get involved. When Molly's mother is arrested and detained, Molly is shunned by the girls at school; again mothers drive off, leaving Molly standing alone. The imprisonment of women in the higher echelons of South African society is captured most visually in a scene where Molly, overwhelmed by her loss, runs to Yvonne's house and sees Yvonne and her new friends swimming in the pool. On the fence surrounding the house is a sign with an attack dog crossed by a diagonal red bar. As Molly, shut out, tries to be let in, Yvonne's father arrives home and turns on her in a frenzy—shouting at her to leave and then chasing after her in his car while Yvonne and her mother, summoned by the commotion, stand by helplessly watching from behind the fence. Is this, the film asks implicitly, an example of good mothering? Only for a moment is Yvonne's mother distracted from her daughter by the

Carol Gilligan is the author of In a Different Voice: Theological Theory and Women's Development *(Harvard University Press 1982). She is a founding member of the collaborative Harvard Project on the Psychology of Women and the Development of Girls, and is a professor in the human development program at the Harvard Graduate School of Education. This review appeared in* Tikkun, January/Febuary 1989.

political situation. Or, to put it differently, isn't this daughter also shut out (or shut in) from what is going on in the world which she as an adult woman will enter?

In the recent book *Mothers in the Fatherland*, Claudia Koonz observes that the word *Lebensraum*—literally living room or space for living—was initially the call of German feminist movement members, symbolizing their wish (presumably in the name of motherhood) not to become involved in the corrupting world of politics, power, and men. This policy contributed to women's paradoxical willingness to vote for the openly misogynistic Nazi party. But it also contributed, perhaps more insidiously, to the patina of normal family life which women provided for Nazi husbands and fathers, so that systematic murder could be integrated with happy families.

It is a tribute to Shawn Slovo, and perhaps to her mother, that she resists the kind of judgments which are made so readily about mothers in our contemporary psychologically minded culture, the easy statements about good and bad mothers which abound in clinical case conferences and case histories, as well as in the media. In *A World Apart* an adult woman revisits the thirteenth year of her life when her mother was imprisoned to ask a different question: What does it mean to be a good mother to an adolescent daughter coming of age in South African society, and what can women teach girls about resistance and courage and love in the face of violence? We would need to see South Africa and mothers through the eyes of Yvonne and the other students who turn on Molly before we evaluate Molly's mother or the consequences of Molly's childhood sadness. But then, instead of judging the goodness and badness of mothers, we might question more generally whether a life without sadness is possible in contemporary South Africa and whether women—as mothers or teachers—can stay with their daughters without joining the resistance, especially once the daughters are able to see beyond their enclosure. □

Drawing by Noga Wizansky

Abortion: Bad Choices

Larry Letich

How has legal abortion, something that over fifteen million American women have undergone, remained controversial enough that its future remains in doubt? Has there been a backlash against feminism? Perhaps, but backlash can't provide a full explanation. It's clear that the idea that women can and should be equal to men has permeated our culture. Typical middle-class fathers, even among conservatives, go to their daughters' Little League games and dream of their future careers. Pat Schroeder could think seriously about running for president. Our society has barely begun to institutionalize this new attitude, and we've yet to make any progress in valuing more traditionally feminine contributions to our society; but the momentum is toward more equality of the sexes, not less.

What about the usual suspects—Reagan, the Republicans, and the religious right, with their excellent political organization? These people, so goes the theory, form a very loud and vocal minority that somehow drowns out the will of the majority.

Some truth here, too. But it's also a sad refrain that progressive and liberal movements have used too often to avoid accepting responsibility for failing to capture the American political imagination.

The disturbing fact that the pro-choice movement must face is that it has failed to communicate effectively to middle Americans why women must keep the right to abortion.

According to a study done by the National Opinion Research Center, which has been polling Americans about abortion for over twenty years, there is a core of people—about 10 percent—who are deeply convinced that abortion is wrong in almost all circumstances. There is a larger group of Americans—30 percent—who are equally convinced that abortion is a right that must be protected. But the vast majority of Americans, including the majority of baby boomers, are ambivalent about the right to a legal abortion. This moral ambivalence has been strengthened by the anti-abortion movement's daily hammering and its ever more creative publicity tactics.

What has the pro-choice movement done in return? It has *ignored* this ambivalence. It has blinded itself to the need to develop a dialogue with the American people, to understand the roots of this ambivalence and respond to it. The pro-choice movement has focused (at least until recently) only on the superficial aspects of the polls—such as the fact that 69 to 73 percent of the population supports the right to an abortion. It has acted as if abortion rights were being hijacked from a complacent but totally supportive majority by a small band of right-wing religious fanatics. Over and over again, however, the public has shown its ambivalence about abortion.

Much of the American public believes that liberalism is amoral and that it has contributed to the ethical decay of our society. This attitude, of course, doesn't reflect the way most liberal and progressive people live or believe. But for a variety of reasons, some good (the value progressives place

Larry Letich is a free-lance writer and public-relations consultant interested in forging new communication strategies for progressive issues. He is currently developing a new alternative men's magazine: Animus: Men in an Era of Change. *This article appeared in* Tikkun, *July/August 1989.*

on tolerance) and some bad (a reaction against the hypocritical morality of the right wing, a holdover from the "I do my thing, you do your thing" attitudes of the late sixties), progressives have failed to articulate a clear moral, values-based vision of what they want for America. Without such a vision, Americans can be forgiven for feeling that progressives stand for no morality at all.

Moreover, the abortion issue is right at the core of the public debate between individual rights and old-fashioned moral obligations. It is especially threatening because it calls into question the nature of *women's* role, *women's* morality, and *women's* power in a society that has historically seen women as the "civilizers" of a world run by men.

What can the pro-choice movement do to reach the ambivalent majority? How can the pro-choice movement get off the defensive and begin influencing and molding American opinion?

First, it must understand to whom it speaks. The largest and most important segment of the population is the baby boomers. The fact is, the entire baby-boom generation has grown up. The youngest baby boomers are twenty-five, the oldest forty-three, and the vast majority have gotten past the point where an accidental pregnancy is a serious worry for them. On the contrary, they've been having kids—cute, precious, doted-on little Jennifers and Jasons and Jessicas. Or else they've been spending months with thermometers by their beds and dreams of the baby they're finally ready for. An estimated 1.5 million Americans want a child but can't have one. One can't open a magazine these days without reading about infertility, artificial insemination, in vitro fertilization—and adoption. Somewhere unspoken is the resentment against women who have had an abortion when either oneself or someone one is close to can't conceive and may end up spending thousands of dollars to adopt a child.

Second, the pro-choice movement must confront the ambivalence head on. The anti-abortion messages—"abortion is murder," "a fetus is an unborn baby"—are simple, emotionally powerful, and effective. Moreover, the anti-abortion activists are aided by the medical advances of the past twenty years, which have brought home more vividly than ever the miracle of prenatal development.

Nothing the pro-choice movement is saying or doing is powerful enough to counter these statements. It is focusing almost exclusively on "freedom of choice" and "privacy" arguments—and they're very important and effective arguments, certainly the most important ones from a legal perspective. But alone they're not enough. It's true that the pro-choice movement tested these messages and found that "rights" and "freedom of choice" have positive connotations. But these terms also remind people of all those sixties-liberal-ACLU rights that middle America loves to hate. To many people, compared with even the *possibility* that abortion is "murder," a woman's "rights" seem very unimportant.

The problem with an exclusive focus on the "right" to abortion is part of a bigger problem facing liberals and progressives. "Reproductive freedom" and "the right to choice" are rejected by many Americans because these slogans seem to emphasize the primacy of the individual and neglect other moral considerations. Sadly, these phrases conjure up a vision of self-indulgence and selfishness, which leads many Americans to think that those who favor choice are insensitive to other moral concerns.

Americans do not accept the philosophy that each person is an atomized owner of personal rights, a person unconnected to other human beings. Even as they have lived according to this philosophy, they have suffered and are so desperate for messages validating human community that they'll buy anything—cereal, soda, presidents—based upon commercials that deliver these messages. These "community commercials," with their picturesque farmhouses, smiling old people, and families gathered around a table are one of the hottest trends in TV advertising. People are yearning for community. Liberals and feminists seem to be promising people exactly what most Americans don't want any more—a lonely and empty freedom.

For that reason, it is extremely important that the pro-choice movement begin to reframe its arguments in terms that underscore the fundamental moral vision from which its politics emerge. One way for the pro-choice movement to make its moral commitments more explicit is to focus on the experience of women with unwanted pregnancies. The most vulnerable aspect of the anti-abortionist message is the way it ignores women, treating them as if they were mere vessels for the fetus. The right-to-lifers' underlying assumption (one that fits right in with middle-class experience) is that pregnancy and childbirth are always positive (or at least not destructive) experiences. It is on this false assumption that the anti-abortion movement is most morally vulnerable.

The pro-choice movement should focus on the experience of a woman who is pregnant against her will. It should argue that forcing women to stay pregnant against their wills is abusive. In this way, the difference between a wanted and unwanted pregnancy is similar to the difference between wanted and unwanted sex. In both cases, an experience that in one situation is beautiful and wonderful in another situation is horrific. As difficult as it may be morally for some people to accept abortion, there is a greater wrong—a greater immorality—in forcing a woman to undergo experiences as demanding, intimate, and at times life-threatening as pregnancy and childbirth.

It's fine in the rarefied atmosphere of East Coast intellectual circles to talk simply of a woman's "freedom of choice." But the right-to-life movement (and the right wing in general) has shifted the moral base. The message coming from the heartland is that there has to be a moral calculus involved in the decision about abortion. The argument that unwanted children will live miserable lives, or that nobody will take care of these children properly, or that they'll end up on the welfare rolls, is too easily manipulated into a charge that eugenics is the hidden agenda of the pro-choice movement. But the claim that forced pregnancy will cause extreme pain and suffering, so much so that some women will risk and lose their lives by having back alley abortions rather than carry the pregnancy to term, has the moral justification for abortion that Americans demand. What's more, it gets the anti-abortionists off their moral high horse and reveals the true lack of compassion in their stance.

This message must be articulated forcefully. Advertisements with words like "forced pregnancy," "suffering," and "violation" not only pack an emotional wallop, but also capture the moral issues that the anti-abortionists ignore. Furthermore, every woman has either had forced sex or else lives with the nightmare that someday it might happen. To link "unwanted pregnancy" to "unwanted sex" is to connect it to a universally hated and morally repulsive experience.

The pro-choice movement needs to focus more on the pregnant woman in general. Until the recent outpouring of articles on abortion, we hadn't heard much about the women who get abortions. We mustn't forget that the people who would be forced to carry their pregnancies to term, who would be forced to endure immeasurable suffering, are precisely that—people, not mere statistics. More specifically, they are women, and only women can humanize the abortion issue. Women, and women's lives, must be heard—in magazines, on television, throughout the media. People must be made to confront the humanity of the pregnant woman.

People also need to be reminded that criminalizing abortion will kill women. Unfortunately, such poor statistics were kept about fatalities from illegal abortions (partially because these abortions *were* illegal) that there are no reliable figures about how many women died and who they were. Still, it would be worthwhile to go into the archives and find the story of *one* woman who died of an illegal abortion. Perhaps a huge funeral march could be organized in her memory, if only to remind Americans that women die from abortions—not nameless women, but women of flesh and blood, women with friends and loved ones, women whose lives were cut short while they were still young.

The next issue is the most difficult but most important one of all. The anti-abortionists have spent sixteen years and countless dollars telling America that "abortion is murder." Watch any anti-abortionist rally or listen to any abortion debate, and you will see that the anti-abortionists' entire argument rests on the idea that a fetus is an "unborn baby." In the latest twist, in a "National Town Meeting" debate on abortion rights televised by PBS on April 9, 1989, the anti-abortionists repeatedly referred to fetuses as "preborn babies."

If one accepts that a fetus is a "preborn baby," however, one *has* to agree with the anti-abortionists. There is simply no argument.

So, what does the pro-choice movement say in response? On the question of the human status of the fetus, the pro-choice movement's reaction has been a resounding "no comment."

But the American people are *demanding* a forthright answer to this question from the pro-choice movement, and the movement's failure to respond lends tacit support to the anti-abortionist position. The last ten minutes of the hour-long debate was reserved for questions from the audience. Three out of the five questioners brought up the issue of when life begins. The first was a right-to-life woman who said, "Let's just get biological. I would like to ask ... each of you to respond to the question, If it's not a baby at the moment of conception, what is it?" Then an older man—someone I would count as a member of the ambivalent majority leaning over to the anti-abortionist side—said, "There's a basic question that nobody has really answered on the pro-abortion side of the fence. *When does life begin?*"

OK, let's get biological. Most abortions take place between the eighth and twelfth weeks of gestation. At that time the fetus is two to three inches long and weighs less than 1.5 ounces. Its brain, still in the very early stages of development, weighs at most ten to fifteen grams, compared to 350 grams for a newborn infant's and 1200 to 1400 grams for an adult's. A fetus, especially a fetus in the first trimester, when 91 percent of all abortions are performed, is no more a baby than an egg is a chick.

The pro-choice debaters, good liberals that they were, kept saying that the point when human life begins is a religious issue that honest people can disagree about—that some people may feel that human life starts at conception. This answer sounds like—and frankly is—a wishy-washy cop-out. The question is not simply a religious question; it's a moral one as well. In any case, the pro-choicers' response is unnecessarily conciliatory. Of course "human life begins at conception"—just as a building begins when you lay a cornerstone. But the belief that a full human life exists at conception is simply nonsense, no more a question of differing opinions, religious or otherwise, than the statement that the world is flat or that the earth was created in the year 4004 B.C.E.

If human life is something more than a human body, a human form; if it entails a quality of consciousness or existence; then somewhere in the second trimester a human life begins. Before that a fetus is the potential for human life, absolutely precious as such, but without the neural equipment to experience anything we would recognize as a human life.

This is not to claim that there's no moral component to abortion. Most women considering abortion do realize that a potential life must be treated seriously. Yet they also recognize that a zygote and an eight-month-old fetus are in no way morally equivalent. Still, Americans constantly hear the argument that there is no moral way to separate the two, and in light of the fact that the pro-choicers have been unwilling to address the question, these people are beginning to believe the anti-abortionists. The pro-choice movement must be willing to rise above euphemism and speak truth.

Especially if abortion again becomes a matter for each state to decide, the distinction between a zygote and an eight-month-old fetus may become pivotal in the battle to save abortion rights. The viability argument has always rested on shaky ethical ground. In essence, it says that as long as the fetus is totally dependent on its mother for survival, the mother has the right to terminate its existence. This is a hard position to defend morally; the right to survival should not be based on questions of dependence. But if we change the terms of the debate so that it deals with the fundamental question of when life begins, we start to create possibilities other than the yes-or-no choice offered by absolutists on both sides. Legislators, in an eager mood to compromise, will begin to negotiate cut-off dates for legal abortion. Some states' cut-offs will be very early, some will be late; but the overall effect will be to reduce the power of the fundamentalists to mold the debate.

This two-pronged campaign, focusing on women's *need for* (as opposed to *right to*) an abortion, and entailing a serious public inquiry into the human status of the fetus at various stages of development, would be the fastest way to reach consensus about abortion, one that takes into account the moral issues most people feel. It might defuse the civil war that we seem to be approaching, and it would also isolate the extreme right wing and set the stage for acceptance of RU486, the pill that induces early abortions.

The communications problems of the pro-choice movement are only a reflection of the broader difficulties that liberal and progressive movements are having in America today. In many ways, liberals and progressives have given up trying to *persuade* the American people to agree with their point of view.

Back in the sixties, the right wing was as popular as—well, as the left wing is now. There's nothing mysterious about this change in political fortune. In the sixties, the right wing morally discredited itself through its opposition to civil rights. Right-wingers looked pretty venal to the average American; they argued for segregation while Blacks in suits and ties and Sunday dresses were shown on evening television getting attacked with police dogs and fire hoses. Then came abortion (along with pornography and the exaggerated evils of suspects' rights), and the right wing was truly born again as the protector of the good and the innocent against the wicked and the licentious. While progressive people offered legal and technocratic answers to America's ills, the right wing grabbed the moral high ground in America's debates.

Liberals and progressives have also experienced a strange failure of the imagination. They seem to be struck by a need to communicate their vision in only the most earnest and humorless way imaginable—a sort of homegrown "socialist realism." With depressingly few exceptions, their brochures, pamphlets, and advertisements fall into one of two categories. They're either bland, apolitical exhortations that self-consciously try to appeal to Yuppies, or they're tomes that seem to say, "Here is three times more information about this subject than you've ever wanted to know. Now that you know the Truth, you'll agree with us or you're a heartless idiot."

Americans *will* listen to a progressive movement willing to reach them. As a whole, Americans are a compassionate people with a deep sense of justice and a great deal of sympathy for the underdog—and, by and large, the American people have failed us because we have failed them. We've stopped listening to their concerns, and most of all *we've stopped speaking their language.* As in any relationship, all the love and goodwill in the world don't make up for an unwillingness to listen and communicate.

The moral vision that we progressives hold can be the most important weapon in our arsenal. We must not focus on narrow legal and procedural concerns; we need to be up front about our moral commitments, finding ways to articulate them and relate them to political concerns. Americans are most responsive to that which makes the most moral sense. For that reason, what is deepest and truest is also what is potentially most popular.

America has been talking to us all along. It's up to us to find the right words to say in return. If we can listen to what America is telling us, be humble enough to see what we have misunderstood, and express our ideals and our compassion in words that speak to the American heart, then a new political era may begin. ☐

Abortion: Historically Compromised

Ruth Rosen

In times of crisis feminists never know whom to trust. The good news is that, at both the San Francisco and Washington, D.C. pro-choice marches in April, about 15 percent of the marchers were men—not half, but a considerable improvement over rallies that have taken place during the last twenty years. The bad news is that many men are simply ducking the question or, in the extreme case, becoming fashionably preoccupied with the rights of the fetus.

Take Christopher Hitchens, for example, whose biweekly column in the *Nation* regularly supports all manner of leftist struggle. Hitchens rarely takes up women's issues, but when he does, he sure knows how to stir up controversy. Across the country, feminists felt a depressing sense of betrayal as they read Hitchens's "Minority Report" in the April 24, 1989 issue of the *Nation*. As hundreds of thousands of women and men descended upon the capital to protect women's right to choose abortion, Hitchens came out of the closet as a left-wing pro-lifer to offer a grand historic compromise on abortion.

You may ask: Just what is a left-wing pro-lifer? Hitchens has provided an example. It is someone who would swap socialist reforms for women's right to abortion.

Appalled by abortion, Hitchens asks: "What if there were to be a historic compromise between pro-choicers and pro-lifers?" His grand compromise requires that pro-lifers offer a national health service that guarantees free contraception, prenatal care, nutrition and health care for children, sex education in the schools, and a national adoption service.

In return for this (rather short) list of concessions, Hitchens would have pro-choicers give up women's right to abortion—except (à la Bush!) in the case of rape or incest, or if the woman's "mental or physical health is threatened."

So what is wrong with Hitchens's grand historical compromise? Plenty. If Hitchens is interested in pragmatic considerations, then he should know that his historic compromise is, and will be, completely unacceptable to pro-lifers and to the right in general—who don't seem inclined to augment the welfare state. Hitchens's short list of concessions, moreover, constitutes an inadequate response to the many economic and social conditions that discourage women from bearing—and rearing—children. Lack of child care, lack of housing, and men's unwillingness to raise children are also at issue.

But let us leave pragmatism out of it and assume that Hitchens is simply searching for an acceptable ethical position. In that case, his blind spot regarding women's rights and the experience of being female is of embarrassing proportions.

The first problem with Hitchens's historic compromise is that it converts biological difference into a justification for the subordination of women. To state the obvious, women get pregnant; men do

---

Ruth Rosen, professor of history at UC Davis, is author of The Lost Sisterhood: Prostitution in America *and a regular contributer to the* Los Angeles Times. *She is currently writing a history of contemporary American feminism. This article appeared in* Tikkun, *July/August 1989.*

not. And when women do, their lives are changed forever—not only for nine months. Giving up a child for adoption is no easy psychological matter. To achieve equality between the sexes, women, like men, must be able to determine the course of their lives. Hitchens fails to see that the right to abortion is integral to the entire complex of women's rights. His historic compromise creates a two-track society in which women alone must bear the burden of the double standard imposed by biology.

The second problem is that Hitchens's compromise in effect allows the state to enforce coercive childbearing, a kind of involuntary servitude. Granting the state such power over women's lives—in the name of socialism, no less!—comes perilously close to creating a left-wing version of Margaret Atwood's brilliant *A Handmaid's Tale*, a totalitarian society in which women's abject subordination is achieved through coercive childbearing.

Hitchens's argument for a historic compromise is also riddled with faulty logic and factual error. At one point he states that "one of the century's most positive developments [is] the sexual autonomy of women." But how can women exercise that autonomy if the state has the right to coerce childbearing? With great authority, Hitchens also announces that "in order to terminate a pregnancy, you have to still a heartbeat, switch off a developing brain, and, whatever the method, break some bones and rupture some organs." This is certainly true during the later stages of pregnancy, which is why I personally advocate that abortion take place before the end of the first trimester. But at four weeks? At six weeks? Just which textbooks on embryology has Hitchens been studying?

At another point, Hitchens states that "obviously the fetus is alive, so that disputation about whether or not it counts as a life is casuistry." Yet just a few paragraphs later, Hitchens joins Bush in arguing that he would exempt women who have been victims of rape or incest. Why? "Because not all taking of life is murder, and ... it is immoral and unscientific to maintain otherwise..." Aha. Now it is clear. It is murder if a woman has consented (and God forbid, enjoyed) sex, but it is not murder if she has been coerced. (I have much greater respect for the consistent pro-lifer who doesn't care how it happened but simply wants to save life.)

Such is the logic of a left-wing pro-lifer who thinks women's sexual autonomy is one of the century's most positive developments. But positive for whom? Hitchens's historic compromise reminds me of the naive young left-wing men who at first welcomed the women's movement, thinking it was about greater sexual freedom. It was not. It was about equality. One way of obtaining equality was to make sure that the sexual revolution did not remain on men's terms. At the height of the sexual revolution, too many women found that they, not their partners, paid the price for the sexual autonomy Hitchens so admires. That is why women's movements all over Western Europe and the United States have clamored for abortion rights.

As a historian, I grow suspicious whenever men try to discredit the effort to secure women's rights by denouncing women as selfish. This is a long and dishonorable tradition throughout history. The not-too-hidden assumption is that women should sacrifice their own needs and rights in order to service men and the family. When women sought the vote, anti-suffragists called them selfish. When women sought the right to education, men called them selfish. When women demanded birth control, society called them selfish. During the 1950s, critics pilloried working women as the epitome of selfishness. When socialist feminists in China, Russia, Cuba, and Nicaragua argued for women's rights, the revolutionary male elite called them selfish. Hitchens joins this tradition as he concludes his essay: "It is a pity ... that the majority of feminists and their allies have stuck to the dead ground of 'Me Decade' possessive individualism...."

It is true that some of the most radical visions of the women's movement—redistribution of wealth, class transformation, collective advancement—were transformed and redefined by the Me Decade into an acquisitive individualism celebrating self-realization and self-promotion. But women didn't start having—or demanding the right to—abortions during the 1970s. Throughout history women have resorted to abortion. Poor Jewish women on the Lower East Side during the early years of this century didn't seek abortion because they wanted to advance a career. Nor did the struggle to secure safe and legal abortions during the 1960s have much to do with "possessive individualism." It was a serious effort to prevent women from dying from botched abortions. Hitchens fails to address this issue at all.

Even if Hitchens's historic compromise were accepted, women would still seek illegal abortions. They always have; they always will. There will always be reasons why women want to end pregnancies; legislation will not change that. A longer list of socialist—and feminist—reforms would probably encourage fewer abortions, a prospect I heartily welcome. But women should maintain the right to make this personal decision; it should not be swapped in some grand patriarchal compromise.

Strange that a writer who has written so eloquently of the Palestinian right to self-determination should fail to acknowledge women's right to control their own lives. But the Left's blind spot regarding women is nothing new. That Hitchens has revealed it all over again is a scandalous reminder of why the women's movement arose in the first place. □

Drawing by Noga Wizansky

Beyond Egalitarianism

Judith Plaskow

An interesting paradox is emerging in non-Orthodox Jewish communities. The very success of egalitarianism—the gains in equal access for women to educational opportunities, and fuller participation in Jewish religious life—has generated new questions and uncertainties about whether egalitarianism is enough. Over the last twenty years, barrier after barrier has fallen before women. We have found ourselves being counted in *minyanim*, going up to the Torah, leading services, becoming ordained as rabbis, and studying Talmud alongside boys and men. These new opportunities, however, have brought women up against the *content* of the tradition, and in doing so, have pointed to the need for changes far deeper and more frightening than the process of simply making available to women what all in the community acknowledge to be of value.

A rabbinical student finds herself studying a text that renders invisible her existence and experiences as a woman. A woman is called to the Torah and reads that daughters can be sold as slaves (Exod. 21:7-11) or that a woman's vow can be annulled by her father or husband (Num. 30). Women seeking to expand our Jewish lives discover that a tradition that seems to have a blessing for everything offers no Jewish forms for marking menarche or menopause. Ironically, it is only in gaining equal access that women discover we have gained equal access to a male religion. As women read from the Torah, lead services, function as rabbis and cantors, we become full participants in a tradition that women had only a secondary role in shaping and creating. And if we accept egalitarianism as our final stopping place, we leave intact the structures, texts, history, and images that testify against and exclude us.

Many non-Orthodox Jews are now stuck in a position of acknowledging the justice of women's claims to equality, but not knowing how to bring about deeper changes. Or feeling content that in some institutions the goal of equality has been achieved. Or feeling uncomfortable because even where the goal has been achieved, something is not quite working. If none of the steps toward equal access is easy, at least each is definable and measurable; one change opens to the next, and each is concrete and generally linked to a specific context of struggle (e.g., the Conservative movement, a particular synagogue). Beyond egalitarianism, the way is uncharted. The next step is not nearly so obvious as fighting for *aliyot* or ordination. Beyond egalitarianism, Judaism must be transformed so that it is truly the Judaism of women and men. It must become a feminist Judaism: not a women's Judaism or a Judaism focused on women's issues, but a Judaism that all Jews have participated in shaping. But how do we move from here to there? How does egalitarianism become the starting point for a fuller process of transformation?

I would suggest that there are at least five stages that any community has to move through on the path from egalitarianism to feminism or genuine equality....

Judith Plaskow is a professor of religious studies at Manhattan College. She is the author of Standing Again at Sinai: Judaism from a Feminist Perspective *(Harper & Row, 1990). This article appeared in* Tikkun, *November/December 1990.*

• The first stage is *hearing silence*. Indeed, the impetus to move beyond egalitarianism stems from hearing the silence of the Jewish tradition and of particular Jewish institutions and events concerning the history and experience of women. Silence is difficult to hear. When a silence is sufficiently vast, it fades into the order of things. We take it for granted as the nature of reality. When I went through three years of graduate school without reading a single word written by a woman, it took me a long time to notice. After all, men are theologians; who else should we study? Women have a long history of reading ourselves into silence. From childhood bedtime stories to the biblical narratives, from male teachers to male books on male Judaism, women learn to people silences with our own shadowy forms.

Rebekah, Bruriah, and other individual women, a class on women in the Bible or a panel at the Y, are not disproofs of women's silence in Judaism. These are names and occasions we need to turn to *after* we have listened to silence, not in order to fill or deny it. Otherwise we miss the jolts against whose background particular women and events emerge: "You shall not covet your neighbor's wife" (Exod. 20:14) (who is the community being addressed?); the absence of Miriam's prophecy or the record of Huldah's teaching (the hints in normative sources that there is so much more to women's leadership than the sources choose to tell us); a talmudic discussion of whether a girl penetrated before age three should receive her full *ketubah* (*Ketubot* 11a,b) (would women scholars ever have asked this question?); *a contemporary discussion of this talmudic debate that assumes this is a reasonable question.* Women were agents throughout Jewish history, fashioning and responding to Jewish life and carrying its burdens. But women's perceptions and questions did not give form and content to Scripture, shape the direction of Jewish law, or find expression in liturgy.

• The second stage is *making a space to name silence*. Both hearing and naming silence can refer to the large silences of Jewish history or the smaller silences within any particular movement or community. Hearing silence is often a private experience. Whether a community will move beyond egalitarianism is in part determined by whether or not it creates the space for people to name the silences they hear. Often in particular egalitarian communities women's silence is interpreted either as accidental or as personal choice, or it simply leaves people resentful or befuddled. "We just don't happen to have many women who feel competent to lead Torah discussions." "I don't know why more men than women speak. A woman is leading the discussion; anyone can participate." The historical and structural impediments to women's speech thus get dismissed or overlooked, and the community is absolved from responsibility.

Communities need to set aside the time for members to speak the silences they hear. This might happen in an open meeting specifically called for the purpose. Participants might be asked to name the places where they feel silenced or hear women's silence. Discussion must take place initially without judgment and without challenge or cross talk, simply as an opportunity for people to speak their pain and their experience.... The list of silences provides a concrete agenda for a community to address.

• The third stage is *creating the structures that allow women to speak*. What these structures are in particular contexts will emerge from the list of silences. In congregations where men dominate the Torah discussions, it might be decided that men and women will call on each other in alternation. In a Talmud class where women feel that the text ignores their questions and experiences, it might be agreed that women will lead the discussions for a certain period, with the understanding that the class is there precisely to hear women's questions of and responses to the text. In any context in which women are apparently free to speak but seldom take the opportunity, a program on gender differences in socialization, discourse, and learning styles may help both men and women to understand the personal and institutional barriers to women's participation, and to analyze the gender style of their own institution and events.

Crucial to allowing women to speak are women-only spaces—not women-only spaces that are auxiliaries to male ones, but spaces in which women meet to discuss and explore their experiences as women. Men can listen to women, but, by definition, they cannot be the ones to end women's silence, and there are many forces that prevent women from finding their voices in situations in which men are present. Women's discussion groups, Rosh Hodesh groups, retreats, and spirituality collectives are spaces in which, to use Nelle Morton's phrase, women "hear each other into speech." These spaces are sources of energy, empowerment, and creativity that potentially enrich the whole Jewish community.

• The fourth phase is *taking the authority to fill in silence.* Once silence is named and space created, there is nothing to do but to take courage to speak. This is what is happening all over the country as women compose new blessings and liturgies, create rituals to celebrate important turning points in our lives, research our history and write new midrashim, reclaim our sexuality and explore our concepts of God. This is the phase where we create the content of feminist Judaism, and its time frame is open-ended, its agenda sufficiently broad to include every facet of Judaism.

Much of this exploration and creativity, however, is taking place outside the boundaries of particular Jewish movements or institutions. Whether feminist innovations will ultimately be integrated into the tradition depends to some extent on the earlier phases I have discussed. It is difficult for women to dare to take the authority to speak. But that authority will be acknowledged and welcomed only when members of the larger community open themselves to hearing silence and thus recognize the need for the inclusion of women's voices. Thus, to take one concrete example, through midrash, storytelling, and historiography, women are creating women's Torah. But women's Torah will be accepted and taught as Torah only as Jews acknowledge that at least half of Torah is missing. Will Hebrew Union College or the Jewish Theological Seminary confront the contradiction of educating women in institutions in which Torah is still defined entirely on male terms? That depends on whether they hear the silence built into their curricula.

• The last phase is *checking back.* Speaking into silence entails enormous risk. It involves changes that are uncharted and whose direction is finally unpredictable. Not everything spoken into silences will be true or worth saying, and not everything said will finally feel Jewish. Any change that a community takes in the direction of transforming Judaism will necessarily involve feedback and evaluation. Did a particular liturgical or curricular change work? Whom did it empower? Did it create new areas of silence? Did it open new areas of Jewish experience and exploration? Did it feel Jewish? Why or why not? What is our operative understanding of "Jewish," and does it need to be expanded? Would we want to continue our change or experiment again? Would we want to teach the change to our children?

While such evaluation is crucial, it is equally crucial that it *follow* speaking into silence rather than precede it. Too often, questions concerning the appropriateness and boundaries of change are the first ones raised when feminists begin to alter tradition. Judgment is demanded in advance of any real experimentation. Will it be Jewish? is asked as a way of maintaining silence and continuing the status quo. But once we hear the silence of women, it becomes clear that repairing that silence will take all the creativity Jews can muster. Experiments in form, in content, in new relationships between women and men will all be necessary to make Judaism whole. There is time to decide the shape of the Jewish future—but that time is after those who have been silent have spoken. □

Anti-Judaism and Christian Feminist Theology

Susannah Heschel

I first started reading feminist theology while I was saying Kaddish for my father. Those eleven months of Kaddish hit me hard. I was devastated by my father's sudden death and took on the twice-daily trip to the synagogue as much to comfort and distract myself as to fulfill what I felt was an opportunity to express my love of both my father and my Judaism. But the experience turned out to be very different from what I expected.

I remember thinking during the week of *shiva*, while I fluctuated between periods of catatonic grief and overwhelming tears, that at least I would have the Jewish community to turn to. Some of the synagogues where I went to say Kaddish were filled with mourners—men and women—and the services went smoothly. But not one of these Conservative and Orthodox congregations counted women in the minyan, or gave women aliyot, or allowed women to lead the services. All too often there were nine men present with me—and the minyan was canceled....

Every now and then came a real blow. One afternoon, while driving from Boston to New York, I stopped in New Haven for *minkha*, and found the local Young Israel synagogue. The weekday services were held in a classroom. I arrived early, sat down, and waited. When the men arrived, I was told I would have to leave because there was no *mekhitza* in the room. I offered to stand in the back of the room, near the door, and explained that I had to say Kaddish. To no avail. I remember the words distinctly: "We cannot pray as long as you remain in the room." So I left.

That same year, 1973, feminist philosopher Mary Daly's book, *Beyond God the Father*, was published. Reading it both terrified and comforted me. I felt comforted because Daly explained to me the root of all the rage I had felt—the condescension, the meannesses, the exclusions—whenever I complained about my experiences in Jewish life. At the same time, I felt something rip. Daly destroyed my optimism that solutions could be found. She argued that the treatment of women was not the result of laws that could be changed, or teachings that could be modified, but of root symbols, of God as Father, of morality as male-created and fundamentally patriarchal. There were no more easy answers, it became clear, no way to modify a sexist husk and retain a just core. And no more reason to struggle for simple changes. If women were excluded from aliyot "for the sake of the honor of the congregation," the problem was no longer the word "honor" (that men's honor not be offended by women's presence) but the word "congregation," which now appeared to be identified solely with men. Not only was I excluded from an occasional minyan, but I now saw myself excluded from the Jewish people. Reading Daly and saying Kaddish for my father took away my sense of home....

Susannah Heschel is the Abba Hillel Silver Assisitant Professor of Jewish Studies at Case Western Reserve University. She is the editor of On Being a Jewish Feminist: A Reader, *and the author of a forthcoming study of Abraham Geiger and the German-Jewish view of Christianity. This article appeared in* Tikkun, May/June 1990.

More and more I turned to feminists for support. I started to read more books on feminist theology, most written by Christian women, and felt a tremendous sense of excitement: Here was something new and fresh and original, ideas that had never been stated before. Or had they? At first I didn't want to pay attention to the articles or book chapters that would set my heart racing with their explanations of patriarchy, passages that blamed the Old Testament, "Yahweh," or Judaism and its law codes. Jesus, I read, fully intended to liberate women, but Paul the Pharisee was full of Jewish misogyny and squelched the feminist impulse. Once upon a time, I read elsewhere, we all worshiped a Goddess and lived in a world without violence. But then along came the ancient Israelites and their jealous, exclusive, monotheistic father God. He killed the Goddess and introduced violence and war, patriarchy and exploitation.

Blaming the Jews for all sorts of societal problems is certainly nothing new in the history of anti-Semitism, including that of leftists. Jewish blame for patriarchy seems to have been introduced hand in hand with the feminist theology that emerged during the 1970s. It was accepted readily by many Christian women who were angered by their religious communities. After all, blaming Judaism provided a convenient explanation for patriarchy, together with a prescription for its cure: Just get rid of the Jewish influences and Christianity will be rescued, in all the pristine feminist glory of Jesus.

At Harvard Divinity School, where I studied, Jewish responsibility for patriarchy became a new dogma among the feminists. In their rejection of traditional male-authored Christian theology, they still kept certain aspects, including the anti-Judaism. The radical, post-Christian feminism they espoused was not all that radical, nor all that post-Christian, since it retained classical anti-Semitic motifs found in Christian theology. But when the obvious was pointed out, particularly after Judith Plaskow published a short article, "Blaming the Jews for Patriarchy," the reactions were disappointing. Some feminists refused to see the anti-Semitism, others claimed we were simply mired in our Judaism (lacking full feminist consciousness), and some charged that we were actually undermining feminism.

Losing my sense of Jewish home was devastating; realizing that the women's movement was infested with anti-Semitism made me furious. With all the sharpness of the feminist critique of Christian theology's maleness and its treatment of women, anti-Semitism was rarely discussed by feminists. Instead, Judaism was emerging as kind of "fall guy" for the problems feminist theologians found with Christianity.

I can find three general motifs of anti-Judaism in Christian feminist theology: first, a scapegoating in which Judaism is blamed for the origins of patriarchy because the ancient Israelites, together with the Father God of the Hebrew Bible, murdered the ancient Goddess and destroyed the peace-loving society that worship of her had promoted; second, a motif in which Christianity is said to be the ultimate solution to the problems of feminists, regardless of their religious background; and third, a motif that affirms early Christianity's positive treatment of women by negating first-century Judaism's negative treatment. The motifs should be familiar—long before feminism, anti-Jewish motifs played an important role in traditional male Christian theology.

The first motif, blaming the Jews for killing the Goddess and introducing patriarchy to the world, echoes the old Christian charge that the Jews killed Jesus. The argument entered feminist writings beginning in the early 1970s and is repeated by Elizabeth Gould Davis in *The First Sex*, Sheila Collins in *A Different Heaven and Earth*, Merlin Stone in *When God Was a Woman*, and Gerda Lerner in *The Creation of Patriarchy*.

In what became one of the most popular feminist books in West Germany several years ago, *Ich Verwerfe im Lande die Kriege* ["I Denounce the Violence of the Land"], Gerda Weiler repeated the argument: "Patriarchal monotheism developed through the elimination of the cosmic Goddess; there is no father in heaven without the murder of the mother." The dominance of patriarchy has left us, these feminists continue, with a society that is dualistic and disunified, in which body stands apart from soul, mind from nature, men from women. Worship of a male deity sets forth a pattern of social control of men over women. Moreover, the male religion described in the Hebrew Bible is said to legitimate violence and destruction.

On one level, the argument that an ancient Goddess-worshiping society once existed is important to feminism because it asserts the historically accidental nature of a patriarchy, in opposition to those who claim that patriarchy is biologically rooted. In addition, the argument tries to legitimate feminist goals by showing that they were once realized in an ancient woman-centered society. If patriarchy is a historical phenomenon, it can also be overcome by historical progress.

These assertions, however, are problematic. That a male Father God sanctified patriarchy is clear, but the corollary is not necessarily true: that the simple presence of female deities will guarantee a feminist social order. Patriarchy has existed, and continues to exist, even among peoples who worship female deities. That the Hebrew Bible makes a strong case against worship of the Goddess is uncontested, but the relation between Her suppression and the actual role of women in biblical society has not been clarified. Women's real power in the agricultural society of ancient Israel was, according to Carol Meyers's recent study, *Rediscovering Eve*, much greater than we can realize from biblical narratives. Finally, just as feminists have tried to reconstruct ancient female spirituality based on relics of Goddess figurines, the biblical texts have also been interpreted by feminists to show that Israelite women may have had their own spiritual traditions. Reading between the lines of the Hebrew Bible, feminists suggest that prophetic condemnations of Goddess worship are evidence for the persistence of Goddess worship by Israelite women. Future research might indicate the persistence of women's unique religious traditions throughout the course of Jewish history.

What troubles me more, however, is when the argument extends beyond an affirmation of feminism to an historically unverifiable assertion that the Jews introduced patriarchy and violence into the world....

How do we respond to such arguments? Even a casual survey of the mythology of other cultures yields evidence for the early introduction of patriarchy in other parts of the world. Curiously, this comparison has been ignored. Beyond that, however, it is obvious that women do "speak to God" in the Hebrew Bible, and we can point to women leaders, such as Deborah, and prophets, such as Hulda. On the other hand, such apologetics are not a real answer. Biblical religion is clearly in the hands of men, beginning with the patriarchal accounts and continuing through the classical prophets, the priests, and the scribes. Yet the real issue at stake here is not the actual lives of Israelite women, but whether the Hebrew Bible (the Jews) can be held responsible for inventing patriarchy.

According to Elizabeth Gould Davis, when God accepted Abel's offering of meat, "the new male God was announcing his law: that thenceforth harmony among men and beasts was out, and killing and violence were in." Emphasizing the violence described in the Hebrew Bible has often been used throughout history to denigrate Judaism. At times, that violence is contrasted with the supposedly peaceful actions of Jesus reported in the Christian Scriptures. But the biblical reading is often distorted. The rape, murder, and other violence described in the Hebrew Bible is not intended prescriptively, but descriptively, as a picture of a social reality that scripture as a whole discovers, seeks to understand, and condemns. And the Jesus of the gospels is hardly a peaceful fellow; what he doesn't like he overthrows (literally, when he enters the Temple) or curses (the fig tree).

An old anti-Jewish motif has characterized the God of the Hebrew Bible as a God of wrath, in contrast to the God of love of the Christian Scriptures. While early Christians rejected the distinction as heretical, it remained a strong motif throughout the history of Christian theology, and it emerges in feminist theology as well. From a Jewish perspective, though, the God of the Hebrew Bible is a God of passion who expresses love and anger out of a sense of caring for human beings.

The Jewish God is not remote and impassable, but passionate and affected by human action. The view that the Hebrew Bible introduced violence into the world is as absurd as the accompanying claims by Christian theologians that Jesus introduced love. Ancient Near Eastern documents predating pentateuchal materials make it clear that war, violence, and patriarchy predated the Bible and coexisted with a pantheon of goddesses as well as gods.

For all their claims to be post-Christian, these feminists are setting forth a schema that seems to follow the traditional Christian model of the Fall: first there was an idyllic state in the Garden of Eden (worship of the Goddess), then a fall through human sin (rejection of the Goddess), and now a state of evil in which we await a future redemption (return to the Goddess). In the feminist schema it is not women who brought about the Fall, as in traditional Christian theology; it is the Jews. How ironic that the old anti-Semitic association of Judaism and deicide should resurface here in feminist writing. What is operating in these arguments is not historical evidence—because the Garden of Eden is a myth, not a historic reality—but a new theodicy that blames the Jews for the suffering of women and the existence of violence.

The distinction between a misogynist Old Testament and a feminist New Testament is expressed in nontheological feminist writings as well. Carolyn Heilbrun and Catherine Stimpson describe two types of feminist literary theory, an "Old Testament" approach that "looks for the sins and errors of the past," and a "New Testament" approach that looks "for the grace of imagination ... the grace to see what, until this moment, the masculinization of society has prevented us from seeing." The Old Testament approach, in other words, is concerned with the misogyny expressed by the male literary tradition, while the New Testament approach explores where a feminist aesthetic might lead. Old Testament is male, New Testament is female.

Similarly, Carol Gilligan's research concerning gender difference concludes that in responding to moral dilemmas males are concerned with establishing universal rules and principles, while females are concerned with fostering close relationships. Her oppositional categories of analysis repeat a classic distinction of Christian theology: law versus gospel. Christianity traditionally viewed Judaism as a religion of law, and itself as a religion of love. That opposition is now continued by feminists, who imply an identification of maleness (and patriarchy) with Judaism and femaleness (and feminism) with Christianity.

A second motif of feminist anti-Judaism appears in the work of Christian feminists who proclaim that Christianity is the solution to feminism, and not just to the problems of Christian feminists. Patricia Wilson-Kaster, in her book, *Faith, Feminism and the Christ*, writes

> The cosmic vision of feminism is not an illusory dream of naive individuals, but in its most thoroughgoing and radical form is the vision of the gospel, the promise made by God to the world through Jesus Christ. The struggles of feminism find their fullest context and their strongest promise of fulfillment in the risen Christ.

This is a curious argument: if Christ is the answer, why are Christian feminists so critical of him? Mary Daly has called the centrality of a male savior "christolatry," and argues that Christ's elevation reinforces the denigration and scapegoating of women.

Similarly, Barbara Brown Zikmund, in an essay from *The Christian Century*, identifies Easter with feminism because, she argues,

> the doctrine of the Trinity sets forth a radical ethic of justice and care very similar to the ethic that psychologists see within women's lives.... Women's experience invites us all to take the doctrine of the Trinity more seriously.

But if only Christianity can solve the problems of feminism, what happens to feminists who are Jewish, Muslim, Hindu, Buddhist, and so forth?

Ultimately, such arguments are a cover for Christian supremacy, an old canard asserting that Christianity represents the sole and ultimate religious truth, thereby denying the legitimacy of religious pluralism and making its goal the conversion of all humankind. Among the world religions, Christianity has probably had the greatest difficulty with religious pluralism because of its claim that salvation comes exclusively through Jesus Christ. Recently, some Christian theologians have tried to develop a view that allows other claims to religious truths the right of theological legitimacy alongside Christianity. These feminists, unfortunately, have not joined that effort, but limit their concern to reconciling feminism with Christianity.

In trying to overcome the challenge of feminism, both Zikmund and Wilson-Kaster try to distinguish between a problematic male Jesus, who is a human figure, and a redemptive Christ, who by transcending earthly gender can be saved as a divine figure for feminists. Yet the distinction would seem implausible, and even heretical, since central to Christian teaching is the claim that Jesus Christ is both human and divine, and any denial of his human or divine nature is considered a heresy. Of course, that combination points back to the problem of Jesus' maleness, which is the central dilemma of Christian feminists. Far from having solved the problem of feminism and Christianity's male divinity, Zikmund and Wilson-Kaster have avoided it.

The third motif of anti-Judaism is unquestionably the most prevalent, not only among feminists but also among Christians eager to defend Christianity against the very need for feminism. This motif affirms Christianity through a negation of Judaism. It is a technique common to Christianity ever since Paul, and it is particularly dangerous because it assures Judaism a central role in Christian theology, but only when that role is negative.

The "negation" motif first became influential among feminists with the publication in 1971 of "Jesus Was a Feminist," an article by Leonard Swidler. While Jesus is not reported in the gospels to have claimed to be a feminist, his rather ordinary interactions with women can be made to seem remarkable if they are brought into comparison with a picture of a highly patriarchal, misogynist Jewish society in which he lived and preached. By painting a negative picture of first-century Palestinian Judaism, Swidler, as well as the others who followed his lead, could make a claim for Jesus' message of feminist liberation.

Swidler's argument has been employed both to denigrate and support the contemporary feminist movement. Sometimes it is used to prove that Christianity has no need for feminism because Jesus already liberated women. In other contexts, the argument is used to legitimate the contemporary feminist movement, since Jesus himself was a feminist. In both cases, it is Judaism that ends up taking the blame....

In some feminist accounts, Jesus (or Paul) was a feminist, compared to the misogynist Jews of their era; or Jesus (or Paul) would have been a feminist, had it not been for their Jewish upbringing. A classic example comes in the writings of Elisabeth Moltmann-Wendel, a German Protestant feminist whose books have also become popular in the United States because they represent a "moderate" feminism. Moltmann-Wendel is able to rescue Jesus and Christianity from the more serious feminist criticisms by contrasting Jesus with early Judaism. She writes, in *Freedom, Equality and Sisterhood*:

Jesus and his message are to be seen against the background of this world. Palestine, where Jesus appeared, was in no way already the great world with progressive views, emancipated women and insightful men who tolerated independent women. Palestine ... was a small, conservative enclave. Jewish tradition and interpretation of the law still determined the people's consciousness and the customs of the country, despite some attempts at reform. The pious Jew still thanked God every morning that he was not an unbeliever, a slave, or a woman.... Women sat on the balcony of the synagogue and so never entered the inner sanctum of the house of God. The integrity of a worship service according to orthodox Jewish practice did not depend on whether or not women were present. Women were not permitted to say confession or thanksgiving prayers; only saying grace after meals was allowed them. The Jewish patriarchy was severe, although some of its traits were favorable to women. Naturally, there was no question of any emancipation of women.

She then concludes, "This background makes Jesus' appearance and message even more impressive."

Moltmann-Wendel's account of Jewish women's position in the first century is not supported by historical evidence. Recent studies have established, for example, that archaeological remains do not show the existence of a women's gallery in first-century Palestinian synagogues. That Jewish women of the first century—or any century—were only permitted to say the prayers of grace after meals is simply false.

At issue, however, is not only the reality of Jewish women's lives in the first century but also the structure of Moltmann-Wendel's argument. She paints a deliberately negative picture of the situation of Jewish women not to sympathize with Jewish feminists but to highlight the alleged superiority of Christianity. Jesus is made to seem "even more impressive" by contrasting him with the allegedly wretched, discriminatory treatment of women by other first-century Jewish males. It is difficult to respond to this charge from a Jewish feminist perspective because we are placed in a position of defending what we have grown used to criticizing: the position of women in Judaism during the Second Temple and rabbinic periods. Moreover, we are accustomed to Jewish apologetics which try to defend the classical treatment of women by comparing it to an allegedly worse situation for women in the ancient, non-Jewish world—an argument that is structurally the same as Moltmann-Wendel's.

Both Jewish and Christian feminists are trying to look between the lines of the available evidence to recapture a positive picture of women's lives. For example, Christian feminists have read Pauline injunctions against women speaking out in church as evidence that women were taking active leadership roles in early Christian communities. Similarly, Mishnaic statements that women danced in the forests of Jerusalem on the 15th day of Av and on Yom Kippur can be read as indicating that at least some independent religious activities were undertaken by Jewish women in the period of early Judaism. Each constituency is trying to reconstruct a positive, redemptive picture of women's reality underlying whatever repressive, patriarchal measures emerged in rabbinic Judaism and in the Church. It is also striking that Moltmann-Wendel uses the word "Jew" to refer only to Jewish men. Often in feminist writings there are subtle indications of an attitude that all Jews are male, and all feminists are Christian.

The negative depiction of Second Temple and Mishnaic Judaism is also used in arguments by some West German feminists regarding the nature of nazism. They argue that nazism is a patriarchal phenomenon and therefore not a movement for which women bear responsibility. Perhaps the most outrageous statement is found in the work of Christa Mulack. In *The Female Ethics of Jesus* she asserts: "We can say that the relations of Jesus with the law corresponded to typically female ideas, while those of the Pharisees and Scribes were at home in a typically male mental world." Mulack further argues that under patriarchal ethics, men absolve themselves of responsibility for their actions. In the following paragraph she draws a parallel between the Pharisees and the Nazis:

Under patriarchy no one has responsibility for his deeds, because he behaves at the command of someone higher. They themselves wash their hands in innocence. These men would have done exactly as Pilate, if Jesus had let them, but also exactly like Rudolf Hess or Adolf Eichmann, who pleaded "not guilty," because in the last analysis they had only followed the command of a führer. And if this führer commanded murder, then his followers would have to murder. With all the differences, that are certainly present here, the inner methods of argumentation are still the same. It always shows the same obedience to authority that is so typical for the male gender.

By contrast, Jesus, according to Mulack, never used a law or another authority in order to secure his own deeds. Quite the contrary, his perspective was divine, regardless of what the law said about it. Jesus began neither with the law nor with God, but with the people themselves. What is the result? Mulack tells us: Women are liberated!

Mulack's argument is that ethical appeal to God or to a law, which, she says, characterizes Judaism, represents patriarchal thinking. Rejection of external authority is the female mode of ethics, a mode which Jesus also possessed, although he happened to be male. Judaism is male, patriarchal, and misogynist; Christianity is female, feminist, and liberating. The internal contradiction in Mulack's argument is clear: Why does she require an external authority, in the figure of Jesus, to legitimate feminism?

But all of these considerations pale next to the consequence Mulack is drawing: that Hess and Eichmann are typical examples of this patriarchal (Jewish) morality that disclaims responsibility by appealing to a "higher authority." In an assertion almost too extraordinary to believe, Mulack blithely maintains that Jewish adherence to divine commandments is equivalent to Nazi obedience to the criminal orders of their superiors. What is nazism, in Mulack's logic? The domination of Jewish morality over Christian morality. German Christians are thus in no way responsible for the Holocaust; Jews are made by Mulack into victims of their own religion. And who is washing her hands here in innocence?

The late feminist theologian Nelle Morton wrote that for women, the feminist journey is home. When I read the arguments of Mulack and others I don't know where to find my home, in the feminist community or in the Jewish community. I have a sense of exclusion from both, and yet each represents, at least partially, the values for which I struggle. It's not easy to be a Jew, any more than it is to be a woman, not only in the face of anti-Semitism and sexism but also in the face of the uncertainty of modern identity. In large measure, that is the purpose of the feminist movement: to allow us to define ourselves as women, and not simply accept the worn-out, often misogynist definitions of the past.

The same goal is at stake in Jewish feminism: a refusal to allow the male-authored definitions of the past to define who we are, or what Judaism is. It is inevitable that, as Jewish women, we experience profound rage and resentment. What I find remarkable is the extent to which I, and so many other Jewish women, are also deeply moved and exhilarated by Jewish ideas, stories, and history. It amazes me sometimes when I find myself in tears of sorrow or joy when I read certain Chasidic texts, or when I teach aspects of Jewish history, or when I'm asked to lead a minyan. I'm amazed that the rage has not overtaken me, that I am still able to feel so strongly as a Jew. But the ambivalence we feel as Jewish feminists is a problem we must resolve ourselves. We can't walk away from Judaism because of its sexism any more than we can walk away from life itself. What we do demand, though, is the right to examine the problem without the distorted anti-Judaism of Christian feminists whose problems, ultimately, are so similar to our own. Their problems will not be resolved through a manipulative ideology that projects Christian problems (or human problems) onto Jews.

Speaking out against feminist anti-Semitism is rarely received well; some feminists charge that I am undermining feminism, others that the issues are not really very important, still others are sympathetic but concerned with different problems. Similarly, some Jews seem to thrive on reports of anti-Semitism but often trivialize or simply ignore feminist analyses of sexism. In West Germany, where I have lectured frequently on feminism and anti-Semitism, reactions have often been hostile. Insistence on the patriarchal roots of nazism becomes an excuse to discourage German women from taking responsibility for anti-Semitism and fascism.

Discussions of anti-Semitism should not proceed in the same old way, with Jews throwing out a list of accusations against Christians. Jewish awareness of Christian motifs of anti-Judaism should force us to address Judaism's sexism and also eliminate our denigrations of other groups. After all, one of the perennial popular defenses of Judaism remains negation of paganism. Judaism's treatment of women, we are often told, is really not so bad—compared to that of the pagans. Christian feminists have to understand the history and structure of anti-Judaism and how to cease perpetuating it, while Jews who are sensitive to anti-Semitism have to realize that sexism within Judaism is equally destructive. If there is any single most important point promoted by feminism, it is to cease the projection of evil onto others.   □

Written in Pencil in the Sealed Railway-Car

Don Pagis; translated by Stephan Mitchell

i am eve
with abel my son if you see my other son
cain son of man
tell him that i

Nazi Feminists?

Linda Gordon

Mothers in the Fatherland: Women, the Family, and Nazi Politics, By Claudia Koonz. St. Martin's Press, 1987, 556 pp.

I first turned to this book, by a professor of German history, out of my interest in nazism, the Holocaust, and right-wing movements in general; a study of Nazi women, I knew, would also illuminate a great deal about Nazi men. As I expected, _Mothers in the Fatherland_ demonstrates the significant contribution of feminist analysis to our understanding of conservatism and authoritarianism. As I did not expect, however, it also raises troubling and stimulating questions about feminism.

Koonz discusses many aspects of women's participation in Nazi life but focuses particular attention on Nazi women's organizations. Over four million women participated in the _Frauenwerk_, Nazi government-sponsored women's activities; five million belonged to the women's division of the Nazi Labor Front. The Nazi purpose in encouraging such organizations was to mobilize women for all aspects of the Reich's programs: production, social control, "purification of the race," war. Nevertheless, many of these women joined in the belief that they were thereby working for the advancement of women. They believed that promoting womanly virtues and achievements—motherhood and service, above all—could provide for women the respect they deserved. Women leaders often protested the slighting of women's interests by the Nazi party and government. Indeed, one of Koonz's central arguments is that women joined these organizations for many of the same reasons they have joined progressive and feminist movements: They were rebelling against the low status and confinement of women's conventional role and were seeking recognition, an arena for political activism, and power. She does not dismiss these conservative women as dupes of men, inauthentic to a true female character, but emphasizes the degree of genuine conviction among them.

This argument—indeed the whole study—takes risks which I initially doubted could be carried off. Koonz attempts to portray the world from the perspective of these often repulsive characters. Although the book contains two substantial chapters with important new material about Jewish and non-Jewish victims and resisters and pays close attention to anti-Semitism among the Nazi women, it does not place Jews centrally in the picture and hazards the intellectual and moral disadvantages of seeing problems from the myopic point of view of oppressors. The perspective of Nazi women is particularly distorted because it was in support of one of the most woman-hating regimes of the modern world. Yet not to adopt the perspective of one's subjects constricts insight and prevents depth. Much critical work about oppressors is disappointing because it is limited to muckraking, listing atrocities and corruptions, failing to uncover deeper meanings. Koonz's book easily overwhelmed all my misgivings.

Linda Gordon is a professor of history at the University of Wisconsin. Her book, Woman's Body, Woman's Right: A Social History of Birth Control _(Viking Penguin) was released in its second edition in 1990. She is also author of_ Heros of Their Own Lives: The Politics and History of Family Violence _(Viking Penguin, 1988). This review appeared in_ Tikkun, _July/August 1987._

Koonz maintains distance by interlacing the perspective of her subjects with her own author's voice. In an extraordinary opening she describes her discovery in 1980 that Gertrud Scholtz-Klink, chief of the Nazi Women's Bureau, was still alive. (She found Scholtz-Klink's book in a feminist bookstore in Berlin, a store that did not carry Richard Evans's good history of German feminism because it was written by a man.) Scholtz-Klink agreed to an interview. Doubting whether this important ex-Nazi would speak openly, Professor Koonz expected denial, evasion, and contrition. Instead, Scholtz-Klink was loquacious and opinionated, offering advice to contemporary leaders:

"You know, if our politicians learned from the past, they would not have to complain about the unruly youth of today. Why don't they ask us for advice on social problems?... In the Depression, we sponsored a national labor service that took teenagers off the streets and taught them patriotism.... Mitterand is on the right track, but he doesn't go far enough. He created a ministry for women's rights. My own women's division concerned itself with women's responsibilities...."

"Then you were not concerned about Hitler's policies on the Jews?"

"Of course, we never intended that so many Jews would disappear. I had grown up in an anti-Semitic family so the ideas did not seem unusual.... Besides, until the war with Russia, all of our policies were strictly legal...."

Once she had sent money to a Jewish woman who went into exile. "What ingratitude! After I helped her out ... she publicly accused me after the war...."

Koonz soon realized that she was not interviewing an ex-Nazi but a Nazi. This presentism pervades *Mothers in the Fatherland*. Nothing in the book is safely past. In its meanings for feminism, Jewishness, and the appraisal of conservatism, the book seems to send periodic projectiles, many of them sharp, into the present. There is pain in reading this, not mainly from the description of atrocities, but from having certain intellectual comforts torn away, as if an old and beloved quilt is being shredded.

One such loss is the idea that there is something about femaleness that can insulate us from nazism and its like. For two hundred years, one strain of feminism has emphasized the moral superiority of women. This is not necessarily a biologistic view; many modern feminists believe that women have been *made* different from men, but that these differences are nevertheless deep and thorough. Women have been acculturated, they argue, to be more nurturing, less violent, less aggressive, more cooperative than men. The history of Nazi women belies such views in several ways: There were many women responsible for substantial brutality, and many more enthusiastically supported men's brutality. Indeed, adopting for the moment the view that men and women are deeply different, one might say that as the masculine style (at its worst) produces violence and brutality, so the female style (at its worst) produces submission to authority that is an equally important base for fascistic regimes. Hitler himself believed that his regime, the obedience and adoration he required, depended on the feminization of the population:

Someone who does not understand the intrinsically feminine character of the masses will never be an effective speaker. Ask yourself, what does a woman expect from a man? Clearness, decision, power, and action.... Like a woman, the masses fluctuate between extremes.... The Crowd is not only like a woman, but women constitute the most important element in an audience. The women usually lead, then follow the children and at last ... follow the fathers. [from a letter by Hitler to Ernst (Putzi) Hanfstangl].

If femaleness does not protect us from nazism, what about feminism? Germany had a relatively strong feminist movement—not, perhaps, as strong as in the U.S. but stronger than elsewhere in Europe. Why, then, was there no evidence of feminist or woman-centered resistance to the Nazi takeover? Koonz tells many ugly stories of women's organizations agreeing without protest to the expulsion of their Jewish members, for example. Part of the answer lies in the fact that the German women's movement was deeply split between its bourgeois-liberal and its socialist varieties. The former organizations were so driven by their class interests that they could not experience the world through the eyes of their poorer sisters. Putting it another way, their feminism, like all feminisms, had class as well as gender content. Another historian of German women, Renate Bridenthal, has written about the *Reichsverband Deutscher Hausfrauenvereine* (RDH—German Housewives' Assn.), part of the main umbrella organization of the German women's movement, the primary purpose of which became resisting unionization and higher wages among domestic servants.[*] Many working-class German women were organized into socialist women's organizations, but these tended to follow the Socialist and Communist party strategy and did not promote an independent, feminist opposition to nazism.

These class and religious divisions may explain the lack of unified resistance, but they do not explain why so many women activists were attracted in the first place to nazism, a political movement with an openly anti-feminist platform. It stood for the submission of wives to husbands, the restriction of women to domesticity, the exclusion of women from the public sphere. During the war, Koonz relates, Hitler called upon SS men to produce as many illegitimate babies as possible, and asked the women's organizations to endorse this project.

This is not to say that there was no gender gap in Nazi support. Before the panic caused by the Depression, the women's Nazi vote was fifty percent lower than men's. In 1932 boys in the Hitler Youth outnumbered girls by almost two to one. This gap, however, disappeared by the end of the 1930s, and the reasons for this equalization deserve further study.

The most delicate part of Koonz's interpretation is her identification of elements in Nazi ideology that were attractive to some aspects of feminist sensibility. A pause here to describe what I mean by feminism is necessary, in order not to overstate what Koonz means or what I infer from her work. Today many political groups try to define a specific ideology that is feminism and criticize women's groups with whom they do not agree for being non-feminist. As an historian I have been forced by the evidence to adopt a definition broad enough to encompass a great variety of changing feminisms, movements whose common denominator is that women are subordinated and disrespected, and that something can and should be done about it. I do not for a moment suggest that the Nazi women leaders were feminists; the title of this article is wholly ironic. The Nazi women themselves considered feminism their main enemy and did not agree that women were subordinated. Nevertheless, in some of their grievances and programs they were like some types of feminists, and it is difficult to define the boundary. The entrance of women into a wage-labor force and into modern politics produced resentment among women themselves against the devaluation of their domestic and maternal labor. The conservative ideology that women *should* be maternal and domestic can appear as an expression of respect for women and for the maternal and domestic arena. And vice versa, expressions of respect for women's domestic labor and nurturing capacities often contain disapproval of women who choose otherwise. There is a feminist orientation which calls for greater respect for women precisely on the basis of their traditional roles and looks askance at women who desert these roles.

---

[*] Bridenthal's article can be found in an excellent anthology on this topic, *When Biology Became Destiny: Women in Weimar and Nazi Germany* (Monthly Review Press, New Feminist Library, 1984), edited by Bridenthal, Grossmann, and Kaplan.

In Germany the contribution of this sort of feminism to conservatism, even military expansionism, can be seen in the history of the term *lebensraum*. Literally "living room," the phrase came to be associated with the Nazi justification for eastward territorial expansion, but had been used earlier by the bourgeois women's rights movement to refer to a woman-dominated space—nurturing, refined, insulated from the masculine world of money and politics. It was women's responsibility to protect this space for Germany and to nurture the men who would create this "civilized" space for Germans in "barbaric" Czechoslovakia, Poland, and the Ukraine.

Feminism is not only complex and varied but also contains contradictory perspectives: there are, for example, feminisms that assert women's difference from men, and those that assert their essential human similarity; those that call for ending the sexual division of labor and gender difference, and those that prefer to claim and defend different roles for men and women. At its edges feminism shades imperceptibly into non-feminist women's movements. One may disagree with many, but I would be loathe to label any of them inauthentic without a serious attempt to understand their motivation. In some of the most conservative, intolerant rantings, we may nevertheless recognize the same thwarted but unstilled aspirations that drive our own movements. The goal is not reconciliation, but a better explanation of conservative women's activism.

Recognizing these political differences helps identify not only women's different interests but, perhaps more importantly, the ambivalence and conflicting interests within individual women. Industrial societies have presented women with countervailing pressures, even double binds. Women's employment and economic independence represent both opportunity and increased burdens. Women's new roles, combined with the continuation of traditional responsibilities for child-raising and domestic labor, offer autonomy while heightening exploitation. Naturally, women have differing and ambivalent responses.

The ambivalence in women's situation is a problem not only for feminists but may be one of the most important conditions of modern conservative politics. Another message of Koonz's book is that widespread anxiety about the place of women—and also therefore about masculinity—pervaded the whole society, male as well as female, the powerful as well as the powerless. She shows that this anxiety was fundamental, intense, and extremely influential in the rise and maintenance of nazism. She uses to great effect a survey of working-class Germans conducted by Erich Fromm just before the Depression. Virtually the only finding that surprised him was the vehement reaction against women's changing roles. People not only complained about bobbed hair, makeup, and women's employment, they blamed most social problems on these changes. Presciently, Fromm wrote, "Here is an opportunity for political propaganda writers ... to use for their purposes." The Nazi promise to restore women to their place in the family, and thereby to restore stability to the family and authority to men, was a vital part of its appeal, as it has been in many conservative social movements. As Koonz suggests, the apparent traditionalism of Nazi family policy helped mask the radicalism of its other policies. Moreover, as in the US today, the accommodation of liberal, socialist, and even feminist movements to these mythically nostalgic yearnings weakens their ability to resist conservative and authoritarian "solutions."

This gender analysis of nazism—seeing it, in part, as a movement for the restoration of patriarchy—offers insights about anti-Semitism, particularly connections between anti-feminism and anti-Semitism. The rhetoric of conservatism is rich with such connections: Jewishness = modernism, individualism, cosmopolitanism, internationalism—all of them the breeding ground of women's rights. As Gottfried Feder, a Nazi ideologue, put it, "The insane dogma of equality led as surely to the emancipation of the Jews as to the emancipation of women. The Jew stole the woman from us...." But these connections must not be oversimplified. German gentile feminists did not see anti-Semitism as hostile to their own interests. Judaism has been as patriarchal as the other religions.

Some Jews, particularly those of the business class, were attracted to nazism themselves, and for the same reasons as gentiles of their class: an approval of authority, order, German nationalism, and family stability. (This attraction to nazism has been neglected in discussions of why German Jews were so slow to believe the Nazi threat to them.) And the Nazis were as hostile to other groups, not particularly associated with individualism and modernity, which threatened their domination; a case in point is the Jehovah's Witnesses who were near unanimous in their total noncooperation. Still, Hitler's greatest personal intensity and consistency was arguably his anti-Semitism, and the success of this hate in organizing German support can hardly be considered marginal.

Of course nazism was by no means consistently anti-modernist, committed as it was to the rapid development of military and industrial technology. Koonz shows, in fact, that the Nazi regime was unable to turn around even those modernizing, feminist tendencies it most deplored. The birth rate, for example, despite the government's incentives to maternity, never even rose to equal that of the pre-Nazi 1920s. The abortion rate rose, which can be taken as an indicator of the overall birth control rate. The divorce rate increased faster than the marriage rate. Nazi social conservatism had aimed to restore not only male authority over women but also parental authority over children, and that, too, failed. On the contrary, the Nazi ideological and patriotic mobilization subjected children to influences independent of their parents, even encouraging defiance. The Nazi leadership found itself in a double-bind with respect to women's employment: during the war, facing a serious labor shortage, managers still found it hard to coerce women into the factories because they were faced with contradictory policies which lauded and rewarded domesticity. Hitler's rigidity regarding traditional sex roles continued to the end, and the war only redoubled his view that women were more valuable to the state in maintaining men's domestic privileges than for their own industrial labor.

Ironically, the Nazi regime itself hastened the destruction of this idealized domesticity. It did so through its expansion of state control of many apparently private activities: through its eugenics and reproduction policies, its drive for ideological conformity, its control over youth. This contradiction appears most intensely in the activities of organized Nazi women. There is always an irony inherent in the role of conservative women activists—to wit, Phyllis Schlafly—who spend their lives traveling, speaking in public, and vying for public power as they instruct other women to make domesticity and the private sphere their first priority. They joined a movement that directed women to a special, exclusively private role, but which also called upon women to mobilize and provide public leadership toward achieving those ends. The contradiction is not simply in the mixed motives of the Nazi women; it is a contradiction in the very nature of conservative politics in a period of women's emancipation.

Koonz's book is sprinkled with implicit comparisons with the contemporary Right. To articulate them is tricky because the specialness of the time and place of nazism was extremely important. For example, the pro-family content of Nazi ideology is very similar to that found in virtually all socially conservative movements—nineteenth-century anti-woman suffrage campaigns, early twentieth century "social purity," Italian fascism, Vichy patriotism, the contemporary "Moral Majority." Yet the intensity of the Nazi panic against women's "selfishness," men's "emasculation," and women's "mannishness" was unparalleled. During the Depression in the U.S., there was also a pro-family reaction against women's employment, sexual freedom, birth control, and cultural modernism, but it did not provoke so much nationalism, racism, anti-feminism, and anti-communism as in Germany. (The closer resemblance is to the US in the 1950s, when those tendencies were more virulent, but, in part because of a healthier economy, they did not become a mass movement.)

Two generalizations arising from this book can safely be ventured. First, anxieties about the erosion of traditional gender arrangements can contribute to mass susceptibility to authoritarian solutions. Indeed, among all the anxieties created by the destruction of peasant society and its patriarchal order, and its replacement by big cities, industrial labor, and individualist values, those associated with women's new roles and claims to individual rights are often most vivid. In the U.S. the most consistently controversial domestic issues for the last one hundred and fifty years have been women's rights and reproductive rights. Second, women, too, have anxieties about these changes, and the process of modernization has by no means meant reliable and steady improvements for women. While women's movements have in the main been more progressive (that is, leaning more toward greater democracy, equality, and civil liberties) than men's, there is no guarantee that this is always the case, and many women have been attracted by authoritarian promises to restore traditional (albeit usually mythical) stability.

If there are lessons here, they include reminders that the enemy is within us as well as outside us. The vulnerability and manipulability of the citizenry is a function of anxieties already present in us, created in large part by instability in "personal" life—family and community. Conservatives are not entirely wrong in viewing women's individual aspirations as hostile to family stability *on the old terms* (e.g., coercive marriage and childbearing, male authority often enforced by male violence). But a return to the "traditional" family is no more possible now than it was during the Nazi regime. We must expect repeated bouts of intense reactionary responses to these instabilities until there is some new modicum of stability—which can only be achieved on the basis of recognizing women's aspirations.

Koonz's book reveals the limitations of the work of liberal and socialist feminists in Weimar Germany. Both groups focused on individual reforms—absolutely necessary reforms, such as political rights, legalized contraception and abortion, equal pay, homosexual rights—but neither offered a coherent vision of a new society based on sexual equality and freedom. They could not conceive of new bases of stability. That task remains ours today: to articulate a society that meets people's needs for stability as well as adventure, community as well as individual freedom, difference without domination. □

IV. Israel

תיקון

The New Historiography: Israel Confronts its Past

Benny Morris

On July 11, 1948, the Yiftah Brigade's Third Battalion, as part of what was called Operation Dani, occupied the center of the Arab town of Lydda. There was no formal surrender, but the night passed quietly. Just before noon the following day, two or three armored cars belonging to the Arab Legion, the British-led and trained Transjordanian army, drove into town. A firefight ensued, and the scout cars withdrew. But a number of armed townspeople, perhaps believing that the shooting heralded a major Arab counterattack, began sniping from windows and rooftops at their Israeli occupiers. The Third Battalion—about four hundred nervous Israeli soldiers in the middle of an Arab town of tens of thousands—fiercely put down what various chroniclers subsequently called a "rebellion," by firing in the streets, into houses, and at the concentrations of POWs in the mosque courtyards. Israeli military records refer to "more than 250" Arabs killed in the town that afternoon. By contrast, Israeli casualties in both the firefight with the Arab Legion scout cars and the suppression of the sniping were between two and four dead (the records vary), and twelve wounded. Israeli historians called the affair a "rebellion" in order to justify the subsequent slaughter; Arab chroniclers, such as Aref al-Aref, did likewise in order to highlight Palestinian resolve and resistance in the face of Zionist encroachment.

Operation Dani took place roughly midway through the first Israeli-Arab war—the War of Independence, in official Israeli parlance. The Arab states' invasion on May 15 of the fledgling state had been halted weeks before; the newly organized and freshly equipped Israel Defense Forces (IDF) were on the offensive on all fronts—as was to remain true for the remainder of the war.

On July 12, before the shooting in Lydda had completely died down, Lt. Col. Yitzhak Rabin, officer in command of operations for Operation Dani, issued the following order: "1. The inhabitants of Lydda must be expelled quickly without attention to age. They should be directed towards Beit Nabala. Yiftah [Brigade HQ] must determine the method and inform [Operation] Dani HQ and Eighth Brigade HQ. 2. Implement immediately." A similar order was issued at the same time to the Kiryati Brigade concerning the inhabitants of the neighboring Arab town of Ramle.

On July 12 and July 13, the Yiftah and Kiryati brigades carried out their orders, expelling the fifty to sixty thousand inhabitants of the two towns, which lie about ten miles southeast of Tel Aviv. Throughout the war, the two towns had interdicted Jewish traffic on the main Tel Aviv-Jerusalem road, and the Yishuv's leaders regarded Lydda and Ramle as a perpetual threat to Tel Aviv itself. About noon on July 13, Operation Dani HQ informed IDF General Staff/Operations: "Lydda police fort has been captured. [The troops] are busy expelling the inhabitants [*oskim be'geirush ha'toshav-*

Dr. Benny Morris works for the Jerusalem Post, *is a former senior associate of St. Antony's College, Oxford, and is the author of* The Birth of the Palestinian Refugee Problem, 1947-49 *(Cambridge University Press, 1988). This article appeared in* Tikkun, *November/December 1988.*

im]." Lydda's inhabitants were forced to walk eastward to the Arab Legion lines, and many of Ramle's inhabitants were ferried in trucks or buses. Clogging the roads (and the Legion's possible routes of advance westward), the tens of thousands of refugees marched, gradually shedding possessions along the way. Arab chroniclers, such as Sheikh Muhammad Nimr al-Khatib, claimed that hundreds of children died in the march, from dehydration and disease. One Israeli witness at the time described the spoor: The refugee column "to begin with [jettisoned] utensils and furniture and, in the end, bodies of men, women and children...." Many of the refugees came to rest near Ramallah and set up tent encampments (which later became the refugee camps supported by the United Nations Relief and Works Agency (UNRWA), and the hotbeds of today's Palestinian rebellion which current Defense Minister Rabin is trying to suppress).

Israeli historians in the 1950s, 1960s, and 1970s were less than honest in their treatment of the Lydda-Ramle episode. The IDF's official *Toldot Milhemet Ha'komemiut* (History of the War of Independence), written by the General Staff/History Branch and published in 1959, stated, "The Arabs [of Lydda], who had violated the terms of the surrender and feared [Israeli] retribution, were happy at the possibility given them of evacuating the town and proceeding eastwards, to Legion territory: Lydda emptied of its Arab inhabitants."

A decade later, the former head of the IDF History Branch, Lt. Col. Netanel Lorch, wrote in 1968 in *The Edge of the Sword*, the second revised edition of his history of the war, that "the residents, who had violated surrender terms and feared retribution, declared they would leave and asked [for] safe conduct to Arab Legion lines, which was granted."

A somewhat less deceitful, but also misleading, description of the events in Lydda and Ramle is provided by Lt. Col. Elhannan Orren, another former director of the IDF History Branch, in his *Ba'derekh El Ha'ir* (On the Road to the City), a highly detailed description of Operation Dani published by the IDF in 1976. Orren, like his predecessors, fails to state anywhere that what occurred was an expulsion, and one explicitly ordered from on high (originating, according to Ben-Gurion's first major biographer, Michael Bar-Zohar, from the prime minister himself). Orren also repeats a variant of the "inhabitants asked, the IDF graciously complied" story.

Yitzhak Rabin, ironically more frank than his chroniclers, inserted a passage into his autobiography, *Pinkas Sherut* (Service Notebook), which more or less admitted that what had occurred in Lydda and Ramle had been an expulsion. But the passage was excised by order of the Israeli government. (Subsequently, to everyone's embarrassment, Peretz Kidron, the English translator of *Pinkas Sherut*, sent the offending passage to the *New York Times*, where it was published on October 23, 1979.)

The treatment of the Lydda-Ramle affair by past Israeli historians is illustrative of what can be called, for want of a better term, the "old" or "official" history. That history has shaped the way Israelis and Diaspora Jews—or, at least, Diaspora Zionists—have seen and, in large measure, still see Israel's past; and it has also held sway over the way gentile Europeans and Americans (and their governments) see that past. This understanding of the past, in turn, has significantly influenced the attitudes of Diaspora Jews, as well as the attitude of European and American non-Jews, toward present-day Israel—which affects government policies concerning the Israeli-Arab conflict.

The essence of the old history is that Zionism was a beneficent and well-meaning progressive national movement; that Israel was born pure into an uncharitable, predatory world; that Zionist efforts at compromise and conciliation were rejected by the Arabs; and that Palestine's Arabs, and in their wake the surrounding Arab states, for reasons of innate selfishness, xenophobia, and downright cussedness, refused to accede to the burgeoning Zionist presence and in 1947 to 1949 launched a war to extirpate the foreign plant. The Arabs, so goes the old history, were politically and militarily assisted in their efforts by the British, but they nonetheless lost the war. Poorly armed and outnumbered, the Jewish community in Palestine, called the Yishuv, fought valiantly, suppressed the Palestinian "gangs" (*knufiyot* in Israeli parlance), and repelled the five invading Arab armies. In the course of that war, says the old history—which at this point becomes indistinguishable from Israeli propaganda—Arab states and leaders, in order to blacken Israel's image and facilitate the invasion of Palestine, called upon/ordered Palestine's Arabs to quit their homes and the "Zionist areas"—to which they were expected to return once the Arab armies had proved victorious. Thus was triggered the Palestinian Arab exodus which led to the now forty-year-old Palestinian refugee problem.

The old history makes the further claim that in the latter stages of the 1948 war and in the years immediately thereafter Israel desperately sought to make peace with all or any of its neighbors, but the Arabs, obdurate and ungenerous, refused all overtures, remaining hell-bent on destroying Israel.

The old historians offered a simplistic and consciously pro-Israeli interpretation of the past, and they deliberately avoided mentioning anything that would reflect badly on Israel. People argued that since the conflict with the Arabs was still raging, and since it was a political as well as a military struggle, it necessarily involved propaganda, the goodwill (or ill will) of governments in the West, and the hearts and minds of Christians and Diaspora Jews. Blackening Israel's image, it was argued, would ultimately weaken Israel in its ongoing war for survival. In short, *raisons d'état* often took precedence over telling the truth.

The past few years have witnessed the emergence of a new generation of Israeli scholars and a "new" history. These historians, some of them living abroad, have looked and are looking afresh at the Israeli historical experience, and their conclusions, by and large, are at odds with those of the old historians.

Two factors are involved in the emergence of this new history—one relating to materials, the other to personae.

Thanks to Israel's Archives Law (passed in 1955, amended in 1964 and 1981), and particularly to the law's key "thirty-year rule," starting in the early 1980s a large number (hundreds of thousands, perhaps millions) of state papers were opened to researchers. Almost all the Foreign Ministry's papers from 1947 to 1956, as well as a large number of documents—correspondence, memoranda, minutes—from other ministries, including the prime minister's office (though excluding the Defense Ministry and the IDF), have been released. Similarly, large collections of private papers and political party papers from this period have been opened. Therefore, for the first time, historians have been able to write studies of the period on the basis of a large collection of contemporary source material. (The old history was written largely on the basis of interviews and memoirs, and, at best, it made use of select batches of documents, many of them censored, such as those from the IDF archive.)

The second factor is the nature of the new historians. Most of them were born around 1948 and have matured in a more open, doubting, and self-critical Israel than the pre-Lebanon War Israel in which the old historians grew up. The old historians had lived through 1948 as highly committed adult participants in the epic, glorious rebirth of the Jewish commonwealth. They were unable to separate their lives from this historical event, unable to regard impartially and objectively the facts and processes that they later wrote about. Indeed, they admit as much. The new historians, by contrast, are able to be more impartial.

Inevitably, the new historians focused their attention, at least initially, on 1948, because the documents were available and because that was the central, natal, revolutionary event in Israeli history. How one perceives 1948 bears heavily on how one perceives the whole Zionist/Israeli experience. If Israel, the haven of a much-persecuted people, was born pure and innocent, then it was worthy of the grace, material assistance, and political support showered upon it by the West over the past forty years—and worthy of more of the same in years to come. If, on the other hand, Israel was born tarnished, besmirched by original sin, then it was no more deserving of that grace and assistance than were its neighbors.

The past few months have seen the publication in the West of a handful of "new" histories, including Avi Shlaim's *Collusion Across the Jordan* (Columbia University Press, 1988); Ilam Pappe's *Britain and the Arab-Israeli Conflict, 1948–51* (Macmillan/St. Anthony's, 1988); Simha Flapan's *The Birth of Israel* (Pantheon, 1987); and my own *The Birth of the Palestinian Refugee Problem, 1947–1949* (Cambridge University Press, 1988). Taken together, these works—along with a large number of articles that have appeared recently in academic journals such as *Studies in Zionism*, *Middle Eastern Studies*, and *The Middle East Journal*—significantly undermine, if not thoroughly demolish, a variety of assumptions that helped form the core of the old history.

Flapan's work is the least historical of these books. Indeed, it is not, strictly speaking, a "history" at all but rather a polemical work written from a Marxist perspective. In his introduction, Flapan—who passed away last year and who was the former director of the left-wing Mapam party's Arab department and editor of the monthly *New Outlook*—writes that his purpose is not to produce "a detailed historical study interesting only to historians and researchers," but rather to write "a book that will undermine the propaganda structures that have so long obstructed the growth of the peace forces in my country...." Politics rather than historiography is the book's manifest objective.

Despite its explicitly polemical purpose, Flapan's book has the virtue of more or less accurately formulating some of the central fallacies—which he calls "myths"—that informed the old history. These were (1) that the Yishuv in 1947 joyously accepted partition and the truncated Jewish state prescribed by the UN General Assembly, and that the Palestinians and the surrounding Arab states unanimously rejected the partition and attacked the Yishuv with the aim of throwing the Jews into the sea; (2) that the war was waged between a relatively defenseless and weak (Jewish) David and a relatively strong (Arab) Goliath; (3) that the Palestinians fled their homes and villages either voluntarily or at the behest/order of the Arab leaders; and (4) that, at the war's end, Israel was interested in making peace, but the recalcitrant Arabs displayed no such interest, opting for a perpetual—if sporadic—war to the finish.

Because of poor research and analysis—including selective and erroneous use of documents—Flapan's demolition of these myths is far from convincing. But Shlaim, in *Collusion*, tackles some of the same myths—and far more persuasively. According to Shlaim, the original Zionist goal was the establishment of a Jewish state in the whole of Palestine. The acceptance of partition, in the mid-1930s as in 1947, was tactical, not a change in the Zionist dream. Ben-Gurion, says Shlaim, considered the partition lines of "secondary importance ... because he intended to change them in any case; they were not the end but only the beginning." In acquiescing to partition schemes in the mid-1930s, Ben-Gurion wrote, "I am certain that we will be able to settle in all the other parts of the country, whether through agreement and mutual understanding with our Arab neighbors or in another way." To his wife, Ben-Gurion wrote, "Establish a Jewish state at once, even if it is not in the whole land. The rest will come in the course of time. It must come."

Come November 1947, the Yishuv entered the first stage of the war with a tacit understanding with Transjordan's king, Abdullah—"a falcon trapped in a canary's cage"—that his Arab Legion would take over the eastern part of Palestine (now called the West Bank), earmarked by the UN for Palestinian statehood, and that it would leave the Yishuv alone to set up the Jewish state in the other areas of the country. The Yishuv and the Hashemite kingdom of Transjordan, Shlaim persuasively argues, had conspired from 1946 to early 1947 to nip the UN Partition Resolution in the bud and to stymie the emergence of a Palestinian Arab state. From the start, while publicly enunciating support for the partition of the land between its Jewish and Arab communities, both

Ben-Gurion and Abdullah aimed at frustrating the UN resolution and sharing among themselves the areas earmarked for Palestinian Arab statehood. It was to be partition—but between Israel and Transjordan. This "collusion" and "unholy alliance"—in Shlaim's loaded phrases—was sealed at the now-famous clandestine meeting between Golda Myerson (Meir) and Abdullah at Naharayim on the Jordan River on November 17, 1947.

This Zionist-Hashemite nonaggression pact was sanctioned by Britain, adds Shlaim. Contrary to the old Zionist historiography—which was based largely on the (mistaken) feelings of Israel's leaders at that time—Britain's Foreign Secretary Ernest Bevin, "by February 1948," had clearly become "resigned to the inevitable emergence of a Jewish state" (while opposing the emergence of a Palestinian Arab state). Indeed, he warned Transjordan "to refrain from invading the areas allotted to the Jews."

Both Shlaim and Flapan make the point that the Palestinian Arabs, though led by Haj Amin al-Husayni, the conniving, extremist former mufti of Jerusalem, were far from unanimous in supporting the Husayni-led crusade against the Jews. Indeed, in the first months of the hostilities, according to Yishuv intelligence sources, the bulk of Palestine's Arabs merely wanted quiet, if only out of respect for the Jews' martial prowess. But gradually, in part due to Haganah overreactions, the conflict widened and eventually engulfed the two communities throughout the land. In April and May 1948, the Haganah gained the upper hand and the Palestinians lost the war, most of them going into exile.

What ensued, once Israel declared its independence on May 14, 1948, and the Arab states invaded on May 15, was "a general land grab," with everyone—Israel, Transjordan, Syria, Iraq, Lebanon, and Egypt—bent on preventing the birth of a Palestinian Arab state and carving out chunks of Palestine for themselves.

Contrary to the old history, Abdullah's invasion of eastern Palestine was clearly designed to conquer territory for his kingdom—at the expense of the Palestinian Arabs—rather than to destroy the Jewish state. Indeed, the Arab Legion—apart from one abortive incursion around Notre Dame in Jerusalem and the assault on the Etzion Bloc (a Jewish settlement zone inside the Arab state area)—stuck meticulously, throughout the war, to its nonaggressive stance vis-à-vis the Yishuv and the Jewish state's territory. Rather, it was the Haganah/IDF that repeatedly attacked the legion on territory earmarked for Arab sovereignty (Latrun, Lydda, Ramle).

Nevertheless, Shlaim, like Pappe in *Britain and the Arab-Israeli Conflict, 1948-51*, is never completely clear about Egypt, Syria, Iraq, and Lebanon's main purpose in invading Palestine: Was their primary aim to overrun the Yishuv and destroy the Jewish state, or was it merely to frustrate or curtail Abdullah's territorial ambitions and to acquire some territory for themselves?

Flapan argues firmly, but without evidence, that "the invasion ... was not aimed at destroying the Jewish state." Shlaim and Pappe are more cautious. Shlaim writes that the Arab armies intended to bisect the Jewish state and, if possible, "occupy Haifa and Tel Aviv" or "crippl[e] the Jewish state." But, at the same time, he argues that they were driven into the invasion more by a desire to stymie Abdullah than by the wish to kill the Jews; and, partly for this reason, they did not properly plan the invasion, either militarily or politically, and their leaders were generally pessimistic about its outcome. Pappe points out that Egypt initially did not seem determined to participate in the invasion, and all the Arab states failed to commit the full weight of their military power to the enterprise—which indicates perhaps that they took the declared aim of driving the Jews into the sea less than seriously. In any event, Transjordan frustrated the other Arabs' intentions throughout and rendered their military preparations and planning ineffective.

One of the most tenacious myths relating to 1948 is the myth of "David and Goliath"—that the Arabs were overwhelmingly stronger militarily than the Yishuv. The simple truth—as conveyed by

Flapan, Shlaim, Pappe, and myself—is that the stronger side won. The map showing a minuscule Israel and a giant surrounding sea of Arab states did not and, indeed, for the time being still does not accurately reflect the military balance of power. The pre-1948 Yishuv had organized itself for statehood and war; the Palestinian Arabs, who outnumbered the Jews two to one, had not. And in war, command and control are everything, or almost everything. During the first half of the war (December 1947–May 14, 1948), the Yishuv was better armed and had more trained manpower than the Palestinians, whose forces were beefed up by several thousand "volunteers" from the surrounding Arab states. This superior organization, command, and control meant that at almost every decisive point in the battle the Haganah managed to field more and better-equipped formations than did the Palestinians. When the Yishuv put matters to the test, in the Haganah offensives of April and early May 1948, the decision was never in doubt; the Arab redoubts fell, in domino fashion, like ripe plums—the Jerusalem Corridor, Tiberias, Haifa, Eastern Galilee, Safad. When one adds to this the Yishuv's superiority in morale and motivation—it was a bare three years after the Holocaust, and the Haganah troopers knew that it was do-or-die—the Palestinians never had a chance.

The old history is no more illuminating when it comes to the second stage of the war—the conventional battles of May 15, 1948–January 1949. Jewish organization, command, and control remained superior to those of the uncoordinated armies of Egypt, Syria, Iraq, and Lebanon; and throughout the Yishuv also, the IDF had an edge in numbers. In mid-May 1948, for example, the Haganah fielded thirty-five thousand armed troops while the Arab invaders fielded twenty-five to thirty thousand troops. By the time of Operation Dani in July, the IDF had sixty-five thousand men under arms, and by December it had eighty to ninety thousand—outnumbering its combined Arab foes at every stage of the battle. The Haganah/IDF also enjoyed the immensely important advantage, throughout the conventional war, of short lines of communication, while the Iraqis and Egyptians had to send supplies and reinforcements over hundreds of kilometers of desert before they reached the front lines.

Two caveats must be entered. First, Transjordan's Arab Legion was probably the best army in the war. But it never numbered much more than five thousand troops, and it had no tanks or aircraft. Second, in terms of equipment, during the crucial three weeks between the pan-Arab invasion of Palestine on May 15 and the start of the First Truce on June 11, the Arab armies had an edge in weaponry over the Haganah/IDF. The Haganah was much weaker in terms of aircraft, and had no artillery (only heavy mortars) and very few tanks or tracked vehicles. For those three weeks, as the Haganah's officer in command of operations, Yigal Yadin, told the politicians, it was "fifty-fifty." But before May 15 and from the First Truce onward, the Yishuv's military formations were superior both in terms of manpower and in terms of weaponry.

Apart from the birth of the State of Israel, the major political outcome of the 1948 war was the creation of the Palestinian refugee problem. How the problem came about has been the subject of heated controversy between Israeli and Arab propagandists for the past four decades. The controversy is as much about the nature of Zionism as it is about what exactly happened in 1948. If the Arab contention is true—that the Yishuv had always intended "transfer" and that in 1948 it systematically and forcibly expelled the Arab population from the areas that became the Jewish state— then Israel is a robber state that, like young Jacob, has won the sympathy and support of its elders in the West by trickery and connivance, and the Palestinians are more or less innocent victims. If, on the other hand, the Israeli propaganda line is accepted—that the Palestinians fled "voluntarily" or at the behest of their own and other Arab leaders—then Israel is free of original sin. As I have set out in great detail in *The Birth of the Palestinian Refugee Problem, 1947–1949*, the truth lies somewhere in between. While from the mid-1930s most of the Yishuv's leaders, including

Photo by Oliver and Steinberg

Ben-Gurion, wanted to establish a Jewish state without an Arab minority, or with as small an Arab minority as possible, and supported a "transfer solution" to this minority problem, the Yishuv did not enter the 1948 war with a master plan for expelling the Arabs, nor did its political and military leaders ever adopt such a master plan. There were Haganah/IDF expulsions of Arab communities, some of them with Haganah/IDF General Staff and/or cabinet-level sanction—such as at Miska and Ad-Dumeira in April 1948; at Zarnuqa, Al-Qubeiba, and Huj in May; in Lydda and Ramle in July; and along the Lebanese border (Bir'im, Iqrit, Tarbikha, Suruh, Al-Mansura, and Nabi Rubin) in early November. But there was no grand or blanket policy of expulsions.

On the other hand, at no point during the war did Arab leaders issue a blanket call for Palestine's Arabs to leave their homes and villages and wander into exile. Nor was there an Arab radio or press campaign urging or ordering the Palestinians to flee. Indeed, I have found no trace of any such broadcasts—and throughout the war the Arab radio stations and other press were monitored by the Israeli intelligence services and Foreign Ministry, and by Western diplomatic stations and agencies (such as the BBC). No contemporary reference to or citation from such a broadcast, let alone from a series of such broadcasts, has ever surfaced.

Indeed, in early May 1948 when, according to Israeli propaganda and some of the old histories, such a campaign of broadcasts should have been at its height, in preparation for the pan-Arab invasion, Arab radio stations and leaders (Radio Ramallah, King Abdullah, and Arab Liberation Army commander Qawuqji) all issued broadcasts calling upon the Palestinians to stay put and, if already in exile, to return to their homes in Palestine. References to these broadcasts exist in Haganah, Mapam, and British records.

Occasionally, local Arab commanders and/or politicians ordered the evacuation of women and children from war zones. Less frequently, as in Haifa on April 22, 1948, local Arab leaders advised or instructed their communities to leave rather than stay in a potential or actual war zone or "treacherously" remain under Jewish rule. But there were no Arab blanket orders or campaigns to leave.

Rather, in order to understand the exodus of the 600,000 to 760,000 Arabs from the areas that became the post-1948 Jewish state, one must look to a variety of related processes and causes. What happened in Haifa is illustrative of the complexity of the exodus (though it too does not convey the full complexity of what transpired in the various regions of Palestine at the time).

The exodus from Haifa (which initially had an Arab population of seventy thousand), as from the other main Arab Palestinian centers, Jaffa and Jerusalem, began in December 1947 with the start of sporadic hostilities between the various Jewish and Arab neighborhoods. The exodus slowly gained momentum during the following months as the British Mandate administration moved toward dissolution and final withdrawal. The first to go were the rich and the educated—the middle classes with second homes on the Beirut beachfront, in Nablus or Amman, or those who had either relatives abroad with large homes or enough money to stay in hotels for long periods. The Palestinians' political and economic leadership disappeared. By mid-May 1948, only one member of the Arab Higher Committee, the Palestinians' shadow government, was still in the country.

The flight of the professionals, the civil servants, the traders, and the businessmen had a harsh impact on the Haifa Arab masses, who already were demoralized by the continual sniping and bomb attacks, by the feeling that the Jews were stronger, and by the sense that their own ragtag militia would fail when the test came (as, indeed, it did). The Arabs felt terribly isolated and insecure—Arab Haifa was far from other major Arab population centers and was easily cut off by Jewish settlements along the approach roads. Businesses and workshops closed, policemen shed their uniforms and left their posts, Arab workers could no longer commute to jobs in Jewish areas, and agricultural produce was interdicted in ambushes on the approach roads to the city. Unemployment and prices soared. Thousands of people left.

Then came the Haganah attack of April 21 to April 22 on the Arab districts. Several companies of Carmeli Brigade troops, under cover of constant mortar fire, drove down the Carmel mountain slopes into the Arab downtown areas. Arab militia resistance collapsed. Thousands of Arabs fled from the outlying Arab neighborhoods (such as Wadi Rushmiya and Hailssa) into the British-controlled port area, piled into boats, and fled northward to Acre. The leaders who remained sued for a cease-fire. Under British mediation, the Haganah agreed, offering what the British regarded as generous terms. But then, when faced with Moslem pressure, the Arab leaders, most of them Christian Arabs, got cold feet; a cease-fire meant surrender and implied agreement to live under Jewish rule. They would be open to charges of collaboration and treachery. So, to the astonishment of the British officers and the Jewish military and political leaders gathered on the afternoon of April 22 at the Haifa town hall, the Arab delegation announced that its community would evacuate the city.

The Jewish mayor, Shabtai Levy, and the British commander, Maj. Gen. Hugh Stockwell, pleaded with the Arabs to reconsider. The Haganah representative, Mordechai Makleff, declined to voice an opinion. But the Arabs were unmoved, and the mass exodus, which had begun under the impact of the Haganah mortars and ground assault, moved into top gear, with the British supplying boats and armored car escorts to the departing Arab convoys. From April 22 to May 1, almost all the Arab population departed. The rough treatment—temporary evictions, house-to-house searches, detentions, the occasional beating—meted out to the remaining population during those days by the Haganah and the IZL (Irgun Zvai Leumi) troops who occupied the downtown areas led many of the undecided also to opt for evacuation. By early May, the city's Arab population had dwindled to three or four thousand.

The bulk of the Palestinian refugees—some 250,000 to 300,000—went into exile during those weeks between April and mid-June 1948, with the major precipitant being Jewish (Haganah/IZL) military attack or fears of such attack. In most cases, the Jewish commanders, who wanted to occupy empty villages (occupying populated villages meant leaving behind a garrison, which the units could not afford to do), were hardly ever confronted with deciding whether or not to expel an overrun community: Most villages and towns simply emptied at the first whiff of grapeshot.

In conformity with Tokhnit Dalet (Plan D), the Haganah's master plan, formulated in March 1948, for securing the Jewish state areas in preparation for the expected declaration of statehood and the prospective Arab invasion, the Haganah cleared various areas completely of Arab villages— in the Jerusalem corridor, around Kibbutz Mishmar Ha'emek, and along the coast road. But in most cases, expulsion orders were not necessary; the inhabitants had already fled, out of fear or as a result of Jewish attack. In several areas, Israeli commanders successfully used psychological warfare ploys ("Here's some friendly advice. You better get out now, before the Jews come and rape your daughters.") to obtain Arab evacuation.

The prewar basic structural weaknesses of Palestinian society led to the dissolution of that society when the test of battle came. Lack of administrative structures, as well as weak leaders, poor or nonexistent military organization beyond the single-village level, and faulty or nonexistent taxation mechanisms, all caused the main towns to fall apart in April and May 1948. The fall of the towns and the exodus from them, in turn, brought a sense of fear and despondency to the rural hinterlands. Traditionally, the villages, though economically autarchic, had looked to the towns for political leadership and guidance. The evacuation of the middle classes and the leaders, as well as the fall of the towns, provided the Palestinians in the hinterlands with an example to emulate. Safad's fall and evacuation on May 10 and May 11, for example, triggered an immediate evacuation of the surrounding Arab villages; so, earlier, did the fall of Haifa and the IZL assault on Jaffa.

Seen from the Jewish side, the spectacle of mass Arab evacuation certainly triggered appetites for more of the same: Everyone, at every level of military and political decision-making, understood that a Jewish state without a large Arab minority would be stronger and more viable both militarily and politically. Therefore, the tendency of local military commanders to "nudge" Palestinians into flight increased as the war went on. Jewish atrocities—far more widespread than the old historians have indicated (there were massacres of Arabs at Ad Dawayima, Eilaboun, Jish, Safsaf, Hule, Saliha, and Sasa besides Deir Yassin and Lydda)—and the drive to avenge past Arab wrongs also contributed significantly to the exodus.

The last major fallacy tackled incidentally or directly by the new historians concerns an Israel that in 1948 to 1949 was bent on making peace with its neighbors, and an Arab world that monolithically rejected all such peace efforts. The evidence that Israel's leaders were not desperate to make peace and were unwilling to make the large concessions necessary to give peace a chance is overwhelming. In Tel Aviv, there was a sense of triumph and drunkenness that accompanied victory—a feeling that the Arabs would "soon" or "eventually" sue for peace, that there was no need to rush things or make concessions, that ultimately military victory and dominance would translate into diplomatic-political success.

As Ben-Gurion told an American journalist in mid-July 1949: "I am prepared to get up in the middle of the night in order to sign a peace agreement—but I am not in a hurry and I can wait ten years. We are under no pressure whatsoever." Or, as Ben-Gurion records Abba Eban's telling him: "[Eban] sees no need to run after peace. The armistice is sufficient for us; if we run after peace, the Arabs will demand a price of us—borders [i.e., in terms of territory] or refugees [i.e., repatriation] or both. Let us wait a few years."

As Pappe puts it in *Britain*: "... Abdullah's eagerness [to make peace] was not reciprocated by the Israelis. The priorities of the state of Israel had changed during 1949. The armistice agreements brought relative calm to the borders, and peace was no longer the first priority. The government was preoccupied with absorbing new immigrants and overcoming economic difficulties."

Israel's lack of emphasis on achieving peace was manifested most clearly in the protracted (1949–51) secret negotiations with Abdullah. Israeli Foreign Minister Moshe Sharett described his meeting with Transjordan's king at the palace in Shuneh on May 5, 1949, in the following way: "Transjordan said—we are ready for peace immediately. We said—certainly, we too want peace but one shouldn't rush, one should walk." Israel and Jordan signed an armistice agreement, after much arm-twisting by Israel, which British and American diplomats compared to Hitler's treatment of the Czechs in 1938 to 1939. (As Abdullah put it, quoting an old Turkish saying: "If you meet a bear when crossing a rotten bridge, call her 'dear Auntie.'") But the two sides never signed a peace treaty or a nonbelligerence agreement—something that was proposed at one point by Abdullah.

Shlaim—who in *Collusion* expands the description of the secret Israeli-Jordanian negotiations first provided in Dan Schueftan's *Ha'Optziya Ha'Yardenit* (The Jordanian option), published in Hebrew in Israel in 1986—more or less lays the blame for the failed negotiations squarely on Israel's shoulders. A more generous, less anti-Israeli interpretation of the evidence would blame the Israelis and the Jordanians equally.

Israel refused to offer major concessions in terms of refugee repatriation or territory (Abdullah was particularly keen on getting back Lydda and Ramle) and was for too long unwilling to offer Jordan a sovereign corridor through its territory to the sea at Gaza. Throughout, Israel was prodded if not guided by the "blatant expansionism" of some of Ben-Gurion's aides, such as Moshe Dayan. As Yehoshafat Harkabi, one of Dayan's military colleagues, put it (according to Shlaim): "The existential mission of the State of Israel led us to be demanding and acquisitive, and mindful of the value of every square metre of land." In any case, Ben-Gurion refused to meet Abdullah, and the Israeli leaders often spoke of Abdullah with undeserved contempt.

Shlaim writes that "two principal factors were responsible for the failure of the postwar negotiations: Israel's strength and Abdullah's weakness." Nevertheless, Shlaim seems to attribute too much weight to the first and too little to the second. Shlaim does not sufficiently acknowledge the importance of the "Palestinization" of Jordan following the Hashemite annexation of the West Bank, which quickly resulted in a curtailment of Abdullah's autonomy and his freedom of political movement both within Jordan and in the Arab world in general. The twin pressures exercised by the Arab world outside and by his successive cabinets inside the kingdom successfully impeded Abdullah's ability to make a separate peace with Israel. He almost did so a number of times, but he always held back at the last moment and refused to take the plunge. It is possible, Shlaim argues, that more generous concessions by Tel Aviv at certain critical points in the negotiations would have given Abdullah greater motivation to pursue peace as well as the ammunition he needed to silence his antipeace critics, but the truth of such a claim is uncertain. What is clear is that Abdullah, though showing remarkable courage throughout, simply felt unable in those last years to go against the unanimous or near-unanimous wishes of his ministers and against the unanimous antipeace stand of the surrounding Arab world.

What happened with Abdullah occurred in miniature and more briefly with Egypt and with Syria. In September to October 1948, Egypt's King Farouk, knowing that the war was lost, secretly sent a senior court official to Paris to sound out Israel on the possibility of a peace based on Israeli cession of parts of the Negev and the Gaza Strip to Egypt. Sharett and the senior staff at the Foreign Ministry favored continued negotiations, but Ben-Gurion—bent on a further round of hostilities to drive the Egyptian army out of the Negev—flatly rejected the overture. Shlaim summarizes: "[Ben-Gurion] may have been right in thinking that nothing of substance would come out of these talks. But he surely owed his cabinet colleagues at least a report on what had taken place so that they could review their decision to go [again] to war against Egypt on the basis of all the relevant information."

New Egyptian peace overtures in November, after Israel's Operation Yoav, again came to naught.

As for Syria, in May 1949, its new ruler, Husni Za'im, made major peace proposals which included recognition of Israel as well as Syrian readiness to absorb hundreds of thousands of Palestinian refugees. Za'im wanted Israel to concede a sliver of territory along the Jordan River. He asked to meet with Ben-Gurion or Sharett. Again, Ben-Gurion rejected the proposal, writing on May 12: "I am quite prepared to meet Colonel Za'im in order to promote peace ... but I see no purpose in any such meeting as long as the representatives of Syria in the armistice negotiations do not declare in an unequivocal manner that their forces are prepared to withdraw to their prewar territory [i.e., withdraw from the small Syrian-occupied Mishmar Ha'yarden salient, west of the Jordan]."

Continued feelers by Za'im resulted again in Israeli refusal. As Sharett put it on May 25: "It is clear that we ... won't agree that any bit of the Land of Israel be transferred to Syria, because this is a question of control over the water sources [i.e., of the Jordan River]." Shabtai Rosenne, the legal adviser at the Foreign Ministry, put it simply: "I feel that the need for an agreement between Israel and Syria pressed more heavily on the Syrians." Therefore, why rush toward peace? A few weeks later Za'im was overthrown and executed, and the Syrian peace initiative died with him. Whether the overture was serious or merely tactical—to obtain Western sympathy and funds, for example— is unclear. What is certain is that Israel failed to pursue it.

What was true of Israel's one-to-one contacts with each of the Arab states was true also of its negotiations with the Arabs under UN auspices at Lausanne in the spring and summer of 1949. There, too, Israel was ungenerous (though, needless to say, the Arabs were equally obdurate). For months, UN officials and the U.S. pressed Israel to make what they felt might be the redemptive gesture: to proclaim its willingness to take back several hundred thousand refugees. As the months dragged on and Israel remained inflexible, the Arabs became just as obstinate. When, at last, Israel offered to take back "one hundred thousand" which, in reality, as Sharett explained to his colleagues, was only sixty-five thousand (Sharett told his colleagues in Mapai that some thirty-five thousand refugees had already returned to Israel illegally or were about to return as part of the family reunification scheme, and these refugees would be deducted from the one hundred thousand), it was a case of too little too late. And Israel's more realistic offer—to take the Gaza Strip with its resident and refugee populations—was never seriously entertained by Egypt. Lausanne was probably the last chance for a comprehensive Israeli-Arab peace.

In *Pirkei Avot* it is written: "Rabbi Shimon Ben Gamliel was wont to say: On three things the world rests: On justice, on truth and on peace" (1:18). And he would quote Zechariah: " ... execute the judgment of truth and peace in your gates" (8:16). Telling the truth thus seems to be an injunction anchored in Jewish tradition, and the scriptures apparently link truth to peace in some indeterminate manner.

The new history is one of the signs of a maturing Israel (though, no doubt, there are those who say it is a symptom of decay and degeneration). What is now being written about Israel's past seems to offer us a more balanced and a more "truthful" view of that country's history than what has been offered hitherto. It may also in some obscure way serve the purposes of peace and reconciliation between the warring tribes of that land. □

'67 Remembered

Irena Klepfisz

for Khane

In '67 you visited with your sister.
I was in Chicago. Richard Speck had just murdered
seven nurses. We were scared. The war was only
a few days over   and everyone said
how well you and Gitl looked. Who would
have thought   you'd just come
from a war-torn country
dressed chic   in late '60s fashion
smiling   easy   relaxed
confident   the worst was over?
I still have the photographs.

How different   that war
from that other   in your life:
Siberia   the Germans at your heels
your father chopping trees in the forest.
You learned Russian in the street
spoke Yiddish at home   wrote Polish
in the segregated schools. You were
a linguist at eight   ready to master
even more tongues   for the sake of survival.

But in '67   you'd already mastered
it all. You were so relaxed   so easy.
It was a   joke this war   despite
the casualties. It was a joke
how relaxed   you were.

And wasn't I too?   Weren't we all?
Didn't we all glow from it
our sense of power finally achieved?
The quickness of the action
the Biblical routes
and how we laughed over
Egyptian shoes in the sand

how we laughed at another people's fear
as if fear was alien
as if we had known safety   all our lives.

And the Bank?
I don't remember it mentioned
by any of us.
We were in Chicago—it was hard to imagine.
But twenty years later
I hear how they picked up what they could
placed it on their backs

how they marched through the hills
sparse   coarse grass   pink and yellow flowers
rough rocks   defying cultivation
how they carried   clumsy packs
clothing   utensils   images of a home
they might   never see again.
A sabra told me   who watched
their leaving as she sat safe
in an army jeep: it looked no different
than the newsreels at school
of French   Belgian roads. It was simple
she said: people were fleeing   and
_we_ egged them on.

Time passes. Everything changes.
We see things differently.
In '67 you had not married yet   and we all
wondered why   never worrying about
marriage laws   or rabbinic power.
And now more than 20 years later
you live in Jerusalem   ruling
from your lacquered kitchen   and sit
in that dream house   trapped:
enough food   in your mouth
in your children's   and enough warm things
for winter (coats   shoes   woolen stockings
good for Siberia)
and there's no way out   no one to call
about a bad marriage. It's simple:
a woman   without bruises
your lawyer says   there's not much hope
and you accept it:
I can't say I'm happy   but
I've got a truce.

Things fester. We compromise.
We wake up   take new positions
to suit new visions   failed dreams.
We change. Power does not so much corrupt
as blur the edges
so we no longer feel   the raw fear
that pounds in the hearts
of those trapped   and helpless.
In '67 in Chicago   we thought we'd be safe
locking the windows   till Speck was caught.
We did not know   there was a danger
in us as well   that we must remain vigilant
and open   not to power
but peace.

What Kind of State is a Jewish State?

Michael Walzer

"Wait and see" may well be the best answer to the question posed by my title. The citizens of Israel (Jews and non-Jews alike) are actively engaged in a political process through which the meaning of their statehood will emerge. The process has no fixed or necessary endpoint; the "emergence" of meaning is continuous, incomplete, always contested. But at some point in the future, probably the near future, we will see more clearly than we now can what the weight of Jewishness will be in the life of the state. Conceivably Israel will simply be an Israeli state, Jewishness a feature of its founding but a declining influence on its existence. Or, by contrast, Jewish statehood may turn out to be as normal as early Zionist writers hoped it would be, providing a center for Jewish life and opening the way for a new national culture. Or, by contrast again, Jewish statehood may turn out to be as abnormal as (some) religious Zionists believed it would be—"the dawn of our redemption." In any case, the contest will continue through our lifetime, and while only Israeli citizens can participate in the successive decisions (for the third outcome, however, they would require divine assistance), Jews in the Diaspora can hardly help but have hopes and opinions. What follows is my own opinion. I put it forward with the humility of an onlooker and the passion of an interested party.

I

How should the adjective "Jewish" modify the noun "state"? The view of religious Zionists is that "Jewish" is a strong or authoritative modifier, so that a Jewish state is one governed, so far as possible, by the requirements of Halakha, by the laws of traditional rabbinic Judaism. But this is a curious view, since rabbinic Judaism first took shape as a response to the collapse of statehood. It represented a creative adaptation to new and difficult circumstances (the Roman Conquest and the destruction of the Temple), and one might think that further adaptations are required as circumstances change. What is today called "Orthodoxy" provided the hegemonic structures of Jewish life from the loss of independence until the beginnings of emancipation—but not before and not since. Even during those long centuries of statelessness and oppression, Orthodoxy's hegemony was never total. The authority of the Rabbis was challenged by Karaite schismatics, Sabbatean messianists, Hasidic pietists, and an ever-renewed succession of rationalists and mystics. But in the politics of exile—in communal government and in the legal control of everyday life—the rabbinic understanding of Judaism was dominant. It was the rabbis who held the Jewries of exile together.

Before the exile, national independence provided the necessary conditions for partisan conflict and political opposition—thus the struggles for power between Sadducee aristocrats and Pharisee sages, and the fierce sectarianism that marked the two centuries before 70 C.E. And today emanci-

Michael Walzer is a professor of social science at the Institute for Advanced Study in Princeton, New Jersey. He is coeditor with Irving Howe of Dissent *and author most recently of* The Company of Critics: Social Criticism and Political Commitment in the Twentieth Century *(Basic Books, 1988). This article was originally given as a talk at the Shalom Hartman Institute in Jerusalem. It appeared in* Tikkun, *July/August 1989.*

pation provides the necessary conditions for dissent and separation—by Reform congregations, for example, whose members decline to be ruled by Halakha, or by individual Jews or members of *havurot*, who design their own Judaism, protected by a secular and liberal state. In the years between independence and emancipation, however, the possibilities for Jewish life were cramped and limited. The scattered communities were small, vulnerable, beset by enemies; unity was the first prerequisite of their continued existence. Though there were many conflicts within the communities—between rich and poor, rabbis and lay leaders—sustained political opposition would have been very dangerous. And separation was virtually impossible short of conversion; even intimations of separation—the resort to non-Jewish courts, for example—were viewed as a threat to communal security and were strongly condemned.

So each exilic community was, in a sense, a "Torah state"—but only because of the statelessness and unfreedom of Jewry as a whole. Gentile rulers, who simultaneously tolerated and exploited these Jewish communities, found their unity convenient; it made for easy tax collection and cheap government. The great premodern empires practiced a kind of corporate pluralism, and sometimes, at least, the Jews were allowed to organize themselves as one corporation among many and to live according to their own traditions, subject to their traditional leaders. Though the tradition certainly changed over time—more than contemporary Orthodox Jews are ready to acknowledge—it was also remarkably stable, for the conditions of corporate life were repeated in one Diaspora home after another. But emancipation, and now statehood, has changed all that. Shouldn't it also change the role of the modifier "Jewish"?

II

The Jewish state has its origins in the disruption of the old Jewish ministates—the autonomous communities that first took shape in Babylonia and finally disintegrated, several millennia later, in czarist Russia. No doubt, these communities served the Jewish people well, but it is important to recognize that their disintegration was welcomed by a great many, perhaps by most, of their members. The old corporate structures, already in decay, were now felt to hinder rather than protect individual and collective creativity. "Emancipation" was not a sectarian label; nor was it, by and large, a merely partisan choice. The generally liberal-leftist politics of modern Jews expresses first of all a strong preference for states and parties committed to freedom and equal opportunity. Certainly, Jews seized upon the new possibilities of the emancipated life—not only economically but also politically and intellectually. The last two centuries have seen a proliferation of sects, parties, movements, and schools of thought unlike anything in Jewish history except, perhaps, for the sectarianism and party conflicts of the Second Commonwealth.

Having been emancipated by choice, Diaspora Jews are now liberals by necessity. Our commitment to civil rights and liberties, to individualism and pluralism, derives partly from the fact that we are, in all the countries of our exile, a small and still vulnerable minority. But it derives also from the fact that we are now a *divided* minority. The liberal state not only protects us against coercion by non-Jews: special taxes, the denial of political rights, limits on economic activity, intermittent violence, social degradation—all the things that made the old communities so important to Jewish survival. It also protects us against coercion by other Jews, against the community itself. I will offer only easy and familiar examples of this double protection; the list in fact is very long. In the United States today, Orthodox Jews are not compelled to send their children to state (secular) schools, and, at the same time, secular Jews are not compelled to send their children to religious schools. Conservative and Reform Jews organize their congregational life without constraint either by state officials or by Orthodox rabbis. Jews who wish to do so submit themselves to the rabbinic courts; those who don't, don't.

American Jewry can be conceived of as a voluntary association; or as a series of voluntary associations, loosely connected; or as a collection of individuals, differentially committed and identified. In any case, it isn't a corporation, a single, self-governing community, or a ministate. And this is true throughout the Diaspora, even where such old corporate offices as the chief rabbinate still survive. Everywhere, the Jews are divided; the forms of Jewishness (and of Judaism too) are many and various; the institutional structures of Jewish life are independent of one another; no central or authoritative leadership exists. The liberal state tolerates all the versions of Jewishness. It doesn't judge their relative value, nor does it act to enhance or reinforce whatever internal discipline particular groups of Jews accept for themselves. This is what it means to be emancipated.

Only in Israel do Jews now have a corporate existence. But this is a highly problematic corporatism, for the emancipated Jewishness of the Diaspora has been "ingathered" by, and must now be accommodated within, the new state. All the vibrant variousness of contemporary Jewry has come home, and as a result Jews in the Third Commonwealth are as divided as they were almost two thousand years ago in the Second. And political independence provides once again a public space within which these divisions can be acted out. What kind of an adjective can "Jewish" be in these circumstances? Those who believe that "Jewish" should be a strong modifier would use state power to reverse the process of emancipation, that is, to favor, sponsor, and eventually enforce a single version of Jewishness; or, less ambitious and a little more realistic, they would ask the state to set clear limits on the range of difference. The crucial sign of their intentions (and of their partial success) is the rule of religious courts in matters of personal status: one set of courts, legally authorized to apply halakhic law, with jurisdiction over all of Israel's Jewish citizens. But these courts confront more than one set of Jews.

What the Diaspora has bequeathed to Israel is a number of ways of being Jewish. (Zionism was originally one of the ways, though it soon became apparent that there was also more than one Zionism.) The number includes what was once unimaginable—not only different nonreligious ways, emphasizing language or culture or nationality or politics, but also different religious ways. For obvious reasons, though nonreligious difference is politically more significant, religious difference is intellectually more threatening to the Orthodox—hence the heatedness of the battle over Jewish identity and membership. Should Israel set out to reduce the number of ways of being Jewish? Is that what it means to come home? These questions are not so easy to answer; they point toward a dilemma. If that's what home means, then Jews could "come home" simply by restoring the corporate rule of the old Diaspora communities. And if that isn't what it means, then Jews can stay home (as they are in fact doing) wherever they already enjoy the fruits of emancipation. What difference do statehood and sovereignty make?

In practice, the restoration of corporatism is not a real possibility, not in the Diaspora and not in Israel. Emancipation is an irreversible experience, very much like the Reformation in Christian history: There is no way back to a single unified faith. Hence the establishment of Orthodoxy as the only legitimate version of Jewishness (or as the only legitimate version of Judaism) would make Israel into something other than a Jewish state. We would need a second adjective: an *Orthodox* Jewish state, which is to say, a state for some Jews, uncongenial to the greater number, who would be more free to express their Jewishness in the (liberal) Diaspora than in the homeland. "Jewish" cannot be a strong modifier without also being a divisive modifier and itself requiring modification. A state that was simply "Jewish" would have to reflect the experience of the entire Jewish people, not simply of some subgroup within it. But can there be any substance in such a reflection— anything we can put our hands on, *takhlis*, concrete, practical—given the extraordinary diversity and the internal contradictions of that experience?

III

A brief digression on Who-Is-a-Jew—the issue is politically and intellectually unavoidable. And it is in answering this question that we are forced in the most dramatic way to recognize the impact of Diaspora experience upon Israeli state policy. The question has to be answered because of the Law of Return, which establishes Israel as a refuge for Jews in trouble anywhere in the world. Zionism isn't only a rescue operation, but it is importantly that. Nor does the Zionist state rescue only Jews; it participates along with other states in international efforts to help different groups of persecuted or stateless men and women. Still, it acknowledges a special commitment to Jews. Hence, who is a Jew? To whom is the commitment made? Who benefits?

The most obvious answer is that the benefit belongs to anyone who meets the traditional requirements of Jewish law—who has a Jewish mother or who has been converted according to Halakha. But there is one overwhelming difficulty with this answer. The people who make trouble for the Jews have never felt themselves bound by Jewish law. And if the persecutors ignore the halakhic criteria, how can the rescuers adhere to them? Anti-Semitism has regularly extended to people who have only Jewish fathers (or only Jewish grandfathers) as well as to "irregular" converts. And surely all those to whom it extends are entitled to the refuge that Zionism promises. It may sound perverse, but in deciding who is eligible for Return, the Nuremberg laws are more relevant than Halakha.

And if those upon whom Jewish identity has been forcibly imposed are eligible, all the more so are those who voluntarily join the Jewish people and agree to share its destiny. Recall the case of Rina Eitani in the 1960s—a woman who had followed her Jewish husband into a German concentration camp but was denied admission to Israel under the Law of Return because her subsequent conversion did not meet halakhic standards. I would suggest that she became a Jew the moment she entered the camp, for that act bespoke a commitment above and beyond the law: *Your people shall be my people....* To put the matter less dramatically, the Law of Return must cover all those men and women in the Diaspora who suffer or who might suffer *as Jews*, whether Orthodox rabbis think they are Jews or not. Admissions policies can't be governed by the need to preserve the purity of the refuge, only by the need to help the refugees.

IV

Beyond the requirements of the Law of Return, there is no reason for the Jewish state to take an interest in the religious status of its citizens. But then, again, in what sense is it a *Jewish* state? What can "Jewish" mean if it is a weak or, perhaps better, a liberal modifier? Contemporary American political theorists commonly believe that a liberal state must be neutral in matters of religion, indeed, in all matters (cultural, historical) in which particular forms of life might find expression. That view is right to this extent: that the state provides a frame, a protective structure, and that within this frame individuals and groups cultivate diverse forms of life. The State of Israel, insofar as it is a liberal state, sponsors and underwrites a rich, lively, contentious civil society—which is made up, in its largest part, of Jews arguing with one another. There is no need for the state to resolve the arguments; they can be settled, if they have to be settled, in nonpolitical ways or, at least, without coercion.

But this is not the whole meaning of statehood. A state also provides public places and public occasions for a common life, and this is always a life of a particular sort, determined by the dominant culture of civil society. Every state has a particular character; a literally neutral state, a state whose common life was evacuated of all content, while (perhaps) not conceptually impossible, is radically improbable in practice and without example in history. So even if the adjective "Jewish" is a weak adjective, it still must modify "state" in *some* determinate way (that's what adjectives do). Not that "Jewish state" must take on a meaning something like "Islamic republic" in its present

Iranian usage. "Islamic" is currently a strong modifier, but one can imagine its being weakened, much as "Jewish" has been weakened through the effects of emancipation, sectarian division, and modern secularism. In any case, given these effects, a Jewish state today cannot enforce a singular and uniform Jewishness. It can, however, express in public places and on public occasions—in its official calendar, its evocative symbols, its formal ceremonies, its historical celebrations, its school curriculum—a version of Jewishness (loosely structured, latitudinarian) common or potentially common to all the varieties of Jews. I suppose I should say "almost all," for there are bound to be ideologically driven refusals of commonality: sectarian schism, alienation, and withdrawal. Under conditions of freedom, Judaism will produce its own versions of Amish and Mennonite sectaries, say, just as it once produced the Essenes.

But won't this "common" Jewishness represent the lowest common denominator of Jewish life? Yes, that is exactly what it will and should do, though it need not be "low" in the sense of base or coarse; nor need it be simplistic, sentimental, and empty. Israel's common Jewishness should be, to change my metaphor, a distillation of Jewish history and values in which all (or almost all) Jews can recognize themselves. What content the distillation will have, how rich it will be, depends on the creativity of Israeli Jews—on the continuing work of poets, philosophers, artists, historians, and novelists. Bialik's poems, studied by schoolchildren, suggest one possibility; the appropriation of the Amalek story by right-wing politicians suggests another.

The rabbis and halakhic sages of Israel will also participate in this construction of a common Jewishness. But the effectiveness of their participation must depend upon their persuasiveness. They shouldn't be able, any more than the poets are able, to call upon the coercive power of the state. The sages can be legislators for Israel only in the extended sense given to that word by Shelley, when he called poets the "legislators of the world." Under the conditions of statehood, Halakha must become a speculative endeavor, an articulation of a certain kind (not the only kind) of Jewish idealism or even of Jewish perfectionism. It has a possible influence on the common life—of roughly the same sort that Catholic natural law doctrine has on American life when it is applied by American bishops to nuclear deterrence or to the ordering of the economy. Statehood gives the rabbis a new reason to extend and elaborate halakha and to address as wide a range of issues as the bishops do. But the rabbis cannot claim, in the open society that the state frames and protects, the same authority that they once exercised in the closed society of the medieval commune. They have only the authority of their arguments.

What this means in practice is that in a Jewish state, where "Jewish" is a weak or liberal modifier, the religious courts (Islamic and Christian, of course, as well as Jewish) can judge only those who agree to be judged. The judicial system should be like the educational system, with parochial institutions always available but never compulsory. State courts will of course be influenced—though to what degree we can't predict—by the Jewish legal tradition; but they will also be influenced, given the history of the Middle East, by Ottoman and British traditions. And, similarly, state schools will teach the history of the Jews but also a more general history. The contrast between what goes on in the parochial institutions and what goes on in the public institutions will never be an absolute contrast between Jewish particularism and civic neutrality. Rather, there will be a variety of particularisms and an always un-finished but nonetheless recognizable common life. The contrast is partial and endlessly contested.

One can imagine a number of stopping points in this ongoing contest, all of them temporary. Jewish Israel may one day look like Catholic Ireland in the days of Joyce—priest-ridden and parochial, the largely negative inspiration of its greatest writers. Or it may look like Catholic France in the age of Jaurès and Clemenceau, anticlerical and secularist, home to the cultural avant-garde. The adjective "Jewish" doesn't by itself rule out these (or many other) possibilities. But if we give it its broadest sense, allow it to incorporate the full range of Jewish experience in the modern world, then it points toward a liberal state in which clerics and anticlerics, rabbis and secular intellectuals, peacefully (I don't mean harmoniously) coexist.

V

Liberalism, however, isn't only for the Jews. We still need to ask how the adjective "Jewish" can modify a state that includes Arabs as free and equal citizens. Obviously, if "Jewish" is a strong adjective, the inclusion of Arabs is impossible; at best, they would be granted the same kind of corporate autonomy that Jews enjoyed (some of the time, in some places) in the centuries before emancipation. Like the Jews again, they would be denied civil rights. But we have reason to know that arrangements of this sort make for a precarious and vulnerable existence; having ourselves escaped from them, we would have difficulty explaining why we were prepared to impose them on another people. In any case, corporate autonomy works best under conditions of benevolent absolutism or imperial rule; it isn't compatible with democratic self-government.

So: How can a Jewish state, committed to democracy, include Arabs? Some people, worrying about this question (it needs to be worried about!), decided long ago that it was necessary to find another adjective. Since states need adjectives, since political communities must be identified in some determinate way with their own citizens, we must look, they argued, for an identity that predates or transcends the Arab/Jewish distinction. The number of possibilities is fairly limited—Semite, Canaanite, Hebrew, Israeli—and none of them is quite satisfactory. For names of this sort are not matters of mere willfulness, used and disused as we please. Of course, they don't correspond to essences; names and identities are social constructions. But they are constructed over many years and many generations; they tap into the deepest levels of collective self-consciousness. There is no contemporary (or, for that matter, historical) group of Arabs and Jews that answers to the name of Semite or Canaanite; Hebrew is the name of a language that Israeli Jews and Arabs speak, but not the name of a people or a culture; and Israeli is a name still to be tested, an indication of civic status, not yet of cultural or (for the Arabs at least) of national belonging.

It is probably better to acknowledge the separate identities of the two peoples rather than to search for some artificial unity. The Arabs are a minority that should be included in Israel much as Jewish minorities, after emancipation, are included in states where most of their fellow citizens are non-Jews. Or, more generally, Arabs should be included much as any national minority is included in a "liberal" state shaped by, and in some sense for, the majority nation. There are many examples of such inclusion, enough of them problematic, however, so that some further description is required. I will try to indicate the conditions that might justify this particular kind of majority rule. But I don't mean to suggest that these conditions already exist, either in Israel or anywhere else.

Consider, then, the life of an ethnic minority in a country, say, where the public calendar, the evocative symbols that mark public occasions and public spaces, the history taught in the public schools are all of them alien to the minority members, all of them determined by another ethnicity. The minority members are citizens, nonetheless, with full rights not only of ethnic association and religious worship but also of political participation; they are not discriminated against in either public or private employment, nor are they subject to any special laws that don't apply to everyone else. They can organize, publish, petition, agitate, and vote. But because they are a small group, easily outvoted, they have a very limited capacity to shape the culture of their "own" country. There are, I suppose, kinds and degrees of "own-ness." Arabs and Jews in France do not expect to find their own history taught in the public schools—as they would, say, in Algeria or in Israel. French men and women who have stayed behind in Algeria and chosen Algerian citizenship do not expect public celebrations (or a holiday from work) on Bastille Day or on Christmas. But none of these

Photo by Marke Darul Webb

people are degraded by their negative expectations, nor does liberalism require us to deny the place of French history in French schools or of the Islamic calendar in Algerian public life.

Standard American liberalism holds that the state is allowed its civic symbols and historical celebrations only so long as they are narrowly political, focused on itself. But it must not appropriate the symbols and celebrations of any subgroup of its citizens. The citizens have their own social, cultural, and religious life, which the state systematically ignores. This is a view that nicely fits the American experience, where the state is, almost from the beginning, independent of the groups that supply its citizens and where all its citizens belong, so it is commonly said, to one or another minority. But the American experience is historically uncommon; most states are closely connected to a particular national majority; symbols and celebrations are shared by the state and the nation, and it is hard to mark off what is civic or political from what is social or cultural or even religious. A state of this sort can still be liberal, open, and pluralist, guaranteeing the rights of individuals and groups without discriminating among them. But it will have a particular identity that isn't shared in the full sense by all its citizens. Members of minority groups will argue about this identity—as "Third World" Americans do, for example, when they hold that Western culture should be deemphasized in the public school curriculum (an argument suggesting that even the United States has its public particularism). But they cannot be guaranteed victory in such arguments: they have only the right to make their case as persuasively as they can. To study someone else's history in school, so long as the student is free to study his or her own history outside of school, is neither degrading nor oppressive. The particularities of public education can certainly be made degrading for this or that minority, but that is an outcome relatively easy to avoid.

There is, then, nothing necessarily discriminatory in the inclusion of Arabs in a Jewish state (where "Jewish" is a weak or liberal modifier). The fact that the Jews are a religious as well as a national entity, however, makes for special difficulties. Who can imagine, for example, Muslim and Christian Arabs ever joining with goodwill in the singing of *Hatikvah*, a song that expresses a peculiarly Jewish yearning for Zion, as much religious as nationalist in spirit? How does one teach the history of the Jews, which is also, but not only, the political history of the State of Israel, to both Jewish and non-Jewish citizens? I can't answer such questions, though I can imagine a number of accommodating and liberal answers. The greatest difficulty, however, lies in the constant temptation to find some institutional match for the coexistence of nation and religion, to move Judaism to the center of the political stage—and so to drive non-Jews to the margins. The Jewish equivalent of the church-state conflict pits those who would yield to this temptation against those who would resist or repress it. Though the conflict is obscured by external dangers, it is likely to grow more intense in coming years. But it doesn't have to be resolved (nor does the state have to be triumphant) before there can be a liberal regime. As the history of the French Third Republic suggests, the conflict can itself be acted out in a liberal fashion, through the characteristic arrangements of democratic politics. This means, of course, that Arab citizens will play a part in determining its outcome, just as Jews and Protestants played a part in the French case.

But this defense of the liberal nation-state will succeed only in countries where national minorities are relatively small—like the Jews in the United States or the Arabs in France, or if we turn to near-liberal though non-democratic Third World countries, the Copts in Egypt or the Chinese in Indonesia. What we might think of as liberal particularism won't work or won't readily work with very large minorities. For then statehood would need two distinct and possibly inconsistent modifiers—that is, it would have to be binational in character. Binationalism is obviously not impossible; Belgium is a relatively successful example of it. But Cyprus and Lebanon are examples closer to the realities of the contemporary Middle East. The alternative to binationalism is partition: two states, each with its own adjective. In both these cases, politics follows culture; and follow it must, unless the state undertakes a Kulturkampf against some subset of its own members.

Hence the choice that faces Greater Israel today: it can become a non-Jewish or a half-Jewish state (whatever binationalism means), or it can become a small Jewish state living side by side with a small Arab state—"Little Israel" and littler Palestine, each including an Arab or a Jewish minority while also claiming its own national identity.

There is, of course, a third possibility: Greater Israel can become an illiberal or an antiliberal Jewish state. Then the Arabs would have to be wholly excluded, not only culturally but also politically, their fate either subordination or expulsion. For the Arabs of Greater Israel can't plausibly be called a national minority; they are substantially a nation. Hence there is no way, so far as they are concerned, in which "Jewish" can be a liberal adjective; it doesn't indicate merely an unfamiliar public culture but an actively oppressive politics. I am inclined to argue that, given current conditions, it can't be a liberal adjective for the Jews either; that is, as the Jews' relationship to the Arab minority now stands, it can't represent a distillation of Jewish history and values in which all Jews might recognize themselves. Jews who are fully aware of their own (Diaspora) history might well come to identify with the Arabs rather than with the Jews of Greater Israel. Indeed, if the policy euphemistically named "transfer" were ever put into effect, wouldn't the exiled Arabs be more like the Jews of Spain in 1492, and the Jews more like the Spaniards?

VI

Years of exile and persecution have bred among the Jews, or rather among some Jews, a burning desire for a turnabout of just this kind. This desire has left its mark on religious literature and also on some versions of secular—for example, Revisionist— politics. Religiously, this desire takes the form of a messianic triumphalism, a vision of redemption as hegemony, the rule of Israel over the "nations." All this, thankfully, only in the end of days, after Armageddon; and, like one of the rabbis cited in the Talmud, I hope not to live to see it. If there is redemption short of Armageddon, it will have to take a very different form, more like those pastoral and peaceful visions that also figure in the Jewish tradition. In any case, the dichotomy between exile and redemption isn't very helpful in our present circumstances. The Jewish State of Israel is neither the one nor the other. It really represents, as the early Zionists hoped it would, a triumph of the ordinary—which is to say that it occupies the largely unexplored theoretical landscape between exile and redemption. One has only to visit Israel to learn what most of its citizens know very well and are more than ready to say: these are nothing like messianic times. All that the present moment offers is a chance, a *chance,* for a normal Jewish life.

For many Orthodox Jews, however, Jewish normality includes religious coercion—much as Christian and Islamic normality does in the eyes of zealous believers. What can we say to such people? There are two arguments against coercion. The first, which I have not tried to make here, holds that religious commitment and personal freedom are closely, perhaps necessarily, connected. Faith must be free. This is an argument that can be read into the Jewish tradition, on some nonstandard interpretations of that tradition. But it probably presupposes a liberal understanding of both religion and personality, and it won't appeal much to people with different understandings.

The second argument is more practical and institutional in character: it holds that coercive methods, in the aftermath of emancipation, are radically ineffective. There is no going back, as I have already said, to medieval corporatism; nor does coercion offer any way forward to a redemptive politics. It can make only for local ugliness: cruelty and high-handedness tempered by hypocrisy and corruption. What is necessary now—what life in a Jewish state both requires and makes possible—is halakhic revisionism. Just as the Rabbis reconstructed biblical law to meet the conditions of statelessness, so now rabbinic law must be reconstructed to meet the conditions of liberal statehood.

This reconstruction will leave Judaism without an overt political role—without a claim on the resources of the state to punish blasphemy, say, or idolatry, or violations of the Sabbath, or to enforce the rulings of rabbinic courts on such matters as marriage and divorce. Halakhic observance will be, as is true in the Diaspora, entirely free. Still, I have tried to deny what many liberals take to be the necessary corollary of religious freedom—that is, absolute state neutrality. I see no reason why Judaism, and secular versions of Jewishness too, should not play a part in shaping the political culture of the Jewish state. It should be an occasion for pride, not moral anxiety, for example, when talmudic conceptions of equity are invoked in the course of a Knesset debate about taxation. We should be eager to have the Hebrew Bible read and critically discussed in the state schools. The public celebration of a holiday like Chanukah should not be taken as an affront to liberal sensibilities. At the same time, of course, talmudic conceptions of equity will have to compete with other conceptions; Plato's *Republic* should also be required reading; no one can be compelled to celebrate Chanukah. Jewish statehood requires nothing more than this. But we can also say, without embarrassment or apology, that emancipation, liberalism, and pluralism don't require anything less. □

In Defense of Settlement: An Interview with Professor Yoseph Ben-Shlomo

An Interview by Adi Ophir

Adi Ophir: Can you expound on the essentials of your philosophy of history, and show how two events—the Holocaust and the Six Day War—fit into it?

Professor Yoseph Ben-Shlomo: I won't talk about the Holocaust. It is too early to relate to that event, and I object to attempts to interpret it. The Satmar Rebbe's explanation of the Holocaust as a punishment for Zionism is disgraceful. Nor do I accept the interpretation by Zionist circles that the Holocaust played a dialectical role in the establishment of Israel. I think it's too shallow-minded. Don't forget that only seventy years after the great catastrophe of medieval Jewry—the expulsion from Spain—the first spiritual reaction took shape. Lurian Kabbala was a great success, it dominated Jewish mystics, and this was because it represented a metaphysical expression of the historical event which was the expulsion from Spain. The expulsion was reinterpreted into a voluntary self-contraction of God's presence in the world—a divinity that expels itself. Yet R. Isaac Luria makes no explicit reference to the expulsion from Spain, not even a single word. Compared to the Holocaust, the expulsion from Spain was a trifle. Do you expect me to respond appropriately to the Holocaust only fifty years later, while some of the victims are still living among us? So I won't talk about the meaning of the Holocaust.

One can understand history in two ways: as a continuity of events succeeding one another in time—the descriptive and analytic attitude of the historian—or as a process of meaning and laws. The latter I call historiosophy, the great innovation of Judaism. It is historiosophy, including the messianic idea, that marks the Western Judeo-Christian culture that grew out of the Bible. Ernest Renan, for example, viewed the philosophy of history as the great achievement of Judaism. Even Sartre, at the end of his life, said this about the messianic idea.

Unlike the Greek and Roman historians, the Bible was "weak" in historiography. In a manner that looks "provincial" it ascribes central importance to events that are marginal in the history of the ancient East. Deutero-Isaiah, for example, describes all the conquests and wars of Cyrus in Babylon as leading to Cyrus' proclamation that Jews may return to Zion. Historiographically, this is absurd. After the fact, however, it seems that Isaiah was right: Of everything he did, Cyrus will be remembered in human history as the man whose proclamation made the Return to Zion possible, and thereby Christianity, and the matter is well known. Events such as the Exodus or the Hasmonaeian rebellion were local, and left no mark on the historiography of their time. The Exodus is not mentioned in any Egyptian document. But these events are of supreme importance in history. Even

---

Professor Yoseph Ben-Shlomo teaches Jewish philosophy at Tel Aviv University. He was a student of Gershom Scholem and is one of the prominent intellectuals of the Right in Israel. Adi Ophir teaches philosophy at Tel Aviv University. This interview appeared in Tikkun, March/April 1987.

opponents of Judaism such as Nietzsche admitted as much.

But the Bible does have historiosophy. That is, it understands events according to inner laws and meaning. This is an idea running directly from the Bible to Marx, and it is not by chance that a doctrine phrased in this manner was not produced by the great civilizations of China and India. The perspective that history is a fulfillment of certain precepts reached China from the West, and ultimately from the Bible, via its secular incarnations in Hegel—who still phrases his creed in a pseudo-religious way—and Marx.

In such a view of history, contemporary events affecting Judaism must also be given meaning in historiosophy. In principle, this includes the Holocaust.

It is self-evident that there can be different meanings, insofar as there may be different historiosophies. The ascendancy of Zionism, for example, is perceived differently by Marxists and Zionists. However, Zionism itself did not have a philosophy of history; even Ahad Ha-am did not have one. Marxist Zionists such as Syrkin and Borochov are exceptions. Zionism had a positive role in their Marxist historiosophy. The anti-Zionist Marxists believed the Jewish people were at the end of their role in history, and would be obliterated through the world revolution. The Bolshevik Revolution, it has been argued by many, was but a secular-cosmopolitan incarnation of the Jewish messianic idea, and it is therefore no great wonder that the presence of Jewish Marxists in the Bolshevik elite—from Rosa Luxembourg, to Trotsky, Zinoviev, Kamenev and others—was immeasurably greater than the proportion of Jews in the population.

All Jewish historiosophers, except for A.I. Kook, and, to a certain extent, Buber, rejected Zionism on philosophical grounds. Hermann Cohen and Franz Rosenzweig view Judaism as a faith of the spirit that needs no political fulfillment. Consider Cohen's famous pronouncement on Zionism: "These people want to be happy." Since they cannot be happy, according to Cohen, Zionism is doomed to be a passing episode. American philosophers such as Salo Baron and many East Coast Jewish-American authors think the same way. Saul Bellow, Bernard Malamud, and Philip Roth all stress the element of an outsider perspective in Judaism. This has to be taken seriously, because these attitudes are enjoying a great revival today.

One left Hegelian philosopher who became a portender of Zionism is an exceptional example in this context. He is Moses Hess, a socialist and a teacher of Marx. In his book *Rome and Jerusalem* he contends that a world center will develop in Palestine that will once again bring the Good News to the world, as did the Bible and Jesus. Hess views the return of the Jewish people to the Land of Israel as a matter of world significance.

Ophir: What about Martin Buber?

Ben-Shlomo: Although he favored the establishment of Jewish institutions in Palestine, Buber objected to the establishment of a state. Only A.I. Kook reserves a place for Zionism as an element of substance in a comprehensive system that embraces the interpretation of the relationship of God to the world and relates this to contemporary events.

Ophir: Do I understand that you consider yourself a disciple of A.I. Kook?

Ben-Shlomo: Absolutely. If his doctrine is correct, then the process clearly did not end with his death, and his disciples continue to understand subsequent events in the spirit of his teaching. The Holocaust and the Six-Day War (which is a direct continuation of the War of Independence) are part of a dialectic process preceding Redemption, a progression of precipitous descents and broken paths—three steps forward and two steps back, as Lenin said. This is neither militaristic chauvinism nor simplistic optimism. It is an interpretation that follows a philosophical system, as do Marxist, and Hegelian interpretations.

Ophir: Since you've mentioned Hegel, he holds that the identifiable and intelligible stage of the process has already ended, whereas in contemporary Orthodox Judaism, the emphasis is placed on active involvement in history.

Ben-Shlomo: Certainly. "The owl of Minerva flies at dusk," and the historian who describes our era has not yet been born. For anyone who accepts Hegel's doctrine, every action is a gamble whose results will become apparent only in the future. You believe you know in what direction things will develop, and you go with it. Man cannot sit on the sidelines altogether; he is an active historical creature. If you don't believe this, you are neither a Hegelian nor a Marxist, and you do not even belong to the Judeo-Christian tradition, for this is the idea that makes the tradition distinct from that of Oriental civilizations (which I do not disparage). Here, too, Jews depart from the Greeks. For Aristotle, man is a *political creature*, but in Judaism man is an *historical one*.

The problem of the relation between the "lawfulness" of the historical process and the freedom of man participating in it is not particular to A.I. Kook's historiosophy; it perturbs every Marxist, and is not substantially different from the general problem of freedom of the individual (in the metaphysical sense): Some things are permanent, and others can be changed. The Sages were puzzled by the contradiction between two terms applied to Redemption: "speedy," and "in due time" (cf. Isaiah 60:22). They resolved it as follows: "If they merit [it], [the Lord] will speed it. If they do not merit [it], it will [occur] in due time." The historical process can be accelerated or slowed, but natural law is objective and acts on its own. As Hegel emphasized, understanding the logic of a process plays a positive part in the process itself.

Ophir: Can one discuss and predict the substance of Redemption?

Ben-Shlomo: It's impossible to describe Redemption concretely. There are, of course, literary visions: "Every man under his vine and his figtree," or "And they shall beat their swords into plowshares." But there is no point in trying to prophesize; it is not even fair. In any event, visions of Redemption are always the Biblical-classical ones. Most important of all—from the Bible through Moses Hess to Gershom Scholem and Buber—it is clear that the Jewish people have a special role in the process; they are a chosen people. The idea of chosen people can be interpreted in contradictory ways. Franz Rosenzweig, a man of the most profound philosophical thought, takes this idea, adds Hegelian and Existentialist considerations, and arrives at a rejection of Zionism—whereas Buber lauds it. Sartre, too (and I deliberately mention names that are not suspect of primitive religiosity), understood by the end of his life the need for a "singular people"—a historical entity with the special avant-garde role of causing fermentation. This typifies that trend in modern Judaism (alone) that the literary critic B. Kurzweil called "anti-destiny." One can argue as the writer Hazaz does in *Ha-Drasha* (the Sermon): "I'm sick of being chosen and afflicted; there is no Jewish history, let's go out and play soccer." This is how early Zionist thinkers like Berdyczewski and Klatzkin—not Ahad Ha-am—looked at the matter, and this is how Israeli politicians like Abba Eban or Amnon Rubinstein think. But there is no ignoring the idea of a chosen people, and anyone who understands it does not confuse it with racism. One reason is that one of the basic elements built into the idea as early as the Bible is an added measure of suffering, not of benefit.

The problem, as I said, is that modern perspectives in Judaism do not view the State as part of the fulfillment of the chosen people idea, but rather as something of a contradiction to it. Only A.I.

Kook thinks differently, and he is religious and Orthodox. Hence the anti-Zionism of American Jewish thought, and what is left of Jewish thought in England and France. For this reason I'll follow the coming issues of *Tikkun* magazine with interest. Perhaps they'll provide a new perspective in this field.

Ophir: I understand that in your view Zionism has not come to an end; it continues to exist, and its most conspicuous manifestations today are found in Gush Emunim.

Ben-Shlomo: Not only in Gush Emunim, but in anyone who views Zionism both ideologically and practically and not just pragmatically. Gush Emunim does stand out, because it surfaced at a time— 1973—when Zionism was in the doldrums. It is a matter of pioneerism. It was not confined to Gush Emunim alone; it embraced the entire "Greater Israel Movement," which represented non-Orthodox people and included not only a man like Uri Zvi Greenberg—a great poet who was labelled a "Fascist"—but great luminaries of the spirit like Alterman, Agnon, Hazaz, and Dob Sadan, as well as a political leader like Tabenkin and the Ahdut ha-Avoda Movement. Individuals like M.K. (Member of the Knesset) Shulamit Aloni and Amnon Rubinstein view Zionism pragmatically—a movement aiming to set up a state like all other states. Not an Albania, to be sure, but a Denmark. But the fateful question is why bother to establish a state *like* Denmark, when one can live in Denmark. We all believe in democracy, freedom, justice, and order, but these are pan-human values, not Zionist ones. You can't persuade a Jew to leave the country he's living in and come live in Israel on their basis alone, for in such a perspective Israel forgoes its Jewish uniqueness.

This is the "normalist" trend in today's Judaism, and it is leading back to the territorialism of Herzl and Pinsker. "It doesn't matter where the Jewish State is established," they said. "We'll take Eretz Israel (the Land of Israel) wherever we go." They look on Eretz Israel as a random piece of land that serves the State of Israel.

Ophir: I believe we can now turn from historiosophy to history—to the events themselves.

Ben-Shlomo: The turning point was the Six-Day War. I would like first to stress the importance of May, 1967. While waiting for the war, many *sabras* underwent a psychic upheaval—identification with Holocaust Jewry and determination that "It won't happen here." Suddenly the peril of annihilation was in the air, and a decision was taken: Even if we are killed, we won't return to Auschwitz. May, 1967 added a historical dimension to the *sabra*'s mindset, as well as an existential comprehension that we have no one but ourselves. There are other memories, too: George Steiner sitting on the sidewalk in London wailing for Israel, Rimmon Aron saying he wouldn't want to go on living after Israel was no more, and Arthur Rubinstein telling Piatagorsky, "Come, let's die with them."

In June, both religious and non-religious Jews felt they had witnessed a miracle.There were leftists who didn't think kindly of the victory from the very beginning. George Steiner said, "So sorry we won." But spirits really did soar at first, and the Six-Day War was understood as an important stage on the way to Redemption. Very quickly, however, the process of erosion with regard to Eretz Israel and Jerusalem began to set in. The erosion does not stop at the Green Line. When you begin to doubt our moral right to Judea and Samaria, you can only agree with Professor Dan Miron and Professor Haroshovsky, who doubt the very justice of the War of Independence and our right to be here. Alterman makes the point beautifully in his last poem, "Thus Spake the Devil." The Devil realizes he cannot vanquish the nation by direct means, so he decides to infect its heart with gnawing doubt, causing it to forget that justice is on its side.

Those who forget justice is theirs in Hebron go on to forget it in Galilee—and certainly in Jerusalem, too. M.K. Yossi Sarid said it in so many words. The "Occupied Territories," as the world defines them, include not only Kedumim, where I live, but neighborhoods in Jerusalem such as Gilo and Ramat Eshkol! Half the Arabs in Galilee and the 100,000 Arabs in Jerusalem—we are lording it over them, too, against their will. The poet Wieseltier says "When the Arabs reach the shore of the Yarkon, then I'll pick up a rifle and fight them." But why stop them at the Yarkon? Why not Jaffa?! If you have no right to Hebron, you have no right to Jaffa; it's a question of ethics, not politics. I have not yet heard any serious answer to this argument, which seems infantile. Why is the Jews' "right of distress" valid in Jaffa and not elsewhere? If the essence is lacking—that Eretz Israel is your homeland, not the Palestinians'—you're just as much a colonialist in Jaffa as in Hebron! Does the Palestinian have to hand you his homeland—Jaffa, Beersheva, Acre—because there was a Holocaust?

You can sum it up in one sentence: What happened in the Six-Day War was either the liberation of territories in Eretz Israel or the beginning of the "corrupting" occupation. Only time will tell which of the two proves to be correct. I believe in the former and have rational arguments on my side. The arguments of the other side can be adduced in Abba Eban's article in Vol. 1, No. 2 of *Tikkun*. He uses the same arguments and tone about Eretz Israel that Chamberlain used about Sudetenland in 1938.

Ophir: There are general social processes associated with the Occupation, and they cannot be swept aside by calling it "liberation." I'm referring to the side effects of the Occupation: anti-democratic phenomena, moral weakening of the army, a Jewish underground that emerged in the territories. I believe you should relate to the profound discomfort in Israel, the feeling Emanuel Sivan calls "colonialism with a bad conscience."

Ben-Shlomo: Let's differentiate. If people feel bad because they're dominating a foreign people, Jaffa and Jerusalem should make them feel just as bad as Hebron does, and what such a feeling means is that Zionism is rooted in error. Respectable people hold this opinion, but it is simply anti-Zionist. As for the rest, I definitely agree with you. If the phenomena are not brought to a halt, the State of Israel will be laid to waste just as the Second Temple was. If the erosion does not stop, Hermann Cohen will have been right, and Zionism will have been a passing episode in Jewish history.

The fundamental error in your question is that it obfuscates the distinction between issues of personal ethics (like attitudes taken toward the Arabs who live in Shechem and Hebron) and the issue of our historical right to Shechem and Hebron. On the personal level, it is unethical to drive an Arab off his land. But that was done by the Hashomer Hatzair kibbutzim, not by Gush Emunim. Arabs were driven away in Jaffa and Abu-Tor, not in Kedumim! The personal side—the fact that I will not expel an Arab from his home if he does not endanger me—is obvious. But I'm speaking of parts of my homeland, which I am entitled to incorporate into my state; and I have every right to expel anyone who objects to this and compounds his objection with terror. Is it conceivable that an Englishman would part with Wales or Scotland for the sake of peace with the separatists?! The example of Sudetenland applies to the defense aspect of the problem, while the Wales example applies to the ethical side.

True, these are not pleasant matters, but if you do not understand that they are the birth pangs of a homeland, you are an out-and-out colonialist. The French were colonialists in Algeria, but not in Marseilles. Beating up or throwing out an Arab is not "colonialism with a bad conscience," but pure and simple thuggery. But this is precisely the point. If you agree that this is an occupation, then it certainly is, and behavior follows suit. If you do not believe that the Israeli army in Hebron is an occupying force, you object to Jewish acts of thuggery. For this reason, Rabbi Levinger, a leader of the settlers in Hebron, is a leading opponent of Kahane. He understands that if he wants to live in

Judea and Samaria, he must relate to his Arab neighbors as human beings and citizens.

The thought that the Occupation ends at the Green Line represents weakness of mind. The Arabs never said anything like this. They sing about returning not to Nablus but to Jaffa, and how "With blood and fire we'll liberate Galilee." Will they forget about the "plundered lands" once they're sitting in Palestinian Kalkilya, a stone's throw from Israeli Kfar Saba? Occupation prevails within the 1967 borders, too, and a concession would only elicit a greater hail of stones and bombs because it would prove that justice isn't ours. Occupation is just as unpleasant for a million Arabs as for 50,000, and after the pullback we'll have to beat up and throw out Arabs in Kalkilya. Those of "beautiful soul"—and I don't say that disparagingly—whose stomachs turn at the thought of these phenomena can only conclude as Hermann Cohen did, that Zionism was a mistake through and through. Some have indeed reached this conclusion. The only way to avoid unpleasant actions is to live in New Zealand (as the poet Dalia Rabikowitcz writes). War, however justified it may be, and the patriotism that we still consider vital, involve unpleasant deeds—as long as Redemption has not arrived. I know that some of our best people, our best pilots and warriors, are leftists. They still think it possible to avoid the decision, to claim that Occupation takes place in Hebron alone and not in Jaffa, and to create a normal state here. But the Jewish people is not a normal one, and Israel will never be a normal state! Gershom Scholem, who cannot be suspected of Gush Emunim affiliation, said: "I have never accepted the silly claim that the House of Israel is like all the nations."

I have a brother who's ultra-Orthodox. He gambles that the Jewish people can preserve itself the old-fashioned way, the ghetto and self-sequestering way. He may be right. The ultra Orthodox alternative is available now as always. True, statistics show that only three percent of the Jews are ultra-Orthodox, but M.K. Rabbi Shapira was maybe right when he said that these three percent are the ones who will survive. For the ultra-Orthodox Rabbi Shach there's no border problem; he objects to Zionist Tel Aviv as well, although you'll never hear him insinuate that we are an occupying or malicious people. He believes we ought to study Torah and wait for the Messiah. I do not accept the stance of Rabbis Shapira and Shach. I espouse the alternative offered to me by the historiosophy of A.I. Kook, and believe secularism is part of the dialectic process of history. You on the Left fail to understand that the only serious and reasonable option you still have is the anti-Zionist one, the position of Hermann Cohen or Franz Rosenzweig. It's a serious position! I have yet to hear serious arguments for an in-the-middle stance of the kind you're trying to adopt.

This is no abstract theoretical discussion; these are the visible facts. Retreat from Zionism is a psychic process, and the psyche has no "green line." We must ask ourselves: When did Zionism ever take the Arabs into account? Take, for example, the establishment of the Etzion Bloc, or settlement of the Beit Shean Valley. Those were genuine incursions into the heart of settled Arab areas (and a price was certainly paid; almost all the Etzion Bloc settlers were killed). It was the essence of Zionism. The only reason for settling there was that there were no Jews there. These reasons, ideology and security, are valid today, too, for Gush Emunim. Ethically speaking, I simply don't understand the claim: Jews settled in Hebron, twenty-nine were slaughtered in riots, so Jews aren't allowed to live in Hebron today? Pragmatically speaking, anyone who believes the Arabs will forgo the "plundered lands" when they're sitting in Kalkilya is the real "oddball mystic." If the erosion process goes on, the Palestinians will vanquish us, and rightly so. History knows no mercy, and we are collapsing from within.

Ophir: Gush Emunim criticizes the emptiness and materialism that the Left imported from the West, and professes to offer an alternative. In particular it criticizes the quest for instant solutions expressed in the name "Peace Now." Do you share this criticism?

Ben-Shlomo: Peace Now is made of individuals. Some of their best people are extremists about instant solutions in the sense you mentioned, and some are not. Politically, Peace Now is just as "now-ist" as Chamberlain at Munich. Why this historical short-sightedness? The Swiss, the Dutch, the Yugoslavs, the Greeks—all of them needed centuries to attain peace.

My basic contention is that man is not a creature contained in his present reality (a "now-ist"). By nature, he has a tendency to transcend himself. "Man searches for meaning," as psychologist Victor Frankl writes. As for simple people who are not artists or men of spirit, one of the great ways of infusing life with meaning is, of course, religion. I cannot argue against Peace Now by claiming it is a "now-ist" movement, but I can contend positively about Gush Emunim that it offers an alternative— not necessarily a religious one—to that cultural "now-ism" you mentioned, an alternative to stand alongside ultra-Orthodoxy, or Marxism, or Fascism.

Ophir: Territorial compromise is not necessarily a "now-ist" solution. Surely one can claim that the process may take decades or centuries, but that the only conceivable solution, when it comes, is compromise—a partitioning of Eretz Israel.

Ben-Shlomo: One can certainly argue that way, but I have summoned arguments that demonstrate why the path you're proposing is highly dangerous. Now the burden of proof is yours: Why will the Palestinians give up the idea of conquering the "plundered lands" once they get a state in Judea and Samaria? You will have to justify risking another war, this time fought within the 1967 borders.

I've got a solution, and here I represent myself alone. I do believe in territorial compromise. I am willing to forego three-fourths of Palestine—Mandatory Palestine. That is: Transjordan. I'm not referring at all to Biblical Eretz Israel. The historical connection to Amman is not as deep as to Hebron, and I am willing to make a concession in hopes of gaining peace. The Palestinian people were born in fraud, but a successful fraud. Today there is a Palestinian people, and we will know no quiet until a Palestinian state comes into being. Well, let it arise in Jordan. Perhaps in a vast country, at a healthy distance from Jaffa and Jerusalem, and helped along by their own internal disputes, the Palestinians will finally leave us alone.

But the discussion is purely theoretical. I have no doubt that the victory will ultimately be yours, men and women of the Left, and that will be a sorry day for us. Victory is yours because the Left dominates all the instruments of education and communication. Lies like "Settlements are supported at the expense of development towns" have become common currency in the development towns. Almost all the educators of this generation are on your side. The lie about the Palestinian people has become real, the Zionist malaise deepens, and, with it, so does the world's pressure and the temptation of peace. In the end, everyone will be ready to relinquish Judea and Samaria, probably to Hussein. The only legal basis we've got is the 1947 partition borders, and I'm convinced we'll find ourselves in a dispute about the 1947 borders "in order to prevent war, in order to spare the blood of youth." And then—in the inevitable war—we'll either reach the end of the line or reconquer Judea and Samaria (and perhaps Sinai, for the Egyptians may be tempted to get off the fence in such a situation). Then, perhaps then, we'll sober up.

Ophir: The idea that the Left is about to triumph is surprising. Any thinking person on the Left will express the exact opposite. Look at Benvenisti's conclusions about the processes of integration between Israel and the territories. Look at the *de facto* partition between Israel and Jordan of spheres of influence and control in the territories. Look at the growing numbness of the Israeli public toward the Occupation and its ethical price. Just as you ask me to argue against the risk of war, you've got to explain how we can avoid becoming the South Africa of the Middle East.

Ben-Shlomo: We'll find ourselves within fifty years in South Africa, even inside the Green Line. The same demographic forces are at work there, too. If faith in Zionism is dead, the State of Israel is a lost cause in any case. There's no way of knowing. The indications are not good, I know: Jews are leaving South Africa for Canada and Australia, not for Israel, and Western Jewry is showing no sign of a spiritual awakening. But if fifteen years ago someone had said that 170,000 Soviet Jews would settle and acculturate themselves in Israel, he would have been thought insane. The same problem existed in 1947: How could you declare a state with a million and a quarter Arabs and 600,000 Jews? "There was a miracle," said Moshe Sharett, "and the Arabs fled." You can't rely on miracles when you plan, but as Ben-Gurion said, in our history a total realist is simply a pessimist.

I, like Benvenisti, believe we ought to annex the territories. Ethically, all the Arabs in Eretz Israel should be given the right to vote. They'll have equal rights if they have equal duties. They'll pay taxes, and if they cannot serve in the army, they'll do national service and pledge allegiance to the Israeli flag, just as every American citizen pledges allegiance to the American flag. It's a risk I've got to take, and I believe in the inner dynamic of the process. Just as there are now fourteen Arab Members of Knesset today—although there should be more according to the proportion of Arabs in Israel's population—so the Jewish majority will not be undermined if the territories are annexed. Some Arabs in Judea and Samaria would certainly prefer to leave voluntarily, rather than suffer the unpleasantness of pledging allegiance to Israel. I am willing to help them. The ones who remain will be a minority that can be lived with, on condition, of course, that there is aliya. It's the same gamble we took in 1948.

Ophir: Do you consider it a reasonable gamble?

Ben-Shlomo: I consider it less risky than the pragmatic rationale. Furthermore, your gamble involves the erosion of the whole Zionist idea.

Ophir: Your gamble involves the erosion of the values of ethics and democracy.

Ben-Shlomo: Please, argue with *me*, and do not mistake me for Kahane. I, like M.K. Geula Cohen (of the right wing "Tehiya" party), favor suffrage for the Arabs in the territories. Then there's no ethical problem in pledging allegiance. The plan is obviously part of an overall rubric including a Palestinian state in Jordan. I am the one who is considering the Palestinian problem, and it is clear to me that it won't be solved with Hussein. If so, the idea that we'll augur peace by making a concession to Hussein is irrational. The gamble on Sinai was justified not only because the security risk was less, but mainly because there are no Palestinians in Sinai, and the dispute is with Egypt. Giving up Sinai was admittedly a security risk, but Judea and Samaria are a historical risk.

I am aware that the issue here is one of basic faith and a gamble. Both of us are gambling. Do not depict me as a gambler and yourself as standing on solid ground. That's not how it is. I can argue with Hazan (the venerable leader of the Zionist Left), who says, sure, Hebron is Eretz Israel, my heart bleeds, but I'm willing to give it up for peace. But Abba Eban in his latest article (in *Tikkun* Vol. 1, No. 2) doesn't discuss Eretz Israel at all. He doesn't even argue with human beings, but with imbeciles in need of medical care. I am no imbecile, and in terms of philosophy I'm no less erudite than he is. This is my claim: I'm definitely capable of seeing myself on your side, but you are unwilling to see yourselves on mine; you dehumanize me. Of course Gush Emunim has its primitive types, but you have them too, and the Bolshevik Revolution is judged by Lenin, not Stalin. You [the Left] are in error by not dealing with Gush Emunim's stance at its best; it's a stance that deserves deliberation on its own merits. You of all people, who try so hard to see things through the other side's eyes, who are capable of identifying even with Arafat, are not prepared to consider our side—and it's a great pity. ☐

Dangerous Land

Yehuda Amichai, translated by Sabina Lask-Spinac

Dangerous land. Land of suspicious objects
and booby-trapped beings. And anything can be
the beginning of a new religion: every birth, every death,
every brushfire, every wisp of smoke.
Even lovers must watch what they do and say,
hands held out for a hug, whisper at midnight,
hidden sobs, a glance into the distance, a descent
down the stairs in a white dress. All these the beginning
      of a new religion.

Even the migrating birds know this
when they come in spring and fall and do not tarry
like the gods of the earth who likewise do not tarry.
And he who says there was is a prophet of consolation
and he who says there will be is a prophet of wrath.

And from north to south there is no end to summer joy
and warnings of deep and raging waters
with warnings of drought upon the land,
and tombstones lie over the land, like weights
so annals of history won't scatter, like papers in the wind.

The Occupation: Immoral and Stupid

Michael Lerner

The widespread moral outrage at Israel's policies in Gaza and the West Bank—the sense that Israel is violating the basic values of Judaism—is coupled with a growing realization that these policies are also bad for Israel and bad for the Jewish people. Granted, some of Israel's current critics have been unfair, both in their failure to acknowledge the role of Palestinian leaders and Arab states in creating the conflict, and in their tendency to judge Israel by standards that they rarely apply to the rest of the world. Nevertheless, from the standpoint of Jewish ethics and Jewish survival the Occupation is unacceptable. There are plausible solutions to the Palestinian problem that must be tried. But they won't be tried unless American Jews unequivocally tell Israel that the Occupation cannot continue. This message must be conveyed forcefully to Prime Minister Shamir and to the Israeli public.

The pain and sorrow many American Jews feel about Israel's policies on the West Bank and Gaza are rooted deep in our collective memory as a people. Israel's attempt to regain control of the refugee camps by denying food to hundreds of thousands of men, women, and children, by raiding homes and dragging out their occupants in the middle of the night to stand for hours in the cold, by savagely beating a civilian population and breaking its bones—these activities are deplorable to any civilized human being. That they are done by a Jewish state is both tragic and inexcusable. We did not survive the gas chambers and crematoria so that we could become the oppressors of Gaza. The Israeli politicians who have led us into this morass are desecrating the legacy of Jewish history. If Jewish tradition has stood for anything, it has stood for the principle that justice must triumph over violence. For that reason, we typically have sided with the oppressed and have questioned the indiscriminate use of force. We, who love Israel, who remain proud Zionists, are outraged at the betrayal of this sacred legacy by small-minded Israeli politicians who feel more comfortable with the politics of repression than with the search for peace.

Any policy that requires the immoral tactics currently being used against an unarmed and militarily subjugated population must be rejected. If the activities of the Israeli army since December really are necessary, that in itself would be sufficient to discredit the Occupation. We do not diminish our loyalty to our own people by acknowledging our profound sadness at the suffering of Palestinians. Those who have grown up in camps or in exile have experienced homelessness in much the same way that Jews have experienced it throughout history. Even if this suffering were the absolutely necessary consequence of our self-preservation, we would still be deeply upset by the pain that thereby was caused to another group of human beings. We have been too sensitized by our own history of oppression not to feel diminished when others are in pain. That is why we dip drops from our wine cups at the Passover seder, in memory of the pain of our Egyptian slaveholders. But when that pain is largely unnecessary, we feel not only sadness but also anger and a deep determination to do what we can to stop the suffering.

This editorial appeared in Tikkun, *March/April 1988.*

Our outrage is shared by many Israelis. Over fifty thousand of them gathered in Tel Aviv on January 23 1988 in one of the biggest antiwar demonstrations in Jewish history to protest Israel's policies. Joined by hundreds of thousands of others who could not attend the demonstration but who share their outrage, they are asking American Jews to speak out. To be silent, or keep our criticisms safely "in the family," would be to betray our Israeli brothers and sisters.

That is why we say in unequivocal terms to the Israeli government: Stop the beatings, stop the breaking of bones, stop the late night raids on people's homes, stop the use of food as a weapon of war, stop pretending that you can respond to an entire people's agony with guns and blows and power. Publicly acknowledge that the Palestinians have the same right to national self-determination that we Jews have, and negotiate a solution with representatives of the Palestinians!

But our anger at Israel's current policies comes not only from moral outrage but also from deep concern about Israel's survival and the survival of the Jewish people. From a strictly self-interested position, the Occupation is stupid. Here's why:

• The longer the Occupation exists, the more angry and radical young Palestinians will become. The possibility of negotiating a two-state solution will decrease since these young Palestinians will come to regard a West Bank state as a "sell-out" of their dreams for a fully liberated Palestine, and PLO leaders willing to settle for a such a state will be seen not as "moderates" but as betrayers of the struggle. This attitude is becoming more prevalent, but it has not yet achieved dominance. Yitzhak Rabin's policy of "the iron fist" only quickens this radicalization. In years to come we may wish that we had dealt with the PLO before the Palestinians embraced some radical form of Islamic fundamentalism that makes it a religious sin to live in peace with Israel.

• Even those Palestinians who now live within the pre-1967 borders of Israel are being drawn into the struggle. Faced with the repression of their own people in the Occupied Territories, they participated in the general strike in December. Some have rioted in protest of Israeli military action. The longer the Occupation lasts, the more they will be drawn into the struggle—with disastrous consequences for Israel. Unless the Occupation is speedily ended, Israel may soon resemble Beirut or Northern Ireland.

• As the Occupation continues, the logic of domination and repression of Palestinians will require that Israelis adopt an increasingly insensitive view towards those whom they must control. Israelis will inevitably be pushed to the political Right. In the past few years we have seen the right-wing Tehiyah party and even some sectors of Likud advocate Kahane-like ideas. Today, right-wing members of the Labor Party such as Yitzhak Rabin act in ways that would have made them scream at Ariel Sharon only a few years ago. This move to the right is likely to accelerate the already large emigration (*yeridah*) rate plaguing Israel—only this time those who leave will be going, not to find their "fortune" in America, but to escape a political situation that they cannot morally justify. Increasingly, it will be the scientific, technical, and professional personnel who leave—people whose contributions have been essential to the defense technology, economic strength, and intellectual creativity of the country.

• Because most of the pro-Zionist Jewish leadership in the United States has remained quiet, the only voices articulating clear moral criticism have been those of Israel's enemies. For the anti-Semites and the anti-Zionists these are wonderful times. Reports already exist of campus demonstrations with posters denouncing "Jewish murderers"—and many Jewish college students, ashamed of the images of the Jewish state being portrayed in the media every day, are willing, for the first time, to listen to the anti-Zionist propaganda being disseminated. Previously lacking any rational foundation for their attacks on Jews, the voices of hate have gained credibility by their association with legitimate criticisms of the Jewish state. Israel's current policies give credibility to the worst lies about Judaism. And, in the years ahead, the Jewish people may face hard times based not simply on the lies and distortions of anti-Semites, but on the justified indignation of many people who see the Jewish state embodying a viciousness and moral callousness that they would find repugnant anywhere.

• The Occupation threatens to erode the popular base of support for Israel in the United States. As America's economic problems intensify in the coming years, people will inevitably question any large-scale military and economic aid given to any foreign country. Moreover, major American corporations have never been happy with the government's tilt toward Israel. Most corporations understand that their long-term economic interests are better served by friendlier relations with the various Arab autocracies. Opportunities for investment and trade have been limited by America's alliance with Israel. The United States' policy of military support to Israel is one instance in which popular forces, using the democratic mechanisms of the electoral process, have countered corporate interests. Even the power of AIPAC is based less on its fund-raising capacities (does anyone seriously doubt that Arab oil companies could, if they so chose, raise more cash for political candidates than AIPAC?) than on its ability to mobilize a political constituency of Israel supporters. Yet many of these Israel supporters would be much less committed if Israel were perceived as having repudiated its commitment to democratic values and human rights. If Americans continue to be barraged by images of Israelis beating, tear-gassing, shooting, and starving a civilian population, they will be much less likely to stand up to the Arab and corporate interests that argue for "even-handedness" in American policy.

Make no mistake about it: What is at stake for Israel is not only its Jewish soul but its survival. Once the perception fades that Israel stands for moral values, those of us who want to provide for Israel's defense may be unable to convince the United States to supply the latest and most sophisticated military hardware, and Israel may be unable to keep up with Arab armies supplied not only by the Soviet Union but also by Japan and Europe. As a result, Israel may be vulnerable to serious military attack. There is no more pressing Israeli security need than its need to maintain its image as a society committed to just values.

• The Occupation is also a threat to the survival of Judaism and the Jewish people in the Diaspora. The breakdown of authoritarian communal structures increasingly makes every Jew a Jew by choice. In the past two decades there has been a dramatic revival of interest in Judaism from Americans who have found the individualistic and competitive values of American society unfulfilling and morally vacuous. They have turned to Judaism because they rightly sense Judaism's moral sensitivity and its transcendent vision, which stands in sharp opposition to the logic of domination and mean-spiritedness that permeates life in most competitive market societies.

The Occupation may reverse this trend since increasing numbers of Jews will begin to dismiss much of Judaism's moral vision as pious moralizing that lacks substance. A Judaism that has lost its moral teeth and becomes an apologist for every Israeli policy, no matter what its moral content, is a Judaism that not only betrays the prophetic tradition, but also risks losing the adherence of the Jewish people.

Israel is putting its supporters in the agonizing position of either rejecting its current policies or rejecting some of the central teachings of Judaism. While Israel's policies in the West Bank and Gaza are anathema to Jew and non-Jew alike, to secular as well as religious people, they are especially upsetting to those who take Judaism seriously as a guide to life. No rule in the Torah is repeated as frequently as those that, in one form or another, warn us not to respond to being oppressed by oppressing others. Using the term *ger* ('stranger') to refer to anyone who is part of a relatively powerless minority—just as we were in Egypt—the Bible commands us over and over again: "When you come into your land, do not oppress the *ger* who dwells in your midst." "One law shall be for you and the *ger*." And always the haunting reminder: "Remember that you were a *ger* in the land of Egypt!"

The wisdom of Jewish tradition is deep. It recognizes the temptation to do unto others what was done unto us, to engage in a kind of collective repetition compulsion in which we attempt to achieve mastery over the traumas of the past by identifying with our oppressors and becoming like them. We can see this dynamic in many people who were traumatized as children, and who then as adults seem to replicate, in their behavior toward others, much of what was done to them when they were young and powerless. The Torah seems to recognize that this same dynamic can affect an entire people, and it insists that freedom means breaking out of this pattern by consciously resisting it. For the Children of Israel, political freedom from slavery was only the first step. In order to be entitled to the Land of Israel, they had to accept the yoke of moral responsibility not to pass on to the next generations the evils of the past. For that reason, the Children of Israel were required to wander in the desert for forty years until the generation that was crippled by the mentality of slavery died off. The psychological traumas of oppression cannot be made the basis for building a Jewish society. We must transcend this dynamic: We must not do to others what was done to us. God's voice here is unequivocal: There is no right to the Land of Israel if Jews oppress the *ger*, the widow, the orphan, or any other powerless group.

The Torah insists that both physical and psychological/spiritual slavery must and can be broken. This is the liberatory message of Passover. To the extent that Judaism has kept alive this message of hope, it has been a revolutionary vanguard, insisting that the logic of the past, the logic of oppression, is not the only possible reality, that there exists a transcendent and liberating Force that we must foster. For this very reason, Jews must reject every effort to turn Judaism into a cheering squad for Israeli policies. We also must resist the arguments of those who say, "We Jews were hurt so badly in the past and have such a residue of anger for our past oppression that you must understand why we act as we now do." On the contrary, the essence of Judaism is to resist that argument.

Nevertheless, we must have compassion for the people who feel this way. We cannot ignore the specific features of Jewish history that may have conditioned Israeli soldiers to act like a classical colonial force trying to subjugate a rebellious citizen population. The rage that these soldiers exhibit when they beat civilians they suspect have been involved in rock-throwing may be understood, in part, as a response to the two thousand years during which the world systematically denied their right to exist as a people, a denial that culminated with extermination in gas chambers and crematoria. This oppression occurred not only in Europe; many Jews also had to flee Arab lands after hundreds of years of oppression and delegitimation. This same process of delegitimation has been further perpetuated by the Arab states in their refusal to relocate Palestinian refugees in 1948, in their insistence that these refugees stay in camps in Gaza and the West Bank, and in their failure to follow the lead of other countries that resettled much larger refugee populations, such as Pakistan's resettlement of nearly ten million Moslems after the struggle for Indian independence. This conduct by the Arab states was a loud proclamation: "You Jews don't really exist for us. Your presence here is temporary. We don't have to resettle the Palestinians or deal with this problem because you will soon be gone."

For two thousand years the Jews have had to scream in silence, fearful that protesting their delegitimation would lead to an escalation of oppression. Now, with the existence of the State of Israel, these Jews have begun to unleash their pent-up anger on the Palestinians—not a people of innocent bystanders, but a people that refused to accept the State of Israel in 1947, a people whose leadership still views a state as a transitional entity to a "second stage" in which Israel will be destroyed. One can understand the rage of some Israeli soldiers by recognizing this history of delegitimation.

A people this deeply wounded deserves compassion. Yet love for Israelis requires us to do our best to stop them from hurting themselves and others. Just as we understand the frustration that leads Palestinian youths to throw rocks even as we criticize their conduct, so too do we express deep

Photo by Oliver and Steinberg

care for our brothers and sisters in Israel even as we reject their actions.

We do not have to be reminded that the Palestinians themselves played a major role in creating the present conflict. When they were the majority in Palestine and *we* were refugees, they would not allow refugees to share the land. When Jews were desperately fleeing Christian Europe as well as Islamic Asia and North Africa, the Palestinian refusal to grant Jews a haven convinced many Zionists that Palestinian self-determination is incompatible with Jewish survival. When the media focus on Israel's treatment of the Palestinians, they paint an incomplete picture to the extent that they fail to inform their audience that the Palestinians are heirs to a tradition that to this day continues to reject the legitimacy of Jewish claims to a state. Those who throw rocks today may be justifiably frustrated, but if they do not have the courage to match their rock-throwing with the political will to accommodate Israel, if they wallow in their fantasies of eliminating the Jewish state, they will simply prolong their homelessness.

So we say to the Palestinians: Stop the rock-throwing, stop the talk of violently overthrowing Israel, reject the rejectionists, and publicly proclaim your willingness to live in peace with Israel. Begin to talk publicly about peaceful coexistence. You will not be granted genuine self-determination until you allay the legitimate fears of many centrist Israelis that you still are committed to destroying Israel.

Along with many people's failure to recognize that the Palestinians bear part of the responsibility for the present crisis has come criticism of Israel that simply is out of proportion, and that makes both Israelis and American Jews defensive and prevents them from recognizing the genuine injustice of Israel's policies. The worst example of such criticism is the comparison between Israel and South Africa. Israel is not South Africa, and what it is doing is not apartheid. It is true that Israel, like South Africa, is inflicting needless suffering on a population that seeks self-determination. But when it does this, it acts as a colonial oppressor in ways more similar to the Soviet Union's oppression (on a much larger scale) in Afghanistan, or China's in Tibet, or the United States' (acting through local proxies) in much of Central America.

Apartheid is a racist system under which blacks are discriminated against simply because they are black. In Israel the picture is different. Arabs who have remained within the pre-1967 Israeli borders have the same political rights as any other Israeli and are represented in the Knesset. Though Israeli Arabs rightly complain about unfair allocations of the budget and discrimination in housing and employment, these are practices that more closely resemble the unfair realities of Black life in the United States than the formal legal discrimination of apartheid. The fact remains that an Israeli Arab with large amounts of money does not face the kind of discrimination that remained legally instituted against Blacks in the United States until thirty years ago. Israeli Arabs play on the same beaches, eat at the same restaurants, attend the same movie theatres, and are free to stay at the same hotels as other Israelis.

The situation in the Occupied Territories is terrible, but resembles colonial oppression much more than racist apartheid. First, even if the territories were annexed into Israel, we would not be faced with the South African situation of a minority ruling a majority. Israeli Jews would remain a majority oppressing a minority the way Sikhs are oppressed in India, or the Kurds in Iran and Turkey, or the Misquito Indians in Nicaragua, or the Irish Catholics in Northern Ireland, or the Basques in Spain. Second, unlike typical colonial oppressors, many Israelis still favor a solution under which they would rid themselves of the West Bank, provided that they could guarantee Israel's security. Israel's good faith already has been shown in its withdrawal from the Sinai in return for peace with Egypt. This is not the behavior of a colonial power, much less of a South African-type regime. In short, the South Africa analogy distorts reality and allows right-wingers to focus on its flaws instead of dealing with the justified criticism of Israel.

There are solutions to these problems. A demilitarized and politically neutral Palestinian state can be established on the West Bank and Gaza in precisely the same fashion that the Russians and Americans agreed to give Austria independence after WWII. Demilitarization would be guaranteed by the United States and the Soviet Union, and the treaty that establishes this Palestinian state would also recognize Israel's right to intervene militarily in order to prevent the introduction of tanks, heavy artillery, or airplanes. The United States, Soviet Union, and Israel would create a unified force to protect the Palestinian state from attack by Syria, Iraq, Iran, or other hostile powers, and the United States would enter into a collective security agreement with Israel guaranteeing the full power of American military might to defend Israel against attack. The Palestinian state would renounce all claims to the rest of Palestine and would police those remaining Palestinians still desiring a further struggle with Israel. Israel would agree to enter into economic confederation with this Palestinian state after a specified period of peaceful coexistence.

Who could negotiate for the Palestinians? Any group that is willing to recognize Israel's right to exist. If Israel claims that the PLO doesn't represent the Palestinians in the Occupied Territories, let it immediately hold a plebiscite to determine whom West Bank Palestinians want to negotiate for them. And Israel must set no restrictions on who can be a candidate.

What if no Palestinian leadership is willing to accept a demilitarized Palestinian state? Then Israel loses nothing by having offered, and actually gains a great deal. Instead of Israeli rejectionism, we would be back to a clear picture of the Palestinians as the obstacle. It is reasonable for Israel to insist on its own security. If, in the 1930s, Jews had been offered a state under a similar plan guaranteed by all the great powers, they certainly would have accepted it, even on a considerably smaller piece of land. Ultimately, a totally demilitarized Middle East is optimum, but for now a demilitarized Palestinian state is the only kind of state likely to be accepted. We hope the Palestinians prove the skeptics wrong by accepting a demilitarized state.

Israel should publicly offer the Palestinians such a state now. This proclamation will help ensure Israel's political and military survival. It will probably also provoke a crisis in the Palestinian world and bring to the fore the unresolved conflict between those Palestinians who really are willing to accept Israel's right to exist and those who desire a state on the West Bank simply as a launching pad for the total destruction of Israel. If the rejectionists win the struggle, Israel has proved itself reasonable without weakening itself militarily. We hope, however, that the forces of reason among the Palestinians will win and that the kind of peace that most Israelis want can be achieved.

Anything less than such a public proclamation will be seen as stalling—and rightly so. Prime Minister Shamir's attempts to revive Camp David "autonomy" talks are clearly delay tactics. The autonomy being proposed is a sham—the opposite of genuine self-determination. But even an international conference will have limited impact if Israel is unwilling to commit itself to a demilitarized Palestinian state. A "solution" that proposes anything less than this—for example, a Jordanian confederation on the West Bank under which the Palestinians still do not have self-determination, their own flag, or their own passports—will give extremist Palestinians the incentive to expand the struggle. The psychology of the situation is clear: Until the Palestinians feel that they own something, which limited autonomy cannot provide, they have no real incentive to stop the struggle. Once they acheive this sense of ownership, those who advocate continuing the struggle will be seen by fellow Palestinians as putting their own state in jeopardy. If however, Israel commits itself publicly to a demilitarized Palestinian state, it need not yield an inch of land until the demilitarization is firmly in place.

Americans, particularly American Jews, have an extraordinary historical responsibility at this moment. The path of least resistance—privately criticizing Israel but publicly supporting it or remaining silent—is actually a dramatic betrayal of the interests of our people. Americans must use every possible means to convey to Israelis—in private communications, in letters to Israeli newspapers and to members of Knesset, in petitions to the government of Israel, in public rallies and teach-ins, and in statements issued by synagogues and communal organizations—that Israel is in deep jeopardy and that the Occupation must end. What we do now actually may make a significant difference. Israeli centrists are under the illusion that American economic and political support can be taken for granted. Conservative leaders from the American Jewish world have fostered this fantasy. Many of these centrists can be moved to support peace proposals if they are made aware of the precariousness of their position. The ordinary Israeli has no idea how deep American disaffection has become or how such disaffection may threaten Israel's military security in the future. The only way s/he will "get it" is through a combination of public protests and private communications. Since we can't count on Jewish leaders to convey this sense of urgency, we need to do it ourselves.

Many American Jewish leaders have displayed shortsightedness and cowardice in dealing with the current difficulties. Little in their past style of operation or in their intellectual approach gives them the tools necessary to provide leadership now that it is needed most. The neo-cons, the "Israel is always right" crowd, the people with moral blinders—none of these people can provide an analysis or a strategy that will speak to the American Jewish public. A very large number of American Jews are in a state of deep personal crisis. Their identification with Judaism, Israel, and the Jewish people is being fundamentally challenged. This is the moment when they need to hear a different kind of voice from the Jewish world. Let them hear your voice.

The crisis in Israel is a moment of truth for all of us. It should be responded to with the deepest seriousness and with the full understanding that the choices we make now may have consequences that reverberate for centuries to come. □

Psychological Dimensions of the Israeli-Palestinian Conflict

Michael Lerner

All the "objective conditions" seem ripe for peace in the Middle East. The superpowers have no interest in perpetuating the conflict and are willing to lean on their respective client states to make concessions; Iran's fanaticism appears to be less of a regional factor after the defeat of its war efforts against Iraq and the death of the Ayatollah Khomeini; the PLO, abandoning its previous rejectionist platform, has accepted the Shamir election proposal in the version originally developed by Rabin and Labor party hard-liners; most Israelis realize that they must eventually deal with the PLO; and even hard-line American Jewish organizations have decided that they won't be able to block the American–PLO dialogue.

Is peace around the corner? Not a chance.

The problem is that the focus on "objective conditions" overlooks the complexities of feeling and perception that have made this one of the most intractable international conflicts of the past forty years. The actors continually choose paths that are self-destructive and counterproductive to their alleged rational aims. Israelis claim to seek a partner for negotiations, yet they simply ignore every overture made by the PLO to open talks; and, while claiming to seek a moderate Palestinian voice on the West Bank, they have done everything possible to discourage the development of independent Palestinian leadership. The Palestinians, in turn, recognize that their immediate political task is to convince Israelis that they are willing to live in peace alongside Israel—but they have been unable to figure out that launching military attacks over the Lebanese border, or seeming to justify attacks by Palestinians against Israeli civilians within the pre-1967 borders, only enrages Israelis and strengthens the position of the Israeli right wing.

These are not simple mistakes that can be straightened out by rational argument; if face-to-face negotiations ever do begin between Israelis and Palestinians, these negotiations will not be governed primarily by the dynamics of enlightened self-interest. Yet the irrationalities that govern the situation are not mysterious or impossible to deal with. They are, rather, psychodynamically rooted in the histories and experiences of these two very different peoples.

Several years ago I spent half a year at Tel Aviv University doing research on the psychological dynamics that shape the self-perception of Israelis and Palestinians. My work began with a focus on stress at work. In the course of interviewing hundreds of Israelis and Palestinians, I found that the interviewees inevitably drew me into the larger national conflict and the ways in which they interpreted their possibilities. On each subsequent visit to Israel, including one completed in the summer of 1989, I held follow-up interviews and discussed my conclusions both with the interviewees and with psychotherapists, journalists, labor leaders, leaders of the Israeli Sephardic community, political activists from all parts of the Israeli political spectrum, and Palestinian activists and intellectuals.

This editorial appeared in Tikkun, *September/October 1989.*

My central finding was this: although emerging from very different historical experiences, Israelis and Palestinians suffer from a set of historically generated psychological scars that prevent them from acting in accordance with their own rational self-interest. In some respects this is a classic case of surplus powerlessness. Both sides have experienced real powerlessness, but they have developed psychological frames of self-understanding that make them more powerless than the current reality requires. As a result, neither side is able to take the risks necessary to reassure the other side that peace is in fact obtainable. Instead, each side carefully nourishes the memory of its wounds and uses each current development to further confirm for itself the impossibility of transcending the current dynamic.

When we discuss surplus powerlessness as a factor in the collective experience of an entire people, we are directed toward understanding the historical experiences—mediated through family and cultural history—that contribute to the shaping of that people's current perceptions of its possibilities. Those dynamics are typically rooted in a historic experience of trauma generated by the frustration of our fundamental human desire for recognition and confirmation. To the extent that some set of traumatic events convinces a people that its frustrated need for recognition and confirmation will inevitably lead to a repetition of the original traumatic denial, that people will begin to feel frightened whenever the possibility of achieving such recognition arises. Many people would choose to die rather than reexperience the humiliation and degradation associated with the memory of the original traumatic denial of their needs. So people and peoples develop a multiplicity of strategies to avoid ever reexperiencing that initial trauma. Nationalism, for example, may protect us from having to experience the vulnerability we would be subjected to if we were open to the possibility that we might find deep connectedness and confirmation in the "other." Conversely, we can organize a community around our anger at all the "others" who we are sure would act in a hurtful way toward us should we ever open ourselves to them and risk trusting connections.

Those who have been oppressed and traumatized typically find themselves subject to a "repetition compulsion"—the process by which we pass on to others (neighbors, co-workers, the next generation) the very traumatic experiences that were acted out on us. To the extent that the repetition compulsion dominates our unconscious lives, present events will be cast in ways that make it seem appropriate for us to do unto others what was once done to us. These dynamics of surplus powerlessness, played out in part through a repetition compulsion, are shared by all the major parties to the current struggle in the Middle East.

In order to be viable, any strategies for peace in the Middle East must explicitly address the deep psychic wounds that have so crippled all the parties involved. To do that, we need to understand in greater detail how the dynamics of surplus powerlessness are specifically rooted in the historical experiences of the major actors in the conflict: the dominant Ashkenazi political elite of Israel, the Sephardic majority of Israel and the Palestinian national movement.

The Ashkenazim

It is foolish and naive to attempt to understand the Israeli response to the Palestinians without understanding the massive impact of two thousand years of oppression on the Israeli Ashkenazim (those whose families came from Europe and who today dominate the major economic, military, and political institutions of Israel).

American liberals make all sorts of excuses for the intense level of violence that is a daily reality in the American ghettos—violence that is, for the most part, directed by Blacks against other Blacks. The liberals refer to the cumulative impact of slavery and of the subsequent oppression and racism on the collective psyches of the Black community. Yet we are often less aware of the inevitably distorting impact of violence on the Jewish people. Jews did not respond with violence to the violence done to them—they couldn't. Jews had to moderate their response for fear that if they spoke their anger in any clear terms they would simply call down upon themselves greater oppression and slaughter. As a result, Jews often learned to internalize the violence, directing it against themselves in the form of an extremely punishing superego (manifested most dramatically by their attempt to explain their own exile as a punishment for their sins rather than as the result of their failure to win a righteous but futile national liberation struggle against the world's largest imperialist power), in the form of intense internal intellectual rivalries and struggles, and in the form of self-mockery and Jewish humor.

Underlying all of these responses was the incredible pathos and pain of a people that had been rejected by its neighbors. The Jewish people earned the enmity of ruling classes in the ancient and medieval world by building their national identity and religious practice around the weekly retelling of the revolutionary story of the Exodus. Throughout history ruling classes have always explained to their subjects that class domination is necessary, built into the structure of society. The message of the Jewish people, its very existence as a people, seemed to indicate the opposite, that the world can be fundamentally altered. No wonder, then, that ruling elites found the Jews troublesome—and felt it necessary to try to set their own people against the Jews. The fiercely independent spirit of the Jews, their inability, for instance, to accommodate themselves to Roman imperialism, frequently led them to rebel, even against militarily superior powers, and eventually left them as homeless wanderers among the nations of a world whose peoples had been warned not to trust them.

The pain and humiliation of being a nation without a homeland, and of being rejected and treated with derision by many who surrounded them, was more than the Jews could bear. Traumatized by the way the world thwarted their quite normal needs for recognition and communion with others, Jews developed a theological system for dealing with their pain. On the one hand, the Exile was the punishment for their own sins of having abandoned God's ways. On the other hand, they reinterpreted the older notions of their special responsibilities to fulfill God's commandments by now seeing themselves as specially chosen to bring God's word to the world—a compensatory move that both provided an explanation for the moral inferiority of those who oppressed them and simultaneously helped regenerate that oppression by further infuriating the peoples whose ruling classes had already predisposed them to distrust the Jews. Thus psychologically armed against the onslaught of hostility from surrounding Christian and Islamic cultures, no longer willing to reexperience the hope and yearning for connection with others that had so often been frustrated, the Jewish people survived the growing hostilities of the past two thousand years.

The continual instability of daily life, the expulsions from countries where Jews had lived for hundreds of years, the propensity of anti-Jewish racism to reappear even in societies that no longer espoused the Christianity within which that anti-Semitism had originally been fostered, led most Jews to believe that racism against Jews was part of the psychic structure of almost all non-Jewish societies. When the liberatory promise of the French Revolution and the revolutionary upsurges of the nineteenth century failed to eliminate the deeply entrenched anti-Semitism of European societies, Jews responded in four different ways:

1. *Religious Jews* tended to be passive and to believe that the suffering of the Jewish people could not be overcome until the Messiah was sent by God. This approach led to the "marching like lambs to the slaughter" phenomenon of some sectors of European Jewry.

2. *Assimilationists* thought that anti-Semitism could be overcome by losing one's identity in larger Christian societies (a strategy that failed in Europe when the Nazis simply went back through birth records and sent to the death camps even those who had converted two or three generations earlier) or by courting ruling groups in the hope that they would come to our aid when necessary (a strategy

that failed dismally when the American ruling class refused either to bomb the railroads to the concentration camps or to open the immigration gates and allow Jews to escape from Europe).

3. *Internationalists* thought that one could reject one's Jewish identity and count on international working class solidarity to overcome anti-Semitism. Most of these internationalists perished—not only at the hands of the Nazis, but also at the hands of the European proletariat whose anti-Semitism led many to refuse to help the Jews and others to join in the massacre.

4. *Zionists* believed that the only solution was for the Jews to recognize that in a historical period in which most peoples were responding to nationalism, the Jews would need to have their own Jewish state for self-defense.

None of these responses was based on the assumption that it might actually be possible for the Jewish people to live in peace inside Europe with their non-Jewish neighbors and to find in that relationship the recognition and mutual confirmation that they had for centuries been denied. Subsequent experience in a Europe that responded so enthusiastically to anti-Semitism showed that Jewish fears on this score were well founded. It is the Zionist response to which I shall address myself here, since it proved the most congruent with the historical realities of the twentieth century and since it shaped the State of Israel. Moreover, it was the Zionist response that seemed to embody the greatest degree of healthy self-affirmation in its attempt to recover psychological health for the Jews by insisting on the Jewish people's right to be recognized as a nation among all other nations.

Yet, as though to protect themselves from whatever remained attractive in the Jewish past and to justify the personal sacrifices of going to Palestine when they might have sought their personal fortunes by emigrating to the U.S., Zionists adopted an ethos that negated anything that reminded them of the self-limiting dynamics of Jewish accommodation to the Diaspora. Instead of acknowledging the painful life experiences of the Jewish people that had led to many self-limiting choices (not to mention the positive value—derived from our Diaspora experience—of Jews' learning to compromise and live with others), the Zionists saw the entirety of the Diaspora experience as generating a Jewish pathology that could be cured only by living as a strong and independent people in our own land, a people who could no longer be kicked around and that would no longer have to spend its psychic energy "pleasing the goyim."

Underlying all the bravado was the same melancholic resignation at the impossibility of achieving real reciprocity with others that had pushed an earlier generation of Jews to escape into the world of Talmud and fantasies of the coming of the Messiah. Zionist activists shared with the more passive religious fundamentalists the conviction that genuine human reciprocity with non-Jews would always be impossible, but simply adopted a different strategy to effectively deny themselves any memory of the desire for connection or of the pain associated with its denial.

The most problematic consequence of the Zionist response was its call for an Israel that would be a nation like all other nations. The idea of a special moral responsibility of the Jewish people, embedded in the concept of the "chosen people," was bitterly rejected by Zionists. Instead, many Zionists argued, Israel should be judged by the same standards as all other peoples. If the rule of the jungle governed the twentieth century, as seemed obvious to many of these Zionists, then Jews had to get sharp teeth and claws like the other beasts that had been devouring them. If the world was governed by militarism, the logic went on, then Jews had to become militarists. When others responded that in so doing the Zionists would be rejecting the long history and culture of the Jewish people that did self-consciously judge itself by different criteria from those prevailing in other societies, the Zionists responded that this argument reflected a ghetto mentality—that the attempt to apply moral standards was a ridiculous religious fantasy that had nothing to do with the reality of the twentieth century.

In short, playing out the repetition compulsion described above, and having been shaped by a brutal history, a section of the brutalized people adopts the behavior of the oppressors and identifies with those oppressors' moral standards. Barely had this worldview begun to express itself in the Zionist movement of the twentieth century than the fury of European anti-Semitism reasserted itself, seeming to confirm that Jews could never trust anyone.

The trauma of the Holocaust re-evoked the feelings of shame and disgust that many Zionists felt about their own history. Faced with this new trauma, many Jews found it too painful to continue nurturing the hope that they could obtain the recognition and validation we all seek from each other. Rather than lament the tragedy of a world that makes such connectedness impossible, some Ashkenazim had already begun to foster in Israel a culture that rejected the very need for connection with others as a Diaspora pathology. And those who had trusted non-Jews, and hence not prepared themselves for what afterward appeared to many Zionists to be a betrayal, were berated for being naive and scorned for allegedly having walked as sheep to the slaughter.

The Holocaust finally and massively traumatized the Jewish people. Any talk of rational solutions today must be tempered by an understanding that we are dealing with a traumatized people, a people that is only now beginning to acknowledge to itself what it has gone through.

The greatest distortions of the present situation are in part a product of this trauma. The Palestinians have only made matters worse: by talking about pushing the Jews into the sea, by even now having a charter that calls for the elimination of the Jewish state (despite Arafat's personal disclaimers), and by failing to repudiate those people in the Palestinian movement and the Arab world who overtly identify with anti-Jewish racism.

Palestinian bluster and racism would, however, be considerably less important if Israelis could approach the situation with a realistic assessment of their own power. The inability of many Israelis to tell the difference between Nazis and Palestinians, and their inability to recognize their own military superiority so that they could understand that they are no longer a powerless people trembling at the threshold of the extermination camps of Europe, is not willed stupidity. It is, rather, a pathological distortion based on the trauma of victimization not yet overcome. Yet the cries of the Jewish victim can be heard not too far below the surface of arrogant self-assertion. The deep doubts that the PLO has "really" recognized the State of Israel with its latest moves are not simply about a piece of paper or the content of a particular declaration by the Palestine National Council; rather, they mask a cry of pain at a history in which the peoples of the world have never given us the recognition and mutual confirmation to which human beings are entitled. No wonder, then, that Israelis are often unable to hear a similar cry of pain coming from the Palestinian people—our own cries are so loud they drown out those of the other. This pain impedes realistic political judgment and ensures that Israel will misjudge its possibilities.

The Sephardim

The Sephardim (Jews whose families emigrated from Islamic lands) are the majority group in Israel, and their votes for the right wing have provided Likud with its margin of victory in recent elections. The Sephardim shared with the Jews who settled in Europe a common experience of oppression, victimization, and traumatization through the expulsion from their land in the ancient world. For more than a thousand years Sephardim were degraded second-class citizens. They were subject to periodic outbursts of mass murder, and faced daily economic, political, and social discrimination in Islamic countries. The Koran contains many denunciations of Jews and Judaism which set the tone for the relationship that developed. The *dhimmi*, or non-Muslim, was tolerated under strictly regulated conditions. A special *dhimmi* tax was often levied in a systematic attempt to expropriate Jewish property, so that Jews often lived in poverty or near-poverty. Though there were periods in which some Islamic rulers were particularly friendly toward the Jews, and in which individual Jews managed to play important roles as court physicians, moneylenders and political advisers, Jewish life in Islamic states often entailed a careful balancing act whose precariousness created deep tension in daily life. In many Islamic societies Jews were required to wear distinctive pieces of clothing so they could be easily identified; they were not allowed to own horses, not permitted to drink wine in public, and not permitted to perform their religious rituals in public. The cumulative impact of these measures, coupled with periodic outbursts of more severe violence, was to ensure that they would never feel fully secure. Once again, Jews were unable to achieve a sense of confirmation and mutual recognition from their neighbors. The pain and humiliation of this constant rejection at the hands of the Islamic majority, the powerlessness and need to internalize the resulting rage, left deep scars on the Sephardim. These Sephardic Jews feel about the Arabs the way many refugees from the Soviet Union feel about communism—and they find it hard to understand why others who have had no direct experience with the Arab regimes don't take the Sephardic experience more seriously. In the interviews I conducted in Israel I heard many Sephardim argue that their anger at Arabs was not (as in the case of the Ashkenazim) a displacement of an earlier anger (toward Germans or Poles or East Europeans): "We lived in an Islamic society, and we became refugees from *that kind of society*. So our anger is appropriately directed." It is an anger that derives much of its energy from the denial of recognition that Sephardim experienced for a thousand years at the hands of their Arab neighbors.

There is, however, a second and perhaps even more complicated element in the story of the Sephardim. When many Sephardim came to Israel in the 1950s, their entire history and culture was demeaned by the dominant Ashkenazic culture—Sephardim were made to feel as though they were inferior in every way. Moreover, because they had not been subjected to the Holocaust, their own tales of suffering at the hands of the Arabs were construed by the Ashkenazim as being whiny and self-indulgent. Their culture was denigrated and their self-respect assaulted. This created massive resentment that is today a central factor in the political culture of Sephardic life. After a long history of invalidation by their surrounding Arab neighbors, Sephardim returned to the land of their ancestors with the anticipation that they were, at last, coming home. Instead, they were greeted with derision, which was often painful and embarrassing. The humiliation of this experience led to a deep anger that has been displaced onto the most immediately available recipient—the Palestinian people. It is in relationship to the Palestinians that some Sephardim have been able to act out the frustrations they have suffered.

The Palestinians

In the late nineteenth and early twentieth centuries, European nations colluded to carve out a series of national entities in the Middle East in order to divide up the area among the colonizers. The Arab peoples who lived there were seen as primitives whose fate and fortune could be decided elsewhere, whose long cultural and religious tradition could be demeaned, and whose own wishes for recognition and validation could be ignored. Palestinian nationalism, then, emerged first as a variant of a larger Arab nationalism—a reaction to the experience of oppression and invalidation. Like so many other similar anticolonial phenomena, the demand to be recognized as fully human was as much a part of the impulse toward national self-determination as was any intrinsic political, economic, or cultural program.

No wonder, then, that Palestinian national self-determination was from the start marked by strong opposition to those Jews who had begun to return to their ancient land. That early Zionists could describe the land of Palestine as "a land without a people for a people without a land" was an indication to Palestinians who lived there how deeply ingrained was a colonial mentality in the consciousness of these Jewish settlers. The exclusion of Palestinians from Jewish labor unions and communal settlements seemed a further indication that the Zionists had no room in their conceptual scheme for the Palestinian people. In these ways, painful and humiliating experience as a victim of colonialism was identified in Palestinian consciousness with the emergence of a Zionist presence in Palestine—a presence symbolized most thoroughly by the Balfour Declaration, which promised the Jewish people a homeland in Palestine without bothering to consult the desires of those who formed a majority in that land.

I do not mean here to exonerate the Palestinians for their obvious racism, which also played an important role in shaping their response to the Zionists. The racist attitudes toward Jews that were dominant in Islamic societies certainly played a role in preventing Palestinians from being able to see how Jews might be potential allies in undermining British imperialism. The Jews who came as settlers, after all, were not primarily British or enthusiastic subjects of other colonial regimes. Rather, they were for the most part escapees from the oppression of Eastern Europe, and they arrived with internationalist ideas that might have provided a potential basis for alliance and for the cultivation of mutual interests. It was precisely this possibility that frightened many of the feudal leaders of the Palestinian people, and it was through its leaders' eyes that the largely illiterate Palestinian peasantry received its information about the nature and intentions of the Jewish settlers. Playing on the preexisting anti-Jewish attitudes of Islamic culture, the feudal leaders developed a national consciousness that gave the early Palestinian movement a distinctly anti-Semitic reality. Palestinian nationalism gave no recognition to the fact that in the first half of the twentieth century the Jews were landless, homeless, and desperate refugees, while the Palestinians refused to share what land they had. In fact, the Palestinian national movement became increasingly involved with Nazi propaganda and anti-Semitism, and some of its most important leaders openly championed a Nazi victory to deal with the Jewish problem.

But it makes little sense to condemn all Palestinians living at that time; most had little information, and many who did were expressing a legitimate anger at Western imperialism—anger incorrectly but understandably directed against Jewish Zionists. It's more reasonable to understand the situation as one in which two peoples, both victims of international imperialism, were manipulated opposing each other so as to strengthen the hold of the larger imperialist order. We don't need pathological categories to understand the circumstance that led to the collisions of 1945 to 1948.

Yet, when all is said and done, the collision of these two nationalisms led directly to the creation of the Arab refugee problem. Here I think it critical to acknowledge that many of the subsequent self-destructive activities of the Palestinian people in dealing with their situation were a result of the trauma of dispossession and then of life in the camps. I use "self-destructive" here in the same way that I apply it to the current activities of the Israeli government: self-destructive because the PLO fostered a spirit of armed struggle that was then and remains today utterly and tragically futile—and this they substituted for the kinds of political initiatives that might have worked. I believe today that a Gandhian style Palestinian movement, with total Gandhian discipline and Gandhian clarity about accepting a nonviolent solution and a demilitarized state—a strategy that firmly renounces any intention of using a Palestinian state as a launching pad for a second stage of struggle, a strategy that unequivocally denounces acts of terrorism against Israelis inside the pre-1967 borders—would produce a Palestinian state within five years; and I believe that every other strategy will take more time, cost more lives, and involve more pain.

Meanwhile, the psychological trauma of past pain caused by the dislocation of hundreds of thousands of Palestinians in 1948, the devastating impact of forty years of life in the refugee camps, the shame at being mistreated and manipulated and sometimes even murdered by Arab regimes' use of the Palestinians to advance the sectarian needs of Arab power politics, and the daily humiliations that are part of life under Israeli occupation—all combine to traumatize the Palestinians in ways that make them unable to act effectively in their own self-interest. The ultimate triumph of irrationality might come if the Palestinian people, unable to achieve any serious this-worldly gains through their support of the Palestinian Liberation Organization, were to turn toward Islamic fundamentalism and its otherworldly solutions.

Healing the Wounds

The primary task for those who wish to bring peace to the Middle East is to develop a set of confidence-building measures that can help reassure each side that there is a basis for trust. If, for example, the Palestinians were willing to take a dramatic set of steps like those taken by Sadat, the political atmosphere would change instantaneously in a massive way.

A Sadat-like move would entail the following: (1) Amending the PNC charter to eliminate references to the destruction of Israel and substituting in their places references to living in peace with Israel; (2) The PLO's accepting and articulating in detail how demilitarization of a Palestinian state would work and describing in detail the measures it would take against those Palestinian factions that seek to continue terrorist attacks; (3) The PLO's renouncing all forms of violence and insisting that the Palestinian movement model itself on Gandhian resistance; and (4) The PLO's committing itself now to signing, as part of the same agreement that would create a Palestinian state, a public declaration renouncing—in the name of the Palestinian people—all claims to the parts of Palestine within the pre-1967 boundaries of Israel.

If the Palestinians were to implement such changes in one dramatic step, not piecemeal and not quietly, the peace forces in Israel would be dramatically empowered and would virtually be assured of victory in future electoral struggles in Israel.

Similarly, if an Israeli leader were to accept the right of the Palestinian people to national self-determination and to a fully demilitarized state, he or she would quickly help consolidate and strengthen the forces within the Palestinian camp that would be able to lead the Palestinian movement toward a path of mutual acceptance and peaceful coexistence.

Yet before such developments can take place, the relevant players will have to believe that their own willingness to take such risks is likely to produce a change on the other side. Much of my analysis here is designed to show why most of the actors are unlikely to draw such conclusions.

Similarly, the various well-intended plans calling for "education for democracy," "education against racism," and even face-to-face parlor meetings or encounter sessions between Israelis and Palestinians have so far had minimal impact on the larger political realities of the society. No matter how many good ideas are taught, no matter how good one feels after meeting face to face with real human beings on the other side, the abiding psychological legacy ultimately reasserts itself. Even those who have felt absolutely convinced that they could trust people on the other side feel unable to say this in a loud and clear way to their fellow Israelis or Palestinians, aware that they will only discredit themselves among those whom they hope to influence. Given the powerful impact of this psychological legacy, every partial move toward accommodation is interpreted as meaningless by the other side. So, when Arafat says he will come to Jerusalem to talk peace, Shamir says he will arrest Arafat should he arrive at Ben-Gurion—because he is convinced that it is not peace but trickery that ultimately underlies Arafat's moves and that will always necessarily underlie the moves of the other, because the other cannot be trusted.

Effective strategy would, instead, integrate a focus on the pains of the past and provide a way for people to confront and transcend those pains. We can learn here from the remarkable impact of the women's movement and its array of methods for transforming the self-understanding of women in the past twenty-five years. Through group consciousness raising, articles, speeches, rituals, fiction, poetry, and a host of legislative and political struggles, women were able to challenge the long history of sexist conditioning and create a new self-understanding that has begun to succeed in making women feel less like victims while simultaneously challenging the objective sexist social and economic structures that helped shape that consciousness.

In lieu of a Sadat on either side, we need to develop political approaches to mass psychology similar to those of the women's movement but shaped to take into account the specific needs of the realities of the situation in the Middle East.

Let's start by considering one aspect of the problem: how to deal with the trauma of two thousand years of oppression that culminated in the Holocaust.

There are those today, including some who write for *Tikkun*, who think that the solution is to forget the past. For example, they claim that the Jewish people has focused too much on the Holocaust and for that reason have become obsessed. The Jews would be better off, they say, if they could forget their past.

I think they are deeply mistaken. A trauma can be dealt with only by being brought up again and then worked through under conditions in which we have greater mastery.

Hasn't that been done? No—quite the contrary. The first twenty years of Israel were marked by massive denial and shame about the Holocaust—and the people who went through it were told to keep their stories to themselves, because they represented precisely what Israel had been set up to negate and overcome. David Grossman's recent novel *See Under: Love* and Gila Almagor's film *Summer of Aviya* give moving accounts of this period in Israeli life.

After the Six Day War, the Holocaust was put on the front burner—but in a method that was designed to integrate the past into a Zionist historiography that emphasized Jewish power and reviled Jewish impotence. Yom Hashoah, National Holocaust Memorial Day, was titled also "leegvurah"—to emphasize our strength, not our weakness and vulnerability. Museums were built, institutions erected, commemorations instituted—all in the service of avoidance of the actual emotional experiences, and with little focus on the detailed stories of the experiences that people had gone through.

Israel needs a massive retelling of that history through the experience of the survivors—in thousands of small groups, with sympathetic listeners who can tell the survivors that they are secure now, that they are less vulnerable, that they do not need to see Nazis all around them. Training Israelis in how to be good listeners in such a group may be central to this process. It is not just the survivors and their children who need this therapy; most Israelis of European descent have shaped their identity in reaction to the pain and humiliation of this historical victimization, and they would benefit by being able to acknowledge the personal feelings of shame and pain and rage that get displaced onto Israeli political life.

Zalman Schachter has suggested one mass psychology intervention that goes some distance in the direction that we must travel. Rabbi Schachter suggests that the peace movement should create a mikva ceremony for Israelis who are returning to civilian life after a period of serving in the Israeli reserves. The ceremonial immersion in water, a traditional purification act, is meant to convey our notion that the current service in the Israeli army in the West Bank necessarily leads Israelis to perform actions that pollute the soul. At the very least, the mikva is meant as an affirmation that we do not wish to bring the destructive psychodynamics generated by being part of an army of Occupation into the rest of Israeli life. While such a process may not go far enough in asserting our opposition to the Occupation, and while it presents the potential danger of being misused as a symbolic washing of our hands of the moral dirtiness of the Occupation, it has the value, in the hands of a psychologically sophisticated peace movement, of affirming Jewish tradition and using that tradition as a mechanism of critique of current Israeli policy. Similar and more dramatic techniques are necessary to develop a political practice that is sensitive to the psychological realities of the Israeli population, and that incorporates a sensitivity and compassion for the people whose views we hope to change.

A similar kind of thinking will be necessary to deal with the legacy of pain among the Sephardim and Palestinians. For example, if the Ashkenazi-dominated peace forces were to begin their public campaigns with an honest and public recounting of the actual ways that Ashkenazi Israel has demeaned Sephardim in the past, it might then be possible to generate an audience for ideas about how to move beyond the current political impasse. Since the intifada began, Israeli activists have organized gatherings in which Israelis and Palestinians meet in each other's homes for small dialogue groups. It would be an important advance if the peace movement were to arrange similar groups so that they could meet and listen to Israeli Sephardim, listen to their anger and pain, and then move beyond this pain with them. The very act of providing this kind of listening environment, either in small groups or in larger communal settings, would provide a validation to many who still burn with rage at the way they or their parents were treated by the Labor-party-led government of Israel decades ago.

I do not know the Palestinian community well enough to know the specific forms that mass psychological strategy might take. But the analysis presented here suggests that those in the Palxestinian world who are serious about changing the current reality must address this question with the greatest of seriousness and urgency.

There are, of course, dangers with any attempt to deal with the psychological dynamics of the current situation. For one thing, there is a temptation to use psychological categories as a club with which to covertly assert our own moral superiority over those whom we wish to help—in effect, covertly blaming the victims for their own oppression. The current tragic situation in the Middle East was created not by the moral turpitude of either the Jewish or the Palestinian people, but by a configuration of world historical forces over which neither people had much influence. The Jewish people do not need to be told how bad and irrational they are—this will only increase the self-blaming. The core of the problem is that both people have internalized a sense of inadequacy and self-blame—based on the denial of their fundamental human needs for recognition and mutual confirmation—and have compensated for these feelings with massive denial, massive chauvinism and massive attempts to make themselves emotionally and militarily invulnerable. Nothing will be helpful that reinforces the notion that Israelis and Palestinians are *right* to feel bad about themselves, that they really are inadequate, that they are worse than other peoples. What both sides need is a massive dose of self-worth that would replace the pseudo-forms of self-worth they get through posturing and denying the legitimacy of each other's pains.

A psychological orientation should also not prevent us from simultaneously articulating moral outrage at Israeli policies that deny the humanity of the Palestinian people, or outrage at callous and inhumane Palestinian acts (like the bus massacre on the Tel Aviv-Jerusalem highway) that have been justified in the name of fighting oppression.

It's fashionable today to be skeptical of all psychological approaches, to see them as reductive or flaky attempts to avoid "real politics." There are many who believe that dealing with the underlying pains discussed here would take too long, and that solutions are obtainable through diplomatic breakthroughs. I would not be surprised in fact if we see some such breakthroughs in the period ahead. But just reaching the table will not necessarily lead to a resolution of the conflict. Once the U.S. sat down with the Vietnamese in 1968 there were years of meaningless chatter that led nowhere until a series of changes in domestic politics forced the U.S. to change its position. Though U.S. diplomats believe that the very fact of negotiations would generate a new psychological dynamic, it might actually generate a new pessimism and despair if negotiations become merely another vehicle to perpetuate the status quo. It may yet prove true that dealing with the underlying psychological dynamics is the most effective approach to bringing peace to the Middle East. □

Drawing by Anthony Dubovsky

The Uprising: Voices from Israel

Shulamith Aloni, Abba Eban, David Hartman,
Shimon Peres, Hannan Hever, Yaron Ezrahi

Shulamith Aloni
Member of Knesset

Every individual concerned with human rights has the right to respond to every injustice done to people anywhere in the world, regardless of origin and religion. Jews who feel a common destiny with other Jews of the world have the right to express their opinion about the state of their people wherever they are. Such expressions do not constitute illegal interference into the internal matters of this nation. Jews who have an attachment to Israel and a concern for her future have the right to express that concern and their opinion about her policies, as Israel sees those Jews as partners and potential citizens. American Jews, concerned with the events in Israel and her policies toward her minorities, must examine their responses in light of the principles of the American Constitution. They must also consider actions they would take if they were treated as members of a minority group treated as Israel treats the minorities under her rule.

Abba Eban
Member of Knesset

1) American Jews should reaffirm their right to be heard and should boldly reject the attempt by the Israeli or American Jewish establishments to convert them into "Jews of silence." As Americans they bear the right and duty to participate publicly in fashioning American policy. To deny themselves that right in the very arena in which their emotions are most strongly engaged would be to degrade their dignity as Americans. Israelis have no right to intrude on that dignity.

2) American Jews should remind themselves and others that they were partners in Israel's rebirth and consolidation. They worked for an Israel in which the Jewish legacy and a Jewish power of determination would predominate. They were committed to the idea of democracy without which their support of Israel would have lost its roots in the American and Jewish systems of values.

3) Jews reached their present status in Europe and America through the arduous victory of the idea that all men and women living under any jurisdiction should have the same rights as anyone else living under that jurisdiction. This idea entered history as a Hebrew idea: *Chok echad y'hiyeh l'hem* (One law shall be unto all).

4) American Jewish influence must therefore be used against any process that endangers Jewish majority status or that condones inequality of rights between Jews and Arabs in areas under Israel's jurisdiction.

5) Wherever there is a Jewish community in any country in which Jews do not have the same

---

This article appeared in Tikkun, *March/April 1988.*

rights as other residents to vote, to be subject to the same laws as other citizens, and to be immune from any penalties which are applicable to them alone—the Jewish community of the United States is in ferment and uproar. Mass meetings are held, intense Jewish lobbying takes place, and organizations dedicated to the vigilant protection of Jewish rights go into action day and night. Governments responsible for maintaining conditions of such inequality are kept under moral pressure to bring their policies into harmony with American ideals.

6) Jews cannot rationally behave as if rights which pertain to themselves are considered optional when others are involved.

7) In short, American Jews should strongly articulate the values which Americans and Israel and have always fought to uphold; and they must be conferred upon the Palestinians in credible form if our shared values are to be saved from violation.

David Hartman
Director of the Hartman Institute in Jerusalem and professor at Hebrew University

Any criticism of Israel must be sober and balanced and must not divide all those concerned into saints and devils. Overly moralistic criticism promotes self-righteous responses and fruitless discussions as to who is the real victim in this struggle. The concern must not be to ease one's moral conscience but for Israelis and Palestinians, to believe in the possibilities for fruitful negotiation and discussion.

Americans will be listened to and will be instructive if they reflect on and appreciate the deep pain and rage that grows from Israel's having been delegitimized in Arab propaganda for sixty years, Muslim theology for 1,400 years, and Christian theology for 2,000 years. The radios of even moderate countries like Saudi Arabia and Kuwait habitually refer to Tel Aviv and Haifa in the British parlance of "Occupied Palestine" and to Shimon Peres as "the foreign minister of the enemy." Egypt recently rejected a gift of school atlases that showed Israel on the map. Jordan television switches off the live Eurovision song festival when an Israeli pop group appears.

All this reflects an ongoing refusal to accept our existence as a nation. Living in Israel and feeling isolated and rejected by all our neighbors, one cannot escape the impression that they still harbor a deep, elemental wish that we disappear. The joy of our songs must not be heard and our athletic life must not be seen on the channels of Arab television. We live in a geographic area which refuses to note anything of the creative spirit of our culture. Distinctions which PLO spokesmen make between Jews who came to Israel from all corners of the globe, and those born in Israel cut deeply into our souls. They deny our history, and our traditions, which created an internal bond of the soul of each Jew to the land of Israel. Israel is not a post-Holocaust phenomenon, nor was it created because of Western guilt for the destruction of European Jewry. From the perception of Jews who live in Israel, they have come home. They are continuing a long historical commitment and connectedness to this land and its history. As far as our neighbors are concerned, however, we are perceived as an alien growth in the Middle East. We are not indigenous to its soil, history, and culture. Our return is only the temporary mistake and aberration, which will in due time disappear. It is ironic and sad that although we have come home and built a strong country we often feel, because of our neighbors, the exilic pain of alienation and delegitimization.

The tragedy of Palestinian refugees is that they have been used by hostile neighbors to continue in a condition of suffering and homelessness in order to represent the nonlegitimacy of our national existence. Sermons heard in the mosques and the school books that educate youth in Arab countries do not express any desire to find a dignified solution to the Israeli-Palestinian struggle.

Deeply ingrained in our national consciousness is the knowledge that our return did not evoke any joyful responses from our neighbors. We did not hear, "Welcome back home, my brother Isaac. We share a common father in Abraham and a common spiritual monotheistic tradition." Rather, it was only our military power and our determination to be loyal to our national historical memory that made Israel a viable political reality in the Middle East. The hope of the last forty years has been that our presence would gradually seep into the consciousness of our Arab neighbors and evoke a significant degree of acceptance. Tragically, this has not been the case.

The revolt of the Palestinians during the last weeks and the need for the Israeli army to use brutal force to quell the riots has brought home in a way not present before in Israeli consciousness, the fact that Palestinians do not seek membership within Israeli society. The Palestinians are not prepared to disappear. The Palestinian people possess a national consciousness and a will for political freedom. We cannot continue our relationship with them in total denial of their desire for self-determination.

There are two options. Either we in Israel accept their fundamental human needs and seek to accommodate them, while building safeguards so as not to weaken our national security. Or we shall create an Israeli society that will rule with force and intimidation over a million and a half vehemently resentful people. Even if arguments could be presented that this form of rule is militarily and political feasible, it would inevitably eat away at and undermine the moral and religious significance of our national renaissance. We never dreamed of a Jewish nation that would dehumanize and exploit an entire people. This is not what we prayed for or waited for during the past 2,000 years.

To reduce Palestinians to a subject population that lives in dread of Israeli power, is to destroy any significant connection between the moral and spiritual teachings of our tradition and contemporary Israel. To control the Palestinians permanently will justifiably undermine the centrality of Israel for world Jewry. Palestinians will permanently make us feel as strangers and aliens in our own home, as long as we are unresponsive to their urgent need for political freedom.

An independent Palestinian political reality, in which Palestinians will find it necessary to become responsible for the social, economic, and political well being of their citizens, may begin the process of healing the negative and destructive identity of many Palestinians. If we control the Palestinians, then their only identity is the rejection of Israel. They need to develop a positive identity born from living and being responsible for their own society.

There is a vicious dialectic that must be broken: Palestinian as victim, as symbol of our delegitimization, reinforces our anger and rage and in turn leads to the loss of our deeper moral and spiritual values that make us strangers to our own selves and to our own people. We can deal constructively with our anger if we acknowledge the reality of the Palestinians and are supportive of their need for self-determination.

At the same time, we must proclaim with clarity to them and to the world that Palestinian national existence shall not in any way jeopardize our security. We must insist on total demilitarization of any Palestinian national entity.

In doing this, we clearly articulate that we do not seek to subjugate a people but we equally show a healthy appreciation that the Messiah has not come. The spirit of love and brotherhood does not yet exist in the Middle East. We must insist on very clear safeguards for our national security. Our healthy national need to live and to flourish requires that no Arab army exist on this side of the Jordan river. By doing this, we make it clear that we seek to live with our neighbors but that we are fully cognizant that only through a secure and viably strong Israel is there any possibility for a future emergence of good will and understanding between the different nations in the Middle East.

The Palestinian-Jewish struggle is clearly the central issue facing the Jewish state today. Palestinians will not develop a dignified and creative national identity unless they free themselves from the tragic error of calling for the eventual destruction of Israel. We, in turn, will never feel fully at home until we build a national existence that does not require the suppression of Palestinian desires to be a dignified and free nation. The future identity of both national communities hangs on their finding the wisdom and good will to resolve this tragic condition.

Hannan Hever

Hannan Hever teaches Hebrew literature at Hebrew University in Jerusalem

The recent eruptions of violence on the West Bank and Gaza Strip are important, not simply because of the number of Palestinians killed, or because relations between the Israelis and the Palestinians have become more tense than ever before, but because the latest incidents may start to convince Israelis that their government's policies must be radically changed—that the Israeli occupation of the West Bank and Gaza must end immediately. It is hard to tell whether a broad-based political movement for such radical change will arise in the near future, at least in part because Israelis are still in a state of shock from the escalated violence. Israelis are embarrassed, and therefore, many of them have remained silent. In addition, great confusion exists because people are still trying to disseminate the information being reported by the media. Nevertheless, there are growing indications that radical opposition to Israeli policies is mounting to levels far greater than ever before.

This tendency can be seen in several ways. Many Israelis are abandoning the traditional, less bold methods of protest, such as petitions and demonstrations, and are advocating civil disobedience and other more active forms of struggle. Previously, Israelis who opposed the Occupation asked the Israeli government or the Minister of Defense not to send them to the Occupied Territories. Now they are making a declaration. They—some of them are even army officers—are refusing to serve there, and they even are willing to go to jail. Some, in fact, are already sitting in jail. Moreover, there exists a growing number of teenagers who openly state that they are not willing to be drafted into the Israeli army to serve in the Occupied Territories.

Eventually, the public at large may come to support the rights of struggling Palestinians and refuse to unite behind Peres and Shamir, who continually demand "law and order" when what they really want is to maintain the Occupation as it now stands. Ultimately, there never have been fundamental differences between Peres and Shamir. Both of them have always worked under the a priori assumption that some sort of Occupation must continue. The consensus in favor of Occupation has lasted for twenty-one years, and even those who officially have opposed the Occupation have not challenged this consensus, have "played the same game" as the occupiers. Fortunately, this recent turn of events may help us finally to break the consensus and force Peres and Shamir to stop insisting upon continued Occupation.

There seem to be two principal avenues for protest in Israel. One is the more traditional avenue— the avenue of parliamentary debate. Within parliament we see people like Peres pressing for some sort of agreement with the Palestinians and for an international peace conference. People further to the left—in the PLP, for example—are willing to speak about recognizing the PLO, negotiating directly with its members, and establishing a Palestinian state on the West Bank and the Gaza Strip.

But the second avenue of protest is, I think, far more important. This avenue is being taken by a growing number of people, people who have become convinced that parliamentary debate has become largely irrelevant. In this way, there are certain similarities between this crisis and the war in Lebanon. There, too, people began to realize that the Knesset was not dealing with the fundamental issues, and that the important events were happening in the streets, outside of our parliament. Even Peace Now is becoming more forceful in its protests. Recently, for example, it has engaged in a vociferous protest to change the political situation—to end the rule by "iron fist," to stop the cruel treatment of Palestinians, to halt the brutal break-up of demonstrations.

Unfortunately, however, Peace Now is still out of touch with the fundamental problems plaguing Israel. It has nothing new to offer Israeli society, and this fact is becoming particularly obvious today. After all, today we are dealing, not with a war in Lebanon, but with a situation that has been going on for twenty-one years, something that all of us have become a part of. Everyone who is pained by the situation is asking what to do, and Peace Now is not even beginning to give an adequate response. It is doing something very limited and very cautious. Peace Now is saying to Israelis: "Come to the Tel Aviv Museum, come to a square in Tel Aviv, stay here for a half-hour to listen to speeches and go home." Why should anyone come? Why should anyone go to a demonstration held by a group that has failed to deal with the roots of the problem? No one in Peace Now has demanded that Israelis break the consensus for Occupation. No one in Peace Now has bothered to ask whether what's happening in Gaza really is terrorist activity. It's not terror. One can call it a thousand names—war, for example, or a struggle for national liberation—but it surely isn't terror.

There exist today two alternatives to Peace Now, alternatives that are beginning to gain support. One is an organization called Dai La'kibush (Stop the Conquest), and the other is called Yesh Gvul (There is a Limit/Boundary), both of which are much more aggressively opposed to the Occupation and have a clear political program: withdrawal from the territories, establishment of a Palestinian state, and recognition of the PLO, among other things. Moreover, their members are committed to strong non-parliamentary struggles, such as civil disobedience on the part of both soldiers and citizens. The recent wave of teenagers who spontaneously decided not to go to the army, as well as the increasing number of people in reserves who also have refused to serve, can be attributed directly to the organizational efforts of Yesh Gvul. Eventually the efforts of these important organizations may force Peace Now to join in the struggle.

Someone I know has suggested that perhaps our largely non-parliamentary struggle is a moral struggle, not a political one—that we are engaged in a useless campaign simply to soothe our own consciences. Such claims are not only wrong, but offensive. A growing number of Israelis have proven themselves willing to take great risks for the cause of justice, and it is ludicrous to assume that because we emphasize the non-parliamentary components of the struggle that we therefore are engaged in a battle that is not political. On the contrary, we are making a very radical political statement. We alone have been willing both to question and to attempt to destroy the political consensus in favor of occupation—the consensus that has guided Israelis on both the Left and the Right for twenty-one years.

If I were writing a letter to my friends in America I would tell them that if they want to understand the seriousness of the problems in Israel, and if they want to help us combat these problems and genuinely help this country that we all love, then they must regard all silence about the occupation and all support of the current Israel regime as an attack on those of us who are fighting for a moral Israel. I am asking American Jews not to tolerate this injustice in any way. I am asking them not to give money, political support, or any other type of assistance to the Israeli government until it effects fundamental changes in its policies toward the Palestinians. Instead, they should help Israel by providing support for Yesh Gvul, Dai La'kibush, Peace Now, or any other organization that asks for money in order to fight the Occupation.

I have seen a few American Jews interviewed on television who have begun to take this stand. They are making the important distinction between supporting us—the people of Israel—and supporting the government's policies. These people are doing crucial and heroic work. They are making an important moral statement, and they also have succeeded in reassuring us that we have direction, that there is hope for the future of our struggle.

One last thing, I urge American Jews to refuse to participate in the celebration of Israel's 40th anniversary in April/May of 1988, but to instead turn this occasion into an opportunity to debate Israel's policies in Gaza and the West Bank. This year is not a time for celebration—but rather for all Jews who love Israel to let Israeli leaders know that the Jewish people will no longer support an Israeli Occupation.

Shimon Peres
Foreign minister of the State of Israel

The choice today for Israel is to be willing to have less control and more peace. The central task for Jewish life in the 1940s was for Israel to reach independence. The task for Jewish life in the 1990s is to reach peace and to offer it to the whole region. We need to show this region that we can demonstrate talents for construction and friendliness, for cooperation and modesty, for caring for other people—just as we have shown strength in our ability to defend our lives when we were attacked.

What is happening in Judea, Samaria, and Gaza shows that this time is the time for decision. This is the most important topic on the agenda of the Jewish people. When we look at the Palestinians and Arabs who now live in lands currently being governed or administered by Israel, there are several groups. First, there are 700,000 Palestinians who are currently citizens of Israel. They should be equal to everyone else. There should be no distinctions from the standpoint of a state between citizens who are Jewish and citizens who are non-Jewish. They should enjoy equal rights and equal obligations. Then there is another group of Palestinians living in the West Bank, some 800-850,000 people. All of them, without exception, are Jordanian citizens. They carry Jordanian passports and they are represented in the Jordanian parliament. There are close to thirty members of that parliament from the West Bank.

A third group is some 600,000 Arabs in Gaza living without any citizenship or passport. They are called the people who are always late, because wherever they go they are put last in line. With them we have to decide: What do we want? To make them citizens of Israel? They are entitled to have passports, like any other human being. There will be over a million of them in fifteen years' time. Gaza is as crowded as Hong Kong. And density is not necessarily a good way to reduce crime or bitterness. Now they don't have passports, they hardly have a piece of land. They don't have water. They don't have industries. They are cut off from all sides. What are you going to do?

When people say "Let's annex Gaza," what do they mean? To annex the land or to annex the people? Can we really separate the two? The only person who ever did that was Marc Chagall—in his paintings people float in the air. I tell you from the bottom of my heart: We should not escape the moral truth of our political situation. Let us be fair-minded. The people in Gaza are refugees, they live in refugee camps. They are on our conscience and our responsibility. You cannot run away—I cannot run away. Finally, we have a fourth group, people residing in East Jerusalem, 130,000 of them. Almost without exception they are Jordanian citizens, and if these people are now part of Israel, then they must enjoy complete equality—in real terms, not just in declarations. We have to do that not in order to do them a favor, but in order to be true to ourselves.

For the rest, they should be given self-government or eventually be part of a Jordanian-Palestinian framework and run their own lives. I see no advantage in us running their lives. We know how difficult it is to administer a Jewish life—why should we try to administer on top of that a non-Jewish life? Let's make our own society successful.

Photo by Oliver and Steinberg

Yaron Ezrahi
Professor of political science at Hebrew University

In the present situation, the unity and solidarity of American Jews behind the official Israeli government is an empty, convenient gesture which suggests to me a considerable measure of irresponsibility when Israel is divided on matters of life and death. I think it is morally reprehensible to unite behind a paralyzed Israeli government and failed leadership. What type of evidence are American Jewish leaders waiting for to convince them that automatic solidarity with any Israeli government is corrosive to the moral authority of their voice in relation to principal issues of Jewish life as well as to matters of Jewish interest? One would have expected that American Jews would understand better than Jews who don't live in democratic states that consensus forced from the top without debate, without a real consensus of opinion, is a farce which lacks the legitimacy of a democratic consensus that develops only after serious deliberation. If there are American Jewish leaders who believe that we should engage in mass deportations, in limiting the press, and in blocking the political process, and if they believe that we should do these things as necessary measures to further the interest of Israel, let them say so publicly, so they can be exposed to the kind of legitimate criticism that may exhibit the weakness of this position. If there are American Jewish leaders who think, on the contrary, that such measures are self-destructive and that the peace process should be pursued with the utmost urgency without the procrastinations of Mr. Shamir, then why the hell aren't they saying that publicly? There should be a public debate in America about these issues—just as there is in Israel. This debate within America is necessary in order to create the opportunities for new, American Jewish leaders to arise and challenge the present leadership, which is timid, lacks imagination, and thinks bureaucratically. Certainly American Jewry deserves better leadership than those who prefer to rub shoulders with Israeli ministers rather than taking courageous stands on matters concerning Israel's destiny. □

Now is Not the Time to Speak Out

Kenneth Jacobson

Some years back, George Ball wrote an article in *Foreign Affairs* entitled "How to Save Israel in Spite of Herself." Today, we are witnessing others, including the editors of *Tikkun,* taking it upon themselves to save Israel from herself. They call on American Jews to speak out in criticism of Israel because they "know" that Israel has lost its moral bearings and is the obstacle to peace. And they justify this course of action on the grounds that some Israelis encourage them to do so.

The motives of American-Jewish critics of Israel may be different from those of George Ball. But their posture—knowing what's good for Israel—reflects a certain chutzpah and lack of faith in Israel's democracy. Not having made the ultimate commitment to the Jewish state—*aliya*—they now seek to enter the decision-making process from a distance without having to bear the consequences of those decisions.

This piece will argue that we ought to continue to support the people and elected officials of Israel, however *they* choose to resolve the difficult problems before them.

• On February 10, 1988, the *Jerusalem Post* reports that King Hussein of Jordan said on a visit to Europe that the greatest gain for the Arab world from the uprisings in the territories has been the reaction it has provoked in the American-Jewish community.

• Early in March, thirty U.S. Senators wrote a letter to Secretary of State George Shultz that, in part, criticizes Israeli Prime Minister Yitzhak Shamir for his position with regard to the West Bank and Gaza.

These are some of the early results of the growing tendency in the organized Jewish community to engage in public criticism of Israel. If this tendency continues, we may have seen nothing yet.

For most of Israel's existence the Jewish Community has generally accepted the principle that on matters of fundamental security there ought not be public criticism of Israel. The basis for this proposition has been that Israel is a country under siege, that Israelis are the ones that have to live or die with the consequences of Israeli decisions, and that we as a community, as much as we care about Israel, must leave these big decisions to Israel since we have not opted to participate in Israeli democracy through *aliya* and will not suffer the consequences of any one course of action. None of which is to say that there was ever any question about the right to speak; obviously, as Americans we all have that right. Rather, it is a question of responsibility.

Now along come some American Jews among the editors of *Tikkun,* who maintain that things have changed. It is said that one side of the Israeli political spectrum, led by Yitzhak Shamir, is leading Israel down a road that is harmful to the country and is blocking an opportunity for peace. Therefore, it is said, the question of responsibility must be seen in a different light, and American Jews ought to speak out and side with those on the Israeli Left who oppose Shamir.

Kenneth Jacobson is the director of Middle Eastern affairs for the Anti-Defamation League of B'nai B'rith. This article appeared in Tikkun, *May/June 1988.*

But movement away from the long-standing position of Jewish restraint ought not to be taken lightly. We should move in that direction only when there is an absolutely clear consensus among American Jews that Israel's course is self-destructive. There is no such consensus. Take the question of an international conference. It may well be, as Israel's Labor party leaders argue, that Israel should grasp the opportunity for such a conference. On the other hand, the Likud leaders have a persuasive argument of their own: If King Hussein were truly interested in peace he would go the route of direct negotiations, as Sadat did; that to inject the Soviets and Syrians into the peace process would inevitably lead to stalemate and maybe even war. Ten years ago, we may recall, the Carter administration was calling for an international peace conference, when the man of peace, Anwar Sadat, understood that direct talks were the real route to peace. Arguments can be made on both sides. But this very fact impels us to refrain from intervening and trying to "save Israel in spite of herself."

More broadly, let us imagine for a moment that those who are opposed to Shamir have their wish: elections are held early in Israel and Shimon Peres does something that's never happened in Israel's history—wins a majority of the seats in the Knesset. According to those who criticize Shamir, peace would now be at hand.

In fact, there is nothing to suggest that such would be the case. Let us remember that even Peres, who supports an international peace conference, wants such a conference to lead to direct talks between the parties, without a role for the PLO, and critically without preconditions for negotiations. King Hussein undoubtedly has moved closer to such a position himself, but he never could come to the table without legitimation from the Palestinians. For several years prior to the disturbances, the King had been seeking that legitimation. First he sought agreement from Yassir Arafat and the PLO, but he could not bring it off because of the PLO's continued rejection of Israel and of a process of open and direct negotiations. After that, he thought to finesse it through Palestinians approved by the PLO; but in that instance too, no success.

Now come the riots. The suggestion that Palestinians will display a new moderation after the activity of recent months is not supported by any evidence. Hussein is weaker, violence has been encouraged, and radical Palestinian factions as well as Islamic fundamentalists are in control. There are no Palestinians, hence no Hussein, ready to negotiate directly without preconditions for Israel.

Thus, unless one accepts the proposition that Israel in advance of negotiations should agree to long-standing minimal Arab demands—full withdrawal, creation of a Palestinian state, East Jerusalem to the Arabs (a posture which no Israeli leader supports) it is reasonable to conclude that there is no peace process today.

What Israel, including Shamir, might do when facing real peacemakers ready to negotiate openly is unknown. In the early 1970s Moshe Dayan used to say, "Better no peace with Egypt than peace without Sharm el Sheikh;" the same Dayan, with Begin, was instrumental in bringing about the peace with Egypt in which Israel gave up the whole Sinai, including Sharm el Sheikh. The choices of peacemaking generated a new reality.

At least half the people of Israel are ready to make concessions on the West Bank once there are negotiations; one can assume that fraction will grow with the sense of a chance for real peace. In other words, all problems—Israeli security, greater Palestinian control over their own destiny, the demographic issue—can be resolved through negotiations.

Historically, the American-Jewish community has also refrained from public criticism of Israel for another vital reason—to criticize would weaken our ability to influence U.S. policy in a pro-Israel direction. While American Middle East policy has been motivated by strategic and moral interests, we have mattered. We count because the political world and the general public know that when it comes to matters affecting Israel's security, the community will be united, personal opinions aside, in its respect for Israel's right to decide. As a result, in the most basic terms, there is a political price to be paid by those who would turn against Israel.

Now we are in danger of losing what we have built these many years. During recent months, the community, by the willingness of some to break this historic posture toward Israel, has made it easier for political figures and others to discount the cost of their criticizing Israel. All of this criticism is in an early stage and there is nothing that has been lost to date that cannot be recouped. But should the criticism continue and grow, should a free-for-all emerge in the Jewish community, then those who see as their goal the weakening of America's relationship with Israel will find their task far easier.

It is no accident that King Hussein of Jordan and others have focused on the impact of the riots on American Jewish opinion. While they may exaggerate the influence of the community, they understand that to neutralize us might open up all kinds of possibilities. Indeed, let us not forget the analysis by Arab leaders about why they don't have a military option against Israel—because of U.S. military and economic support—and how they can regain it—by working to diminish and eliminate that support. Whatever chances exist for peace, indeed the one part of peace that does exist, depend on the Arabs knowing that the U.S.-Israel relationship is here to stay. A split Jewish community revives hope among the Arabs that a new dynamic in U.S.-Israel relations can be set in motion. The result: Peace opportunities disappear, thoughts of war reemerge.

One more point. One should not be overly impressed by the argument that it is now legitimate to speak out because Israeli political figures come here and call upon us to do so in order to help Israel. This is not so new a phenomenon. It usually is a case of whose ox is being gored. Israelis on the Right opposed to the Camp David accords wanted American Jews to speak out to "save Israel"; and Israelis on the Left opposed to the war in Lebanon wanted American Jews to speak out to "save Israel." Each would have been appalled had we spoken out on the "wrong" issue. They would have told us to mind our business, to leave these crucial matters to Israel. And they would have been right.

In sum, let us maintain our historic approach to this question. Israelis, not we, still have to live with the life and death consequences of their decisions; nothing fundamental has changed to suggest they are not capable of making these decisions in a rational way when facing a choice for peace; and, the critical role of the American-Jewish community in the making of U.S. policies warrants continued support for Israel. □

Jewish Umbrellas and Dissent: Baby, It's Raining Outside

Albert Vorspan

W hat happens to Jewish umbrella organizations when traumatic events in Israel deeply divide American Jews? How can dissenting organizations function under an umbrella without being drenched in a downpour?

One significant umbrella is the National Jewish Community Relations Advisory Council (NJCRAC) which is the coordinating body for the entire field of Jewish community relations. It includes ten national organizations and over one hundred local Jewish community relations councils. Among the national agencies are the American Jewish Committee, the American Jewish Congress, the Anti-Defamation League, and the Union of American Hebrew Congregations (UAHC, Reform). In terms of process, the NJCRAC is the most open and democratic of all umbrellas. Its annual convention is both serious and substantive.

Over the years, the NJCRAC has succeeded in producing an annual joint program plan which is relatively liberal and surprisingly multi-issued, thus refuting both the *Commentary* contention of a Jewish tilt to the right and the liberal-left lament that Jews are becoming a single-issue community. Since 1967, the Israel issue has been the highest priority for the NJCRAC. Prior to the Six Day War, Israel was not even one of the major issues in the field, eclipsed then by immigration policy, church-state separation, and civil rights.

At this year's convention in Los Angeles in February, there were sessions on every major issue; but this year we *were* one issue at heart. The key session was a plenary debate between Ted Mann, president of the American Jewish Congress and a prominent peacenik, and Malcolm Hoenlein, director of the Conference of Presidents of Major Jewish Organizations, but it was too bland to ignite the passions of the delegates.

In all modesty, a forum on anti-Semitism, in which I participated with Earl Raab and Gary Tobin, somehow hit the nerve and the fan. Rabb surveyed the unfolding events in the territories and charted somber scenarios involving a possible backlash against Israel by opinion makers in America and ultimately by Congress. Tobin noted the shallowness and volatility of American public opinion on the Middle East and the disturbing persistence of stereotypes such as Jewish loyalty to Israel taking precedence over Jewish loyalty to America.

I accused the Jewish community relations field of being advocates for social justice on all issues except one—ours. We had lost our role as champions of social justice and had become cheerleaders and amen-sayers for every policy coming out of Jerusalem. By defending even the indefensible, we had hurt our credibility and badly served Israel itself. I said that the Hebrew prophets judged the Jewish people, and not only the Assyrians and the Egyptians. If we pretend that the media are the

---

Albert Vorspan is director of social action and vice-president of the Union of American Hebrew Congregations. This article appeared in Tikkun, *May/June 1988.*

349

heart of our problem and continue to suppress the "P" word—Palestinians—we will not be community relations workers but hired guns for bankrupt policies.

There was loud applause, which I interpreted as a sense of relief on the part of younger delegates and staffers. But so what? Jewish community relations councils are tied umbilically to Jewish federations which are the fundraising and planning arms of every local Jewish community. Federations have a vested interest in Israel and in protecting sacred cows from criticism and controversy lest the spigot be turned off.

So what can one expect from an umbrella when profound diversity exists among many of its agencies? Fair and pluralistic debate. An honest hearing. And procedures whereby an organization's position is not ignored in the name of majority rule.

The NJCRAC is scrupulous about process. The rub comes when such a body as it's Israel Task Force, set up jointly with the Council of Jewish Federations and Welfare Councils, evolves strategies and guidance for local communities that may or may not reflect the nuanced differences among the agencies. Inevitably, the NJCRAC maintains day-to-day relationships with Israeli consular officials that are much more intense than its relations with its own agencies, excepting of course the so-called Big Three (the American Jewish Congress, the American Jewish Committee, and the ADL). If Shamir is prime minister, one should not expect the idea of an international conference to be pressed upon Jewish umbrellas by Israeli consular officials. Thus, the bland lead the bland.

There is another and very powerful player—American Israel Political Action Committe (AIPAC)—that interacts on both policy and daily operations. Apparently it was AIPAC that dreamed up the idea of legislation to close down the PLO offices in both Washington and New York City. Some NJCRAC agencies went along in Washington but thought closing the U.N. office in New York City was illegal and counterproductive. But by that time ambitious legislators were already making hay with fire-eating bravura and anti-PLO posturing—and it was too late. Moreover, the doubters within the Jewish Establishment were afraid to go public after the fact. Thus, dumb policy-making and fear of making waves made the Jewish community look ridiculous in the eyes of Shultz and others in the know at the very height of the Israel crisis. Incidentally, AIPAC is now undergoing a major internal postmortem concerning the recent letter of the thirty senators. How did it happen? Could it have been stopped? Was it erosion or reality? One question that will not be asked: Isn't it chutzpah to think U.S. senators need permission from the Jewish Establishment to comment upon an American peace initiative? And is it beyond our comprehension that these senators, several of them Jewish, are going through the same anguish and questioning that we ordinary people are?

The NJCRAC is careful to avoid becoming an obvious vehicle of propaganda. Propaganda, no. *Hasbarah* (public relations), yes. The NJCRAC is solicitous about the sensibilities of its national agencies, especially the Big Three. When the American Jewish Congress disapproved of a draft of an NJCRAC letter rapping the thirty senators who had criticized Shamir, the draft was dead in the water. But whose idea was it in the first place? How could such a letter even be contemplated by a consensus body that included in its membership organizations that had gone public in favor of territorial compromise and against the status quo?

The truth is that while the NJCRAC is a multi-issue umbrella, its bottom-line issue is Israel, and the dovish and hawkish bodies cancel each other out on the policy level. At the recent convention, an agreement could not be secured to say anything, even in private, about the impending Shultz peace mission. Operationally, day by day, the NJCRAC does an important job of interpreting Israel to the American community—usually better than the government of Israel does.

A second umbrella is even more *pareve* on the Middle East. The Synagogue Council of America (SCA) representing Orthodox, Conservative, and Reform bodies, is invisible on the Israeli crisis.

This coordinating body for the Jewish religious community, far from raising the prophetic moral issues that undergird Judaism itself and that wrench thoughtful Jews everywhere, has chosen to sit this one out. A fragile body at best, living under the sword of a frequently threatened veto by Orthodox bodies, the SCA agrees about very little of serious consequence, except for some areas of interreligious relations (not including the Pope).

How a silent Jewish religious umbrella can meet with Catholic bishops, the Methodists, the National Council of Churches, and other leading organizations in the midst of this crisis boggles the imagination. Perhaps by steering the discussion to hunger in Ethiopia or the old staple of Soviet Jewry.

As a delegate representing the UAHC, I urged the SCA to address the "moral issues" in the midst of the uprising. "What moral crisis?" I was asked. "Oh, you must mean the decline of tourism." Another person said that the paramount moral issue was the presumption that Jewish leaders in the Diaspora had a right to speak publicly while Israelis were on the firing line.

A rabbinic leader of the Synagogue Council participated in the recent Presidents' Conference mission to Israel. He publicly urged Prime Minister Shamir to ignore pressures for compromise and flexibility and to dig in his heels against the Shultz peace plan. So much for the Jewish religious mitzvah of pursuing peace and being a light unto the nations.

Indeed, when Amos Oz says that the current crisis is not about the borders of Israel but about the boundaries of Judaism, I start to notice how rare it is to hear rabbis (especially the chief rabbis) talk about the moral imperatives of Judaism, the demands of God, the universality of God's family, and the uniqueness of Jewish ethics. If Israel has become our God, our surrogate synagogue, and our surrogate faith, we are all idolaters.

But it is the Presidents' Conference that is the chief vehicle of support for Israel. Like the NJCRAC, the Presidents' Conference tries to give a hearing to diverse views. Its three-day mission to Israel early in March reflected careful planning and an exceptional mix of contrasting positions. The difficulty is that, in a crunch, the Conference inevitably becomes a useful tool for whichever Israeli government is in the saddle. Thus, when the current drama exploded in the media, with headlines about beatings and deportations and mass arrests, Morris Abram, current president, inexorably emerged as the defense attorney. In effect, he became another Israeli ambassador to the public, and, despite virtuosity and great skill, the bestower of a communal kosher stamp upon Israeli conduct and policies.

Thus, when Shamir came to New York City to report to the Jewish community on the results of his meeting with Shultz in Washington, he was received by Abram and three hundred leaders of the Presidents' Conference not as a failed diplomat who had blundered into saying "No" to an American peace initiative, but as a conquering hero, fresh from the wars. Having hoisted and shackled the Shultz plan, he skewered Jews in America who presumed to criticize Israel. Two of us rose to challenge him, urging him to consider that difference of opinion on policy should not be equated with disloyalty to Israel and the Jewish people, reminding him that if the government and public of Israel are divided, American Jewry will be divided as well. From the audience's response, one would have imagined we had presented a brief for Jesse Jackson to the Jewish Defense League. Mr. Shamir lowered the boom on us, suggesting that public criticism of Israel by Jews plays into the hands of the anti-Semites and helps the government of the United States pressure Israel. Thunderous ovation. It was an atmosphere hostile to diversity and more akin to mass hysteria than to pluralism.

So how can one function within an umbrella like this? With difficulty. Organizations of the Left and of the right must have the courage to fight for their positions, however unpopular at the moment. It is good to remember that Israeli public opinion was antagonistic to Egypt and the prospect of peace with Egypt only months before Camp David. It is vital to keep the Conference from preemption, either by Israel or by a grouping of member organizations within the Conference. Our commitment to the Jewish people means that we need instruments of Jewish cooperation. The alternative to the Conference is chaos. But in the name of unity we must not paper over the deep philosophical and political principles that divide us on issues like the disposition of the territories. We should not destroy our credibility by blaming everybody else and exempting Israel from any accounting. We are not ambassadors who either carry out orders or get fired. We are loving and honest Jews who are joined at the hip with our people and are full partners (and not silent partners) in the Jewish enterprise.

Each of our organizations retains its own autonomy and sovereignty. By joining an umbrella, we do not cease developing our organizational resolutions, or expressing our conscience and our judgment. Schindler-bashing may have become the chic indoor sport of American Jewish leaders— they now have Woody Allen and thirty Senators to savage as well. But the real debate is about the nature of our Jewish identity, the quality of our ethics, and the Jewishness of the Jewish state. That debate resonates in every conscience and in every broken Jewish heart. In that sense, a meeting of the Presidents' Conference is an Alice in Wonderland exercise in self-delusion, because it pretends that debate raging everywhere occurs only on the margins of Jewish life.

Credibility and integrity are at risk. When Alex Schindler publicly criticized the Rabin policy of beatings, Rabbi Harold Schulweis, one of Conservative Jewry's compelling moral voices, indicated that he agreed with Schindler but attacked him for going public. The dichotomy between our public utterances and our true beliefs is becoming a form of communal schizophrenia. Check the last few presidents of the Presidents' Conference. Most said publicly what they disbelieved privately. The evidence is the dramatically different views they expressed after they left office.

And what difference does it make? Who can take such leadership seriously? Why should an American official meet with a Presidents' Conference delegation—Ten Little Sir Echoes—when he can meet much more simply with the Israeli ambassador? What is the particular role of the Presidents' Conference? If U.S. and Israeli interests are not totally identical, then are American Jewry's and Israel's interests absolutely the same? With reference to Irangate? Pollard? Relations with South Africa? The Iraqi Pipeline?

After the tumultuous events of recent months, a sea of change is taking place beneath the surface. American Jews no longer accept Israeli leaders as infallible or even wise in many matters. They see a mediocre leadership in all parties, totally gridlocked. Our institutions will not turn away; we will intensify our efforts in Israel in the belief that its very soul is in jeopardy. The Reform movement has responded by developing a Religious Action Center in Jerusalem. Our joint task is not to stand around singing *Hatikvah* while Israel may be headed for disaster. Despite Shamir and our umbrellas, the relations between Israel and the Diaspora will never be the same again. They will be more reciprocal, more quarrelsome, more candid, more public and more plural. How the Jewish umbrellas respond to this new reality will determine whether they will endure as worthy servants of the Jewish people or be discarded like the leaky and broken umbrellas one sees littered on the sidewalk after a storm subsides. ☐

Between the Lines:
A Journey to Beit Sahur and Back

Sidra Ezrahi

asual conversation at a cocktail party in July 1989 with an actor from California on a sentimental family pilgrimage to Israel: "What places will you be visiting?" "Masada. And Yad Vashem and the Diaspora Museum." "Will your guide also be taking you to the Intifada?" "The *what*?!" "You know—the Palestinian uprising on the West Bank and Gaza." "Oh. I thought that was over." (Quick, talk about the cholera epidemic in Odessa. Or the War of the Roses. Or Dustin Hoffman. Don't be impolite. Israel is a monument. A symbol. A museum. Martyrs and heroes. Simple, neat, well-packaged.)

Shall we dare to ruffle our brothers' and sisters' feathers by arranging alternative tours of the Land of Israel—featuring Nahalin, where townspeople were taunted for days last year by border policemen who then shot four of them dead outside a mosque early one Ramadan morning; or Beita, where a resident who broke the gun of one settler during a bloody skirmish was given an eight-year sentence; or the refugee camp where a woman died after being deprived of medical treatment during a curfew? Day trips can be arranged to the detention centers at Dahariya and Ketziot. The road to Dahariya passes Dehaisha, a town behind barbed wire. A few kilometers further, the road passes Elazer, a town behind barbed wire. The first, a Palestinian refugee camp, and the second, a Jewish settlement, are the landmarks of a warped Zionist territorialism. "Welcome to the Dahariya Installation," reads the cheerfully painted sign in front of the prison....

But I would like to offer yet another sort of tour—a walking tour through the streets of Beit Sahur, visiting the homes of Ghassan Andoni and Jamal Hilal, where on numerous occasions over the past year we would sketch our visions of the future over cardamom-spiced coffee. Beit Sahur is one place where the efforts of a small but determined group of Israelis and Palestinians committed to ending the Occupation and accepting a Palestinian state alongside Israel seem to have made a difference.

Today, Ghassan and Jamal won't be there to greet us; they are in administrative detention at Ketziot, along with more than a thousand other Palestinians. In between prison stints this summer, Jamal managed to taste the first ten days of matrimony. Since in these cases there are no such amenities as charges or trials or verdicts, we can only speculate that Ghassan and Jamal have suffered for the crime of talking peace with Israelis. We might be hosted by Eleas Rashmawi who, today at least, is outside prison. It is a short walk from his pharmacy, with its empty shelves, to his home, where the scuff marks on the floor signify the place where the sofa should be. The summer months provided a heated environment for the inevitable escalation of hostilities in the Occupied

Sidra DeKoven Ezrahi is a member of Tikkun's *editorial board and the author of* By Words Alone. *She teaches comparative Jewish literature at Hebrew University and is writing a book on exile and the modern Jewish imagination. This article appeared in* Tikkun, *January/February 1990.*

Territories. The "masked youths" now roaming the streets of the West Bank and Gaza are a sure harbinger of the unbridled violence that will, sooner or later, erupt if the present impasse is not broken. But the one place that has been singled out for irregular treatment is the town of Beit Sahur. Primarily known until a few months ago as the site of Shepherds' Field, where the Star of Bethlehem appeared to the three wise men, this predominantly Christian, middle-class town of twelve thousand people who have lived for generations just a stone's throw from Bethlehem has become the focus and the symbol of a hitherto invisible aspect of the intifada: the tax revolt and the government's concerted effort to crush it.

The dialogue between residents of Jerusalem and Beit Sahur, which celebrated its first anniversary this past September, originated out of resistance to the forces of depersonalization and mutual demonization that had begun to grip the Israeli and the Palestinian communities. Soon after the onset of the intifada—a seismic tremor that exposed deep layers of self-delusion—dialogue groups initiated by a few Palestinians and Israelis proliferated in the Occupied Territories. Most of these groups were meant to be convened only once or twice—just enough to begin to dislodge grossly stereotyped notions of the other. Those groups that have persisted are an anomalous presence in a place still largely immured within hermetic codes. Behind their mufflers, the masked Palestinian youths afoot in the streets echo (or parody) the menacing anonymity of Israeli soldiers behind their visors and helmets. The clothes of your neighbors are as varied as their personal tastes; the clothes of your enemy are uniform.

Within the semiotics of segregation in this region some of us appear, then, as cross-dressers. Often mistaken for settlers heading for the town of Tekoa, our people, many with head coverings, are waved through Beit Sahur (the most direct route to the Jewish settlement) by Israeli soldiers on the alert for the seditious appearance of "the peace forces." On one of our visits to Beit Sahur, the young son of our Palestinian host looked around the crowded room impatiently and asked his father what had happened to the Jews who were supposed to arrive. His father pointed to the people sitting on the couch. "No," the boy insisted. "They're not Jewish; they don't have guns." The *kaffiyeh* on the dashboard of a car driven by an unarmed Jew with a beard and skullcap can be as much a sign of the permeability of his lines of defense as of camouflaged or forfeited identity.

Dialogue that began in curiosity and mutual suspicion became, over time, an exercise in redrawing geopolitical borders while safeguarding the boundaries of human dignity. At the heart of this enterprise is a "theory of remainders" which defines the struggle in terms of its limits—limits that could leave both sides enough dignity to begin, somewhere down the road, the long task of reconstruction. No one who has watched Israeli society slip back into the grip of an ancient rhetoric of martyrdom and fear of demonic others should minimize the long-term pathological effects of persecution on all the participants and (in communities stricken with long memories) their descendants. Each time the Israeli army crosses another "red line" in the humiliation of the occupied population, the remainder shrinks.

There are, then, lines to be crossed and lines to be held fast. Red lines, green lines. A riot of color. In their quiet rerouting of the main arteries of transportation around the city, many Jerusalemites have effectively reinstated the old Green Line—some, admittedly, out of fear for their own safety, but some as a gesture of respect for the divided territorial claims of two peoples. When such individuals cross the border into what will someday be the state of Palestine, they do so only as invited guests.

The distance from the outskirts of Jerusalem to Beit Sahur is about five kilometers. But just beyond the invisible border, the scenery changes dramatically—armored cars and troops are the semaphores of a novel traffic control system, stopping random vehicles with variegated Palestinian license plates; stone-throwing Palestinian youths are the shadowy presences behind every tree, targeting cars with yellow Israeli license plates; trigger-happy Jewish settlers patrol the roads in their own vigilante groups—so that the fifteen-minute journey, though often uneventful, is negotiated on roads exposed to the ballistics of Palestinians, soldiers, and settlers. We pass Rachel's Tomb (ah, Rachel, where are your tears? Your sons have returned to their borders and forgotten so quickly the pain of homelessness)—and turn left down the hill leading to Beit Sahur.

As we drive, those who understand Arabic strain their eyes to decipher the writing on the walls. Their walls, like ours, are scarred with signs and portents; they stand firm and ominous while elsewhere in the world the walls between the East and West Banks of enmity are crumbling. Traveling through the Occupied Territories one learns, with time, to *read* the landscape. The graffiti on every wall, door, and shutter in Beit Sahur and other towns is a palimpsest of messages inscribed under the cover of night, painted over at gunpoint in the morning ("We use white paint; it provides a good backdrop for the next layer"), and reinscribed that night. The intifada even has its local Tom Sawyer, the Palestinian shopkeeper whose slow-motion swipes at the inscription on his lintel displeased the commanding officer. "Here, let me show you how it's done," the officer said, taking the brush and, with efficient strokes, whitewashing his little corner of Palestine.

Many of the Israeli soldiers on graffiti detail cannot read the Arabic inscriptions. "Do you know what it is you are forcing me to strike out?" one resident of Beit Sahur asked the soldier in charge. "No," the soldier admitted. "It says, 'We Want Peace'." The soldier blushed. "Who could object to that?" he asked. "Shamir, I guess," answered the man. "To hell with Shamir. I want peace too," said the man in khaki, and walked away.

Of course not all the texts are innocuous. Youths whose white hoods glow in the nighttime streets paint slogans and distribute leaflets sponsored by the various factions, including extremist nationalist and fundamentalist groups (Hamas, Islamic Jihad), calling for violence and holy war.

(This war is being fought over texts almost as much as over territory. An Arab student from Beersheba was discovered to have removed the parchment from a mezuza and replaced it with passages from the Koran ...)

In a land so saturated with the authority of scriptures, one learns both the power and the intractability of conflicting narratives. Stereotypes of the other prove easier to relinquish than the incompatible chronicles of the history of this land. Eventually we found a way, as the long winter of the intifada gave way to spring, to direct our dialogue away from the vast and exclusive dreamlands of our youth to the possible territory of an inclusive future.

Given the private, often clandestine nature of our meetings and the absence in the early stages of any media coverage, the initial posturing could yield over time to less ritualized gestures. Within the rhetoric of the conflict, the incredulous, then grudging acknowledgment by the Palestinians of "Jewish fear," along with the equally hard-won Jewish acknowledgement of a Palestinian claim to the vocabulary of exile and homecoming, transformed the formulas of coherent competing narratives into fragments of discourse making their way into new domains. Fully invested in our role as neighbors engaged in dialogue, rather than politicians engaged in negotiations, we also allowed ourselves the luxury of exploring but not attempting to resolve some of the more stubborn points between us, such as the Right of Return and the status of Jerusalem.

Significant distinctions can be drawn between these local discussions in Beit Sahur and elsewhere in the Occupied Territories, and parallel encounters between Israelis and Palestinians abroad. There is a palpability to claims to homeland that we make—or forfeit—in each others' homes, especially when the houses of some of the Israeli hosts have dubious biographies. (As does lemon tree in the yard, whose fruit nobody refuses.)

Dialogue led to a series of exchange visits between the two communities—one in a church in Beit Sahur in December 1988 (at which the mayor declared a day of peace—and not a stone was thrown) and another, several weeks later, at a synagogue in Jerusalem (where the teenage *shebab* of Beit Sahur and the soldiers-to-be from Jerusalem squared off on the basketball court). Even the landscape took on softer contours; coming for a visit, we could be touched again, after so many years, by the magic of the setting sun over the terraced hills.

Of course the horizon never remained clear for very long. Intimidation took the form of repeated arrests and, it appears, physical harassment as well. Between jail terms, Palestinian members of the dialogue group reported being warned by the military authorities not to resume their contacts with Israelis.

And yet, life in Beit Sahur began to assume a kind of normalcy, if punctuated by harassment and occasional tragedy. An "intifada economy" had evolved when the people began boycotting Israeli products and raising their own crops. (Granted, the authorities did not look favorably on such enterprises; Jad Is'hak, professor of biology at Bethlehem University, was imprisoned in Ketziot for assisting the townspeople in planting backyard gardens.) It began to seem, though, that the real hero of the intifada was a cow. Declared illegal by the military authorities, she was "deported" to an unknown destination. After her departure, the continued appearance of local milk and freshly churned butter in the homes of the residents of Beit Sahur was that much more of a miracle, even in a corner of the world so practiced in miracles.

Suddenly, in September, the miracles ceased. A crackdown began that has added another mark of shame to the visage of modern Israel. The refusal to pay taxes to the occupier for services never rendered may be the most natural and at the same time the most remarkable strategy in the Palestinian uprising. It had reached the point where there was almost no civil activity in the West Bank and Gaza that was not contingent upon the payment of a special surcharge. There were even "stone taxes" and "broken glass taxes." It became clear to the residents of Beit Sahur that they were, in effect, helping to defray the costs of the Occupation. Their economic boycott met with massive retaliation. Under siege, their telephone lines cut and supply trucks turned back from the heavily patrolled entrances to the town—even as moving trucks bearing their goods and means of livelihood rolled out of town daily—the people of Beit Sahur managed to send a communiqué to their Israeli friends:

Today we are meeting you under circumstances which differ from those under which we met throughout the year of our dialogue.... You have told your own people of our protest against Occupation and our commitment to a national Palestinian identity. You have seen how Beit Sahur is a safe and welcoming place where any Israeli who comes as a visitor and not an occupier can sleep and pray and break bread. Today we must meet you halfway between your homes and ours, for your army will not let you into our town while its tax raids continue.

In their manifesto entitled "Taxation Without Representation," the citizens of Beit Sahur declared their resolve to continue their civil disobedience, at whatever personal costs to themselves:

Taxes are paid by people to their legitimate [elected] political bodies to cover the cost of services provided.... The services provided to the Palestinian people by the occupying authorities include: opening new jails and detention centers to humiliate and terrorize us and our children; purchasing and developing weapons and equipment to kill and maim us; the deliberate retardation of development of our economic, health, and social institutions.... The Israeli tax authorities are robbing the Palestinian people and depleting their economic resources in the name of tax collection.

The response of the Israeli authorities demonstrated the propensity of misdirected power to disengage from the most elementary restraints of human compassion—a failing reflected in the faces of the children for whom even a confiscated teacup can leave permanent symbolic wounds. One family that had recently acquired a used piano for their young daughter reported pleading futilely with the soldiers to take their new dining room set, of far greater value, in its place. The child watched helplessly as Jews carried her instrument into the waiting truck. The chattel of Beit Sahur— the sofas and refrigerators, the televisions and pharmaceutical drugs and carpenter's bench—sitting at Lod airport waiting to be auctioned to the highest bidders, are the randomly dispersed icons of disrupted lives.

As of this writing, both the six-week tax siege and nightly curfews in Beit Sahur have been lifted. Still, the interdenominational "Prayer for Peace" on November 5 was conducted in a Catholic church totally surrounded by Israeli troops who denied access to their own compatriots, including rabbis, who had come to pray along with the Palestinians, and to those journalists from around the world who had come to bear witness. The town's priest, addressing the handful of Israelis who had managed to cross the barricades, spoke in Hebrew and referred to the Israeli peace camp as "the conscience of the Jewish people." When Hillel Bardin, an Israeli of American origin, rose to speak, he was greeted by deafening applause. Why, he asked, were journalists barred from attending this event at which three thousand Palestinians who had been subjected to the most relentless humiliation, were demonstrating *peaceably* for their rights? Why is it that messages of peace are consistently intercepted by the military authorities to prevent them from reaching the Israeli and the international public? (Why, indeed? Can it be that the gospel that goes forth from Jerusalem these days is that *good* news is *no* news?)

I think we can say that the people of Beit Sahur, denuded of nearly all their worldly possessions, have won this battle—for both sides. The massive response of the Israeli authorities that was so disproportionate to the provocation underscored the struggle for *control* which is the very essence of the intifada. As Beit Sahur began to take its fate into its own hands, the government, in turn, attempted to reassert its control through force. If peaceful resistance ultimately fails and violence comes to rule the streets, both our peoples will be the losers. At least let the record show, then, that on both sides of this Green line, our *fault line,* there were people who dared to explore alternatives to carnage and xenophobic visions of indivisible space.

Today the newspapers are right.... After the months of summer drought, the rains have finally come. Rain is general all over the Middle East. It is falling on Jerusalem and Beit Sahur, on every part of the dark central plain, on the treeless, rocky hills, on the vineyards and olive orchards, on the lonely graveyards, on the villages and settlements, on the prisons and detention camps, on the army bases and the storehouses of confiscated goods. It is falling upon all the living and the dead, on those who are alive today and will be dead tomorrow, and on all the unborn. □

Faisal Husseini: A Conversation

An Interview by Michael Lerner

Michael Lerner: *Tikkun* has called for the creation of a demilitarized Palestinian state. One of the arguments used against us is the claim that Palestinians would not accept demilitarization as a condition for obtaining a state.

Feisal Husseini: Well, if we want to create peace, then let's talk peace and not a scenario for war. It doesn't make sense to try to create a plan for a new state based on some scenario for creating a balance of forces—let's instead talk peace. Nor do I see that an army for a Palestinian state would guarantee its security. Our security would have to be obtained through guarantees—I don't think it would come through us having a big or strong army, because we would be surrounded by other states, like Israel, Syria, and Jordan that all have big armies, and our army would not be big enough or strong enough to protect us. So our security could not be achieved through military force. To have real security, the following would have to happen: Either we and Israel should have no arms—but I know Israelis would refuse this idea—or we would be without an army but Israel would have one. Imagine the scenario. We don't have any mines or raw materials. All we would have is agriculture. So we would develop a technology for agriculture, and because we would not be spending our money on armaments or supporting an army as Israel is doing, we would instead spend our money on research laboratories to develop our technology and our industrial capacity. Within thirty years we would be able to sell our computers on the international market. The Israelis would not be able to match this, since they are spending their money on armies. So who could guarantee us that Israel would not come with its big army standing on our borders and forcibly raise the cost of our computers? So we will need international guarantees that no one will attack our borders!

I am sure that if the Palestinians do create a demilitarized state, the Israelis, within two or three years, will come to us and ask us to build an army and buy some tanks and some airplanes from Israel. So all this talk has to be placed within the context of a more fundamental question: Are we trying to build peace or are we still talking war? If we are talking peace, then the issues can be resolved.

Lerner: From my analysis of the situation in Israel, one of the critical things that needs to happen is that we need to build confidence among Israelis that peace is really a possibility. After decades in which the Palestinians refused to recognize Israel, and a long history outside this area in which people have continually tried to destroy us, it is understandable that there is a certain distrust. Those of us who wish to build peace must seek ways to eliminate that distrust.

Husseini: Yes, it's true that for years we refused to recognize the State of Israel. But from the other

Michael Lerner talked with Faisal Husseini at his home in East Jerusalem. Husseini is the chairman of the Arab Studies Research Center in Jerusalem and is considered the leading spokesperson for the PLO on the West Bank. This interview appeared in Tikkun, *March/April 1990.*

side, Israel is preventing us from having a state. Maybe theoretically we may have been against an Israeli state; practically speaking, Israel is now against a Palestinian state. Saying "no" to a Palestinian state has generated much suspicion among Palestinians about Israeli intentions—some people think Israel's goal is to destroy the Palestinian people. So we need to build confidence not only among Israelis but also among Palestinians.

To help the process, we produced a Palestinian peace initiative which accepted the Israeli state, accepted a two-state solution, accepted UN resolutions 242 and 338, and said we are ready for negotiations. Now we would like to have the same thing from the Israelis. We'd like to hear from them that they are not against a Palestinian state. We'd like them to say, "We are not against you. We are afraid that your state would endanger us, so let us talk to see how we can build this state without endangering Israel." *This* I would accept as confidence building from the Israelis. But to tell me, "It is forbidden to you to have a state because we are afraid that it will endanger us"—this is not acceptable.

Lerner: I don't think it is a fair account of the history to say that there was theoretical opposition by Palestinians to an Israeli state while now there is practical opposition to a Palestinian state by Israel. The Palestinians engaged in armed struggle in order to prevent the creation of an Israeli state.

Husseini: But since 1948 the Israeli state has been there.

Lerner: But people have not forgotten '48.

Husseini: If we start talking about memories, I'll tell you I can't forget about De'ir Yassin, I can't forget that Jaffa was an Arab city, and we will not get out of this circle. But I'm talking about the more recent period, the last several years. During that period we were saying, "We are not going to recognize Israel, because that's our last card."

Lerner: So you think now that you've played that last card, that you've granted recognition?

Husseini: Yes.

Lerner: Many of us who oppose Shamir's policies and have been subjected to considerable abuse for our willingness to do so in public, in other words those of us who strongly support the creation of a demilitarized Palestinian state, are still not really convinced that what happened in Algiers constituted a clear statement of recognition. Even when Arafat met with Jews in Stockholm, it appeared to me that he was pushed into uttering the right words; I never had a clear sense that he was genuinely committing himself. Nor did I have a sense from Algiers that people were saying in a clear and forthright way, "We are recognizing Israel and want peace with Israel." Instead, there was legal mumbo jumbo, which made it possible for some of the people there to deny they had made a commitment to abandoning the notion that someday Israel would be replaced by a Palestinian state that would "liberate all of Palestine." If Arafat were to go on American television and unequivocally say, "Look, we recognize Israel, we want to live in peace with Israel, I want to go to Jerusalem to negotiate peace...."

Husseini: Arafat already said that he is ready to go to Jerusalem to sit down with Shamir. And Shamir responded, "If Arafat arrives at Ben-Gurion airport, I will arrest him immediately." We've already taken the steps you ask for. What more do you need?

Lerner: I could write you a paragraph which, if passed by the Palestine National Council (PNC), would change the whole dynamic and give irresistible momentum to the Israeli peace forces.

Husseini: Yes, what would it say?

Lerner: It would have several clauses:

1. We amend the Palestinian National Covenant to remove any references, direct or indirect, to the idea that Israel should be eliminated.

2. We would accept a *demilitarized* Palestinian state.

3. If you give us a demilitarized state with international guarantees to protect that Palestinian state, then—once the state is set up—we will commit ourselves to publicly renouncing, in the name of the entire Palestinian people, all claim to the part of Palestine that remains within the pre-1967 borders of the State of Israel.

Husseini: But what you are saying now would be the *result* of negotiations, not *conditions* for negotiations. Because if we started out saying that now, then we'd be asked to make *further* concessions during the actual negotiations.

Lerner: This is the exact same argument that right-wingers in Israel give when I say, "Let Israel offer a *demilitarized* Palestinian state." They say, "If we offer that as a starting point, we'll have to give more in the actual negotiations."

So I say to both sides: state your whole position now. You have to realize that most Israelis simply cannot believe that the Palestinians would ever really accept demilitarization.

Husseini: But I said that when I said that a Palestinian state would live beside an Israeli state.

Lerner: That word "beside" is still consistent with the fear of many Israelis that eventually such a state will be used as the launching pad for a second stage of struggle in which you attempt to eliminate Israel altogether. Why not say explicitly: "We used to have the idea of a two-stage solution, in which gaining a state would be a first stage, leading to a second stage in which we would attempt to liberate the rest of Palestine. We now repudiate that two stage notion."

Husseini: But what did 242 say?

Lerner: It didn't say it in a way that anyone could believe. You can hide behind legalese and the language of international diplomacy. But I'm talking about how to change the political situation. We need to create a majority of Israelis who could really believe that it would be possible to live in peace. To do that, you must speak to the heart, not just to the head.

Husseini: The Palestine National Council is a body which adopts resolutions that speak to the legal community and therefore it speaks that language. To speak to the heart, I can't make it through the PNC—but we can do it through other resolutions, statements of high officials of the PLO, and statements from Palestinian institutions. And we'd like to hear such a thing from the Israelis— that they want to hear this kind of language and that then they'd be prepared to give us something back.

Lerner: You'll never get it from Shamir. But in Israel there is a democratic process, and if you make these kinds of statements we can change the democratic alignment of forces—we can change who has power.

It would be useful if you would pay more attention to influencing the outcome of that democratic process. It's too bad that the PNC didn't issue its statement before the 1988 Israeli elections, instead of waiting until they were over. Instead, a day before the election Israelis heard about a terrorist attack on a bus in which a mother and her children were burned alive. Obviously all this pushed the whole dynamic to the right. If you are going to accept 242 and 338, why not do it before the 1988 elections?

Husseini: It was my assessment that had the PLO issued any statement before the elections, both sides would have discounted it. In the pre-election days Labor and Likud had built a dynamic in which the real question was, "Who is most against the PLO?" The most successful propaganda that Likud used was to picture Peres with Arafat; and the Labor party spent much of its energy trying to defend itself against this image. So the atmosphere was *not* conducive. Moreover, I felt that if we took a new position during the elections, once a new government came into power it would view that as a position from the past and would seek some new concessions. We are always trying to shape our policies to help the Israeli peace movement, but in the end we are discovering that they can't deliver the vote. After all, they told us that if we accepted 242 and renounced terrorism this would create a huge advance. America tells us this, you in the peace movement tell us this, but when we do change, neither America nor you can actually deliver the appropriate changes in Israel.

Lerner: This is one of the limits on a democratic system: you have to win people's minds and hearts, and people have been terrified by a long history.

Husseini: But really, where is the end of this? First they said to us, "Recognize the right of Israel to exist in peace with recognized borders and security." Then someone came to us and said, "No, we need more. We want you to accept *the historical right* for Israel to exist." Then someone came and said, "No, that would not be enough—we want the Palestinians to accept the moral right for Israel to exist." I don't know where it will stop. Will it stop only when I finally have to say, "OK, I admit that I have no right to exist"?

Lerner: I understand that you are saying that you want something in return. I understand the legitimacy of your position. But I think about this *politically* in terms of how to change the situation, rather than in terms of who is right or wrong. Politically it is necessary for the PNC to change the charter and for the PLO to say that it would prosecute people who engage in terrorism against Israeli civilians. This is a principle recognized by the Israeli army. We might both criticize the sentences against Israeli soldiers who have committed brutal acts—they are too light. But *in principle* the Israeli army recognizes that these acts should be punished—it doesn't, as the PLO did in the past, issue statements claiming credit for attacks against uninvolved civilians. So people who beat up Palestinians can and do get prosecuted, even if the sentences aren't stiff enough. Finally, suspend military actions of PLO forces trying to infiltrate Israel through the northern border. And say that you would accept a demilitarized state.

But you are right to say that we can't guarantee immediate results—there's a political process in Israel. We don't have a dictatorship there—people's minds have to be changed. The alternative is to keep the present situation in which every little concession made by the Palestinians isn't even noticed. Make one big concession of the sort I'm describing, let the PNC take this kind of action in a clear way, and you could change the political dynamics in Israel. It's not fair to ask you to do this;

but it's smart. And it's time to begin to distinguish between "fair" and "smart." ...

Husseini: But we are already saying that we are ready to give up the borders of the 1947 UN resolution and that we are now accepting the 1967 borders, which in effect means giving up very large parts of what we understand to be part of our homeland. It will be equal when both sides recognize that we have here two peoples fighting each other, and that the conflict will be resolved when we both reach the decision that we should not destroy each other, but must live together in peace. From our side, we've reached this point—we've declared we are willing to live with a two-state solution. The other side does not acknowledge that they would be willing to live on equal terms with the Palestinian people as a people—they insist instead on dealing with us not as a people, but as a minority group that is inhabiting foreign land. Mr. Shamir is willing to negotiate with a Palestinian living inside the Occupied Territories, even if he is more extreme, than he is with someone who is a Palestinian who doesn't currently reside inside the Occupied Territories; but he won't sit with members of our people who reside outside that territory. He won't sit with Edward Said or Abu Lughod just because they are from outside—because if he would sit with them he could no longer say he was dealing with a minority, he would have to thereby acknowledge that he was dealing with a people.

So the real question remains, "Is Israel willing to deal with us as a people, or does it insist on dealing with us as a minority that has no right to self-determination?" What we want from Israel is that they recognize that we are one people, and those people who are living outside are not coming from the moon. I am in Jerusalem, so Israel says they can talk to me. But what about my other three brothers, who are outside—why can't they also participate in determining the future of this land? Why do they have no right to be here—who made that determination? So, the only way to get out of this is to have mutual recognition of the principle of self-determination for each people. But it makes no sense to ask the Palestinians to make further concessions unless we can start with both sides acknowledging the right of the other to self-determination. And from our side, I believe we have done our steps, by passing the resolutions at Algiers, by Arafat saying he is willing to come to Jerusalem—we have done our job. The peace camp in Israel is asking us not only to do our job, but also asking us to do for them their job. The peace camp in Israel needs to change Israel. Because if people like the right-wing Israeli leader Gandi—who calls for expulsion of all Palestinians—continue to operate, eventually Israel will lose its own democracy, it will lose its freedom, it will go on to create a very perilous situation....

Lerner: Let's consider the issue of Israeli settlers in the West Bank. *Tikkun* has taken the position that there is no country in the world that has a right to say, "This country must be *judenrein*—which is to say, Jews can't live here in this country." On the other hand, we recognize that there is some dispute about the legality of the way some of the land taken by the settlers was acquired, and that some of the settlers are interested in provocations and would be a provocative force inside the new Palestinian state. So we've suggested some kind of international force that would supervise the borders and set up an international tribunal to decide which land was taken fairly and which land was taken unfairly. This force would also have the responsibility, for some transitional period, of enforcing law on the settlers, so that the Palestinian state would not risk creating "provocations" that would be used as justifications by the Israeli Right for military incursions against the Palestinian state. But all this thinking is based on our assumption that in principle not all settlers would have to give up land, because some of the land was legitimately acquired. Jews have a right to live on such land, just as Palestinian Arabs have a right to remain on the land that they currently inhabit inside the State of Israel.

Husseini: Just as we would not accept any other state excluding us on principle, our state will not exclude Jews or Christians. We will let anyone live here—but as part of the Palestinian state, as Palestinian citizens, not as refugees and not as part of a group that considers itself citizens of another state. Now, in the settlements that have already been set up by Jewish settlers, we will have to insist that they become open to Palestinian Arabs for settlement as well—just as we will not accept that there should be any area that prohibits Jewish settlement, so we will not accept that any area of our state would prevent Arabs from moving in. Jews would live here as citizens, as equal individuals, but not as a corporate body or as a ghetto.

Lerner: I wonder if the Palestinian movement has developed tensions and differences of perspective between those Palestinians who live on the West Bank and Gaza and those who live outside the boundaries of historical Palestine. These kinds of tensions are apparent in the Zionist movement— there are often clear differences of perspective between Jewish American Zionists and Zionists living in Israel—so I wonder how analogous differences are manifested in the Palestinian movement.

Husseini: Our movement today does not really have those fundamental differences, because our movement is like the Zionist movement before 1948 when there was a fundamental unity about the need to establish a state. Once a Palestinian state *is* created, then people in our diaspora will face the same issue that faced Zionists: Do they make use of their right of return? From that point on, the decisions about the fate of the Palestinian state will be in the hands of those who make that decision. But until they have the *right* to return, the direction of our national movement will be determined not only by those who have been allowed to remain here, but by our entire people.

Lerner: Perhaps many Palestinians who have built a more comfortable life for themselves in the U.S. or England or France or some other countries will, like many Jews in our diaspora, choose not to return.

Husseini: As long as they have the choice. At that point, fine, not everyone has to return. It may be good for us to have some people living in other places—they can still help us, not only financially, but morally and politically. Maybe if someday we develop a policy in some matter in our Palestinian state that is offensive to the rest of the world, those Palestinians will come and say to us, "Look, I'm a Palestinian just like you, but now I want you to listen to my advice."

Lerner: But isn't there a difference between those who live here in conditions that they consider oppressive and at least some of those who live in other countries under conditions that aren't so terrible? Many analysts report that those Palestinians living here are more interested in working out a solution, while many who live outside feel that they can hold onto more maximalist solutions because they don't face the daily pressure of life under Occupation.

Husseini: No, we have a majority here on the West Bank and Gaza who favor a two-state solution and a minority who still do not accept that we must live in peace with Israel. And we have a similar majority that favors a two-state solution among Palestinians elsewhere—and a similar minority. Now, if you consider the people in this Palestinian majority who seek peace with Israel, I cannot say that I am more moderate or have more understanding of the path toward a solution than, for example, Nabil Shaath or Abu Iyad or other Palestinian leaders. Sometimes I hear statements coming from them that are more conciliatory than I might have thought to make, and I have to think about their positions and sometimes explain them by telling myself, "Maybe they've come to their ideas before I came to them because they are thinking about the interests and needs of the whole Palestinian people while I'm reacting just on the basis of what I feel living here." But while this may occur in reacting to a particular situation, there is no fundamental political difference as far as I can see.

Lerner: Isn't there a danger that a growing number of Palestinians are becoming attracted to Islamic fundamentalist positions like those of Hamas, and that if the PLO doesn't win some concessions soon and doesn't have something to show for its current policies, more Palestinians will move in that direction?

Husseini: Some will, yes, but a majority of Palestinians will continue to be committed to a two-state solution.

Lerner: So you don't see that Hamas is a serious danger?

Husseini: No, I don't see that they are a serious danger. I know the people in Hamas and I know that the majority of people in Hamas are also ready to accept the idea of two states....

Lerner: You were recently quoted in the *New York Times* saying that you opposed the settlement of Sovet Jews on the West Bank. How do you understand the issue of Soviet Jews?

Husseini: We support the right of Soviet Jews to leave the Soviet Union if they want, and also their right to choose where to go. Americans fought hard for the right of Soviet Jews to leave the Soviet Union, but once America succeeded in getting this right for Soviet Jews, then America closed its border to the Soviet Jews. This is not fair. So first, the United States should open its border. But then it's the right of Soviet Jews to decide where they want to go, and they can choose to come to Israel. We are not against them coming to Israel. But they should not be settled in the West Bank or the Gaza Strip or East Jerusalem, because this is an area where we Palestinians wish to settle our own refugees. We do not oppose Israel solving the problem of the Jewish people of Europe—but not at the expense of the Palestinian people. There is a way to do it that recognizes the needs of both peoples.

Lerner: So you recognize the right of Israel to bring in Jewish refugees?

Husseini: Yes, I do, and I do not want to be told in the future that we in a Palestinian state don't have a similar right to bring back our own people from their exile. Similarly, I want the Palestinian people to have the right to choose either to come to their homeland or not, and to have other options available to them as well.

Lerner: Looking at it today, the end of January 1990, what do you think are the chances of the Shamir election plan going forward?

Husseini: The main problem with the Shamir plan is that it is trying to address us not as a people but as a minority or as a refugee problem. We are a people. We are a people with the rights to national self-determination. A people who can negotiate our own future for ourselves. If he continues to insist that he will not talk to Palestinians who live in East Jerusalem or Palestinians who live outside the West Bank or Gaza, if he insists on choosing our negotiators for us, his plan will not succeed □

Anti-Semitism Parading as Anti-Zionism

Daniel Landes

Lovers of Zion who are critical of Israel's policy on the West Bank face a dilemma. They feel duty-bound by their Judaism and by their Zionism to continue the criticism—believing that it is in the best interests of Israel and the Jewish people that criticism be made. At the same time, they know that much of the worldwide uproar against Israel is not inspired by true concern for Israel's safe, secure, and morally correct future. It is important for us to become aware of the problematic nature of the growing anti-Israel forces.

Many people tend to dismiss the various hateful expressions against Israel that one frequently hears as only overheated rhetoric that will disappear as soon as the Palestinian crisis is resolved. But many of the anti-Israel sentiments being expressed today are not produced by the current situation nor will they disappear once the Palestinian issue has been resolved. Rather, many leftist anti-Israel sentiments must be understood for what they are—a structural extension of earlier forms of anti-Semitism.

To understand the contemporary anti-Israel stance of the Left, one must first understand the specific forms that anti-Semitism has taken in the past. Let us start by considering the anti-Jewish hatred of the Greco-Roman world. The root cause of this hatred seems to be the prominence of Jewish "no's." The Jews in the classical world said "no" to a variety of appealing offers. They said "no" to intermarriage, the sharing of holidays, communal sacrifices, the perfect body (since Jews insisted on retaining the "mutilation" of circumcision), shared meals, and especially to the gods of the Empire. From the standpoint of the Empire, the Jews were guilty of racial pride, religious exclusiveness, and contempt for their neighbors. How could a Jew fail to become part of the great Roman self-celebration? How could a Jew reject the incredible accomplishments of Greek and then Roman culture? The Jews benefited from the scientific, technological, and eventually even the artistic and philosophical advances of the Empire—how could they reject the invitation to become a full, equal part?

Yet, from a Jewish worldview, Rome was the embodiment of evil. Rome had enslaved most of the civilized world. A society built on oppression and exploitation, a brutal military force as the core instrument that held the Empire together, gladiators and humans forced to fight bare-handed against animals in the Roman arenas, an ethos of power as the ultimate justification—this was the Rome that Jews saw behind the friendly invitations to "become like everybody else." The Jews saw the Empire as Edom, the spiritual descendant of the capricious and murderous hunter Esau—a social order that denigrated the human, both through the hedonistic and self-serving lifestyle of the ruling elite and through the cruel, demeaning, and destructive treatment of the powerless. The Jews thought of themselves as the keepers of the promise that humanity was created in the image of God—*tzelem elohim*. Their refusal to join the universal club of the classical world was

Daniel Landes, an Orthodox rabbi, teaches at Yeshiva in Los Angeles and is the director of the National Education Project at the Simon Wiesenthal Center. This article appeared in Tikkun, May/June 1989.

Photo by David Solin

based on their seeing through its superficial openness and their witnessing the moral bankruptcy at its core....

Later, left anti-Semitism, emerging from the Enlightenment, was based on similar ideas. Jews were egotistical and dangerous because they wanted to continue their own existence and refused to merge with the larger mass of humanity. Marx, looking forward to the emergence of a universal class, talked of liberating Jews by having them abandon their Jewishness ("the social emancipation of the Jew is the emancipation of society from Judaism").

The ultimate rejection of the Left's plan for universal revolution was the Jews' decision to return to the Jewish homeland, giving credibility to nationalism at the very moment when the Left was calling for a new internationalism. No wonder that the Left vented its rage on the Jews, now updating the ancient charges—converting the claim of "racial pride" into the charge of "racism," religious exclusiveness into theological fanaticism, and contempt for one's neighbors into persecution of the non-Jewish minority and refusal to make peace. It is important to recognize that this way of thinking about Zionism predates the present crisis and even the establishment of the State of Israel. It is the source of the Left's opposition to Zionism from its very beginning. This hostility to Zionism is anti-Semitism, and one recognizes it as such the moment one realizes that the Left does not level similar criticism at any other ethnic or religious group, but rather lionizes and identifies with the national liberation struggle of virtually every other people but the Jews.

Zionism emerged out of two realizations made by modern Jews: that the world has no place for Jews to actualize their autonomous social vision and that the world might simply have no place for Jews at all. The collapse of Western civilization upon the heads of European Jewry in the years 1933 to 1945 tragically confirmed these two notions. The creation of the State of Israel is the final attempt on the part of Jews to establish a place where they can attempt to actualize their own vision and where they can physically survive.

Yet the Left does not accept the legitimacy of these two concerns. Its active support of, or quiet acquiescence to, the United Nations' "Zionism is Racism" declaration is the legal manifestation of its charge that Zionism is really misanthropy. In effect, the Left calls for the Jew to assimilate or perish. This is a classic manifestation of anti-Semitism.

Leftist anger at Zionism must be understood also in terms of the cultural legacy of the second major historical manifestation of wrath against the Jews: Church anti-Judaism. Christians attacked Jews not for their failure to join in the social and cultural framework of the here and now, but rather for their refusal to accept the Kingdom of God beyond the dictates of Torah law. These Jews, children of Abraham, rooted in the Flesh, were unable to accept the Spirit and thereby lost their covenantal destiny. The Church presented itself as the Israel of the Spirit, thus the verus Israel, the true Israel. The Jews' continued focus on the need to transform this world and their insistence that ethical action in this world is of fundamental importance, seemed to indicate a Jewish tilt toward the world of the flesh as opposed to the otherworldly realm of the spirit.

Indeed, it was this insistence on changing this world that made the various left-wing approaches to salvation feel like a continuation and culmination of Jewish ethics. The Left's emphasis on liberating people resonated with a Jewish ethical impulse and the desire for *tikkun olam*. Jews who joined the Left could feel that they were being true to the best ideals of their heritage and to the lessons learned from their history of suffering. At the same time, the Left, like the Church, had no tolerance for those who should have known better but refused the Messiah anyway. So the Left was angry at the Jewish people for refusing to be swallowed up by communism or socialism....

The Zionist enterprise has been a necessary affirmation of Jewish particularism for the sake of self-protection. As part of this process, Jews have managed to create within the State of Israel some very wonderful things; and hopefully, as Israel's security increases, Israel will become a place where Judaism's more universal message can increasingly manifest itself.... The more secure the Jewish people feel about their own physical safety, the less central the issue of survival will be to their daily consciousness. Consequently, Jews who remain true to a traditional Jewish conception of being chosen will have even more of their energy available for the task of *tikkun olam*.

The Left's difficulty with the Jews is linked to its approach to the Holocaust. Unlike the Neo-Fascist right, which claims that Jews invented the Holocaust to hoodwink the world into granting them a state, the Left takes the Holocaust very seriously and has misappropriated it in at least three ways. First, the USSR has misused the Holocaust by converting the graves of brutally murdered Jewish victims at Babi Yar into a memorial to the children of Mother Russia fallen in the valiant fight against fascism. While no one doubts that there were many non-Jewish victims of World War II, the self-described Communist countries of Eastern Europe have felt a need virtually to erase the memory of the specifically anti-Jewish campaign of mass extermination and thereby to bury all memory of the deep anti-Semitism that the invading Fascist armies appealed to during the war.

Second, in a related way the Left has universalized the Holocaust, as though it had nothing to do with anti-Jewish racism specifically, but was rather merely a manifestation of some global potential for human destructiveness. It's as though the people who want to warn about the danger of nuclear war, the destruction of the ecosystem, and other potential global disasters are afraid that they can't make their case on its own terms, so they must appropriate the Holocaust in order to bolster the moral legitimacy of their position. In the process, the specific campaign of extermination against Jews gets obliterated, and we who insist on remembering that reality are seen as too parochial.

A third (and more sickening) abuse of the Holocaust by some leftists comes from those who equate Jewish Israelis with the Nazis, and Arab Palestinians with the persecuted Jews. This reversal uses the full force of a personal and national tragedy to make a polemical point and to relieve the Left of its own guilt for its many failures during the Holocaust.

Leftist guilt is based on the following realities: 1. the Stalin-Hitler pact; 2. the failure of the Left in the Soviet Union and in the United States to make opposition to the destruction of European Jewry a central part of their political and educational work during World War II; 3. the very real anti-Semitism inside Communist and Socialist parties that made many of their members unwilling to provide substantial assistance to Jewish resistance efforts; 4. the failure of the leftist dream of proletarian solidarity, caused in part by the working classes of Europe allowing their anti-Semitism to take precedence over their class consciousness when they were faced with the rise of fascism....

Rather than come to grips with the fact that, had it abandoned its early opposition to Zionism and encouraged people to go to Palestine in the 1930s, many hundreds of thousands of Jewish lives would have been saved, the Left prefers to excuse itself by "discovering" that Zionism has transformed the Jews into little Hitlers and their state into a mini-Reich.

Tikkun magazine is living proof that one can be critical of Israel without being a self-hating Jew. Indeed, the term "self-hating Jew" has been thrown around as a way of suppressing all dissent, and hence many people think it is essentially meaningless. But it is not meaningless. There really are Jews who have internalized the anti-Semitism of the societies in which they live, and who feel angry at the parts of themselves that are distinguishably Jewish. The self-hating Jews have a quandary. On some level they identify as Jews, but they simultaneously deny an essential part of that definition: either peoplehood, religious culture, or the Jews' historical relationship to the land of Israel. The Israel/Nazi analogy relieves the self-hating Jews of this tension: they can be good prophetic Jews by opposing exclusivistic Jews, fanatical Judaism, and the "Fascist" Jewish state. The attack on the Jewish state thus gives them an explanation for why they are not involved in Jewish concerns and simultaneously allows them to claim that they are still connected to their Jewishness.

Leftists also try to delegitimate all references to the Holocaust in the context of assessments of contemporary political reality. Anyone who shows concern about the possible destruction of Israel and the Jewish community is accused of paranoia or "Holocaust obsession." The Holocaust, it is charged, has clouded these people's judgment....

As the Holocaust imagery is inverted upon the Jews, so once again do the Christian symbols of Jewish perfidy emerge from the substrata of the Western unconscious. Israel becomes Judas— betraying both humanistic values and the Jewish people. Israel is a hateful, suspicious people, interested only in grabbing land for itself. Israel is obdurate, stupidly refusing to realize where its salvation lies—in giving up its existence. And Israel, ultimately, is the crucifier of the innocent. All the ancient lies now dressed up in contemporary garb by the Left!

Now that Jews have abandoned a position that the Left respects (a position of Jews as victims), the only other way to see Jews is as victimizers. The Left has no neutral category, no way of imagining the Jews as simply another people wanting to live their own lives. For this reason, everyone who settles on the West Bank must be seen as evil, and the physical attacks on them are automatically regarded as legitimate. Every one of these people becomes a trigger-happy messianist ready to hurt anyone in his or her way. There is no room in leftist categories for people who moved to the West Bank settlements with the hope that Jews and Arabs might live together in peace. As a result, leftists end up supporting a *judenrein* West Bank in which Jews would be prohibited from staying in the homes they have built for themselves—a policy of racial exclusion that these leftists would not support if aimed at any other racial, ethnic, or religious community in the world.

What I have tried to show here is how easily the attacks on Israel's policies turn into anti-Zionism, and how anti-Zionism becomes a contemporary manifestation of a long tradition of anti-Semitism. I have great respect for the integrity of many of the people who are now criticizing Israeli policy, but I do think that they are on a slippery slope. For that reason I find it particularly important for a Jewish Left to examine itself carefully, to eliminate all self-hatred, and to combat all those who make the illegitimate move from criticism of Shamir to criticism of Zionism itself. *Tikkun* is on the right path in making these distinctions. But I think it needs to remind itself over and over again that, without consciously and publicly facing up to these issues, it will have difficulty getting a respectful hearing from many others whom it hopes to influence in the Jewish world. □

Kitsch 22: On the Problems Between Majority and Minority Cultures in Israel

Anton Shammas

Cyril Connolly, the English writer and critic, writing in the 1960s, discussed the relationship between art and climate. Cocking a British eyebrow, he stated that art is a sun substitute and that excessive sunshine casts out art. Therefore, he claimed, there is no worthwhile painting south of Rome or Madrid, there being a point where it gets too hot to hang pictures on the walls—unless air-conditioning should contribute to creativity in the torrid zones, just as central heating moved the creative limit northward. He concluded by stating, "The literature, painting, music, architecture, sculpture produced between latitudes 40° and 60° in the last two thousand years under seasonal conditions can justify existence to me while I also live between latitudes 40° and 60°, and am subject to a similar awareness of the seasons."

Unfortunately, Israel still extends between latitudes 29° and 33° and ceaselessly seeks to link up with the twilight zone of latitude 40°, like a heart which has been separated from its body—or, as Milan Kundera, winner of the Jerusalem Prize in 1985, said in his acceptance speech, "Israel, the newly-found homeland, appears to me to be the true heart of Europe, a strange heart which lies far from the body." This state of affairs worried its founding fathers in the very earliest days of Zionism. In his *Judenstaat* Theodor Herzl stated that "we shall form part of Europe's fortified wall against Asia, and fulfill the role of cultural vanguard facing the barbarians." Vladimir Jabotinsky, in his essay "The Vogue of the Arabesques" (1927), quoted Nordau, who said, "We are going to the land of Israel to carry the moral boundary of Europe as far as the Euphrates." Fortunately, this boundary still languishes somewhere along the Jordan, and it is not easy to discern its moral aspect.

Likewise, Ibn-Khaldun, the fourteenth-century Arab historian, in the chapter dealing with the effect of climate on civilization in his *Muqaddimah*, offers an instructive explanation to the question, Why does man sing in the bath? According to Ibn-Khaldun, the hot air in the baths warms the spirit and causes the bather to feel elated, so that he may express joy in singing. The Sudanese, he noted, are a light-headed people, given to song and dance, because the powerful sun in their places heats up the spirit which lies in the chambers of the heart, thinning it and causing its volume to expand, so that it rises into the head and confuses it. That is why the Sudanese are known for their merriness, which is only a hair-breadth away from folly. And if you are not convinced—here Ibn-Khaldun lands his *coup de grâce*—observe how melancholy are the denizens of the cold countries in the north, whose spirit is congested and weighs heavily on their heart.

Incidentally, Ibn-Khaldun (who was born in Tunis) wrote his *Muqaddimah* in the province of Oran, Algeria, which lies on latitude 35°, five degrees south of Cyril Connolly's "creative limit," and some six hundred years earlier.

Anton Shammas, author of Arabesques, *teaches Near Eastern studies at the University of Michigan. This article was translated from the Hebrew by Yael Lotan. It appeared in* Tikkun, *September/October 1987.*

Some years ago I visited a certain house in my village—which lies on latitude 33°02'—to console the bereaved. The man whom I was to console, as he had just lost his wife, was in his seventies and was considered in the village to be one of the pillars of "rural culture." He was known, on the one hand, as a dignified collaborator, close to the powers that be, yet loyal to the villagers, and, on the other hand, as a generous, hospitable person known to almost everyone in the Galilee. I had never before set foot in his house, and this visit was something of a journey back in time for me. After the words of consolation and the sipping of bitter coffee, which was appropriately served in a demitasse on a gleaming copper tray, and during the prolonged silence which ineluctably falls on these occasions, my gaze wandered over the walls, classical Arab walls, untouched by the hand of progress. Walls dazzling in their bluish-white limewash. About three meters from the floor, about a meter below the ceiling, hung various pictures—mostly wedding photographs of the children and grandchildren, alongside pictures of saints and decorated, embroidered rugs. They hung all around, in restrained coloration, their crowding suggesting what the History of Art Department at the Hebrew University in Jerusalem would call the *Horror Vacui*. Very few Arab houses have been preserved in this state, and fewer still keep their pictures hanging so high. It would not be inaccurate to suggest that the exposure of the picture level of the Arab wall to another culture lowered it by at least a meter, to eye level, those eyes which have lost their visual confidence and no longer know what may be called "beautiful." Is beautiful the bare wall, whose white limewash was usually tinted with laundress's blue and frequently hung with a multitude of pictures close to the ceiling; or is beautiful the wall which has obeyed the command of aesthetic loss of nerve vis-à-vis the majority culture, and which is hung with cheap reproductions (often of a weeping child) or tapestries depicting imaginary gardens in imaginary places or ornamental wallpaper, a distant and pathetic echo of the walls of the Alhambra?

One way or the other, the Arab wall, the mirror in which I see reflected the changes in Arab culture since the early 1950s, is not what it used to be, and the people who face it and look at it are no longer the same people—not to mention the alterations in the climate, cultural and otherwise.

Milan Kundera, in the aforementioned speech, quoted the words of Herman Broch on the modern novel, which tried to stem the tide of kitsch but in the end was overwhelmed by it. Kundera said, "The term kitsch, which originated in Germany in the middle of the century, describes the desire to please the greatest number of people at any cost. To please, one must say what everyone wants to hear, to cater to the widely held views. Kitsch translates the foolishness of the widely held views into the language of beauty and sentiment." (Here I shall overlook a certain puzzlement regarding the speaker, in my opinion one of the finest writers of our time, who chooses in Jerusalem to speak of Israel as "the true heart of Europe, a strange heart which lies far from the body." Does not this suggest "a desire to please the greatest number at any cost"?)

The Arab house in Israel, between whose walls I wish to examine the impact of the majority culture upon that of the minority, is one of many monuments to the "overwhelming" of the culture of the Third World by the European kitsch—which, of course, does not acknowledge the "culture" of the Third World. (This last sentence is unquestionably a typical product of the Third World.) Before collapsing under the onslaught of the terrible kitsch, the Arab wall in our parts underwent several phases, which I shall divide schematically into three: the wall of the father, the wall of the son, and the wall of the grandson. We have said that there are very few Arab walls preserved from the beginning of the century, from the days before the Zionist fathers sought to push Europe's moral and cultural border eastward. The classical Arab wall is a creation in which the functional and the aesthetic coexist in a delicate balance. The wall divides and separates, defines and supports, while at the same time its white limewash, tinted with laundress's blue, inspires the space called "home" with an atmosphere of tranquility which characterizes not only the walls but all the components of classical Arab construction: The arch is functional (it supports the ceiling) as well as aesthetic; the keystone, which is the topmost stone that binds the other arch stones together, symbolizes better than anything else the balance which binds and consolidates all the elements of structure into one entity, from which the removal of a single component part may jeopardize the whole.

In the traditional Arab houses, such as you find mostly in the villages, there are rarely any pictures on the walls, but rather objects which are also functional-aesthetic, and insofar as there are pictures, they are usually hung well above eye level, close to the ceiling. A possible explanation is that since the seating in the father's house is generally close to the floor—on mattresses, stools, padded shelves—the angle of vision tends to reach higher, in the direction of the ceiling. Or it may be an expression of respect: the higher the object hangs, the further out of reach, the greater its honor. For honor, generally, implies a certain awe, and things which inspire us with awe are usually placed high. Arab culture regarded the imitation of reality with awe. The transmission of reality via the artistic vision entails for the villager an element of defiance against the supreme power. Having overcome this awe and hung a single picture on the wall, he feels threatened by the remaining blankness and hurriedly piles any number of other things on the wall—and everything, of course, above eye level.

But then the son married and built his own house. The neighbors who came to call after the wedding and after the birth of his children, and on other festive occasions, brought various things which they felt were suitable to hang on his walls, whether he cared for them or not. Thus if you were to visit a house which has preserved its character since the 1950s you would be amazed by the peculiar conglomeration of tastes which populates its walls.

The son's wall has been expropriated by the neighbors. For surely it would be unthinkable to offend the giver of a gift, no matter how horrid it is in your own eyes, and refrain from hanging it on the eastern wall of your house. That was the beginning of the onslaught of kitsch upon Arab culture in Israel, and the villager wished to please the greatest number of people, as Kundera put it. The son's house was, in reality, the house of the orphans of 1948, of all those who had been abandoned by the generation of fathers who had been exiled, and remained exposed to that new and fearsome being, the State of Israel, a state which defined itself, politically and culturally, as a "Jewish State." This sudden exposure knocked the ground—both figuratively and literally—from under the son's cultural confidence and left him naked and helpless to face new challenges. Given this reality of a cultural and political threat, in the atmosphere of military government and land expropriations one can hardly expect a man to devote much attention to the inner decoration of his walls, his house, and himself. Metaphorically speaking, the Jewish-Israeli reality, under its new guise of power, not only expropriated the son's walls, with the help of his neighbors, but forced him to hang upon them things he never thought to hang on them—a poster of Ben-Gurion hung in my father's cobbler shop—much as it forced him to carry a permit of passage from place to place.

The Arabs of the 1950s needed those permits in order to travel from place to place in their native land which had become "the homeland of the Jewish people." But no such permits were available for moving about the cultural spaces in which they had grown. The severance from the existence which had been cut away and ended up in the refugee camps was complete, and so was the severance from their cultural milieu in the region, leaving them in a prolonged state of cultural quarantine.

Some two-thirds of the 156,000 Arabs who remained in the State after its establishment and the great upheaval were of the rural population and were thus spared the fate of the wanderers. This population was less prepared and less confident in the face of the new reality, and was thus a fertile ground for the growth of the multifarious kitsch. The son's generation was also that of the writers who sought to continue the Palestinian literature, when they had recovered, or believed they had recovered, from the shock of the rupture. These writers tried to sprout new roots after the shock of losing ground from under their feet. And while the 1950s were arid years for Arab literature in Israel, they only reflect the condition of a body trying to breathe with one lung when the other lung has been amputated. The hesitant syllables, the limited expression, nevertheless arouse respect for the ability to survive, the ability to contend, however inadequately, with the encroaching kitsch from within and without.

At the end of the fifties the Druze were declared a recognized religious community and in 1962 the Knesset passed the "Druze Religious Courts Law," in exchange for which two acts the young Druze men were required to serve in the Israeli army. This step, made at the apogee of the military government, symbolized more than anything else the nature of the relationship the young State offered its non-Jewish citizens—the recognition of the ethnic distinction of a certain group in return for that group's unconditional commitment to the State's self-definition as a "Jewish State." This recognition of the ethnic distinction of the Druze community also gave it the privilege of writing "Druze" under the heading "Nationality" in the Israeli identity card. Thus, as if by magic, the Druze were separated from the Arab nation of which they were, and still are, a part. Through the young Druze men who were recruited into the Israeli army, a tremendous, if unperceived, change took place in the Druze villages. The Hebrew language began to be heard in its streets and gradually displaced the Arabic. The Druze community was so thrilled to be recognized as a "nationality" that its leaders forgot that in return for the military service they might have demanded to be recognized as "Israelis," as belonging to the "Israeli nationality." But the Israeli nationality, then and now, did not exist as a legal entity. And what is all this if not a pure political kitsch—a group which seeks to please everyone to the point of overlooking its main purpose and which ends up creating in the Druze villages on the Carmel a "Druze Zionist Movement," which is surely the most ludicrous and shameful product that the State of Israel as a Jewish State has succeeded in extracting from the confused national minority in its midst.

At this time the Druze house served as a vulgar testimony to the changes that have occurred in the Druze culture. Pictures of Theodor Herzl, of the president, and of members of the government hang in the living room alongside family photographs, and polished mortar shells stand beside the traditional coffee pot, which is likewise made of gleaming copper.

Yet the Druze simply fell victim to the cynicism of the government and should not be entirely held to blame for their predicament. Nobody ever warned them that their active participation in the life of the State, in its extreme form of service in its armed forces, did not entitle them to the status of citizens with equal rights, both social and political, as promised to all the citizens of Israel in the Declaration of Independence. Nobody ever explained to them that their contribution was to be strictly a one-way relationship, one that did not offer them immunity from land expropriation or security for the future of the demobilized Druze soldier, as if he were part of the Jewish-Israeli social framework. The "Druze Action Committee," which has been active in the community in the past decade, has called for the reconsideration of the matter of military service and has encountered angry reactions on both sides of the issue—the reactions of the deceived, refusing to acknowledge their failure, and the reactions of the cynics, who still believe that you can demand that the Israeli Arabs carry out faithfully all their duties to the State and yet remain content to be defined as a "national minority" in a Jewish State, that is to say, a minority which is effectively devoid of all nationality.

And this is, in effect, the position of all the Arabs in Israel, regardless of specific community. The position, which we may call "Kitsch 22," can be described as follows: The State of Israel defines itself as a Jewish State (or even "the State of the Jews") and demands that its Arab citizens fulfill their citizenship, but, when they do so, promptly informs them that their participation in the State is merely social and that for the political fulfillment of their identity they must look elsewhere (i.e., to the Palestinian nation); when they do look elsewhere for their national identity, the State at once charges them with subversion, and, needless to say, as subversives they cannot be accepted as Israelis—and so on, in circles, ad infinitum.

Now we come to the house of the grandson, which is the most confused of them all.

The grandson's house was built in the shadow of the 1967 war. The military government had only recently come to an end, and the direct contact between the Israeli Arabs and the Arabs beyond the "green line" had just begun. The shock of the encounter between the one-lunged Arab, who had been living under the restrictions of the military government, and his "national oxygen" led to a profound upheaval in his conceptual world. For the military government had served to delegitimize the Arab in Israel—he was, in effect, only transiently a citizen, and as such his every attempt to set foot outside the boundaries imposed on the national minority was an illegal act. Thus, for example, the lands were expropriated and the Arab local councils were given no development plans, so that an Arab who tried to build a house in Israel inevitably engaged in illegal construction. Once the "Green Line" was erased, however, and the State itself began to engage in illegal construction in the Occupied Territories, the bent spine of the Israeli Arab acquired some added vertebrae, and he began to feel at last that his belonging to the Palestinian nation legitimized him where he lived, even if this feeling of legitimacy amounted to crime in the eyes of the government.

By now the house of the Arab in Israel has become a regular festival of kitsch. The wall, which had in any case been illegal, has now become a fertile ground for what may be called a crime against the laws of Arab aesthetics.

Jabotinsky, in his essay "The Vogue of Arabesques," from which I have already quoted, stated, "The arabesque was invented because the Qu'ran forbade the depiction of real things—not only the image of man, but even a cat or a table. Therefore they contented themselves with painting by allusion, in which one cannot recognize either the cat or the table. This means that the arabesque is not at all a special, independent artistic conception, but only a retarded art form." Fifty years after this essay was written, Professor Jacob Bronowsky, in his book *The Ascent of Man*, discussed the Alhambra palace in Spain, one of the masterpieces of Arabic architecture, in connection with the achievements of Arab mathematicians in the field of two-dimensional symmetry. In the Alhambra palace, says Bronowsky, tranquility overcomes the adventurous impulse, and one discerns the lassitude of an empire past its peak and devotes itself now to a sensuous observation of the world. The ornamentation in that palace (to wit, those arabesques described as "a retarded art form") are in fact the summation of all the possible symmetries in two-dimensional space, the product of a thousand years of mathematics, "a magnificent finality ... the perfect finish."

Today the Arab house is torn between these two opposite views of the arabesque. The Israeli Arab, the grandson of the late 1960s, is no exception. For, having been denied permission to build his own house in Israel, he turns to his grandfather's house and "remodels" it, so as to conform with the "aesthetic demands" of his day. The tranquility of the whitewashed walls, the sensuousness of the supporting vault, the weary harmony among the diverse components of the structure—all these are now set aside, to be replaced by new elements. The gate, whose stones had for many years displayed their carvings and ornaments, is replaced with a decorative iron gate. The arch, which had borne the weight of the house, is hidden by a new wall which divides the old space into many small ones. The walls are, at best, covered with wallpaper that dimly recalls, to the collective Arab memory, the walls of the Alhambra, thus legitimizing the kitsch and creating a false sense of being at peace with the past. The future looks in through the window—a false window in the form of a landscape-wallpaper, opening from the desolate living room upon a view of faraway worlds, usually a fairytale forest in Switzerland—which, as we know, lies between latitudes 40° and 60°. And between the mountains of Switzerland, on the one hand, and the pseudo-arabesques, on the other, the Israel Arab must contend with the complicated reality of the Jewish State, with the complexity of living between two languages, both of which are written from right to left, a vestige of the good old Semitic days, but one of which, Hebrew, flows also from left to right, as a language must to be language of "Europe's torn heart" in the agonized carcass of the Levant.

Some years ago in Jerusalem, in my wanderings from one rented apartment to another, I found myself residing in an old Arab house in the old Katamon quarter. In addition to the handsome furniture, which was marvelously appropriate to the Arab structure, there stood in the bedroom a shining, brightly polished piano, cunningly left there by my Jewish landlady, who was also my friend. At first we were mutually indifferent, for I had never played the piano, nor any other musical instrument. But gradually a dim hostility arose between us, which before long became open and incomprehensible. I spent many restless nights, for I had never slept in the same room with a piano. Now alone with a polished piano in a single bedroom, I found dormant impulses awakening in me. What could a piano be doing in an Arab house? It struck me that its very presence was an intolerable contradiction, a tension I could never cope with. Finally one evening I took courage and began to hit the keys, an act which disturbed the rest of the delicate-eared neighbors but brought sweet sleep to my eyes.

The tension in the tales of *A Thousand and One Nights* resembles the tension of piano playing (as I am told by better pianists than myself): The left hand provides the background, the framework, while the right hand plays in and out of the framework, just as in the stories of *A Thousand and One Nights* the subsidiary tales depart from and entwine with the central story, in the end returning to it. So it is with the arabesques of the Alhambra: Out of the basic pattern of the ornament subsidiary patterns branch off, like variations on a theme, and in the end all harmonize together in a single arabesque. But when the left hand of this equation was replaced by a European hand, the Arabs contented themselves with the right and returned to two-dimensional creativity. This may explain why it is not at all fair to compare the writings of, say, Nagib Mahfouz with the writings of Gabriel García Márquez. For Mahfouz took *A Thousand and One Nights* for granted, as something readily accessible, whereas Márquez was influenced by it through the filter of generations of Spanish culture. In Mahfouz's work one senses the lack of the left hand, as one senses it in most of contemporary Arab culture. And this, presumably, also expresses the relationship between the culture of the majority and the culture of the minority in Israel today—how are the Arabs in Israel to play their culture with the right hand, when the left hand of the Jewish majority sets the framework chords, which they must, willy-nilly, go in and out of?

As for me, I chose to contend with the piano that I was living with, face to face, and used both hands to write my first novel, *Arabesques*, an Arab story in Hebrew letters. This was not easy at all. A certain Hebrew writer, who was very pleased with my attempt at piano playing, so to speak, recently urged me to take my belongings and move one hundred meters to the east, to the Palestinian state-to-come, if I wish to fulfil my whole national identity. But he does not realize that his left hand is already part of my Israeli being, just as at least one finger of his right hand is one of mine.

For the Arab in Israel to contend with all the above, he needs, as Emil Habibi suggested in his *Opsomist*, only "a large dose of oriental imagination," an imagination which can carry its owner far from the Levant, to those regions of culture that lie between latitudes 40° and 60°, where all of us, presumably, would rather be. □

Talking About Torture in Israel

Stanley Cohen

I n *The Body in Pain,* her dense meditation on the vulnerability of the human body, Elaine Scarry keeps returning to the political consequences of the "rigidity" of pain, its sheer inexpressibility. "Physical pain does not simply resist language," she writes, "but actively destroys it, bringing about an immediate reversion to a state anterior to language, to the sounds and cries a human being makes before language is learned."

There are many situations in which the experience of pain has to be rendered into words: patients talking to doctors, artists depicting suffering, human-rights organizations reporting on torture, injured parties claiming legal damages. Of all these contexts, torture is perhaps the most problematic, and the consequences of even using this word are the most profound. Torture is the calculated infliction of pain, but it is also an emblem of state power. To talk about torture is not just to talk about pain, but to enter a complex discourse of morality, legality and politics. As Scarry notes, the very structure by which pain is produced within the body of the prisoner entails denial, "a perceptual shift which converts the vision of suffering into the wholly illusory but, to the torturers and the regime they represent, wholly convincing spectacle of power." All talk about torture becomes a contest between different observers—the victim, the state, human-rights organizations—over how to reproduce this vision. Indeed, even to attempt any reproduction can be a way of subverting the spectacle of power.

The event itself should be simple enough to describe. For all the different contexts (religious inquisition, nationalist conflict, political thought control), for all the different techniques (crude blows, burning rods, psychotropic drugs), the primal scene is simple, and sickeningly identical from case to case. There is a room in which one or more persons (the "interrogators") deliberately inflict pain on another (the detainee, suspect, enemy of the state).

But the technical problems inherent in representing this scene—how the experience is memorized, conveyed to others, corroborated, translated into a public language—are only compounded by its political context. There is always a struggle to define reality, an epistemological politics. On the one side, there are the forces to whom torture is real, to be denounced, to be abolished: the victim, international prohibitions and laws, human-rights organizations. On the other, there is the organized power of the state, denying that "it" happens, calling it something else, or justifying it as necessary, or even as something that serves a higher moral good. A history of torture is a history of talking about torture.

In the higher reaches of postmodernist theory (which, in this case, serves the interests of the powerful very nicely), no common, universal definition of torture is possible. It all depends. It depends, postmodernists tell us, on context, on the observer's values, on the truth-rules of the prevailing discourse. It depends, the powerful tell us, on context, on the interests of the state, on how you interpret those universal definitions. But in the struggle for social justice and human rights—however

Stanley Cohen is a professor of criminology at Hebrew University and one of the founders of the Public Committee Against Torture in Israel. This article appeared in Tikkun, *November/December 1991.*

tarnished we are told these master-narratives are—some pragmatic, commonsense definition of the word must be attempted. The historian Edward Peters is surely right to say that if we reject the purely moralistic or sentimental uses of the term, then "the longest and surest definition is a legal—or at least a public—one." The common historical thread, "torment inflicted by a public authority ostensibly for public purposes," is captured in the standard 1975 United Nations Declaration Against Torture definition:

> Any act by which severe pain or suffering, whether physical or mental, is intentionally inflicted by or at the instigation of a public official on a person for such purposes as obtaining from him or a third person information or a confession, punishing him for an act he has committed or intimidating him or other persons.

But what is meant by "severe"? What is meant by excluding (as the UN definition goes on to do) pain and suffering "inherent in ... lawful sanctions"? Is the mere threat of inflicting pain to be included? What does it mean to declare oneself to be "against" torture? How can information or confession be obtained from unwilling persons if not by causing them some suffering?

There is a massive discourse—human-rights reports, judicial rulings, government commissions, philosophical tracts—that depends on the continued salience of these questions. And if there ever was a call for a shared public language, this is the place for it. However indeterminate the boundaries—between moderate and severe pain, between permissible and impermissible sanctions—the notion of boundaries assumes that there is an area that can be talked about.

Talk as Exposure

Talking about torture is difficult enough in general; it is even more so in Israel. In the depressing global league of torture drawn up by organizations like Amnesty International, Israel ranks far below Syria, Iraq, Turkey, and dozens of other countries all over the world. The methods of torture used in Israel are less elaborate, less systematic, and less intense than those favored by more brutal authoritarian regimes. But there are deep-seated ideological barriers to talking openly about the cases that do exist. Within the tiny (and diminishing) liberal enclaves of Israeli society, there is the self-serving myth that "things like this can't happen here"—and if they do, they are isolated abuses that will be dealt with properly. The ideological Right, as we shall see, perceives any attempt to expose gross human-rights violations as anti-Israel propaganda. The rest of the society—the majority of which has no moral unease about what happens to Palestinians and will justify anything in the name of national security—pays no attention to any such talk.

Just what is the record? In the first decade after the Occupation began in 1967, some allegations surfaced about the ill-treatment of Palestinian political detainees. These stories circulated mainly among political activists and a few lawyers, and were not given wider exposure or deeper credibility. In 1977, a number of well-grounded claims were published in the *London Sunday Times*. In the late 1970s, immediately after the first Begin government, torture clearly declined—apparently because of restraints ordered personally by the prime minister, to whom the General Security Service (Shin Bet or Shabak) is formally accountable.

By the mid-1980s, though, new reports were surfacing. From that period on, Israel has possessed the basic requirements for making the question of torture an official public problem: first, the objective record of events; and second, the subjective awareness on the part of a growing human-rights community and an increasingly brave Israeli media that there is something to be talked about. By 1990, even the U.S. State Department review of human rights in the Occupied Territories could record that "physical and psychological pressures are particularly severe during incommunicado detention in investigation." Note, though, the inhibition about using the taboo word "torture" in writing about Israel (an inhibition that even Amnesty International overcame only in its 1990 report). The political causes of this inhibition are obvious. In very few other country-entries does the State Department identify the sources of claims merely as "critics" and make no attempt to evaluate them.

The crucial year for the construction of torture as a public problem was 1987. One dramatic case triggered the discussion. Izzat Nafsu, an Israeli Circassian army officer, had been sentenced in 1982 to an eighteen-year prison term for espionage and treason. He continued to claim that he was innocent and that his confession had been extracted by force during a Shin Bet interrogation.

In May 1987, the High Court accepted his claim, along with the corollary charge that the investigators had lied to the court, and ordered his release. A government commission, chaired by former Supreme Court president Justice Moshe Landau, was set up in June and issued its report four months later.

It is impossible to talk about torture in Israel without referring to the Landau Commission report. Indeed, this text is so rich and resonant that even a superficial reading reveals every major contradiction of Israeli society. The report arrived at three main formal conclusions. First, it concluded that since 1971, Shin Bet agents had systematically lied to the courts by denying that they had used force to extract confessions. Second, it ruled that the officials responsible for these sixteen years of torture and perjury should be exempt from any prosecution, on the grounds that they were "ideological criminals" doing their sacred national duty, and that too many criminal cases would disrupt the agency's normal work.

Finally, the commission decided that although perjury was to be utterly condemned, the actual methods of interrogation used in the past were "largely to be defended, both morally and legally." According to the Landau report, not only are methods of "nonviolent psychological pressure" justified to extract information, but "when these do not attain their purpose, the exertion of a moderate amount of physical pressure cannot be avoided." A secret second part of the report lays out the precise "operational guidelines" for permissible "moderate physical pressure."

This is not the place to consider the legal and moral reasoning by which the commission arrived at these extraordinary conclusions, nor to review the deluge of criticism that they have aroused. This has already been done in a special issue of the *Israel Law Review* and in the report on torture in the Occupied Territories published recently by B'tselem (the Israel Information Center for Human Rights in the Occupied Territories; see "The Wrong Arm of the Law," *Tikkun,* September/October 1991). The main lines of criticism cover the spurious adaptation from criminal law of the "necessity defense" to authorize in advance the use of force by government officials; the lack of distinction between preventing possible future harm and testifying about supposed past offenses; and the elastic and wholly political definition of the enemies of the state against whom "special means" are permissible (the commission's definition of "hostile terrorist activity" or "subversion," which could include flying a PLO flag). For the purposes of this discussion, however, we need to focus on the clear prospect that the advance licensing of physical pressure—that is, lifting the absolute moral and legal taboo on the sanctity of the body—will open the door to the routine resort to other, graver abuses. This was indeed the peril that the Landau Commission professed itself so eager to avoid: "the danger of sliding toward methods practiced in regimes that we abhor."

Throughout the report, the commission avoids the word "torture" except in references to international conventions and methods used by the British in Northern Ireland. The less vivid and emotive phrase "moderate physical pressure" (or a set of similarly euphemistic equivalents) has to be used as long as Israel continues to hold on to a democratic self-image. In order to circumvent international prohibitions and the provisions against torture in Israeli law, the commission had to work within, rather than outside, the discourse of legal liberalism. We could see this not as a deliberate attempt to deceive, but as either self-deception or deception of the commission by the Shin Bet. In any event, whatever the Landau Commission's intentions (and let us read them as benevolent: to avoid excesses, to regulate, to place limits and restrictions, indeed *not* to allow torture), what follows from its recommendations is the institutionalization of abuse. The Shin Bet received the stamp of kashrut it requested. This is hardly surprising, given the commission's definition of its "principal function": to "guide the essential process of rehabilitation and healing" of the GSS, thus restoring to its agents "inner conviction in the rightness of their way which they require for their work."

The Israeli legal community, not usually given to public moral indignation, received the report with dismay. Mordechai Kremnitzer, dean of the Hebrew University Law School, summed up this reaction at the end of a sixty-two-page legal critique published in the *Israel Law Review*:

It is difficult to live with the Landau report. One is tempted to shake oneself free of it, to awaken as if from a bad dream and say: perhaps it never was, perhaps the confidential part of the report does not contain a license for physical pressure in interrogation.

The shock that torture can indeed be justified in apparently democratic language is, as Kremnitzer is aware, not unique to Israel. Totalitarian states, military dictatorships—"regimes that we abhor," in Landau's words—don't have to talk about torture in any complicated way. They do it, deny it, and need not lay down any limits. George Orwell anticipated the awful truth fifty years ago, when he predicted that our century would be the time when practices like torture "which had long been abadoned, in some cases for hundreds of years ... not only became common again, but were tolerated and even defended by people who considered themselves enlightened and progressive."

The emblematic case was France during the Algerian War. As Rita Maran shows in her recent book *Torture: The Role of Ideology in the French-Algerian War* (Praeger, 1989), France's colonial government defended the use of brutal, systematic torture—much worse than anything practiced in Israel—as part of its historical mission to maintain the French presence, to uplift and civilize native Algerians.   France's 1955 Wuillaume Report (an investigation into allegations about torture in Algeria) could have been copied by the Landau Commission: Yes, torture ("excesses," "violence") had been used in Algeria; no, responsibility should not be fixed on individuals; in the future, "less brutal methods" or "special procedures" should be used under careful supervision; and it is important to "restore confidence in the police." Maran stresses the importance of democratic discourse in the Wuillaume Report: A state that acknowledged itself or any of its agents as torturers would stand discredited before its citizenry and the world. And so its agents spoke not of "torture" but of "abuses" and when arguing either for or against torture, did so in the lexicon of colonialism's civilizing mission.

Some two months after the Landau Commission issued its report, the intifada began, creating a political context that, of course, the commission could not have anticipated. Initial waves of mass arrests were followed by batch trials, which convicted prisoners on the basis of "evidence" no more substantial than the testimony of the soldiers who had arrested them. Court cases became (and remain) cruel parodies of judicial norms. At least twenty-five thousand Palestinians were arrested during each of the first three years of the intifada. Either the army or the Shin Bet has subjected at least eight thousand of these detainees to some form of formal interrogation, and at least a quarter of these eight thousand to what professional jargon euphemistically refers to as "intensive methods."

Repeated allegations circulated about gross ill-treatment of Palestinians during detention and interrogation: severe beatings, various forms of verbal and physical humiliation, being tied up in painful

Photo by Yehudit Elani

positions, long confinement in "closets," "coffins," or "refrigerators." In 1988 and 1989, eighteen Palestinians died during detention; in five of these cases, death apparently resulted from interrogation methods. In December 1989, Khaled al-Sheikh Ali was beaten to death by his interrogators in Gaza Central Prison. (His family's attorney was informed that Ali died of a heart attack.) Two Shin Bet agents were eventually sentenced to six months' imprisonment for causing death by negligence. Against this background, the Public Committee Against Torture in Israel was established at the beginning of 1990; it continues to work on publicity and education and take up individual complaints. In the summer of 1990, B'tselem also decided to investigate the subject. Research director Dr. Daphna Golan and I began to investigate methods of interrogation used against Palestinian political detainees since the beginning of the intifada. We worked for six months; in March 1991, B'tselem published our report, entitled "The Interrogation of Palestinians During the Intifada: Ill-Treatment, 'Moderate Physical Pressure,' or Torture?"

In talking about torture, we immediately faced intertwined technical and political problems. Torture is a unique form of human-rights violation in two respects. First, the international prohibition is absolute. No contingencies can be invoked to justify the use of torture: neither superior orders nor exceptional circumstances, such as war or a perceived threat to national security. This absolute ban creates strong requirements of proof. Allegations cannot be thrown around carelessly. Torture is too potent, too special a word to be debased by rhetorical use. But this leads to the second problem: Indisputable proof is difficult to obtain. Torture represents the public—in the sense that it is perpetrated by the State, which claims to protect the public—but it does not occur in public, as it did in the spectacle of torture that prevailed in the premodern era. Modern torture is invisible. There is the victim and the interrogator in that closed room. The victim very rarely makes a formal complaint and if he does, he is seldom believed. The interrogator remains silent and unaccountable—except in those rare cases when the regime gives way to a more democratic successor.

As a result, great care has to be taken in checking stories. The moment the word "torture" is used, rather than pressure, force, ill-treatment, abuse, even violence, the talk takes on a dimension absent in standard human-rights documentation. Other human-rights abuses at least can be submitted to common criteria of observable fact: house demolitions, shootings, teargassing, deportation, land confiscation, administrative detention. In each case, the event can be documented as a matter of public record and its semantics are not disputed. A house is blown up—and the issue is not whether this happened, but whether this is justified or not. In the case of torture, however, the value position is preceded by first-order questions: Is this happening? Can it be happening here? Is torture the proper word to use?

These questions appeared even before the report was published. The B'tselem board (lawyers, law professors, politicians, human-rights experts) read various drafts of the report more intensely than any of the organization's previous reports and scrutinized its language, sources, and methodology. By all standards of the genre, the B'tselem report is a conventional human-rights document: We review international definitions and prohibitions, Israeli law, the status of the GSS, the Landau report, and previous allegations. We then describe each of the eleven methods of interrogation reported by our forty-one interviewees; this is followed by longer stories from seven individual detainees. Some common methods of torture are illustrated with drawings—like the "banana tie," in which the suspect's legs are bound to the front and his hands to the back legs of a stool, the body bent over like a banana, to be beaten. These drawings were our main departure from the normal genre. We wanted to undermine the function of political language ("moderate physical pressure") that Orwell pointed to: "Such phraseology is needed if one wants to name things without calling up mental pictures of them."

But even the drawings, even the vivid testimonies of deliberate abuse, humiliation, and violence over periods as long as forty-five days, even the medical documentation on six detainees injured so badly by their interrogators that they needed hospital treatment—all this knowledge enters a discourse in which nothing can be taken for granted.

Here is Mohammed Jit, in the Shati Detention Camp in Gaza: "They put a sack over my head, choked me with their hands around my throat, let go, put my head in a pail of water up to my neck. The sack was stuck to my face. They did this six or seven times.... When they took my head out of the pail of water, they beat my head with their fists." Here is "Hassan," with the interrogator known as "Maradona" in Dahariya Detention Center: "He began to hit me on the head with the pole [a bolt about twenty centimeters long with a rubber handle]. He hit me twice and I fell down. When I came to, they were still beating and kicking me. I tried to get up and got more beatings on the head. I fell down. While I was lying down they continued to beat me all over my body.... I thought that I was going to die then and there—I couldn't move. Two stood over me and began to spit all over me, again and again without stopping. They stepped on my face with their shoes." And here is "Barakat," in the Russian compound off Jaffa Road, which every tourist in Jerusalem passes: "Someone held a pipe of Tippex [correction fluid]. Another grabbed me by the hair and poured Tippex into my mouth. I immediately spat up everything and his face was covered all over with spit and Tippex.... Then they really got mad and beat me harder. They continued beating me and because of all the beating I lost control and began urinating in my clothes and I noticed that my urine was full of blood. I saw blood on my pants and blood and urine on the floor. They wiped up the blood with my beard and hair."

Ill-treatment, "moderate physical pressure," or torture? Our subtitle recognized the linguistic ambiguities that attended these descriptions.

Talk as Self-Correction

Of the many contradictions in Israeli society, one of the strangest for the outsider to understand is that the same political space is shared by brutal repression and democratic institutions. As much as the denial of Palestinian rights is total, as much as racism and militarism penetrate civil society, so—

for Israeli Jews, that is—the terrain of democracy, legality, and civil rights remains more or less open.

This means that the work needed to expose human-rights violations can be done in relative free-dom and that there are open arenas for talking about this work, such as the media, universities, and political meetings. Human-rights organizations—Israeli, international, and to a lesser extent, Pales-tinian—can do the sort of documentation impossible in societies where gross human-rights violations take place under a regime of total state control with no access or accountability. In Israel, the formal mechanisms of liberal legality are intact, if vulnerable. There are special sections in the Foreign Min-istry and the Ministry of Justice that painstakingly handle complaints from bodies such as Amnesty International and the International Committee of the Red Cross. There are officials whose entire working lives are spent meeting with endless delegations from all over the world. And the press is re-strained more by its own sense of the national consensus than by direct state censorship.

None of this freedom, of course, is enjoyed by the Palestinians—and this, in itself, corrupts and compromises the heart of Israeli democracy. It also means that these officials are engaged in ritual denials, accusations of worldwide bias against Israel, uncheckable promises to "investigate each alle-gation," or appeals to preposterous legalistic sophistry to explain why, for example, the Geneva Con-vention does not apply to the Occupied Territories. It means that allegations coming from Palestinian, or international, or suspect Israeli sources are easily discredited—while exactly the same information from a mainstream Israeli organization like B'tselem has to be taken seriously. Despite all these lim-itations, though, the freedom to talk is real and should not be taken for granted.

The consequence of this freedom is to create the impression of a self-correcting social system. The image is of a society where departures from democratic norms are exposed, recognized only *as* de-partures, and then automatically corrected by built-in mechanisms of restraint and regulation. There are reports, complaint investigations of allegations, commissions of inquiry, routine procedures, ques-tions in the Knesset, an independent state-comptroller office, and prosecutions of individual officials who go too far. During the first two weeks after the B'tselem report was published, we saw extesive reaction from the liberal bloc of Israeli society. The Hebrew papers—particularly *Ha'aretz* and the influential mass-circulation weeklies—gave detailed coverage to our report; they printed extracts of testimonies, descriptions of interrogations, and the drawings (which made a special impact). Edito-rials and articles carried demands for an inquiry into the allegations. Sixteen Knesset members—all from RATZ, MAPAM, Shinui, and Labor—appealed to the prime minister either to deny or confirm the conclusions of the report.

This coverage was generally sympathetic and fair. The impression was that people were genuinely perturbed. This, remember, was the period after the Gulf War, when there was hardly any sympa-thy for the Palestinians even among liberals. But the question "Can this be happening here?" drew forth the liberal anxiety about how these patterns of violence might spread to Israeli society itself. Even a right-wing journalist, Dov Goldstein, joined the front and demanded: "Is it or is it not true that the Shabak, or the police, or the army ... is breaking the arms of Palestinian prisoners by torture ... as happens in South America, Africa, and Asia?"

How did the official system respond? At first, there were standard techniques of official-talk: The Israel Defense Forces (IDF) criticized B'tselem for releasing the report without prior notice; the Min-istry of Justice claimed (falsely) that it had not been sent allegations to check; assurances were given that individual complaints were always followed up. But clearly the subject was not going to be buried. Two powerful Knesset committees (Foreign Affairs–Defense and State Comptroller) demanded and planned debates. A vivid testimony by Ari Shavit, an Israeli reservist who had served in Ansar 2 (the army detention facility at Gaza Beach), was published in *Ha'aretz* (an English translation later ap-peared in the *New York Review of Books*). The sounds of pain that Shavit recorded—the "hair-rais-ing human screams" from the interrogation block—could not be easily shut out.

A week later, no fewer than three separate official inquiries were announced: one by the IDF (to cover allegations about ill-treatment in army prisons), one within the GSS itself, and another coordinated by the Ministry of Justice. As I write, we are still waiting for the results of these investigations. A press release in August that reproduced part of the IDF report suggested that the report's authors at least took our allegations seriously: They recommended that some interrogators be prosecuted but also (curiously) that all interrogations be transferred from the army to the Shabak. The other investigations are totally secret. Overall, there is likely to be some discrediting of our evidence and criticism of our refusal to identify informants whose anonymity we guaranteed. Our careful reservations about not being able to vouch for every detail might backfire. And the limitation of all such official inquiries is that they remain within a legal model of checking individual testimonies, rather than looking for general patterns.

To what extent can the system correct itself through such mechanisms? Clearly there are major limits to what the "watchdog" mode of human-rights work can achieve when it is running against the dominant political current. In fact, the conditions that allow ill-treatment and torture are endemic rather than incidental. These conditions are, first of all, political: a perceived threat to national security; the need to process large numbers of suspects; dehumanization of the out-group; high-level authorization (provided formally by the Landau Commission) to violate normal moral principles; the invocation of a sacred mission to justify anything. Second, there is a set of legal conditions: a prolonged period of incommunicado detention without access to a lawyer (two weeks is the norm, a month common, three months possible); the fact that detainees cannot identify their interrogators by name or number; trials under military regulations rather than in regular courts; the absence of independent medical examinations; procedural rules that do not automatically exclude evidence obtained by force.

The political will needed to eradicate such conditions does not exist in Israel today. I don't want to sound too cynical about self-correction. The traditional rationales for human-rights intervention remain valid: humanitarian help for individuals; the possibility of redress; the inhibiting effect produced by the knowledge that one is being watched; the chance to make violations more (and hopefully, unbearably) costly for the authorities. Even on general principles, the Israeli legal system still retains some flexibility. In June 1991, for example, attorney Avigdor Feldman (acting on behalf of the Public Committee Against Torture) won a notable case in the High Court by obtaining a restraining order calling on the government to justify the legality of the Landau recommendations. There have been limited victories on limited terrain; law can be a shield if not a sword.

A more depressing event, on wider political terrain, took place in April. At the annual Independence Day ceremony, Landau was awarded the prestigious Israel Prize. The citation noted that, as president of the Supreme Court, Justice Landau had written decisions that translated "basic values of freedom, equality, and fairness into a way of life"; it extolled his role in advancing the "principles and values of an enlightened society ... and human rights." The citation was signed by the two leading Israeli liberal figures, former attorney general Yitzhak Zamir and Justice Aharon Barak. The citation made no reference to the Landau Commission—only to Landau's previous distinguished record. (A newspaper advertisement by the Public Committee drawing attention to this was denounced as "bad taste.")

Talk as Treachery

For the Right—which claims, quite correctly, to speak for the national consensus—there is nothing to correct. Indeed, in their view, the problem with Israeli society is that too many concessions are made to universal principles such as legality and civil liberties. This is just the Hellenism that Kahane used to denounce in every speech. To respond to internal and external criticism is to be too sensitive to a "foreign" ideology, to worry too much about what the goyim think. And for those on the Right who genuinely understand human-rights principles, the doctrine of national security overrides other considerations.

A graphic statement of this position came not from the Right but from a political journalist identified with the liberal center. In an article in *Ha'aretz,* Dan Margalit told his own atrocity story. His daughter and her friends were walking along a Jerusalem street. Some Palestinians in a Mercedes drove toward the girls and kept stopping near them; when they started getting out of the car, the girls ran and screamed for help from a soldier. The Palestinians drove away and the girls complained to the police. What was Margalit's message? "One of these young girls is my daughter and as far as I'm concerned, the Shabak can use as much 'moderate physical pressure' as the Landau Commission says in order to find the gang. I don't care what the B'tselem report will write about it." Yes, there must be some controls; yes, deviations must be punished; but a democracy cannot deal with its violent political enemies as it does with ordinary delinquents.

The range of explicitly right-wing opinion was revealed in a series of interviews published in *Ha'aretz.* Only three of the eleven right-wingers interviewed had read the report, but all tried to discredit information based on Palestinian sources and disseminated by an organization like B'tselem. More fundamentally, right-wing critics saw the whole enterprise of talking about human-rights violations as suspect. For Limor Livnat, member of the Likud Central Committee, even to read the report would mean being contaminated by the "moral obscenity" of its source. Those who talk about human rights are denounced as traitors, enemy agents, or self-hating Jews. In a letter I received from one "Blanche Tannenbaum, New York" after talking about the report on WBAI radio, the exact description of me was a "Jewish anti-Semitic piece of shit."

But the most extraordinary of all such terms of abuse is "informer" (the Hebrew word *malshin*). Can there be another country in the world where whistle-blowers—those who expose not just human-rights abuses but also fraud, corruption, and malpractice in government agencies—are routinely branded as "informers"? The dovish Knesset members who toured the United States in June to draw attention to the government's expansionist settlement plans were also denounced by Arik Sharon and the Right as a "commando of informers." According to this rhetoric, talk is treachery. ("Careless talk costs lives" was the wartime slogan in Britain.) An important subtext is "Don't let the goyim know." Even if the picture is true, it should not be allowed to circulate. A peculiarly Israeli theme, articulated clearly by former Chief Rabbi Goren, is that Jews (and particularly the "holy and pure" Jews who work for the GSS) are simply incapable of doing anything bad. Right-wingers and centrists have also questioned the accuracy of the allegations or assigned them the status of "exceptions," departures from the norm. These objections have to be responded to seriously by human-rights organizations anywhere, especially if they are presented in an open-minded way, rather than as a technique of denial.

All these statements, however, express a single, if internally contradictory, message: "It can't be happening here, but if it is, it must be all right." Let us call the two elements in this message denial and justification.

A common form of denial finds expression in self-protective homilies, such as "You can never believe what Palestinians say." An extreme racist version of this position appears in an interview reprinted in our report, in which two retired Shabak agents claim that Arabs have a "mental problem," a "genetic difference" that prevents them from telling the truth: "A Bedouin cannot pass a polygraph because his moral level is different from yours." A more sophisticated version says that because Palestinians are the enemy, they deliberately lie and exaggerate for the purpose of political propaganda. Critics have also discredited B'tselem as politically biased and gullible, or else downplayed the seriousness of the injuries: This is not "really" torture; there is no permanent damage; what is a couple of days without sleep, or being spat at, or being tied up and beaten compared with what happens "elsewhere"? And after all, they don't really feel it; look at the violence they inflict on each other.

Justifications of torture draw first on the idea of "necessity," which appears in a sophisticated form in the Landau report. There is no other way, this argument goes; national security requires these methods. A second, more elevated version, appeals to a sacred mission, a higher set of values that transcend the rule of law. (As Livnat argues, "Zionism is above all. If a group like B'tselem had existed when Israel was being established, a Jewish state would not have come into being.") A third appeal—deeply ingrained in the collective Israeli psyche—is to the Darwinian struggle for survival: It's us or them; it's our fate to be locked into a cycle of violence that has no end. And finally, a fourth line of defense is to reproduce wholesale the self-image of the security services: good people doing their job as best they can under difficult conditions. Somebody has to do the dirty work; "you can't chop wood without splinters flying"; every palace has its dirty corners.

Many of these reactions were publicly expressed not by the far Right, but by no less than Justice Landau, the bastion of Israeli liberal legalism. In response to a private (but admittedly provocative) letter from the director of B'tselem asking if he saw any connection between the methods revealed by our inquiry and those permitted by the commission, Landau published an open letter in the mass-circulation daily paper *Yediot Achronot*. Understandably sensitive to what he saw as unfair criticism, Landau took two main lines of defense. The first was to repeat the commission's argument that international definitions of torture cover only methods that cause "severe" pain and suffering. These were not approved; "moderate physical pressure" is obviously something different, since it does not destroy the subject's dignity. The second was to requote the commission's conclusion that "false claims" and "wild exaggerations" are "part of the systematic campaign conducted by terrorist organizations against the GSS, with the aim of weakening it in its war against Hostile Terrorist Activity, and tarnishing its image in the eyes of well-wishing individuals and organizations by presenting it as a ruthless organization engaged in torture and maltreatment of innocent 'freedom fighters.'" He poured scorn on our methods of checking sources for internal consistency and validating them through external evidence such as medical reports.

Lest his political subtext remain unclear, Landau went on to accuse B'tselem of having caused prejudice and animosity toward the Shin Bet investigators, "as if the torture of people under interrogations was their daily bread. The B'tselem report viciously maligned a service whose function is to defend the residents of the state and the Territories (Jews and Arabs) against mass and individual terror. Ultimately you therefore assisted—unintentionally, I assume—those evil-mongers of the State who conduct psychological warfare against it, in addition to other kinds of warfare, with the purpose of undermining its existence."

The question of terrorism is, in fact, irrelevant: Not a single one of our forty-one subjects was charged with or even suspected of committing or planning an act of terrorism. But the real irrelevance of Landau's letter, as we noted in our reply (which *Yediot Achronot* refused to publish), is that nowhere does he decide between two possible alternatives: either that these practices (or something like them) occur—but they fall within the commission's secret approved guidelines—or else that such practices (or something like them) lie outside the approved guidelines, and therefore should be condemned as torture. Neither alternative, of course, can be publicly confirmed unless the secret guidelines are disclosed.

Talk as Discursive Practice

The public criticism we least expected came from our own side. In a series of articles in the weekly supplement to *Davar*, Adi Ophir, a philosopher from Tel Aviv University and a founder of the anti-Occupation group the Twenty-First Year, launched a sardonic attack on the B'tselem report. His thesis is complex and became qualified in response to countercriticism, but its essence is clear enough to anyone immersed in current postmodernist theory and anti-positivist philosophy.

Ophir argues that radical intellectuals should know better than to work within the standard genre of human-rights documentation. The B'tselem report, for Ophir, is just another text—a text with a pretense to representation that it cannot sustain. Ophir sees any claim to objectivity—checking the facts ("I was tied up for twelve hours") or their representativeness ("Most detainees are tied up ...")—as merely a "rhetorical strategy" designed to give the document legitimacy. Behind this strategy, he writes, lies a worldview, liberal and positivist, according to which facts exist on their own and one can really distinguish between facts and values, description and interpretation and, above all, one can disconnect a description of social reality from the power struggle that attempts to shape this reality. In a postmodern world, in a culture that rejects the possibility of a transparent descriptive language or an objective spokesperson, this worldview appears naive, if not ridiculous.

Intelligent radicals such as the writers of the report, Ophir allows, could hardly be so naive. Their strategy surely must have been different, more complex, less ridiculous; we must rather have assumed that torture is such an obvious case of evil that there is no need to differentiate (or pretend to) between description and interpretation; that all we have to do is say that the events happened—and invite the authorities to confirm or deny that. The facts would speak for themselves and every reasonable and sensitive person would find them shocking. But if this worldview is more epistemologically sophisticated than the first, it is just as politically wrong. For there is no general consensus about the evil of torture.

In any event, Ophir argues, whatever our rhetorical strategy, the results are devastatingly the same: We simply reproduce and thereby strengthen the culture of the Occupation. The report by necessity "joins the hegemonic political discourse that the regime of the Occupation creates as if this were the natural order of things, a discourse whose function it is to normalize relations between the occupier and the occupied." The very attention that the report generated—the official inquiries, questions in the Knesset (talk as self-correction)—only proves that it posed no serious challenge. Although organizations like B'tselem aim to provide alternative knowledge, the genre they are forced to use is far too limited; it shuts out too much and compromises too much in trying to adapt itself to the dominant discourse.

To emphasize the limits of the genre—and the costs paid by radicals for using it—Ophir compares the report unfavorably with the recently published volume *Poets Will Not Write Poetry,* edited by Ilana Hammerman and Roly Rosen (Am Oved, 1990). This is a collection of texts (soldiers' testimonies, legal protocols) that makes up a collage of impressions, a montage that abandons any pseudoscientific pretense to objectivity, as a way to challenge the hegemonic culture. Such a montage invites the reader to make an active choice (resist or collaborate) rather than—like the B'tselem report—merely placing responsibility on the regime and leaving the reader as a passive observer. The fact that *Poets Will Not Write Poetry* did not sell and received little media coverage compared with the report, needless to say, vindicates its radical status.

In a later response to his critics, Ophir notes that he is just making a division of labor; each genre has its place. His dividing line, however, is clearly between the mere liberalism of RATZ or Peace Now—the discourse into which he claims the B'tselem report is locked—and the true radicalism of the montage. Moreover, the report is not even authentic liberalism, but the work of fellow subversives who, out of despair with radical politics in Israel, have deflected their energy and talents into an inherently defective strategy.

No one exposed to the astonishing twists in critical theory over the last two decades can afford to ignore the intellectual sources from which Adi Ophir's critique derives. Anyone who works in a field such as human rights must share some of his theoretical doubts. Yes, we make compromises and pay prices. No, such reports will not end the Occupation. But a critique that aspires to this type of translation or "application" of theory to the case in question, torture in Israel, is just too facile and self-indulgent. It is victim of two ironies (that favorite postmodern attribute): At the theoretical level, it uses a perspective that rejects any totalizing meta-narratives precisely to construct a totalizing critique that lacks any openings, that offers no possibility of multiple meanings other than the fixed hegemonic structure into which all attacks are gobbled up. And at the political level, it is symptomatic of the very despair of which he accuses us.

The genre, the rhetorical strategy, is seen as limiting and restrictive. There is no sense of its possible advantages or effects. First, there is the immediate humanitarian possibility: As long as the terrain of democracy, legality, and accountability continues to exist in Israeli society, it has to be exploited to its absolute limit. Every such strategy of intervention—prevention of individual suffering, redress, tightening legal controls, holding officials accountable—depends on a mode of knowledge that must use the language of facts and universal human-rights standards. An autopsy report shows whether a prisoner died from a beating rather than a heart attack; there is no question here of another "genre" being more effective. As Hammerman and Rosen would be the first to concede, if they had included such an autopsy report in their collage, it would only have been because a human-rights organization had struggled (with the only rhetorical strategy possible) to obtain an independent inquiry to discredit official lies.

Second, there is the admittedly more remote but genuine prospect of delegitimization. People, especially political elites, can be persuaded to change if they pay too much of a price for staying the same—not only a material price (standard of living, loss of life) but a moral price, a sense that what is being done in their name is no longer legitimate. No doubt, material damage is more threatening than moral damage. But as a case like South Africa shows, the combination of external pressure (sanctions, isolation, disinvestment) and internal fragmentation, which finally led to political change, was informed by decades of "liberal positivist" exposure of the evils of apartheid. Or take a closer case, the French withdrawal from Algeria—in which the intellectual campaign against torture was decisive.

The exquisite aesthetics by which politics becomes text and pain beomes semiotics leaves us with a bitter taste. The problem is not that we are too ready to place our theoretical doubts aside becuase of political expediency and despair. Nor are we saying that these intellectual worlds—whether those of Quine, Davidson, and Rorty, or of Derrida and Foucault—do not belong in the Middle East (that the Left Bank is not the same as the West Bank, as one of Ophir's critics suggested). The problem lies in sorting out which strands in these theories make any sort of political sense in general and in our local situation in particular. The solution is not to use so inherently (and intentionally) ambiguous a body of ideas to prescribe some "correct" rhetorical strategy. Deconstruction itself does not necessarily undermine the utility of any political practice, nor the power of the master narratices from which it draws value.

These master narratives—social justice, national liberation, human rights, the struggles against racism and sexism—have not sunk into some historical black hole. A scene that I often like to think about is Michel Foucault at a press conference in Geneva in 1981, joining activists from "humanitarian" organizations to announce a new human-rights initiative in defense of Vietnamese boat people. Here stands that most profound archeologist of the link between knowledge and power, that most skeptical critic of leberal humanism, talking about "facts," "rights," and the "duty of international citizenry." Foucault uses the opportunity to theorize about political action itself: how organizations like Amnesty International are trying to create a new right (the right to speak about the unspeaka le), a will of individuals "to inscribe itself in a reality over which governments have wanted to reserve a monopoly for themselves—a monopoly that we must uproot little by little every day." I don't see any inconsistency here between theory and practice—or at least no more than is inherent in all life.

Silence

There were moments—when we were collecting testimonies, writing the report, dealing with our critics, or giving evidence to the investigating committees—when we felt that all these words were superfluous. This feeling of hopelessness came not from the avant-garde conceit that the only role for the progressive intellectual is a dignified silence, a refusal to enter the dominant discourse. My inclination to silence came rather from the sense that all the empirical, legal and moral niceties we were trying to convey added little to the moral issue at stake. Here we were—in company with thousands all over the world who face risks we do not face and expose still worse horrors—still trying to convince our fellow citizens about the importance of *torture?* At the end of the twentieth century, why should anyone still have to explain all this? As a Salinger character says of the Gettysburg Address: Lincoln should just have stood in front of the crowd, shaken his fist at them and walked away.

As with slavery, the only morally defensible position about torture is abolitionist. It simply is not the task of human-rights organizations to talk about alternatives, even to begin to ask, "What would you do if you were in our place?" But even abolitionism needs words. The untalkable has to be talked about because in all societies at all times (and Israel is no exception), and for the vast majority of the population, the contours of daily life depend on ignorance, silence, and passive collusion. Most people exercise what Daniel Ellsberg nicely calls "the right not to know."

There is another very special obstacle to talking about torture, and not just in Israel: The pervasive myth that while such practices are undesirable and unfortunate, they are, alas, necessary. This is the classic utilitarian justification, as old as torture itself: that it is only a method (and the only possible method) of obtaining information, intelligence, testimony, confessions, or evidence. If our findings or those of any other investigation leave only one memory behind, it should be this: Whether the utilitarian defense is morally justifiable or not is not what torture is about.

Orwell saw this in *1984*. No one can ever forget O'Brien's terrible explanation of why Winston must be tortured rather than simply killed: "The object of persecution is persecution. The object of torture is torture. The object of power is power. Now do you begin to understand me?" ☐

When Palestinian Rocks Shattered My Windows

Michael Lerner

I can't pretend I wasn't scared. I had always driven this road alongside the walls of the Old City, turning up through a few blocks of East Jerusalem as the fastest way to get to the Hebrew University, but today I stopped to ask an Israeli policeman if this was still the best way to go. "Yes, straight ahead," he had told me. A few blocks later the barrage of rocks began, thrown by what appeared to be a few dozen Palestinian youths. When the glass of my car window shattered all over me I was lucky not to have been cut. But luck was not on my mind as I stepped on the gas and sped away, shaken, confused as to which way to go to safety, and not yet sure that I was all right.

A few minutes later I found an Israeli army patrol that led me to the Jerusalem police. No one at the police station had the slightest interest in going back to that corner opposite the Rockefeller Museum where my car had been attacked. "Happens all the time," I was told. There was a standardized form for Palestinian attacks in cars, which I dutifully brought from the police to my car rental company, who in turn replaced the shattered window without charge.

Conventional wisdom in the early 1980s was that a neo-conservative was simply a liberal who had been mugged. I shared the feeling of anger and upset at the sudden, terrifying indignity of violent assault. But I had no political conversion. Rocks may not bring freedom for Palestinians—but neither have their pleas to Shamir to negotiate. When Yassir Arafat said he would come to Jerusalem, Shamir announced that he would be arrested the moment he deplaned at Ben Gurion airport. Daily reports of jailings and torture of Palestinian activists add to their frustrations. Had I been born a Palestinian, I could easily imagine myself being tempted to join that crowd of rock-throwing teenagers.

But rocks are not the solution. The Israeli population must be won over. The Israelis I meet are often sensitive, intelligent, and caring. Even those who do not side with the peace movement often talk about the complicated nature of the problem, and of the absence on the Palestinian side of anyone who shows sensitivity to the fears of Israelis.

I confront several Palestinian activists on this question. Why don't they understand that Palestinian support for Saddam Hussein, and the image (however blown out of proportion) of Palestinians standing on the rooftops cheering as Scuds landed on Tel Aviv, have done incalculable damage to the possibilities for peace? Surely they must understand that Israelis need to hear a Palestinian voice that condemns all this, and that unequivocally distances itself from Saddam and all that he stands for. Yes, they assure me, they do understand.

So why not say so publicly? Don't they understand how much it would help the Israeli peace movement to have this voice as a prominent factor in public debate?

Yes, they do understand. But do I understand that every Palestinian moderate who might take such

---

This editorial appeared in Tikkun, *July/August 1991.*

a stand gets harassed, beaten, and jailed by the Israeli police?

But surely this is not enough to account for the silence. You wouldn't let the police silence you on other matters vital to the survival of your national liberation movement. A strong Palestinian voice of rationality would make a tremendous impact on Israeli politics—why not speak out?

And then, the sad answer: We can't speak out, because there are others who would kill us. There is no tradition of free speech or minority dissent in Palestinian society. If the PLO in Tunis decides to change its line, fine. But otherwise, for any individual to take a stand that absolutely defies the PLO line—a stand that would look to fellow Palestinians as pandering to Israelis and playing to their concerns—is to sign her own death warrant. An Israeli friend intercedes: Don't even suggest such a thing to these people. We need them to be alive so that they can play a leading role when a Palestinian state eventually is created.

Sure, I respond. But what will keep them from being killed even after such a state is created? If Palestinian society does not tolerate dissent, why will that change once they obtain freedom?

There will be problems, Palestinian activists concede. But it will be different—because the violence imposed on us by the Occupation will no longer be there, and hence the justification for unanimity in face of external oppression will be gone. It's precisely the process of obtaining a Palestinian state—through the sustained political struggle that is empowering an entire population—that helps create a Palestinian constituency who will not be willing to accept undemocratic practices once we have the power.

But, I counter, that is just what worries me. If the process is undemocratic now, what reason do we have to think it will be more democratic later?

Have you ever tried to create democracy under a military occupation? they respond. We get arrested and thrown into jail, precisely when we try to show moderation or caring for the Israelis. And none of what we say gets reported on the Israeli television, and little even in the Israeli newspapers. Under these conditions, you can't expect us to be saying what Israelis need to hear.

Shamir's tactics seem to be working. Following the logic of Zeno's paradox, Shamir has managed to divide the space between any two points into an infinite number of pieces. Each move forward is divided in two so that the ultimate end is never reached.

Meanwhile, Secretary of State Baker seems to be locked into a strategy that is almost certainly a nonstarter. Whatever hoopla and media hype may accompany the opening of the international conference Baker still hopes to engineer, the most likely long-term consequence will be a continuing stalemate. We should take Shamir at his word when he promises his Israeli supporters that such a conference will never lead to an exchange of land for peace.

Baker and the State Department crew believe that once the conference starts, it will generate an unstoppable dynamic toward peace. I doubt it. Shamir and the Israeli Right will portray themselves as having made the major compromise just by showing up at the conference—and will expect in return that the U.S. will reward Israeli participation by refusing to apply any pressure for substantive compromises. Unlike Camp David, which was preceded by Sadat's Jerusalem visit and a sudden switch in Israeli public opinion, an international conference under the present circumstances will yield little.

The only thing that could change this prospect would be for the U.S. to put forward a substantive vision of a Middle East peace solution. *New York Times* State Department correspondent Thomas Friedman argued this same case in an article in April probably aimed at catching the attention of Baker: If the U.S. is to generate support for a peace process in Israel it must offer some specific picture of what peace could look like and exactly what its role would be in guaranteeing and sustaining that peace.

Shamir knows that this is true—which is precisely why he has insisted that the U.S. play an entirely neutral role in any conference with himself and the Palestinians and that the U.S. agree from the outset that it will not put forward its own plan.

Shamir is an expert at deadening public debate, squelching hope, and generating mass cynicism in Israel. After the Gulf War, many in Israel expected that there would soon be a major break-through in the stalemated peace process. By focusing the entire discussion on the logistics of setting up a conference, rather than the conference's possible outcomes, Baker has played into Shamir's hands perfectly. One important result has been that the Israeli public has lost all interest in the daily reports of this or that nuance in the negotiations over the conference's logistics, and hence does not feel betrayed or even upset when Shamir blocks forward motion. In the U.S., Baker's efforts get plenty of attention—they represent one of the only positive initiatives of U.S. foreign policy. But in Israel the media do not make a big deal of the Baker trips—so increasingly the public pays little atention to their progress. If Baker's efforts fail, Shamir will not pay too heavy a political price. But if they succeed in creating an international conference, we are likely to face a long period in which Shamir will be attempting to obstruct any positive outcome that might emerge from such a conference.

Virtually all the people I meet in the peace camp in Israel tell me that they can't imagine changing the current deadlock unless the U.S. brings external pressure to bear. So imagine my surprise when I hear that a group of Knesset doves visiting the U.S. in May are vociferously denying the charge raised against them by Israeli rightists that the doves are trying to legitimate U.S. pressure on Israel. The word "pressure" is itself ambiguous, because it can mean anything from political lecturing to economic boycott. Those who argue for America to use moral suasion obviously haven't been watching Israeli politics over the past years. Over and over again the U.S. has made statements calling for Israel to bring an end to settlements, has repudiated Israel's annexation of Jerusalem and the Golan, and has asked for adherence to UN Resolution 242, which calls for an exchange of land for peace. All of these statements, however, mean absolutely nothing in Israel. In fact, their impact is worse than nothing—they create a backlash of support for the government, which can play on the fierce pride and sense of independence that has traditionally characterized the mass psychology of Israeli society. It is now all the easier for the Right to build on this backlash since U.S. credibility—at an all-time high during the Gulf War—has taken a nosedive in the face of its betrayal of the Kurds.

But if political backlash is to be avoided, wouldn't any suggestion of economic pressure be worse? Not necessarily, according to some peace movement activists. The worst thing, they argue, would be a little bit of economic pressure. This would reinforce the "we are once again being be-trayed" syndrome that dominates Israeli consciousness. But a lot of economic pressure might have very different consequences. The peace movement has long argued that Israel's intransigence on the Territories will eventually have bad consequences. These warnings have seemed empty to the Israeli public as long as the Reagan and Bush administrations have accompanied their moral warnings to Israel with increases in aid and military support. If, instead, there was a real and immediate possibility that the Israeli standard of living might seriously decline because of the Occupation, many sectors of Israeli society who today believe they can have both financial security and the Occupied Territories would be shaken, and would likely force the government to change course. Where symbolic cuts would create backlash, massive economic pressure could produce positive results, these Israelis argue.

Whatever the general validity of this position, I'm not yet ready to support this kind of approach. When I see the economic difficulties facing Israelis today, and when I realize that the brunt of cuts in U.S. aid would most likely fall on the poor, I'm very reluctant to support any program of aid cuts. But economic pressure can take other forms. Lately I've been floating a different idea—pressure through incentive. My specific proposal is this: Let the U.S. publicly promise Israel that it will give 10 billion dollars of aid per year for five years. This aid would be aimed at helping Israel absorb and settle Russian and Ethiopian immigrants, and would be contingent upon Israel meeting two conditions: It must begin direct negotiations with Palestinian representatives (chosen in free elections in which members of the PLO are allowed to run) before the first year; and it must conclude an agreement for a demilitarized Palestinian state by the end of the second year of the aid.

Some people might argue that the incentive program itself is unfair to Israel—after all, why should the plight of Soviet immigrants be held hostage to Israeli moves on the Palestinian front? But the answer is simple: The U.S. has its own problems with poverty and homelessness, and Americans have every right to wonder why massive escalations in aid should go to Israel before these internal problems are solved. On the other hand, it might reasonably be argued that the stabilization of the Middle East that would arise out of the resolution of the Arab-Israeli conflict might allow for important cuts in U.S. spending in the short run, and preclude the need for U.S. military intervention in the long run. This kind of an expenditure might actually be a net savings for the U.S., if Israel were willing to accept this kind of linkage. Incentives of this sort could have a massive impact on Israeli politics. The Russian immigrants are expected to vote for the Right. But if the hard-line policies of the Right were understood to be the reason why monies for jobs and housing were not available, the peace movement would have a new basis of appeal in the next elections. A peace movement that adamantly supported continuation of the current levels of aid, but that also endorsed the notion of incentives, would have a good position from which to argue.

But for U.S. supporters of the Israeli peace movement, calling for any such incentives, or any other form of economic pressure, is very hazardous. Many elements of the Jewish establishment have labeled us "traitors" and "self-hating Jews" for our willingness to support the Israeli peace movement's calls for negotiations with the PLO to establish a demilitarized Palestinian state. Our response has traditionally been that we were merely articulating here what many Israelis have been saying publicly in Israel. But if we were to call for economic pressure on Israel—something that *Tikkun* has never done and which we are not doing in this editorial—we would be in the position of pushing for a policy that leading Israeli doves have carefully eschewed, a position that would greatly increase our own political vulnerability.

Yet what makes this so complicated is that many of these doves are privately telling us that they see no solution, no possibility of forward movement in Israeli politics, until this kind of economic pressure is forthcoming—and at a level that is dramatic enough to make it credible.

I understand the dilemma of many of the elected Knesset doves. They want to change Israeli policy. But they also want to ensure their own short-term political viability (a reasonable and not unprincipled desire). I feel a deepened respect for those South Africans who supported sanctions— only now do I fully understand the tremendous pressures they must have faced in making that choice. Looking back now at the powerful impact of sanctions in changing South African governmental policy, it's easy to forget how only a few years ago the right-wingers were telling us that de Klerk would never yield to sanctions, and how political moderates in the U.S. and South Africa warned us that nothing but backlash and further suffering would ensue.

But is economic pressure the only way that the peace movement could change Israel's internal politics? Not so, according to many Sephardic and Mizrachi activists with whom I am meeting. Their criticism runs along these lines: "If these Knesset members and Peace Now people were willing to send fewer delegations to New York and Los Angeles and more to the poor sections of Tel Aviv or the settlement towns, they might have a much bigger impact. The problem is that they feel more comfortable dealing with New York liberals and wealthy Hollywood stars than dealing with those of us Israelis who are not fancy Ashkenazim. Peace Now [Shalom Achshav] has a big name in the U.S.—it's done a great marketing job there and has plenty of money to back it up. But in Israel, Peace Now has largely discredited itself, precisely because of its elitist manner and its alienation from the Sephardic majority."

This charge, I think, is partly unfair. Shalom Achshav has given some attention recently to outreach efforts aimed at the Sephardim. And some of the anger at Shalom Achshav is the historical legacy of a generalized anger at the way Ashkenazim treated the Sephardim when the Ashkenazim first arrived in Israel some forty years ago.

But Sephardic critics feel that hiring a few people to do part-time outreach in settlement towns is not a strategy capable of undoing the damage of decades in which the Left was perceived as hostile or indifferent to Sephardic interests. To do that, the peace forces would have to come to agreement on an economic program that paid attention to the problems of the poor. And that, it turns out, might be very complicated for some of the well-to-do elites who currently play a major role in the peace movement.

To understand the problem, consider the differences in the economic perspectives of the peace parties. Mapam, deeply rooted in the socialist Kibbutz Artzi movement, has been a major supporter of both peace and justice. Recognizing that the major task of the moment is to strengthen the faltering peace camp, Mapam members have been calling for a united "Peace Party" for the next election. But who are their possible allies? Ratz, the Citizens Rights Movement, has distinguished itself through its courageous work on behalf of the Palestinians. Yet apart from MK Ron Cohen, whose populist views have made him a much-admired figure among the Sephardim, Ratz is often associated with economic policies that appeal more to the upper middle class than to Israeli workers. This is even more true of the dovish Shinui party of Amnon Rubenstein, which is led by well-known free-marketeers. An alliance with these dovish parties would allow activists to articulate a peace perspective far more coherent than anything that Mapam could achieve in an alliance with Labor. But it would also be a peace party that reinforced the widespread impression within Sephardic circles that the peace camp cares little about the economic oppression that many Oriental Jews suffer.

Americans who remember that the movement against the war in Vietnam was led by two separate major antiwar coalitions (one devoted exclusively to the single issue of opposing the war, and the other a National Coalition for Peace and Justice) may wonder why the Sephardim have not yet set up a Peace and Justice Now movement as a popular alternative to Peace Now. But in the U.S., the multi-issue coalition was financed primarily by church groups. Israel has no comparable sources of funding. The New Israel Fund strictly eschews support for political organizations; and more traditional funders would never consider aiding a Sephardic-led peace movement. So the Sephardic leaders who might have played a major role in attracting people to the peace camp can do little more than work on the sidelines, hoping to offset the damage done to peace consciousness that arises from the association of the peace message with Ashkenazic leaders who seem insensitive to the problems of Oriental Jews.

"It's not the message, but the messenger that is the problem," say many Oriental Jews. This observation is borne out in Israeli opinion polls, which indicate considerable support for the peace perspective, but also reveal that Israelis remain deeply alienated from the peace movement, and little inclined to trust it. It's the same dynamic that has bedeviled Left movements around the world. Few are willing to face the implications of this astounding reality: that though they have been very successful at communicating their message, they've been unable to win power because the people don't like them and don't trust them.

Part of the reason for that distrust is that many people feel that the Left doesn't understand them and doesn't respect the way they have chosen to live. Nowhere is this clearer than in Israel, where Sephardic Jews have often clung tenaciously to their religious and national heritage as a way to protect themselves from the cultural elitism of Ashkenazic Jews. Many Sephardim experience the aggressive antireligious secularism of the Left as yet one more Ashkenazic attempt to invalidate the culture and traditions they brought with them from the Arab lands from which they fled.

Not that the Left has no reason to be antireligious. Indeed, most Israelis have been rightly angered by the oppressive imposition of religious restrictions by legal fiat at the behest of the ultra-Orthodox parties. However, the Left has been unable to clearly distinguish between a justified assault on the religious establishment on the one hand, and contempt for Jewish religious tradition on the other. Similarly, the Left has suffered from an inability to distinguish between the right wing's chauvinistic appropriation of nationalist symbols and the deeper and potentially liberatory meanings those symbols hold for the people as a whole. As a result, the Left has developed a culture that appears to outsiders to be insensitive to the national heritage of the Jewish people.

Ironically, the Israeli Left makes the same mistake here in its attitude toward religion and Jewish nationalism that others make in their attitude toward left-wing ideas. The form of reasoning that leads leftists to dismiss Judaism and Jewish nationalism as fundamentally reactionary ("Just look at what those Gush Emunim people are doing!") is identical to the reasoning that has led many people to dismiss all socialist ideals because Eastern European totalitarians used the language of socialism to justify their oppressive regimes. ("Since that's what revolution always leads to, we'd better just reconcile ourselves to the flaws of capitalism.") The Israeli Left might have been considerably more successful had it been able to develop a politics that built on the liberatory possibilities within the Jewish historical experience.

But it's always easy to preach about what someone should have done. The fact is that the liberal and progressive forces in the U.S. and throughout the Western world face very similar problems, and for very similar reasons. Part of the reason that the Left can't make the appropriate practical leaps in its politics is because it is stuck, as much in the U.S., Britain, and France as in Israel, with an ideological framework that fails to seriously address the human need for transcendence and meaning. Thus the Left simply has no place to understand the deep human yearnings to be part of loving relationships embodied in spiritually sensitive communities devoted to a larger ethical vision of human life on earth.

Facing the rocks of Jerusalem, one is reminded of the Jewish vision articulated through the Prophets of a new world that could embody such communities of meaning and ethical purpose. If we do not articulate such a vision—or worse, if we allow such a vision to be appropriated by the Right for nefarious purposes—the Left will be unable to grasp the opportunities within its reach. And meanwhile, I am faced with an Israel that oppresses Arabs, leftists who oppose this oppression but who render themselves impotent and largely irrelevant, and Arab kids throwing rocks through my car window. □

V. Being Jewish in the Contemporary World

Don't Take Your Daughter to the Extermination Camp

Eleonora Lev

We walk, embracing, down the paths of the Maidanek extermination camp. She complains that she's hot and cold inside her body. Her head presses against my shoulder, nestling in my embracing arm, working nonstop in its complicated, invisible way. What is she building in there? Into what secret language is she translating what she sees with her eyes? She is still sheltered by the blessed ignorance of her age; ultimate despair still falls outside her spectrum of familiar emotions. Her powers of imagining have not yet faltered under the effort to imagine things that really happened. She still hopes I'm omniscient and already suspects I'm not; for now, however, this suspicion brings only a good-hearted smirk to her lips.

To her I am transparent. As fully understood as the seasons, as essential as the weather, and to the same extent nothing special, merely what's available. Thus she clings to me, the child who is usually as casual with me as with her bedroom slippers. The forced, self-conscious effort, the doubts, the ever-present feeling of not-up-to-the-job—all these, it seems, come from my side. It is she who teaches me compassion, humility, a life of constant attention to every detail, a compelling concern and a trusting devotion. From her I have come to know the magnitude of my power to destroy, to inflict pain. The difficulty of controlling that power. And the fact that I can wreak this destruction so easily, with a word, a glance. And that blunders and negligence can hurt as much as willful malice.

Her hands are long and thin, usually dirty: black crescents of sand under the fingernails, glue stains, felt-pen doodlings, water-soluble Donald Duck tattoos. Her hair is thick and smooth, that caressable hue somewhere between honey and light brown. It gets darker every year; when she was very little, she was straw-blond. The quick glinting gold scattering and disappearing from her hair is one of the certain sweetnesses of my life, like the shape of her head in my palm, the roundness of her forehead. The look in her eyes is bittersweet chocolate, a look she had even as an infant, a wise and pensive look set in a little elongated face. Hidden dimples in her cheeks emerge only when she laughs hard. And now her body is blossoming with the first signs of approaching womanhood. When I gave her a bath in the hotel in Warsaw, she sang loudly, gaily, a "soap song" she invented on the spot, a made-up melody with nonsense words, and explained, choking with laughter between "stanzas": I don't know what it is, it's the song the soap makes. If I had a son, would I love him differently?

The burden I bear, sometimes with pleasure and always with a hundred regrets, is this desire: to be forever very sane for her, very, very good. As André Gide said, "I intend to give you strength, joy, courage, perspicacity, defiance." And how shall I give her all these when they are forever eluding my own grasp? The thing I always try to keep secret from her—out of shame, out of fear of

---

Eleonora Lev emigrated from Poland to Israel in 1956. She writes for the Israeli daily Maariv. This piece is taken from a forthcoming book entitled A Sort of Orphanhood, 1983. *This article appeared in Tikkun, January/February 1987.*

hurting—is the rabid dog, the drooling, worm-infested beast, eyes inflamed, who races about madly in a corner of my mind, gnawing on rotten bones, ridden with leprosy, wailing in the dark from its stinging wounds as it pisses on itself. The essence of its madness is its vehement refusal to die. DeathFear, that's its name, and there are nights when I have nowhere to escape from its howling. Then I am really alone and cold. But if she suddenly appears by my bed in the middle of the night, I immediately make her a warm, soft refuge under the blanket; I wrap and curl myself around her and put her to sleep. The front of my body, concave to her, radiates confidence and serenity as if nothing were the matter, as if the hateful dog isn't still crouching, panting at my arched back—like the dark side of the moon—lying in wait for an opportunity to bare its teeth, to suck my very marrow. Thus we curl together, three crescents tightly sandwiched in the dark: tiny Effie, going back to sleep, I curling around her in the middle, and DeathFear grabbing me from behind and breathing down my neck.

Why on earth are you taking the girl to Auschwitz, people asked me. How old is she? Are you sure it's for her? I had no good answer, as if I had been accused of taking my only daughter to a brothel, a bad mother, what a scandal. I invented some macabre smart-aleck answer: and the children who arrived at Auschwitz forty years ago, was it for them? It's not a place for people of any age, if you ask me. The discomfort did not go away.

I never raised my hand at her in my life, not even once. This was a deliberate commitment I assumed when I was about her age: When I have children, I vowed then (my body burning from one of my hot-tempered mother's painful outbursts of rage), I will never beat them, never. Thus I expunged violence altogether from my life. I do not hit and do not get hit. I always say, I don't understand women who hang on for years with a man who beats them. Let someone dare just once to give me a light slap, just one little slap, I will not stay around to hear the end of the story, I will walk out for good then and there. Never mind how much I love him, no one will control me by force. That's rather hysterical, people tell me. What are you afraid of? That a little slap you give your daughter will lead to murder? And I agree, something's out of whack here. All the laws of psychology tell us that the thing we detest most fiercely is precisely that which we are attracted to in our subconscious—the most righteous and moralistic types are the biggest lovers of lechery.

Must I take these rules upon myself? Is my anxious abhorrence of violence passive or active, a psychic stop-sign against my own drives? I, who shut my eyes in goose-pimple fright at any fight scene in a movie—what have all the murderous apparitions of the Nazis been doing in my nighttime dreams all these years? What do you think they represent, all the Nazis you dream about, Yasmine asked me. I tried to study the question with an open mind. I've read the literature, haven't I; they've got to stand for some hidden facet of my character. It's a fact that these Nazi dreams are much more frequent when I am depressed, and less so when I am in a better mood. Thus I considered Yasmine's question carefully and at length, and finally said: I think they represent Nazis. In other words, absolute evil. In other words, something which I am wholly unwilling to acknowledge in myself. It is a fact that in these dreams I am usually the persecuted, murdered Jewess, sometimes the desperately fighting Jewess, and, less often, the onlooker who does not lift a finger. But never, never did I dream I was one of the black-uniformed Nazis, the absolute sovereigns, who bash an infant's head against the wall without batting an eye, who have high, gleaming boots, whips, cold blue eyes, the supreme calm of those who are sure nothing will ever touch them, who know their supremacy, their invincibility. And something forces me to ask, what makes me so sure even when awake, that I am not like this, that I couldn't—if the circumstances were right? Where is the breaking point at which I would join them, in mind or in body? How do I know I will forever be a victim, always, automatically in the right?

When I was little I had a dream of knowing the world encyclopedically. The names of every country and river, every people and civilization, every flower and insect, every shade of blue and clear glass, every book written in every language, and the experience of flying in every flying machine—especially a balloon. There was no place at all to sort the reflections of evil which seeped, in a constant septic trickle, into the exciting multicolor world I looked forward to. They came from a source which seemed at first external, random, banishable with a bit of effort. When every evening the radio carried a summary of reports about the horrors revealed at the Eichmann trial, I used to steal the World War II "Stalag" thrillers my older sister was reading furtively. Hot all over, I would consume the imaginary tales, the orgies of the SS officers, the whippings (the skin on the victim's back always peeled off "strip by strip"), every kind of rape and erotic humiliation. It was disgusting and it was frightening and it was arousing, and I was unaware of the relationship between this literature, penetrating-to-the-clitoris, and the *nicht schuldig* which echoed in my ears from Jerusalem. Only years later, of course, did I hear of Wilhelm Reich's theories.

Sometimes, when I open my kitchen cupboard or the drawer where I keep my socks, I am an occupation-army soldier searching my house—isn't there any food here, or something to loot, maybe concealed jewelry or something? The soldier who rifles through my things down to the last corner of the house (my corpse is splayed on the floor, gushing blood, or else I'm very, very far from here, the train has already taken me) is neither a Syrian nor an Egyptian nor a Palestinian; he is always a Wehrmacht soldier of the Second World War. All the black demons who have the power to claim my soul, who terrify more thoroughly than any terrorist, have German names.

("All the black demons who have the power to claim my soul have Jewish names," thought Hitler to himself. And the rest, as they say, is history.)

How long my handicap will last, I don't know. It's a matter of generations, I suppose, perhaps many generations—perhaps as long as anyone bothers to ferret out details, to read documents. The scourge is fading away. There are Israelis who visit Germany as tourists, some even settle there. Even so, it's not just me. I am Alice in Horrorland, alternately growing and shrinking, living in a shadow which does not pass, the ground treacherous under my feet. When I walk, kick a stone, tread on an anthill, watch the ants scramble blindly to save themselves—I can wipe them out to the last ant with a single squirt of spray—I think-not-think about the time when people were ants, when hobnailed boots burst through doors. It was no use to scramble; they were taken away in mid-everything-work, lunch, love, scheming, gossip, prayer—and exterminated with insecticide.

When I get on Bus No. 5 and they push me from every side, shoving me all over, sour, short-tempered people, crowding like sheep under the ticket-taker's staff as he arbitrarily slams the door in their faces, I half-remember how very easily this could have been a cattle-train heading "east": the same desperate shoving, the same selfish backs turned on the aged and the weak. In a momentary flash of hate, I assess the ticket-taker as a fit candidate for the job of kapo once we reach the final destination. When I pass the show window of a Tel Aviv electric shop and see heaters made by Krupps (Krupps!) made-in-West-Germany, and the shopkeeper has added a handwritten note: "Just the thing for the bathroom." I say to myself yes, sure; the main thing is to take a deep breath as ordered.

When we were setting out for Auschwitz we hesitated for a moment at the rent-a-car place: for this of all trips, would we take a Mercedes? So what, we deserve it, we thought childishly. Hate is not an exact science. (If it were, Hitler would not have decided to kill our families, who did him no harm.) The idea of pulling into Auschwitz in a Mercedes was a piece of magical thought, an attempt to armor ourselves against fear by dressing in wolves' clothing. I have a Holocaust survivor friend who is dying to screw German women, the blonder, the better. Like everyone else, we were under the spell of the evil charisma which this place radiates—which even the name radiates. Ozwiezcim in Polish, Auschwitz in German, "Oshvitz" in the hybrid abbreviation of Israelis who have trouble with foreign pronunciation. For those who were there, the supreme horror goes by various names, those of the camps or the ghettos where it happened to each of them. Some of these names mean very little if anything to us today: Stutthof, Neungame, Trawniki, Grîss-Rosen, Sachsenhausen, and so on—hundreds of names. There were little places, and places where no one survived to tell the tale, even though each of them was one hundred per cent Auschwitz for its prisoners. So Auschwitz, this camp of all places, has become a trademark, a symbol, an astonishing page out of the Guinness Book of Records. "The world's greatest anything" grips people's attention and casts a shadow on everything else in its field. And if the trip to Poland, the whole of it, was first of all a trip into a myth—the myth of my birthplace and that of my father and Nathan's mother, the myth of the city of Lodz, the War, the Warsaw Ghetto, Graf Potocki, Galicia, Solidarity, Gefilte Fish, and so forth—Auschwitz of course is the greatest myth of all, the very Heart of Darkness.

In a dispirited world, dissolute in mediocrity, where the old dividing lines between good and evil are gone forever and the dominant emotional tone is a perplexed ambivalence, if not total indifference, one point of reference remains constant. We belong to a generation that has lost sight of the origin of absolute good, even though our hunger for it survives. The old illusions of being satisfied become faded, threadbare (we can perhaps get by without a God, but not, it seems, without some kind of prayer). So we cling, at least, to the only absolute we've still got, the only word without a "maybe," without an "on the other hand:" Auschwitz, the focal point of absolute evil. At the backstage of consciousness it functions as a metaphor, the raw material of nightmare, a negative reflection of every hope for a Kingdom of Heaven on earth.

And so we are going to Auschwitz (not in a Mercedes), sixty short kilometers west of Cracow where we spent the previous night. We are in Silesia, Shlonsk in Polish, the disputed mining district. I expected a bare, gloomy landscape, mountains of industrial waste, an accursed, mosquito-infested land. But the tender greenery of early Polish spring lies on everything like a festive down blanket, and the places of human settlement along the way look no more God-forsaken than their counterparts elsewhere. (Had I been brought here blindfolded and were suddenly allowed to see, I wouldn't have known this was the way to Auschwitz.)

When they went, in the trains, they did not know they were going to Auschwitz. Not even when they arrived did they know. Nor when they died. (Like Stendhal's soldier at Waterloo—with a difference!—who never got to see the Emperor, history happened to them without their realizing it.) For them, everything broke down into a physical continuum of moments of terror and pain beyond any known or knowable experience: hunger, thirst, excrement, suffocation, slow dying in the locked cars, Raus, Schnell, Schnell, dogs barking, the cracking of whips, and on the platforms "porters" in striped prisoners' clothing, skinny, heads shaven, turning furtively in a hoarse urgent whisper to this or that one of the new arrivals: "Have you got any food? Jewelry? Give it to me, you won't be needing it anyway." The wails of children, Mommy where are you? Occasional gunfire, blood, no time to stay behind with the fresh corpses, Raus, Schnell, Schnell.

The road skirts the town of Ozwiezcim: cute two-story houses, budding potted plants in the windows, and signs directing you "to the Museum." A giant parking lot for the convenience of visitors, next to railroad tracks which still appear to be in use.

Roland Barthes tells a parable of the ship Argo: the argonauts gradually replaced all its parts over the years, ultimately producing a ship which was wholly new, though un-changed in name and shape. Amazingly, it was the very same Argo. Identity—of a space, of an object—is therefore determined by the structure and the name an object bears, says Barthes. If he were right, we would indeed, now, in April, 1983, be approaching Auschwitz: the name is unchanged, the structures are faithfully maintained, with most of the original parts carefully preserved. Yet obviously it is not Auschwitz to which we have come. The Argo, for all those years and for all those parts replaced, continued to be the same ship, wandering the seas in quest of the golden fleece. But Auschwitz ceased to exist—even though the name and site have been preserved—the moment it stopped serving its intended purpose. Auschwitz is dead (yes yes yes yes may it be so). The place we are visiting is only the bottle of formaldehyde where the corpse of memory is kept. Identity is determined, after all, by the human function an object or space fulfills; without that, all that remains is matter, neutral, always tending toward insignificance.

(And if Auschwitz' function still exists, it exists not here but is dispersed throughout the world, in fragments, in the survivors' memories. There, Auschwitz still lives day and night, continuing to strangle and gnaw and consume, without refuge.)

The first thing missing here, of course, is the odor, one of the first strong impressions mentioned in most accounts. The stench of tens of thousands of corpses wafted from this place for years, spreading into

Drawing by Leo Glueckselig

the atmosphere for kilometers around. This cool and fresh spring day, its air gentle and peaceful, has lost all memory of that overwhelming stench.

The large structure standing at an angle outside the fence, just off the parking lot, is the reception hall where certain lucky arrivals checked in (all were young and healthy-looking, most were men; even so, youth, health, and maleness did not guarantee a thing—not here), got a tattoo on the arm, that is, a stay of execution for another few weeks or months of torture, beatings, starvation, endless lineups and grueling labor, while fully conscious. This, in fact, was the choice you had—which was not yours at all—once you reached this place: to get a reprieve and become, for the moment, a blue-numbered walking skeleton who knows what they are doing to you—or, so fast you don't know what's happening, to become a little heap of ash to be scattered the next day in the fields or into the Sola, a tributary of the Vistula a few kilometers south of here.

The moment we park and climb out of the car, a sudden numbness comes over me, as if a thin layer of intelligence has evaporated and left only a bare crocodilian field of sensation. I lose the ability to focus; my vision goes flat and cloudy, riddled with scales. My thoughts wander weakly down the blurred lines left in my memory by the reading I have done, the maps I have seen: "The structure at an angle at the front of the camp was the reception and registration building." The half-fainted crocodile in my head notices, through the thickness of its dense stupidity, that the building has become a youth hostel. Groups of school children come here on their annual field trip; tourists drop in from all over the world.

The Auschwitz Youth Hostel. They've also got a kiosk where they sell color postcards to tourists: "Vacation in Ozwiezcim"—sailboats on the lake, modern hotels, flags fluttering in the wind. Only in the afternoon, when we returned to Cracow—outside the circle of death—did we gather our thoughts, open the Ozwiezcim maps we had bought, and learn: pop. 45,000, a lake, a Town Hall, churches, libraries, hospital, two stadiums, even an old Jewish cemetery (for there was a Jewish community here, before the deluge. At the beginning of the occupation, its last members had to prepare the original structures for the camp about to arise at the edge of town.) The former I.G. Farben factories have become Poland's largest chemical plants.

In its heyday Auschwitz held 200,000 prisoners or more. But even today, as a mere museum of horrors, it continues to dwarf the town beside it sprouted like a virulent cancer. It is stronger than the town, its life, and everything which preceded it; its grip over the future as well, for generations on end, is total. Ozwiezcim, robbed of its name, its innocence, will never free itself from the shadow of this camp, just as the city of Versailles will never slip away from the shadow of Louis' chateau and garden. It was selected—one of Himmler's random orders—because it was small, faraway and nevertheless close to a junction of railroad tracks from four corners of Europe. And how does it go on existing there, as if it were nothing, a blemish of normality beside that mammoth malignancy? Why is it the town, with its human face, that looks shameful, monstrous in its insistence on staying and brazenly pursuing its ordinary life? From here Israel looks surprisingly virgin, innocent of the malice of memory: look at what the Poles have to live with day in and day out.

Along with a throng of visitors we enter the gate (the maps show it at the lower left-hand corner of the peripheral fence), and overhead passes a thin shadow of the words cast in iron: *Arbeit Macht Frei*. This inscription, apparently conceived by Rudolf Hoess, the kommandant, was used in several other camps. The background slide they use on Israeli TV whenever Haim Yavin talks about Auschwitz (a true-blue German Jew, he pronounces the name in the German original) was taken at a gate built into the wall of a different camp. Here in Auschwitz the inscription is cast in metal, a lettered arch over the iron gate. Auschwitz did not hide behind a stone wall; people outside could see right into the yard. The notorious double electrified fence: I am afraid to touch it, to make sure the current is really off. *Achtung*. I always found this the most terrifying word in the world; I thought it was the skull and crossbones' first name.

Outside the camp fence, not far from the gate, is Gas Chamber No. 1. That's the "little" one, where they killed about 70,000 people until 1942. It was plainly not equal to the ambitious goals of annihilation set at the Wannsee Conference: 11,000,000 Jews from all countries of Europe. So they built Birkenau a few kilometers to the west, and the bulk of the extermination was carried out there. But Birkenau's four big gas chambers, each with a capacity of thousands, were blown up—one by its Jewish operatives in their last-minute desperate insurrection, and the others by the Germans themselves before their retreat. Only this one, the "little" one, still stands.

What do you do when you visit a gas chamber, what do you do? When you go in, you gauge the dimensions of the sealed room (about one and a half average Israeli living rooms? No, larger? Rather dark in there.) You tell yourself this is it, this is the place, here's where it happened. You repeat it to yourself. Here. You take your daughter's hand and go on to the next room, for a look at the massive crematoria (made by Topf). Little trolleys used to carry the corpses from the gas chambers to the mouths of the crematoria, which blazed and thundered with fire, and now are cold and dark; you can put your hand in, if you have the guts. You recall that the extermination in Birkenau's great gas chambers took place in an underground hall, and that the corpses were hauled in a special elevator to the crematoria at ground level. Auschwitz, you make a mental note, had everything on one level. For years you've been imagining, haven't you, that studying the technical details would help you understand, digest it, lance the inner abscess which fills with pus each time anew. Why did you imagine that, what secret did you think the technical details might hold? We step outside and climb the dirt bank to the flat roof. There we find several square chimneylike openings. Nathan lifts the cover of one of them by its handle, and we look down at the tourists wandering around in the gas chamber. They look up, surprised at encountering our eyes in the sudden gaping hole. It was from right here that the German on duty observed the naked people packed erect in the locked room below, after they had been forced in with beatings and shoving—or with soothing words, promises that it was only a shower before going out to work. Afterwards (wearing a gas mask for the sake of good hygiene) he opened his little boxes and dropped the bluish crystals down this chimney, this hole in the roof, and quickly slammed the cover shut. Then he went away to wash his hands. Removal and cremation of the bodies, after all the screaming inside had stopped, were entrusted to prisoners, the *Sonderkommando*, who unlike the other prisoners, ate well and enjoyed regular rations of schnapps. After several months at this labor they, too, were exterminated and replaced by a new *Sonderkommando* detail which was annihilated when its time was up, and so on. The first duty of every new gas chamber squad was to cremate the corpses of its predecessors....

We reach the entrance to Birkenau, a pointed tower over a yawning arched gated inside the elongated, fortified structure, a little like a fairy tale castle.... The fence between the boulevard and the bloc compounds has been left open here and there for the convenience of visitors. The view inside does not confirm what the imagination has portrayed, and the crocodile issues a muted groan, as if out of duty. But it does not seem possible that nine people were crushed onto each bunk like this—there isn't room even for three. But it does not seem possible that they drank the foul soup from the same pail the *kapo* used as his chamber pot. But it does not seem possible that assignations were arranged in the outhouse, and that, despite strict separation of the sexes and liberal use of the death penalty, women took every opportunity to make themselves available next to the pit of excrement for anyone (who still had the strength and the mind for such matters), if he only gave them a rotten potato or some such in return. But it does not seem possible that an inscription on the inside wall of the hut states, in stylized Gothic lettering—I see it with my own eyes—"One louse can kill you." (Had I been here forty years ago, I would have found my way quite well: the German for "louse" and "death" resembles the English.) This is how the hygiene-loving Germans reminded the public to take extreme care in avoiding typhus-carrying lice. But the slogan had a different and much more realistic reading in this place forty years ago: In their all-out war against epidemics, the Germans sent anyone found carrying even a single louse straight to the gas chambers.

But it does not seem possible that we would be so dependent on the body—always wont to get filthy, to stink, to betray—on its hysterical insistence on staying alive; that we would depend on the demands of the stomach, a blind, wet, acid-emitting red sack: What has it to do with us? And the intestines, a few meters of slimy tubing, rolled up in the dark— *they* would turn us into wild beasts? (The camp rejoiced when the transports from Hungary began to arrive in the spring of 1944. Unlike the Polish Jews, who arrived destitute after years in ghettos, the Hungarians had enjoyed relatively normal conditions almost to the last moment. Since they usually set out well-equipped for their "resettlement", the starving camp gorged on dozens, hundreds of parcels of choice salami, preserves and alcohol whenever a transport was liquidated—it was a dream. The sorters always defied mortal peril by doing business with part of the booty. Thus the beginning of the annihilation of Hungary's Jews meant several months' reprieve for some of the veterans of Auschwitz and Birkenau.)

So, the body. A certain question irked me for years: What did they do when they had a period? It concerned me already at the age of eleven, when I listened to broadcasts of the Eichmann trial. Even then I understood that the Germans were not so kind as to provide the women of Auschwitz with cotton wool and sanitary napkins, that was obvious. Just the same, there were women there, yes, some spent years there, so what did they do, how did they get along? I never dared to ask. No one, of course, ever explained it to me by his own initiative.

The uncontrollable dripping, the sublime humiliation, my body with its bleeding and discharges. Certain troglodyte rabbis and their flock often "explain" the Holocaust as the result of Jews having "gone astray" and neglecting the rituals concerning menstruation. So much do they hate me and the "defilement" my body produces, that this is the punishment they think I deserve for my disgraceful bleedings—Auschwitz, no less!

Then we have the revealing appellation the language of my country has applied to me—*nekeva*, "hole". From the outside, it suggests a constant penetrability, a standing invitation to any maniac; from the inside, it bespeaks an inability to control the incriminating drip, drip, drip. Little boys and girls learn with much effort to control their emissions "like grown-ups", and they are praised for it. Ten years later, the little girl learns to her horror that her body has taken her back to a smelly, sticky, infantile helplessness, as least as bad as soiling her pants. (The girls in class used to whisper hair-raising tales about girls who "got it"—"right there in the middle of the street.")

What did the women in the ghetto do when the Judenrat handed out an announcement from the Germans to the effect that births in the ghetto were permitted only up to a certain date, and that "the Jewesses are asked not to give birth any longer thereafter"? There was such an order in one of the ghettos; it's in writing. The text often flashes through my mind, ever since I first saw the document. I automatically contract my thighs, in the street, at work, standing in line, trying to close the incriminating holes, control them by force of will.

At night, cold sweat. DeathFear is not a dog but a bitch, a leprous, contemptible female, her hole dripping ceaselessly dirtying her entire surroundings. DeathFear lies supine, her legs splayed wide, tied in stirrups in the air, in a room awash with strong surgical light, and she writhes with waves of pain and no one stands beside her. She feels it coming out of her, big and scary and wet. I cannot get up, cannot escape, and she screams, it's coming out, it's coming out, look, it'll fall to the ground, and the grinning faces in the white cloaks tell me nonchalantly not to be hysterical, there's lots more time, and she howls no, it's coming out, and she's right: At the last moment they come on the run, they couldn't even get the rubber gloves on, grabbing with their bare hands the baby girl who bursts like a missile into a void and rips me to shreds.

DeathFear remembers: Dr. Mengele could help a woman give birth, take up the infant, inflate its lungs, and cut the umbilicus while observing all the rules of antisepsis—an attentive, concerned physician. Half an hour later he sent mother and child together to the gas chambers. DeathFear is an expert at minutiae, forwarding them to consciousness at just the right moment; she is a wizard at drawing hysterical comparisons, analogies as hoarse as a shriek. With her hate, her rancor, her constant sad wail, DeathFear still tries to fight for her supremacy; now she wants to continue to hurt, to bite, to grip the consciousness, and to bury it somewhere like a bone she has found and will never cough up. Bitter, sputtering again and again with rebellion, she gradually shrinks back into her corner. Only slowly, slowly does she finally grasp that for all that, something more important than she is happening here. This body with its secretions, this despised and embarrassing thing, has produced a gift from within: a pink, wrinkled baby girl, and she is breathing, and she is crying, and she has these dark and wondering eyes, and her name is Effie.

(Two days after I gave birth to her I sat up—it was hard, with my dozens of stitches—in the dining room in the maternity ward and watched television. Eleven Israeli athletes had been murdered by Black September terrorists at the Munich Olympics. All the announcers and all the politicians stressed how horrible it was that this had happened "on German soil, of all places." I grasped what was being said only with great difficulty, as if through constant static. My thoughts were on the tender bleating bundle they brought me every four hours from the baby ward. I was like a deposed queen, stunned by the Copernican blow I had taken: that's that; never again will I be the most important person in the world.)

So, Effie. She has reached the age now when she asks profound questions, and she is checking me out (it's got nothing to do with the trip to Poland): How would you like to die? And I answer: To tell you the truth, the deathless way. That gets her mad; I've broken the rules of the game. Oh really, but let's say you've got to, so what way is best?

We talk it over: Let's say I've got to die, let's say. How do we picture the various ways— drowning, burning, hanging? It's a talk about the facts of death. Long ago, and not only once, we had talked about what the women's magazines used to call, when I was a girl, "the facts of life." I wanted to spare her the female self-contempt and I am not sure I succeeded (against all logic, however, I am still sure that this really was my role, that I should have been perfect, that it should have been possible to save her). Before we set out on this trip I packed sanitary napkins for her, just in case, even though she's still a little young. For her part, she reviewed her menagerie of dolls, and finally selected the woolly lamb Jo, a pink-faced, wall-eyed, very genial creature. Sometimes Effie lets Jo look out the car window and asks her what she thinks of the scenery, and Jo gives erudite long-winded answers in Effie's voice. The lamb-monologue is our backseat driver. At night she sleeps with Jo in our Polish hotel beds.

It's hot and cold in my body, she says again at Birkenau, as she said at Maidanek, and I hug her, caress her head, her hair, and under it my fingers automatically search for the fontanelle, which has long since come together and hardened. It was a terrible thing to discover and feel it when I first held her—nothing but a thin layer of baby skin between my fingers and her tender brain. I did not trust myself to be careful and gentle enough; I would bite my lips sharply and cry with fear and pity for her, how her skull was open to the big evil world, and she had only me to protect her.

Had we been brought here by train (with Effie clutching her woolly lamb, Jo) we would have been sent, together, in the very first selection, to the line heading for the "showers". (Reading the testimonies, I got somewhat confused which side was life and which was death; the Germans chose "Left!" for the gas chambers in some accounts, and "Right!" in others. It may be a matter of point of view: Was it the German's left, or that of the person whose fate had been sealed?) She has accompanied me on this imaginary journey since she was born. Parents, relatives, friends, loved ones—I lose sight of them as the train clatters inside my head. I am jounced in the car with strangers, and they are groaning, collapsing, crushing, crushed, their eyes radiate hate and fear. (Shared humilia-tion does not make for intimacy. The sense of community has already vanished; we reach that degree of terror where it's every man for himself.) Only Effie, so familiar and be-loved that there is no escape, gazes at me, clings to me the whole way, and cries: Mommy, water. And I say: soon, soon, we're almost there. Thus she clings to me for days and nights until the bitter end, when we arrive, half-dead, and the SS doctor orders us to go "Left". I clutch her hand and say Come, Mommy's with you; everything will be all right.

Each and every one of my friends who live abroad assured me, in his or her turn, that he or she would take Effie in and raise her "if something happens in Israel"—if one of the wars here is serious, if we are ever really in danger of being thrown into the sea, or whatever. Though I pretend I am not quite serious in these conversations, I demand that the promise be made in utter seriousness: my friends, some sniggering at my Israeli paranoia (I snigger along, of course) promise as requested. It's obviously nothing more than a Russian-style declaration of boundless friendship, valid only at the moment it is given, for who knows how the future will strike us, when its time to strike comes.

My fear of the future always wears the face of the past, and, in these talks with my overseas friends, I strive perpetually to keep Effie off my last train ride. □

The Philo-Semitic Face of Christian Anti-Semitism

David Biale

The Wrath of Jonah by Rosemary Radford Ruether and Herman J. Ruether. Harper & Row, 1989, 277 pp.

Some books are part of the solution. *The Wrath of Jonah* is part of the problem. Under the pretense of trying to effect a reconciliation between Israelis and Palestinians, the authors have only thrown more oil on the already burning tires of the Middle East. This is an anti-Zionist diatribe cloaked in the sweet light of Christian universalism; as such, it stands as a singular warning of how a Christian critique of Israel can slide unwittingly into the swamp of anti-Semitism. The question prompted by the dubious book is how it could come from the pen of Rosemary Ruether who, fifteen years ago, exposed the Christian roots of anti-Semitism in her pathbreaking *Faith and Fratricide.*

There is, to be sure, much in the Ruethers' polemic against the state of Israel with which progressive Jews might agree. Many, both in Israel and the Diaspora, have paid no small personal price for attacking Israel's occupation of the territories and the abundant human rights violations that have accompanied the Occupation since 1967. Many have called for Israel to sit down at the negotiating table with the PLO in order to arrive at a two-state solution. Many would agree with the Ruethers that Israel bears a share of the responsibility for creating the Palestinian refugee problem in 1948 and for pursuing policies that have discouraged the emergence of Arab moderates. Many might even agree with the Ruethers' far-reaching calls for a restructuring of the state of Israel to make its Arab citizens truly equal.

But the Ruethers' criticisms of Israel are embedded in a subtext that is so lacking in balance and so unremittingly hostile to the very notion of Jewish national self-determination that their book loses all credibility. Despite gestures toward a two-state solution, the Ruethers clearly do not believe that the Jews have the right to a state. They fail the minimum litmus test for any progressive solution to the Israeli-Palestinian conflict by viewing the conflict as right against wrong rather than as a clash of two equally legitimate rights. By systematically denying the legitimacy of the Jewish position they become the flip side of Israeli rejectionists such as Yitzhak Shamir who believe that the Palestinians have no rights. Against such rejectionism from both camps, it needs to be asserted, again and again, that the only viable solution must rest on mutual recognition. The Ruethers are so wedded to the Palestinian side of the story that they are unable to evince the barest sympathy for the historical experience of the Jewish people. In their cursory survey of Jewish history, they naturally mention

---

David Biale is the director of the Center for Jewish Studies at the Graduate Theological Union in Berkeley. His most recent book is Power and Powerlessness in Jewish History *(Schocken Books, 1987). This article appeared in* Tikkun, *May/June 1989.*

the Russian pogroms and the Holocaust, but they fail to exhibit even the slightest understanding of why, after this recent history of oppression, Jews might feel the pressing need to achieve political sovereignty. Instead of empathizing with the instinctive response of Jews to the Nazi nightmare, the Ruethers regard the Holocaust as a "shock" that "made it possible for Zionists to capture control of Jewish organizations in the Diaspora and cement the official loyalty of world Jewry to the Jewish state." How can the author of *Faith and Fratricide* fail to grasp why most Jews have responded to modern anti-Semitism by demanding the right to defend themselves in their own state? Do the Jews deserve Ms. Ruether's sympathy only when they are down, not when they are trying to defend themselves?

The Ruethers make a series of tendentious and unsupported claims that often border on the conspiratorial or outright fanciful. They write, for example, that "it has been suggested that the Abu Nidal group has actually become a front for the Mossad [Israeli Intelligence]." The authors muster no evidence to support this grave allegation that one of the world's most ruthless murderers is an Israeli agent; the footnote that precedes the sentence refers to two works, neither of which corroborate the claim. Similarly, the Ruethers describe the assassination attempts on the Palestinian mayors in the West Bank as "incidents that have been officially blamed on settler extremists (but are *generally believed* to have been coordinated by the Israeli military and secret police." [emphasis added]) Generally believed by whom? On what grounds? The authors give no reliable source. Instead, they simply reproduce the kind of feverish rumor that has led many Palestinians to believe that the Mossad placed the bomb on the Pan Am plane that recently blew up over England.

But there is more. The Ruethers hold that Ben-Gurion devised a plan between 1944 and 1947 to terrorize

> the Arab towns and villages [in order] to encourage most of the middle-class leadership to leave. Once the British departed and the Jewish forces were fully in command, then there could be a more forcible mass expulsion of Palestinian villagers, either razing their villages or transferring their property to Jewish immigrants.

This alleged plan was put into effect in early December 1947, and it culminated with the Deir Yassin massacre. Later, the Ruethers describe the conquest of Ramle and Lod as a "blitzkrieg" (one wonders why they don't come right out and call the Israelis Nazis).

There is no mention here of the widespread attacks by Palestinian guerrillas against Jews in the weeks after the United Nations partition resolution—attacks that resulted in hundreds of Jewish civilian deaths. The Arab side bears no responsibility whatsoever in their account for the civil war that engulfed Palestine between December 1947 and May 15, 1948. Moreover, the Ruethers' discovery of a prior Jewish "plan" to expel the Arabs has never been supported by a shred of evidence (and the Ruethers do not offer even a footnote). The Israeli historian Benny Morris, whose recent revisionist history of the creation of the Palestinian refugee problem contains material that is highly critical of the Haganah for inflaming the Palestinian-instigated civil war (see *Tikkun,* November/December 1988), asserts that no such evidence exists. Even the left-wing Israeli historian, the late Simha Flapan, whom the Ruethers quote approvingly elsewhere, also found no evidence for such a plan. That the Ruethers continue to advance such a claim shows that they are on one side of the propaganda war rather than in the business of mediation.

But by far the most outrageous distortion with respect to modern Israel is their argument that, were it not for the Zionist transfer agreement with Nazi Germany, the Holocaust might not have happened. The Ruethers claim that, by trading with the Nazis as a way of utilizing the blocked accounts of German Jewish immigrants to Palestine, the Zionists effectively destroyed the boycott of Nazi Germany. Had the boycott succeeded, they argue, "the German economy might have cracked and Hitler's regime toppled." As a result of Zionist perfidy, "Hitler remained very much in power, rearmed Germany and embarked on the conquest of Europe.... The economy of Jewish Palestine thrived, building the infrastructures of the future Jewish state, while European Jewry was being murdered."

Needless to say, this preposterous claim not only inflates the economic power of the Yishuv (whose population was between 400,000 and 500,000 during the 1930s) but also ignores the intense moral dilemma posed by the Nazi regime. The transfer agreement, about which one may legitimately argue, made it possible for Jews to leave Germany at a time when the freezing of bank accounts effectively prevented many from emigrating. These Jews survived the Holocaust. No one who reads the Hebrew press from the Yishuv in the 1930s can doubt that the transfer agreement had as much to do with saving Jews as it had to do with building the Yishuv. Don't the early Zionists deserve some credit for saving these lives, or were the Zionist leaders motivated solely by political self-interest?

For the Ruethers, Zionism is a conspiracy designed to dupe the Jewish people, who otherwise would remain peacefully in the Diaspora. That Zionism might have the same deep roots in the Jewish people's historical experience as Palestinian nationalism has in the experience of the Palestinians seems beyond the Ruethers' comprehension. That the enmity between the Jews and the Arabs is the tragic result of a conflict between two equally legitimate nationalisms also has no place in their conspiratorial view.

Why, then, bother with this book, when it appears, on the face of it, to differ little from a whole library of pro-Palestinian propaganda? The story, however, is much more complex, for the Ruethers also propose an interpretation of Jewish history and of Judaism that removes the question of Israel's existence from the dusty battlefields of the Middle East to the ethereal realms of Christian theology.

The Ruethers believe that it is their role to "liberate the Jewish community [so that it can] regain its prophetic voice toward its own system of power." As Christians, the aspect of Judaism with which the Ruethers identify is the so-called voice of prophetic universalism. In their view, rabbinic Judaism is the genuine continuation of biblical prophetic Judaism because it is universalist and ethical, unlike the ethnocentric nationalism of the Zealots. They also claim that rabbinic law developed primarily in Diaspora settings rather than in Palestine. "True" Judaism is the Judaism of the Diaspora, the Judaism that renounces national exclusivism and presents itself as "a light unto the nations." Jews are not a nation, but a religion; the Zionists are the ones who try to impose alien nationalism on the Jewish people.

Much of this argument looks like nineteenth-century Reform Judaism. But it is scarcely history. The Rabbis were, in fact, part of the Palestinian Jewish governing hierarchy and were strong nationalists who supported the first part of the Great Revolt against the Romans, as well as the later Bar Kokhba rebellion. Jews in the Greco-Roman Diaspora considered themselves, and were considered by Hellenistic and Roman law, to be an *ethnos* rather than a *religio*. The passage that the Ruethers quote (from Tractate Pesachim of the Babylonian Talmud) in order to support the view that the Rabbis wanted Judaism to be a "light unto the nations" is, in fact, a call for proselytism throughout the Roman Empire, hardly a product of pluralist universalism!

Throughout the Middle Ages, the Jews were not universalists, nor was Judaism purely a religion, either in the Jews' self-conception or in the view of the nations among which they lived (in medieval law, they were viewed as *foreigners*, not simply as non-Christians). In modern times, the definition of Jews as a religious group was an innovative construct that became untenable in Eastern Europe where, in fact, Jews constituted a nation long before the rise of Zionism.

But all of this history will hardly make a dent in the Ruethers' analysis. Their view of Jews and

Judaism really has more to do with their own peculiar view of Christianity than with actual Jews and Judaism. They identify fully with the position of certain Arab Christian theologians, giving them totally uncritical celebration. In a curious argument, they hold that only anti-Zionist Christians can respect Judaism as an equal religion because their Christianity is based on universalist tolerance—"true Christianity" for the Ruethers. Such universalism has no place for ethnocentric nationalism (does this include Palestinian nationalism as well?). According to the Ruethers, the "only" Christians who, as a group, support the state of Israel are the evangelicals, but they do so out of a desire to convert the Jews.

It now becomes increasingly clear how the author of *Faith and Fratricide* could have written this book. The purpose of *Faith and Fratricide* was to divest Christianity of its own form of chauvinism, namely, anti-Semitism, so that it might become its true universalist self. The purpose of *The Wrath of Jonah* is to do the same thing for Judaism, the parent religion of Christianity. Christian universalism comes from the "true" Judaism, but the Jews have strayed from their calling by espousing tribal nationalism. The correct role for Jews is to fight for these universal, pluralistic values in the countries of the Diaspora, the true Jewish homelands.

Faith and Fratricide was a bold and welcome attack on "Christian imperialism" as well as a call for Christians to reexamine their very core beliefs in light of their culpability for anti-Semitism. With the publication of *The Wrath of Jonah*, however, it becomes necessary to ask whether Rosemary Ruether has in fact overcome the very anti-Semitism she so eloquently pilloried. She and her husband will no doubt indignantly protest that anti-Zionism is not the same as anti-Semitism, and on that score they are, in principle, correct. To object to the existence of a Jewish state on political grounds need not involve anti-Semitic myths: the acquisition of Jewish sovereignty has created real political questions that should not be confused with the fantasies of the anti-Semites.

But the Ruethers have gone far beyond a mere political critique of Zionism. Their wild and unsubstantiated conspiracy theories, which inflate Zionist power beyond recognition, smell suspiciously like the older myths of a world Jewish conspiracy. More important, their attack on the Jews' right to self-determination, while couched in universalist rhetoric, smacks of the old double standard; for they apply none of the same criticism to the Palestinians, whose nationalism they celebrate.

Here, in the final analysis, is Christian anti-Semitism with a philo-Semitic face. Having disposed in her previous book of the belief that the Jewish exile is a punishment for rejecting Jesus, Rosemary Ruether can now embrace the Jewish existence in the Diaspora as a positive vocation. *She*, after all, is willing to fight for Jewish rights in the Diaspora. But the Jews—that stiff-necked people—are (once again) ungrateful and prefer to defend themselves with their own arms in their own state. Having betrayed their calling to remain dispersed among the nations, Jews surely deserve the wrath of the righteous Christians.

As has been true for two millennia, the Jews are not allowed to be themselves. They are neither purely a religion nor purely a nation, neither strictly universalists nor solely exclusive nationalists. For Judaism is all of these things and more, and the struggles and tensions between these strands are the essence of Jewish history. The Ruethers' definition of true Judaism as the precursor to Christian universalism is exactly the same as the old Christian definition of Judaism as a *preparatio evangelica*—valid only as a precursor to Christianity. Theirs is the liberal version of the old Christian imperialism, that spiritual colonialism that presumes to tell the Jews who they really are.

The Ruethers have entitled their book *The Wrath of Jonah*. According to their interpretation, the Book of Jonah is a prophetic critique of Jewish ethnocentrism, represented by Jonah's anger upon hearing that God renounced His vow to destroy the city of Nineveh when its inhabitants repented. Jonah could not accept a universal God who loved the Ninevites as much as He loved the Israelites. This may or may not be a plausible interpretation of the Book of Jonah, but in taking it as the leitmotif and title of their own book, the Ruethers have repeated Christianity's oldest offense against Judaism: they have stolen a Jewish book and told us how to read it. They have turned the Hebrew Bible into a stick with which to beat the Jews.

There is, without question, a place for a prophetic critique of the State of Israel, just as there is a place for such a critique of all nation-states. But a Christian author attuned to the history of Christian anti-Semitism should be the first to exercise caution before assailing the Zionist barricades with Bible in hand. In a recent article in *Christian Century,* the Protestant theologian Robert McAfee Brown laid out a set of reasoned principles for how a Christian should criticize Israel if he or she expects to receive a Jewish hearing. Brown does not shrink from invoking the prophetic tradition in opposition to the idolatry of the nation-state. But he makes it clear that such criticism must never be applied to Israel alone. And he understands that criticism will register only if it is presented as part of an affirmation of the Jewish right to self-determination. The Ruethers have failed on these counts, and they have consequently forfeited the audience they claim to seek.

Progressive Jews are engaged today in a fateful struggle over the future of Israel and, indeed, the future of the Jewish people. We desperately need all the allies we can get. But the last thing we need is modern versions of the medieval sermons that Jews were forced to listen to in Christian churches, or "well-meaning" attempts to "liberate the Jewish community." We wish to be neither oppressors nor victims, neither heroes nor puppets in someone else's theology. We wish, in short, to be a normal people. □

Drawing by Anthony Dubovsky

Jewish Romantic Relationships

Estelle Frankel

"Mating," the Talmud tells us, "is as difficult as the splitting of the Red Sea." What once was rabbinic hyperbole, however, now understates the problem. In my work as a counselor, I hear Jewish men complain that Jewish women make them feel less manly. By the same token, Jewish women assert that their femininity is not appreciated by Jewish men as it is by non-Jewish men. Behind these gripes lies more than the standard war between the sexes. For when it comes to mating practices between Jewish men and Jewish women today, the struggle is compounded by a hornet's nest of psychohistorical and cultural factors.

Why is it so hard for Jews to love each other? Because, say Jewish men, Jewish women are too complicated, controlling, materialistic, and demanding; Jewish women counter that Jewish men are self-centered, "in their heads," needy, and "nebbishy." Some young Jews are put off by a feeling of incestuousness or a lack of mystery with a Jewish partner. Others simply don't find Jewish partners to be attractive or sexy and prefer classically non-Jewish-looking mates. Even those who would rather be with a Jewish partner express frustration over their difficulty in finding the "right" Jewish partner and often end up in relationships with non-Jews. In the U.S., intermarriage has doubled during the last two decades, and current estimates suggest that it stands somewhere between 40 and 50 percent. The antipathy that exists between Jewish men and women is cited as a significant factor in that rate.

The Role of Jewish Self-Hatred

Internalized anti-Semitism, or Jewish self-hatred, is responsible for much of the trouble. Kurt Lewin's studies on different minority groups found that aggression increases as members of lower-status minority groups are frustrated in their attempts to become part of the higher-status majority group. Instead of directing the aggression toward the "idealized" and more powerful higher-status group, minority-group members tend to direct their aggression against themselves and other members of their group. One way that minority group members do this is by taking on the projections and the negative stereotypes that the majority culture has about its minority members. Theodore Herzl aptly described this tendency among Jews of his time. "There are more misconceptions in circulation about the Jews than about any other people," he said. "And our age-old sufferings have made us so depressed and so discouraged that we ourselves parrot and believe these canards." Even many Zionist leaders exhibited this aspect of Jewish self-hatred in their use of classic anti-Semitic images, such as the "Jew as parasite," in order to motivate Jews in the Diaspora to make aliya. Like the classic anti-Semite, they blamed the Jewish victims for their own misfortune.

Estelle Frankel is a psychotherapist in private practice in Berkeley. She teaches courses and leads workshops on the relationship between Judaism, Jewish identity, and psychology. This article appeared in Tikkun, *September/October 1990.*

411

The phenomenon of Jewish self-hatred was almost unknown prior to the Emancipation. Only as Jews rapidly stopped identifying with Jewish values and attempted to assimilate into their host culture did they become subject to the dynamics of internalized anti-Semitism. As Raphael Patai points out in *The Jewish Mind* (Scribners, 1977), so long as Jews were strongly identified with the Jewish community, they were for the most part immune to the damaging effects of anti-Semitism. Though economically and politically a disempowered minority group, they were happy to remain a separate, "chosen" people, and so Lewin's rule did not apply to them. The oppression that Jews experienced throughout their history in exile was interpreted by the rabbis as the unfortunate by-product of Israel's "chosenness." The Talmud goes so far as to interpret Jewish suffering as a sign of God's love for the children of Israel. These religious beliefs, along with feelings of superiority, provided a form of psychological protection for pious Jews, which shielded them from fully internalizing the hatred they encountered, though of course the persecution left profound scars.

With the advent of the Jewish Enlightenment and Emancipation in the eighteenth and nineteenth centuries, however, European Jews began to leave the religious fold en masse. As they disowned their Jewishness in order to succeed in non-Jewish society, they lost their immunity to the psychologically damaging effects of anti-Semitism. No longer seen as a privilege or blessing, Jewishness came to be viewed as a stigma—a barrier to full acceptance into the mainstream society. Jewish youth abandoned the yeshiva or Talmud Torah in order to pursue secular education, and knowledge of what it means to be a Jew was gradually lost. Lacking in Jewish self-definition, these highly assimilated Jews became even more vulnerable to the negative definitions of others. The assimilated Jew has no protection from anti-Semitic rhetoric, except to move further away from his or her Jewishness. Such a move, however, can cause considerable damage to one's self-esteem, because it involves a turning against part of oneself.

Ethnic self-hatred also affects the image of one's romantic partner. In order to fall in love, one must be able to form an idealized image of one's partner, though in time this idealized image must be replaced by a more integrated and realistic view of the beloved. Jewish men and women who feel ambivalent about their Jewishness often find it impossible to see love in the mirror of a Jewish relationship, because a disliked and disowned part of the self—one's Jewishness—will be reflected in a Jewish partner. Moreover, Jews who suffer from unconscious self-hatred often find themselves as well as members of the opposite sex unattractive, because their "Jewish" looks don't fit the mainstream cultural ideal of beauty. Since we live in a culture where women, more so than men, are objectified and valued according to their looks, Jewish men tend to look for non-Jewish partners more often than Jewish women do. Complicated psychological dynamics, which I'll describe in a moment, make matters even worse for Jewish women.

Extreme ambivalence about Jewish identification is also found in the people who avoid Jewish partners as a way to remain in "hiding" Jewishly. Underlying this dynamic is a deep unconscious fear of the potential danger to one's life if one is easily identifiable as a Jew. As one woman at a recent workshop on Jewish relationships said: "To be with a Jewish partner makes me feel very vulnerable—I actually fear for my life, though I don't really know why." Another participant quoted her parents as saying, "You're lucky you don't look Jewish." The implication was that she could easily pass as a non-Jew if the need arose. For the Jew in hiding, having a non-Jewish mate is tantamount to having a safe refuge when the Nazis or Cossacks return for the rest of us.

Many such "Jews in hiding" had parents who were victims or refugees of the Holocaust. Others grew up with parents who, in response to anti-Semitism and discrimination, chose to go into psychological hiding by detaching themselves from the Jewish community and its religious and cultural traditions. Remaining distant from the Jewish "victims," they hoped to avoid a similar fate; in fact, they are simply avoiding the need to deal consciously with their own fears of anti-Semitism as well as their cultural ignorance. Children growing up in such families often know extremely little about what it means to be a Jew apart from inherited notions of suffering and victimization. As a result of rootlessness, they belong to neither the mainstream culture nor the Jewish community. Denied a Jewish education, such children are often limited in their Jewish identity to the feeling of shame over belonging to a historically despised minority group. Not surprisingly, intermarriage appeals to them.

Jews in America have historically been subject to varied forms of direct and indirect discrimination, including exclusion from many professional and social groups. We learned that by "passing" we were more likely to be accepted, more likely to succeed in our pursuit of the American dream. Marrying a non-Jew in order to disguise one's Jewishness, or changing one's obviously Jewish name (or nose) are just a few of the ways in which Jewish self-hatred is masked in contemporary American culture. This pressure to conform or assimilate not only influences our physical or social image of ourselves, but deeply affects how we value each other as men and women.

The Impact of Internalized Anti-Semitism on Masculinity and Femininity

The aversion that many Jewish men and women feel toward one another also derives from the fact that traditional Jewish ideals of masculinity and femininity are very different from those of mainstream American culture. When not appreciated for their uniqueness, these differences become another source of mutual devaluation. For instance, unlike the American macho ideal of masculinity, Judaism teaches an inner form of strength based on restraint of impulse. In *Pirkay Avot*, one of the earliest compilations of Jewish ethical teachings, we find such dicta as "Who is strong? He who uses restraint with his impulses." This attitude developed in response to historical circumstances, as Jewish men generally had little power to control their own destinies. Barred from tilling the soil and many other respectable "male" professions, Jewish men learned to live by their wits. Wisdom and piety were valued above physical prowess and material success. In the Bible, Jacob, the thoughtful introvert, is chosen over Esau, the hairy (masculine) hunter; young David, the poet and musician, overpowers Goliath, the giant Philistine warrior.

It's interesting to note that many anti-Semitic thinkers described Jewish men as being both inferior and feminine. But If Jewish men were "feminized" by the conditions of exile, one might say that Jewish women were "masculinized." The struggle to survive under extremely difficult conditions placed an additional burden on Jewish women to be strong and stand by their men. It was also considered a virtue for the Jewish woman to work in order to support her husband's Torah study. So Jewish women traditionally exercised power not just in the home, but also in the family business. In the post–World War I era, as American families were able to be supported by a single income, many wives stopped working outside the home. The energy that these women once divided between family and work became focused solely on the family. Barred from creative spiritual expression in the synagogue, and unable to exert power in the world of work, stifled Jewish women began stifling their husbands and children. Or so the standard explanation goes. In any event, Jewish men and women alike are now faced with the stereotypes of the overly controlling Jewish woman who lives vicariously through her children, and of the Jewish man as inadequate, weak, or "nebbishy." These stereotypes reinforce Jewish self-hatred, further undermining romantic attraction.

Yet we must face not only the distortion but also the relative truths of these stereotypes. I have repeatedly seen Jewish men and women enlist one another in the playing out of these roles. The nebbish's problems with self-assertion and the expression of anger, for instance, result in his chronically seeing himself as "the victim" in relationships. Instead of expressing his own anger, he may induce it in his mate by means of the psychological mechanism of projective identification.

Drawing by Anthony Dubovsky

Enlisting his mate to enact his own internal conflicts, he will treat her in such a manner that she begins to actually feel angry toward him. He feels more and more like a hapless victim, while she slowly and unwittingly becomes a bigger "bitch" than she knew she could be. In "Lifting Up the Shadow of Anti-Semitism: Jewish Masculinity in a New Light," Barbara Breitman suggests that when Jewish women take on the projected aggression of Jewish men, together they re-enact the dynamics of anti-Semitism by acting out the roles of victim and oppressor. The net effect of these destructive dynamics is that Jewish men may feel and act less masculine, and Jewish women feel and act less feminine.

In the stereotype of the "Jewish American Princess" we find a particularly destructive image of Jewish women. Undoubtedly, there are some Jewish women who may fit aspects of the JAP stereotype, but they are a small minority. The daughter of wealthy, overly indulgent parents, the classic JAP feels that the world owes her a great deal. In fact, many Jewish women have difficulty feeling even a healthy sense of entitlement. They focus on caring for others, more than nurturing themselves. Those Jewish women who actually do fit the description of the JAP often use the characteristic attitude of entitlement as a defense against deep feelings of emptiness and unworthiness. They turn to an indulgent consumerism hoping to cover up these painful feelings. Like the narcissistic individual who constantly seeks attention but never feels seen, these Jewish women vainly attempt to fill an emotional-spiritual void with external representations of love. Often they had parents who were unable to express love to their children, except through money .

But the JAP dynamic isn't that simple. Beneath the vicious use of the label lurks a more hidden projection of Jewish men's painful feelings of inadequacy onto Jewish women. Again and again I hear Jewish men using the JAP stereotype as an excuse for why they choose not to go out with Jewish women. Instead of really confronting the sources of their feelings of inadequacy, (namely, historic oppression, the current trend of downward mobility, and growing up with critical Jewish parents who had unrealistically high expectations of their children), Jewish men have blamed Jewish women.

Displaced Jewish Anger

The name-calling that goes on between Jewish men and women seems to have provided a new outlet for stifled Jewish aggression. Jews appear to have a strong tendency to internalize rather than externalize anger because of the unique interplay between Jewish history and theology. Judaism reinforced the internalization of aggression both by its moral aversion to the expression of anger ("One who gets angry is like an idol worshiper"—Zohar: Genesis 2 and Maimonides, De'ot: 2) and by its doctrine of guilt and self-reflection. This theology of guilt comes directly from Deuteronomy, which blames Israel's sinfulness for the prophesied exile. The notion that we are responsible for our own suffering was further developed in Rabbinic Judaism and is reflected in such sayings as the following, from the Talmud (Berachot 5a):

> If you find yourself suffering, search your ways. If you search and do not find any sin, maybe you haven't studied enough Torah.... If you search and find that also not to be true, assume your suffering is from God's love.

Moreover, for centuries Jews were hardly in a social or political position to express anger and outrage over their plight. So instead they classically learned to direct aggression at themselves.

Freud described another psychological aspect of this dynamic—the need to preserve the image of God as a benevolent and involved parental figure. In order to let God off the hook, we blamed ourselves for our repeated misfortunes. The unexpressed aggression, according to Freud, became channeled into the Jewish superego, which grew in size and stature to its currently enormous dimensions. The more Jews were oppressed, the more stringent were the laws and forms of holiness they created in order to atone for their sense of guilt. In *Civilization and Its Discontents* Freud says:

> For the more virtuous a man is, the more severe and distrustful is his behavior, so that ultimately it is precisely those people who have carried saintliness furthest who reproach themselves with the worst sinfulness.... The people of Israel had believed themselves to be the favorite child of God, and when the great Father caused misfortune after misfortune to rain down upon this people of his, they were never shaken in their belief in his relationship to them or questioned his power or righteousness. Instead, they produced the prophets, who held up their sinfulness before them; and out of their sense of guilt they created the over-strict commandments.

The psychological mechanisms employed in the dynamic described above bear great resemblance to those employed by abused children and other victimized individuals: in both we see the interplay of "painful experience" and an attempt at control and mastery of trauma through self-blame.

These coping strategies have had adaptive as well as neurotic results. They enabled Jews to elaborate a unique capacity for introspection and a highly developed ethics. They also enabled Jews to find meaning in their painful fate and to develop the messianic vision of a time in which the forces of good would overcome the forces of evil—if people did their part to bring that time near. In secular Jewish society this same tendency toward high expectations and perfectionism has empowered Jews to achieve high levels of excellence in a variety of pursuits. The downside of this same tendency is that as a people we are more prone to self-blame and neurotic guilt than many other minority groups. Since neurotic guilt is the result of internalized aggression, a more healthy attitude toward the expression of anger would be tremendously healing for this Jewish neurosis.

Familiarity as a Challenge to Sexual Attraction

Because of the pronounced enmeshment commonly found in Jewish families, intimacy with a Jewish partner can easily remind us of the "smothering" or overprotectiveness we may have experienced growing up. This "closeness" seems to pose a more difficult challenge for men than for women. Gender identification for boys involves a more radical separation and disidentification with mother. For the grown man, intimacy with a woman threatens to stir up not only fears of childlike dependency but also fears of losing his sense of maleness. For a Jewish man, these fears can be exacerbated with a Jewish partner who is more likely to remind him of his earliest dependent bond with mother than a non-Jewish partner might. The physical and cultural difference experienced with a non-Jewish partner, at least initially, may serve to reassure him of his otherness or masculinity, whereas with a Jewish woman he may find himself feeling more like mommy's little boy and less like a grown man. Feelings of familiarity seem to pose less of a problem for most women; in fact, the very experience that can be a turn-off for Jewish men is often a turn-on for Jewish women. This basic gender difference may be another one of the reasons that more Jewish women seem to want Jewish men than vice versa.

Positive and Negative Aspects of Refinding

What we are touching on here is connected to the way "refinding" is experienced in Jewish romantic relationships. Refinding—the desire that propels us to rediscover in a contemporary love qualities and dynamics that were present in our early love relationships—is intensified in Jewish romantic relationships because partners are more likely to remind one another of the painful as well as the nurturing aspects of early familial dynamics.

On the positive side, with a Jewish partner one is likely to refind "heimishness," a warmth or emotional expressiveness, and a familiar sense of humor. Jewish partners are also likely to share common values and ethics, including a strong valuation of family. And they are likely to find their child-rearing attitudes to be similar—a quality not to be underestimated in its importance for long-term compatibility. Beyond these psychological and emotional commonalities, Jewish partners can potentially partake in shared cultural traditions and rituals, which root them in a common history. Jewish holidays and rites of passage provide the couple with access to archetypal healing symbols and connect them deeply to the cycles of nature and the stages of the life cycle. The shared experience of these rites can be deeply bonding for the couple.

Also of tremendous significance to the life of the couple is the importance of a shared community. Couples in social isolation have greater difficulty surviving the internal stresses of emotional intimacy. Regular contact with community offers the couple a place to release hostilities, and it reinfuses the couple with new vital energies. The community also provides the couple with a larger context of meaning, thus reducing the overload on the relationship that occurs when one expects a relationship to provide all of one's needs.

The negative aspects of refinding affect both falling and remaining in love. The initial sense of "mystery" that fosters romance is diminished by the instant replay of old emotional conflicts. Once in an intimate relationship, Jews tend to be haunted by the voice of their critical parents. Unresolved anger due to excessive parental criticism tends to find an easy outlet with a Jewish partner. Inevitably, as one partner finds fault or is critical of the other, intense anger and hurt begin to surface. Specific criticisms are experienced as complete character assassinations because they are amplified and exaggerated by one's internal critical voice. Thus, superego conflicts of the individual are acted out interpersonally....

It's no wonder that Jewish couples complain that their relationships require "higher mainten-ance." Other factors contribute to this perception as well. Because Jews tend to be verbally expressive of their feelings, there's more out in the open to deal with. While this high level of emotional expressiveness may facilitate a deeper experience of intimacy, it brings with it an increase in openly expressed conflict. Furthermore, as the result of overly gratifying Jewish parents, one or both partners may have unrealistic expectations of what to expect from a mate. Partners may find themselves competing with each other for unconditional nurturance, inevitably disappointed with what they actually can receive.

If this weren't enough, subtle forms of jealousy and competitiveness between Jewish men and women are sown in the Jewish family by the different ways in which boys and girls are treated. In addition to the sexism present in the culture at large, Jewish women growing up in more traditional families have to contend with the religious attitudinal preference for the boy child. The absence, until quite recently, of a ceremonial ritual to mark the birth of a baby girl is a clear example of Judaism's "second-best" attitude toward women. Unequal celebration of bar and bat mitzvah rites is another. Many Jewish women feel angry that their educational and professional aspirations were taken less seriously by their parents than were their brothers'; remaining "marriageable" was seen as more important than being successful in one's own right. Though these sexist trends have already begun to change in most American Jewish communities, I've encountered many Jewish women who still harbor resentment toward their brothers over their envied position. These feelings of resentment easily get transferred onto and acted out with a Jewish mate.

How can we enhance *the promise* of Jewish romance? Bleak as the picture I've painted might seem, Jewish romantic relationships do hold considerable promise. But in order to enhance that potential, Jewish men and women must heal their mistrust of one another with mutual understanding and compassion. We need to come to terms with our own internalized anti-Semitism and face the way in which negative stereotypes have distorted our view of ourselves and each other. In order to get beyond destructive relationship dynamics, we must resolve the internal conflicts that drive our perfectionism. This involves sorting out healthy and realistic expectations from those that are excessive. We need to differentiate between the authentic Jewish vision of *tikkun olam*—which may motivate one to actualize one's highest potential—and neurotic perfectionism, which compensates for feelings of inferiority or guilt and is a derivative of internalized oppression.

Where in all this is the promise of Jewish romantic relationships? Couples who draw upon the richness of Jewish culture and spirituality find that the opportunity for fulfillment in love is immeasurably enhanced. Beyond the positive aspects of "refinding" that are inherent in Jewish relationships, there are aspects of the Jewish tradition that offer the couple a wellspring of meaning and creative spiritual expression.

Consider, for example, the Jewish Sabbath ritual—twenty-five hours of special time removed from the world of work, mastery of the physical world, and other outer-directed activity. Shabbos, an oasis in time, offers the couple freedom from the overwhelming details of mundane reality, and a chance to re-center emotionally and spiritually. It's a sacred time in which couples can reconnect with their yearning for the experience of unity and transcendence. In the Jewish Mystical tradition, sexual union on Shabbos is celebrated as a mirror of the divine union, and is also the gateway to apprehending this greater unity. We live in a world of division and dualism, and sharing one's life with another person at times entails painful conflict and struggle. The spiritual experience of unity that can be attained through observing Shabbos offers couples an opportunity for healing these splits.

Jewish myths and rituals open doors to the transcendent or sacred dimension of life. They offer the couple the deep bond of a shared spiritual experience and root the couple in a historic legacy. As part of the movement for Jewish spiritual renewal, both Jewish women and men today are creating innovative rituals. They are rediscovering the healing power of our ancient rites while imbuing them with new and psychologically relevant meaning. This renewal can strengthen the bonds of the couple by providing families with a larger, richer context of meaning and identity. □

Killing the Princess:
The Offense of a Bad Defense

Elisa New

The Death of a "Jewish American Princess": The True Story of a Victim on Trial by Shirley Frondorf. Villard Books, 1988, 320 pp.

Mass art, routinely maligned for distorting social reality, is often guilty only of mirroring it too truly. The tabloid tale of bunny born to mom cuts straight to our anxiety about bioengineering; the contemporary horror novel exhumes communal nightmares of feminist empowerment, single-parent homes, peer pressure. Even supermarket sci-fi, which projects Reagan's Evil Empire somewhere beyond our fraying ozone, sheds uncanny light on fears that "Meet the Press" somehow leaves dark. Mass art—not unlike cubism—skips syntax, qualification, and the weighing of claims to display on one flat plane its logic of feeling. Shallow, yes. But in its very shallows one can sometimes discern—as from the air—the true grade and contour of what we think before we think about it. Thus it is that our current wisdom about that oft-blamed victim, the Jewish American Princess, is disconcertingly reflected in Shirley Frondorf's current page-turner, *The Death of a "Jewish American Princess": The True Story of a Victim on Trial.* The interest of Frondorf's book lies in this: by credulously parroting the best arguments of Jewish feminists, Frondorf unintentionally exposes the weaknesses of these arguments as defenses either of Judaism or of women. Wholly unaware of where her advocacy shades into apologetics, her feminism into sexism, her tolerance and pluralism into sellout, Frondorf ends up celebrating a Jewish fulfillent that depends on female disempowerment. Her book is an object lesson in the ways a well-intentioned but unsophisticated Jewish feminism can backfire.

In May of 1981, a man named Steve Steinberg killed his wife Elana by stabbing her with a carving knife taken from the kitchen of their Scottsdale, Arizona, home. Elana's children heard their mother's screams as she was stabbed twenty-six times in her silver and white bedroom, and though Steve Steinberg himself disclosed the murder, calling the police with the story of two bushy robbers, it wasn't long before the police discovered that his story was false. He was put on trial for the first-degree murder of Elana Steinberg. But less than a month after the trial began, Steve Steinberg went free, declared temporarily insane by reason of sleepwalking, and thus innocent of killing his wife— whose alleged extravagance, shrewishness, and sexual parsimony made her the prototypical JAP, and, as the defense implied, a menace better-off dead. Though defense attorneys saw no reason why Steve Steinberg should not return to a society to which he posed no further hazard, they left jurors with little doubt that society was safer minus the woman whose postmortem diagnosis their paid forensic psychiatrists obligingly produced: Jewish American Princess....

Elisa New teaches American literature at the University of Pennsylvania. This review appeared in Tikkun,
March/April 1989.

For Frondorf, the idea of the Jewish American Princess is a chimera, the slur a term of opprobrium hardly deserving the dignity of comment. That is why when she engages the issue made so prominent by the title of her book, she falls apart. Though she is certain that Jewish American Princesshood is neither grounds for murder nor a psychiatric malady, she is lost when it comes to any deeper understanding of the term, especially of what it might mean for Jews. As if to entertain even the semantic intelligibility of so noxious a term were to admit that Elana Steinberg deserved to die, Frondorf holds the term at arm's length by putting it in quotes. This gesture is symptomatic of the automatic and undigested nature of Frondorf's analysis. For one senses that though she is herself a veritable stranger to Jewish American culture, she has been well briefed in the contemporary arguments of Jewish feminists who debunk the idea of the Princess.

Not that the arguments Frondorf cribs are without merit. Take her two central tenets, tenets one finds rehearsed all over the best-intentioned protest literature about the Princess. Tenet one specifies that the epithet is sexist inasmuch as it allows Jewish men arbitrarily to project their own self-hatred onto women. This is undoubtedly so. One female Jewish lawyer I know recounts how male colleagues greet her return from lunch with inquiries about where she spent it—at Bloomingdale's? Such a taunt reveals the sexism of some Jewish men, who try to deflect their uneasiness not only about their own love of loot, but about female competition—and female competence.

Tenet two suggests, trenchantly enough, that the term is anti-Semitic, only a new twitch to the old Christian reflex that couples the Jew with a dollar sign. Like the sexist motive, the anti-Semitic motive is concealed by an artful projection. By disparaging Jewish materialism, Christians can jettison their own ambivalence about worldly gain. Moreover, as proponents of tenet two often point out, Judaism is nowhere ascetic. Blessed with the bounties of this world, Jews may enjoy with clear consciences what Christians enjoy at the peril of their souls.

As helpful as these theses may be in pointing to the sources of the term "Jewish American Princess," they fall far short of explaining its peculiar potency. Try, for example, to synthesize the two tenets into an argument, and they self-destruct: Even as the argument that JAP-bashing is anti-Semitic celebrates Jews' robust enjoyment of the material world, the argument that JAP-bashing is sexist implicitly delegitimizes such enjoyment when it passes off the hot potato of that gusto to the materialistic Jewish man. Such contradictions nestle at the heart of the Jewish American Princess problem, a problem not to be solved by surgically excising the term....

The evidence before her is chilling: a man and wife who seem matched by little more than their spending habits, a network of friends brought together by the thresholds of their credit cards, Jewish men enraged at their wives, Jewish women illogically testifying to the stupendous excesses of a woman each protests "was one of my very best friends." Even as the Steinbergs zealously preserve the Jewishness of their social circle, living in a so-called Jewish "ghetto," and even as the murder of Elana takes place only a few weeks after a family trip to a bar mitzvah, the Steinberg's Judaism is not just supported by but realized in their lifestyle. Defining their Jewishness through observances of display and consumption, Steve and Elana's identities are likewise attenuated in twinned, cameo roles: the Gambler, the Shopper.

Need it be emphasized that nowhere are Jews commanded to gamble or shop? Shopping and gambling are, on the contrary, secular activities of sacral mystique, activities that live off our homesickness for awe, for miracle, for release, even as they invest us more and more heavily in a culture where the House always wins. But beyond their connections to magic, gambling and shopping synthesize the American dream of winning in an afternoon's rush. To gamble is to have a career in five minutes, to freebase one's parents' struggle for success all in one day. It is no coincidence that Steve Steinberg is recalled as a frequenter of banks and other financial institutions which he "played" for the capital to finance his real vocation; nor is it contradictory, as Frondorf points out, that Steve was described by coworkers as a workaholic. Gambling, speculating, and business are all spawn of one American mythology that prizes best the success that risks the most: hence, the man who "loses his shirt" is our portrait in virility; hence our recent obsession with the entrepreneur. Similarly, anyone who has shopped compulsively, or knows compulsive shoppers, understands the shopping high, the promise of self-transformation, of the "make-over" that complements the "self-made" man's autogenesis. Exchanging the old her for the new me, one enjoys a charged interval wherein having substitutes for being.

Now, if "professional" shopping is no more a crime than legal gambling, neither is it a terribly reliable means to a stable sense of self. Both activities put a maximum of strain on identity: gambling ruthlessly separates winner from loser, rending self from self as the chips fall, while shopping shears the self to an appendage of what it buys, clipping identity to performance. It is both telling and poignant that without knowing the effects their words would have, friends of Elana's testified without subpoena not only to her supernal "glamour" but to how that glamour was driven by a ruthless worship of appearances. Upon sharing with Elana the news that her business was failing, one friend told Frondorf how Elana seemed shocked, finally urging: "Don't tell anybody that! Just say that you sold it." ...

We can look straight at the values that made Steve Steinberg so unhappy and Elana his miserable victim without calling them Jewish values. What Frondorf misses, in her scramble to glorify as Yiddishkeit the Steinbergs' consumerism, is an understanding of the vexed relationship of American Jews to material culture; of their belated discovery of that culture in a Gilded Age already recoiling from itself; and finally, of the dynamic that a whole tradition of Jewish American writing has recognized: a naively driven materialism defining itself as Jewish.

To begin with, the Jewish American Princess who has caused us so much grief is only lately Jewish, grafted onto a much older character, the American Princess, herself sprung full-grown out of the wreckage of the Southern Belle. Preserved flower of a New World weakness for the aristocratic, the American Princess graces the rising class that Thorstein Veblen described in 1899 in *The Theory of the Leisure Class*, where he coined the term "conspicuous consumption" to describe the vocation of a class that separates itself from the world of labor by cultivating an ever-greater uselessness, by perfecting the art of flamboyant waste. Such a class defines itself, Veblen argued, not by blood, nor even by purchasing power, but by an indolence relieved in exercises of "taste," that same "taste" so mysteriously fetishized by Elana Steinberg's friends and so ubiquitous among the leisure—that is to say, female—classes of American Jews.

Indeed, what Veblen did not anticipate—though Henry James did when he noted the "growing divorce between the American woman (with her comparative leisure, culture, grace ...) and the male American immersed in the ferocity of business"—was that, in a country without a landed class, it would fall to women to exercise the tastes their husbands labored to support; that the leisure class in America could only be a female class whose lifestyle is preserved through intrafamilial class warfare. It is this warfare that we see explode in the comedy of the fifties, where the American man as Provider is a disgruntled or bemused prole, shackled to supporting his wife's conspicuous spending. And it is this warfare that is, not incidentally, so standard in the repertoire of those Borscht Belt comics who are our mainstream American comics. When Rodney Dangerfield, Shecky Green, and Alan King pillory their wives, it is not to reveal that the wrangling over the Visa card is unique to the Jewish marriage. It is rather to point, with rueful humor, to the Americanization of that marriage.

And yet this hegemony of the family's Princess is won at a stiff psychic price. Late-nineteenth-century American literature is bursting with female characters who, made fancy ladies by their husbands' money, eroticize that money, perhaps as a gesture of protest against a culture that makes sex their only job. But the text that best dramatizes my point, even as it prophesies the forms of an ever-growing American materialism, is *The Great Gatsby*. Fitzgerald's Daisy Faye Buchanan is the ultimate American Princess whose frigid passions are slaked only by things, and the seduction scene of that novel is a veritable proto–JAP joke. The scene comes after Gatsby has led Daisy through his magnificent East Egg mansion, won all for her; they have just arrived in his bedroom. Rather than clasp a palpitating Daisy to his breast, Gatsby reads her right: He shows her his shirts. "They're such beautiful shirts!" sobs Daisy as she sinks ecstatically into the imported silks. It is this same cathexis, this same transfer of libidinal energy from the nice man who worships her to Neiman-Marcus, that the cruelest of JAP jokes lampoon; yet the joke is American, the Princess a flapper whose heart is as wilted as her daisylike innocence. Over the years the stereotype of the Princess has gained added potency when married to the troubling figure of the dark lady, the sultry, grasping bitch most recently incarnated in Alexis of "Dynasty." Long before Jews came to America the dark lady was here, the enticing Venus flytrap whose only religion was sexuality, but whose hunger for men was her lust for her own identity displaced.

Poignantly, there is nothing intrinsically Jewish about the Princess absorbed in her nails and her decor except a turn-of-the-century greenhorn credulity that read her straight, that discerned in the role of Princess the *Eishet Khayil's* big break: Over the streets paved with gold, the Woman of Valor might preside, finally coming into her own. One hesitates to gainsay the impulse, for the woman whose price was above rubies had too long shared her shtetl kitchen with the livestock and, even in America, with her piecework. And yet, as the stories of the turn-of-the-century writer Anzia Yezierska reveal, the American *Eishet Khayil* was anachronistic almost from the moment of her realization. Exiled in her modern kitchen while her children went out for Chinese food, she was made superfluous by the same ideology of helplessness and the same laborsaving devices that stranded her Main Street counterpart at home.

The economic dimension is key. In America, the Jewish woman who would aid her husband's ascent to the top had to learn a new relationship to her home: no longer arena for her talents, it was now a showcase, setting for that highly symbolic leisure that served her husband's manly image. In other words, if, at another time, in another place, the Virtuous Woman's rubies were her market value, metaphoric crown of her labor, her vocational usefulness ("She seeketh wool and flax,/And worketh willingly with her hands"), now they functioned to mark her vocational uselessness, to crown the repose whose invisible maintenance preserved her husband's virility. In her cage hung with mirrors, the Jewish woman who defines herself in recursive rituals of self-perfection— (re)decorating, make(overs), and the "functions" that commemorate the movement of other lives— is only as narcissistic as the Yankee Princess she imitates just as her forebears imitated the grande dames of the Four Hundred. And she is only as trapped. Except, of course, to the extent that she believes star quality to be her Jewish obligation, the aristocracy her Jewish niche.

This is a characteristic swerve well documented in Jewish American literature, a literature that tells again and again the story of a Jew who, hungry to belong in America yet incapable of abandoning tradition, makes a pious study of American values only to call them Jewish. The identity crisis such a graft provokes is first dramatized in Abraham Cahan's The *Rise of David Levinsky,* a book whose very title is cloned from William Dean Howell's *The Rise of Silas Lapham*, which points with irony to the phenomenon of ambition learned straight from Horatio Alger. Delmore Schwartz's tragicomedies of the thirties go even further, capturing the warfare of parents and children who have sacrificed their hold on a ritual culture in pursuit of American perks. In Schwartz's families, the culture of materialism is so ritualized, so artfully superimposed onto Jewish tradition, that the children prove their respect for the faith by *buying* the things their parents could not buy, by making the money their parents would have made. The American *apikores* (Jewish apostate) is not the son gone secular but the son who fails to make a million.

The symbiosis that results leaves Jewish parents and children infantilized together in a world bereft of that which sustains Jewish culture: history. Lacking a sustaining code of ritual value to keep history dynamic, Jews maintain their group identity with a garish kind of supermaterialism, an adolescent outconsumering of the consumer culture. The Jew stereotypes himself as American in order to identify himself as Jewish. In other words, the young woman becomes Fitzgerald's needy, languid Daisy Faye Buchanan only in order to become Philip Roth's Brenda Patimkin....

What Frondorf fails to recognize is that the woman who calls herself a "professional shopper" or brandishes "Jewish American Princess" in rhinestones on her bosom is neither a child, nor a bimbo, nor even a study in self-hatred. Often, this woman does these things in order to salvage some identity out of a profoundly compromised situation, out of vocationlessness and the ever-present possibility—through divorce, for example—of being reduced to an impoverished, unskilled serf in the consumer culture she now commands. So that if at first it seems that Frondorf is soft-pedaling, unwilling to indict Elana's female friends whose testimony to her spending habits was as damaging as the testimony their husbands' offered on Steve's behalf, on closer scrutiny it becomes clear that she is doing much worse. Devoted as she is to celebrating Elana's consumerism as traditionally Jewish, Frondorf fails to see the deeply troubled and self-revealing quality of the female responses to Elana's memory. Because anything like skepticism about Elana's Jewish virtue looks to Frondorf like five points for Steve, she chooses to characterize the torn statements of Elana's friends as sour grapes. She hazards:

My guess is that Elana stepped over the line with at least a few of the women, upsetting the very fine balance that was acceptable for this circle. They were all consumers, obviously, but each group has its own limits. Elana was very much a free spirit, and she was breaking out from the mold....

By Elana's side to the very barricades, Frondorf paints a picture of the "professional shopper" as young artist, misunderstood by those philistines unwilling to go to such lengths for their art. It is no more convincing to compare a woman who shops till she drops to a "free spirit" than it is to call a gambler who wins, favored of the gods. At any rate, how can Frondorf call "free" a woman whose self-expression depended so utterly on her husband's unreliable income, and whose option of divorce was no doubt clouded by the prospect of a poverty that offered no means of self-expression?

And notice the divisiveness of Frondorf's feminism. If Elana's onetime friends shut their doors in Frondorf's face, it was probably not that they had forgotten Elana but that they had remembered her all too well. Frondorf might have read in their testimonies not envy and bitchery but a muted, yet eloquent, solidarity. Taken together, the statements compile a vision of economic powerlessness and imperiled identity, all enforced by a communal nostalgia for the Princess that grandma never was. Elana's friends' ambivalence points not to Elana's bold spirit, but to her compromise: to an economic vulnerability so gripping and a self-abnegation so extreme that she could choose to maintain appearances while disregarding what signs there were that the man she lived with would stab her twenty-six times while her children listened, instructed by their father as they burst terrified from their rooms, to "Shut the fucking door."

That Steve Steinberg, murderer of his wife, walks free is a crime for which a cynical forensic psychiatrist and a sexist legal strategist share blame. Elana Steinberg, brutally slain, was innocent of all crimes. She did not deserve to die, and the epithet—JAP—that provided her killer's ticket to freedom has a dangerous power fittingly dramatized by the story *The State of Arizona v. Steve Steinberg*. Yet in our haste to bury the epithet we must be very cautious not to go Frondorf's way, not to naturalize as Jewish those values that happen to be held by Jews, not to shore up those myths of Jewish American culture that call a woman's desperate narcissism her freedom, and her economic helplessness, her tradition. To question the materialism of Jews is not to defame Jewish culture any more than to notice Elana Steinberg's straitened life is to murder her or her tradition. That tradition is accustomed to taking history in stride. □

At the New Moon: Rosh Hodesh

Marge Piercy

Once a two day holiday, the most sacred stretches
in the slow swing of the epicycling year;
then a remnant, a half holiday for women,
a little something to keep us less unsatisfied;
then abandoned at enlightenment along with herbals
and amulets, bubeh mysehs, grandmothers'
stories.

Now we fetch it up from the bottom of the harbor,
a bone on which the water has etched itself,
and from this bone we fashion a bird, extinct
and never yet born, evolving feathers
from our hair, blood from our salt, strength
from our backs, vision from our brains.

Fly out over the city, dove of the light,
owl of the moon, for we are weaving your wings
from our longings, diaphanous and bony.
Pilots and rabbis soared. The only females
to fly were witches and demons, the power
to endure and the power to destroy alone

granted us. But we too can invent,
can make, can do, undo. Here we stand
in a circle, the oldest meeting, the shape
women assume when we come together
that echoes ours, the flower, the mouth,
breast, opening, pool, the source.

We greet the moon that is not gone
but only hidden, unreflecting, inturned
and introspective, gathering strength to grow

as we greet the first slim nail paring
of her returning light. Don't we understand
the strength that wells out of retreat?
Can we not learn to turn in to our circle,
to sink into the caves of our silence,
to drink lingering by those deep cold wells,
to dive into the darkness of the heart's storm
until under the crashing surge of waves
it is still except for our slow roaring breath?

We need a large pattern of how things change
that shows us not a straight eight-lane tearing
through hills blasted into bedrock; not stairs
mounting to the sacrificial pyramid where hearts
are torn out to feed the gods of power, but the coil
of the moon, that epicylcling wheel

that grows fat and skinny, advances and withers,
four steps forward and three back, and yet nothing
remains the same, for the mountains are piled up
and worn down, for the rivers eat into the stone
and the fields blow away and the sea makes sand
spits and islands and carries off the dune.

Let the half day festival of the new moon
remind us how to retreat and grow strong, how to
reflect and learn, how to push our bellies forward,
how to roll and turn and pull the tides up, up
when we need them, how to come back each time
we look dead, making a new season to shine.

A Plain Brown Wrapper

David Mamet

T he periodic arrival of the Charles Atlas material disturbed me greatly. I was nine or ten years old and had answered their ad in a comic book. The ad assured me that there would be no charge for information regarding the system of Dynamic Tension—the system that could and would transform the weakling into the well-proportioned strong man of the ads. The ad further assured me that the material would arrive in a plain brown envelope.

The material did come, as advertised, in the plain wrapper. But it did not make me strong. It terrified me, because each free installment dealt with one thing and one thing only: my obligation to the Charles Atlas Company and my progressively intransigent, incomprehensible, and criminal refusal to pay for materials received.

I dreaded the arrival of those envelopes, and when they arrived I slunk in shame and despair. I loathed myself for ever having gotten involved in this mess.

Was the whole Charles Atlas promotion geared to idiots and children? Looking back, I think it must have been. The method of Dynamic Tension promised fairly instant strength and beauty at no cost to the consumer. And the vicious and continual dunning letters played masterfully on the undeveloped ego of that idiot or child. I, one such child, thought, on receiving their threats: "Of course they are disappointed in me. I am weak and ugly. How dare I have presumed to take these fine, strong people's course? How dare someone as worthless as I aspire to possess the secrets of strength and beauty? The Charles Atlas people have recognized, as they must, my laughable unworthiness, and my only defense against them is prayer."

For they were, of course, God—they offered me transformation in exchange for an act of sacrifice and belief. But I was unprepared to make that act.

The other religious experience of my youth was equally inconclusive and unfortunate. It was Reform Judaism: and though the God Jehovah, the God of Wrath and Strength and Righteousness, spoke through the mouth of Charles Atlas, he was deemed quite out-of-place at the Sinai Temple.

The rabbis were addressed by the title "doctor," the trumpet was blown in deference to the shofar, the ancient Hebrew chants and songs were rendered in Victorian settings, and we went to Sunday School rather than to *shul*. There is nothing particularly wrong with these traducements of tradition, except this: They were all performed in an atmosphere of shame. Untutored in any religion whatsoever, we youngsters were exposed to the idea of worshiper-as-revisionist. Our practices were in-reaction-to. The constant lesson that we learned in our Sunday School was that we must be better, more rational, more up-to-date, finally, more American than that thing that had come before. And that thing that had come before was Judaism.

Chicago-born David Mamet is the author of many plays, including Glengarry Glen Ross, *for which he won both the Pulitzer Prize and the New York Drama Critics Circle Award as the best American play of 1984. Most recently, he has directed Broadway's* Speed the Plow. *He has also directed three movies, the most recent being* Homicide. *This article appeared in* Tikkun, *November/December 1988.*

Judaism, at my temple in the 1950s, was seen as American Good Citizenship (a creed we could be proud of), with some Unfortunate Asiatic Overtones, that we were not going to be so craven as to deny. No, we were going to bear up steadfastly under the burden of our taint—our Jewishness. We were such good citizens that although it was not our fault that our parents and grandparents were the dread Ashkenazi, the "superstitious scum of Eastern Europe," we would not publicly sever our connection with them. We Reform Jews would be so stalwart, so American, so non-Jewish, in fact, as to "Play the Game." We would go by the name of Jews, although every other aspect of our religious life would be Unitarian. Our religion was nothing other than a corporate creed, and our corporate creed was an evasion. It was this: We are Jews, and we are Proud to be Jews. We will express our Jewishness by behaving in every way possible exactly like our Christian Brethren because what they have is better than what we have.

I found the Reform Judaism of my childhood nothing other than a desire to "pass," to slip unnoticed into the non-Jewish community, to do nothing that would attract the attention, and, so, the wrath of mainstream America.

Why would America's notice necessarily beget its wrath? Easy: We were Jews, and worthless. We were everything bad that was said against us; we didn't even have a religion anymore; we'd given it up to placate the non-Jewish community, to escape its wrath.

What of the Wrath of Jehovah? He, too, was better left behind if we were to cease being Jews.

What was it, then, to be Jewish? Heaven forfend that it was to be part of a race, and spare us the wretched image of dark skins, loud voices, hook noses, and hairy hands.

Was it to be part of a religion? Of what did that religion consist? Every aspect of its observance had been traduced. Which of us Reform (which meant and means, of course, reformed, which is to say changed for the better, and, implicitly, penitent) Jews could remember the names, let alone the meanings, of those joyless holidays we attempted to celebrate? Those occasions—sabbath, holidays, bar mitzvahs—were celebrated with sick fear and shame. Not shame that we had forsaken our heritage, but shame that we had not forsaken it sufficiently.

One could both despise and envy Kissinger, Goldwater, and others who, though they had rejected the faith of their fathers, at least had the courage of their convictions.

The lesson of my Reform Temple was that metaphysics is just superstition—that there is no God. And every Sunday we celebrated our escape from Judaism. We celebrated our autonomy from God and from our forefathers, and so, of course, we were afraid.

My co-religionists and I eventually sought out the God we had been denied. We sought God in Scientology, Jews for Jesus, Eastern Studies, consciousness-raising groups—all attempts to explain the relationship between the one and the all, between our powerlessness and the strength of the universe. We sought God through methods not unlike Dynamic Tension—in which the powerless weakling, having been instructed in the Mysteries, overcomes the Bully (the Juggernaut, the World) and so restores order to the Universe.

Here is my question: What was so shameful about wanting a better physique?

Why did such information have to come in a plain brown wrapper?

Why did the Charles Atlas Company know that such an endeavor needed to be hidden?

The answer is that the desire for a better physique was not shameful, but we, the *applicants*, were shameful: We were intrinsically unworthy, and the idea of weaklings such as ourselves desiring strength and beauty was so laughable that, of course, we wanted our desires to be kept secret.

That was why the dunning letters worked. They threatened to expose not the fact that we hadn't paid our bills, but the fact that we had the audacity to want a beautiful life.

And that was also my experience, as a child, of Reform Judaism. It was religion in a plain brown wrapper, a religion whose selling point was that it would not embarrass us.

Thirty years later, I am very angry at the Charles Atlas Company, and at the Sinai Temple. Neither one delivered what it could and should have, and, more important, neither one had the right to instill in a child a sense of shame.

Thirty years later I am not completely happy with my physique, but I am very proud of being a Jew, and I have a growing sense of the reality of God. I say to that no doubt long-demised Charles Atlas Company, "You should be ashamed," and to the leaders of that Reformed temple, "What were you ashamed of?" □

For My Tree in Israel

Julia Vinograd

There is blood on my tree,
on the tree with my name in Israel.
The tears of tear-gassed crowds
water the roots,
and the tears of rage
and the tears of grief for the dead.
Is this the tree I planted
to bring forth life from the desert?
The broken bones of hands throwing rocks
and the rocks they threw
pile around my tree,
the tree with my name in Israel.

It did not begin like this.
Everyone in my class planted a tree in Israel,
filled out a form and sent a letter
with our names.
I could've had pictures sent me of the tree
growing as I grew
but I didn't want to know what it looked like.
The tree didn't know what I looked like.
We shared a name, it was my name,
it was enough.
And now there is blood on my name
on my tree in Israel.

Do not speak to me of self-defense,
of necessity and nations and history.
There is no water in such words
and I need a glass of water before I sleep.
Do not explain, it may be true
but it doesn't help,
it is not in the same language
in which my tree talks to the wind.

There must always be an Israel
because my tree is there
and they shall never come with axes
and cut down my name.
But there is blood on my tree
and the smell of blood
and I want my name to be good again.
I want my good name to grow in Israel
and put out damp new leaves every spring,
as soft as kisses.

Taking Down the Christmas Tree

Anne Roiphe

In December of 1978, the *New York Times* asked me to write a small piece on a Christmas theme for the home section of the paper. I dashed off an essay on being Jewish and having a Christmas tree. The *Times* published it the Thursday before the holiday. I had thought this a small, unimportant piece, a kind of family musing that would melt in the mind of the reader like a snowflake on the tongue. I have made misjudgments in my life but none so consequential for me as this one.

The phones rang at the *New York Times*—it seemed as if all the officers of all the major Jewish organizations were complaining to their personal friends at the *Times* about my piece. Housewives, rabbis, lawyers, doctors, businessmen, all but Indian chiefs phoned or wrote in, furious that the paper had published an article that advocated assimilation, displayed ignorance of Judaism, and seemed to express contempt for the Jewish way of life. At our house the phone calls began on Thursday at noon and lasted for weeks. "I hope your children get leukemia," no fewer than three irate callers announced. "You deserve to die," several heavy-breathing souls saw fit to whisper through the AT&T lines. Far more difficult for me was the caller who announced himself as a survivor and said I had dishonored the dead of Auschwitz and Treblinka. Other survivors wrote with the same comments.

What I wrote in the *New York Times* was this: every Christmas, my family bought a Christmas tree—and it seemed as if every Christmas we ran into the rabbi who lived across the street just as we were bringing the tree into our house. I always felt uncomfortable, embarrassed, and I didn't quite understand why. True, my family was Jewish, and all of us identified as such. But we had made a decision not to celebrate Chanukah—because we were secular Jews, because Chanukah had always seemed to me to be a holiday about an unacceptable miracle. God, I said, should have prevented the war in the first place, saved the lives of those who died in battle on both sides, instead of merely allowing a small can of oil an extended life. After the Holocaust, the miracle of the can of oil seemed pretty weak. At this point in my article, I made an embarrassing mistake. I confused the Romans with the Syrians and revealed to the readers of the *New York Times* that I had learned about Chanukah so many years before and had become so indifferent that even my grasp of Jewish history had grown weak. I aptly, if unconsciously, demonstrated the point that ignorance about Judaism is the ice on the slippery slope to total assimilation. In my essay, I concluded by stating that we celebrated Christmas because it was a way to come together as a family, to pause in our daily efforts, to be with each other, and to give something to each other. In honor of what?

Anne Roiphe is the author of Lovingkindness *(Summit, 1987) and* Season for Healing: Reflections on the Holocaust *(Summit, 1988). Her most recent book is* The Pursuit of Happiness *(Summit, 1991). She is the fiction editor of* Tikkun. *This article appeared in* Tikkun, *November/December 1989.*

In honor of the family, I supposed.

The intense response to the piece made me realize that I had inadvertently offended many people. Rabbis were using the piece as the subject of their sermons, treating me as if I were a female Arafat. Every day, rabbis, scholars, and friends invited me to explore Judaism and see what it was that I had missed.

I accepted those invitations. Why? I realized that I had written the piece out of discomfort with the peculiar form my Jewishness had taken. I had written the article with the knowledge that Christmas without Christ (because that is all we had) was only a commercial break, a huge effort to make the family happy through purchases, large and small, which never seemed to fulfill whatever it was that everyone needed. I knew that Christmas stripped of its religious meaning was a charm on the American bracelet, a potion for homogenization that left one thirsty for identity and meaning and self.

So I began to study Talmud, I read Jewish history, I read about the Jewish mystics, and I talked to every rabbi who would speak with me. I learned about the richness of the Jewish tradition, the arguments between Shammai and Hillel, the centuries of worrying about kindness and the law. After several years, I began to know the Jewish story, which was my story after all, finally my real story. I realized that, although I indeed knew the words to "Good King Wenceslas," I now knew the kaddish and the meaning of the shofar and the names of Rabbi Akiva and Rabbi Nachman. I also knew that I was now tied, by a love beyond understanding, to the fate of the Jewish people. I began to understand the meanings behind the rituals, and I found that I was amazed and proud of what it meant to be Jewish, of the ways Jews have approached intellectual issues, of the ways we have survived, of the ways our rituals blend into the seasons and bind us together in a past that finds its purpose in the future.

My studies made me realize that I had not freely chosen to be less Jewish and more American. I hadn't known that assimilation was something that was happening to me and my family. I hadn't known that a tide of history had borne my family from Central Europe to the shores of the Lower East Side and up to the portals of the best colleges in the land. I had not understood the force of the dominant culture playing against my fragile identity, telling me that I would be more beautiful if I looked like a non-Jew, with straight blond hair and a short nose. I hadn't understood that, growing up in the forties, I had absorbed the anti-Semitism of the culture, and that's why I thought that people who spoke with accents were peculiar, that Jews were outsiders. I wanted to be inside with the others. And where were the others at Christmas? They were gathered around their Christmas tree.

Before I began to learn about Judaism, I didn't realize that assimilation had a dark side. I thought assimilation was a process as natural and inevitable as breathing. That's not quite true. I didn't think about it at all. I now realize that assimilation can produce an identity that is shallow, materialistic, unrooted, and anxious. Assimilation can deprive a person of the pleasure of belonging and the vitality that comes from real knowledge about and interest in that person's own community. To be American and nothing else is to be bland like a McDonald's hamburger, to be flat like the highways that cross Kansas, to be dull like our nightly TV programs. Americans can spout platitudes about the Constitution and brotherly love and the wonder of Paul Revere riding through the night, but the American identity, if it is not grafted onto something firm, turns to vapor, a substance that cannot sustain or nourish.

My studies of Judaism made me understand the conflicts my parents and I had faced. I realized that the concepts of Diaspora and melting pot are directly opposed and that my parents had chosen the melting pot for reasons that were legitimate enough for them.

When I was growing up, Christmas was the only holiday of the solstice that was important. My mother found it hard to resist the twinkling lights, the fir trees, the reindeer, and the presents that were all around her. At that time, no one celebrated Chanukah in a way that could compete with the apparent joyousness of Christmas. This was no small matter, because the power of Christmas—the carols, the Mass, and the commercial hoopla—was very great and made the American mainstream Christian world seem more appealing than the Jewish one. The choices individuals and families make about Christmas are significant statements about assimilation, about how these individuals and families will live as Jews in America and where they will stand on the tightrope between being Jewish and being American. When Jews resist Christmas, we affirm our own separate identity. When Jews resist Christmas, we reduce the hypocrisy in our lives and increase our personal security by deepening our roots within our own traditions. We claim our right to participate as equals and not just as a barely tolerated minority when we insist on not going along with the dominant culture.

The Jewish world has recognized the importance of upgrading Chanukah to compete with Christmas. Jewish children, like their Christian neighbors, can now feel that they have their own holiday exploding with joy. This upgrading of Chanukah, although purists find it somewhat silly, is an important tool in fighting off the appeal of the mass culture, of Rudolph the Red-nosed Reindeer and Tiny Tim and the Little Drummer Boy. There is no question, however, that Christmas with all the angels singing is a powerful matter. When, as a result of my travels, both intellectual and literal, through the Jewish landscape, my family began to celebrate Chanukah instead of Christmas, my children thought I was the Grinch who stole the holiday.

I am certain, however, that the somewhat delirious buying of objects that had occupied me from Thanksgiving to December 25 was not the way to make a family strong and root its members in their communal past and communal future. The Jewish content of my life was rescued by my writing that small piece ten years ago, and for that I am grateful.

I am not so grateful, however, for what I learned through the harshness of Jewish response to the piece. The hostile response was an example of the depth of fear in the Jewish community of the seductiveness of the Christian world, a fear that perhaps is not helpful and is an example of the tendency rooted deep in Jewish culture to declare the other person outside the pale. As long as there is a Diaspora, there will be many Jewish families who continue to celebrate Christmas—because of childhood memories, because of the intermarriage of some member, because of living in an isolated community—without losing all connection to their Jewish roots or their Jewish life. The Christmas tree should not be used as a club with which one Jew assaults another. In each generation, we will lose some Jews to the mainstream culture, and in each generation we will gain others who are returning to the community with renewed passion and connection. We can think of Jewish families as riding on swells of an American ocean—some drowning, some floating, some steering the boat. Which role an individual plays will vary within each family, but no one can necessarily predict who is going under and who is about to be captain of the ship.

The staying power of Judaism is and will remain its ability to provide us with an access to spiritual, political, and moral vision and language that speaks to us more powerfully than any of the competing visions that populate the contemporary world. Strengthening and teaching that vision is the only way to avoid assimilation. Whatever we do to keep the Jewish community strong—and there are many things we can do—we should not make harsh judgments against those who move back and forth between Frosty the Snowman and Esther the Queen. We should not allow our fear of erosion to promote hostility toward anyone, not someone carrying a red and green package all wrapped up in a silver bow, not someone with a package of tinsel in a shopping bag; not anyone at all.

I now see Chanukah not as a celebration of the miracle of the oil, but as a time when, as we light the candles, we pause in awe before the Jewish people whose survival through adversity brings light into the darkness of the human soul. This view makes me Jewish in a different way from the way in which I was Jewish before. It makes me a part of the continuity while allowing me still to be myself,

Goyim Bashing and Jewish Pessimism

Michael Lerner

Hostility toward non-Jews has a long history in the Jewish world, and it may be as prevalent among American Jewish liberals as among Israeli right-wingers. But whether it expresses itself as racism in Israel or suspicion of gentiles here in the United States, goyim-bashing is a powerful sign of our inability to remain true to the revolutionary optimism that was the central meaning of the covenant that Jews received at Sinai.

To the extent that we become overwhelmed by pessimism and despair, we grant a posthumous victory to those who hoped to destroy the Jewish people. Our enemies may not have destroyed the Jewish body, but to the extent that they have created a new kind of Jew who uses the behavior of the world as the criterion for how Jews should behave, to the extent that they have made Jews "realistic," the enemies of the Jewish people may have succeeded in destroying one of the most important aspects of the Jewish soul—our ability to envision and fight for a different and better world. Nowhere does this loss show up more dramatically than in our relationship to non-Jews.

It's no secret that Jews disparage non-Jews behind their backs. Some Jews brag about tricking them in business, others shun them socially. The Yiddish phrase a *goyishe kup* (a non-Jewish head) indicates someone stupid or foolish. In Jewish literature, the non-Jew is often portrayed as someone who is untrustworthy, dangerous, or hateful.

Many younger Jews growing up in the post–World War II era were scandalized by parents or relatives who talked about *shvartses* or who made disparaging references to the civil rights movement. Yet even these younger generations have sometimes imbibed anti-goy sentiments, have been insensitive to converts to Judaism, and have participated in the subtle critique of the gentiles that makes one feel "in" as a Jew. Goyim-bashing may be most intense among Jews who have little in the way of an active daily religious life and who consequently hold on to their ethnic identity all the more fiercely. All that they have to substantiate their Jewishness, apart from some food preferences, is the degree to which they see themselves as different from the non-Jew.

Given the tremendous oppression the Jewish people have endured at the hands of non-Jews, suspicion and anti-goy sentiment are understandable. The anger that many Jews feel is often legitimate. Our relative powerlessness to defend ourselves made it necessary for us to repress our outrage and anger at what was done to us, and to develop instead a quiet anger that evolved into a distinct culture of anti-goyism. Unable to express anger in direct and healthy ways, we Jews sometimes expressed it instead through humor, religious triumphalism, and ultimately a Zionist ideology whose fundamental assumption was that the goyim could never be trusted.

There is no blame implied here. The trauma of the Holocaust may have so deeply scarred us that our current attitude is understandable. There are moments when I become so overwhelmed by the feelings of anger at what was done to my family and my people that I become sympathetic to the most extreme fantasies of Israeli right-wingers. It takes an act of conscious determination to prevent

---

This editorial appeared in Tikkun, *September/October 1990.*

the past from shaping our perceptions of the present. Yet precisely because I do love my people, I feel the need to consciously overcome the pain of the past, so that I can look more honestly at the present.

Today, Jewish anger has been transformed into a deep pessimism about "the other," a pessimism that led many post-Holocaust Jews into a worship of power and now allows them to dismiss all moral criticism of Israel as idealistic baloney. The only thing that Israelis need to worry about, these pessimists believe, is the size of our army and the strength of our state. In the final analysis, they assert, nothing else counts besides strength—and since the goyim will inevitably try to destroy us, the only issue worth worrying about is how strong we can make the State of Israel.

By acting on the assumption that the rest of the world is implacably hostile, Israel helps create a set of responses that then fulfill its worst fantasies. For example, many Israelis are so deeply filled with pessimism that they repeat, almost trance-like, the notion that they would love to find peace, but that no one from the other side is willing to talk. If one mentions the PLO's call for direct talks, or Arafat's announcement that he would go to Jerusalem to talk with Israel (to which Shamir responded by saying that he would arrest Arafat as soon as he arrived at Ben Gurion Airport), then they reply, "We will not negotiate with terrorists."

Many Jews simply cannot register the fact that the enemy is ready to negotiate peace. They cannot take "yes" for an answer. Not that they *should* blindly trust their enemies. When the negotiations start, many of us believe Israel should insist that any Palestinian state be completely and carefully demilitarized, and that continued demilitarization be enforced by both an international force and the Israeli Army. But the difference between asking for reasonable terms when negotiating with your enemy and not being able to recognize that the enemy is ready to negotiate is the difference between rational self-interest and paranoid self-destructiveness. Having been deeply shaped by a consciousness that tells them they will always be alone against the world, many Jews are unable to act in ways that could make their world safer, if in so doing they had to violate their internalized injunction to "Distrust the Other."

This also shows up in the way we have failed to explain Israel's case to the rest of the world. Israeli public relations efforts are usually self-defeating because they assume that everyone is always going to be against us. There is real anti-Semitism in the world today, but much of it is rooted not in the destructive legacies of two thousand years of religious oppression, but in the reaction of many people around the world to Israel's current policies. Many of the peoples of the world who have developed antagonism or suspicion about the Jewish people have no historical legacy of antagonism toward us. In the years since the Second World War they have come to know us primarily through the activities of the state which calls itself the state of the Jewish people. Set up to provide a refuge for the victims of Nazi oppression and the extermination camps, that state is now seen as the cause of the suffering of the Palestinian people.

We know that the historical record is more complex. We could explain to many Third World countries that Palestinian rejectionism in the pre-1948 period was at least as responsible for the current suffering of the Palestinian people as any Jewish intransigence. Had the Jewish people, both in Diaspora and in Israel, taken the goal of explaining Israel's case to the rest of the world seriously, we would have seen a massive effort made to reach Third World communities and Third World opinion makers. Jewish communities in the U.S. would have invited foreign students at local universities to participate in discussions of these issues, Jewish teenagers would have been asked to serve as ambassadors of goodwill when they went abroad, and Jews would have reached out to Third World minorities living in their own communities to explain our case. No such effort was made because Jews assumed from the start that no one would ever listen to us. Our only hope for success, Jewish leaders insisted, was to whisper into the ears of local elites, show them that Jews or

Israel would serve their interests, and thereby gain official support for Israel even when the local populace could not be trusted to be anything but anti-Jewish.

This same strategy dominated the Israeli government's strategy toward Third World countries. Israeli economic aid to Third World dictators was based on this same "realpolitik" assumption: since people would always be against us, or would be too stupid to understand our position, our only hope to win friends would be to give military or economic assistance to ruling elites. No wonder, then, that when military elites toppled, citizens of these nations were angry at Israel for supplying the dictators with military weaponry and advice. Jews could then interpret this hostility as further proof that no matter what we did to help them, the non-Jews of the world would turn on us.

This same sense that the world is implacably hostile also leads to the view that the very raising of these questions is a betrayal. Any talk about mistakes being made by Israel or the Jewish people will, it is feared, inevitably lead to a renewed upsurge of the anti-Semitism that is always lurking around the corner. Criticism of Israeli policy, even criticism in the name of saving the Jewish people from self-destruction, is dismissed as a product of self-hatred: Why else would anyone "endanger" the Jewish people by potentially giving ammunition to our enemies? So the self-correcting mechanisms of loving self-criticism are themselves silenced.

Time and time again we are faced with Jews who present themselves as victims who have "learned the lessons of history" and become cynical about every idealistic notion of what could happen in the world. The Jewish neocons, the Henry Kissingers and Norman Podhoretzes and Charles Krauthammers, present the Jews to the world as a group whose history proved that force and cynical manipulation are keys to survival, and that the U.S. ought to learn these lessons. We have allowed ourselves to be represented by people whose cynical detachment and ironic turns of phrase are calculated to produce in others a reconnection to their own deepest despair and pessimism—now represented to them as high culture and deep wisdom. In Israel, this despair is called common sense. Nothing is more devastating for an Israeli than to be told *"Al tibyeh friar,"* don't be a naive idealist, a crime far worse in the Israeli political lexicon than being a bonebreaking oppressor of a colonized minority population.

The pessimism I have been describing fundamentally rejects Judaism's healing and revolutionary message. Early Judaism proclaimed that the world could be turned on its head, that the powerful could be defeated by the powerless, that a whole new world could be constructed. The Torah never doubted the strong pull of the past and the tendency of people to visit on others the oppression to which they had been subjected—what Freud labeled the "repetition compulsion." Yet its message was truly revolutionary: the repetition compulsion that governs daily life is not the most powerful force in the universe. Human life is governed by a much more powerful force—a God who is the source of transcendence and possibility.

It is this God that Moses encounters at the Burning Bush. When Moses presses God for His/Her name, God responds, *"ehyeh asher ehyeh,"* "I shall be who I shall be." "Tell them," God continues, "that 'I shall be' sent you." The fundamental force ruling the universe makes possible transcendence and freedom, the overcoming of the hold of the past over the present. The force governing the universe is a force of freedom that gives the world the possibility of movement toward a transcendent moral order.

This conception of possibility stood in opposition to the various religious systems that provided the metaphysical foundations for existing systems of oppression in the ancient world. The Egyptian empire that Moses confronted was the world's greatest imperialist power. The Egyptians saw history as a repetition of patterns that were built into the structure of necessity. This sense that the social world could be understood as fundamentally similar to the natural world and its endless repetitions led to a political quietism, an acceptance of systems of oppression as ontologically given and unchangeable. Existing systems of oppression were not the product of human choice, but were part of the fabric of the universe.

No wonder the Jewish worldview was perceived as threatening and no wonder every ruling class had to find some way to marginalize and deal with this troublesome people, to set their subjects against the Jews. For if the Jewish message were to be heard by others, they too might begin to wonder if their world could be radically altered. As the Torah made clear, many other peoples had benefited from the Exodus. It had been a "mixed multitude" that had left Egypt in the great slave rebellion led by the Jews. It was not the intrinsic hatred of Jews that moved ruling elites throughout history to try to stir up anti-Jewish sentiments among their subjects, but rather the fear that the revolutionary consciousness implicit in Jewish thought and Jewish history would spread and undermine the existing social order.

The implications of the claim that YHVH governs the universe, that its fundamental force is not some scientific regularity but moral possibility, are breathtaking. Human beings, according to Torah, are made in the image of God: that is, they too can participate in shaping the world and participate in making it a moral order. Although Torah recognizes the tendency of human beings to act out on others the pain to which they themselves have been subjected, it makes a revolutionary claim: "You do not have to do that." As though it could have anticipated the condition of the Jews thousands of years later, the Torah spells out the implications most forcefully in its injunctions concerning the stranger, the person who is the oppressed minority within any given system. In one form or another, there is no commandment more frequently repeated in Torah than variations on the following theme: When you come into your land, do not oppress the stranger. Remember that you were strangers in the land of Egypt.

Living with the injunction to transcend the pain and oppression of the past is hard to do. The revelation of God's presence was overwhelming to the Israelites at Sinai, and its implications may even be hard for us today. The tendency to let the patterns of the past shape our sense of the possibilities of tomorrow is virtually overwhelming, and so the voice of God that Moses heard at Sinai can easily be lost among the other voices that are more consonant with previous understandings of the world. This process begins within Torah itself, so that even within the Torah we see moments in which the children of Israel begin to hear a very different kind of god, a god of revenge and anger, a god who resembles the tribal gods of other peoples, a god who gives sanction to act out on others the pain that has been visited on the children of Israel. This is the god whose voice is heard in Deuteronomy, when the Israelites are given the instructions to wipe out the people of the land they are about to conquer, and to show no mercy. Because of this voice, religious extremists today can use Torah to justify the passions and hatreds they feel.

So even in Torah the Jewish people's understanding of God is in dispute. Indeed, we may see the entire Bible and the subsequent history of the Jewish people as a struggle between two different conceptions of God. What happens, I believe, is a struggle between the moments in which we can truly hear the voice of God as the force that will allow us to break the patterns of the past and believe in the possibiity of creating a world governed by mutual caring, love, peace, and justice; and the moments in which that voice is drowned out and all we hear is the legacy of inherited pain and oppression which presents itself as the voice of common sense and reality.

This struggle between the voice of God and the voices of the past shapes Jewish history. The Jews do *not* become the embodiments of Torah; they are conflicted, torn between the revolutionary demands of a new way of being and the crippling psychological legacy of the past. As the revolutionary zeal of the Exodus recedes, a new ruling class emerges in ancient Judea and Israel. Judaism becomes a Temple-based system that sometimes turns a deaf ear to the unfair treatment of the poor and the powerless. Yet the older revolutionary legacy is strong enough to produce a powerful response: the Prophets. In the name of Torah, the Prophetic tradition acknowledges that Judaism itself could quickly be distorted by those who follow the letter of the ritual law while ignoring its moral obligation to defend the powerless.

While Prophets were often ignored or persecuted, the message stirred the hearts of the people. Eventually it was included in the Bible and the the Sabbath prayer service. Even so, the revolutionary consciousness continued to be subverted as Jews faced a world increasingly dominated by cruel systems of imperial rule. The talmudic tradition is a monument to the variety of clever ways in which the most revolutionary demands of Torah were subverted or made "more realistic" by scholars and sages who had lost their zeal for confronting the powers that be. Particularly after Rabbi Akiba and his disciples perished at the hands of a Rome whose power they had tried to resist, a quietism and deepening cynicism began to emerge in the Jewish religious tradition. The more that the Jews felt the need to accommodate to the status quo, the less they believed in the possibility of transformation. Their pessimism, defeatism, and cynicism about human nature inevitably led to goyim-bashing. Anyone who reads the talmudic tractate *Avodah Zara* cannot escape the impression that the Jews have come to believe that all non-Jews are so dangerous that they should be avoided. Instead of imagining that the non-Jews would, as in Egypt, become fellow travelers on the road to world transformation, Jews saw non-Jews as obstacles, threats, people who would be manipulated by their rulers into becoming anti-Semites and enemies.

This is what *did* happen—and not because *we* did anything wrong. My contention is not that we should have acted differently in the past, but rather that we can now act on different assumptions about the present. The historical conditions we face are very different from those that faced us through much of our history, yet we continue to see our possibilities as limited by an inevitable repetition compulsion that will always make the non-Jew act in destructive and hateful ways.

A word now on behalf of legitimate anger. One source of the generalized anti-goy pessimism has been our inability to express the legitimate anger we feel at those who have oppressed us. Jews have an absolute right to feel outraged at the oppression we have experienced, and to demand that there be serious recompense. For example, we have every right to ask of those who identify themselves as having historical continuity with the Christian churches, churches which spread blood libels about the Jewish people, that they involve themselves actively in the contemporary struggle against anti-Semitism. It is not enough, for example, for the Catholic Church or various Protestant denominations to eliminate from their teachings the notion that the Jewish people bears historical responsibility for the killing of Jesus. Those religious communities need to educate their own communities to the role that these churches played in fostering anti-Semitism throughout the ages. On similar grounds, *Tikkun* has opposed German reunification until the German people go much farther in acknowledging their responsibility for the anti-Semitic devastations of the twentieth century and in combatting the legacies of that hatred that are reappearing throughout Europe.

When anger is focused and specific it is often salutary and to be encouraged. Some people have argued that Israel or Jewish life is too focused on anger at the Holocaust. I strongly disagree. In fact, the various commemorations and museums are a substitute for legitimate anger. They function to repress the real emotions Jews have every right to feel. The role of the American ruling elite in closing off immigration of Jews, the role of the American-Jewish establishment in caring more about their own position in the eyes of that American elite than in saving the Jewish people, the role of various Zionist leaders in giving higher priority to the enterprise of nation-building than saving Jewish lives in Israel—all these would become central targets if Jews were actually to allow themselves to get angry at the Holocaust.

Goyim-bashing, cynicism, and pessimism prevent us from feeling justified anger at our real enemies: they are depressive substitutes. Because as a people we still don't feel entitled to our own focused anger, because we still follow the neurotic pattern of every oppressed group in unconsciously blaming ourselves for our suffering, we allow ourselves to succumb to a self-fulfilling pessimism about the world. As a result, we blur vital distinctions. As it is, we are no longer able to tell the difference between the anger of a Palestinian teenager who has grown up in a refugee camp and wants some dignity and self-respect, and the maniacal hatred and ruthlessness of a Saddam Hussein or a Hafez Assad. Indeed, unable to really tell our friends from our enemies, we revert to the one strategy that has always failed—tying our fate to that of ruling elites. In so doing we reject the possibility of making friends with those who have also been victims in other societies. And we go on believing that we will always remain a people alone, misunderstood, abandoned, and betrayed.

This theology of pessimism is the ultimate abandonment of Judaism for idolatry. Idolatry is the worship of That Which Is and the abandonment of the consciousness of That Which Could And Should Be. In practice, idolatry is the belief that the way things are in the world is all that can be, the reduction of the *ought* to the *is*, the abandonment of the belief that the world is governed by a force that makes possible the triumph of good over evil. Reflecting a deep pessimism about the Other, goyim-bashing is one of the many varieties of idolatry that dominate contemporary Jewish life.

Israeli politics reflects this same cynicism, which explains in part why some of the most ethically sensitive Israelis avoid political involvement (in the process, ironically, ensuring that the opportunists and pessimists will continue to dominate the public arena). In my view, a religious Zionism still makes sense—but only if it stands as a radical critique of the existing policies of the State of Israel and as a vocal challenge to the chauvinism, pessimism, and cynicism in contemporary Israeli life.

The alternative to realpolitik, of course, is not a Pollyannish idealizing of the Palestinians or of other non-Jews around us. Those of us who watched the New Left attempt to make oppressed groups into the embodiments of revolutionary virtue understand that this, too, was a manifestation of idolatry. We can expect that just as Jews and other oppressed groups have been partly deformed by that oppression, so the Palestinians are likely to reflect their own kinds of deformations—and it will be appropriate for Israel to protect itself from the likely hostility that the occupation of the West Bank helped engender. But their hostility, too, is not necessarily permanent or built into the ontology of the universe. Just as the French and Germans, bitter enemies for centuries, today cooperate as allies, so too a day can come in which Israelis and Palestinians can be allies. But only if we act in ways that make that possibility more likely. We human beings can become partners with God in remaking the world, in healing, repairing, and transforming it. And that means seeing "the others" not as enemies but as potential allies even when they are not acting as such. If we approached the world as though we thought it might be possible for us to win, to be liked, to overcome others' suspicions and irrationalities, we might have considerably more success.

I don't mean that the Jewish people needs to end its struggle with anti-Semitism or to disarm the Israeli army. On the contrary, it is precisely because we have real enemies that we need a strong army that has not been undermined by the insane and hopeless task of repressing the national aspirations of the Palestinian people. As Israel's peace treaty with Egypt has shown, even those who were fighting against us in the past need not always remain our deepest enemies. Even some anti-Semites can be changed (though not most). But more importantly, those who are not yet against us need not be written off in advance.

Even as we need to live in the world with peoples who are unfairly or irrationally against us, and even as we need to protect ourselves accordingly, we also need to search continually for openings and possibilities for transformation. It is the dulling of our sensitivity to the possible that makes us see the world in rigid terms, and this in turn turns us against those who might potentially be our partners in remaking the world. ☐

Random Reflections of a Second-Rate Mind

Woody Allen

Dining at a fashionable restaurant on New York's chic Upper East Side, I noticed a Holocaust survivor at the next table. A man of sixty or so was showing his companions a number tattooed on his arm while I overheard him say he had gotten it at Auschwitz. He was graying and distinguished-looking with a sad, handsome face, and behind his eyes there was the predictable haunted look. Clearly he had suffered and gleaned deep lessons from his anguish. I heard him describe how he had been beaten and had watched his fellow inmates being hanged and gassed, and how he had scrounged around in the camp garbage for anything—a discarded potato peel—to keep his corpse-thin body from giving in to disease. As I eavesdropped I wondered: If an angel had come to him then, when he was scheming desperately not to be among those chosen for annihilation, and told him that one day he'd be sitting on Second Avenue in Manhattan in a trendy Italian restaurant amongst lovely young women in designer jeans, and that he'd be wearing a fine suit and ordering lobster salad and baked salmon, would he have grabbed the angel around the throat and throttled him in a sudden fit of insanity?

Talk about cognitive dissonance! All I could see as I hunched over my pasta were truncheons raining blows on his head as second after second dragged on in unrelieved agony and terror. I saw him weak and freezing—sick, bewildered, thirsty, and in tears, an emaciated zombie in stripes. Yet now here he was, portly and jocular, sending back the wine and telling the waiter it seemed to him slightly too tannic. I knew without a doubt then and there that no philosopher ever to come along, no matter how profound, could even begin to understand the world.

Later that night I recalled that at the end of Elie Wiesel's fine book, *Night*, he said that when his concentration camp was liberated he and others thought first and foremost of food. Then of their families and next of sleeping with women, but not of revenge. He made the point several times that the inmates didn't think of revenge. I find it odd that I, who was a small boy during World War II and who lived in America, unmindful of any of the horror Nazi victims were undergoing, and who never missed a good meal with meat and potatoes and sweet desserts, and who had a soft, safe, warm bed to sleep in at night, and whose memories of those years are only blissful and full of good times and good music—that I think of nothing but revenge....

On the cover of this magazine, under the title, is printed the line: A Bimonthly Jewish Critique of Politics, Culture & Society. But why a Jewish critique? Or a gentile critique? Or any limiting perspective? Why not simply a magazine with articles written by human beings for other humans to read? Aren't there enough real demarcations without creating artificial ones? After all, there's no biological difference between a Jew and a gentile despite what my Uncle Max says. We're talking here about exclusive clubs that serve no good purpose; they exist only to form barriers, trade commercially on human misery, and provide additional differences amongst people so they can further rationalize their natural distrust and aggression.

Woody Allen is a writer, actor, and film director. This article appeared in Tikkun, *January/February 1990.*

After all, you know by ten years old there's nothing bloodier or more phony than the world's religious history. What could be more awful than, say, Protestant versus Catholic in Northern Ireland? Or the late Ayatollah? Or the expensive cost of tickets to my local synagogue so my parents can pray on the high holidays? (In the end they could only afford to be seated downstairs, not in the main room, and the service was piped in to them. The smart money sat ringside, of course.) Is there anything uglier than families that don't want their children to marry loved ones because they're of the wrong religion? Or professional clergy whose pitch is as follows: "There is a God. Take my word for it. And I pretty much know what He wants and how to get on with Him and I'll try to help you to get and remain in His good graces, because that way your life won't be so fraught with terror. Of course, it's going to cost you a little for my time and stationery...."

Incidentally, I'm well aware that one day I may have to fight because I'm a Jew, or even die because of it, and no amount of professed apathy to religion will save me. On the other hand, those who say they want to kill me because I'm Jewish would find other reasons if I were not Jewish. I mean, think if there were no Jews or Catholics, or if everyone were white or German or American, if the earth was one country, one color; then endless new, creative rationalizations would emerge to kill "other people"—the left-handed, those who prefer vanilla to strawberry, all baritones, any person who wears saddle shoes.

So what was my point before I digressed? Oh—do I really want to contribute to a magazine that subtly helps promulgate phony and harmful differences? (Here I must say that *Tikkun* appears to me as a generally wonderful journal—politically astute, insightful, and courageously correct on the Israeli–Palestinian issue.)

I experienced this type of ambivalence before when a group wanted me to front and raise money for the establishment of a strong pro-Israel political action committee. I don't approve of PACs, but I've always been a big rooter for Israel. I agonized over the decision and in the end I did front the PAC and helped them raise money and get going. Then, after they were off and running, I quietly slipped out. This was the compromise I made which I've never regretted. Still, I'd be happier contributing to *Tikkun* if it had a different line, or no line, under the title. After all, what if other magazines felt the need to employ their own religious perspectives? You might have: *Field and Stream: A Catholic Critique of Fishing and Hunting.* This month: "Angling for Salmon as You Baptize."

I have always preferred women to men. This goes back to the Old Testament where the ladies have it all over their cowering, pious counterparts. Eve knew the consequences when she ate the apple. Adam would have been content to just follow orders and live on like a mindless sybarite. But Eve knew it was better to acquire knowledge even if it meant grasping her mortality with all its accompanying anxiety. I'm personally glad men and women run to cover up their nakedness. It makes undressing someone much more exciting. And with the necessity of people having to earn their livings by the sweat of their brows we have a much more interesting and creative world. Much more fascinating than the sterile Garden of Eden which I always picture existing in the soft-focus glow of a beer commercial.

I also had a crush on Lot's wife. When she looked back at the destruction of Sodom and Gomorrah she knew she was disobeying God. But she did it anyway. And she knew what a cruel, vindictive character He was. So it must have been very important to her to look back. But why? To see what? Well, I think to see her lover. The man she was having an extramarital affair with. And wouldn't you if you were married to Lot? This self-righteous bore, this paragon of virtue in a corrupt, swinging city. Can you imagine life with this dullard? Living only to please God. Resisting all the temptations that made Sodom and Gomorrah pulsate with vitality. The one good man in the city. Indeed. Of course she was making it with someone else. But who? Some used-idol salesman? Who knows? But I like to think she felt passion for a human being while Lot felt it only for the deep, pontificating voice of the creator of the universe. So naturally she was crushed when they had to leave town in a hurry. And as God destroyed all the bars and broke up all the poker games and the sinners went up in smoke, and as Lot tiptoed for the border, holding the skirts of his robes high to avoid tripping, Mrs. Lot turned to see her beloved *cinque à sept* one more time and that's when unfortunately the Almighty, in His infinite forgiveness, turned her into a seasoning.

So that leaves Job's wife. My favorite woman in all of literature. Because when her cringing, put-upon husband asked the Lord, "Why me?" and the Lord told him to shut up and mind his own business and that he shouldn't even dare ask, Job accepted it, but the Missus, already in the earth at that point, had previously scored with a quotable line of unusual dignity and one that Job would have been far too obsequious to come up with: "Curse God and die" was the way she put it. And I loved her for it because she was too much of her own person to let herself be shamelessly abused by some vain and sadistic Holy Spirit.

I was amazed at how many intellectuals took issue with me over a piece I wrote a while back for the *New York Times* saying I was against the practice of Israeli soldiers going door-to-door and randomly breaking the hands of Palestinians as a method of combating the intifada. I said also I was against the too-quick use of real bullets before other riot control methods were tried. I was for a more flexible attitude on negotiating land for peace. All things I felt to be not only more in keeping with Israel's high moral stature but also in its own best interest. I never doubted the correctness of my feelings and I expected all who read it to agree. Visions of a Nobel danced in my head and, in truth, I had even formulated the first part of my acceptance speech. Now, I have frequently been accused of being a self-hating Jew, and while it's true I am Jewish and I don't like myself very much, it's not because of my persuasion. The reasons lie in totally other areas—like the way I look when I get up in the morning, or that I can never read a road map. In retrospect, the fact that I did not win a peace prize but became an object of some derision was what I should have expected.

"How can you criticize a place you've never been to?" a cabbie asked me. I pointed out I'd never been many places whose politics I took issue with, like Cuba for instance. But this line of reasoning cut no ice.

"Who are you to speak up?" was a frequent question in my hate mail. I replied I was an American citizen and a human being, but neither of these affiliations carried enough weight with the outraged.

The most outlandish cut of all was from the Jewish Defense League, which voted me Pig of the Month. How they misunderstood me! If only they knew how close some of my inner rages have been to theirs. (In my movie *Manhattan*, for example, I suggested breaking up a Nazi rally not with anything the ACLU would approve, but with baseball bats.)

But it was the intellectuals, some of them close friends, who hated most of all that I had made my opinions public on such a touchy subject. And yet, despite all their evasions and circumlocutions, the central point seemed to me inescapable. Israel was not responding correctly to this new problem.

"The Arabs are guilty for the Middle East mess, the bloodshed, the terrorism, with no leader to even try to negotiate with," reasoned the typical thinker.

"True," I agreed, with Socratic simplicity.

"Victims of the Holocaust deserve a homeland, a place to be free and safe."

"Absolutely." I was totally in accord.

"We can't afford disunity. Israel is in a precarious situation." Here I began to feel uneasy, because we can afford disunity.

"Do you want the soldiers going door-to-door and breaking hands?" I asked, cutting to the kernel of my complaint.

"Of course not."

"So?"

"I'd still rather you didn't write that piece." Now I'd be fidgeting in my chair, waiting for a cogent rebuttal to the breaking of hands issue. "Besides," my opponent argued, "the *Times* prints only one side."

"But even the Israeli press—"

"You shouldn't have spoken out," he interrupted.

"Many Israelis agree," I said, "and moral issues apart, why hand the Arabs a needless propaganda victory?"

"Yes, yes, but still you shouldn't have said anything. I was disappointed in you." Much talk followed by both of us about the origins of Israel, the culpability of Arab terrorists, the fact that there's no one in charge of the enemy to negotiate with, but in the end it always came down to them saying, "You shouldn't have spoken up," and me saying, "But do you think they should randomly break hands?" and them adding, "Certainly not—but I'd still feel better if you had just not written that piece."

My mother was the final straw. She cut me out of her will and then tried to kill herself just to hasten my realization that I was getting no inheritance.

At fifteen I received as a gift a pair of cuff links with a William Steig cartoon on them. A man with a spear through his body was pictured and the accompanying caption read, "People are no damn good." A generalization, an oversimplification, and yet it was the only way I ever could get my mind around the Holocaust. Even at fifteen I used to read Anne Frank's line about people being basically good and place it on a par with Will Rogers's pandering nonsense, "I never met a man I didn't like."

The questions for me were not: How could a civilized people, and especially the people of Goethe and Mozart, do what they did to another people? And how could the world remain silent? Remain silent and indeed close their doors to millions who could have, with relative simplicity, been plucked from the jaws of agonizing death? At fifteen I felt I knew the answers. If you went with the Anne Frank idea or the Will Rogers line, I reasoned as an adolescent, of course the Nazi horrors became unfathomable. But if you paid more attention to the line on the cuff links, no matter how unpleasant that caption was to swallow, things were not so mysterious.

After all, I had read about all those supposedly wonderful neighbors throughout Europe who lived beside Jews lovingly and amiably. They shared laughter and fun and the same experiences I shared with my community and friends. And I read, also, how they turned their backs on the Jews instantly when it became the fashion and even looted their homes when they were left empty by sudden departure to the camps. This mystery that had confounded all my relatives since World War II was not such a puzzle if I understood that inside every heart lived the worm of self-preservation, of fear, greed, and an animal will to power. And the way I saw it, it was nondiscriminating. It abided in gentile or Jew, Black, white, Arab, European, or American. It was part of who we all were, and that the Holocaust could occur was not at all so strange. History had been filled with unending examples of equal bestiality, differing only cosmetically.

The real mystery that got me through my teen years was that every once in a while one found an act of astonishing decency and sacrifice. One heard of people who risked their lives and their family's lives to save lives of people they didn't even know. But these were the rare exceptions and in the end there were not enough humane acts to keep six million from being murdered.

I still own those cuff links. They're in a shoe box along with a lot of memorabilia from my teens. Recently I took them out and looked at them and all these thoughts returned to me. Perhaps I'm not quite as sure of all I was sure of at fifteen, but the waffling may come from just being middle-aged and not as virile. Certainly little has occurred since then to show me much different.

Letters

Maurice Friedman, Judy Greenwald, Janet Kauffman

To the Editor:

Why does Woody Allen imagine that it is possible to write or publish anything at all "without a limiting perspective" ("Random Reflections of a Second-Rate Mind," *Tikkun*, January/ February 1990)? What is specious about Woody Allen's argument is its simplistic either/or: either one writes for human beings in general, an altogether illusory and even undesirable goal, or one writes for "exclusive clubs that ... exist to form barriers, trade ... on human misery, and ... rationalize natural distrust and aggression." One who addresses everybody addresses nobody, and no one knows that better than Woody Allen himself, who cheerfully gives up addressing by far the largest part of the world's population (those who do not know English, those who have never been to Manhattan and don't care about it, those who are not educated and do not enjoy the subtle contortions of neurotics and hypochondriacs, those who are not Jewish and are not interested in things Jewish) in order to reach all the more effectively those who do know and are interested in these things!

The designation of a journal or group as Jewish (or Catholic, Protestant, Buddhist, or anything else), need not at all mean that group is exclusive. In my books I distinguish between what I call the "community of affinity," or "like-mindedness," and the "community of otherness." Only the former is exclusive, since its whole purpose is self-congratulation and self-protection.

The "community of otherness," in contrast, not only is ready to confirm the otherness and uniqueness of each of its members but also stands ready to enter into dialogue with every other "community of otherness." *Tikkun* has helped strengthen the tendency to make Judaism a community that is genuinely sensitive to the needs of others—and to reach out to others without repudiating its own historical roots and legacy. Far from creating artificial divisions, this self-affirmation is the best basis for connections with others.

In his article, Woody Allen characterizes *Tikkun* as "a generally wonderful journal—politically astute, insightful, and courageously correct on the Israeli-Palestinian issue." What does Woody Allen think is the deepest root of this stance that he admires if it is not its very Jewishness? Does Woody Allen imagine that there are general human values that are afforded us simply through the fact that we are human? Many primal peoples did not even regard other peoples as human beings. Ancient Athens, vaunted as the prototype of democracy, not only rested on a slave culture but held that all non-Greek peoples were "barbarians" and therefore slaves by nature. Only the Hebrew Bible in the ancient world postulated the equality of every person before God and held one law for the Israelite and the "stranger" alike Even "an eye for an eye and a tooth for a tooth" (Leviticus 24:20), which most Christians and many Jews in our culture imagine to be a description of the vengeful God of the "Old Testament," was actually one of the earliest statements of social democracy where each person, no matter how great or how insignificant, was equal before the law. As such it was the natural complement of the command to deal lovingly with they neighbor as one equal to yourself, that command which Jesus quoted from the same book of the Hebrew Bible (Leviticus 19:18) yet which most Christians imagine to be a statement of Christian love and forgiveness in contrast to "Old Testament" vengeance!

Although I would not express myself as he did, I share Woody Allen's concern about

Jewish-Arab relations in Israel and the repressive measures connected with the intifada. While a Senior Fulbright Lecturer at the Hebrew University of Jerusalem in 1987- 198, I wrote a six-page letter to the *Jerusalem Post* on that subject and on my return to America signed Michael Lerner's open letter to Shamir in the *New York Times* that caused the self-appointed representatives of "true" Jewish opinion in the United States to brand the signers as "traitors to the Jewish people"! Yet none of our criticisms will ever be of any value, Woody Allen, as long as first-rate minds such as yours fall into the either/or of polarization that destroys al chance of genuine dialogue!

Maurice Friedman
San Diego, California

To the Editor:

Woody Allen is mystified as to why *Tikkun,* a magazine devoted to Jewish perspectives, should exist. For many of us, Judaism and the Jewish community are sources of inspiration and wisdom that enrich our lives. We marry fellow Jews not because we're not allowed to marry non-Jews, but because we want to lead Jewish lives and have Jewish families.

I care what Woody Allen thinks about Jews and Judaism. Because he is such a good filmmaker, and because he makes films about Jews, Allen's images and characters define for many Americans—both Jews and non-Jews—what it is like to be Jewish in America.

Allen has a right and maybe even an artistic responsibility to portray people the way he sees them. I just wish he saw thinks differently. Or, more realistically—now that I've read his article—I wish that some creative, funny, talented filmmaker who had Jewish experiences more like my own would make, say, one movie about Jewish people. In this fantasy movie there might even be a likeable, smart, beautiful Jewish female character (something I've never seen in any of Allen's films). The plot might involve her rejecting an ugly, dumb, non-Jew for a handsome Jewish guy who doesn't wear glasses. None of the Jewish characters would whine. They be would comfortable with, not self-conscious about, their Jewishness. They might have fun, say, celebrating Jewish holidays. And they would have parents who imparted to them meaningful traditions, ethical values, and a proud sense of their history, and didn't fill them with guilt about everything. It would be diametrically opposed to—and just as unbalanced as—Woody Allen's movies.

Judi Greenwald
Silver Spring, Maryland

To the Editor:

Mr. Allen, you tell us that being Jewish has nothing to do with why you don't like yourself very much. Fine. But why, in every single movie you've produced in which you appear, do you portray yourself to some degree as a self-mocking, self-degrading Jew? You're lying to either yourself or your audience if you say that your "persuasion" has nothing to do with it. Forget the chance that you may one day have to fight or even die because you're a Jew. You can proclaim yourself a humanist al you want, but when you die you'll be memorialized as a Jewish director, Jewish producer, Jewish writer, Jewish comedian.

Janet Kaufman
Iowa City, Iowa   □

The Question of American Jewish Poetry

John Hollander

When I confront the question of what American Jewish poetry is, I find myself asking many other questions—questions about what such a question might mean. My colleague Harold Bloom, when asked once to discourse on American Jewish culture, said that the phrase reminded him of the history teacher's line about the Holy Roman Empire: that it was neither holy, nor Roman, nor an empire. What most people mean by Jewish American culture is just as peculiar. Certainly for all serious scholars, the very idea of *culture* is as problematic as the idea of Jewishness. And the ambiguities in both terms generate even more problems when they are conjoined. If by *culture* is meant something like what a Jewish American disciple of Matthew Arnold, such as Lionel Trilling, would have meant by it, then it involves a relation among texts, moral ideas, and the way in which they affect institutions. For most people it would mean, perhaps, Judaized versions of Balto-Slavic or Austro-Hungarian peasant cooking. For anthropologists and sociologists, for fundraisers and political analysts, "culture" would comprise very different areas of behavior, or as I should prefer to say, of life.

I would leave this discussion to social scientists and theorists of tradition were I not unsure how closely related my questions about American Jewish culture and American Jewish poetry might turn out to be. How poetry stands in relation to culture generally is itself a complex matter, and one not to be debated here. But in any case, were I not a poet and scholar, I should find this question far easier to contemplate. For example, in his remarkable book *Alone with America*, the poet and translator Richard Howard selected (in 1969) forty-one of his contemporaries—then roughly between thirty and forty-five years of age—and wrote extensive essays on their poetical works. (His judgments see to have borne up well under time, and nobody now would claim that, even with so considerable a number of poets, Howard had dipped very deeply into mediocrity.) Of his forty-one poets, eleven were Jewish—at least as far as the Law of Return would define them—and two more had Jewish fathers. Howard, himself a poet of considerable distinction, also is a Jew.

I am also by no means sure that a selection of forty American poets of the previous generation would have avoided so much mediocrity. But the list would have included poets ten or fifteen years older than those Howard selected—poets such as Elizabeth Bishop, Robert Lowell, Theodore Roethke, only two or three of whom would likely have been Jewish (Delmore Schwartz, Karl Shapiro, perhaps Muriel Rukeyser). It may be that historians some years hence will look back on the last thirty five years as a time in which Jewish American poetry flourished exceptionally.

But I am burdened by the American imaginative restraint that demands what Emerson called speaking in "hard words." The first hard question is: "Well, do these Jewish American poets write Jewish American poetry?" But that question is itself misleading. And matters are not made clearer by rephrasing it in the apparently sophisticated literary language—"Which of these poets writes

---

John Hollander has been awarded the Bolling and Levinson prizes for poetry and a MacArthur Fellowship. He is A. Bartlett Giamatti Professor English at Yale. This article appeared in Tikkun, *May/June 1988.*

poems with Jewish *content*?" or "Which poems reflect Jewish experience?" Such terms as these mean little to poets and perhaps even less to serious and inquiring literary critics. After all, can anything a Jew experiences—even apostasy—*not* be "Jewish experience"? In any case, the notion of "content" in poetry, the strangely Marxist concept of literature "reflecting" conditions of society, is a rather fumbling notion as far as the teaching and interpretation of literature are concerned. Moreover, poetry always takes concepts such as these and reinterprets them: If something serious and complex is meant by a poem "reflecting" world events, a true poet will reinvent that concept of reflection in each poem he or she writes, will create a new and unique form of distorting mirror. So, too, with the notion of "content": It usually is invoked only in contrast to a notion like "form." Can there be Jewish form and gentile content? Or vice versa? The notion that *form* is what makes a text a poem is a little more adequate than the one that claims that context makes it so, but not much more.

Consider a poem by Moses Ibn Ezra, written in Hebrew, in Spain around the year 1100. It is "about"—its content concerns, if one must—an apple. A contemporary American poet translates and adapts it—makes a new English poem of it. The poet is Jewish, yet there must be hundreds of gentile scholars who know more Hebrew than he does. He grafts his own epigram on to the original one. Is the fact that he writes a new poem by interpreting a traditional text a Jewish act? A Judaistic one? The original says something like this:

The Apple, in truth, God created only for the pleasure
of those who smell and touch it. I see how green and
red are conjoined in it: I see there the face of the
wan lover and the blushing beloved.

The modern poet takes only the conceit of the red and green from the Hebrew and, instead of the medieval Spanish-Jewish poet, who substituted his power of poetic meditation for any fool's ability to take a bite out of the fruit, he imagines an interpreter fully conscious of apples as symbolic and literal fruit at once:

O apple with which—as first fruit of desire—
Our hunger for significance is fed:
Around your globe pale grass borders on fire,
The lovesick green pursues the blushing red.

What is it that makes either of these two texts a poem? Is content a kind of liquor poured into a bottle called form? Is a gentile thought embodied, in the first instance, in the Hebrew language, the literary tongue but not the vernacular of medieval Jews? Modern criticism is properly unhappy with the notion of poetry's having themes or subjects, conceptions derived from composition classes and, when purportedly embraced by poems, only done so in a deep and systematic travesty of thematic discourse. A poem might be Christian, English romantic, or Emersonian American. I could imagine in the last instance, for example, identical stances being taken in the poem by an American Jewish and a gentile writer. Would only the former be writing a Jewish poem, with Jewish content?

It is clear why it might be better to ask, with respect, say, to the American Jewish poets in Howard's collection, "Can you tell from their poem that these poets are Jews? And, when you can, how does each poet's work reveal or conceal or ignore that fact in its own way?" For the essence of true poetry is originality of a mode of expression; that is, a poet will express or figure forth in language not only something totally unique in him/herself, but, as a kind of general metaphor for the holiness of human individuality, will thus reinvent expressing, or poetic telling. Now, many of the poets Howard discusses—Howard Nemerov, Theodore Weiss, Howard Moss, Kenneth Koch (save in what must be one of his more inspired moments in a long comic poem at which specially prepared *matzot* are employed in a visionary South American city as screen in windows against killer bees)—do not reveal much Jewish identity in their work. For some of them, the modernist stance of impersonality was so central to their notion of poetic writing that anything as intimate as their particular sense of "Jewish identity" was irrelevant to what they had to say. As irrelevant, for example, as their blood pressure. Of course, the intimacy associated with Jewish identity would seem to be a condition of certain kinds of exilic assimilation; but, in any case, poetic consciousness always internalizes, makes a peculiar kind of private matter, questions that ordinary language and political life hold to be public.

Of course, Irving Feldman—whose recent work has become stronger than ever—and Edward Field both reconsider and work over some of the ambience of urban American Yiddishkeit with irony and with warmth, but their ways of doing so are original and widely different from each other's. Allen Ginsberg's long—to me, I must confess, turgid—wail about the madness of his poor mother is called "Kaddish". Whether or not one admires this poem, one must recognize that it ignores the meaning—the nature, structure, liturgical function—of the prayer after which it takes its title. The litany of Aramaic predicates of sanctification, conjoined with Hebrew afterthoughts; the fact that its recitation by mourners is only one special occasion of its frequent reappearance throughout the synagogue service; the fact that the text on that occasion does not refer to its use as a prayer for mourners—as if *thereby* (i.e., by having those mourners, instead of lamenting in public, intone sanctifications of God's name) it were being deeply, rather than trivially, appropriate—of none of these facts is the poem's allusion in the title aware. It is as if the poem thought that "*kaddish*" meant only a public plaint or dirge of the bereaved. Furthermore, there is nothing in Ginsberg's "Kaddish" to suggest that he somehow knows all this and is deliberately making his "*kaddish*" his poetic revision of the prose, as it were, a public ritual—into metaphoic anti-sanctification: No matter how blasphemous that may sound, it might have made a true poem, and more truly interestedly Jewish in an antinomian way.

It certainly is true that, from the point of view of a naive notion of *content*, some writer who puts into rhyme sentimental childhood memories of Friday night *kiddush* ending with a cry of self-rebuke for having lapsed from the old ways, would be expressing Jewish content or whatever. But it wouldn't be poetry, and this is the heart of the problem. Most people think that a poem is anything printed with a jagged right-hand edge (the technical term for this, pregnant with appropriate moral overtones, is an "unjustified" right-hand margin, and although obviously no Calvinist, I relish it.) But that is just like saying, fifty years ago, that a poem was anything that rhymes. Free verse has replaced certain kinds of jingling rhymed verse as the mode in which amateurs write what they think are poems. What is Jewish or not Jewish about certain American poems is all tied up in the vexing problem of what is poetic or not poetic about them.

And so I would prefer to draw back for a moment and approach the question from another direction. Let me do so by citing a strange remark by one poet that is quoted as an epigraph to a poem by another one. Neither of the two poets was American. The remark is by the Russian symbolist poet, Marina Tsvetayeva: *Vcye payeti zhyidi*, "All poets are Jews." The poet was not Jewish, and we may surmise that she meant by it that all poets are like Jews in the Diaspora, alienated and in exile from something perhaps irrecoverable, nevertheless having to live with and in and among the rest of society. That is a touching and characteristically modern idea, although hardly as suggestive as the metaphoric extension of Jewish identity to stand for the condition of imaginative fullness and modified incapacity which Joyce or Proust, in very different ways, could evoke. What is interesting for me about her remark is that it is quoted as an epigraph to a profound and difficult poem by the great contemporary poet Paul Célan (born in Bukovina, he wrote in German, survived the Holocaust, and lived in Paris where he taught at the Sorbonne until his death in 1970). Célan is possibly the greatest poet since Rilke to write in German and he is probably also the major Jewish poet of his generation anywhere. As a Jewish poet, Célan takes back the phrase for the sake of a deeper Jewish significance. It is not merely that modern poets and Jews are outsiders, by nature itinerant no matter how locally rooted. It is more that both—and a gentile poet might be less likely to perceive this point—carry the burden of an absolutely inexplicable sense of their own identity and history.

Jewish identity is not so much a mystery as a problem: "People," religion, nationality, linguistic culture—to know anything of these terms, and of Jewish history, is to know how limited their conceptual usefulness really is. If poetry is like Jewishness, it is that both know very well what they are and though with a lot to say on nearly everything, they cannot easily explain *that*. Both poetry and Jewish identity are forever condemned to being misunderstood, to being wrongly interpreted. Clear, effective writing—whether reporting of facts, classifying and interpreting them, making suggestions, giving orders, framing instructions, making laws—aims at being understood. But "To be great," said Emerson, "is to be misunderstood," and even merely very good poetry shares this with greatness.

Poetry always seems to know that it cannot ever fully be understood. It certainly is possible to put a set of instructions for assembling something into rhyme, *viz.* "Turn part B the other way / And into it insert flap A," but that will not make it poetry. Or, in a contemporary equivalent of rhyming jingle, we could write out those instructions in short lines that do not come to the end of the page. Or, if one believes that poetry is not verse, but the expression of sincere feelings, one could drop upon one's toe a very heavy weight or a quantity of boiling water and become—without knowing how to write—a great poet. The major American poet of our age, Wallace Stevens, observed both that "[s]entimentality is a failure of feeling" and that "[r]ealism is a corruption of reality." Poetry is neither of these, but rather a matter of intense meaning, of having so much significance with respect to its own locale and the most general parts of life that it breeds a rereading and further rereading over the years. True poetry—rather than what I might call literature in verse—partakes of what Rabbi Ben Bag Bag said of Torah itself: "Turn it and turn it over again, for everything is in it."

But if intensity of meaning can lead to difficulty of reading, the openness of poetry to easy misconstrual has perhaps another source. Dante, in that remarkable little book about the dawning of his imaginative existence called *The New Life*, talks of what he calls a "*schermo della veritate*," a "screen for the truth." He is referring to an unnamed lady past whom he was looking, in a church full of people, at his secret muse, Beatrice d'Este. This lady sat in his line of sight. Everyone else believed him to have been looking at her, and he half-collaborated with this misprision of his intentions. He thought to make of the noble lady a screen for the truth, he says, and he thereafter wrote poems "to" and "about" her, all the while thinking of Beatrice. This story is about all poetry, really, which always uses its "subject" or "occasion" as "un schermo della veritate," a screen. And it may be very clouded, or very ornate; and each poet will not only construct his or her own screen, but virtually invents the materials and the mode of construction. Yet the result will always be that the *subjects* of poems are no more what they are "about" than their verse-forms are. This fact, too, makes difficult any discussion of Jewish subjects or contents in poetry. A remarkable comment on this question is made in a beautiful poem of Paul Célan's that anyone but a rabid Satmar Hasid or ultra-Orthodox rejectionist would call Jewish. It is titled "Hawdala" and starts out with a meditation on the braided, twisted candle used in the havdalah service which ushers out the

Sabbath on Saturday evenings. In an inadequate translation, it begins:

> On the one, the
> only
> thread, on it
> you spin—by it
> spun about, into the free, there,
> into the bound . . .

> [An dem einen, dem
> einzigen
> Faden, an ihm
> spinnst du—von ihm
> Umsponnener, ins Freihe, dahin,
> ins Gebundne]

This is a strange love poem reminding itself that the literal root meaning of the word "havdalah" is "division" or "separation," and that the spinning around of the twisted strand of light is of the essence of the kinds of twisting of literal meaning (the Greek word for it is "trope," or "turning") that is itself of the essence of poetry. This is hardly a traditional Judaistic observation to make, although in a general sense it is sort of midrash on the text, as it were, of the candle's braided structure, and of how this twisting bears light aloft.

One other way of reading the relation between the condition of being Jewish and that of being a poet has to do with a misunderstanding by others of one's own sense of history. As Yosef Hayim Yerushalmi has shown in his fine study *Zahor: Jewish History and Jewish Memory*, the very notion of Jewish historiography is more or less a modern German one, whereas the internalization of the memory of a people in any individual's consciousness is very traditional indeed. The central metaphor of the Pesach haggadah might be said to reside in the notion that "*I* was there at the Exodus from Egypt." But such a trope is hardly historiographic (it is not even used, for example, to create a first-person narrative of What Happened That Night, etc.) Similarly, poetic history is *not* the literary history or the history of ideas that so many people think it must be. The stuff of tradition is braided into poetry with the stuff of what is often called experience, and every true poet has very complex relations with those who have preceded him or her. In one account of poetic tradition, the poets who have gone before are ancestors, direct family forebears. (Should one think of them now as one's people?) But more and more for me, the account in *Bereshit* about Jacob's wrestling match seems a central fable of poetry.

The man with whom Jacob wrestles by the ford of the river Jabbok—the text designates him merely as "*ish*," "some man"—who cripples Jacob's thigh in order to win; who asks to be released from Jacob's lock on himself because day is about to dawn (shades of Dracula!—even if, Rashi so anxiously hastens to assure us, because whoever or whatever it was had to go to his morning prayers); who, in exchange for being released, blesses him by giving him a new name—Israel (meaning "one who has struggle with "*El*"); and who, when asked *his* name, says that one must not ask such a question—this presence is, for any poet, a figure of his major precursors in poetic history, those great figures who have told all the great and important stories, who have been there first. The only strength one has to wrestle with is the power of one's own language. One always comes away from such a struggle with emotional sciatica from which one suffers until end of one's days. And one is blessed to receive a new name if one comes away victorious from any part of the struggle, but unlike our father Jacob's, it is a name that can be uttered no more than that of the ineffable *El* with whom the struggle has occurred.

The matter of a poet's language is very important. In the first place, it is very private: Stevens once wrote that "every poet's language is his own distinct tongue. He cannot speak the common language and continue to write poetry any more than he can think the common thought and continue to be a poet." How, then, could Jewish poetry be Judaistic in a common way? And how could a poet speak in a common Jewish language, even if his uncommon one, his own poetic word-hoard, were based on a tongue thought of as commonly Jewish? Part of what Stevens meant by the uncommonness of poetic language reflects another aspect of a matter considered earlier. Paul Célan's deeper understanding of Tsvetayeva's comparison of all poets to Jews would seem to say that all poets are in a kind of linguistic *galut*—they are members of a people dispersed and wandering in a realm of ordinary language, a world of the literal. But poets also are, in a way, an interpretive community, internally and eternally expounding and revising, individually working out a *gemara* or completion of the argument about what poetry really must be: a working out given to none of them truly to complete, but from which they are not free to desist.

But Jewish diaspora has always had the Hebrew language—or perhaps, as with the Alexandrians, just the memory of a Hebrew language—as a clew or thread to hold on to amid the mazes of exile. In medieval Spanish and German its constant seraphic presence lurked always in the spirit of the Hebrew letters, the adapted means of writing as well as in significant parts of the vocabulary. The poetic diaspora which affects all poets, though, has only an imaginary idea of a language of its own, and each poet must forge it anew from the common metal, or spin its new thread from the fibers picked out of common speech. Thus it is that the Jewish exilic poet can be seen to exhibit two modes of longing for estranged, original language.

For American poetry, in its way a kind of *gemara* of the history of poetry in the English language, there are other problems. The contemporary Israeli poet—Yehuda Amichai, or the late Dan Pagis, for example—can write in a modern Hebrew that is still the biblical language. A poet whose language is English, whose wrestling grips are English hammer-locks and chanceries, has the English Bible built into the heart not only of the diction and syntax, but also the poetics of his language. The English Bible is a polemically Protestant translation of an orthodox Christian book called the Old Testament, which is itself a Christian interpretative translation of the Torah. A modern poet—and by this I suppose that I mean any poet from Alexandrian times on—is, if Greek, a wrestler with the shade of that fictional but very great author, Homer, if Jewish, with Homer's analogue, Moses, who figures as the author of the Pentateuch, and not merely as a character in Exodus.

Thus there is a profound and ever-present irony in a poet's writing "in" (would "out of" be better?) a language from whose literary tradition Torah is not, in fact, merely absent but rather present in such facinatingly distorted form. The cadences and grammatical constructions of the King James version, the shadows of misunderstanding lurking in the archaic meanings of words that have since undergone semantic change, are always singing an undersong in our language, from Milton through Whitman and in subsequent re-echoings. A British or American poet can engage the fabric of scripture in English or even in Latin and still be working in commonly uncommon ways. And to intensify the Latin presence in English by allusion or quotation has the same touch of the natural that moving into extended Hebrew phrases or clauses does in Yiddish. In any case, the English Bible has a strange power for the poet. For example, the way in which the King James Bible translates the grammar of the construct state of the Hebrew tends to create, in the language of the translation, metaphors and even allegorical personifications, traces of fable and parable, which are absent from the original. The dark or shadowed valley—the *gei tsalmavet*—of Psalm 23 becomes that allegorical region, "the valley of the shadow of death" only in translation. But what *is*, for a poet, "the valley of the shadow of death"? Does some heroic figure called the Shadow of Death live there? Rule it? Did he, or she, or it move hills about to create it and then desert it? Did Death leave its shadow there for eternity? Or are the hills that cast the shadow themselves embodiments of death? Or what? This kind of prepositional phrase—the common form "the X of Y," ordinarily transparent becomes complex, opaque, and problematic in the language of poetry. The language of the King James Bible is poetic primarily because it is so richly ambiguous, forcing listeners and readers to interpret in order simply to construe. For a Jewish poet writing in English, then, the resonances of the English Bible are already full of complex fables.

But if poets are in some way exiled from some irrecoverable original language, and if diasporic Jewish poets are so in at least two ways, it must be said that all poets devote to the matter of their personal uncommon languages a most profound and absorbed attention. It is more than the care of a workman for his tools; for language is both material and implement at once. There is a dangerous power, close to magic, by which it molds its fictions, and, as an object of such devotion and attention, a dangerous iconicity, or image-like quality to it. Particularly for Judaic tradition this creates additional complications.

Poetry, as has been observed, lives in remarkably, almost supernaturally, meaningful language, gaining intensity of significance by consciously working with its own structure. Because of this fact, it can always seem poised on the brink of image-making, in the proscribed Judaic sense—though the figures here are of speech and thought rather than of clay or brass. But for the modern poet, older, previously employed poetic images and fictions have indeed become silent, impotent idols of mental brass. Modern poetry will not be content with the tropes and fables that long usage has turned to clarity. The poet must, if invoking them at all, twist them about into originality and thereby into poetic truth. First Isaiah's (2:4) trope for peace following war is one that almost every literate person used to know: "And they shall beat their swords into ploughshares, and their spears into pruninghooks." The poetic quality here—the way of being poetic peculiar to ancient Semitic literature—comes from its figures and from the way in which one serves to gloss, or revise, the preceding one (in this case it is not only a matter of intensification). But let us consider a more modern poet, using the same image. The Roman Virgil, talking of the twisting of peaceful civilization into the strict violence of warfare, writes (in the *Georgics*, I, 508) that unbending blades are forged from curved sickles; but this works in the peculiar way of Latin poetry, certain words are pushed up syntactically against others in the line to make an additional point. Virgil's *"et curvae rigidum falces conflantur in esenem"*—or, as I'll try to make in work in English, "From sickles curved unbending blades are formed"—says in effect that the curvature of sickles that causes the grain to bend as well during the mowing of peacetime is as nothing to the rigid inflexibilities of the straight swords of battle. The spirit of the Latin language itself makes the metaphor more than another instance of what may have been a Roman commonplace. It is this way of revising an old figure and making metaphor with it as if it had itself been a literal meaning that in part makes for poetic originality.

At this point, one thinks once again of what Tsvetayeva's remark must have meant to Paul Célan: that, among other things, every true poet is in a kind of diaspora in his own language. Célan, who in his later poetry had to invent new German words out of purely German materials, and based on analogies of purely German grammatical structure, probably grew up in a German rather than a Yiddish-speaking home. But he was keenly aware of a poet's distance even from the language with which he thinks to gauge all sorts of other distances. *Sprachgitter*—"the grid of language"—is the title of one of his books, and it evokes images of an infinite regress of Dantean poetic screens, and screens of screens. But all poets, even those without Célan's sense of living and writing in a post-apocalyptic time and space, know what exile inside one's own language might mean. For poetry doesn't *use* words in the way ordinary discourse does; rather it stands back from them, misuses them, plays with them as no grown-up who really *knew* the language would, notices funny things about them that only a nonnative speaker would. Poets know, with Emerson, that every word is a fossil poem, that the history of its meanings, changing over millennia by means of the tropes of metaphor and metonymy which characterize the stuff of poetry, is a kind of fable of transformation. For poetry, etymology is one of the great primal stories, to be told and retold on the occasion of a fresh look at any word. As a Jewish poet, I suppose that Haggadah rather than Halakha, fable and fiction rather than law, is most important to me in Judaic tradition. But as a poet I also note that the word halakha means a way, a going, a walking, and that, as in so many other languages, including English and Chinese, the basic word for ethical procedure on life's journey literally evokes a footpath. I suppose that a scholar might point out that the concern for the interpretative play of etymologies is deeply rooted in Judaic tradition; certainly, portions of the Pentateuch are studded with etymological wordplay, false-etymologies invoked as narrative devices, mysterious and unavowed puns, and so forth. But the poet of a passage in the Pentateuch had more wonder at his own language than did all his commentators.

Hebrew, some dialects of Aramaic, some of Alexandrian Greek, some versions of medieval Spanish and German—these have been the languages of Jewish literature. One might argue that modern German, the language of Kafka, Célan, Freud, Gershom Scholem, Martin Buber, Walter Benjamin, Leo Strauss, must be added to these. But we have as yet had no great Jewish literary culture in English. An American Jewish poet must make his or her own way, making American English his or her own. The first steps of this process always involve, for a young writer, purging one's style of cliché, of empty public gesture; and this entails, of course, the impossibility of, say, versifying rabbinically ordained sentiments. As a matter of fact, the poet's almost idolatrous relation to language cooperates with another more profound Judaic danger. For if Jewishness is to be identified solely with normative rabbinic religion—particularly as it has become sectarian since European modernity—then the poet's path is the road to *herem*, religious destruction.

Consider in this light the stern rabbinic admonition in one of my favorite midrashim on *Bereshit*—Genesis 1:1—which appears to have been directed against a Jewish Gnostic and poetic spirit. It starts out by pondering the significance of the fact that the story of the origination of everything and anything, the opening words of the Torah, begins not with *aleph*, the first letter of the alphabet, but with *bet*, the second one, in the word *be-reshit*. It asks: "Why was world created with a *bet*? Just as the *bet* is closed at the sides but open in front, so you are not permitted to investigate what is above and what is below, what is before and what is behind." One of the amusing things about this passage is that it gives what literary scholars would call an emblematic reading of the image of the letter *bet*, treating it momentarily as a hieroglyph or picture; not a picture of its original pictographic value—"*bet*" of course means "house," and the original Phoenician syllabic sign was derived from such a pictogram—but of an abstract picture of openness and closure. This reading in itself comes dangerously close to being an iconic pun, and therefore open to the charge of image-making. And yet, the forms and numerical values of the letters of the Hebrew alphabet were always exempted from such a prohibition. It is as if all the impulses that, in Greek, Roman, and Christian tradition, went toward the production of significant visual images of the human body, of symbolic objects and eventually landscapes, were, in Judaic tradition, reserved for the imagery of alphabetic letters. But my personal delight at this midrash quite apart, the rabbinic injunction not to inquire about what is above, what is beneath, what was before time and what will come hereafter is a *kherem*, a destructive ban, against the Imagination itself. For it is precisely those forbidden questions that the poet will always be asking and whose answers he or she must continually supply in the form of fable.

I suppose that what I have been saying implies that all poetry is in some way or another unofficial midrash, a revisionist commentary upon some kind of canonical text. At the very beginning of Western literary tradition, those texts were Homer and Torah, but the great poetry that followed them became part of the canon as well. It is not that great poetry is purely original and minor poetry derivative or allusive to prior poetry. Rather, it is, as all true poets and critics have always known, that great poetry is more original in its way of being derivative. Modernism in poetry—by which, in this instance, I mean romanticism—creates the great fiction that there is a fresh, unopened book called "Experience" that all genuine poetry will henceforth proceed to copy. But that book has itself become worn and dog-eared, and people who today ask honestly but naively to hear of how, say, American Jewish poetry reflects American Jewish experience are simply talking about an old book (dating back to the 1790s in English) without knowing it. The true text of the world is always fresh and always renewing itself. But its pages are as full of poems, pictures, stories, philosophies, laws, and songs as they are of mountains, rivers, railroads, cities, and histories. And all poetry is in some way a continuing midrash on such a book.

The great poet of the English language who almost literally avowed this point was the radical Protestant John Milton, himself enough of a Hebraist to know some midrash in the original *Paradise Lost* is so great a midrash on *Bereshit*, and so great a poem, that it remains authoritative whether one is Milton's kind of Protestant or not, and it remains so much part of nature for any true poet writing in English as the Sahara desert or the Mississippi. This is a truth that I myself came to see only in my mid-thirties, when, after having published three books of verse, I began to understand what poetry really was. But to extend this notion further, I would also suggest that a poet's work—and this may be the hardest notion to grasp—is also a midrash upon his or her language itself.

As long as that tongue is Hebrew, or even Yiddish or Ladino, there is nothing problematic about this assertion: Major Yiddish poetry, for example, will frequently call implicit attention to the various Hebraic, Germanic, or Slavic origins of the words in daily use by means of ironies implicit in deeply significant rhyming patterns. But what is an American poet to do? The English language itself, partly Germanic, partly Romance, veined with Latin and Greek special vocabularies, its writing system and early literature shaped by Christendom, its poetic history shaped by the gradual unfolding of the Protestant Reformation first in England and then in America, its great "rabbis" being Spenser and Shakespeare and Milton and Wordsworth and Emerson and Whitman, its character partaking for the Jewish poet of Hebrew and Aramaic and the Yiddish or Spanish or Arabic of daily life over the centuries all at once—the English language itself is as much the language of *galut*, but no more so, than the Greek *koine* of two thousand years ago, or the medieval French in which Rashi also wrote. I also should add modern Hebrew to this list: If it were not one of the languages of *galut*, of the diaspora, it would have undergone the same kinds of linguistic change that all languages do over two and a half millenia, and could be almost unrecognizably related to the Hebrew of the Pentateuch. The very fact of its having been so successfully but artificially resuscitated as a living vernacular has itself attested to the fact of the diaspora, to the interruption of its vernacular history by wave upon wave of conquest and exile. If this is tantamount to saying that modern Israel is still part of *galut*, than I am afraid it must be so. But it is, after all, diasporic language in which all modern poetry—whatever its linguistic or cultural environment—is written. That is why any American—or German, or Russian, or Israeli—Jewish poet must make his or her language his or her own by wandering into it while quite young, and perhaps getting lost in the forest of that language for many years.

It may be, then, that an American Jewish poet has to spend years becoming an American poet and learning what that can mean before being able, perhaps, to cope poetically with his or her own Jewishness, however problematic a notion *that* might be. This uncertain venture may even give the appearance of wandering away from Jewish identity—at least, as other people construe it—when for the poet it is evidence of just the opposite. For in a temporary or apprentice devotion to impersonality, the young poet learns how to be truthful about self in the only way that poetry can be, by being figurative, rather than shallowly literal about it. One must learn to construct and, what is just as hard, to believe in the good of those Dantean screens. So, if an American poet's Jewishness —whatever that might be—is somehow temporarily shelved, this shelving is done as part of something so deep and so intimate that it cannot pause to explain itself.

Thus, one cannot escape the fact that the history of great American poetry up through the present generation has been intimately involved with the history of revisionist American Protestantism; and the question of how Judaistic notions might be woven into such a tradition is profoundly difficult. The touching paradox inadvertently invoked by Emma Lazarus, the first American poet some of whose poems would reveal her to be Jewish, is interesting in this regard. Writing in 1882, she compared Jewish identity in diasporic nations to the *pi'el* form of the Hebrew verb: "Every student of the Hebrew language is aware that we have in the conjugation of our verbs a mode known as the *intensive voice*, which by means of an almost imperceptible modification of vowel points, intensifies the meaning of any primitive root. A similar significance seems to attach to the Jews themselves in connection with the people among whom they dwell. They are the intensive form of any nationality whose language and customs they adopt.... Influenced by the same causes, they represent the same results...." But alas, students of Jewish history will feel that this is a German Jew, and not an American one, talking. Emma Lazarus speaks more for the Sephardic and German immigrants of the 1840s and after than she does for the millions who came from Eastern Europe and whose families led the ways of life that would become the stuff of Jewish-American cliché. Also, Jews were no more the *pi'el* of American identity than were the immigrant Irish, or Italians, or Caribbeans, or West Africans, or Norwegians, or Poles. Her final sentence sounds more like Disraeli than anything else: "... but the deeper lights and shadows of their Oriental temperament throw their failings, as well as their virtues, into more prominent relief."

Still, I would adapt Emma Lazarus' remark by saying that poetry is, among other things, the *pi'el* of ordinary discourse. As for the rest of the matter, let it go. In any case, I don't think that an American Jewish poet can write Jewish poetry without thereby writing American poetry. And since, with regard to consciousness of being Jewish, it is useful to know what a commentator as well as a poet had in mind, I will end by quoting and briefly discussing a poem I wrote when some of these puzzles were especially vivid to me. To frame this ending, I can offer only a final word about beginnings.

My first book of poems, published when I was twenty-eight, had nothing of what normative Judaism would want to call Jewish content—save, perhaps, for a poem that took off from an aphorism of Martin Buber, and save for a sort of Yeatsian dramatic lyric, written for Orpah, Naomi's other daughter-in-law in the book of Ruth, who goes home to her own people and chooses not to enter biblical history. But when if finally came to giving the book a title, I felt the need for some kind of avowal of my ambivalence about publishing a book—that mixture of ambition and reticence that comes from having at least glimpsed what real poetry truly is, and wondering about one's chutzpah in trying to write it, while at the same time knowing that aiming lower wouldn't make the cost of the arrow worthwhile. A text from *Ecclesiastes* that I had always liked—"As the crackling of thorns under a pot, so is the laughter of a fool"—seemed appropriate here, but only through a midrash on it which said that "when all other woods are kindled, their sound does not travel far; but when thorns are kindled, their sound travels far," as though to say: We too are wood. With that epigraph, the book was entitled *A Crackling of Thorns*. But in another sense, midrash came through to me in my childhood, not from formal study (I was never anywhere near a yeshiva), but from the Pesach seder. Even in early childhood, I was made to grasp the fact that the annual scene of rejoicing and remembering was also the scene of interpretation. For me, that may have been an important poetic scene of instruction as well. Over the years I've returned to both the rhetorical form and the interpretive strategy of midrash from time to time.

I suppose that the American Jewish poet can be either blessed or cursed by whatever knowledge he or she has of Jewish history and tradition. I obviously believe in the power of the blessing, but it would be easy for any writer to be trapped in a slough of sentimentality or a homiletic bog. Literalness is the death of poetic imagination, and all groups in the cultural community that speak for Jewishness will always be very literal about what "Jewish experience" is, as will all groups that want to speak for "American experience." Both kinds of experience are for the poet momentary aspects of the protean body of being who one is, and the analogues between American and modern Jewish identity are interesting apart from the almost exponential complications resulting from a combination of the two. These complications of the varieties of experience remain to be explored by practical criticism and cultural history. Being no sort of historian, I have had to invent figures for the kind of Marrano existence that modern poets lead even when they do not seem to. Since such figures are borrowed and reinterpreted from the text of Jewish history, I cannot be sure whether any such figure makes a parable of modern poetic or modern Jewish existence. The invention below will have to speak and withhold, for itself. Some years ago I read of how Cecil Roth, studying the history of the Marranos in Spain, had earlier in this century encountered some ordinary Christian families in part of northern Portugal who burned a candle inside a crock or pitcher on Friday evenings. When he inquired about the significance of this act, he was told that nobody knew why, but that it had always been done their families. Years later, at the end of a long, avowedly Judaic and American poem—an allegorical quest that meditates on the colors of the spectrum and, at the same time, the seven lights of the lost menorah carried from Jerusalem to Rome—this same figure returned to me, and I to it. I was writing "Violet" (the color on my allegorical spectrum closest to black, to darkness, and to death), and thinking of the poet's eternal task of telling a certain kind of truth, at a time too late for such kinds of truth-telling:

How then can we now shape
Our last stanza, furnish
This chamber of codas?

Here in the pale tan of
The yet ungathered grain
There may be time to chant

The epic of whispers
In the light of a last
Candle that may be made

To outlast its waning
Wax, a frail flame shaking
In a simulacrum

Of respiration. Oh,
We shall carry it set
Down inside a pitcher

Out into the field, late
Wonderers errant in
Among the rich flowers.
Like a star reflected
In a cup of water,
It will light up no path:

Neither will it go out ... □

Circumcision: A Painful Case

Lisa Braver Moss

Ask ten Jews a simple question, the saying goes, and you'll get at least eleven answers. But ask the same ten what they think about circumcision and the choral response will be loud and clear: Jewish baby boys should be circumcised—period.

Indeed, Genesis 17 unequivocally states that we must circumcise our sons in order to fulfill Abraham's covenant with God. The uncircumcised Jew shall suffer the penalty of *karet*, which the rabbis understood to mean "excision at the hand of heaven from the community." *Karet* is also the punishment for such transgressions as idolatry, incest, adultery, and the desecration of the sabbath. According to the Talmud (*Shabbat* 137b) the very existence of heaven and earth depends on *brit milah* (the covenant of circumcision).

But most of us these days don't follow Halakha to the letter. Why do we strictly observe this one commandment while ignoring so many others? Probably because medicine, tradition, aesthetics, and psychology influence our decision to circumcise our sons. Very few of us practice *brit milah* solely to obey God's commandment.

Judaism requires that commandments be fulfilled with genuine spiritual intent, and *brit milah* is no exception. In his *Guide for the Perplexed*, Moses Maimonides says that one's decision to circumcise the male child should be based on faith alone. Yet one *mohel* estimates that only 10 percent of his clients request his services for *purely* religious reasons. (This doesn't take into account the large number of Jewish circumcisions done by physicians.) Given the gravity of the circumcision commandment and the overwhelming lack of commitment to the commandments on the part of most contemporary Jews, it makes sense to counter the procircumcision chorus and question our attitudes toward *brit milah* as Jews have practiced it through the ages.

The issue at hand is pain—pain, and what it means to be Jewish. I think it's safe to say that, deep into their eighth-day ritual festivities, most Jewish parents have their pride and sense of solidarity with tradition interrupted by the nagging question: "Why are we doing this?" Our tradition strictly forbids us from causing *tza-ar ba'alei khayyim*, pain to living things. The *Encyclopedia Judaica* points out that "even the necessary inflicting of pain is frowned upon as 'cruel'" in both halakhic and ethical rabbinic literature. Many of us have resolved the conflict between this Jewish principle and *brit milah* by believing that infants don't feel pain when they are circumcised.

The notion that infants don't feel pain has been an accepted medical view for hundreds of years. In the thirteenth century, Maimonides, a physician as well as a rabbi, wrote in regard to circumcision that "a child does not suffer as much pain as a grown-up man because his membrane is still soft and his imagination weak." As recently as the 1980s, premature infants were still undergoing major surgery with *no* anesthesia at some well-known U.S. hospitals.

But in September 1987, largely in response to lawsuits filed by parents whose infants had

---

Lisa Braver Moss is a freelance writer living in San Francisco. She has two young sons. This article appeared in Tikkun, *September/October 1990.*

undergone surgery without anesthesia, the American Academy of Pediatrics (AAP) published a formal statement challenging the assumption that infants differ from adults in their ability to feel pain. The statement recommends that anesthesia be used on every infant undergoing surgery, unless the infant is high-risk or "potentially unstable." According to Nance Cunningham Butler, an ethicist with Yale University's Program for Humanities in Medicine, safe anesthetic agents *are* available for use on infants in most situations; infants demonstrate the same responses to injury that adults do; and even premature infants have the physical capacity for memory and may suffer both short-term and long-term negative effects of early painful experiences. The AAP statement concludes:

> the decision to withhold [anesthesia] should be based on the same medical criteria used for older patients. The decision should not be based solely on the infant's age or perceived degree of cortical maturity.

Local anesthesia has been available for infant circumcisions since the 1970s. The dorsal penile nerve block, consisting of an injection of lidocaine at each side of the root of the penis, has been shown in medical studies to be a relatively safe and effective anesthetic agent for newborn circumcision. Although research about this procedure is still limited, the nerve block has been shown to reduce crying as well as changes in heart rate and blood pressure for most infants during circumcision. Infants who are given the nerve block also exhibit less behavioral distress during the twenty-four hours following the surgery.

One would think that the availability of the nerve block would be of great interest to the Jewish community. On the contrary, despite the fact that local anesthesia for circumcision is halakhically permissible, almost all Jewish circumcisions are still being done without it.

I have found it nearly as hard to generate a dialogue about anesthesia in the Jewish community as to question the practice of *brit milah* itself. And while I have managed to stir some interest in the subject among Jewish peers and leaders, pain relief is still seen largely as a nonissue. Bringing up the topic usually elicits responses ranging from the lighthearted and dismissive ("anesthesia might go to better use on me than on the infant") to the defensive ("I was circumcised without anesthesia and it certainly didn't do *me* any harm"). I sense an underlying anxiety that if we acknowledge infants' pain and discuss anesthesia, we may call the entire ritual into question. And that's taboo.

But suppose we found, after an evaluation of the pain that the ritual entails, that a Jewish argument *against* circumcision could be made. Judaism would not fall apart. The beauty of Halakha is that it has the capacity to recognize and integrate advances in empirical knowledge. Beyond this, the fact remains that most Jews feel themselves bound less by Halakha than by a vaguely defined commitment to be "ethical." But if my own experience is any indication, re-evaluating the ritual may actually strengthen Judaism; I am a far more committed Jew now than I was before I began to question *brit milah*.

Let's look at some common Jewish misconceptions about circumcision and pain:

• *Lack of crying indicates lack of pain.* It is often said that many infants don't even cry during circumcision. The medical explanation for this phenomenon is that these babies are experiencing neurogenic shock, that is, withdrawing into a state of diminished responsiveness in reaction to sudden, massive pain. It is ironic that the absence of crying is used as evidence that circumcision doesn't hurt.

• *History makes right.* It is also said that since circumcision has been practiced without anesthesia for thousands of years, it must be OK. Few of us today would use this reasoning to condone slavery, child abuse, or even the subordinate role of women throughout most of Jewish history.

• *It's the restraint, not the surgery.* Some say that infants are upset because they are held down, not because of the surgery itself. This is pure conjecture, but even if it could be proved, I fail to see how such a distinction justifies the withholding of anesthesia.

• *"I didn't undergo any great trauma."* Jewish men often point out that they were circumcised without anesthesia and they turned out fine. I suggest we cannot establish whether or not they turned out fine. We do not have a control group (an identical uncircumcised group to use for comparison).

• *Pain is part of life.* Some concede that the infant feels pain, but maintain that pain is part of life. Unfortunately, the infant will discover this soon enough even without circumcision. In any case, though pain is undeniably part of life, Halakha does *not* mandate pain as part of the circumcision.

• *Anesthesia is risky.* Some people confuse the risks of general anesthesia with the much smaller risks of local anesthesia. Though research on the subject is limited, complications due to the nerve block appear to be extremely rare.

• *Circumcision is over so quickly, it would be silly to give an anesthetic.* Many are unaware of the painful procedure the baby must undergo in addition to the cutting off of the foreskin. The *mohel* or physician must sever the membrane between the baby's foreskin and his glans, either by inserting a blade or probe all around the glans or by retracting the foreskin very hard. This procedure may well be as painful as the actual cutting. Some *mohels* do this manipulation before the ceremony begins, creating the impression that the procedure involves only the cutting of the foreskin. Circumcision involves more than this.

• *Mohels are so fast, anesthesia is unnecessary.* It is sometimes said that if a doctor does the operation, it may be "worth" using anesthesia, but if a *mohel* does it, it probably isn't (*mohels* are usually faster than doctors). I would argue that surgery is surgery, and that unless one is an accomplished yogi, surgery hurts. And unlike adults, infants do not understand that pain is temporary.

• *But they're given wine.* The ceremonial wine given to infants is sometimes mistaken for an anesthetic agent. It would be dangerous to give an infant enough alcohol to make him unaware of the surgery.

• *It's harder on the parents than on the baby.* While it is certainly important to examine the pressures on parents regarding *brit milah*, discussions of who suffers more at a bris only take the focus away from the obvious: The baby is suffering.

If we are circumcising our sons for reasons that are not purely religious, then circumcision is a medical procedure, and we ought to consider using anesthesia as an appropriate way to do surgery. If, on the other hand, we *are* circumcising our sons for purely religious reasons, we ought to consider using anesthesia as a logical way to protect living creatures from undue pain, as mandated by Jewish law.

Childbirth lore promotes the notion that parent-child bonding occurs just moments after birth. Such was not my experience with either of my sons. Especially the first time, it took me weeks to develop what I would consider a maternal instinct, and months to feel that I truly knew my child.

When my first son was circumcised, I cried not for the suffering of my infant, but because *I* felt bullied by this part of being Jewish. I felt my husband and I were failing our son, despite the fact that we were doing the "right" thing by Jewish standards and despite the fact that I wanted my son to be accepted as a Jew. I blamed myself for letting cultural and social factors affect a decision that I felt should be purely religious. My bond with my son was not yet strong enough for me to experience his suffering as primary and my own as secondary.

I'm sure some people do experience strong instant bonding with their newborns. But no matter how powerful the initial connection, it cannot be as powerful as the connection that develops over time; even the most loved and welcomed and "bonded-to" newborn is a stranger in the family compared to an older infant or child. Maimonides was well aware of this when he advocated circumcision on the eighth day:

The parents of a child that is just born take lightly matters concerning it, for up to that time the imaginative form that compels the parents to love it is not yet consolidated. For this imaginative form increases through habitual contact and grows with the growth of the child.... The love of the father and of the mother for the child when it has just been born is not like their love for it when it is one year old, and their love for it when it is one year old is not like their love when it is six years old.

Maimonides encourages us to take advantage of our natural indifference to our infants, for without this indifference, we might not be able to do what tradition demands.

But is it right from a Jewish point of view to do something to a "stranger" just because one would not feel comfortable doing it to a person one knows well? What about the commandment to love the stranger? According to Rabbi Herbert S. Goldstein, Professor of Homiletics at Yeshiva University, the rabbis interpreted this commandment as a warning "first of all not to pain or annoy him at all." Goldstein continues:

The Talmud mentions that the precept to love, or not to oppress, the strangers occurs thirty-six times in the Torah. The reason for this constantly repeated exhortation is ... that those who have been downtrodden frequently prove to be the worst oppressors when they acquire power over anyone.

Again, *brit milah* without anesthesia conflicts with Jewish principle.

The nerve block does not completely resolve the conflict between *brit milah* and the halakhic ban on the causing of pain. Circumcision is traumatic for an infant whether he is anesthetized or not. Until the wound heals over a few days after the surgery, the skin will be raw, nerve block or no. The injections themselves are painful. And anesthesia does not address the fact that, if nothing else, it is surely unpleasant and frightening for the baby to be held down against his will for the operation.

Why do I think the nerve block is so important? It is the best we have at present to lessen the pain of infant circumcision. But aside from this obvious reason, I believe using anesthesia will help us see *brit milah* for what it is—elective surgery on sentient beings. Only with this perspective can we enter into a fresh discussion not only of how, but of whether we should continue with this ancient ritual.

Letters

Thierrie Cook, Hannah Bat Miriam, Vanessa L. Ochs

To the Editor:

Circumcision is not just a Jewish question; it is fundamentaly about the rights of children, specifically the right of the child to be protected from traumatic pain and to an intact, fully functioning sexual organ. To make those fundamental human rights of less imporatance than Judaic tradition is to lose the very essence of Judaism; the sacredness and preciousness of life itself, especialy very young lives that need our protection from pain, trauma, and deprivation. Pain may occur in our lives. but it is a crime to inflict it, except to save a life.

To hear the age-old fallacy repeated by Rabbi Landes that circumcision, by diminishing the male's sexual feeling, thereby makes men more sexually humane is shockingly ludicrous! Rape and sexual abuse are not caused by overpowering sexual drive—they are caused by strong, sadistic rage toward women. Indeed, many rapists do not experience orgasm during an assault. Are circumcised American men also less sexually abusive toward their women? I am surprised that men are not outraged at being considered to have a "natural propensity" to rape. Sexual abuse is culturally and psychologically rooted and does not depend on the foreskin or lack thereof.

Unfortunately, there are traumatic effects from circumcision. We know that infants do feel pain. In certain psychotherapeutic situations, even adult men have relived the painful tauma of their circumcision—the memory is still there. When the memory is blocked, as it is in most men, the trauma manifests itself by *blocking awareness of infant pain*, i.e., creating a defensiveness vis-a-vis circumcision. This blocked awareness also creates doctors who continue to be blind to infant pain. And what about death and disfigurement as the result of circumcision? One Jewish woman has told me of at least ten cases of hemorrhaging, infection, and death from both, within her family and among her friends. There is also the disfigurement known as the "bent penis" in which too much skin is removed, pulling on the penis during erection. If one child risks death or disfigurement, circumcision should be forbidden according to Jewish law. Now is the time to re-examine this practice. Like many Jewish traditions, this too was adopted from another culture. Circumcision is actually antithetical to the supreme Judaic commandment to do no harm. There will be no harm in stopping it.

Thierrie Cook
El Cerrito, California

To the Editor:

There's a hidden but very deep anti-Jewish-male bias in the writing of most of those who wish to eliminate or radicaly transform the circumcision rite. Their basic supposition is that somehow the pain in that rite has lasting negative psychological consequences. To make this point persuasive, one has to assume that in some way, Jewish men who have been subjected to circumcision are less psychologically sound or healthy than those non-Jewish men who did not undergo cirucumcision. If there is no such distinction psychologically, then there can be no grounds for arguing that circumcision has lasting negative consequences. So the anti-circumcision crowd has to assume that somehow Jewish men are in less healthy psychological shape than non-Jewish men.

This, of course, is what the anti-Semites throughout the ages have been saying about Jewish men. It would be intriguing to speculate on what constellation of forces—assimilation, feminism, humanistic psychology?—now makes it possible for some Jewish women to join in the chorus of Jewish-male bashing. Whatever it is, I think it is fundamentally misguided. The fact is that throughout much of history Jewish men have been less violent, less oppressive, and more sensitive to others than many of the men in the cultures around us. I don't attribute that to circumcision or to any essential feature of the Jewish psyche—but I at least must recognize that circumcision did not make these Jewish men more damaged than the men around them. I doubt, in fact, that it would be possible to establish in any rigorous way what precisely the lasting consequences of circumcision really are. But I find it preposterous to assume, as many anti-circumcision women do, that it is simply obvious that the infliction of this amount of pain has lasting negative effects. Rather, I suspect that many of these Jewish women are, in some covert way, doing their best now to inflict pain on Jewish men by suggesting that some terrible and lasting damage has been done to their psyches.

Hannah Bat Miriam
Jerusalem

To the Editor:

Lisa Braver Moss asks why Jews who don't feel bound by Halakha do, on occasion, treat the business of strict, tradititonal observance with utmost concern. How come moderate and nonobservant Jews turn *frum* [observant] at birth and death? I figure the explanation most often delivered from the pulpits is this: that at remarkable rites of passage, we are moved to affirm our continuity with the Jewish people. And if we won't embrace continuity with the Jewish people of the land of Canaan and Babylonia, then at least we can hook up with the particular *mishpoche* we trace back to Montreal, or the Lower East Side, or Russia. "This is what our people do, and have always done. This is what it means to be Jewish."

This may have been the logic that convinced "thirysomething"'s Michael Steadman—the quintessential unaffiliated Jew—to circumcise his infant son. Ancestor worship, aside from being a source of strength and identity, makes for a cozy, pull-at-the-heartsrings TV moment, drawing in guest stars of the older generation to personify "roots".

But in real life? I think birth and death frighten us out of our shoes. Somehow, we have to tame our amazement at them. Neil Gilman puts it this way in Sacred Fragments: "Whenever we are overwhelmed by natural events and feel powerless to control our destinies, we intuitively seek some device that we believe will enable us to regain control and bend nature to our will."

Does fear truly turn us into bona-fide short-term believers? Do we really believe that a nod to God will increase our good luck? We couldn't be that dopey. OK—the rituals of birth and death, if observed traditionally, can be a Jewish version of crossed fingers. We get out the powerful magic of our people to usher us through the threatening thresholds. Call it superstition, call it paganism. Still, I don't think we believe some hocus pocus we perform can coerce God into giving us what we want.

We who reach out for amulets and ceremonies that will protect and keep a newborn life—and we who structure our funerals and our mourning according to tradition—are reaching for assurance. Everything we can do for our newborns seems insufficient to protect them from their fragility. It's not enought to have engaged the best obstetrician in the most well-equipped hospital and the most respected pediatrician, or to have purchased the crib which has been sanctioned by safety research. Even keeping a cribside vigil to make sure the baby is still breathing is not enough. Our powerlessness is overwhelming. By turning to ancient ritual we turn wisely to a road map to safety. The ceremony steadies us, and we regain some control.

Vanessa L. Ochs
Madision, New Jersey □

"thirtysomething" and Judaism

Michael Lerner

In the fall premiere of "thirtysomething," the show's hero, up-and-coming advertising mogul Michael Steadman, a mostly assimilated Jew, and his non-Jewish wife Hope must decide whether to have a *brit milah* (circumcision) ceremony for their newborn son. While Michael does his best to avoid the issue, Hope insists that if their child is going to be raised as a Jew then both son and father should know what that means. Michael vacillates, but eventually opts for a ritual ceremony on the grounds that he doesn't want to break the chain of the generations linking father to son from time immemorial. His ambivalence and internalized anti-Semitism are so deftly scripted that most viewers probably missed how empty Steadman's reasoning turned out to be.

"thirtysomething" is such a refreshing change from the usual TV pabulum, so psychologically sophisticated and nuanced, that it almost seems a crime to find fault with the details of its scripts. After all, one might argue, "thirtysomething"'s major impact is to legitimate a style of emotionally honest discourse normally absent on prime time television, and this it does admirably. For this alone, we'll continue to urge others to watch the show.

But precisely because we have respect for the crew that has put this television show together, we feel all the more upset with the show's presentation of Jews. And the failures in this realm raise some deeper questions that face everyone who attempts to write for television or the movies.

We have yet to see a single portrayal on national television of a Jew who has some good reason other than family tradition for holding on to Judaism. In a key scene, Steadman has an edifying fantasy that his son chooses football over a thirteenth birthday party and recognizes that something has been lost by missing bar mitzvah. But what, exactly, he can't say.

Ethnicity and cultural identity are likely to be "in" for a while in America—a trend that at least in part reflects the growing ethnic diversity of the American population. In fact, *Tikkun* itself may be one of the beneficiaries, as more Americans realize that speaking "as a Jew" need not relegate one to the cultural or political backwaters. That the mainstream press continually quotes *Tikkun*'s reflections, not just on Jewish life and Israel, but on wider political and cultural issues, is a happy sign that Jewish interests no longer automatically marginalize intellectuals, writers, or artists (though being "too Jewish" remains a term of disparagement in some liberal, progressive, and Left circles).

But what is the *content* and *meaning* of being Jewish? It apparently never occurred to the writers of "thirtysomething" that generations of martyrs died to keep Judaism alive precisely because there was "a there there," a message and a meaning. If Jewishness amounts to little more than circumcision, a bat or bar mitzvah party after a child has memorized a Torah reading that (s)he finds largely incomprehensible, some gifts for Chanukah, and a family meal at Passover, it will remain very difficult to convince friends or partners less sympathetic than Hope Steadman that there is much worth preserving. Much as we love our ancestors, many Jews respect the tradition not simply because it belonged to our ancestors, but because it says something that commands our attention.

This editorial appeared in Tikkun, *November/December 1990.*

In its simplest form, that content is embodied in the Sh'ma prayer. "Hear O Israel, YHVH (the force in the universe that makes possible human liberation and a breaking of the bonds of all the various forms of slavery) is Eloheynu (the creator and of the universe, the organizer of the processes of nature), YHVH is one (that is, the totality of all being and all reality)."

The governing force of the universe is the force that makes for the possibility of human liberation. Moreover, because we have benefited from the workings of that power in history (that is, we have gone from slavery in Egypt to self-governing freedom), we are under an obligation to testify to the possibility of human liberation from every form of slavery. Our religion embodies the memory of that struggle and witnesses the possibility of liberation. The weekly observance of Shabbat, the seasonal holidays, the prayers are all built around retelling the story and reminding us of its lessons.

Understanding Judaism in these terms may also help explain why many Jews were unable to make a compromise with Jesus and the early Christians. When Christianity first appeared, Jews were mounting a massive struggle against the Roman imperialists who dominated our land and who even tried to redefine reality by renaming our land "Palestine." Our struggle with the imperialists was in part rooted in a religious notion that the cruelty and moral depravity of Roman rule were an abomination we had to combat even though we were relatively powerless. To the Jews engaged in this mortal combat, the Christian cult was one of several messianic or mystical movements that diverted energy from the struggle. "My kingdom is not of this world," and "Render unto Caesar what is Caesar's and unto God what is God's" may have had a special or more restrictive meaning to Jesus, but to many Jews these words shifted the focus *away* from the confrontation with Roman imperialism and toward more otherworldly concerns. Jewish reluctance to celebrate Christmas has certainly been overlaid with other meanings arising from the long history of Christian persecution and forced conversion of Jews. But this reluctance originally issued from a refusal to recognize anyone as messiah who did not actually bring peace on earth and did not engage in the this-worldly struggle against slavery in all its guises. When assimilated Jews wonder to what extent they ought to participate in Christmas, they often neglect to ask themselves about the degree to which Jewish existence is committed to the notion that the world has *not yet been redeemed*, that *the Messiah has not yet come*, and that consequently our task is to remind the world to stop celebrating what is and start fighting for what *ought to be.*

Can anyone blame the writers of "thirtysomething" for not knowing or understanding this message? Most American Jews have had little contact with a Judaism that could articulate to itself this kind of truth in anything but the most abstract and cursory way. Even when the words are there in the tradition, how can anyone learn the words of the tradition when they are presented in ways that suggest that the speaker doesn't take the message seriously? The most noble words in our tradition are stated when the most Jews are in synagogue: just before Yizkor (the memorial service for the dead) on Yom Kippur. On that occasion we read the chapter of the Book of Isaiah in which the prophet denounces the Jews assembled for their own Yom Kippur fast. "Is this not the fast that I have chosen," thunders Isaiah in the voice of God, "to feed the hungry, to clothe the naked, to stop oppression, to loose every yoke?" But people come to hear these words and return to a world in which they do not feed the hungry, clothe the naked, or fight against oppression. So the underlying message many young people get is that the prophet's stirring appeal—so central to the essence of Judaism that it has been placed in the liturgy at the moment it is most likely to be heard by the greatest number of Jews—is just a bunch of words that nobody takes seriously. In fact, all too many Jews conclude that the only things Judaism really takes seriously are Israel, Jewish survival, communal fundraising, and a set of ritual incantations to please a God that even most Jews who remain affiliated don't really believe in.

Today the Jewish community is so often stultified by deadening ritual, materialism, conformism, political conservatism, anti-intellectualism, Israel-is-always-right-ism, and Jews-are-better-than-everyone-else-ism that the revolutionary message of Torah can barely be discerned. Why should anyone be surprised if most teenagers find little to engage them in *that kind of a Judaism*? So, as soon as pressure from parents ends (once the bar or bat mitzvah has happened), most of these youngsters flee from any association with Jewish learning. And when they become adults, confronted with the choice of how Jewish they want to be, they can only base that choice on the knowledge of Judaism they acquired till they were thirteen. It is scarcely astonishing that they find it difficult to know why to stay Jewish. They may feel loyalty to parents, or a stubborn refusal to give Hitler a posthumous victory through total assimilation. But these largely symbolic loyalties will not serve to explain to a potential spouse why one wants to raise one's children in a Jewish way, or why one wants to have a Jewish home, if the tradition being passed on has been reduced to a set of ritual, Hebrew prayers that are largely unintelligible to most American Jews. While an older generation could compensate for its lack of attachment to Judaism itself by substituting blind loyalty to Israel, Holocaust memorials, fundraising, and a general ethnic chauvinism that often manifested itself as goyim-bashing, these are unlikely to work to hold future generations in the fold.

Michael Steadman (and the writers and producers of "thirtysomething") might argue here—as those in the media often do—that they are merely describing reality. They didn't create it, so why condemn the messenger? Yet every so-called neutral description is always a selection from reality. And when the television show that most accurately reflects the generation of people touched most deeply by the social change movements of the sixties and seventies makes *its* selections, we want to reflect on what the consequences of those choices might be.

We can see the problem more clearly if we also notice the way that "thirtysomething" represents and misrepresents the legacy of the sixties. Just as the underlying message of Judaism gets trivialized in the "thirtysomething" world, so too the political messages of progressive social change are routinely diluted and misunderstood. Moments of touching nostalgia for the sixties are vitiated by a general cynicism about that past and about anyone seriously committed to a "cause." Though some other characters still have some attachment to progressive political ideals, Michael looks on with the knowing cynicism of having to face "reality," viz. the complexities of making a living. "thirtysomething" manages to depict as neurotic, infantile, self-serving, or narcissistic virtually all those who try to blend their ideals with their attempts to make a living. It never occurs to the writers of "thirtysomething" that there are hundreds of thousands of people (many of them readers of *Tikkun*) who remain committed to the best ideals of the sixties, who do their best to consciously embody those ideals in their work, and whose compromises with the demands of the capitalist marketplace are fraught with the tension that inevitably arises in the lives of morally sensitive human beings. Many of the survivors of the sixties and seventies are now raising families, trying to find economic security, and even enjoying family, good food, sex life, play, and humor. But this doesn't make them one whit less morally pure or less committed to the values of the past. Though there may not be any prominent political movement for them to identify with (given the collapse of any coherent and psychologically sophisticated Left) they have not abandoned their values. In fact, they remain a potent political force—and television for the past two decades has been convincing them that they really don't exist, that no one is like them, that only weirdos still hold on to a progressive vision, and that they'd be smarter to be like Michael Steadman and put most of their energy into having and holding a good job and raising their children.

Just as "thirtysomething" underplays and discounts the idealism that has shaped the generation that is its audience, so it has also missed the emergence of a Jewish renewal movement that has lent considerable depth and vitality to Jewish life in the past twenty years, a movement that finds expression in *Tikkun* and that has helped make us one of the largest circulation independent Jewish magazines in the U.S. Growing numbers of Jews have rejected both the conservative spiritual deadness of the organized Jewish community and the equally dead-end route of assimilation. Ironically, Philadelphia, where "thirtysomething" is set, is one of the powerful centers of our renewal movement.

The problem, then, is that "thirtysomething" tells the truth about only one part of reality: it ignores those who have retained a coherent vision of the good. And by ignoring them, it helps create the reality that it claims to be merely describing. It reflects back to the viewer a world in which Judaism has been emptied of content and daily life has been emptied of political possibility. And each of us, looking at this picture, has the cynical and despairing part of our psyches slightly strengthened, the hopeful and idealistic part slightly undermined. The alternative? "After all, you can't expect us to become advocates for some religious or political orientation," television and movie writers will piously insist in response. Of course not. The alternative is to air the coherent voice of someone who is not portrayed as neurotic or irrelevant, someone who can articulate the vision of those of us who remain committed to Judaism and/or of those who remain committed to progressive politics. Allow that voice to be one of the many that get presented. Until that happens, "thirtysomething" will continue to reinforce and reflect TV's spiritual and political vacuity rather than transcend it. □

In the Coffee Shoppe

Aron Krich

Daughters of Israel Home

Enter a zone of silence and abandonment,
A rubber atmosphere of tips of canes,
Of walkers hesitating like funambulists
In the middle of the wire. And my mother
Who marched 5th Avenue against the Nam
Is pushed around like a paraplegic vet.
And wheeling her as she me in my pram,
We proceed to the kindness of the Shoppe,
Two scoops with maggot sprinkles on the top.
And though she sits like a Hadassah lady
At a lunch, my mother has become a mouth
As I was at the oral stage. "Food is love."
I feed her strawberry sundae from a spoon.
She tries to eat the paper napkin too.

VI. Judaism

A Question of Boundaries: Toward a Jewish Feminist Theology of Self and Others

Rachel Adler

K'nai l'kha chaver: This teaches that a person should set himself a companion, to eat with him, drink with him, study Bible with him, study Mishna with him, sleep with him, and reveal to him all his secrets, secrets of Torah and secrets of worldly things—Avot d'Rabbi Natan 8.

This rabbinic text describes a distinctively Jewish kind of intimacy: the study-companion relationship. The *chaverim* do not simply study Bible and Mishna; the very structure of their relationship and the nature of its boundaries present a Jewish model for the relation between the self and the other. In this relationship, people experience each other as whole, rather than as fragmented, beings. Companionship is simultaneously physical, emotional, intellectual, and spiritual.

Self and other are not sharply separate here. To be *chaverim* is to be neither fused nor counterposed, but to be juxtaposed. The root CH-B-R means to join together at the boundaries. The curtains of the tabernacle, for instance, are *chevrot isha el achotah*, "joined one to another" (Exod. 26: 3).

Boundaries define the shape and extent of an entity, and distinguish between what is inside and what is out. They maintain the integrity of the entity and keep it from dribbling out into everything else. Setting the boundaries of entities and formulating categories for them is the way we make sense of a vast and diverse world.

Some boundaries are barricades—chainlink fences guarded by Dobermans. Others are not primarily barriers but loci of interaction. A cell membrane, for example, is part of the living substance of the cell. It is the perimeter at which the cell conducts its interchanges with other cells—the contacts, the flowings in and out, which maintain its life within its environment. The boundary between self and other in our passage from *Avot d'Rabbi Natan* resembles this living, permeable boundary.

The boundary of *chaverim* requires two entities sufficiently alike to be capable of bonding; it presupposes an other who is experienced as akin to the self. In *From A Broken Web: Separation, Sexism, and Self*, feminist philosopher Catherine Keller contends that the notion of an other experienced as analogous and contiguous to the self is alien to Western philosophy. She asserts that since the time of Hegel, Western thinkers have understood boundaries as barriers that entities erect to protect their integrity in an invasive war of all against all. According to this formulation, opposition and subjugation are the means by which we make the world make sense. In other words, I can only be an I—a subject—by objectifying you and making you less significant than myself.

Keller and other feminist theorists argue that opposition and subjugation particularly characterize patriarchal modes of making boundaries and making sense. Consequently, in patriarchal societies

Rachel Adler lives in Los Angeles and has written extensively about women and Judaism. This article appeared in Tikkun, *May/June 1991.*

the structure of thought itself predisposes us to split and separate rather than to perceive interconnections and interdependencies. Susan Griffin describes how patriarchal category-making carves the universe into dualisms. At the heart of this dichotomous system is a definition of normative humanity as maleness and irreducible otherness as femaleness. And that is how woman comes to be the first stranger.

By exclusively claiming normative humanity, patriarchal man denies that there exists among all the members of his species a human similarity in whose context human difference takes on meaning. He splits himself off, alienating himself from the females of his kind, and an infinite series of dualisms proceeds from this splitting. In each dualism, the superior term is associated with patriarchal man while the inferior and dependent term is identified with woman. Heaven and earth, light and darkness, cleanliness and filth, good and evil, freedom and slavery, sufficiency and lack, all are made to mirror the estrangement of patriarchal man from the woman he has cast out. These dichotomies are then used to justify the subordination and exclusion of all who are consigned to the feminized category of the other.

Keller charges that monotheism is a product of this patriarchal splitting. Pained by the fragmentation of self and world that he has engineered, patriarchal man longs for unity. But he conceives of it not as the reunion of all he has driven apart, but as the conquest and incorporation of the realms of the other. The god of the patriarchal philosophers, omnipotent, passionless, and utterly alone, is simply a projection of the patriarch's own desire for absolute self-sufficiency and self-control. This god serves both as a model and as a justification for all patriarchy's tyrannies and exclusions. The charges in Keller's critique can be substantiated, to varying degrees, by texts and events within all three monotheistic faiths. However, Judaism cannot be reduced to the misconceived monotheism Keller describes. Instead, I would like to argue that as Jews we have available to us a different way to define the relation between self and other: to reconstitute the objectified other as a subject; and to understand a subject as a self with permeable boundaries contiguous with the boundaries of neighbor-selves. This Torah of self and other, which we saw reflected in our text about the study-companions, grounds not only our capacity to be *chaverim* but our capacity to create *tzedek*, justice-as-righteousness. *Tzedek* is a justice far richer and more particularized than the abstracted, objective fairness of Western liberalism. Its goal is to embody the Torah of self and other in a social matrix that allows all human beings to flourish.

However, the one relationship that Jewish tradition has consistently refused to incorporate into this Torah of self and other is the relationship between women and men. Instead, Jewish tradition permits men to define themselves by objectifying women. In Halakha, in narrative, and in liturgical praxis, tradition has sought to construct impermeable boundaries to wall women out. Our text about the study-companions is a case in point. For the man who wrote the text and for the generations of men who learned it and transmitted it, such a relationship between women and men was inconceivable. This refusal to acknowledge the Jewish woman as subject has perpetuated a brokenness, an institutionalized estrangement of women from men in Judaism. We confront this estrangement as soon as we reach out to one another to be *chaverim*.

It is now essential that we claim and integrate the portion of Torah that has remained unfulfilled in the walling-out of Jewish women. As women have begun to describe and critique the social and linguistic structures that have objectified and marginalized them, they have recovered the vantage point of the subject. To be aware of oneself as objectified subject is to be conscious of oppression.

Because there is a Torah of self and other, Judaism possesses within itself the means of relieving the oppression of women. To refuse to integrate this Torah into our man-woman relationships is to claim that there is one kind of human relationship which need not be just, and one kind of human being who cannot be a subject or a *chaver*.

Where did we learn this Torah of self and other, and what do we know? We learned it from being the people other peoples knew as the *ivrim*, the ones from the other side of the river, the boundary-crossers. As boundary-crossers, *ivrim* are bridgers of worlds, makers of transition. The name *ivri* is not resonant of self-perception. It reflects the perspective of those native to this side of the river, those who are at home. Those who do not cross the boundaries may view the relocations of the *ivri* as transgressions against a fixed cosmic order, trespasses into the anomalous and the chaotic.

In our narratives, however, it is God who demands that Abraham and Sarah become *ivrim*. A people rooted in one place experience a God rooted in a particular place. A people that has known transience can experience the translocal nature of God. It is the revelation of a God who is present in every place that makes possible the moral universe of the covenant, where relatedness rather than location becomes the ground of ethics.

If our story about our beginnings as God's *ivrim* were not enough to give value to the project of boundary-crossing, our master-narrative about crossing the boundary from slavery into freedom, and about bridging the boundary between creature and creature in the transaction of covenant has done so. We have valorized these boundary-crossings in our tradition; they shape not only our memories of the past but also our actions in the present and our visions for the future. We are obligated to regard our liberation and our covenant not simply as legacies from our unique history as crossers-over, strangers and slaves, but as events that radically transform the meaning of boundaries in the world; they demonstrate the potential for all objectified others to be reconstituted as subjects similar to ourselves. There is nothing inevitable about this moral understanding of our communal identity. Our special liberation and covenant make equally powerful justifications for subjugation of the other. The admonition in Exodus 23: 9 warns us not to adopt this second interpretation. "You shall not oppress a stranger, for you know the feelings of the stranger, having yourselves been strangers in the land of Egypt." By itself, this commandment could be read as a directive to merge with strangers and to idolize in them the image of our own history as stranger. Instead, Torah demands that we extrapolate from our bond with the stranger to include familiar deviants within our own communities, with whom we may be more reluctant to identify:

> You shall not subvert the rights of the stranger or the fatherless; you shall not take a widow's garment in pawn. Remember that you were a slave in Egypt and that the Lord your God redeemed you from there; therefore do I enjoin you to observe this commandment.
> (Deut. 24: 17-18)

I mean to argue that the central narrative of Judaism thus embodies an implicit challenge to the polarized thought structures of patriarchies—even though patriarchal thinking is embedded in Judaism as it is in the rest of Western culture. This is not to claim that either ancient Israelites or rabbinic Jews had modern sensibilities for dealing with those defined as other. Such a contention would be both anachronistic and demonstrably false. I do claim, however, that the unfolding of the *ivri* identity and its experience of covenant locates at the core of Judaism an implicit challenge to an ethics of alienation and dualism that perceives the world outside its borders as threatening and chaotic. The Torah of self and other that we first encountered as *ivrim*, and later internalized through liberation, covenant, and prophetic admonition, erodes and must eventually obliterate the fixed, impermeable boundaries that define the world of patriarchal dualism. By recognizing a self in all others with a potential like our own for transformation, this Torah transforms the boundaries between self and other and deconstructs the justification for patriarchal boundaries. Contrast, for example, Aristotle's notion that slaves and barbarians had fixed natures suitable to their condition, and that these natures made them qualitatively different from Athenian gentlemen. The subjugation of these inferior beings is justified by their nature as objects—a moral dissimilarity from human beings with value that could not be changed or mitigated by more fortunate circumstances.

But having ourselves crossed the boundaries from slavery to freedom, from dependency to responsibility, from homelessness to home, from powerlessness to power, we know that people have a capacity for transformation. We cannot justify either our privilege or our virtue, such as it is, by arguing that some people are, by nature, flawed in character and intended for subjugation. Having crossed the boundaries Aristotle thought impassable, we are no longer adept at maintaining the impermeability required to keep the alien alien. Biblical narratives illustrate how, even when estrangement is most to our advantage, we are propelled across the boundary where the other lifts to us a human face.

That is why, with our legitimacy as inheritors hanging in the balance, the narrative compels us to follow Hagar and Ishmael through their painful wanderings in the wilderness and then requires us to witness their redemption. We are not spared Esau's anguished cry, "Have you but one blessing, Father? Bless me too, Father!" (Gen. 27: 38). At Nineveh, with the reluctant Jonah, we are forced to watch the moral renewal of an enemy nation and to understand that it too is precious in God's sight. We cannot even kill the archenemy Agag, King of Amalek, without hearing in his last utterance, not the demonic defiance that makes executions easy, but a human cry of fear and regret, "Ah, bitter death is at hand" (1 Sam. 15: 32).

It is not that the meanings liberation and covenant hold for Jews have rendered us incapable of injustices or atrocities. Rather, because liberation and covenant entail such flexible boundaries between self and other, it is more difficult for us to separate from the other sufficiently to inflict hurt without feeling reciprocal pain. Inability to wall out the other explains why the intifada has distressed Jews across the political and religious spectrum. It accounts for a common motif in both Israeli and diaspora novels: the depiction of Palestinians as mirrors or doubles of Jews.

It is important not to mistake this discomfort for an ethical response. It is a symptom of ethical dysfunction just as pain is a symptom of disease. Anguished hand-wringing over the terrible things we are doing is nothing more than a self-indulgent display of symptoms. The flexible boundary that enables us to sense our commonality with the other is the *ground* of justice in Judaism, but it is not justice. Justice is the reshaping of our actions and institutions to express this sense of commonality in our everyday life.

I have been saying that the obligation to do justice is derived relationally, and rests upon a prerequisite obligation to perceive a likeness to self in the other. Taken together, these obligations comprise a fundamental normative principle in Judaism. If this is so, however, why has Judaism consistently estranged and excluded its most intimate others—Jewish women? How shall we understand sacred texts that polarize and subordinate? How shall we determine what authority any text may claim to form our attitudes and to inform our actions?

What perpetuates this intimate injustice in Judaism is that in its deconstruction of dualistic, other-rejecting, patriarchal thought-structures, Judaism stops short and leaves in place the foundational construction—the otherness of woman. This constructed rift is embedded so deeply in our language, in our psyches, and in some of our texts that we reinforce the objectification and estrangement of women without even being conscious of it.

Man names himself *zakhar* in Hebrew, the creature with the male member. And it is perhaps more than coincidence or homophony that the *zakhar* is also the *zokher* and the *zakhur*, the rememberer and the remembered. In a patriarchy, the only memory is the male memory, because the only members are male members. They are the rememberers and the remembered, the recipients and transmitters of tradition, law, ritual, story, and experience. They are the righteous whose memory will be for a blessing and the teachers whose lips will move in the grave.

Zakhar names as his antithesis *nekeva,* the pierced one, the one whose boundaries are penetrated by the invading male. Even her name is held hostage to male memory. How she described herself to herself has been forgotten. *Nekeva* represents not only an objectification but a projection. In this naming, patriarchal man points at the other as the permeable one. He portrays himself as sealed and impenetrable.

We cannot be too surprised to discover that our texts have been marked by male memory and by the alienated, hierarchical relations of the patriarchal self with the other. The rabbis' dictum, *dibra Torah beleshon bnai adam*, "The Torah speaks in human language," implicitly acknowledges the limitations of context-dependent human language and human texts for conveying transcendent truths. There is, however, a very special kind of truth that is captured only in texts.

A text is a mirror. Once you have told a story about your experience, you have an image of it external to yourself into which you and others can look. This makes possible the process of critical reflection. I would like to reflect upon two texts about the origins of women and men that mirror two kinds of self–other relations and teach two different lessons.

The first is the Genesis 1 account commonly ascribed to the P (Priestly) author. In it God speaks in the plural as if out of a diverse and many faceted wholeness: *vay-yomer Elohim na'aseh adam betzalmenu kadmutenu.* "Let us make the human in our image, after our likeness." The gendered humanity thus created represent two varieties of a single species, collectively called *adam: U'vara et ha-adam betzalmo, betzelem elohim bara oto, zakhar u'nekeva bara otam.* "And God created the human in His image, in the image of God, He created it, male and female He created them."

This creation proceeds not by polarization but by differentiation within wholeness. A modern analogy would be the biological process of human development in which a zygote, a diverse wholeness which a sperm and an ovum have merged to create, differentiates into the various cells of a particular human being. Emphasis is placed upon similarities and kinships. The *tzelem*, the image, is a source of connection and continuity between creator and creation. The two varieties of *adam* embody diversity within similarity. Equally human, they share equally in the responsibilities and benefits of the natural world.

In contrast, the Genesis 2 account, generally assigned to the J (Jahwist) narrator, depicts creation as a process of opposition and partialization. Adam in this story is a male individual, and bears a curious resemblance to the motherless asocial resident of the state of nature posited by liberal political theory. He is a competent male adult, endowed with language and reason, engaged from the moment of his creation in the business of mastering nature. Human sociality is recognized as a necessity: *lo tov heyot ha'adam levado*, "It is not good for man to be alone," but the remedy for man's isolation is the creation of an oppositional other: *e'eseh lo ezer kenegdo*, "I will make him a helper who is his counter/part." (The word *kenegdo* carries dual senses of likeness and opposition which I have tried to convey with the translation counter/part.)

Woman in this story has no independent being. She is neither created (b-r-a) nor formed (y-tz-r) but constructed (b-n-h): *vaviven Adonai Elohim et ha tzela aher lakach min ha-adam vavavei el ha-adam.* "The Lord God built the rib into a woman and brought her to the man." A part of the man is separated off, constructed into woman, and handed back to him. He recognizes her neither as similar to himself nor as a different entity with its own boundary. Instead he claims her as a part of himself that he can reincorporate through fusion:

This time bone of my bone and flesh of my flesh ...
Hence a man leaves his father and mother and clings to
his woman and they become one flesh. (Gen. 2: 23-24)

Adam, in this narrative, is both gendered male and generic human. His maleness represents the original human condition, rather than one variety of it. Hence, there is no mention of the creation of maleness, as there is in Genesis 1. The text only alludes to Adam's gender identity as *ish*, man, in the wordplay that establishes *isha*, woman, as a derivative gender. Together they are *Ha'adam ve-ishto*, the human and his woman, for the text never recognizes her as *adam*. It designates her only as *isha*, a creature derived from *adam*, contrasted to him and possessed by him; a construction designed to meet his specifications.

How are we to characterize these two accounts, and what Torah may we learn from them? Genesis 1 may be taken as a description of the creation of humanity. It teaches about kinships, about the continuity of boundaries between God and humanity, and between the two varieties of humankind. Genesis 2 is best understood as an account of the creation of patriarchy. Its depiction of the patriarchs' inner experience—loneliness, and a sense of mutilation—and its account of the attempt to recover the banished other through fusion and incorporation are as perfectly convincing as its disastrous aftermath. An Eden founded upon a fantasy of obliterating the other is bound to be unstable.

Yet nothing in this text speaks to us with normative authority. There is no reason to conclude on the basis of the narrative that relations between men and women in subsequent Jewish societies must adhere to the patriarchal model. In fact Genesis 2 has never been an independent source of normative authority for Jews. The prescriptive language of legal obligation ("be fruitful and multiply") occurs not in Genesis 2 but in Genesis 1. Jewish tradition does not understand the curses that follow the eating of the forbidden fruit as literal prescriptions, although some antimodernist Christian sects read them this way. Hence, it has never been claimed that because the text says "by the sweat of your brow shall you get bread to eat," Jews ought not to use modern farm machinery or labor-saving devices. Similarly, while some Victorian clergymen cited "in pain shall you bear children" as a reason to forbid anesthesia in childbirth, no Jewish authority ever did so. By analogy then, there can be no prescriptive force in the admonition to Eve: "Your desire shall be for your husband and he shall rule over you." Consistency requires us to read the entire narrative as a description of how things came to be the way they are—in other words, as an etiology of the construction of patriarchy and its attendant hardships.

The two creation stories with their divergent accounts of object relations return us to the general question: How shall we determine what authority any text may have to form our attitudes and to inform our actions? Halakha, classical Jewish law, addresses this question by making certain texts repositories for generalized obligations, mitzvot *kollelot*. These are not meta-halachic principles; that is, they are not discourse about the project of Jewish law. They are, rather, intra-halakhic discourse. We might call them orienting mitzvot, because they point out the direction in which our normative perceptions and decisions ought to go. Orienting mitzvot are the most generally phrased, and hence the most dependent upon the particularities of context, of any Jewish obligations. What then orients the orienting mitvot? To determine what is right action or holy behavior for a Jew, we are obligated to begin by recollecting the story that tells us who we are: "Remember that you were a slave in Egypt and the Lord your God redeemed you from there" (Deut. 24:18). Deuteronomy appends this admonition to all its commandments about the welfare of vulnerable others, and to general exhortations to observe the laws of the covenant. A particular ethical orientation must characterize the behavior of a liberated and transformed people. This orientation forbids the oppression of others and urges us to recognize in them a capacity for liberation and transformation akin to our own. This is the principle that orients the content of the generalized mitzvot, and in the context of its flexible boundary with the other we must assess the ethical claims that other texts make upon us.

What implications follow for the boundary with the first Jewish other? Dorothy Sayers once asked, "If women are the opposite sex, then what is the neighboring sex?" By defining woman oppositionally as derivative *isha* or invaded *nekeva,* patriarchal texts refuse to acknowledge a shared reality. We could call this the reality of mutual interpenetration. Interpenetration, interconnectedness, and interdependency attest that not only do we inhabit a single context, but within that context we live deeply within one another's boundaries. The only way to in/habit, one must conclude, is to co/habit. The patriarchal fantasy of the impermeable self is a snare and a delusion. Human beings are profoundly interdependent. We begin life tiny and helpless, utterly dependent on others. We come to perceive ourselves as distinct and particular beings only through experiencing our impact upon others and their impact upon us. Intimacy is a survival need for our species. Babies who lack a caring other to bond with, even if they are fed and cleaned, die in alarming numbers from a syndrome known simply as "failure to thrive." From birth to death we coexist in a great network of others, bound to them by speech, by touch, by labors, quests, exchanges, and stories.

We are in truth no more separate from God than we are from one another. What makes us Jews is not that we subscribe to a dogma which holds that the world is controlled by a deity without needs or desires, upon whom no one and nothing has impact, or that this deity has revealed to us a fixed and objective law. What makes us Jews is that we frame our identities and our commitments by telling and retelling how we came to be *ivrim,* how God freed us from slavery and made a covenant with us. What makes us Jews is that we center our selfhood, both individual and collective, both male and female, around these memories, that we learn from them the living, permeable boundaries that make the other a neighbor and a partner rather than an opposite. When we apply this orientation to our man–woman relationships, then all Israel will indeed be *chaverim.* □

The Book of Ruth and Naomi

Marge Piercy

When you pick up the Tanakh and read
the Book of Ruth, it is a shock
how little it resembles memory.
It's concerned with inheritance,
lands, men's names, how women
must wiggle and wobble to live.

Yet women have kept it dear
for the beloved elder who
cherished Ruth, more friend than
daughter. Daughters leave. Ruth
brought even the baby she made
with Boaz home as a gift.

Where you go, I will go too,
your people shall be my people,
I will be a Jew for you,
for what is yours I will love
as I love you, oh Naomi
my mother, my sister, my heart.

Show me a woman who does not dream
a double, heart's twin, a sister
of the mind in whose ear she can whisper,
whose hair she can braid as her life
twists its pleasure and pain and shame.
Show me a woman who does not hide

in the locket of bone that deep
eye beam of fiercely gentle love
she had once from mother, daughter,
sister; once like a warm moon
that radiance aligned the tides
of her blood into potent order.

At the season of first fruits we recall
two travellers, co-conspirators, scavengers
making do with leftovers and mill ends,
whose friendship was stronger than fear,
stronger than hunger, who walked together
the road of shards, hands joined.

Down-to-Earth Judaism: Food, Sex, and Money

Arthur Waskow

For most liberal and progressive American Jews, Judaism has little to do with the warp and woof of everyday life—little to do with what food we eat, to whom and how we make love, where we spend or invest our money.... Many of us might say that our social concerns are ultimately rooted in our sense that Judaism cares about the poor and the oppressed.... The time in which we work, spend money, eat, sleep—most of our life-time, in fact—has little that is especially related to being Jewish. That we save for a wedding, a funeral, a holy day, perhaps a Shabbat.

It is true that in the last twenty years, some liberal and progressive American Jews have taken the first steps to experiment with walking a more holistic Jewish life-path. But only a few, and only the first few steps. Precisely as liberals and progressives, but rarely as Jews, we have said that "politics" and "culture" and "religion" are not in fact isolated parts of our lives, but the fabric of our whole existence; that what we do about sex, money, and food is indeed more fully and really our "politics," our "religion," and our "culture" than what we do in those isolated moments when we deal with "policy." ...

I want to propose that we now explore in our imaginations what it would mean to take the next step on a more holistic Jewish life-path, a down-to-earth Judaism that addresses our daily lives....

In each of three areas of life, we will look at three questions: how Jewish tradition might mesh with our contemporary concerns, how we might develop the tradition in new paths, and how we might actually initiate and organize those new paths—ground them in continuing reality.

Let us first take up questions of food. It is not by accident that I propose to start here. Perhaps the way in which Biblical Israel focused on food and taught all future generations of Jews to do the same was a distinctive element of Israelite thought.

According to "Biblical Israel's" understanding of itself, as expressed in the Bible, and according to some (not all) of those who have studied the ancient cultures of the land of Canaan, the very divergence between "Canaanites" and "Israelites" may have emerged in part from the divergence between two ways of addressing the Life-Force of the Universe. One path was through sexuality, which obviously transmitted and celebrated life through the generations. In this view, sacred sexual intercourse with sacred sexual priests and priestesses (what the Bible called *kadesha* and *kadesh*—from the root for "holy") was in ancient Canaan a way of invoking and celebrating that ultimate Intercourse that gave rise to all life.

The other path was through the celebration of food. In this view, biblical Israel created a form of prayer and celebration that rejected the path of temple sexuality and focused entirely on bringing

---

Arthur Waskow is a fellow at the Institute for Jewish Renewal, author of Season of Our Joy *(Bantum, 1982) and director of the Shalom Center at the Reconstructionist Rabbinical Seminary. He is also member of* Tikkun's *editorial board. This article appeared in serialized form in* Tikkun, *January/February and March/April 1988.*

the food that sprang from the land—goats and sheep, barley and wheat, olive oil and wine, even water—to the central place of worship. Some was set aside for God the Lifegiver who was the real owner of all land; some for the landless priests; and some for the poor who had little to eat.

In this culture, even the first independent act of human history was described as an act of eating—not as an act of sexuality or parenting or murder. That act of eating from the Tree of Knowledge sprouted into the burden of endless toil that all human beings faced to wring food from the earth. And when the same culture joyfully welcomed Shabbat into the world—the first step in releasing that burden of endless toil—it was also in the context of food, the manna in the wilderness, that Shabbat came.

So it is hardly surprising that this culture generated an elaborate system of kashrut. When the destruction of the Temple and the dispersion of the Jewish community necessitated some new approach to hallowing food that did not depend upon the Temple sacrifices, the Talmud described each family's dinner-table as a holy Altar, and kashrut was elaborated far beyond its Biblical simplicity. Without a separate food-producing land to make them distinctive, the Jews made their Diaspora dinner tables so distinctive that at every meal their separate peoplehood was reaffirmed.

The content of kashrut has puzzled many analysts. Some have claimed that the prohibition of certain meats protected health; others, that it was the compromise a deeply vegetarian ethic made reluctantly with inveterate eaters of meat. Some have argued that the method of ritual slaughter minimized the animals' pain; others, that the separation of milk from meat was intended to strengthen an ethic of distinguishing death from life.

Perhaps the most interesting analysis—because it went to the heart of what the entire halakhic system was about—was the one that argued that the entire system of distinctions concerning food was an integral part of a culture that focused on distinctions.

In our own generation, the strongest defenses of kashrut are simply that it is what we have inherited from the Jewish past, and what therefore defined us as Jews in everyday life. As even the far-flung ghettoes and Jewish neighborhoods dissolved into an even more dispersed Diaspora, kashrut might be practically the only distinctive element in everyday Jewish life. From this standpoint, too, kashrut is about distinctions: distinguishing ourselves from others.

For many Jews in our generation, therefore, the question of kashrut is especially problematic. Most of us want to assert our Jewishness without letting it separate us from others with whom we share basic political, cultural, and spiritual values. Many of us act as if "we are what we eat" when it comes to decisions about vegetarianism, macrobiotic diets, boycotts of food grown by oppressed workers in Chile, South Africa, or the United States. Yet, many of us also resist the imposition of absolute, black- and-white distinction in our lives: this you must and this you must not.

Is there any way to reshape this ungainly bundle of our partly contradictory values so that it makes a coherent whole, affirming and strengthening our lives as Jews?

Most of our strongest social values have their roots (or at least their analogues) in values expressed by Jewish tradition:

Oshek. The prohibition of oppressing workers—and similar prohibition of exploiting customers. Its principles could be extended to prohibit eating the fruit of such oppression or exploitation....

Tza'ar ba'alei hayyim. Respect for animals. It could be extended to prohibit eating any meat, or to prohibit eating meat from animals that have been grown under super-productive "factory farm" conditions. It could also be extended to respect for the identity of plants—for example, by prohibiting the misuse of pesticides and of genetic recombination or the eating of foods that were grown by such misuses.

Leshev ba'aretz. Living with, and not ruining, the earth. It could be extended to require the use of "natural" or "organic" foods—foods not grown with chemical pesticides.

Shemirat haguf. The protection of one's own body. It could be understood to prohibit eating food that contains carcinogens and/or hormones, and quasi-food items like tobacco and over-doses of alcohol. This principle would also mandate attention to the problems of anorexia or overeating that cause us deep physical and psychological pain and make food into a weapon that we use against ourselves.

Tzedakah. The sharing of food with the poor. It could be extended to prohibit the eating of any meal, or any communal festive meal, unless a proportion of its cost goes to buying food for the hungry. An extended version of this approach suggests that, in a world where protein is already distributed inequitably, it is unjust to channel large amounts of cheap grain into feeding animals to grow expensive meat protein—and that it is therefore unjust to eat meat at all.

Rodef tzedek and **Rodef shalom.** The obligation to pursue peace and justice. It might be understood to require the avoidance of food produced by companies that egregiously violate these values—for example, by investing in South Africa or by manufacturing first-strike nuclear weapons.

Berakhah and **Kedushah.** The traditional sense that eating consciously must affirm a sense of holiness and blessing. This might be understood to require that at the table we use old or new forms for heightening the attention we give to the unity from which all food comes—whether we call it God or not. This would help maintain an awareness of the sad fact that we must kill plants and/or animals to live....

The decision to apply these ethical principles to the choice of what to eat would represent a process of consulting the tradition without being imprisoned by it. If we undertook such a study, we would first find that every one of these principles stands as an ethical norm in Jewish tradition—not only in the aggadic sense of symbol, metaphor, philosophy, but also in the law code: Halakha. Then we would find hints in this tradition that one is obligated not only to avoid doing these misdeeds, but also to avoid benefiting from them if they have been done by others. But we would also find that there is no clear legal requirement to bring together the Jewish sense of the importance of food with these principles, by forbidding the eating of the fruits of these misdeeds. We would also find that there is little in the tradition that would stand in the way of adding new ethical restrictions to what we allow ourselves to eat....

Does it make sense for us now to draw on these basic principles to set new standards for what we actually eat—standards for an "ethical kashrut"? If we did, do we run the danger of obsessiveness, or even the danger that applying strict standards might result in drastically reducing the kinds of foods we could eat at all? Perhaps we can learn a lesson from the way different types of Jews practice traditional kashrut today.

Different Jews do maintain different answers to the question, "Is this food kosher?" For example, some will accept only certain types of certification on packaged goods, while others are satisfied with reading labels to verify ingredients as kosher. Some people will drink only kosher wine, while others believe this category is no longer relevant. Some keep "biblical kashrut," only abstaining from biblically forbidden foods. Some are willing to eat non-kosher foods in restaurants and in other people's homes, while others do not eat any cooked foods away from home.

A new kashrut that is rooted in ethical strands of Torah will also demand that people make choices about how to observe. For example: some will treat the principle of *oshek* (not oppressing workers) as paramount, and will choose only to eat foods that are grown without any oppression of food workers (from one's own backyard or neighborhood garden, or from a kibbutz where all workers are also owners and participants). Others may make the principle of *leshev baaretz* (protection of the environment) paramount, and will *oshek* in a secondary place—perhaps applying it only when specifically asked to do so by workers who are protesting their plights.

But there will also be some important differences in the way choices will work in an ethical kashrut from the way choices work in traditional kashrut. According to the new approach, there will be so many ethical values to weigh that it may be rare to face a black-and-white choice in a particular food. This one is grown by union workers, that one with special care for the earth and water, another.... So choices will depend more on a balancing and synthesizing of the underlying values than on an absolute sense of Good and Bad. More on a sense of Both/And than of Either/Or....

This approach to kashrut would be trying to deal with the issue of "distinctions" in a new way: not by separating only, but by consciously connecting. Connecting what is uniquely Jewish with what is shared and universal. Connecting Jewish categories with universal concerns. Consciously asserting Jewish reasons to avoid a food that others are also avoiding for similar but not identical reasons. Choosing not Either/Or but Both/And.

If we were to draw further on the analogy with traditional kashrut, what we would need is a kind of "living Talmud"—a group of people who are Jewishly knowledgeable, ethically sensitive, and willing to become reasonably expert on questions regarding food so that their advice would be taken seriously by large parts of the Jewish community. Such a commission on Ethical Kashrut might periodically issue reports and suggestions on specific matters and specific foods, listing specific foods and brands that it regarded as "highly recommended," and others "to be avoided if at all possible."

How should such a Commission come into being? We will take up this question after dealing with two other areas of "down-to-earth" Judaism.

In the ancient world, food and sex were the two most powerful emblems of the Life-giver in the visible world, and the production of food was the strongest link between human life and the rest of the created world. On the earth-to-human side, this link was governed by kashrut; on the human-to-earth side, it was governed by rules of land use, including provisions for the poor and for periodic equalizations of land-holding, and by intense prayers for rain. Indeed, the provision and protection of water is one of the main concerns of Jewish liturgy.

There were other links between earth and humanity, but none required as much care and regulation as did food. Clothing was one of these other links, and the Torah notes a kind of kashrut of clothes—not mixing linen and wool. But the rabbinic tradition did not greatly elaborate the rule. Breathing was another link. God's most intimate name may have been based on a breathing sound, and breath/wind became the metaphor for life, soul, and spirit. Even in the biblical and rabbinic periods, air pollution was occasionally a problem—downwind of a tannery, for example—but this was rare, and few rules were developed for the correct use of air.

In our own world, food is no longer the only problematic link between human beings and their environment. Our water and air are often polluted, and although food represents the most crucial link to the earth, producing it takes up a much smaller a proportion of our work than it did before the modern age. Today there are many products that we make from the world around us that are crucial to our lives and health. Does it make sense to apply to them some rules of "kashrut," and if so how would we develop such rules? And how would we enforce them?

In this new society, the human-to-earth link is not so much through the use of land as it is through the use of money. Rules about reserving the gleanings and the produce of the corners of a field for the poor, redistributing land once a generation, letting the land rest from its work every seventh year—all these need to be translated into the use of money and of "technological capital" if we are to preserve the same functional relationship of holiness between human beings and their environment....

There are some religious and cultural traditions that view money itself, or the effort to amass it, as intrinsically evil. There are others that see the possession of money—or large amounts of it—as intrinsic evidence of holiness and blessedness. Most of Jewish thought sees money as a powerful tool for evil or for good—depending on how it is used. There is deep Jewish experience with the mitzvah of *tzedakah*—sharing the just and righteous use of money not only to alleviate poverty but to help end it and create shared wealth—and with the use of money to protect Jewish rights, assist Jewish refugees, and help create the Jewish community in Israel. All this experience suggests that as the Jewish community stirs itself to protect its own survival and that of the planet, the wise use of money is an important tool. Knowing where *not* to spend money, as well as where it *should* be spent, is important both morally and politically.

Let us look at the different areas of possibility:

Work. How do we choose what companies to work for and what work to do? Should engineers, secretaries, scientists, public-relations experts, and nurses, be asking whether their work contributes to or reduces the danger of a nuclear holocaust? Do Jewish tradition and the Jewish community offer any help in making such judgments? What help is most needed? ...

How could the Jewish community, or parts of it, decide whether specific jobs were "kosher"? Suppose a community decided a specific job was not kosher; should and could the community provide financial help—temporary grants, low-interest loans, etc.—to Jews who decide to leave such jobs for reasons of Torah and conscience? Should organizing toward such a fund be a goal of the Jewish community?

Investments. How do we judge where to invest money—in which money market funds, IRAs, etc? What about institutional funds in which we may have a voice or could make for ourselves a voice—college endowments, pension funds, city bonds, etc? In the last ten years, there has arisen in the United States a network of people and groups concerned with "socially responsible investment," that is, working out how to apply ethical standards to investment decisions. Demands for divestment from businesses that operate in South Africa are one—but by no means the only—example of this approach. Labor relations, degree of involvement in the arms race, and health and safety concerns have been others. The network has now brought into being socially responsible "screened" investment funds, which avoid investing money in what each considers the most socially irresponsible firms, and affirmative socially responsible investment funds that seek to invest in new or small but financially viable businesses that in their eyes have major positive factors for social responsibility.

In the Jewish community, investment funds that might become "socially responsible" include community-worker and rabbinical association pension funds, synagogue endowments, building campaign accounts, pulpit flower funds, seminary endowments, etc. How would the community decide which investments are "kosher"?

Purchases. Should we as individuals, when we choose which companies to buy consumer goods from, use as one factor in our choice the facts of what else a specific company is producing? Are operations in South Africa, the USSR, Chile—or in making nuclear weapons, dangerous petrochemicals—relevant? Should we ask our synagogues, our pension funds, our city and state governments, our PTA's, to choose vendors on the same basis? Rabbi Zalman Schachter-Shalomi has suggested that since in our era we consume many items other than food, the notion of kashrut should be expanded beyond food to many other products that we use. Is electric power generated by a nuclear plant "kosher," he asks? And, even more to the point, could we call into being a broader commission for Eco-Kashrut that could reach out far beyond the Jewish community to define what products are so damaging to the earth that they ought not be bought or consumed?

Taxes. Is it legitimate to challenge, protest, or prevent the use of our tax money to carry on activities that profoundly contradict Torah? If so, how do we define "profoundly contradict"? What weight do we give to the fact that our taxes and government expenditures are defined by elected representatives?

Tzedakah. How do we decide how much money we should give to "charity" and to which enterprises to give it?

In the last twenty years, there have grown up among Jewish liberals and progressives not only new channels for tzedakah, such as Mazon (intended to feed the hungry) and the Jewish Fund for Justice (intended to help groups of the poor or powerless organize to win their own footing in the world) but also a relatively new (and old) form for tzedakah—the "tzedakah collective." These groups meet together, face to face, to discuss possible recipients of tzedakah; the participants agree in advance on what proportion of their incomes they will give, and on a more or less collective process for deciding how to give it. The ambience is very different from what happens when individuals write checks to a national tzedakah organization, whether it is the United Jewish Appeal or the Jewish Fund for Justice; and usually the involvement of the participants is much deeper in learning about tzedakah and the Jewish tradition's teachings on tzedakah, as well as in learning about projects that might be tzedakah recipients.

Participants in these tzedakah collectives report that their involvement feels inspiring and their field results seem good; yet the number of such collectives seems still to be much lower than the number of *havurot* for study and prayer. What would be ways of encouraging this process?

It would take two steps to encourage such direct involvement in tzedakah. One would be face-to-face organizing by rabbis, Jewish teachers, and similar local Jewish community workers to get groups of families to meet together to do tzedakah. The other would be providing such groups with information not only on tzedakah decisions that groups like them are making, but also on Jewish aspects of the everyday use of money in their non-tzedakah lives: the "kashrut of money" for investment, purchasing, tax, and workplace choices. If a packet of newsletters with such information were made available every month or two first to rabbis to pass on to "tzedakah activists" and then to tzedakah collectives as they appeared, the chances would be much greater that Jewish values would be consciously applied to the use of money in many aspects of life.

What about the issues of sexual ethics that for many Jews today pose extraordinarily puzzling and painful dilemmas in their daily lives? Few progressive Jews—indeed, few Jews of almost any political and religious hue—turn to the traditional Jewish code of sexual behavior as an authoritative or practical guide to their own actual behavior....

But many of us do not feel we are doing so well when we try to act totally on our own, either. Indeed, the problems many liberal and progressive Jews now face in shaping their sexual ethics is one of the strongest pieces of evidence that a wholly individualistic ethic, not in some sense shaped by interaction between communal and individual needs, is destructive to individuals as well as communities. So even here it may be useful to see whether aspects of Jewish practice might help many of us sort out deep doubts and confusion in our sexual lives....

For most of Jewish tradition, the link between sex and procreation was very strong—though not absolute. This connection strongly influenced rabbinic attitudes toward masturbation, homosexuality, contraception, abortion, and marriage. The rabbis paid great attention to the first of all the commandments: "Be fruitful and multiply, and fill up the earth."

In our generation, however, it is possible to argue that the commandment has been so thoroughly fulfilled by the human race as a whole that it no longer needs to be obeyed by all human beings as individuals. The earth is filled up; we have done Your bidding; what comes next?

Since "Be fruitful and multiply" is the command that comes at the outset of the Garden of Eden story, perhaps what comes next is Eden for grown-ups: the garden of the Song of Songs. The sexual ethic of the Song of Songs focuses not on children, marriage, or commitment, but on sensual pleasure and loving companionship. What if we were to take this as a teaching for our epoch? What if we were to look at the human race as a whole as if it had entered that period of maturity that a happily married couple enter when they no longer can (or want to) have children? They continue to connect sexually for the sake of pleasure and love—and so could the human race, or the Jewish people. Without denigrating the forms of sexuality that focus on children and family, we might find the forms of sexuality that focus on pleasure more legitimate at this moment of human and Jewish history than ever before.

With this broader understanding in mind, let us turn to the specific areas in which ethical doubts and questions have arisen.

First, in regard to sexual activity by unmarried people: most Jews reject in their own practice and in theory, the traditional adherence to early marriage and the traditional opposition to sexual activity by unmarried people. The two are connected; few American Jews believe that early marriages are wise in our complex society, where personalities, careers, and life-paths almost never jell in the teens and often not till the mid-thirties, sometimes come unjelled during the forties and fifties and usually are changed again with long-lived retirements beginning in the sixties or seventies. It is hard enough to make stable life-long marriages when one partner is changing in this way; when both are, it is extremely difficult.

There are several different conceivable responses to this situation:

a) Reverse the basic situation, and restore the kind of society in which life patterns were set close to the onset of puberty and did not change much. Few American Jews believe this can be, or should be done. The Hassidic communities, however, may be showing that for a sub-community it can be done.

b) Accept that first marriages will come many years after sexual awakening and that most marriages will end while the partners are sexually active and alert—and practice celibacy for long periods of unmarried time. This is the solution that almost all American Jews have rejected. It is also, however, the solution that they identify as the "official" position of Jewish tradition and religious authority. There are certainly few public assertions by religious authorities or communities that this is not the "correct" Jewish view, and almost no public Jewish way of honoring or celebrating sexual relationships other than marriage.

This chasm between practice and understanding of the tradition may be one of the most powerful elements driving most Jews in their pre-married, sexually active years—from 16 to 31— and in their "post-married" sexually active years away from Jewish life. Who wants to be part of an institution that looks with hostility or contempt on the source of much of one's most intense pleasure, joy, and fulfillment?

c) Accept that life-patterns will change several times in any person's lifetime, that marriages will change accordingly, and greatly change our expectation of "marriage" so that it carries fewer burdens of financial, emotional, and other involvement. In other words, make it easy for sexually active people from puberty on to enter and leave marriages—make marriages much "lighter" acts unless children emerge in them. But to make marriages "light" enough that 16-year-olds or 18-year-olds can easily enter them, expecting easily to exit from them at 20, and to enter and exit again at 21, 25, 28, 32—would make that kind of "marriage" so different from one that could give an adequate context for child-rearing that it is hard to imagine that the two should have the same name. (But note that many American marriages are dissolving even during the child-rearing years. Should leaving marriages be "light" then too? Or is the distinction one that most Jews would want to keep?)

For those Jews who try to abide by Halakha, it might be easier to use the traditional labels and forms of marriage and redefine the content than to follow the paths listed above or those listed below. The Talmud, for example (*Yebamot* 37b), mentions that a few of the rabbis, when they went on what we would call lecture tours, would marry a woman one night and divorce her the next morning. In that period, of course, men were permitted polygamy, so such a practice of "light" marriage did not undermine simultaneous "heavy" marriage—at least not in law.

d) Accept and publicly honor the present practice that many unmarried people are sexually active—that there are likely to be periods of "fluidity" in sexuality during any life-path— without creating standards of ethical behavior for unmarried sexual relationships or creating ceremonial or legal definitions of them. This is basically the pattern followed by the burgeoning *havurot* (participatory and relatively informal congregations of prayer and study). In many of them, married couples and unmarried people who are fluidly coupled and uncoupled have shared the same communal space. Acceptance of unmarried sexual activity has been high and public, with little effort to set standards or to deal with painful experiences except among close friends or with the help of psychotherapists who themselves use only such "Jewish" sources as Freud, Reich, Fromm, and Perls.

This solution is not as opposed to Jewish tradition as many of us suppose; for there are many references in the traditional literature that legitimate sex between unmarried people. (See, for example, in the 13th century Nachmanides—#2 in Responsa and in the 18th century Rabbi Jacob Emden, cited in Gershon Winkler, "Sex and Religion: Friend or Foe?" in *New Menorah*, second series, Number 7, pp. 1-3.) But the main definitive statements of traditional law in the last four centuries—particularly in the popular Jewish consciousness in Eastern Europe whence most of our grandparents came—ignored these permissive authorities.

e) Redefine marriage and create new Jewishly affirmed forms of sexual relationship that are to be publicly defined with certain standards and are to be ceremonially honored. There are certain vestiges of ancient tradition that might even be drawn on for such new forms—the *pilegesh* relationship for example, which is usually translated "concubine" but has great openness to legal, practical, and ceremonial definition.

We could imagine three different basic forms of sexual relationship:

Times of great fluidity, when the community might affirm only such basic norms as honesty and the avoidance of coercion without expecting monogamy or emotional intimacy;

Times of commitment without great permanence, when notice of a *pilegesh* relationship is given to a face-to-face Jewish community—not to the state—and is defined by the people entering it (explicitly monogamous or not, explicitly living together or not, explicitly sharing some financial arrangements or not, etc.). In this pattern, the community joins in honoring, acting in accord with, and celebrating such arrangements, and there is an easy public form by which either of the parties may dissolve the relationship.

Times of marriage, which may also be partly defined by the couple through the *ketubah*, but which are expected to be more long-lasting, to be essential for child-rearing (though used also by couples who do not expect to have children), and to be dissolved only by joint agreement of the couple and by serious participation of the Jewish community as well as the civil order in arranging the terms of separation.

This last approach, it seems to me, takes the complexity of our present situation and the resources of Jewish tradition most fully into account. But it would take more than a piece of paper announcing *pilegesh* for this approach to begin functioning. Let us come back to the necessary institutional processes after we have looked at the other arenas of doubt that exist in our practice of sexual ethics.

About sexual relationships between men, or between women, there is much less agreement in the Jewish world than about heterosexual relationships between unmarried people. Many American Jews—probably a majority—support guarantees for the civil rights and employment rights of gays and lesbians. What seems to be a growing minority is ready to assert that a gay or lesbian life-path can be a fully and authentically Jewish life-path. Somewhat fewer are ready to act in such ways that publicly gay and lesbian Jews would allow to become rabbis, communal Jewish leaders, members of broad-spectrum congregations, celebrants of life-cycle transformations like weddings, etc.

The written texts of Jewish tradition and most of the actual practices of most Jewish communities are more heavily weighted against the public acceptance of gay and lesbian life-paths than they are against the acceptance of heterosexual relationships between unmarried people. When we look at the most ancient texts, some of them may turn out to be slightly more ambiguous than we are used to assuming. For example, what are we to make of the fact that the biblical text gives us no obvious command against lesbian relationships? What are we to make of the Bible's celebration of David's love for Jonathan—whose "love was more pleasing than the love of women"?

During the rabbinic era of Jewish history, there can be no doubt that most communities and rabbis were strongly hostile to homosexuality, on the part of men or women. Yet even in the rabbinic era, Jewish practice may not have been so single-valued as we usually assume. During the Golden Age of Jewish culture in Spain, more than one of the greatest liturgical poets of the period, whose poems grace our traditional Siddur, also wrote poetry of homosexual love. Did these poems rise out of life-experience, or only out of literary convention? Even if the latter, what does that say about our assumptions regarding Torah-true Jews and Judaism?

For us to think intelligently about these questions today, we must go beyond biblical texts and rabbinic rulings—even beyond our own midrashic understanding of the texts—to try to hear what may have been the hopes and fears that were at stake; to take them seriously; and then to see where we ourselves come out, trying to hold together all the values that are bespoken by Torah and Jewish life.

Two of the strongest strands of Torah are hostility to idolatry and urgency to have children. Indeed, one of the deepest traumas of the Jewish psyche seems to have been the fear of not being able to have children—as expressed in the stories of Abraham and Sarah, Isaac and Rebekah, Jacob and Leah and Rachel. The story of slavery in Egypt focuses on the danger that children would be murdered. So do the attacks on Canaanite religion—claiming that in it, children were "passed through the fire to Moloch." Whether or not these descriptions are accurate, they bespeak a deep Israelite concern for procreating the next generation.

In such a culture, homosexuality might have seemed a dangerous diversion from fecundity. If, as seems likely, the practice of sacred homosexuality was also part of the worship of the surrounding "idolatrous" cultures of Canaan, then the hostility of the Israelites to homosexuality would have been redoubled. As the rabbis encountered Hellenism, with its non-theistic or polytheistic philosophies, its emphasis on the body as an end in itself, and its approval of homosexuality, the Jewish hostility to homosexuality might have been intensified.

If these are the concerns that underlie the traditional view, then we may see the issue differently today—perhaps in a way closer to that of the Golden Age in Spain. We too, in the era of the H-bomb, are concerned over whether there will be a next generation. But we live also in the era of population explosion. It is clear that the human race as a whole has much more to fear from violence and environmental destruction as a threat to its children, than from the failure of biological reproduction. It is true that the Jewish people is not experiencing a population explosion, but in an era when conversion to Judaism is at an extraordinarily high level, even for Jews the literal needs of childbirth are not so extreme. What is more, gay and lesbian Jews have themselves been exploring the possibility of having children and rearing them Jewishly. So the birth issue is not nearly so problematic for openness to homosexual practice as it once was.

As I have already suggested, we may live in the era when the sexual ethic celebrated by the Song of Songs—an ethic of sexual pleasure and love—comes into its own alongside the sexual ethic of family. It may seem ironic that the Song of Songs, one of the greatest celebrations of heterosexual sexuality in all of literature, might be taken to affirm the homosexual community's bent toward sex as pleasurable and loving rather than as procreative. But sometimes ironies bear truth. If any community of Jews has in our epoch embodied the values of the Song of Songs (taken at its literal meaning, not allegorically), it is the community of gay and lesbian Jews. Perhaps in our epoch, then, the despised and rejected gay subcommunity turns out to be the unexpected bearer of a newly important teaching. As the tradition teaches, sometimes the stone that the builders rejected becomes the cornerstone of the Temple.

In this light, it is especially poignant that the sexual ethics of commitment and family have taken on new seriousness within the gay community, as a result of the impact of AIDS. It is as if the two ethics, which had been ghettoized from each other before, each embodied in a separate community, have now begun to be intertwined into a more holistic vision of a sexual ethic that can incorporate the

values of family, commitment, procreation, sensual pleasure, and loving companionship.

If another of the ancient Jewish objections to homosexuality was the belief that it was connected with idolatry or Hellenistic philosophy—today it seems clear that homosexual practice accords with the same range of dedication to and rejection of honesty, modesty, fidelity, intimacy, spiritual searching, holiness and God as does heterosexual practice. If reports of certain specific gay male subcultures of extremely multiple sexual partnerships seem incompatible with most Jewish values, then care must be taken both to avoid blanketing all homosexuality into that subculture, and to note that there are similar heterosexual subcultures in our society as well. In other words, if the basic value at stake is some level of stability and focus in sexual relationships, then that value ought to be affirmed without regard to the gender of the partners; and it is also important to be clear about whether we respect a "time of fluidity" in sexual practice of the kind we have already sketched.

Even aside from the possibility that in our generation the whole framework of sexual ethics needs to shift, two other factors have recently come into play that have their own connections to values of Torah. One is the discovery that for some large proportion of gay men and some (perhaps smaller) proportion of lesbians, homosexuality is not a matter of choice—but of identity set either genetically or very early in life. For those who continue to accept the traditional understandings of Halakha, this discovery has put into discussion the halakhic principle that absolves of "sin" those who act under compulsion. At a more Aggadic level, this relatively new discovery raises the question of whether a community that has celebrated the Song of Songs as "the Holy of Holies," imagined its own relationship with God as that of spouse and lover, and refused to make a virtue of heterosexual celibacy, ought to be insisting that someone whose deepest sexual identity is homosexual and who cannot experience sexual pleasure with a partner of the other gender, should choose a life of celibacy or of privatized, closeted, stifled sexuality rather than one of publicly affirmed homosexuality.

The other new factor is an increasing sense that gay men and lesbians are an oppressed community, "strangers in the land" as we were strangers in the land of Egypt, fellow-victims (though not in the same way) of the Nazi Holocaust, and therefore to be treated as the Torah commands that "strangers," the excluded and oppressed, be treated: with love, respect, and equality.

Once we have noted the demand of the Torah that the stranger be treated with justice and love, we should also note that it may be precisely the "strangeness" of gayness that is at the root of the fear and hatred that has been expressed toward it. Perhaps it is not the desire for children, not the hatred of idolatry, that has been the root of the rejection of homosexuals—but rather the fear of what is different, strange, queer. ("What do they *do* in bed, anyway?") Especially the fear that "I myself" am somewhat different, strange, queer—different from the person I have advertised myself to be. The deep fear that when I take a close look at the strange face of the stranger, it will turn out to look a great deal like the strange face in my mirror. The Torah repeats the command to love and respect the stranger 36 times—a hint that this command is not so easy to obey. We could honestly face the difficulty, and then persevere in our perennially difficult task of embodying Torah.

So in our generation it may be necessary for the Jewish community as a whole, in the light of *all* these values, to reexamine its attitudes toward gay, lesbian, and heterosexual Jews. Is there a way to reaffirm the importance of raising the next generation of Jewish children without denigrating homosexual practice—indeed by affirming the right, the ability, and the duty of *all* Jews to join in that work? Is there a way to develop an ethic of sexual relationships that takes into account the experience of gay and lesbian as well as heterosexual relationships, while the ethic itself addresses the quality of the relationship—not the gender of the partners? Is there a way of celebrating God as Lover and Spouse with images that work for Jews of all sexual orientations?

In my own judgment, it is possible and desirable to move in these directions—to reexamine ways in which all the values of Torah can be upheld, rather than upholding some—such as fecundity—while shattering others—such as free and equal participation in the community—for part of the Jewish people. On such a path, the values that seem to have been the reasons for celebrating heterosexuality do not need to be discarded. On such a path the choices do not need to be Either/Or—but Both/And-What-Is-More.

If this is the path that a new Jewish sexual ethic is to take, we will need to work out ways for congregations and communities to open up prayer, life-cycle celebration, tzedakah, *shalom bayit*, and other aspects of Jewish life to full and public participation by gay, lesbian, bisexual, and heterosexual Jews. No matter what sexual ethic we develop about the nature, techniques, and celebration of different forms of sexual relationships, it could be applied equally to sexual partnerships regardless of the gender of the partners. Homosexual marriages, homosexual *pilegesh* relationships, homosexual "fluid" time could all be treated in the same way as their heterosexual equivalents.

The question of what sexual ethic should operate within a marriage is another arena of doubt. The asserted norm, for most Jews, continues to be sexual monogamy and fidelity for married people. But a sizeable number violate this norm in practice, and the community is certainly unclear what sanctions to apply. Should known adulterers be expelled from congregations? denied leadership offices? denied honors such as being called up to read Torah? admonished privately? treated as if their sexual behavior were irrelevant?

The question gets more complicated when some argue that the norm is disobeyed in practice not because people are perverse, but because the norm is untenable—at least for many couples. Should couples then make their own decisions whether their particular *ketubah* requires monogamy? Is sexual relationship outside marriage "adultery" only if the partners entered a commitment to monogamy, and one then betrays the commitment? Or does the community as a whole have a stake in affirming that a "marriage" should be monogamous?

Very few voices have suggested approaching the question by drawing on one of the oldest strands of Jewish sexual ethics—the openness to certain forms of polygamy. Until one thousand years ago among Western Jews and until a few years ago among Eastern Jews, it was legitimate, though unusual, for men to have more than one wife. Was there any wisdom in allowing this possibility? Since one of the main reasons it was abandoned was the protection of women who were in a deeply unequal status, does the reason for the prohibition of polygamy still stand, or do changes in the status of women suggest that instead the prohibition be ended and the possibility be opened as well that a woman can take several husbands? (For those who would like to avoid a radical break from traditional Halakha, the latter decision would be a great deal harder to accomplish.) Or, since the other main reason that polygamy was forbidden to Western Jews was that it exposed them to contempt in Christian eyes, does the incredulity or ridicule that the notion provokes in many people suggest that polygamy is still viewed with contempt in the West and should still be avoided—that *de facto* adultery is less dangerous than *de jure* polygamy?

To point out how hard some of the questions about "adultery" might be, consider the following hypothetical case: A well-known leader of the Jewish community approaches his rabbi and the lay leaders of his synagogue. He has been lovingly married for many years. His wife has for several years been institutionalized with a debilitating and disabling but not fatal illness. He has cared for her with love and devoted attentiveness. Her illness has now been diagnosed as incurable. He does not wish to divorce her, for that would damage her both financially and emotionally. Yet he cannot bear to live forever lonely. He has come to love another woman, and wants her to live with him and be his sexual and emotional partner. What is the view of the congregation?

Should the Jewish community force him to retire rather than let its leader carry on such a relationship, considering his high visibility in Jewish and public life? or simply on the ground that adultery is forbidden? Should the community tolerate his life-path, provided he leads it in secret? Should it insist he divorce his wife? Should it affirm his choices as Jewishly best under the circumstances? Or should it perhaps refuse to decide at all, and leave the whole matter to individual conscience?

Even in less agonizing situations, some who assert that they do in fact live by the monogamous norm and some who assert that they have agreed to "open," non-monogamous marriages both report enormous social pressure against their decision. Among the monogamous some report that in a society suffused with sexual attractions, even close-knit Jewish communities do not act fully supportive of their commitment to monogamy but that some members of the community act both sexually seductive and politically contemptuous, as if such a commitment were old-fashioned and repressive. Some also report that when they seek emotional intimacy with others than their marriage partners, not intending to include a sexual relationship as part of the intimacy, both they themselves and their friends find it hard to draw the lines.

As for those who assert that their marriages are "open" and non-monogamous, some also report that their communities treat them with derision or fear, and some report that they themselves experience deep inner conflicts with jealousy and fear of loss. In both groups, some say ruefully that hypocrisy turns out to be more comfortable to live with than either a clear commitment to monogamy or non-monogamy in theory as well as practice.

Finally, there is the arena of doubt about specific sexual practices in any relationship, without regard to who the partner is. Here again, the tradition is more permissive in some areas than some modern Jews assume—though in other areas a great deal more restrictive than most modern Jews would accept in their life-practice. For example, some of the rabbis for centuries have approved both of oral and anal sex where the partners find these the source of greatest pleasure. (See, for example, Maimonides, *Mishnah Torah Hilkhos Issurei Biah*, 21:9, cited in Winkler, *New Menorah, Second Series, Number 7.*) On the other hand, the rules of *niddah,* prohibiting sexual relations during the menstrual period (and a good many days afterward) have been a clear Biblical-rabbinic tradition. Most liberal and progressive Jews see *niddah* as a regressive rejection of femaleness in that it rejects menstruation as an "unclean" time and process; but in our generation it has been explained by Rachel Adler as a way of honoring the uncanny edge of life-and-death that is involved in menstruation's casting off of a viable egg cell, and by others as a way of creating a rhythm of separation and renewal between two sexual partners. Similarly, the opposition of much of Jewish tradition to the use of some forms of contraception has been rejected by most liberal and progressive Jews.

Discussions of *niddah,* however, have turned up suggestions of ways to affirm some of the values that may be at stake without denigrating women. When one couple who were in deep disagreement about the question asked for help from a feminist leader of the movement for Jewish renewal, she suggested that they explore separating sexually for the days of Rosh Chodesh—the new moon—rather than at the time of menstruation. In this way they could experience the rhythm of separation and return without focusing on menstruation. Others have suggested refraining from sex for just a day or two of the menstrual cycle, thus honoring its uncanniness without defining it as unclean.

The more basic possibility underlying these responses is that they came not from a place of law or judgement but from a place of nurturing wisdom, seeking to reconcile deeply held values that did not need to be seen as contradictory and to draw on Jewish tradition in new ways without rigidly obeying strictures that have risen in the past. In a sense, the feminist whom the couple consulted acted as a rabbi not judging as part of a *beit din*—"house of legal judgment"—but as part of a *beit rachamim* or *beit chesed*—"house of nurturing love," or perhaps a *beit seichel*—a "house of prudence." Pursuing this approach on matters of sexual ethics could be one of the most important steps that Jewish communities and congregations could take. Imagine how different attitudes toward the rich fabric of Jewish thought and practice might become and how unnecessary the desperate loneliness of people now faced with decisions they see as utterly individual, if every synagogue and havurah were to create a panel of women and men noted for their practical *chesed* and *seichel,* from whom a person or a couple in an agony of doubt and pain over sexual issues could choose one or a few people with whom to counsel.

We might even consider making it a matter of communal ethical agreement and obligation that before undertaking a major change in sexual relationships, congregants were required—not simply encouraged—to consult with such a *beit chesed*. Whether they followed its recommendations would be up to them. The legal obligation would go not to the content but to the process of consultation. Such an understanding suggests one way to resolve the tug between individual and communal desires.

The decision to create such *b'tei chesed* might begin in any congregation—and if it worked, would spread. Some of the other decisions I have suggested—for instance, a clear and public affirmation that there are three different "times" or kinds of legitimate and holy sexual relationships, the clarification of *pilegesh* relationships, the clear legitimation of homosexual relationships—would require statements by authoritative individuals or groups in Jewish life. Even the clarification of the process of ending a Jewish marriage would require not only a new decision by the Reform movement to insist that a *get* or Jewish divorce is necessary along with a civil divorce, to end a Jewish marriage—but a decision by *all* branches of Jewish life to issue a *get* not simply as a formula, but after serious consultation with the couple on the conditions of the end of the marriage.

How do we get these processes of change going? ... Who will organize the organizers? Who will bring into being a Commission on Ethical Kashrut, a network of wise and loving *b'tei chesed* and *b'tei seichel*, a network of tzedakah collectives? I think we need to have what might be called a "Center for Down-to-Earth Judaism"—a center for infusing the daily nitty-gritty of the lives of Jews with Jewish content drawn from a creative response to Torah.

Such a Center would pull together the information, the mailing lists, the newsletters, the practical "*shylahs* and *tshuvahs*" (questions and answers in a new version of the rabbinic mode) that could help weave a fabric of Jewish living in the workaday time that is not Shabbat or festival, not wedding-day or funeral....

As we have looked at specific issues and specific new approaches, we have kept noting that an atmosphere of Both/And-What-Is-More might emerge, quite different from the atmosphere of Either/Or that for many of us seems linked to the traditional Jewish life-path. If indeed there is some way to "institutionalize" this atmosphere, then the demons and nightmares of a generation of Jews who fled from narrowness and "command" might be exorcised. For in this atmosphere, there is neither rigid command nor utter fluidity, utter antinomianism, utter individuality. There is structure, there are boundaries, there are communal institutions to give communal guidance—*not* command.

In this new atmosphere, the new kashrut is understood to come not from a "commander" outside and above us, but from a sense of loving connection between humans and the earth, among those who do the work of growing, moving, shaping, and cooking food, among those who sit to eat it and between them and all these others. These sexual ethics emerge from the need to make worthy, honest, decent, and stable loving connections among us. So too with a new financial ethic.

So these new approaches may lead us toward a redirection of our spiritual searchings, a relocation or re-imaging of what is God and Godly—indeed a reconnection of our sense of spiritual wholeness with our sense of social justice. For here the sense of justice, of ethical behavior, springs precisely *not* from rules but from the yearning for wholeness, for harmonious connection between the different parts of a whole that is yearning to be whole, to be *Shalem*.

This is a new approach, but its seeds are ancient. As we walk this path, we can remind ourselves that Judaism does see the mundane, the down-to-earth, and it is suffused with a sense of community, a sense of intellect, and a sense of the spirit.... □

Speaking in Thunder

Arthur Green

Among Jews in North America, Shavuot is surely one of the least-known and least-observed Jewish holidays. Another irony of Jewish history: the holiday of the book, forgotten by the people of the book. Shavuot, which commemorates the giving of Torah at Mount Sinai, should by rights be the apex of the Jewish festival cycle. Passover, the time of liberation, leads up to it. We count the days from Exodus to Sinai, as though liberation itself were just a prelude. In order to be wedded to our God at the Mountain, we have to be free from bondage to all our inner and outer pharaohs. Sukkot, the third partner in the pilgrimage cycle, basks in the afterglow of Sinai. In it we celebrate our wandering through the wilderness and eternal preparation to enter the promised land. Neither of these makes any sense without the Main Event, the revelation of God at the Holy Mountain.

Sinai takes us to the heart of Jewish faith: it claims that God communicates to humans; that such communication took place between Y-H-W-H (the unutterable Hebrew name for "God," understood here as an impossible form of the verb "to be" best translated "Is-Was-Will Be") and Moses and Israel at the mountain in the wilderness; and that this revelation makes known the divine will. In one form or another, this set of claims pervades all of classical Judaism. I believe it is necessary both to deny and to affirm the claims of Sinai.

My denial of literal faith in Sinai will undoubtedly seem to some too distant from the simple notion of revelation they had in childhood. For many more contemporary Jews, my affirmation will doubtless sound too strong. My theological tone may sound to them too much like a "real" belief in revelation after all. I seek a mature and believable Jewish faith based on an ultimate commitment to a nondualistic vision of the universe, one that denies the radical separation of "God" and "self." Modern Judaism has conveniently buried the truth the Jewish mystics knew centuries ago: All God "reveals" at Sinai is God's own self, the self of the universe. The entire Torah is nought but this, God's own name. All the rest is commentary.

If the revelation and commandment at Sinai are the heart of Jewish faith, they are also the most difficult and "scandalous" claims made by the religious traditions of Israel. Taken at face value, they form the very essence of Jewish "supernaturalism" and seeming theological arbitrariness: Y-H-W-H, the Creator of the universe chooses at a particular moment to reveal "Himself" uniquely to the Jewish people, addressing them in words and pledging eternal loyalty in covenant with them if they will accept "His" specific will as manifest in the practice of Judaism. Both mind and conscience reel at such a thought! What does it mean to say that God speaks? Does God speak to Israel in a language that Israel understands, commanding a Torah made up of laws, ethics, rites, and traditions that seem remarkably related to those of the pagan nations in whose midst Israel lives? Can we

Arthur Green is the president of the Reconstructionist Rabbinical College. This article is excerpted from Seek My Face, Speak My Name: A Contemporary Jewish Theology, *(Jason Aaronson 1991). This article appeared in* Tikkun, *May/June 1991.*

imagine a God so arbitrary as to choose one nation, one place, and one moment in human history in which the eternal divine will was to be manifest for all time? How can we attribute to Y-H-W-H, who becomes "person" only through our encounter, this sort of arbitrary willfulness? For these reasons and others, thinking Jews in our time, including many who seek a serious approach to questions of the spirit, balk at accepting the "yoke" of Sinai.

But hear another voice from within the tradition. "Moses spoke and God responded in a voice" (Exod. 19:19). The rabbis comment: God responded "in the voice of Moses." This seems to say that the only voice heard at Sinai was that of Moses, sometimes speaking on his own and sometimes possessed by the divine spirit, God responding from within Moses' own voice. Rather than a "voice from heaven," there was the voice of a prophet transformed by an inner encounter that can only be characterized as "heaven." Jews over the centuries have debated how to refine the naive biblical depiction of Sinai and the experience of revelation. The phrase "Shekhina [divine presence] speaks from within his throat" was often applied to prophets.

The fact is that any sophisticated theory of revelation recognizes a moment in which the Divine and human minds flow together. Indeed, we speak of the "mind" of the Divine only by analogy with the human mind. If Y-H-W-H is the incorporeal essence of the universe, and mind or soul is the incorporeal essence of the person we *call* God the mind or soul of the universe. God as Y-H-W-H knows no distinction between "matter" and "spirit." In seeking to comprehend revelation we may, however, speak of Y-H-W-H as a cosmic mind, present in the depths of each human mind, and impressing itself in a unique way upon consciousness. The universal One seeks to be known by the human, this manifestation of its own self that is also, paradoxically, its "other." Its "seeking" or "calling out" to its "other" (the human) is not of language. It is only humans who can make the divine articulate in words, since words themselves are a human invention. In fact, the most recent translations of Exodus 19:19 render it, "Moses spoke and God responded in thunder." Y-H-W-H speaks in thunderclaps; it takes a Moses to translate God's thunder into words.

If the Jewish imagination regards the divine and human as separate, God living in "heaven" and humans on earth, revelation is the act that comes closest to bridging this separation. Moses goes up to the top of Sinai, according to the Torah, and God comes down upon the mountain (Exod. 19:3, 20). But at that moment the entire top of Sinai is covered by thick cloud—as though to say that the border between the "upper" and "lower" realms is lost. Later accounts of the revelation are more fanciful; they actually depict Moses as riding on the clouds, entering the heavenly realms, and holding on to God's Throne of Glory. Moses returns from the revelation still human, but his face glows with the light of that encounter in which the upper limits on human spiritual attainment had been momentarily cast aside. He returns to the "world of separation" from an experience of transcendent unity, the Torah now "translated" within him. God's thunder and Moses' words are now one.

But the God who speaks in thunder is still the sky god, still the one who dwells in heaven and atop the highest peak. We are seeking a more fully internalized version of that foot-of-the-mountain experience. Remembering that our earliest ancestors were diggers of wells in the desert, suppose we allow ourselves to turn the high mountain into a deep well. Abraham observed Torah, say the rabbis, before it was given at the mountain. Let us try to imagine Torah as it was seen by that digger of wells. Instead of coming "down" from the top of the mountain, his wisdom or Torah flowed forth like water from deep within the earth. We thus try to understand revelation as the most profound of inner experiences. Seen this way, Moses' experience has much in common with the creative act, the inner mental activity of the artist, the musical composer, the mathematician, and others along with the religious figure. The core experience of creativity reaches a depth that necessarily contains an element of mystery, something "other."

We are talking here about an inner straining of the human mind to the breaking point—but rather than a breakdown that leads to madness or confusion, we envision a breakthrough to new creative achievements. This may come in the form of a novel insight, a flash of intuition instantaneously translated into the medium in which the creator works: into music, into mathematical formulae, into words. The creative energy, like the divine light, is undifferentiated. Only the tools and mindset that lead one to that flash of intuition draw on that mysterious inner reserve and direct each to be creative in a specific way. (The rabbis say that at Sinai the very senses were confused, and Israel "saw the audible and heard the visible." We can only imagine a state of creative elation from which Einstein would return with a symphony and Beethoven with a mathematical formula!) At this level of inner experience, lines between "creativity," "discovery," "inspiration," and "revelation" are impossible to draw. The language we have for drawing such fine distinctions belongs to a level of consciousness other than that at which these inner events occur. The free flow of inner energies that characterizes such moments does not admit clear borders between "I" and "Thou" or between "mine" and "thine."

When the soul (the human capacity to love and tremble in awe) as well as the mind (the human capacity to understand) participates in the creative, inspirational, or revelatory event, that event takes on a religious character. The human striving for revelation involves joining the emotional and the intellectual life fully. We Jews assert that Moshe Rabbenu—Moses our Teacher—had such an experience. The religion of ancient Israel, as embodied symbolically in that moment at Sinai, continues to represent for us the result of one of the great human encounters with Divinity. For us as Jews, it is, in existential terms, the greatest such encounter of all time. It is the only encounter we know. Others that may exist are not existentially open to us; they are not ours. True participation in a spiritual language requires the whole of the human heart. Each heart can speak only one such language. Our heart is given wholly to this one. While we recognize that there may be others, we cannot know them, cannot "set them upon our heart."

The Jewish people throughout its history has accepted the task of forming a communal religious existence and creating a civilization that stands in response to the event at Sinai. This is what I mean by "accepting the Torah." What we accept is the reality that Divinity is present in humans, manifest in human language and human institutions. We accept the challenge to create a society, with all its institutional trappings, that embodies this presence. We are no less charged with that task today than we were thousands of years ago. Part of our charge is to maintain and keep trust with the traditions of the past. We are here to be faithful bearers of our heritage. But every generation will have to create some new forms and reinterpret many old ones in order to keep the fire of Sinai alive, to keep it from becoming mere ash. Maintaining a sense of balance between these two, and not losing our awareness of Y-H-W-H while we are engaged in that balancing act, is no small task.

Generations of believers have invested boundless emotional and spiritual energy (*kavana*) in the forms of Jewish devotional life, including the words of prayer, the cycle of the calendar, its sacred music, and tales and commentaries. I believe that the power of this *kavana* is never lost. The intensity with which a form is used as a vessel of spiritual life grows and builds through each generation of devotion to it. The spiritual riches borne by the words of prayer or the form of offering increases in richness over time. A latter-day Jew, especially one coming from outside the tradition, who opens him or her self to that form may discover the tremendous riches of *kavana* that lie waiting within it. The Jewish people has both created and accepted these forms in love. That love is never lost or diminished, but is only hidden until we discover it again. The forms may not have been given by God from Sinai. But they are what we bring to the mountain; we invest them and forever associate them with the holiness we encounter there.

The relationship between the memory of Sinai and our ever-evolving religious lives as Jews is not a simple one. There is divinity to be discovered within the mitzvot (commandments), but this is not the divinity of a commanding God who insists on their proper performance. Judaism is a way of reaching inward and outward toward the One, a way sanctified not by divine fiat but by generations of those who have walked along the path. The light that lies hidden within our Torah, made up of the countless points of love and devotion placed there by our ancestors, is also the hidden light of Y-H-W-H.

Is it then imperative that Jews seek out this light? Does the God who has dwelt within the hearts of so many generations, and who has been given expression through these forms, become an immanent metsaveh, a "commanding one," who will stand behind the mitzvot as the indwelling embodiment of religious authority? I find myself to be rather close to this position, but I am not ready to assert it in any but the most personal and subjective ways.

In my own religious life, I have come to recognize the need for submission to Y-H-W-H (remember to say "Is-Was-Will Be," and not just "God"!) as a part of religious devotion. I fought long and hard against this aspect of religious life, but I now, perhaps with long-delayed maturity, have come to accept it. I believe there is no room for God—however defined—in our lives until we can overcome our own willfulness. To thus submit, to "negate your will before the divine will," is essential to accepting our covenant as I understand it, to be ready to serve as a channel for divine presence in the world.

In Judaism, this submission, usually described as *kabbalat 'ol malkhut shamayim* "accepting the yoke of divine rule," is joined to *kabbalat 'ol mitzvot*, "accepting the yoke of commandments." For myself, I recognize the necessity of this link, the sense that religious awareness only becomes constant in life through the regularity of religious discipline. But I also remain constantly aware of the pitfalls of submission as a religious value. It can lead to the cultivation of an overly submissive personality. Some expressions of submission, in our tradition as well as elsewhere, border on self-hatred. Most seriously, from a devotional point of view, the emphasis on submission may be at the expense of the true joy and exultation that are the heart of religious awareness. I turn to religious language to express the fullness of my heart. Let me be wary that religion itself not serve to diminish that fullness and joy.

Here the non-Orthodoxy of my theology is critical to my religious life. Because I know of the human role in the origin of the commandments, and because I know that all human creations are fallible, I never hand myself over entirely to the commandments. I know that they are but a means, and an often arbitrary one, to a greater end. Out of my love for our ancestors and the divine spirit who dwells within these traditions and who asks that Jews not abandon them, I choose to be faithful to the religious discipline they represent. I will do so wherever this discipline does not bring me into conflict with religious principles I hold even more deeply: I recognize all humans as embodying the divine image and I follow the seven Noahide commandments as I have chosen to understand them. (The rabbinic list of basic universal norms for human behavior, the Noahide commandments are Judaism's closest parallel to "natural law." They are prohibitions against murder, theft, idolatry, incest, and adultery, blasphemy or denial of god, dismemberment of living animals even for food, and an admonition to establish a society ruled by law.) I seek to affirm this commitment anew each day, to keep it an act of faith ever chosen in freedom. I need to cross the Sea each day, a reminder of my freedom, before I can renew the covenant. I am helped in this struggle with authority in religion by the very helplessness of God. The One who is present in these mitzvot is really no longer the frightening commander on the moutaintop. I thank the ever self-revealing Y-H-W-H for the gifts of biblical scholarship and historical study of religion, which have helped to break the excessive yoke of religious authority, making our generation a post- rather than a premodern one. The Presence that remains within the forms is the still, small voice of our people's deepest inner self. The God I know is a Divinity that cannot act or be realized in the human world at all except through human actions. Knowing full well that I live in an age of choice and freedom, one in which I can opt to leave the domain of this religion at any moment, I choose to remain "at home" with the life rhythms of the Jewish people. In doing so, I let myself hear that pleading voice of the One who has so long inhabited these traditions, and who asks not to be abandoned by yet another one of Israel's children.

Such an "imperative" is, of course, an entirely personal one. I share it with the reader without advocacy. I have seen too much of the dark and dangerous side of religion to dare prescribe submission for anyone but myself. Though I take delight in others who join us on this path, I will not permit myself to become anyone else's surrogate "commander." You who seek to stand before that mountain, to hear the voice, to be commanded—you must get there by your own path. There is no better time to start than the night of Shavuot, a time when the heavens of your heart can open, and Torah can be given all over again. □

The Chosen People

David Curzon

The Hebrews in Egypt who chose not to leave—
mostly those holding responsible positions—
refused to be part of a stampeded populace
led by a mad stuttering murderer
who discoursed in the desert with burning bushes.
These realistic skeptics expected the worst;
they could predict worship of golden calves.
It made sense to them to stay civilized slaves

and not be witness to the separating sea,
the pillar of cloud as guide by day,
the pillar of fire as guide by night,
the struck rock that gushed water,
the thunder and lightning as signs over Sinai,
the countenance of Moses descending the mountain.

Not By Might, Not By Power:
Kahanism and Contemporary Orthodoxy

Chaim Seidler-Feller

Meir Kahane's assassination was abhorrent. But so were the reactions of some highly visible Jews. Only Leon Wieseltier got it right when he wrote in the *New Republic* that "Kahane's contribution was verbal and physical violence. This man only poisoned.... He did not save anybody from anything. He was directly responsible for the killing of innocent people. His killing was a repulsive act. But the Jewish community lost nothing."

It is incomprehensible that responsible individuals, including Seymour Reich of the Conference of Presidents, Abraham Foxman of the ADL, as well as a representative of the Israeli consulate (all three of whom attended Kahane's funeral) and Alan Dershowitz of Harvard, found it necessary to pay their respects to a man they claimed to loathe. Once again, American Jewish leaders and Israeli officials appeared unable to maintain a moral stance when confronted with populist chauvinism and an outcry for ethnic solidarity. They not only reduced Jewish moral capital, but also showed themselves to be not very different from the leaders of other ethnic communities and political bodies whom the Jewish establishment routinely condemns as weak-kneed and unprincipled.

Even more troubling, however, was the host of commentators who were careful to denounce Kahane's racism but who then credited him for important contributions to Jewish life and for the pointed questions that only he, putatively, dared to face squarely and directly. Such self-indulgent apologetics were reminiscent of the attempt by African-Americans to convince themselves that Farrakhan's anti-Semitism was but a minor—and exaggerated—component of a generally constructive social message. Indeed both men have shown a passion for hatred, and a penchant for demagoguery. And both could deftly inflate their own group's pride at the expense of another group's honor. What apologists in both camps seem to ignore is the profoundly simple teaching that evil cannot be neatly set apart from any wider "social" message.

Far more disturbing than the rationalizations of these revisionists is the way Kahane has been embraced as a Jewish hero by a large segment of the Orthodox community. The Orthodox rabbi of the Young Israel of Ocean Parkway, where Kahane's funeral was held, referred to him as a *tzaddik*, or saint. Rabbi Moshe Tendler, a prominent Yeshiva University talmudist and biologist, declared in his eulogy that "God spoke to Rabbi Kahane clearly," but that his "prophecy" had gone unheeded. The Orthodox Yeshiva of Flatbush where Kahane received his primary education saw fit to display its grief by placing an obituary for him in the *New York Times*. And among the thousands who attended his funeral, both in the U.S. and in Israel, the Orthodox formed an overwhelming majority. Of course, this is consistent with the preponderance of Orthodox Jews among Kahane's supporters

---

Chaim Seidler-Feller, a member of the Tikkun *editorial board, has ministered to students and faculty at UCLA Hillel for the past fifteen years. This article appeared in* Tikkun, *January/February 1991.*

and sympathizers. In other words, a key feature of Kahane's popularity, and one often overlooked in the discussions of the Kahane phenomenon, is the Orthodox connection.

What predisposes Orthodoxy to Kahanism? Why were so few prominent Orthodox rabbis willing to publicly condemn and ostracize him? Why, after all, is Orthodoxy amenable to a theology of vengeance and violence? Herein, we can only sketch tentative responses to such questions.

First, consider the demographic distinctiveness of the Orthodox community. Orthodox Jews tend to live in urban areas and, due to the rampant crime and threat of assault in inner-city neighborhoods, readily view themselves as victims in need of a champion. The Orthodox community was also devastated by the Holocaust. And many survivors, in the wake of the Holocaust, have identified themselves as Orthodox. This makes for a community with little or no trust in the "other." These survivors took to heart Kahane's message that "all goyim [sic] are out to get you" and "you can only rely on yourselves."

Second, one needs to take into account the psychological characteristics of Orthodox belief. Decades of public disparagement of Orthodoxy and predictions of its imminent demise have left Orthodox believers with a reservoir of smoldering anger toward other Jews and the world at large. And due to their particular experience, Orthodox Jews have internalized the negative stereotype of Jews as totally powerless. Kahane exploited these feelings of shame and anger, and, since he spoke the language of Orthodoxy, was accepted as a savior who restored Jewish pride to the downtrodden Orthodox.

Finally, in matters of theological doctrine, Orthodoxy proved to be a congenial setting in which Kahane could lend religious credibility to his racism. Since Kahane consistently quoted biblical and rabbinic sources to bolster his arguments, Orthodox rabbis were reluctant to criticize him. For to do so would have meant admitting that some Jewish teachings are indeed racist, hateful, and immoral, and therefore must be reinterpreted—either changed or rejected. For some, this basic failure of theological nerve merged with a deeper feeling that Kahane had accurately pinpointed the primitive underbelly of Judaism; that his reading, based as it was on tradition, was actually correct.

And Orthodoxy has seized upon those elements of our tradition that lend themselves to such interpretations. The Book of Joshua and the commandment to conquer the land have invested traditional Judaism with a rationalized violent impulse. In fact the only manifestations of organized Jewish violence since the establishment of the state of Israel have come from within the ranks of Orthodoxy: I refer to the Shabbat stone-throwing practiced by ultra-Orthodox Jews; and to the Jewish underground (*mach teret*) that plotted to blow up the mosques atop the Temple Mount and murdered several Arab students in cold blood.

Moreover, the typical Yeshiva curriculum has little to say to its students about ethical approaches to the non-Jew. When the question of other faiths is broached, it is usually only to demonstrate the superiority of Judaism and the vanity of any competing tradition. More often than not, Yeshiva students are taught to regard other religions—particularly Christianity and Islam—with contempt. Under these circumstances the results of a recent survey of the attitudes of Israeli high-school students toward Arabs are not at all astonishing: the data reveal that the level of intense hatred of Arabs is almost twice as great among religious students as among secular students.

These lessons are learned in the synagogue as well. Orthodox worshippers chant a memorial prayer almost every Shabbat that calls forth God's vengeance: "May our God remember them for good with the other righteous of the world, and render retribution for the blood of God's servants which has been shed." And many Orthodox children learn tossing the opening words of Psalm 94:1—"God of vengeance, Lord, God of vengeance, appear!"—to the tune of a rousing march. Is it not possible that the ease with which Orthodox Jews call for *nekama* (revenge) unconsciously primed them to respond to Kahane's vengeful anger? *Nekama* was forever on Kahane's lips, and he frequently led crowds in a *nekama* cheer. Kahane's funerals in Brooklyn and Jerusalem teemed with signs calling for revenge.

The changed complexion of world religion—notably the fundamentalist movement—has made Orthodoxy still more vulnerable to Kahane's message, producing a bitter backlash against modernity among Orthodox believers. One component of that fundamentalist revival is the emergence of an uncharacteristic literalism within the heart of rabbinic Judaism. The ability to formulate principles based on a literal reading of texts (both biblical and rabbinic) further bolstered ultra-nationalists, Kahane among them, with traditional proofs that substantiated their chauvinism. In addition, the growth of Orthodox fundamentalism aroused the already fervently nationalistic Orthodox masses to seek a messianic figure—or more correctly, an anti-messiah—whose divine pretensions ran contrary to the Torah-of-this-world and whose absolutism was, by definition, idolatrous. Here too, it comes as no surprise that Lubavitch, with its messianism, was consistently tolerant of Kahane, and that a lubavitcher rabbi from Los Angeles was among his eulogizers. Apparently one *avodah zarah* (idolatry) is comfortable with another.

For all these reasons, Orthodoxy has proven a fertile breeding ground for Kahanism. This partnership is especially destructive for Judaism, since Kahanism not only defiles the God who is the creator of humanity; it also undermines the basis of a Jewish religious humanism. Kahane's theology of vengeance has transformed the God of love and peace into a pagan god of hatred and war.

The death of Kahane will not stop this process. The challenge for all Jews is to reclaim their tradition and decisively uproot, once and for all, the Jewish teachings of contempt that have attracted so many followers to Kahane's message. □

Al Cheyt עַל חֵטְא

Michael Lerner

We invite you to use this as a supplement to (not a replacement for) the traditional High Holiday confessional prayer "Al Cheyt."

On the Jewish High Holidays we take collective responsibity for our lives and for the activities of the community of which we are a part. Although we realize that we did not create the world we were born into, we nevertheless have a responsibiity for what it is like as long as we participate in it. Despite the ending of the cold war and the growing recognition that there is no longer any serious external threat to America's security, we live in a society that pours huge sums of money into meaningless military expenditures while ignoring the plight of the hungry, the homeless, and the poor. We participate in an economy that squanders the world's resources and destroys the life-support systems of the planet, all in the name of the "freedom" of individual corporations to amass endless profits without concern for the well-being of the rest of the human race. Our Jewish heritage teaches us that even though we may not have personally created these policies and this social system, to the extent that we participate in this society and benefit from its wealth and power, we are also morally respnosible for these sins.

The requirement to take collective moral responsibility for our world makes it necessary for us to atone for what is being done in the name of the Jewish people. This year we are particularly hopeful that peace negotiations will bring lasting peace and security to Israel. But we are also aware that the government of Israel refuses to acknowledge the rights of Palestinians, refuses to allow them to choose their own representatives to engage in negotiations, and maintains that Israel will never exchange land for peace. Given these positions, the Occupation is likely to continue—and so too will the suffering of the Palestinian people and of the many Israelis who attempt to enforce the Occupation. The most recent B'Tselem report of torture (printed in *Tikkun*, September/October 1991) cannot be ignored. Israel claims to be acting in the name of the Jewish people—and it is as proud Jews that we must take collective responsibility for Israel and repent for its misdeeds even as we rejoice in its many virtues.

We understand that the Jewish people did not create the circumstances that now place Israel in the role of governing more that one-and-a-half million Palestinians. Jews needed a haven from the oppression they faced in Europe and in Arab lands—but in order to create that refuge, Jews' own needs for national self-determination were set in opposition to the Palestinian peoples' need for their own homeland. The growth of anti-Semitism in the Soviet Union and Eastern Europe reminds us how important it is to us to have a strong and secure Israel. Yet as Jews we must also take responsibility for not having done all that we could to resolve the conflict with the Palestinian people in these past years, and for allowig the government of Israel to speak in an insensitive way and to act in an arrogant manner toward those Palestinians who for decades have languished in

---

This supplement appeared in Tikkun *September/October 1991.*

refugee camps and in exile from their homeland.

While the struggle to change ourselves and our world may be long and painful, it is our struggle. No one else can do it for us. To the extent that we have failed to do all that we could on either the personal or social fronts in the past year, we ask God and each other for collective forgiveness—and commit ourselves to acting differently this next year.

וְעַל כּוּלָם אֱלוֹהַּ   *Ve-all kulam Eloha*
סְלִיחוֹת, סְלַח לָנוּ,   *selikhot, selakh lanu,*
מְחַל לָנוּ, כַּפֶּר לָנוּ.   *mekhal lanu, kaper lanu.*

For all our sins, may the force that makes forgiveness possible forgive us, pardon us, and make atonement possible.

For the sins we have committed before you and in our communities by being so preoccupied with ourselves that we ignored the social world in which we live;

And for the sins we have committed by being so directed toward the political and social world that we have ignored our own spiritual development;

For the sins of accepting the current distribution of wealth and power as unchangeable;

And for the sins of giving up on social change and focusing exclusively on personal advancement and success;

For the sins of feeling so worn out when we hear about oppression that we finally close our ears;

And for the sins of dulling our outrage at the continuation of poverty and oppression and violence in this world;

For the sins of participating in a racist society and not dedicating more energy to fighting racism;

And for the sins we have committed by allowing our food and our air to be poisoned;

For the sins of allowing our government to continue the arms race;

And for the sins of squandering the resources of the planet in order to produce frivolous goods;

For the sins of not doing enough to challenge sexist institutions and practices;

And for the sins of turning our back on—or participating in—the oppression of gays and lesbians;

For the sins of allowing our society to give low priority to fight aginst AIDS, cancer, Alzheimer's and other disease;

And for the sins of allowing homelessness, poverty, and world hunger to continue;

For all these sins we ask God and each other to give us the strength to forgive ourselves and each other.

For the sins we have committed by not forgiving our parents for what they did to us when we were children;

And for the sins of having too little compassion or too little respect for our parents or for our children;

For the sins of not seeing the spark of divinity within each person we encounter and within ourselves;

And for the sins of not learning from and giving adequate respect to our elders;

For the sins of being jealous and trying to possess and control those who we love;

And for the sins of being judgmental of others and and ourselves;

For the sins of witholding love and support;

And for the sins of doubting our ability to love or to get love from others;

For the sins of fearing to lose ourselves in a commitment to another person or to a cause;

And for the sins of insisting that everything we do have a payoff;

For the sins of not allowing ourselves to play;

And for the sins of being manipulative or hurting others to protect our own egos;

וְעַל כּוּלָם אֱלוֹהַּ   *Ve-all kulam Eloha*
סְלִיחוֹת, סְלַח לָנוּ,   *selikhot, selakh lanu,*
מְחַל לָנוּ, כַּפֶּר לָנוּ.   *mekhal lanu, kaper lanu.*

For the sins we have commited by not publicly supporting the Jewish people and Israel when they are being treated or criticized unfairly;

And for the sins we have committed by not publicly criticizing Israel or the Jewish people when they are acting as oppressors;

For the sins of not recognizing the humanity and pain of the Palestinian people;

And for the sins of not recognizing the humanity and pain of the Israeli people or for blaming the conflict with the Palestinians entirely on the Jewish people or Israelis or Zionism;

For the sins of not fostering a dialogue between Israelis and Palestinians;

And for the sins of ignoring the racism of Jews toward Arabs;

For the sins of allowing the beating, gassing, shooting, and killing of Palestinians to continue;

And for the sins of denying Palestinians in the Territories fundamental human rights;

For the sins of focusing only on Israel's sins without also acknowledging the intransigence and insensitivity of the PLO and the violence against suspected collaborators;

And for the sins of ignoring the victims of Palestinian terrorism;

For the sins of allowing conservative or insensitive leaders to speak on behalf of all America Jews;

And for the sins of being critical of Jewish life from a distance rather than from personal involvement and commitment;

For the sins of not learning more of our Jewish heritage and tradition;

And for the sins of not giving enough time and energy to building the kind of Jewish community we desire but instead expecting things to happen without contributing to make them happen;

For the sins of thinking we are more conscious or more intelligent or more ethical or more politically correct than everyone else;

And for the sins we have committed by being insensitive or insulting to non-Jews;

For the sins of not sharing responsibility for child-rearing;

And for the sins of not taking care of each other;

For the sins of not having compassion for each other;

And for the sins of always having to be right;

For the sins of focusing only on our sins and not on our strengths and beauties;

And for the sins of not adequately rejoicing and celebrating the beauty and grandeur of God's creation;

For all these, Lord of Forgiveness, forgive us, pardon us, grant us atonement. ☐

וְעַל כּוּלַם אֱלוֹהַּ   *Ve-all kulam Eloha*
סְלִיחוֹת, סְלַח לָנוּ,   *selikhot, selakh lanu,*
מְחַל לָנוּ, כַּפֶּר לָנוּ.   *mekhal lanu, kaper lanu.*

The Problem with Halakhic Ethics

Moshe Ish Shalom

I t is 1996 at the Hadassah Hospital in Jerusalem. Either Israel has been transformed into a complete theocracy, or the religious political parties have become strong enough to get a series of laws passed, including a law stating that no one may be criminally prosecuted for observing Halakha (Jewish religious law). Sounds innocent enough, especially to assimilated Jews who are returning to their roots. In fact, it makes them damn proud (in a romantic sort of way) that, after two thousand years, a Jew can never be hurt again for observing ancestral rites and customs. So most Jews have supported the legislation.

One of the most brilliant surgeons on the ward is a very presentable Jew, quite religious, with a long but well-groomed beard. Quite by accident, it is discovered by someone in the mortality statistics department that over the past ten years this surgeon has operated on three thousand patients. Seventy percent of the Jews have survived. Seventy percent of the non-Jews (most of whom are Christians) have not survived. Furthermore, of the Jews who have died, 90 percent were secular.

The doctor is arrested on suspicion of mass murder, and the case is brought to trial. His defense attorney has a simple argument. He cites the authoritative sixteenth-century compendium of Jewish law, the *Shulkhan Arukh* (Yoreh Deah 158), which states quite clearly that it is forbidden to save the life of an idolater or of a Jew who brazenly rejects the kosher dietary laws or any other religious law. This prohibition applies also to a Jew who is an *apikores*—someone who does not believe that the dead will be resurrected someday or that a descendant of David will be the Messiah. The law is directed especially at doctors, who should withhold treatment from such people. In fact, the *Shulkhan Arukh* suggest ways to get rid of such people, including spreading rumors about them that will eventually lead to their being killed, or removing a ladder from a place to which they have fallen and have no other means of escape (in this way, the man or woman simply starves to death). The attorney cites supporting evidence that the rights of an idolater in Israel are nonexistent and adds that Maimonides asserted (in his Laws of Idolatry) that, when Jews have a secure military hold on Israel, the above-mentioned laws do not go far enough. Idolaters must not be permitted to be in the land at all. It is not clear from the context whether, if they refuse to leave, idolaters are to be "transferred" (to quote a popular euphemism for expulsion) by force or simply killed.

In light of these halakhic precedents from the greatest of the codifications of Jewish law, the case against the surgeon is rather weak. The prosecuting attorney makes a feeble attempt to raise the issue of *mishum aivah*—the law, cited by the *Shulkhan Arukh* itself, that if such action will cause hatred of the Jew then it is not to be done. But the defense attorney neatly rejects this charge

---

Moshe Ish Shalom is a pseudonym being used by an Orthodox rabbi who was ordained by Yeshiva University. In explaining his use of a pseudonym, Rabbi Shalom says, "I'm not prepared to sign this piece because there has been a decrease in openness within the mainstream of the Orthodox world toward discussing difficult issues such as these, and I would be unable to remain unscathed by people's anger and adverse reactions were I to give my name." This article appeared in Tikkun, March/April 1989.

because *mishum aivah* expresses an exilic concern with Jewish safety in the midst of an idolatrous host society and therefore is clearly not halakhically relevant in a militarily strong Israeli state.

The prosecuting attorney also attempts to echo the sentiments of Jewish religious liberals (there are still a few) who state that compassion is an essential component of what it means to be Jewish. In fact, he cites the same Maimonides, who says that one of the essential characteristics of a Jew is his compassion. Of course, all this argument does is impugn the character of the defendant; it cannot possibly make him criminally liable. But the defense attorney disputes even this point. He puts his client on the stand, and the doctor tells the judges that he is a man of great compassion. He works with windows and orphans, and he offers personal assistance to the poor. Of course, all of those he helps are religiously observant people, since he is obligated to hate those who are not, because they fall under the category of *rasha*—the wicked. Furthermore, he gladly confesses his actions in the hospital and feels that he was simply fulfilling his halakhic obligations. Finally, he claims that even · though idolaters are wicked, he had compassion for them and did not allow them to bleed to death slowly. Rather, at the risk of being discovered, he made sure to eliminate key steps in the operations so that they would die quickly.

The case is dismissed. The non-Jews and secularists of Israeli society scramble to establish their own hospitals, and, in the back of their minds, they make plans to leave. And so the horror begins...

Is this scenario impossible? I do not know, but I do know that we who are committed to Halakha have not even begun to face some very tough questions about what it means to be religious and ethical in the twentieth century. And if we are not careful, the rule of the mob or the forces of history—not our great tradition of ethics—will determine our spiritual consciences. The fundamental question for a contemporary halakhist must be how s/he responds to laws that, by standards of personal conscience, are morally repugnant. This is not the place to prove it, but it seems clear to me (from studying Jewish texts for the past fifteen years) that now is not the first time in Jewish history that halakhists have had to struggle with this issue. It seems that , at some juncture, the laws about killing a wayward son; wiping out whole cities of idolatrous Jews; forcing a woman suspected of adultery to drink a potion; allowing capital punishment, polygamy, and slavery; and prohibiting women from going out in public all become problematic to many rabbis.

The major problem, however, is that rarely, if ever, did halakhists categorically state that a law was wrong or morally problematic. Instead, the rabbis effectively eliminated the Deuteronomic extermination laws, for example, by claiming that they referred to the seven nations of ancient Canaan and that those nations no longer exist. But this method of modifying the law is extremely dangerous, since it eliminates honest discussion of the moral problem of the mass murder of men, women, and children. The law is conveniently consigned to the dustbin of halakhic history and is not attacked from the universalist perspective of fairness, tolerance, and compassion, or from the broader Jewish perspective embodied by the many other prophetic and rabbinic texts that display extraordinary moral sensitivity and deep respect for all human life, which is created in the image of God.

To take account of this broader Jewish perspective is to confront the agonizing contradictions that I, a halakhic Jew, struggle within the *Shulkhan Arukh*. Specifically, the *Shulkhan Arukh*, in addition to the aforementioned problematic laws, also contains an extraordinary discussion about protecting one's life in situations of danger. That discussion is intimately related to a whole series of laws, codified by the *Shulkhan Arukh*, about not being permitted to put someone else in danger. In fact, one critical law states that one must not sell weapons to those who will use them to kill, because one ends up being an accomplice to the crime—murder being one of the seven prohibitions that all people, regardless of religion are halakhically bound to observe. (This law, incidentally, makes a large chunk of the taxes collected by every modern state for the purposes of weapons production and sales halakhically questionable—yet another Halakha conveniently ignored.)

Technically, the law against selling these weapons comes under the halakhic rubric of not putting a stumbling block before a blind person, which is a powerful example of a compassionate, moral law of ancient Judaism.

How does one struggle with such deep ethical contradictions in the halakhic system? I think the only answer is to do it honestly, and halakhists make a tragic mistake when they continue to gloss over these problems by apologetically claiming that this or that law is not relevant in such and such a circumstance of contemporary life. Another favorite method used by halakhists to quote the small portion of the laws of idolatry that states that one must support the idolatrous poor as well as the Jewish poor for the sake of peace, while completely ignoring the surrounding laws which are neither humanitarian nor peaceful.

We cannot avoid these tough problems anymore, the stakes are now too high for apologetics because apologetics leaves open a moral Pandora's box. Imagine that instead of the United States' having said unequivocally that nonwhites and women have the right to vote, it had said that the Blacks who came from Africa were not really human and the women of yesteryear had minds like children, but that today's Blacks and women are no longer that way, so they have voting rights. Doesn't this claim leave the door open for racist senators in the year 2000 to destroy civil rights in this country?

If we as halakhists do not struggle with laws that are morally problematic, if we do not honestly confront the paradoxes of the halakhic system, we are bound for disaster in the new age of halakhic power. We must unequivocally acknowledge, despite the miserable moral track record of Western civilization, that there are universal moral principles (many derived from our own prophets) that dozens of great minds have agreed upon and to which we owe allegiance. We must acknowledge that great moral ideas come from great moral minds created in the image of God. The human mind is not our sole allegiance, but to replace the mind with obedience to the written word *alone* is extremely dangerous. To do so is to be untrue even to the halakhic system, itself, which allows for honest ethical struggle that can, when necessary, lead to the overriding of something morally repugnant from the past. The old adage continues to be relevant: the Torah is like water; it can grow either beautiful flowers or weeds.

When I was in yeshiva I had some extraordinary teachers. Two particularly memorable ones taught me Talmud and Bible. Both men were survivors of World War II, and both were the gentlest men I have ever known. I remember how we never seemed to dwell on the portions of Genesis that involved Jewish cruelty, such as the section about the sons of Jacob wiping out the city of Shekhem. And I was told time and again that Abraham was the father of our people because he showed so much compassion for the stranger and even for the cruel people of Sodom. I remember that I never learned about the Ten Plagues without also learning that we do not say Hallel, the prayer of praise, on the last six days of Passover because the midrash states that God reproached the Israelites for singing at the Red Sea while His creatures (the Egyptians) were drowning. And the list of moral ideals that I was taught goes on. I know that the people who teach in yeshiva now are not emphasizing these principles. The essential teaching today focuses on survival, angry survival. And I shudder to think of what might be taught tomorrow.

Moreover, I have to say that, despite my love for those teachers, they were wrong for not discussing in class what was in their heart of hearts—namely, that there are elements of the tradition that do not coincide with the ideal Jewish way of life that they believed in; that the *erlekh*, good Jew that they loved and admired would not have, indeed could not have, mass murdered a city of idolaters or put someone to death for violating the Sabbath. It was wrong to shove the issue under the table because doing so left the door open for a generation today that is profoundly influenced, even impressed, by the weaponry and violence of the world of nation-states; this generation openly embraces the very values that these saintly Jewish rabbis of old found most repugnant in their exilic host societies. When I sat in a minyan (quorum for prayer) with these rabbis and I said with them, at the end of the prayer service, "These with chariots and these with swords, but we will trust in the name of God," I knew very well with whom I was praying and to which God we were praying. Now I am not so sure on either score. Now I am sure only that I must call upon my religious colleagues to build a contemporary halakhic structure that is not a desecration of the Divine Name but, on the contrary, is a sanctification of that Name—the Name that brings this world closer to redemption.

The hypothetical case that I have raised is not an isolated problem of one difficult law regarding idolaters. People who are well-versed in Jewish law know this to be true. The problem involves a huge body of Jewish law that has been rather carelessly applied to all non-Jews both in ritual and in civil law. Most important, this body of laws will, in these years ahead, be used by some people, with increasing frequency, as a battering ram against Palestinians and anyone else, Jewish or gentile, who gets in the way of an amoral ultranationalism.

We already see a Jewish world in which everyone picks and chooses the central elements of his or her religiosity. For many, the laws governing the observance of Sabbath are not relevant to their lives, while for others, who are fanatical about observance of the Sabbath and the kosher dietary regulations, the laws governing business ethics and pursuit of peace are nonexistent. We have to be prepared for the likelihood that in the near future some people will make laws governing the elimination of idolaters from the land of Israel a central tenet of their Judaism. These laws have already become a great excuse for abusing the Palestinians.

Certainly, blame for Jewish hatred of the gentile, particularly the Palestinian, cannot be placed squarely on the Halakha. The reasons are numerous, many of them understandable if not justifiable. We did not ask for two thousand years of senseless persecution, right up to and including the brutality of the PLO, but the psychological damage that such persecution has wrought is unmistakable. Sometimes, as I read a popular Jewish newspaper, I get confused by the overwhelming number of articles telling me whom I am supposed to hate most: Palestinians; Arabs; Russians; Nazis; neo-Nazis; Black Muslims; Democrats; nascent anti-Semitic groups in the West, the South, Connecticut, Argentina; Jimmy Carter; anyone not Israeli who indicates obliquely that even one Palestinian is suffering, or who in fact even uses the words "Palestinian" or "Arab refugee," (self-hating Jews); and so on…. There is no doubt that we have a right to be sick of persecution, but we are increasingly sick *from* persecution, and it is time to admit that this sickness has blinded many of us to the concrete steps that can be taken to resolve conflicts with non-Jews, especially Palestinians.

We must not allow Halakha to become a vehicle of murderous or suicidal illness, and we can easily accomplish this goal in two ways. First, we must continue what enlightened Orthodox and Conservative halakhists have already begun—namely, the articulation of the many high moral standards that the traditional texts demand of Jews. Second, we must not acknowledge the context in which much of the Halakha concerning non-Jews was written, and face squarely what we are to say and do about the morally problematic laws. There was a very sad mutual hatred between Jew and Christian that prevailed for thousands of years, and this mutual hatred made it extremely difficult for Jews to develop an objective, moral, halakhic perspective on the status of the gentile.

I know that for most Jews the issue of the divine origin of Jewish law is of little consequence. But for some Jews, myself included, the notion that Jewish law is of divine origin is extremely important. Consequently, I agonize tremendously over anything that I find problematic in Jewish religious tradition. One thing that I cannot do—and that we as a people cannot do—is ignore the fundamental religious assumption that lies at the core of the biblical and rabbinic corpus, an assumption that serves as a beacon of eternal truth. And that assumption is that there is a God; a God who created a magnificent, awesome universe and who is good and compassionate for having

Photo by Oliver and Steinberg

given us that universe; a God who wants us to be the same—creative, compassionate, and good. We cannot allow certain laws to be revived by irresponsible people in the name of a spiritual "authenticity" when these laws by themselves actually call into question the moral and spiritual message of a three-thousand-year tradition.

I am fully aware that I have not, in this short essay, even scratched the surface of these complicated laws, indeed, it was not my purpose to do so. My purpose was to alert us to the potential danger that lies ahead if Halakha begins to play a more dominant role in Israeli life, and also to stimulate discussion about the possibility of the growth of halakhic ethics. I am aware that there are counterquotes and that some halakhic theorists and *poskim* (rabbinic authorities) have more humane treatments of the gentile, the idolater, and the righteous and the wicked than do the actors in the theoretical case I've described. However, the interpretation I have presented is a real factor in the religious word and threatens to have a growing influence unless a counterdefinition of an ethically informed Halakha is created. There are two possible reactions to the increasing role of Halakha in political and social life. One is to reject it and its proponents as ethically ill-suited to confront the problems that we face. Another reaction, however, is to refuse to leave Halakha in the hands of those who do not care about the horrifying possibilities of the above-mentioned laws and instead to develop it and struggle with it as has been done for three thousand years. The latter approach would be a far healthier and more authentic Jewish response and would wrest authenticity from those who have extraordinary attachment to ritual observance but little knowledge of Judaism's many moral laws and insights.

It is high time we developed, out of the embarrassingly dusty stock of ethical Halakhas, a serious ethic of social responsibility. The results of such a development, wedded to the best moral insights—both Jewish and gentile—of our day, could have a profound impact on the popular and intellectual life of the Jewish people. □

Can Judaism Survive the Twentieth Century?

Jacob Neusner

T he twentieth century, until practically our own time, has produced no important and
influential Judaic systems. The well-established Judaisms that flourish today—Reform,
Reconstructionist, Orthodox, and Conservative Judaism—all took shape in the nineteenth
century, and in Germany. Secular Jewish socialism and Zionism also arose in the nineteenth century.
How is it possible that one period produced a range of Judaic systems of enormous depth and
breadth, systems that attracted mass support and changed many people's lives, while the next three-
quarters of a century did not? And, further, what are we now to expect, on the eve of the twenty-
first century? I think we are on the threshold of another great age of system-building in Judaism.

Why No New Judaic System for Seventy-Five Years?

Why no new Judaisms for so long? The stimulus for system-building surely should have come
from the creation of the first Jewish state in two thousand years. Yet the creation of this state yielded nothing more interesting than a flag and a rather domestic politics, not a worldview and a way of
life such as the one the founders of the American republic, Madison and Hamilton, enunciated.

American Jewry presents the same picture. War and dislocation, migration and relocation—in
the past these phenomena generated and sustained system-building in Jewish societies. But the
political changes affecting Jews in America, who became Jewish Americans in ways that Jews did
not become Jewish Germans or Jewish Frenchmen or Jewish Englishmen and women, have yielded
no encompassing systems.

Millions of people moved from one world to another, changed their language, their occupation,
and virtually every other significant social and cultural aspect of their lives—and produced nothing
more than a set of recapitulations of four Judaic systems, serviceable under utterly different
circumstances.

I see three reasons why no Judaic systems have emerged since the end of the nineteenth century. I
do not claim that they provide all-encompassing explanations, but I do think they help us answer the
question before us.

1. *The Holocaust*. First of all, the demographic reason, which has two components. The most productive sector of world Jewry perished. Also, the conditions that brought about the great systemic
creations vanished with the six million. Not only too many (one is too many!), but the wrong Jews
died. What I mean is that Judaic systems emerged in Europe, not in America or in what was then
Palestine; and, within Europe, these systems came from Central and Eastern European Jewry. The
Jewish population in Eastern Europe was vast. It engaged in enormous amounts of learning; and
what's more, it formed a self-aware community—not scattered and individual, but composed and

---

*Jacob Neusner is a member of The Institute for Advanced Study in Princeton, New Jersey, and a professor of
religion at Brown University. This article appeared in* Tikkun, *July/August 1989.*

bonded. In short, for the Jews that perished, being Jewish constituted a collective enterprise, not an individual predilection.

In the West, people tend to identify religion with belief, to the near exclusion of behavior, so religion is understood as a personal state of mind. Jews in the West tend to be concerned more with self than with society, less with culture and community than with conscience and character. Under such circumstances, system-building doesn't flourish, for systems speak of communities and create worlds of meaning, answer pressing public questions and produce broad answers.

Yet the demographic explanation cannot, by itself, suffice. After all, today's Jewish populations produce massive communities, 300,000 here, half a million there. Both American Judaism and Israeli nationalism testify to the possibility of system-building even after the mass murder of European Jewry. When we consider, moreover, the strikingly unproductive character of large populations of Jews, the inert and passive ideology (such as it is) of the Jewish communities in France, Britain, South Africa, and the Soviet Union, for instance, it becomes clear that even where there are populations capable of generating and sustaining distinctive Judaic systems, none is in sight. So we must turn to yet another explanation.

2. *The Demise of Intellect.* The as-yet-unappreciated factor of sheer ignorance, the profound pathos of Jews' illiteracy in all books but the books of the streets and marketplaces, is a second explanation for the decline of Jewish system-building. The Judaisms that survive focus on emotional or political concerns—readily available to all. They offer nothing of taste and judgment, intellect and reflection; nothing of tradition and traditional culture; nothing of the worlds in which words matter.

The systems of the nineteenth and twentieth centuries made constant reference to the Judaism of the Torah, even when rejecting it. Jews received and used the heritage of human experience, captured as in amber, in the words of the Torah. So they did not have to make things up afresh every morning or rely only on that narrow range of human experience that is immediately accessible.

By contrast, Israeli nationalism and the American Judaism of Holocaust and Redemption—the two most influential systems that move Jews to action in the world today—scarcely concern themselves with this traditional focus. They emphasize only what is near at hand. They work with the raw materials made available by contemporary experience—emotions on the one hand, politics on the other. Access to realms beyond requires learning in literature; but the Judaic systems of the twentieth century do not regard the reading of books as a principal part of the Jewish way of life. The consequence is a strikingly abbreviated agenda of issues, a remarkably one-dimensional set of urgent questions.

The reason for this neglect is that today's Jews, especially in Western Europe, the Soviet Union, and the United States, but also in Canada, Australia, South Africa, Argentina, Brazil, and other areas, have lost all access to the Judaism of the dual Torah, oral and written, that sustained fifteen centuries of Jews before now. Jews in the European, African, and Australian worlds no longer regard "being Jewish" as a matter of intellect, and, to the extent that they have a Jewish worldview, it has little connection to the Judaic canon.

American Jews specifically have focused their imaginative energies upon the Holocaust, and they have centered their eschatological fantasies on "the beginning of our redemption" in the State of Israel. But they have not gone through the one, nor have they chosen to participate in the other. Not having lived through the mass murder of European Jewry, American Jews have restated the problem of evil in unanswerable form and have then transformed that problem into an obsession. Not choosing to settle in the State of Israel, they have defined redemption—the resolution of the problem of evil—in terms remote from their world. In short, American Judaism is plagued by focusing on a world in which its members do not live.

3. *The Triumph of Large-Scale Organization.* Third and distinct from the other two factors is the bureaucratization of Jewry that has resulted from its emphasis on immediately accessible political

and emotional concerns. Jews who place little value on matters of intellect and learning are placed in organizational positions of power, while those more reflective Jews are given little influence. This stratification prevents system-building because intellectuals are the people who create religious systems. Administrators do not, and when they need ideas they simply hire publicists and journalists who churn out propaganda.

This emphasis on bureaucrats is hardly surprising. In an age in which, to survive at all, Jews had to address the issues of politics and economics, and build a state (in Israel) and a massive and effective set of organizations capable of collective political action (in the United States), politicians, not sages, were needed. And though these politicians did their task as well as one might have hoped, we should not lose sight of the cost. The end of the remarkable age of Judaic system-building may prove to be a more calamitous consequence of the destruction of European Jewry than anyone has yet realized. Not just Jews, but the Jewish spirit as well, may have suffocated in the gas chambers.

The End of the Judaisms of the Nineteenth Century

Among the six great Judaisms of the first third of the twentieth century, all have lost nerve and none retains vitality. Jewish Socialism-cum-Yiddishism is a victim of the Holocaust. Zionism has no important message that is not already available from the Judaism of Holocaust and Redemption. Reform, Reconstructionist, Orthodox, and Conservative Judaisms have all lost power.

Reform Judaism, having sold its soul to the Judaism of Holocaust and Redemption, has lost the source of its energy in the prophetic tradition of Judaism. Western Orthodox Judaism answers questions about living by the Torah in modern society that few people wish to ask anymore. Those who want tradition and also a place in an open society find the answer in a variety of Judaisms. The diverse Orthodoxies now concur, with the exception of the minority around Yeshiva University, that to be Orthodox is to live segregated from and with scarcely veiled hostility to the rest of the Jewish and gentile worlds. Accordingly, everyone wants a place in the center; everyone espouses the ideal that we now identify with Conservative Judaism: that we wish to be Jewish in an integrated society and that we want our Judaism to infuse our lives as Americans with meaning. It is a mediating, healing, centrist, and moderate ideal; an ideal that teaches us to look to the Judaic religious tradition for guidance but to make up our own minds, to live by something we call Judaism but to accept the possibility of change where appropriate, necessary, or desirable.

The institutions of Conservative Judaism, however, are weak. They do not enjoy the financial support of Jewish lay people, and much of the Conservative rabbinate is alienated from the movement's central institution, The Jewish Theological Seminary. In fairness, however, the younger generation of Conservative rabbis is starting to overcome this alienation.

What of Reform Judaism? If I had to choose two words to characterize the contemporary state of Reform Judaism, they would be sloth and envy. I call Reform Judaism slothful because it has become lazy about developing its own virtues and so deprives all Judaisms of its invaluable gifts and insights. I call it envious because it sees virtue in others and despises itself. The single greatest and most urgent idea in the Jewish world today is the one idea that Reform Judaism has made its own and developed for us all, and that is the idea that God loves all humanity, not only holy Israel.

Yet the movement still regards itself as second-class and somehow less than a fully legitimate form of Judaism. By "the movement" I do not mean a few theologians at Hebrew Union College who have set forth a solid and substantial rationale for Reform Judaism in both history (Michael A. Meyer) and theology (Jakob J. Petuchowski). I mean the vast number of pulpit rabbis and laypeople who see more observant Jews and think of themselves as somehow inferior, who meet more learned Jews and think less of themselves.

Though less observance and less learning weaken Reform Judaism's claim to Jewish authenticity, I think Reform Judaism has a message to offer all Jews, including the most Orthodox of the Orthodox and the most nationalistic of the nationalists—one that is more important than studying the Talmud or not eating lobster. Reform Judaism defines Judaism as a religion of respect and love for the other, as much as for the self. Reform Judaism teaches that God loves all people, emphasizes the parts of the Torah that deliver that message, and rejects bigotry and prejudice when practiced not only by gentiles but by Jews as well.

The single most urgent moral crisis facing Jewish communities today is the Jews' hostility toward the other, the outsider. The novelist Norman Mailer, writing in the *New York Times* in language reminiscent of the prophetic tradition, stated what I conceive to be the great contribution of Reform Judaism to the life of Jewry everywhere:

> What made us great as a people is that we, of all ethnic groups, were the most concerned with the world's problems.... We understood as no other people how the concerns of the world were our concerns. The welfare of all the people of the world came before our own welfare.... The imperative to survive at all costs ... left us smaller, greedier, narrower, preternaturally touchy and self-seeking. We entered the true and essentially hopeless world of the politics of self-interest; 'is this good for the Jews?' became, for all too many of us, all of our politics.

Mailer concluded: "The seed of any vital American future must still break through the century-old hard-pack of hate, contempt, corruption, guilt, odium, and horror.... I am tired of living in the miasma of our indefinable and ongoing national shame." I find in Mailer's comments that morally vital prophetic tradition that Reform Judaism—alone among contemporary Judaisms—espouses. All the worse that today Reform Judaism has lost its nerve. Just when Jewry needs what Reform Judaism has always stood for, the message is muffled.

Speaking to the Council of Reform and Liberal Rabbis in London last year, Israeli Professor Ye-hoshafat Harkabi said that there is a crisis in our relationship to the gentiles. In a stunning public statement, Harkabi raised the possibility that "the Jewish religion that hitherto has bolstered Jewish existence may become detrimental to it." Harkabi pointed to manifestations of hostility against gentiles, formerly repressed, but ascendant in the past decade. In the State of Israel, in particular, that hostility takes such forms as these: Chief Rabbi Mordekhai Eliahu forbade Jews in the State of Israel to sell apartments to gentiles; a former chief rabbi ruled that Jews must burn their copies of the New Testament; Rabbi Eliezer Waldenberg, a scholar who has received the Israel Prize in Judaic Studies, declared that a gentile should not be permitted to live in Jerusalem; and the body of a gentile woman who lived as a Jew without official conversion was disinterred from a Jewish cemetery.

Explaining these and many other expressions of anti-gentile prejudice, Harkabi pointed out that these sentiments are not limited to the State of Israel, and he called for "discarding those elements" of Judaism that instill or express hostility to outsiders. He said, "Demonstrating to Orthodoxy that some of its rulings are liable to raise general opprobrium may facilitate the achievement of a *modus vivendi* between it and the other streams in contemporary Judaism."

Where are we to find the corpus of ideas concerning gentiles to counter these appalling actions and opinions of the pseudomessianic Orthodoxy of the State of Israel? I find them, these days, mainly in Reform Judaism—a corps of rabbis bearing a moral concern and, more important, an intellectual system and structure that encourage the Jewish people to think of both itself and the other, to love not only itself but also the outsider. For this reason it is particularly tragic that the Reform movement has become lazy and envious, that it is insecure and accepting of views it should abhor.

And what of Orthodoxy? If the Reform movement exhibits a failure of nerve, Orthodoxy displays a failure of intellect. It is not that the Orthodox are stupid or wrong or venal—merely that their views are irrelevant to the great issues confronting today's world. Except for Yeshiva University Orthodoxy, all of the Orthodox Judaisms of the day (the *haredim*, or ultra-Orthodox, in various guises) exhibit the same enormous incapacity to speak to the Jewish condition.

This is not to suggest that the Orthodox are ignorant of the classical texts of Judaism or that they misrepresent their content. To the contrary, the representation of Torah-true Judaism by the *haredim* is sound on nearly every point. Knowledgeable people can quote chapter and verse of talmudic writings in support of their position on all issues.

And that is precisely why the policies and program of the *haredim*, and therefore of the Judaism of the dual Torah, offer no meaningful option for Jews today. We must ask whether the Torah in its received or authentic or accurate version, as the *haredim* represent it, can serve in the twenty-first century. I think it cannot.

The Torah omits all systematic inquiry into the three critical matters of contemporary life: politics, economics, and science. Thus, any Judaism today that authentically realizes the Torah, oral and written, demands that Jews live only a partial life and that those Jews living in Israel dismantle the Jewish state. Jews living in the Diaspora, for their part, lacking a position on politics and economics and science, must simply retreat into ghettos, having no way to cope with the formative forces that shape the world today. The *haredim* want to make us all Amish, and the Jews are not going to agree, even though, right now, more than a few would like to walk out on the world as it is.

The three most powerful and formative forces in all of human civilization today are democracy, capitalism, and science; and on these three subjects the authentic, classical Judaism, accurately represented by the *haredim*, either has nothing at all to say or says the wrong things. The *haredim* can make their extravagant claims on the rest of us only by being parasites: we do the politics, the economics, and the science so they can live their private lives off in a corner.

If we are going to live in the twenty-first century, we require not only the Torah but also economics, politics, and science. World Jewry has no choice but to turn its back on the *haredim*. Would that God had made the world so simple as the *haredim* think it is. So fond farewell to the fantasy that the authentic Torah of Sinai, as the framers of the Babylonian Talmud read it in the seventh century, is, or can ever be, the authentic Torah of the twenty-first century. We shall do and we shall hear, indeed: *today*.

And Yet Tomorrow

Were the story to end with the creation of the new Judaisms of the nineteenth and early twentieth centuries, we would face an unhappy ending. But the advent of the twenty-first century marks the beginning of a new age of Judaic system-building. The vital signs are beginning to appear. I point to the formation of a distinctively Judaic politics, taking shape around *Tikkun* magazine, and another among the intellectuals of the Right as well. These two intellectual perspectives present two of the three prerequisites of a vital Judaism: a worldview and a way of life. Both of them join the everyday and the here-and-now to an ideal in which people can find meaning in their life together. Whether these political Judaisms can take root in the social worlds of large numbers of Jews and thus constitute not merely theologies and life patterns but "Israels"—that is, social entities—remains to be seen. Reform, Conservative, Reconstructionist, and Western Orthodox Judaisms, as well as Zionism and Jewish Socialism-Yiddishism, all formed not merely intellectual positions but social worlds. Their strength lay in transforming organizations into societies, so to speak. So far, *Tikkun* and *Commentary* express more than a viewpoint but less than a broad social movement. I point further to the *havura* movement, the renewal of Reconstructionism with Arthur Waskow and Arthur Green, the development of an accessible Judaic mysticism by Zalman Schachter-Shalomi, the development and framing of what we may call a feminist Judaism. Each of these extraordinarily vital religious formations gives promise of establishing a Judaism: a worldview, a way of life, realized within a social entity that calls itself (not necessarily exclusively) "Israel." All of these religious formations have identified urgent questions and presented answers that, to the framers, prove self-evidently valid. So I think the long period of no new Judaisms is coming to an end, though it is much too soon to tell which Judaisms, in North America at least, will inherit the greater part of Jewry.

The new Judaisms of the acutely contemporary age will succeed as we increasingly overcome the demographic and cultural catastrophe of the Holocaust. We have in North America a vast Jewish population increasingly capable of sustaining a variety of Judaisms, and we are facing a renewal of Jewish intellectual life in a way that might have stirred envy in even the proudest Jews of Germany and Poland between the Wars.

The possibility of the development of new Judaisms is helped by the decline of the power of the political and communal organizations that have dominated American Jewish life in the twentieth century. The corporate model for organized Jewry has shown its limitations. The decay of B'nai B'rith; the demise, on the local scene, of organizations such as the American Jewish Congress; the retreat of the Federations from the ideal of forming "the organized Jewish community" and their transformation into mere fund-raising agencies—these are all indications of decreased organizational power. Jews no longer find interesting a Judaic existence consisting of going to a meeting to talk about something happening somewhere else. Merely giving money, for instance, to help another Jew help a third Jew settle in the State of Israel has lost all credibility. People want hands-on engagement, and the corporate model affords the opposite.

The rejection of the corporate model and the affirmation of the place of the individual at the center of activity now marks the mode of organization of every important new Judaism today. The *Tikkun* conference in New York City is an example of that fact. I see no clear counterpart in the political Judaism of the Right, which seems to me to be fragmented in social circles such as those surrounding *Commentary*, the *National Review*, and *Chronicles*. Professors of Jewish origin in the new National Association of Scholars, for example, hardly form the counterpart to the social formation made visible at the *Tikkun* conference. In this regard the Left has provided the Right with a model.

We no longer live in what Max Weber called a bureaucratic "iron cage," and the fulfillment of our calling to be Israel comes only through our immediate and complete engagement with our highest spiritual and cultural values—whatever our Judaism tells us these are. We have, in other words, survived the twentieth century. □

Haggadah Supplement

Michael Lerner

Have you ever been to a boring Passover Seder where people mechanically read through the text? This happens only because many of us have abandoned the tradition of heated argument and discussion about the meaning of the stories connected with Passover. In fact, from the time that Rabbi Akiba used the Seder to plan a revolutionary struggle against the Romans to the moment that inhabitants of the Warsaw ghetto celebrated the Seder before beginning their historic revolt, the Jews have used the Seder as a time to grapple with their current reality—applying the message of the historical struggle against the Pharaoh. It is in this spirit that we encourage you to make any Seder you attend a lively and spirited occasion to address the problems of the present moment in light of the lessons of our past. This year particularly the Jewish people must address its relationship with the Palestinian people.

Kiddush

Before the Kiddush (the first blessing over the wine).

We are gathered here tonight to affirm our continuity with the generations of Jews who have kept alive the vision of freedom inherent in the Passover story. We proudly affirm that we are the descendants of slaves—the first group of slaves in recorded history ever to wage a successful rebellion against their slaveholders. Ours was the first historical national liberation struggle, and the prototype of many struggles that other nations would wage against those who oppressed them.

There are others who would have done their best to forget their humble past. There are other peoples that saw themselves as descendants of gods or of superhuman heroes. We are proud that our people has clung to its vision of itself as a slave people and has insisted on telling its story of liberation as the central founding event around which its culture was built.

Ruling classes have traditionally tried to convince their subjects that domination is inevitable and is built into the very structure of the universe. The Jewish people's Torah, telling the story of our liberation struggle, has been a perpetual thorn in the side of these ruling classes. Not only was our very existence a proof that the world could be changed, but every Passover, and every Sabbath, we insisted on recounting the story and drawing the lesson: The way things are is not the way things have to be; the world can be radically altered. While ruling classes, slave owners, and bosses want no limits on how much they can exploit human labor, the Shabbat institutionalizes the first absolute limit and is the prototypical worker's victory over the power of bosses. For twenty-four hours the Jewish people declare that they are withdrawing from anything connected with labor—the activity of acting on and changing the material world. Getting and spending, using money, lighting fires, building, harvesting, and writing are forbidden. For twenty-four hours we stop attempting to dominate and control the world, and instead celebrate its grandeur—and celebrate the victory in

This supplement appeared in Tikkun, *March/April 1991.*

our struggle for freedom which allows us to rest and rejoice in this way.

No wonder that the constant recounting of our struggle for freedom has predisposed Jews throughout the ages to support the liberation struggles of other oppressed groups. While there have been Jews in every age who thought that they best served the interests of our people by cuddling up to the powerful and allying with them, most Jews have rejected this strategy and instead have sought ways to ally themselves with the oppressed.

In recent years the Jewish people have themselves become the symbol of oppression to another people: the Palestinians. We have no sympathy with those Palestinians who recently rejoiced at the missiles falling on our sisters and brothers in Tel Aviv, and no sympathy with those Palestinians who cheered on Saddam Hussein. Yet we understand the frustration that they have felt as year after year the Israeli government officially and loudly proclaimed that it would never negotiate with those the Palestinians designated as their leaders, would never negotiate on the basis of "land for peace," and would never give up any part of the West Bank for a Palestinian state, no matter how many assurances they might get about Palestinians being willing to live in peace. We understand how angry it makes our Israeli brothers and sisters when they see Palestinians rejoicing at Jewish suffering. Yet misguided as those Palestinian political choices have been, and outraged as we are that these people could embrace a dictator like Saddam, we nevertheless will keep in mind that these are the distortions generated by the powerlessness and oppression. In our Seder tonight we will joyfully celebrate our own liberation—but, at the same time, we will remember the suffering of the Palestinians. Righteous though our indignation may be at the political choices they have made, we still understand that most of them live in exile, many in refugee camps, and in conditions that we would not tolerate for our own people. We pray that their liberation and freedom be achieved without harm to the safety, security, and freedom of the Jewish people living in the State of Israel. This is the radical message of our tradition: Our freedom celebration reminds us to affirm the Jewish vision that all other peoples must be allowed to live in freedom and in dignity.

After a decade of selfishly squandering the resources of our society, we now find it without the will or the resources to eradicate the vast inequalities that the past years have deepened. We are glad that the United States has the military power to challenge expansionist dictators; but we still know that the military budget could be decisively cut and tens of billions of dollars could be redirected to fight hunger and homelessness. Any celebration of our own freedom is incomplete unless we use this occasion to rededicate ourselves to redistributing the world's resources—and to remedying the inequalities that allow many of us in the United States to live in luxury and self-satisfaction while turning our backs on and shutting our ears to the thirty million children who will die of hunger this year. We are mindful that the very international economic arrangements that have brought comfort and wealth to the United States have simultaneously brought increasing poverty and suffering to peoples in the Third World. Indeed, tyrants like Saddam Hussein win a mass following precisely because they have learned to skillfully manipulate legitimate anger many in the Third World feel at the legacy of Western exploitation—and to use these feelings to bolster their narrow, power-oriented agendas.

When we see Islamic fundamentalists, various Third World nationalisms, and other ideologies used to mobilize masses of people into armed struggle, we realize that those mobilized are often decent people who have not found a more humane way to express legitimate anger. We will never condone the way this anger then gets linked to anti-Semitism, racism, and other reactionary belief systems. But we also understand the complexity of world oppression, we remember that even our real enemies are also human beings, and we understand that American selfishness and materialism is part of the problem faced by the peoples of the world. Passover, then, is not just a celebration of our own freedom—it is a moment in which we rededicate ourselves to the struggles for peace, justice, and equality for all peoples.

Bless the Vegetation of the Earth in Times of Ecological Crisis

Add to the section where we dip the parsley or greens of the earth in the salt water and say the blessing "boray pree ha-adamah."

Our holiday of freedom is also a time to rejoice in the bountiful blessings of the earth. The earth pours forth its riches, allowing us and a myriad of God's creatures to flourish and enjoy the splendor of life. Each spring we witness the miracle of renewal as vegetation returns to the planet.

This Pesach we pause to reflect on the ways that we have failed to take adequate care of the earth. The free market, in a relentless fury to amass profits without regard for ecological consequences, has generated tens of thousands of corporate ventures and products that have combined to do incalculable damage to the life-support systems of the planet. Willing to let corporate concerns for profit count more than the general interest, we have restricted our responses to the ecological insensitivity.

Our biblical injunction to work and to exercise stewardship over the earth has been transformed into a notion that the earth is simply a resource for exploitation. If we construct a society in which people are encouraged to look out for themselves and advance their own interests without regard for the consequences to others, an ecological crisis becomes almost inevitable.

As Jews, however, we recognize that our own fate is closely connected to the fate of others. The peasant in Brazil who has no other way to make a living but to cut down the rain forest, the Japanese fisherman who has no way to live but to harvest the sea, or the auto manufacturer who uses political clout to block funds for mass transit or for stricter environmental policies—all are acting rationally, given the logic of the competitive marketplace. Nevertheless, their actions have dire consequences for the rest of us. Our task is not to put these people down, but to construct an economic and social system in which people no longer have to choose between their own best interests and the best interests of the environment. This is not a question solely of learning as individuals to be more ecologically aware—though this is also important—but also of transforming the social system that makes it possible for some people to profit on activities that destroy or endanger our planet Earth.

We approach the earth not only as our sustainer, vital to our survival, but also as a sacred place, worthy of our respect and awe. The Bible teaches us that the whole earth is full of God's glory—that every part is alive, holy, and miraculous. Today, as we rededicate ourselves to saving the earth from the ecological damage that has been done, we also rejoice in the earth and thank God for its beauty and wonder.

Blessed are you, God, King of the universe, who creates the fruit of the earth.

Drops from Our Cup of Joy

Before reciting the Ten Plagues.

It is traditional to spill a drop of wine from our cups as we recite each plague. Our cup of rejoicing cannot be full if our enemies are suffering. The Talmud recounts that when the heavenly angels sang songs of praise to God as the Egyptians were drowning in the Sea of Reeds, God reprimanded them for celebrating the suffering of his children the Egyptians.

Our cup of joy also cannot be full this year. The tragedy of the destruction of European Jewry seemed to bring in its wake a new redemption: the creation of the State of Israel. But that new homeland, a renewal of ancient dreams, has been restored to us at the expense of another people. The hundreds of thousands of Palestinians who fled in the midst of an armed struggle in 1948 have turned into millions of people, many living in refugee camps, most desiring to return to their homeland. A million and a half Palestinians now live under the direct military rule of the Israeli army.

Our people did not return to its ancient homeland with the intention of displacing or oppressing another people. The historical responsibility for the tragedy is two-sided; when we were refugees fleeing from the oppression of Christian Europe, the Palestinian leadership did all it could to block our return and refused to consider sharing the land. When the UN offered a two-state solution in 1947, Israel accepted and the Palestinians refused. Yet most Palestinians who fled were not involved in these decisions; they were peasant farmers with little knowledge of or involvement in the affairs that would eventually lead to displacement from their homes.

Our tradition teaches us compassion—and from this teaching we can also learn that if we really want peace in the Middle East, we will have to approach the conflicts with compassion for all sides. Peace is impossible as long as we hold onto the idea that one side has all the good and the other has all the bad.

In Every Generation

After reading "vihee she'amda" (that in every generation there have been those who rose up against us, but God ultimately saved us from their hands).

Why the Jews? Why should we have been the subject of persecution for thousands of years?

Was it perhaps our exclusiveness, our separateness, our insistence on being special—or some other aspect of our internal collective pathology? No!

To counter this, we affirm our Jewishness today. We have not been the cause of our oppression. We have been a very convenient tool for various ruling classes: a separable and recognizable minority that could be used as a scapegoat, a convenient target upon which to vent their hostility.

Jews have not been the only scapegoats to be used in this way. But in Western Europe they were the primary and most consistent scapegoat.

Our target status was largely responsible for our headlong rush into assimilation once that was legally possible. The Judaism that was abandoned, full of tears and suffering, was a Judaism whose sense of joy and inner confidence had been replaced by a narrow defensiveness—itself a response to external oppression. Even Hasidism, born as a protest against the joylessness of a rigidifying Eastern European Judaism, eventually lost much of its spontaneity and its earlier creativity, increasingly reproducing the dogmatic spirit it sought to replace. It is only now, decades after one-third of our people was wiped out, that we can begin to imagine reclaiming the more joyous and life-affirming aspects of our Jewish heritage.

Yet even here we are not free of the dynamics of world oppression. In class societies, virtually everyone is enmeshed in a web of oppression, in some respects by forces outside our control, in some respects by participating and benefiting from the oppression of others. Whether as tax collectors and small tavern owners in Eastern Europe, or as shopkeepers, government bureaucrats, social workers and teachers interacting with people in American ghettos, Jews are sometimes perceived as representatives of the established order in their dealings with other oppressed groups. In the process, and quite unfairly, anti-Semitism is regenerated. It is understandable why we Jews would become angry at the groups who participate in these dynamics—the peasants in Eastern Europe or some African-Americans in the U.S. We wish that they would understand that we too are victims, yet it's understandable why they may see us otherwise.

Similarly, when people point to the relative material prosperity of Jews compared to other ethnic groups in the U.S. and use this as a reason to claim that Jewish oppression is a matter of the past, they fail to understand the history of that oppression. Jews were doing well from a material standpoint in prewar Germany as well. Anti-Semitism, like sexism, cannot be reduced to an economic category—there are other unique forms of oppression besides material deprivation. Jews who sympathize with the oppression of every other group but who have little understanding or knowledge of the history of their own people may be engaged in a massive denial of reality. This denial is sometimes inspired by internalized anti-Semitism and the resulting need to convice oneself and one's non-Jewish friends that Jewishness "really isn't very important," and that it's "really just an interesting historical relic of the past."

There is no easy way out, no way for one people to make a separate peace with a world of oppressors or assimilate successfully and without moral compromise into that world. Our own liberation and our own mental health require the liberation of all, and the end of all oppression.

Pour Out Thy Wrath

After the meal, before opening the door for Elijah and before saying "Shefokh Chamatkha."
Tonight we remember our six million sisters and brothers who perished at the hands of the Nazis and at the hands of hundreds of thousands of anti-Semites who assisted those Nazis throughout Europe. We remember also the Jewish martyrs throughout the generations—oppressed, beaten, raped, and murdered by European Chrisitans.

It's not fashionable to speak about these atrocities—particularly since some reactionary Jews use these memories to legitimate the current oppressive tactics of the Israeli government. But tonight we recall in pain and in anger what was done to our people. We do not think it appropriate to use this past as a blank check to justify what right-wing Jews do to others. Yet we understand the pain that has led many of our fellow Jews to be deeply suspicious of a non-Jewish world that turned its back on us at the moment we were being systematically annihilated.

To get beyond the pain, we must first be allowed to express our anger. Permitting ourselves to articulate our anger, rather than trying to bury it or forget it or minimize it, is the only way that we can get beyond it. So, tonight it is appropriate to speak about our history, about the Holocaust, and about the ways that the American government and peoples around the world failed to respond to our cries and our suffering. What was done to us was wrong, disgusting, an assault on the sanctity of human life and on God. It is with righteous indignation that Jews have traditionally called out "*Shefokh Chamatkha ha'goyim aher lo yeda'ukha,*"—pour out your wrath, God, on those people who have acted toward us in a way that fails to recognize Your holy spirit within us as it is within all human beings. [This might be an appropriate place to pause for discussion.]

Yet, even as we speak our anger, we reaffirm our commitment to the messianic vision of a world of peace and justice, a world in which inequalities have been abolished and our human capacities for love and solidarity and creativity and freedom are allowed to flourish, a world in which all people will recognize and affirm in each other the spirit of God. In that day, living in harmony with nature and with each other, all peoples will participate in acknowledging God's presence on earth. We remain committed to the struggles in our own time that will contribute to making that messianic vision possible someday. □

The Virgin in the Brothel and Other Anomalies

Rachel Adler

"Some events do take place but are not true; others are although they never occurred."
  –Elie Wiesel

"A true story is one which helps us to go on."
  –Stanley Hauerwaus

Those who teach us inevitably teach us themselves, since all learning flows through the medium of relationship. Our teachers bind us to them with their stories. We take into ourselves their Torah sealed inextricably in narrative and with it their blunders, their blindness, their brutalities. God may heal the broken-hearted, but it is our teachers who break those hearts. Our teachers break our hearts when they do not see how their Torah is bounded by their context.

And should that break our hearts? A story has to take place somewhere, and every somewhere has its context, its frame of assumptions about what is real and unshakable and safe. Usually we inhabit this frame without feeling constraint. But sometimes a context becomes a cage. Suffocating, we burst its walls and step out into a new world. It is in the retelling in this new world that some of our teachers' stories break our hearts.

The legend of Beruriah is just such a story. Retelling it from the world in which we stand, we can see how character strains against context, how it shakes assumptions about what it means to be a woman, a Jew, a sexual being. It is precisely this tension of character and context that makes the Beruriah legend anomalous. It is a story about a woman, although at the time of its formation, women seldom were held to have stories. Beruriah was viewed as unlike other women although women were, as far as the storytellers were concerned, alike in all the ways that mattered. And is it a true story? Say rather that the shards of truth are in it, but by the power of the Torah that it contains I hope to understand it and go on.

I call it a story, though in fact it is many stories from many times and many texts, flotsam and jetsam thrown up by the unsounded seas of rabbinic and post-rabbinic lore. Probably until nineteenth century Wissenschaft compilations, few people could have told them all. But teachers and preachers driving home some lesson must have told one and then another, until in the imaginations of tellers and hearers one story shaped itself, the story of a life. Women told bits and pieces of this story to other women. I know, because that is how I myself first heard a story about Beruriah—from an older Orthodox woman, unable to read it in a book. And if she could have told it to me in its entirety, it would have gone like this:

Rachel Adler lives in Los Angeles and has written extensively about women and Judaism. This article appeared in Tikkun, *November/December 1988.*

Once there was a woman named Beruriah, and she was a great talmudic scholar. She was the daughter of the great Palestinian rabbi Hananyah ben Teradyon, who was martyred by the Romans. Even as a young girl, she far outstripped her brother as a scholar. It was said she had learned three hundred laws from three hundred teachers in one day. She married Rabbi Me'ir, the miracle worker and great Mishnaic sage.

One time when Rabbi Meir prayed for some robbers to die, Beruriah taught him to pray that their sin would die, that they would repent. She also taught Meir resignation when their two sons died. Loving and gentle as she was with Meir, Beruriah could also be arrogant and biting. She ridiculed a Sadducee, derided an erring student, and made a fool of Rabbi Yose the Galilean when he met her on the road.

Finally, she mocked the sages' dictum that women are easily seduced and came to a shameful end. Rabbi Meir set one of his students to seduce her. After long denial she yielded to him. When the plot was revealed, she strangled herself, and Rabbi Meir fled to Babylonia because of the disgrace.

What is arresting about the portrayal of Beruriah is the vividness and solidity of her selfhood. She is, in literary terms, a rounded character rather than a flat or stylized one. She does not illustrate a single virtue like Rachel, the magnanimous wife of Rabbi Akiva, nor does she appear in a single role like the learned maidservant of Rabbi Yehudah Ha-Nasi. In some texts she is the ideal daughter or wife, in others simply the source of a legal opinion, and in still others a caustic and formidable figure. What integrates the Beruriah traditions into a complex and ambivalent tale is the tension between a self portrayed as morally significant and a sexually polarized society in which moral significance belongs to the opposite sex; the conflict, in other words, is between character and context.

It is unusual for rabbinic legends to depict women in a rounded or complex way. Since they are exclusively male creations or redactions, rabbinic legends are necessarily androcentric. Women appear in cameo roles at best. At worst, they are shadowy utilities like the black-garbed stagehands of the Japanese Noh drama. But Beruriah is no utility. Mastering, defending, even mocking the tradition that shapes her context, she embodies, as do the most memorable of the male sages, a distinctive moral destiny. The problem of Beruriah—what we will have to understand in order to go on—is what it means that male rabbis transmitted a legend about a woman with a moral life like a man's, and how that legend breaks our hearts.

Paradoxically, it is precisely the anomaly of such a creature as Beruriah that renders her interesting to the rabbi. In their search for universally applicable principles, the sages continually formulated cases that burst the bounds of their generalizations. So, for example, it is written in the Talmud, Tractate Ketubot: "He who forfeits his life pays no monetary fine." But what would happen, they ask, if one managed to do two separate but concurrent acts, one a capital crime, the other a tort. Could one be sentenced both to die and to pay?

The effort to imagine such an occurrence leads the rabbis to propose such improbable situations as a man first devouring forbidden priestly food and then stealing it, or loosing an arrow in the public domain on the Sabbath, which in its trajectory plows through someone else's silk garments before coming to rest in the private domain. What do these surrealistic situations represent if not a passionate attempt to capture some elusive truth by smashing context? Imagining Beruriah must be regarded as just such an effort, a straining for a broader, more encompassing context; an outrageous test case proposed as a challenge to all contextually reasonable assumptions: *"What if there were a woman who was just like us?"*

Beruriah's story is thus imbued with profound ambivalence. On the positive side are Beruriah's brilliance, her special usefulness as a woman who vindicates rabbinic Judaism, and the uniquely appealing depictions of her relationship with her husband. On the negative side, Beruriah is viewed as a threat, a competitor, an arrogant woman contemptuous of men and of rabbinic tradition.

This negative pole of the rabbinic attitude toward Beruriah, which culminates in the tale of her adultery and suicide, is filled with malignant power. It so pervades the legend retroactively that we cannot mention Beruriah's intelligence or accomplishments without adding, if only mentally, "But she came to a bad end." This mental reservation brings the iron bars of the rabbinic context crashing down upon the anomalous woman, indeed, upon all women.

If we consider for a moment the position of women in the rabbinic system, the context-breaking nature of a creation like Beruriah is immediately apparent. In the world of the rabbis, received tradition teaches that women are the intellectual and moral inferiors of men. Tractate Ketubot tells us that "women are flighty," that is, easily seduced, and, because of their looseness, inherently seductive. "Whoever converses overmuch with women brings harm to himself, neglects the study of Torah, and in the end will inherit perdition," write the rabbis in Mishnah Avot (m. Abot 1:5). Women's hair, women's movements, women's voices, women's garments are all enticements to sexual license, according to the Talmud. And, because contact with menstruants is ritually defiling, contact with even a man's own female relatives is circumscribed with prohibitions.

It is no exaggeration to say that women are viewed as aliens inhabiting a different culture that at certain points intersects male culture while remaining distinct from it. This must be the meaning of the adage attributed to Ulla that "women are a separate people." The very lives of women can be viewed as intrinsically less valuable than those of men, since, Mishnah Horagot teaches that when a choice must be made about whose life to save first, a man's life takes higher priority.

Since women are most praiseworthy when they are least visible, a woman's occupation of a central role in a story must be explained. The most reasonable explanations is that she has displaced a man. Thus, in several texts identified with Beruriah, the woman is portrayed as having bested a less competent man.

In one of the earliest of these stories, her competitor is her own brother. The Tosefta poses a legal question concerning the purification of an oven. Hananyah's son says it becomes pure when it is moved from its place. His daughter (Beruriah) says it becomes pure when its parts are disassembled, a more elegant solution, since as soon as its parts are disassembled, the oven reverts to a pile of stones. Since it is no longer a cultural object, it is not susceptible to ritual impurity. The two opinions are told to Rabbi Yehudah who remarks, "His daughter said better than his son." ...

Beruriah's displacement of men is also achieved by confuting them. The Tractate Berakhot describes a dispute between Beruriah and a Sadducee. The Sadducee challenges the verse, "Rejoice, O barren one who has not given birth" on the grounds that a barren woman has no cause for rejoicing. Since this is a Pharisaic narrative, the plot requires that the Sadducee, seeking a theological alliance by basing his objection on "women's experience" be stopped in his tracks by a woman learned enough to direct him to read to the end of the verse: "For more numerous are the children of the forsaken than the children of the favored wife." But Beruriah then presses her advantage. "Why 'barren one who has not given birth'?" she questions. "Rejoice, O community of Israel, which is compared to a barren woman, which has not borne children for perdition like you!" Not only does Beruriah resist the Sadducee's temptation to argue that the text does not represent women's experience, she vehemently rejects all kinship with him. Like her Pharisaic creators, the Beruriah of this story views herself as a representative of the normative tradition. It is not she but the Sadducee who is marginal: the implication of her taunt is that he is not a member of the community of Israel at all....

In a text from Tractate Eruvin, Beruriah herself rebukes a student for his ineffective study habits. She predicts that because he studies silently and passively, he will be unable to retain what he hears.

In an ironic reversal, the woman is a scathing and authoritative scholar, the scholar silent and passive like a woman.

This irony is doubled and tripled in an encounter between Beruriah and Rabbi Yose the Galilean in which all the rabbinic ambivalence and fear about Beruriah is encapsulated:

> He asked her, "By what road do we go to Lydda?" She replied, "Silly Galilean! Didn't the sages say, 'Do not converse too much with women'? You could have said, 'How to Lydda'?"

The story is laden with ironies. Rabbi Yose, fearing a superfluous pleasantry will open him to lust, rudely asks directions without a greeting. Beruriah obligingly demonstrates how he might have made the conversation briefer yet, thereby prolonging their contact. Not only must Rabbi Yose converse with a woman, he must be rebuked by her; not only rebuked, but taught Torah; and not just any Torah, but precisely the dictum he had been trying so zealously to observe.

But the ultimate joke, if it must be called a joke, is on Beruriah. The Torah she has taught Rabbi Yose is genuine, and clearly discriminates against her. The originators of this text have thus come to the crux of the problem: Were there a woman like Beruriah, schooled in and committed to a tradition that views her as inferior, how could she resolve the paradox inherent in her loyalty to that tradition?

The irony through which the potential explosiveness of this paradox is conveyed is itself multileveled. Irony is, first of all, a language that the self speaks to the self over the heads of the unwitting. That is how it functions within the text. Beruriah speaks ironically to the obtuse Rabbi Yose. In response to his zeal, she exposes the sexist dictum and teasingly reproaches its adherent for not observing it.

But irony is also a code by which the knowing can speak to, and make alliance with, the knowing. The Beruriah of this text sends an ironic message of defiance to like-minded readers. For what can her behavior mean, if not that she rejects the rabbinic dictum she purports to teach?

There is, however, a third level to this irony—a third secret message that is conveyed. This is the message the rabbinic transmitters of the story convey to their audience, the message that Beruriah is subversive and unmanageable, a fifth column in the patriarchal domain in which she has hitherto enjoyed the privileges of a resident alien.

This story with its ironies within ironies, epitomizes the negative pole of the rabbinical ambivalence toward Beruriah and adumbrates the story of her downfall. Other texts, however, illustrate the positive pole. For, while it is threatening to imagine being ridiculed and exposed by a woman too learned and powerful to be controlled, it is also moving to imagine being loved and befriended by her. Thus, the rabbis, in describing the domestic life of Beruriah and Meir, portray Beruriah as a feminine version of the ideal study partner.

In one episode, Rabbi Meir prays for the demise of robbers who are plaguing the neighborhood. Beruriah addresses him in the language of talmudic dispute:

> On what do you base your opinion that it is permissible to pray for the robbers' deaths? Because it is written, "Let sins end" (Ps. 104:35)? Not "sinners" but "sins" is written! Moreover, read to the end of the verse: "And the wicked shall be no more." Pray rather that they should repent and not be wicked any more.

Meir prays as Beruriah directs, and the robbers repent.

It is interesting to compare this story with the medieval representation of the virtuous wife of Meir as depicted in Midrash Mishlei in Proverbs 31:10. Although Beruriah's name is not mentioned, the story has become one of the homiletic classics of the Beruriah legend. In this story, Meir's two sons have died on the Sabbath. Their mother evades Meir's questions about their whereabouts until the day has ended. She then proposes a legal case to him, addressing him as a student would a teacher. "Master, a while ago a man gave me an object in trust. Now he wishes to take it. Should we return it to him or not?" Meir quotes the law: The object must be returned.

The wife, thereupon, shows Meir the dead children. When he begins to bewail their loss, she reminds him, "Master, did you not say to me that I must return the trust to its owner?" He responds, quoting Job, "The Lord has given and the Lord has taken away. Blessed be the name of the Lord."

One virtue attributed to the wife of the second story is restraint. Because God is owed a Sabbath unmarred by mourning, she restrains her grief as a mother and her concern for her husband. Her second, less apparent virtue is a distinctive *hesed,* a sort of lovingkindness that only one scholar can offer another. This scholar-wife breaks the terrible news to her husband by asking a question framed to address the subtext of his grief. The metaphor of the owner reclaiming the object left in trust prevents Meir from interpreting the deaths as punishment for parental sins. Consequently, it allows the bereaved parents to grieve without self-reproach.

But how can Beruriah be a man's intellectual and spiritual intimate when women, simply by reason of their womanhood, continually emanate sexual invitation. Rabbi Yose the Galilean was not alone in believing that women were ineluctably sexual beings, and therefore were dangerous; all the other rabbis agreed. Thus, the rabbis in Mishnah Avot made a clear dichotomy between sexuality and love:

> All love which is dependent on sexual desire, when the desire is gone, the love is gone. Love which is not dependent on sexual desire never ends. What is love dependent on sexual desire? The love of Amnon and Tamar. And love which is not dependent on sexual desire? The love of David and Jonathan.

If Amnon and Tamar and David and Jonathan represent the two ends of a continuum, the fact that one end is represented by an incestuous rape and the other by a relationship presumed to be nonsexual does suggest a dichotomy between sexual desire and true love. More significant, the love of David and Jonathan evoked for the rabbis their own study partnerships—passionate relationships, yet devoid of conscious sexuality.

The study partnership was one of the defining social structures of rabbinic society and one of the most idealized. As it is written in Avot d'Rabi Natan:

> "Yehoshua ben Perahyah says: Appoint for yourself a teacher, and get yourself a companion." This teaches that a man should get himself a companion, to eat with him, drink with him, study Bible with him, study Mishnah with him, sleep with him and reveal to him all his secrets, secrets of Torah and secrets of worldly things.

From the rabbinic perspective, the study partners' lack of sexual motive is what safeguards these intimacies. What is eroticized instead is the study. Hence, it is not surprising that the Talmud describes ordination celebrations that mimic weddings. At Rabbi Zera's ordination, for example, the sages sing him the traditional praise-song for a bride: "No kohl, no rouge, no waved hair and still a graceful gazelle." Rabbi Ammi and Rabbi Assi, who are mentioned together at least eight times in the Talmud, are given a joint celebration even more reminiscent of a wedding.

It also is not problematic for the rabbis to appreciate one another's physical attractiveness. Yohanan ben Napha's beauty is celebrated in several stories. In one, the sight of Rabbi Yohanan's bared arm lights up the sickroom of Rabbi Eleazer ben Pedat, who weeps unashamedly over the mortality of his friend's beauty.

Another text narrates the lovers' tragedy of Rabbi Yohanan and his partner Resh Lakish. Resh Lakish, a bandit chief, happens upon Yohanan swimming in the Jordan and is struck by his beauty. Yohanan is equally struck by the bandit's strength. He teaches Resh Lakish Torah and gives him his sister as a wife.

One day the two study partners have an academic dispute which becomes a bitter quarrel. Resh Lakish then falls ill and dies unreconciled with Rabbi Yohanan. After Resh Lakish's death, Yohanan mourns him wildly and dies of grief.

Attachments between teachers and students may be equally passionate. Several stories recount Rabbi Meir's continued loyalty to his teacher Elisha ben Abuyah, who turned heretic. In one, Meir declares "if God will not save him, I will." He spreads his garment over his teacher's grave, aflame with infernal fire, until, by morning, the flames have ceased.

It is precisely Beruriah's inability to provide herself with a teacher and get herself a companion that leaves her isolated in the rabbinic world. The crucial difference between Beruriah and the male sages is that no teacher claims her as student, no student quotes her as teacher, and Beruriah herself quotes texts but never names teachers. Whatever her gifts and capacities, they funnel, ultimately, into a void because Beruriah lacks authority.

Authority in rabbinic Judaism flowed through the medium of rabbinic relationships, and the rabbis could not imagine how to give Beruriah authority without including her in the web of rabbinic relationships—the web of teachers and students and study partners. And they could not imagine doing that without imagining her sexuality as a source of havoc. Sexuality was regarded as women's most compelling characteristic, and it constituted, in the rabbis' opinion, an insurmountable barrier to any relationship other than a sexual one. Women could create great disorder with their rampant sexuality. Not only did this sexuality function as a metaphor for the disequilibrating potential of female power, but it represented to the rabbis all that is untameable, unpredictable, and lawless in human beings.

Two closely related stories about Beruriah address the problem of sexuality—one, a talmudic narrative; the other, an addendum by the eleventh century commentator Rashi, recounting the scandal of Beruriah's death. An analysis of these two stories will show us both how the rabbis tried to break context and how they failed.

The talmudic narrative begins by recounting the martyrdom of Hananyah ben Teradyon at the hands of the Romans. Hananyah himself is burned, his wife is exiled, and his daughter is sentenced to serve as a prostitute. But when the talmudic evolution of the legend fused Hananyah's daughter with Beruriah, identified as the wife of Meir, the story of her consignment to a brothel required major adjustments.

The motif of the virgin in the brothel (generally treated with lip-smacking salaciousness lightly overlaid with pathos) was a popular theme in Latin literature and was easily accessible for Jewish writers. It did, however, both from the Roman and from the Jewish point of view, require a virgin. Were Rabbi Meir's wife to sojourn in a brothel, however briefly, the legal questions about the status of her marriage would be no laughing matter. Hence, Tractate Avoda Zara endows Beruriah with a sister who is sentenced to the brothel and rescued by Rabbi Meir in the course of a picaresque narration that explores the connections between sexuality and power.

The narrative is set in motion by Beruriah. "I am ashamed that my sister sits in a brothel," she tells her husband. So Meir goes to Rome and, disguised as a Roman legionnaire, tests the chastity of his imprisoned sister-in-law. Because she passes the test, he redeems her from the apprehensive procurer, teaching him the magic plea, "O God of Meir, answer me!" which ultimately saves him from execution.

Meir evades his pursuers more farcically. In one version, he darts into a pagan temple, where he pretends to eat from the idolatrous feast ("he dipped in one finger and sucked another"). In a second version, he enters a brothel where Elijah the Prophet appears to him, conveniently disguised as a whore, and Meir embraces him in order to throw the pursuers off the track. They see Rabbi Meir but are convinced it is not he. "Heaven forbid that Rabbi Meir would act like this!" they exclaim.

After her removal from the brothel, Beruriah's sister disappears from the narrative. She is never mentioned again in this or any other text. The story ends with Meir's flight to Babylonia, either because of this episode, it is explained, or because of an unspecified incident about Beruriah.

What have we here? The fugue-like structure with its dissolves and transformations reminds us of a dream, but, if it's a dream, it's a political one—a dream about power and the presentation of the self. Both the woman in the brothel and her rescuer are endangered because they are Jews allied with or related to other Jews in resistance to the empire that governs them. Both are faced with situations where, to preserve their lives, they must pretend to be what they are not; while, to preserve their integrity, they must not be what they pretend. The captive in the brothel must seem to be a whore, but she must also defend her chastity against her clients. The fugitive must evade his pursuers' attempts to unmask him as an outlawed Jew, but he also must behave like a saintly rabbi.

The pretense inherent in the experience of oppression is dramatically expressed in the setting of the brothel. Only the metaphor of the sexual embrace between whore and patron can convey so powerfully the sense of intrusion and humiliation, of involuntary collusion with the oppressor, of merger. To be in the oppressor's power but not yet to have yielded to his will is to be a virgin in a brothel.

At the outset of the story, Rabbi Meir has gone to rescue a virgin from a brothel. Disguised as his own oppressor, a Roman legionnaire, he tries to conquer a trapped woman. Under the disguise is Jewish power. Meir, the wonder-rabbi can provide a terrified procurer with a miracle formula that will shield him from all attack.

But as the story progresses, power is stripped away. Meir, the sham Roman, must flee the real Romans. Transformed from oppressor to oppressed, and unable to save himself with miracles, he must appear to yield, to compromise himself, but resist internally. Meir becomes, as it were, a virgin in a brothel. The rules in Rabbi Meir's brothel are less stringent than those in his sister-in-law's, however. Unlike the woman whose chastity he tested rigorously, Rabbi Meir can actually participate in the forbidden act and emerge innocent: In his brothel, the sexual aggressor is, providentially, Elijah. Moreover, Meir is allowed to contrive his own escape. The loopholes provided in the rabbinic fantasy reflect a context in which male sexual temptations are more sympathetically viewed, and in which men have greater freedom of action and mobility.

What can such a story reflect if not an attempt by the sages to draw an analogy between their own experience of marginality and stigmatization in an often hostile empire, and women's vulnerability and powerlessness under patriarchal institutions? It is significant that the episode breaks off with both Rabbi Meir and his sister-in-law in limbo. Escape brings neither security nor relief. Meir is forced into a new flight, a new exile. The fragmentary structure of the episode mirrors the failure of the story's transmitters to reach some resolution, to bring it home. And, they hint, something to do with Beruriah has made "home" proscribed.

The eleventh century commentator, Rashi, offers the following explanation for Rabbi Meir's flight to Babylonia:

Once Beruriah mocked the rabbinic dictum, "Women are flighty" [i.e., easily seduceable] Meir said, "By your life! You will end by affirming their words." He commanded one of his students to tempt her to immorality. The student urged her for many days before she agreed. When it [the plot] became known to her, she strangled herself. Rabbi Meir fled because of the disgrace.

It is no coincidence that the story Rashi recounts is juxtaposed with the text that we just discussed. The two stories share several motifs. In both, Meir conducts a chastity test, and female sexuality brings shame and causes Meir to leave home. Also, in both, women are assumed to be solely responsible for sexual behavior, even when pressured, deceived, or entrapped by men. Chastity is the measure of women's worth, and there are no extenuating circumstances.

But are there extenuating circumstances for rabbis? Is Beruriah judged by a different standard? While there exists both in Talmud and Midrash an extensive literature of temptation stories about scholars, the ideal comparison to Beruriah's temptation would be the temptation of her own husband. During a discussion in which the rabbis mention the dictum that Beruriah mocked, the following story is told:

> Rabbi Meir used to scoff at [sexual] transgressors. One day Satan appeared to him in the guise of a woman on the opposite bank of the river. As there was no ferry, he [Meir] seized the rope and proceeded across. When he had reached half way along the rope, he [Satan] let him go saying, "Had they not proclaimed in Heaven: 'Take heed of Rabbi Meir and his learning,' I would have valued your life [virtue] at two ma'ahs."

Similar stories are recounted of Rabbi Akiva and of Rabbi Hiyya bar Abba. Having a place in the rabbinic authority structure, then, entitles one to the help of Heaven when one's own defenses against temptation have proven inadequate. Hence, Meir and Akiva are rescued. By contrast, no heavenly voice protects Beruriah by proclaiming, "Take heed of Beruriah and her learning." Like the virgin in the brothel, she is judged by more stringent standards, but, unlike the virgin, Beruriah will fail the chastity test.

The analogy has even richer implications. Like the virgin in the brothel, Beruriah is an anomaly, a person wildly out of place in her context, a paradox that may at any moment be violently resolved. A virgin in a brothel cannot expect to withstand any concentrated attempt to violate her. Her exemption from molestation lasts exactly as long as men's respect for her integrity outweighs their resentment of her autonomy and separateness. Beruriah's an anomaly among the scholars only as long as the scholars permit her to be. And, it is easier in an androcentric universe when there are no anomalies, when women are all alike, when men can easily make them alike by treating them in the same way.

It is significant that in Rashi's story about Beruriah, as in the brothel story, male superiority and patriarchal power are reinforced by reducing women to their sexual function. It is precisely a sexual humiliation that cuts Beruriah down to size.

Rashi's story is also thematically contiguous with the earlier portions of the Beruriah legend. Like many other Beruriah stories, it focuses on the irresolvable dissonance between the character and her context. Had not the author pushed on to prove Beruriah wrong and to punish her for challenging the rabbinic dictum, this could have been a sister story to Beruriah's ironic encounter with Rabbi Yose the Galilean.

Twentieth century readers have been extremely uncomfortable with this final Beruriah story. They have baselessly attacked its unity with the rest of the legend and have objected that, literarily, Meir and Beruriah's behavior is out of character. In a legend, however, new units are admissible only if they succeed in adhering to the legend. If people believe them, to put it simplistically, their integration with the rest of the legend is accomplished.

We might question how it is that sophisticated readers have expended a great deal of energy attempting to discredit this story without succeeding in budging it from its place in the legend. If Beruriah and Meir's behavior were truly inconceivable, the story wouldn't work for us; it would simply be one of the many bizarre or incoherent rabbinic legends that do not speak to us in our context. The ugliness of this story haunts us precisely because it is credible, because we can imagine not only Beruriah's rage and rebellion against the tradition, but also the great scholar and miracle-worker, the charismatic Rabbi Meir, playing the pimp for his own wife in order to vindicate the Torah.

This is the story through which our teachers truly break our hearts. For at what price is the Torah vindicated? Once our teachers had brought into being the Beruriah of the legend, this outrageous hypothesis, the woman with a moral life like a man's, they could not imagine her initiating an affair or falling into casual promiscuity. The only way they could envision Beruriah's adultery was by imagining the guardians of the Torah entrapping her into violating the Torah with them.

The discrediting of Beruriah, then, is accomplished only by means of a betrayal that profanes every relationship rabbinic Judaism holds to be holy: the bond of marriage, the bond between teacher and student, the very covenant with God that the commandments of the Torah express. The cost of discrediting Beruriah is cosmic.

Ironically, this disreputable tale, often dismissed as a fabrication, testifies to the ultimate truthfulness of the legend. The answer to the question the rabbis posed—What if there were a woman who was just like us?—is that the institutionalized denigration, subordination, and exclusion of women would destroy her, and that in the process the keepers of the tradition would besmirch themselves and profane the Torah they sought to protect.

I would like to believe, because of the violence done to the Torah in that final story, that the tellers broke their own hearts as well as their students', but I doubt it. The curse of scholars is the delusion of transcending context, being trapped, all the while, in a frame to which they are oblivious.

The story of Beruriah is not without comforts, although they are sober comforts. To imagine and transmit a legend about a female scholar through a thousand years of patriarchal culture is nothing if not a transcendence of context. But such insights are precious and fragile. They can survive only if we build a new world to sustain them. The task that we inherit from our teachers is to make a world in which a Beruriah could thrive.

And our heartbreak? It is part of our inheritance, a bitter hopefulness in the face of our estrangement from one another and from our world, matrix of the shattered spheres. Heartbreak is what moves us to the work of redemption, which is called *tikkun,* mending. And it is on this account that the Chasidic masters taught, "the wholest heart is a broken heart." □

Ayin: The Concept of Nothingness in Jewish Mysticism

Daniel C. Matt

How can God be defined? It cannot. To define ultimate reality would be to deny and desecrate its infinity. Though language brazenly insists on extending the semantic realm, God escapes its noisy clutches again and again.

The mystics, who celebrate divine ineffabilty, are quite comfortable with a God who refuses to be trapped by language. Yet even they need to refer to this nameless one—at least to communicate their awareness to others, to express a bit of what they have uncovered. One of their favorite strategies is to call God "Nothing." We hear this paradoxical divine epithet in the East and the West: Meister Eckhart's *niht*, St. John of the Cross' *nada,* the Taoist *wu,* and the Buddhist *sunyata* and *mu*. I will focus here on the Jewish mystical concept of *ayin,* "nothingness." *Ayin* is first found in medieval Kabbalah as a theological concept. Later, in Hasidism, its psychological significance is emphasized and *ayin* becomes a medium for self-transformation.

The word *nothingness* connotes negativity and nonbeing, but what the mystic means by divine nothingness is that God is greater than any *thing* one can imagine: it is like *no thing*. Since God's being is incomprehensible and ineffable, the least offensive and most accurate description one can offer is, paradoxically, *nothing*. David ben Abraham ha-Lavan, a fourteenth-century kabbalist, insists that "nothingness [*ayin*] is more existent than all the being [*yesh*] of the world." David's mystical Christian contemporaries concur. The Byzantine theologian Gregory Palamas writes, "He is not being, if that which is not God is being." Meister Eckhart says, "God's *niht* fills the entire world; His something, though, is nowhere."

I

The kabbalists did not invent this negative style of theology. Philo taught that God is unknowable and indefinable. The Gnostics address the hidden God as "ineffable, inexpressible, nameable by silence." Trying to outdo his predecessors, the Alexandrian Gnostic Basilides states that even the word "ineffable" says too much. God "is not even ineffable," but rather totally "nameless and nonexistent." Another Gnostic explains this final negation: "Nor is he something that exists, that one could know. But he is something else ... that is better, whom one cannot now.... He has nonbeing existence." The mystical philosopher Plotinus attacked the Gnostics, but he too maintains that the One surpasses our most basic and cherished categories: "Even being cannot be there."

Daniel Matt is a professor of Jewish Studies at the Graduate Theological Union at Berkeley. His Zohar: The Book of Enlightenment *was published by the Paulist Press in 1984. His more extensive study on ayin can be found in* The Problem of Pure Consciousness *edited by Robert K.C. Forman (Oxford University Press 1990). This article appeared in* Tikkun, May/June 1988.

John Scotus Erigena, a ninth-century Christian mystic influenced by Plotinus, was perhaps the first to apply the term "nothing" to God. Writing in Latin, he calls God *nihil*, by which he means not the lack but the transcendence of being. Because of "the ineffable, incomprehensible and inaccessible brilliance of the divine goodness ... it is not improperly called 'nothing.'" For John, creation out of nothing, *ex nihilo*, means the procession of differentiated being out of divine nothingness. In its essence, the divine is said not to be, but as it proceeds through the primordial causes, it becomes all that is. "Every visible creature can be called a theophany, that is, a divine appearance." Medieval Christian mystics who speak of divine nothingness, such as Meister Eckhart and Jacob Boehme, are indebted to John Scotus.

The kabbalists may also have been influenced by John Scotus, but their immediate teacher in the field of negative theology was Moses Maimonides. Building on the Islamic philosophers Alfarabi and Avicenna, Maimonides taught that God has nothing in common with any other being. God "exists but not through existence," he wrote in *Guide for the Perplexed*. In fact, Maimonides developed an entire system of negative attributes and encouraged his readers to discover what God is not:

Know that the description of God ... by means of negations is the correct description.... You come nearer to the apprehension of Him with every increase in the negations regarding Him.

The Jewish mystics adopted Maimonides' theory of negative attributes, at least as it pertains to the infinite nature of God. The thirteenth-century kabbalist Azriel of Gerona notes the similarity between the mystical and philosophical approaches: "The scholars of inquiry [philosophers] agree with the statement that our comprehension is solely by means of 'no.'"

The very strategy of negation provides a means of indicating the ineffable. Negative attributes carve away all that is false and leave us with a positive sense of nothingness. Here the mystics claim to surpass the philosophers. Joseph Gikatilla exclaims: "How hard they toiled and exerted themselves—those who intended to speak of negation; yet they did not know the site of negation!" *Ayin* is revealed as the only name appropriate to the divine essence.

This reevaluation of nothingness is bolstered by the intentional misreading of various biblical verses in which the word *ayin* appears. In biblical Hebrew *ayin* can mean "where," as in Job's rhetorical question (28:12): "Where [*me-ayin*] is wisdom to be found?" The first kabbalists of the thirteenth century transform this question into a mystical formula: "Wisdom emerges out of nothingness." Asher ben David writes, "The inner power is called *ayin* because neither thought nor reflection grasps it. Concerning this, Job said, 'Wisdom emerges out of *ayin*.'" As Bahya ben Asher puts it, the verse should be understood "not as a question but as an announcement." Refracted through a mystical lens, Job's question yields its own startling answer. In the words of Joseph Gikatilla,

The depth of primordial being ... is called *ayin*.... If one asks, "What is it?" the answer is, "*Ayin*," that is, no one can understand anything about it.... It is negated of every conception.

The kabbalists identified *ayin* with *keter 'elyon* ("supernal crown"), the first of the ten *sefirot*, the stages of divine being. Moses de Leon explains this identification and then draws an analogy between divine and human ineffability:

Keter 'elyon is ... the totality of all existence, and all have wearied in their search for it.... The belt of every wise person is burst by it, for it ... brings all into being.... Anything sealed and concealed, totally unknown to anyone, is called *ayin*, meaning that no one knows anything about it. Similarly, no one knows anything at all about the human soul; she stands in the status of nothingness, as it is said [Ecclesiastes 3:19]: "The advantage of the human over the beast is *ayin*"! By means of this soul, the human being obtains an advantage over all other creatures and the glory of that which is called *ayin*.

God and the human soul share an infinite, inherent indeterminacy. If the human soul could be defined, it would lose its divine likeness. By our nature, we participate in *ayin*.

II

For the kabbalist, one of the deepest mysteries is the transition from *ayin* to *yesh*, from "nothing" to "something." Following in the footsteps of John Scotus and others, they have reinterpreted creation *ex nihilo* as emanation from the hidden essence of God. There *is* a "something" that emerges from "nothing," but the nothing is brimming with overwhelming divine reality. The something is not a physical object but rather the first ray of divine wisdom, which, as Job indicates, comes into being out of *ayin*. It is the primordial point that initiates the unfolding of God. In the words of Zohar (1:15a):

The flow broke through and did not break through its aura.
It was not known at all
until, under the impact of breaking through,
one high and hidden point shone.
Beyond that point, nothing is known.
So it is called Beginning.

The opening words of Genesis, "In the beginning," allude to this first point, which is the second *sefirah,* divine wisdom. Though second, it "appears to be the first" and is called "beginning" because the first *sefirah, ayin*, is unknowable and uncountable. In the words of Moses de Leon, the point is "the beginning of existence."

When that which is hidden and concealed arouses itself to existence, it produces at first something the size of the point of a needle; afterwards, it produces everything from there....
This is the primordial wisdom emerging from *ayin*.

The transition from *ayin* to *yesh* is the decisive act of creation, the real context of Genesis. As time proceeds, nothingness serves as the medium of each transformation, of every birth and death. *Ayin* represents the entirety of potential forms that can inhere in matter, each one "invisible until its moment of innovation," when it issues as a pool spreading out from a spring. As matter adopts new forms, it passes through *ayin*; thus the world is constantly renewed. In the words of one kabbalist, "Form is stripped away by the power of *ayin*." In every change, in each gap of existence, the abyss of nothingness is crossed and becomes visible for a fleeting moment.

III

The mystic yearns for this depth of being, this formless source of all form. Though humans "walk in the multiplicity" of the material world, "one who ascends from the forms to the root must gather the multiplicity ... for the root extends through every form that arises from it at any time. When the forms are destroyed, the root is not destroyed."

Can one know this reality beyond forms? Only by unknowing or, in the words of David ben Judah he-Hasid, "forgetting":

> The Cause of Causes ... is a place to which forgetting and oblivion pertain.... Why? Because concerning all the levels and sources [the *sefirot*], one can search out their reality from the depth of supernal wisdom. From there it is possible to understand one thing from another. However, concerning the Cause of Causes, there is no aspect anywhere to search or probe; nothing can be known of It, for It is hidden and concealed in the mystery of absolute nothingness. Therefore forgetting pertains to the comprehension of this place. So open your eyes and see this great, awesome secret. Happy is one whose eyes shine from this secret, in this world and the world that is coming!

The *sefirot* are stages of contemplative ascent; each one serves as a focus of mystical search. In tracing the reality of each *sefirah,* the mystic uncovers layers of being within himself and throughout the cosmos. However, there is a higher level, a deeper realm, beyond this step-by-step approach. At the ultimate stage the kabbalist no longer differentiates one thing from another. Conceptual thought, with all its distinctions and connections, dissolves. Ezra and Azriel of Gerona call the highest *sefirah* "the annihilation of thought" (*afisat ha-mahshavah*): "Thought ... rises to contemplate its own innerness until its power of comprehension is annihilated." Here the mystic cannot grasp for knowledge; rather, he imbibes from the source to which he is joined. In the words of Issac the Blind, "The inner, subtle essences can be contemplated only by sucking ... not by knowing."

Ayin cannot be known. If one searches too eagerly and pursues it, one will be overtaken by it, sucked in by the vortex. Ezra of Gerona warns:

> Thought cannot ascend higher than its source [the *sefirah* of wisdom]. Whoever dares to contemplate that to which thought cannot extend or ascend will suffer one of two consequences: either he will confuse his mind and destroy his body or, because of his mental obsession to grasp what he cannot, his soul will ascend and be severed [from the body] and return to her root.

Issac of Akko balances the positive and negative aspects of the experience of return. He describes *devequt* ("cleaving" to God) as "pouring a jug of water into a flowing spring, so that all becomes one," yet he warns his reader not to sink in the ocean of the highest sefirah: "The endeavor should be to contemplate but to escape drowning.... Your soul shall indeed see the divine light and cleave to it while dwelling in her palace."

The mystic is vulnerable. Moreover, she is responsible for the divine emanation. She must ensure that the *sefirot* themselves do not collapse back into nothingness. Through righteous action the human being stimulates and maintains the flow of emanation; wrongdoing, on the other hand, can have disastrous effects: "One who sins returns the attributes to *ayin*, to the primordial world, to their original state of being, and they no longer emanate goodness down to the lower world."

The depths of nothingness are both a lurking danger and a reservoir of power. "Out of the depths I call you, YHVH." Mystically understood, this verse from Psalms (130:1) describes a human cry not *from* one's own state of despair but *to* the divine depths in which God lies hiding, from which God can be called forth. This is not to deny the reality of human suffering. On the contrary, adversity leads one to appreciate the resources of *ayin*. "Human beings must quickly grasp this *sefirah* to secure healing for every trouble and malady, as it is written [Psalm 121:1]: 'I lift up my eyes to the mountains; my help comes from *ayin*.'"

IV

In eighteenth-century Hasidism, the kabbalistic material is recast and psychologized; now the experiential aspect of *ayin* becomes prominent. The emphasis is no longer on the *sefirot,* the inner workings of divinity, but on how to perceive the world mystically and how to transform the ego. Dov Baer, the Maggid ("preacher") of Mezritch, encourages his followers to change *aniy* ("I") into *ayin,* to dissolve the separate ego in nothingness. As we shall see, this is not a destructive but rather a dialectical and ultimately creative process. According to Dov Baer:

> One must think of oneself as *ayin* and forget oneself totally.... Then one can transcend time, rising to the world of thought, where all is equal: life and death, ocean and dry land.... Such is not the case when one is attached to the material nature of this world.... If one thinks of oneself as something ... God cannot clothe Himself in him, for He is infinite, and no vessel can contain Him, unless one thinks of oneself as *ayin.*

We must shed the illusion that we are separate from God. To defend an independent sense of self is a sign of false pride. True humility involves the consciousness of *ayin.* In the words of Issachar Ber of Zlotshov:

> The essence of the worship of God and of all the mitzvot is to attain the state of humility, namely ... to understood that all one's physical and mental powers and one's essential being are dependent on the divine elements within. One is simply a channel for the divine attributes. One attains such humility through the awe of God's vastness, through realizing that there is no place empty of Him. Then one comes to the state of *ayin,* which is the state of humility.... One has no independent self and is contained, as it were, in the Creator.... This is the meaning of the verse [Exodus 3:6]: "Moses hid his face, for he was in awe...." Through his experience of awe, Moses attained the hiding of his face, that is, he perceived no independent self. Everything was part of divinity!

The experience of nothingness does not induce a blank stare; it engenders new mental life through a rhythm of annihilation and thinking. "One [should] turn away from that [prior] object [of thought] totally to the place called 'nothingness,' and then a new topic comes to mind. Thus transformation comes about only by passing through nothingness." In the words of one of the Maggid's disciples, "When one attains the level of ... gazing at *ayin,* one's intellect is annihilated.... Afterwards, when one returns to the intellect, it is filled with emanation." The creative pool of nothingness is described as the "preconscious" (*qadmut ha-sekhel*), that which precedes, surpasses, and inspires both language and thought. According to Dov Baer:

> Thought requires the preconscious, which rouses thought to think. This preconscious cannot be grasped.... Thought is contained in letters, which are vessels, while the preconscious is beyond the letters, beyond the capacity of the vessels. This is the meaning of: "Wisdom emerges out of nothingness."

The mystic is expected to trace each thought, each word, each material object back to its source in *ayin.* The world no longer appears as essentially distinct from God. In the Habad school of Hasidism acosmism has become a fundamental teaching: "This is the foundation of the entire Torah: that *yesh* [the apparent "somethingness" of the world] be annihilated into *ayin.*" "The purpose of the creation of the worlds from *ayin* to *yesh* was that they be transformed from *yesh* to *ayin*." This transformation is realized through contemplative action: "In everything they do, even physical acts such as eating, the righteous raise the holy sparks, from the food or any other object. They thus transform *yesh* to *ayin*."

This mystical perspective is neither nihilistic nor anarchic. Matter is not destroyed or negated, but rather enlivened and revitalized. The awareness that divine energy underlies material existence increases the flow from the source (*ayin*) to its manifestation (*yesh*). Dov Baer explains:

> When one gazes at an object, he brings blessing to it. For when one contemplates that object, he knows that it is ... really absolutely nothing without divinity permeating it.... By means of this contemplation, one draws greater vitality to that object from divinity, from the source of life, since he binds that thing to absolute *ayin*, from which all beings have been hewn.... On the other hand ... if one looks at that object ... and makes it into a separate thing ... by his look, that thing is cut off from its divine root and vitality.

World, mind, and self dissolve momentarily in *ayin* and then reemerge. *Ayin* is not the goal in itself; it is the moment of transformation from being through nonbeing to new being. The Maggid conveys this thought with the image of the seed that disintegrates before sprouting:

> When one sows a single seed, it cannot sprout and produce many seeds until its existence is nullified. Then it is raised to its root and can receive more than a single dimension of its existence. There in its root the seed itself becomes the source of many seeds.

Ayin is the root of all things, and "when one brings anything to its root, one can transform it." "First [each thing] must arrive at the level of *ayin*; only then can it become something else." Nothingness embraces all potentiality. Every birth and rebirth must navigate the depths of *ayin*, as when a chick emerges from an egg: for a moment "it is neither chick nor egg." As long as the human ego refuses to acknowledge its divine source, it is mistaking its part for the all and laying false claim to that which cannot be grasped. In the words of Menahem Mendel of Kotsk, "The I is a thief in hiding." When this apparently separate self is *ayin*ized, the effect is not total extinction, but the emergence of a new form, a more perfectly human image of the divine. Only when "one's existence is nullified ... is one called 'human .'"

Ayin is a window on the oneness that underlies and undermines the manifold appearance of the world. The ten thousand things we encounter are not as independent or fragmented as they seem. There is an invisible matrix, a swirl that generates and recycles being. One who ventures into this depth must be prepared to surrender what he knows and is, what he knew and was. The ego cannot abide *ayin*; you cannot wallow in nothingness. In *ayin*, for an eternal moment, boundaries disappear. *Ayin*'s "no" clears everything away, making room for a new "yes," a new *yesh*.

Our familiar and confining images of God vanish in *ayin*. This "*Nichts* of the Jews," writes the poet Henry Vaughan, exposes "the naked divinity without a cover." *Ayin* implies the God beyond God, the power that is closer and further than what we call "God." It symbolizes the fullness of being that transcends being itself, "the mysterious palace of *ayin*, in which everything dwells." The reality that animates and surpasses all things cannot be captured or named, but by invoking *ayin* the mystic is able to allude to the infinite, to *alef* the ineffable. □

VII. Fiction

VII. Fiction

Ghirlandaio

Francine Prose

Not long ago, in the library, I happened to glance through a book on Renaissance painting which someone had left on the table. I saw the Ghirlandaio portrait of the old man and his grandson and immediately closed the book. After a while I turned back to the Ghirlandaio, and then I kept looking until, for a moment, I quite forgot where I was. I was remembering the year when that painting was on loan at the museum and my father took me to see it; remembering how, as a child, I couldn't stop staring at the old man in the painting, at his bulbous grapey nose. And I could almost hear my father's voice telling me once again that what the old man had—what made his nose look like that—was lupus erythematosus.

My father was a doctor, he loved medicine and art and loved especially those places where the two seemed to him to coincide: Van Gogh with his digitalis-distorted color sense, Monet, whose retinal degeneration my father pronounced to have influenced his later works, paintings of saints curing lepers, and most of all astigmatic El Greco, his *View of Toledo* that we lingered before, gazing at the roofs and spires and nighttime sky which El Greco with his bad vision had seen and painted as squiggles. My father walked briskly through the museum, visiting his favorites as if he were making hospital rounds, and in my slippery party shoes I skated after him. The Ghirlandaio double portrait was my father's idea of what art should be, and I was glad that it gave him such pleasure, that year when nothing else did.

I remember that winter so clearly that I can say with both certainty and amazement: I never imagined that by the next year my parents would be divorced. It seems incredible now that they never argued in front of me. But it was also the very last year when, ultimately and beyond all rebelliousness, I chose to take my parents' word for what was real and what wasn't. I believed life was as they told me, as it seemed, and what seemed to be happening on those Sundays was that my father wanted to go the museum and my mother didn't, and she argued against his taking me because this was 1955, at the height of the polio scare, and she was afraid I would catch it in the damp overheated galleries.

But polio, my father said, was a summer disease, and besides, the European painting wing wasn't exactly the community swimming pool or a movie theater showing *Dumbo* to a thousand runny-nosed kids. He made it seem silly to worry about this, and only much later did I understand that this was not my mother's real fear. I have often wondered if, at some time on those trips, my father and I might have run into the woman he would soon leave my mother for. How would I have known? She was no one a child would have noticed in a museum full of adults, and even if my father had seen her, by accident or design, and reacted, I don't think I would have noticed that either. I was eleven, and the drama of my life was happening elsewhere.

Several times, as we stood before the Ghirlandaio, I asked, "Could someone die from that?" And

Francine Prose's most recent novel is Primitive People *(Farrar, Strauss & Giroux, 1992). This story appeared in* Tikkun, *May/June 1988.*

my father, his love for the subject outweighing his customary wariness about what he had told me and I had obviously not paid attention to, said "Well, not immediately." There was a secret conversation beneath this, what he and I did not say: my sixth grade teacher, Miss Haley, had pretty much the same nose. The reason I kept asking was because—though I couldn't have admitted it, not even to myself—I half-hoped Miss Haley might die of it, if not instantly then sometime during the school year.

It is difficult now to remember how large our teachers loomed. Each grade-teacher was our fate for a year that lasted so much longer than any year does now; they were the only future we believed in. We collected the rumors, the gossip, the reputations, studied their passions and personality tics for clues to our future happiness. What you heard about Miss Haley was that her nose looked that way because she was a Christian Scientist and wouldn't go to a doctor, and after a while you got used to it. We heard that you did ancient Egypt, that she had strong, inexplicable, immutable loves and hates—either she loved or hated you, and you knew which it was right away.

From the first day of school it was perfectly clear that Miss Haley hated me, and sixth grade unrolled before me in all its grim, unendurable length. Miss Haley was a stocky, energetic elderly woman who drew fearlessly on the blackboard in very long straight lines which I recognize only now for the marvels they were. By lunch we felt as if hers were the most normal nose in the world, and we realized the truth of what the former sixth graders told us. Something in her presence made it clear that her nose was not to be spoken of—not even among ourselves, in private—and it truly was remarkable, how deeply we took this to heart. The only thing that explains it is that we were at an age when we watched very carefully—to see what you said and kept quiet, what you showed and concealed—and this was especially crucial in regards to things of the body.

Many times that first day she repeated, "Of course, when we study Egypt...", and she drew an enormous pyramid on the far side of the board. Each day, she explained, one well-behaved student would be called up to write his or her name in a brick. The Good Behavior Pyramid was much too young for sixth grade, when anything that smacked of the babyish embarrassed us beyond words. Even so, I longed—without hope—to write my name in a Good Behavior brick.

Miss Haley's unfriendliness might simply have been the result of that chemical friction which sometimes springs up between teacher and student, so that nothing between them goes right. I was a sallow, skinny girl, alternately know-it-all and mopey—it certainly might have been that. It might have been that I was half-Jewish and had a Jewish name in that small, suburban private school where hardly anyone did. Any of that seems more likely now than that Miss Haley disliked me for the reasons I thought—because she and my father (and by extension me) were opposites, because my father represented everything her religion was against, because my father smiled, compassionate and superior, when I told him about her being a Christian Scientist, and because on Sundays my father and I stood before the Ghirlandaio and discussed her disease.

She couldn't have known that, but I imagined she did, and in fact was so certain of it that I never complained to my parents. Enough seemed wrong at home without my adding that. I never suspected the truth—that my father had fallen in love and didn't want to be, and fought it while my mother waited helplessly for him to decide—no more than I recognized our trips to the museum as almost the only things he could still do for comfort and without guilt. Still I sensed danger, some mood that hung over our breakfasts and dinners and even the once-happy moments like watching Sid Caesar's *Your Show of Shows*, some drifting of attention that made it necessary to repeat what we said to my father several times before he heard. I misread my mother's attempts to charm him and make him laugh, her expecting me to do the same; briefly I worried that my father might be sick, or that he was losing his hearing. And I refused to bring home one more bit of bad tidings for my parents to think was their fault.

I too realized the difficulty and great importance of keeping my father interested—but I hesitated to say anything which might accidentally reveal my unhappiness at school. At meals, when my father asked what we were studying, I'd mumble something like, "Egypt."

"What about Egypt?" my mother would say.

"I don't know," I'd say. "Pyramids. The Pharaohs."

"What about the Pyramids?" said my father.

"I don't know," I'd say.

"*We're* the guys who built the pyramids," he'd say. "Actively *shlepped* the stones." Then catching my mother's eye he'd add, "On my side, that is. On your mother's side, Cleopatra."

Sundays, at the museum, my father often suggested a walk through the Egyptian wing. How it would have pleased him to read me the captions and hear what little I knew. There was so much we could have discussed—embalming techniques, anthrax powder, the ten plagues. But I feared that the artifacts themselves would somehow betray the only information that mattered: I'd never been called on to tell about Osiris being hacked up in chunks and thrown into the Nile, or to make a clay man for the funeral barge our class was constructing, or to fill in, with colored chalk, the scarab Miss Haley outlines each day on the board.

By then our class was well launched on what Miss Haley called our little journey down the Nile, and when she pulled the heavy dark-green shades and showed us slides of temples and sarcophagi, I did feel just a bit rocky, as if we were floating past everything that I knew, and the dusty metallic smell of the projector became the salt, garbagey odor of river water and sand. Pretending to watch the slides, I stared at the dust motes streaming in that wedge of light until my eyes went out of focus and the classroom disappeared and a scary chill of aloneness startled me back to myself.

There was no one in whom I could confide; it would have been foolish to let my friends know I cared about something which, without my prompting, they seemed not to notice. We were at that age when much is secret, much is embarrassing, when certain questions—what to do with our shoulders and knees, and whether people like us—assume an intensity they will never have again. At that age, everyone and everything is both love object, mirror and judge, and we go around frantically wasting ourselves on whatever is nearby.

On top of my other problems, that year I fell in love. This, too, I had no one to tell. It was one thing to love Elvis—all the girls loved Elvis except a few who were famous for *not* loving Elvis, and there were a couple of upper school boys we all agreed were cute. But we were late-bloomers, love was still something you did in a group, by consensus, and the consensus was that we hated sixth grade boys.

But there was one I liked. His name was Kenny something. I remember that his last name changed between fifth and sixth grade, when his glamorous actress mother remarried—but I don't remember either name. I have only the fuzziest sense of what he looked like—red hair in a spiky fifties kids' crewcut—which is strange, because our love was so purely physical, so exquisitely located in those angular shoulders and knees, in our skins, in inches of distance between us, and all we asked was to look at each other or brush, accidentally, his hip or his elbow grazing me as we ran out to the playground. This happened perhaps twice or three times a week; the rest of the time, I replayed our moment of contact in my head. For days we didn't look at each other, and I thought I had been dreaming anything else. Then a weekend would pass; on Monday the looks and collisions began again. Everything was unspoken, potential and in constant flux.

Ours was a doomed love. To have acknowledged it, even to each other, would have meant taking on the world—and for what? We might have been forced to have a conversation. In fact we could barely manage a sentence. My greatest dream and greatest fear was being alone with him, and I liked to terrify myself by imagining occasions where this might occur. One place where it seemed this might happen was the museum; our class was scheduled to visit the Egyptian wing. For weeks before the trip I invented impossible scenarios of escaping with him into the shadows of the church-like, stone medieval hall which I alone among the sixth-graders knew about. And what would we do then? My mind refused to go further. Just thinking that far gave me chills, so I thought it again and again until I came up with a plan to arrange what I wanted and dreaded most.

On the morning of the trip I woke up shaking with fever. I still remember staring down into my dresser drawer, wondering how many sweaters I could get away with wearing. I must have put on three or four, but nothing felt warm. At breakfast, I shivered and tried to hide it. How strange that my parents didn't notice; normally, one sniffle and they were feeling my forehead. But sometime during the night we must have entered that world of mischance that parents so fear, with its history of catastrophes occurring in eye-blinks when parental vigilance lapsed.

Briefly I wondered if maybe I did have polio, as my mother so dreaded, but I was still a child, and didn't know what was worth fearing; children rarely fear airplanes but, almost always, the dark. The prospect of missing the trip scared me far more than polio. Besides, I already knew that first principle of everyday magic: Once you say something, give it a name, then, only then, can it happen. So I kept quiet and shivered and wrapped my hands around my cocoa cup and everything around me slipped in and out of focus.

This is how I recall that day—at moments the edges of things would be crisply, painfully sharp; then they would blur and turn wavy. Kissing my parents goodbye, I was so confused I imagined my father would be interested to hear that the world looked to me like an El Greco painting. But just in time I caught myself and climbed onto the steamed-up bus.

Our classroom was in chaos, but through it all rang Miss Haley's strained voice, yelling, "Hang on to your coats," which struck me as the most deeply kind, the most thoughtful thing she'd every said. There was one moment, as we lined up to leave, when I knew I was in danger, that I should tell someone and go home. But then I felt someone bump into me, and even through all those sweaters, I knew who it was. Kenny was right behind me in line, and as we pushed toward the narrow bus door, he whispered, "Can we still go see it?" It took me a while to think what he meant, though for days it was all I had thought of.

What he meant was the Ghirlandaio painting, which he'd heard about from me. It had required astonishing bravery to approach him in the school yard, to speak to him for so long, but that was minor compared with the courage it took to mention the unmentionable—that is, Miss Haley's nose. I don't recall how I'd phrased it, how precisely I'd make it clear that there existed a work of art with a nose like our sixth grade teacher's. It had left us both feeling quite short of breath, as if we'd been running, and had gotten our second wind and were capable of anything, and in that light-headed state I offered to take him to see it. It would be easy, I said—I knew the museum so well we could sneak off and get back before anyone noticed.

Yet now the idea of walking even the shortest distance exhausted me, and my plan (which I'd never expected him to agree to) seemed to demand impossible stamina—though less than it would have taken to shake my head no. I told him to be on the lookout for the right moment, and my voice dopplered back at me through an echo chamber of fever.

At the museum, a guard instructed us to throw our coats in a rolling canvas bin. And this is my sharpest memory from that day—the panic I felt as my coat disappeared, how it looked to me like someone jumping, vanishing into a sea of coats. Suddenly I was so cold I felt I had to keep moving, and I caught Kenny's eye and we edged toward the back of the crowd and dimly I heard my fever-voice telling him: Follow me.

Not even running helped. I just got colder, wobbly and unsure; of course we got lost and criss-crossed the damp medieval hall, where the shadows climbed the chill stone walls, pretending to be doorways which vanished when we got close. At last we found the staircase, the right gallery, the Ghirlandaio. And I gloried in the particular pride of having done what I'd boasted I could.

Kenny stared at the painting. Then very softly he said, "Wow. Disgusto." Disgusto was the word all right. And yet I felt strangely hurt, protective of Ghirlandaio's old man, as if he and his grandson were relatives of mine, and Kenny had passed judgment on my family, on my life, on those afternoons when I stood here with my father as if this were something compelling and beautiful and not what it clearly was: disgusto.

At that moment we heard footsteps, angry taps on the parquet floor, and we knew whose steps they were, though not how Miss Haley had found us. Instinctively, we moved to the center of the gallery, so no one could tell what painting we'd been near, and I thought—as fast as the fever allowed—that if she noticed the Ghirlandaio, I would direct her eye to the grandson, at how he gazed at the old man, how trustingly and with what love. But she just stood there, glaring at us in the silence of the gallery.

Then Kenny burst into tears. Miss Haley and I looked away from him, embarrassed and upset, though I doubt that she could have been feeling the same emotions that I was—revulsion, and the strong desire to be anywhere, with anyone else but with him. Sometimes, in later years, I ran into old loves and wondered what I saw in them; but that day, in the whirl of eleven-year-old love, this shift of emotion happened instantaneously. The love I had felt just a few hours before now seemed grotesque and absurd. I caught Kenny's smell of hair oil and damp wool, and for a second I gagged.

Was it the tears that so turned me against him? I think it was something more: we were at the age when love cannot stand exposure, when to be caught brings humiliation so profound we can only blame the beloved. We were, in that way, not much older than Adam and Eve, whom we must have resembled as Miss Haley chased us through the galleries, past those paintings of the expulsion from Eden which my father always rushed by—perhaps because the couple was naked or, more likely, held no interest for him, having nothing physically wrong.

Meanwhile my fever was climbing, the chill in my bones transforming itself into needles of ice in my skin. When we rejoined our classmates in the Egyptian wing, I hardly recognized them. Shuffling obediently, gazing morosely at their feet, they could have been the funerary procession which the docent was describing. Miss Haley had prepared us for the highlight of the tour—a trip through the vast Egyptian tomb which the museum had imported brick by brick, from Luxor. But as we approached it, the docent narrowed her eyes and dropped her voice to an ominous register and warned us to stay together because the tomb had been built as a maze to foil robbers. And then it hit us all at once—we were entering a grave.

Inside the temperature dropped. I had never been so cold. Perhaps the docent was chilly too, or didn't like it there; in any case she walked faster until the children were practically trotting to keep up. I knew I couldn't do it—and then the urge to curl up and lie down quite suddenly overwhelmed me. I let the others push ahead through the twisting corridors, and when we passed a roped-off room, I ducked into it and found a corner where I couldn't be seen from outside.

I crouched in a cul-de-sac, surrounded by glass-covered walls. Beneath the glass were friezes, lit with a soft golden light. Figures in a procession surrounded me. It was a funeral procession, extending into the afterlife to follow the dead and their gods, and it gave me a strange sense of comfort that I knew who everyone was. First came the mourners, shedding their broken-line tears, then the cows, the oxen dragging the carts with all the dead's possessions, then the boats which ferried them across the waters of the other world. And now came the lesser gods, Bes, the dwarf, Tauret, the hippopotamus, frog-headed Heket, the lioness Renenet, the scorpion, Selket.

Slowly the line began to move forward, and I watched it, steadily and without surprise, moving across the glassed-in walls like an animated cartoon—the goddess with the balances for weighing the souls of the dead, then Thoth, Isis, Osiris to receive the lucky spirits. And all at once it seemed to me that the figures were leaving the walls and marching straight at me, coming for me and for everyone that I loved. In silence came the fifty-two judges, then Horus, Bast, Anubis, the hawk, cat, the jackal streamed toward me through the air, and at the end of the line stood Amement, the Devourer, crocodile, hippo, lioness, receiver of the souls who had been tried and found guilty.

But really, the goddess I saw was Miss Haley, who stood looking down at me, her white hair backlit, flaming around her head. She must have come searching for me, and yet she seemed not to recognize me. Her face was opaque, her eyes looked visionless and dead, and that seemed strange because it had just occurred to me I had been wrong, that all this time I had been thinking Miss Haley and I were opposite, when in fact we were opposite sides of a coin—she and her Christian Science, me and my father and our Ghirlandaio. We had precisely the same concerns. We did the same things in our spare time. This thought made me strangely, inexplicably happy; I was suffused with affection, not only for Miss Haley but for my father and me, a compassion much deeper than anything we credit children with and so consider the exclusive province of adults. I felt like someone who had solved a hard problem and now could imagine relaxing. I was sleepy and closed my eyes.

It was not, as it happened, polio, but a kind of meningitis that did no lasting damage but kept me in the hospital three months. I came home to two separate houses. Since then I have often wondered why my parents—who were always so careful of me— failed to consider the effect on me of a homecoming like that. Why couldn't they have waited? But I think that they must have considered it, considered waiting, and found that they had no choice.

My father and I were never so close again. For a long while I was angry at him, and somewhere in that time stopped wanting to please him and tell him interesting things, including something I remembered, a thought I had but couldn't say when he came to pick me up at the museum.

I remember very clearly lying on a cot in a room with adults gathered around. I looked up and saw my father's face, all wavy and distorted and extraordinarily beautiful, and I wanted to tell him something but couldn't speak, wanted to say it so badly that I can remember it now.

What I wanted to say was this: that he had been wrong about El Greco, that if something were straight and you saw it curved, you would actually paint it straight; your hand would correct what your eye had seen wrong, so it finally came out right. Then the objects in your painting would appear to you just as everything always did—distorted, buckled and curved. But anyone else who looked at it would see what you never saw—a perfect likeness of the world, the world as it really was. □

One More Wave of Fear

Frederick Busch

I did not grow up despising nature on Argyle Road, at the far southern edge of Prospect Park, in Brooklyn in the 1950s. But I did come to hate the upper-case initial with which my parents said the word. Our house was set back from a street on which few children but a lot of lean, straight men and women lived. As I remember them, most were white and Protestant and wealthy, and apparently convinced that their long black cars should frequently be washed but rarely driven. My parents also called it Natural History, or The-Out-of-Doors. My father taught science in a junior high school on Nostrand Avenue, and he loved his work. It didn't seem ever to stop. Lanky, almost thin, with great swollen knuckle joints and knees, with elbows that were sharp and a chin nearly pointed, a nose that led him as he was leading us, my father with his Ed.D., was considered a master teacher by his colleagues and his principal and many of his students and himself. While my mother cooked, he lectured on asparagus. When I rode with him in our DeSoto, he talked about the flowers that grew in vacant lots and through the sidewalk cracks. And on weekends we took wearying walks with the Audubon Society or the Brooklyn Bird Club and, when I grew older, we hiked with the Appalachian Mountain Club on trails in upstate New York. I remember those trips as a blur of similarities: the same swarms of insects at the nose and eyes; the same wet heat that was pooled about us by the same clinging brush; the same unnatural, galloping pace that suggested flight from the birds and plants and marshes we had come to pursue.

I sulked, at 11 and 12 and 13, when they forced me to stroll through Prospect Park while searching, say, for the pileated woodpecker: 18 adults, in various stages (to me) of decomposition, and one slouching kid, who hunted through touch football games and horizontal lovers and the droppings of unleashed dogs, for a bird. My mother hit me after the woodpecker trip. She swung her fists against my back, chasing me up the stairs and into my room, shouting that I'd ruined Nature for her. That night we made up. She explained, my small and never-placid mother, that her difficult childhood in the slums of east Manhattan had led her to marry my father, and to read many books, and to seek the consolations of The-Out-of-Doors. In the darkness of my unkempt room, my mother sat on the chair at my desk, and I lay on my bed, and she told me how little fresh air she had breathed as a girl, and how she had longed even then for Brooklyn, and such a neighborhood as ours—"You know, the suburbs," she said—and how she felt at peace when she was with my father on what she called A Field Trip. Those words were another signal for me, like the phrase The-Out-of-Doors, to long to get as far inside and close to walls as I could.

We forgave each other, sometimes almost daily, and my father lectured, my mother wrote her books about the children of the slums—aimed at children, and written in medicinal sentences (they were good for you, but unpleasant), and published at last by a vanity press, and finally piled in our

Frederick Busch is Fairchild Professor of Literature at Colgate University and was given the 1991 PEN/Malamud award for excellence in short stories. His most recent novel is Closing Arguments *(Ticknor & Field, 1991). This story appeared in* Tikkun, *September/October 1988.*

basement, under heavy pack frames and canvas rucksacks and three sets of snowshoes that we'd never used. My father, the heir of wealthy parents, was a socialist who'd used to be a communist. The more his colleagues turned each other in to education vigilantes—those were the days of naming names to such as the House Un-American Activities Committee—the less communist, the more socialist, and the more secret about each, he became. I think he feared to lose his job because, like many compulsive teachers, he was a voice in search of ears on which his voice might fall. He forgave America, I forgave my mother, and she forgave the need to have to make me understand her. And we walked the hundreds of acres of Prospect Park, and my father pointed at leaves, and told me which were diseased and which could be brewed as tea, and which would make me itch. I played at Captain Video, my favorite television show—"Hand me the atomic hammer!" he would cry to the Video Ranger, as they waged their war against the evil Doctor Pauli—in the farthest place from Nature I could find: my mind. And they *all* made me itch.

One Sunday morning, when I should have been playing stickball with other 13-year-old boys, or—better—looking at Don Winslow of the Navy on TV, I was entering Prospect Park with the rest of the bird club, walking from the assembly point in Grand Army Plaza, under the great arched monument. My mother wore her 9x30 binoculars, and my father his, on thin leather neck-straps. I had been loaned a pair, which I kept in its case and carried, like a book, in my hand: I didn't want to be mistaken for someone who cared about birds. My expression, I am certain, was that of a recent lobotomy patient; it was crucial to me that no reflection of feeling or thought be visible on my flesh. Demonstrating nothing, and looking at nothing, I followed the Leader, as he was called, a man named Ted who pointed at birds and named them.

Ted, fat and roundfaced and sweaty, as he looked through his binoculars suggested to me the attentiveness of U-boat captains in war. "Nothing," he said, lowering his glasses. "Garbage stuff."

"Well, a towhee," my mother said, noting its existence in a little spiral book she carried.

"No," my father said. "No. Sparrow. A tree sparrow."

"You mean eastern sparrow," Ted said.

"Well, they're one and the same," my father said entering the bird in his own spiral book.

My mother said, patting my father's arm in a friendly way, while breezes blew her hair, "I think it's a towhee." She chanted it.

My father shook his head. He smiled at her, but I knew that smile. Its ferocity kept me in check on trips such as these. I stood with my hands in my pockets, and waited. He said "Sparrow."

My mother smiled and shrugged. I guess my father knew what the shrug said. He blushed, and his voice deepened. He said, "Your towhee is too small by an inch, lacks a round black spot on its breast, and is making the strange mistake of *calling* wrong. Listen."

Ted moved closer to my parents, while the others in the group moved on, making do without Leadership. Ted and my father cocked their heads; my mother didn't, but she stared at my father, as if he were another curious bird.

"There!" my father said. "You hear? *Teelwit*! he's calling. *Teelwit*! *Teelwit*! Am I right?"

My mother nodded.

He asked, "And your towhee?"

"All right," my mother said.

"Your towhee?"

"Fine," she said. "You're right."

"What does your towhee sing?"

My mother looked at him, and then she turned and walked to the rest of the group. Ted looked away from my father and followed her; the group moved along.

My father, his face still red, turned to me and looked, with no sign of seeing *me* in his eyes that I could find. He lifted his binoculars, then lowered them gently on their strap until they hung. They seemed to be heavy on his neck. He said, "As your mother well knows, your towhee calls *Chewink! Chewink!* You can't mistake *Chewink!* for *Teelwit!* Can you?"

In those days, there were waves of fear in Brooklyn neighborhoods—anyway, in ours. There had been a wave of fear about Germans possibly landing at night at Plum Beach, near Sheepshead Bay. There had been a wave of fear about the shabby men spotted chalking arrows in the street and on the curbs of certain blocks, one of them ours; the fear had been that Gypsies or tramps would be flooding the streets of Brooklyn, begging for food and clothing, hiring out for work they'd never perform. The men, we had finally learned, were marking routes for the delivery of new telephone directories. And of course there had been waves of fear over polio epidemics and the arrival on the block of Negro families. The wave of fear when I was six was squirrels. Brooklyn was filled with pigeons and squirrels, and the squirrels, with their thick gray pelts, their long graceful tail, their clever paws and large dark eyes, had been part of my childhood, like curled cats and wandering dogs. But to householders they were like the rats to which they were cousins. They scrabbled in attics and ate the insulation of electrical wires, it was said. They stored nuts uninvited. They were invaders. They were part of all the movies of my childhood. James Arness and James Whitmore in *Them*. Giant ants, atomic mutation, man's meddling with nature. It invaded a small western town. Just like the squirrels in Brooklyn. Or *The Invasion of the Body-Snatchers*. Or *Plan Nine from Outer Space*. Or how about all those Japanese things with one American actor and a huge *moth* running amok, everybody milling around, talking Japanese a mile a minute, which gets dubbed as "Remain calm. Tranquility is better than dying of fear and disorder. Get your guns." It was as if the *squirrels* were pillaging and looting. In *Brooklyn*.

At breakfast, my parents discussed the attic-noises they had heard at night. My mother's lips curled with loathing. My father frowned with distress, and his voice deepened. "We can deal with this," he said. "I know how to control a situation like this. I'll be home from school late, and then we'll see."

That day, he drove off to P.S. 240 with a certain harried look that I later came to associate with serious thought; he was showing my mother that he was working. And he did come home late that night, long after we had eaten dinner without him. He carried under each arm a long rectangular machine made of what I think was tin. There were tilted doors inside each contraption, and wires that banged as he walked from the back door through to the kitchen.

"Traps," he announced, slamming them onto the kitchen counter. "*Humane* traps. We catch 'em, but we don't kill 'em."

Above us, as my father in the attic labored to bait and arm the traps, the small gray squirrels ran beneath the eaves and in the walls. They had grown confident, and at night I heard their claws unhesitatingly march on our wood. At first I had been frightened that a squirrel would chew through my walls and enter my room and bite me. And then I remembered my barefoot days in the back yard during the summer—I was never allowed to go barefoot on the sidewalks because, as my mother summed matters up, "Where I haven't looked before you walk on it is dirty. That's the rule." The squirrels had never bothered me out back, and the house, I figured, was still more ours than theirs. So I grew too confident, myself, and I listened to them racing in the woodwork at night, and I smiled for my parents' despair. Cataclysm was really all a kid had going for him until he was taller than his parents.

When I woke, and heard my father going to the attic to check on the traps, I fancied that I had heard them going off at night, and that I'd heard the shrill cries and frantic searching of trapped gentle Disney creatures, prisoners in my house. Then my father would descend and say, "Nope. Nothing."

More and more, my mother greeted his report with a low and guttural wordless statement of woe—as if my father had struck her. He took to coming down in silence. I would listen to their soundlessness as he dressed for breakfast while she, always in her robe at breakfast-time, sat with him in their unstated failure. And at night, they would work again on the bait. They went through cheese, Ritz crackers, soda biscuits, Arnold bread, then cups of Planter's peanuts, then cups of nuts that my mother cracked in the afternoon while we waited for my father to come home. Finally, because peanut butter was my father's favorite food, I suggested that he use it in his traps. I was watching him eat a peanut butter and jelly sandwich, and I was thinking that, with his thin fingers at his mouth, he seemed to nibble like a squirrel. My mother shrugged, and my father raised his brows; that night, they baited with Skippy. Smooth. I recall thinking how gummy the mouths of the squirrels would be.

It worked. There had been no strangled squirrel-cry, no slam of gates into place, but in the morning, as my mother waited in her gathering tension, my father went up to the attic, scrambled about a bit, and then came down slowly, clanking, and bearing trapped beasts. "Yes!" he called, carrying Natural History. "Yes!"

When I came to breakfast, I expected to find them happy. But they were—if not outright huddled—concentrated at the far end of our kitchen table, as far away from the traps on the kitchen floor as they could be. Inside each trap was a squirrel, shivering. The slanted doors had dropped to perpendicular, and the squirrels were walled inside them. Now, my father told us, sounding as if he were trying to sound buoyant, but talking in a way that made me look at him as sharply as I looked at the squirrels, *now,* all that had to happen was that someone take the squirrels to the Park—far away from the house, as far as someone might feel like walking—and then set them free.

"Someone," my mother said.

"You," he told her. "I have to teach."

"I don't *know* anything about squirrels—you're the scientist."

"Yes," he said. "And I told you everything you need to know. You carry the cages by the handles on top. The squirrel can't reach you, no matter how he tries. Then you trip the door in each cage when you're a good long distance from the house. The squirrels run away. Then *you* run away."

"That part I know about," my mother said.

So I did not wait for the school bus that morning. I dressed for autumn weather in my brown corduroy jacket and peaked brown corduroy hat. My mother, who chose to wear gloves that morning, hefted each cage by its handle—her face suggested that she carried each squirrel by its tail—and we slowly made our way up Argyle, across Church Avenue into the Parade Grounds, where kids skipping school played ball, and across which we were going to walk to reach the lowest tip of Prospect Park, near the Lake.

Brooklyn in those days, and especially in parts around our neighborhood, was filled with trees and rich bushes, thick hedge, undeveloped fields that weren't even vacant lots yet—they were more like scraps of leftover forest—and everyplace in the giant trees, it seemed to me that morning in fall, squirrels swarmed, their tails floating behind them, softly-flicked pennants of my mother's dismay.

We had to pause a lot, because my mother carried the traps away from her body, and her arms grew weary. I offered to carry one and was refused in the way parents decline the assistance of children—a signal that sacrifice of some considerable quantity is going on. We made our slow unhappy progress over the Parade Grounds, walking across baseball diamonds, and having nothing to do with play; when I ran down the first-base line and waited for my mother to catch up, her face informed me that second base was not in my immediate future. We were on business, her frown made clear, and as far as I was concerned, from that moment on, the day was one more Field Trip.

We had a long distance to go, were still rather far from the Park itself, but the trees grew thicker, and the squirrels on them seemed to multiply. I noticed them, and I noticed that my mother noticed them. How could she not? They crawled, they scurried, they sat up and nibbled, they ran; sometimes, scrambling up a tree, one would stop, then turn, then hold there upside-down, like a salamander on a stone wall in *National Geographic*. The squirrels made chattering sounds, and long loud squeaks, and some of them silently ran, in bursts, along the tree limbs. I remembered my parents talking of how squirrels hunted down birds, and I did cheer them on, though silently.

My mother said, "Enough."

"Daddy said—"

"If Daddy wants to say, then he can come and carry the squirrels and tell them. Mommy says enough. Get back where it's safe. Go back."

I retreated obediently, so that no vengeance-seeking, human-devouring squirrel, mutated by nuclear testing, or inhabited by invisible beings from another world who sought our blood or souls or air supply—or which were simply part of the enormous danger my parents always discovered—could attack. My mother, in her gloves and long, tent-shaped tan tweed coat, bent above the cages. I saw the squirrels shrink from her. I watched her shrink from them.

I heard a sharp snapping sound, and then something clicked, and a squirrel was paused at the end of a trap. It moved back inside.

"Shoo," my mother said. "Go *on*." She waited, then kicked at the side of the trap. "Shoo!" The squirrel remained. My mother said, "Go on!" With the tips of her fingers, she picked up the closed end of the trap and shook it. She shook it harder, then banged on its side with a fist. "*Go!*"

The squirrel scampered down the incline of the trap and ran away, pausing to inspect; it ran again, paused, then ran farther. It went to a nearby tree and disappeared. The second squirrel went at once, and then my mother sat heavily down on an empty trap.

I watched the tree to which both squirrels had run. It was extremely broad at the base of the trunk, and its heavy thick branches were alive with squirrels. They ran, they paused, they hung upside-down and right-side up, they chattered and made their high-pitched sounds. As I watched them, they became the central object of vision; the tree they ran on was secondary to what inhabited it, and the tree receded, the squirrels advanced, and that was true of neighboring trees as well. The ground, too, seemed to ripple with their motion at the base of every tree.

My mother sat on her trap on the endless green-going-ochre of the Parade Grounds, looking up at the trees, the ceaseless motion of the squirrels as they worked and as the winter came upon them. "They'll come back," she said. "You can't keep that—that"—she swung her arm in its heavy coat, she pointed with her finger in its glove, indicating trees and what swarmed in them—"there's no *way* of keeping them under control, believe you me." She diminished, staring up at them, like the pretty girl in the horror film who at last understands what has come for her. ☐

People Want Everything

Leonard Michaels

It was a summer evening in the fifties. My friend Dmitri Harris, who studied physics at Cornell, had come to town. We arranged to meet for dinner in Greenwich Village, at the San Remo. I hardly ever ate out, but I hadn't seen Dmitri in months so this would be an occasion. I left work earlier than usual and walked uptown, from Chambers Street to Bleecker Street. Dmitri was always late, but I liked sitting in the bar, staring about at the San Remo's tile floor, brown wood booths, and ceiling fans. The mirror behind the bar reflected colorful whisky bottles and a row of windows that looked out on the traffic of MacDougal and Bleecker Streets. Separate from the bar was a small dining room. Dark, serious Italians waited table; efficient men, never obsequious. When Dmitri arrived, he said, "I'm starving," and we went directly into the dining room. He ordered antipasto, minestrone soup, some kind of veal. I ordered clams Casino, salad, and a glass of wine, which probably came to less than ten dollars, but I had to think about it. I had to think about money.

I worked after classes at NYU, as a file clerk in a collection agency. I made three dollars an hour. The office had no technology, no computers. The only machine was me. Looking through the mail, I'd store names and addresses in passive memory. Then, reading through new letters that arrived daily, I'd spot a name or street address that sounded familiar, and I'd go search, try to match the clue in a letter with a file I had seen days or weeks before.

Dmitri asked, "You still have the same job?" Then he asked what I did exactly, forgetting he'd asked the question before. "I know it's a collection agency...."

I said my job was like the children's card game where you put the deck face down, spread cards in every direction, then start turning them over, trying to remember where you last saw a jack or queen or a three so that you can pair it with the jack, queen, or three you'd just plucked out of the spread.

"Oh yeah, yeah. I remember. Sounds like fun," said Dmitri.

"It is."

It was no fun. I felt sorry for debtors who weren't confidence men or deadbeats, but just unlucky, sick, broke, ashamed, miserable, hoping to be forgotten, if not forgiven. There was no forgetting, no forgiveness. There was no hiding from us. We had connections everywhere in towns and cities around the United States, investigators who lusted to collect. We wanted our clients made whole. We wanted our thirty percent plus expenses.

Dmitri never worked. Money came to him in scholarships. But he could have put himself through college. He won regularly at poker and bridge, picking up money from fellow students, and he hustled in Manhattan pool halls and ping-pong parlors. You'd hear people say, when Dmitri shot pool, "The ball has eyes."

Leonard Michaels is the author of two story collections and a novel, The Men's Club *(Farrar, Straus & Giroux, 1981). His most recent book,* Shuffle *(Farrar, Straus & Giroux, 1990), is autobiographical. This story appeared in* Tikkun, *November/December 1990.*

He played. I worked for small pleasures and worried about the price of dinner. I boasted of him to other friends. Amazing guy. What a brain. Maybe there was faint resentment in my heart, but what the hell—Dmitri had a special chemical structure in his chromosomes. It gave him superior hand-eye coordination and let him solve problems built into the physical universe. As if from God, money came to him. He gave no thought to it that evening in the San Remo. He gorged on rum cake.

"Good?"

"Great." Munching, nodding. It was his due. He had chromosomes.

His eyes, wide apart in the flat broad bone of his upper face, carried a diffuse focus, dull, almost sleepy. As he chewed, his nostrils distended slightly, smelling the tastes. His complexion was dark and smooth, yellowish, nearly bronze. The neck of a wrestler. Thick trunk. Ape arms. His parents were first-generation Americans; his grandparents, from Odessa and Istanbul, were Russian Orthodox, except for a grandmother who was Jewish.

During dinner, Dmitri mentioned a party uptown to which he'd been invited by Nina Winslow. "Did you know we broke up?"

"You broke up?"

"Yes. Do you want to go to the party?"

"Sure. So you broke up with Nina Winslow?"

Unfortunately, he had misplaced the address. Three times he left the table to phone Nina. He stood abruptly, in the middle of a sentence, went to the phone, returned. "What were you saying? Go on. By the way, do you want to go to the party?"

Again, I said, "Sure."

He was preoccupied, but still, his concern for the party was maybe a touch rude. I could have had dinner with my mother, saved some money. Anyhow, Nina wasn't answering.

Leaving the San Remo, we walked to Washington Square Park. Street lights were on, calling the darkness. It came to them, swarming about the glow. Above the line of rooftops, you could still see blue air, but mountainous dark clouds had begun gathering. It would be a moonless night.

Dmitri talked about his psychiatrist whose name was Jerry. He'd begun seeing Jerry for help in breaking up with Nina Winslow. He was still seeing Jerry.

"I'd have picked Nina."

"Yeah, you can always get another psychiatrist." He laughed. He didn't think it was funny.

"And Nina doesn't cost as much."

"Come on, Herman, it's no joke."

I wasn't joking. I thought both a lover and a psychiatrist captured your heart and introduced you to the dark forces within.

"I did the hardest thing in the world. Can't you sympathize with your old friend, Saint Demitrious?"

He'd told me on previous visits that he couldn't let a day go without phoning Nina. He'd beg her to skip work and come up from the city. Once, he took off in a blizzard, driving from Ithaca to New York to spend a few hours with Nina. Now he was telling me different. No crazy yearning, no fucking. They were friends.

"I couldn't think, couldn't do my work. The department was going to throw me out of the lab. I was risking my life, Herman. For what? There is no future in death. You think that's a joke?"

"Nina is great. A lot of class."

Dmitri's mouth, half-open with a feeble smile, made a look of bemused surprise. His big hands lifted, pressed to his chest. "Herman, this is me."

"I know who you are. I'm sorry you broke up with Nina. I think she's great."

"I did it," he said, "after much work with Jerry."

"Work?"

"It's an expression."

Dmitri invested too much in Jerry, I supposed, but then Jerry was a doctor, he had knowledge, understanding. Nina was what she was, totally instinctive, every feeling instantly apparent. She didn't understand anything. Just walking down the street she caused trouble. People would feel a horrible rush of happiness. She had too much life. Who could live with it? Dmitri had a career. I understood completely, but I didn't sympathize. He wanted me to say I did.

People want everything.

In the park we found a bench and sat. Nearby, a woman was playing guitar and singing folk songs. A small crowd collected. She had curly brown hair and a high, sweet, quavering, plaintive voice. It seemed to say, "I am suffering."

Dmitri—preoccupied, restless, not listening to her—made me uncomfortable. He still hoped to reach Nina, get the address of the party. He had a compulsive streak, and was giving off nervous impatient signals, like a kid who needs to pee.

I ignored him for a moment, surrendering to the spell of the woman's singing. He noticed. Nudging me with his elbow, he proposed a math problem. I had no interest in math problems. He insisted: "An idiot could solve this problem. Listen.... "

I listened. He repeated himself, emphasizing crucial elements, but I couldn't understand the problem, let alone solve it. "We know different idiots," I said.

He wanted me to feel stupid. Why? I hadn't said what he wanted to hear. Is a friend required to lie about feelings? He knew I liked Nina. She made a picture of contrasts, big green eyes and sharp bones—knees, elbows. Long fine neck.

Dmitri was saying something. I heard his voice. Beyond his voice, I listened to the woman singing. She created an effect of prettiness, though her face was irregular; too interesting to be pretty. I succumbed to the pleading in her voice and gave her what she wanted. I gave feeling, I felt close to her. She suffered. She wore a lavender dress and green shoes, colors of sensibility, heartbreak, love, art. Dmitri's knee bumped mine. He leaned toward me and revealed four matchsticks lying in his palm.

"Let one match touch another. Then try to make any two of the other matches ..."

I said, "Enough. No more. I don't even know how to begin to think about these problems."

The singing ended.

Dmitri said, "Let's get out of here. I'll phone Nina again."

He said it as if conceding to me, phoning Nina for my sake. The phone booth, in a corner drugstore, had greenish sheet-metal walls with a quilted imprint. He dialed, listened, saying nothing for long minutes. Apparently, Nina still wasn't home. He smacked the receiver into the cradle. Hands in his pants pockets, he went strolling up Fourth Street toward Sheridan Square. I went after him. His shoulders were held high, packed with tension, his posture stiff. People got out of his way. The big neck and deep slope of his shoulders, bunched, explosive looking. He was walking in the middle of the sidewalk.

I was too conscious of Dmitri's moods. I felt tension in my shoulders. Neither of us spoke. We walked, the minutes passed. At last I said, "Tell me something. How come you and Nina didn't get married?"

"She didn't want to get married."

"No?"

"She wants to be out there. In the action. I told you I went to a doctor. Can you believe I did that? We evaluated my needs for a woman like Nina. Jerry said, 'I'd like to meet her.' Nina agreed to come up to Ithaca, but then, the day of the appointment, she says, 'What for? There is nothing for me to talk about.' She was there in Ithaca, five minutes from Jerry's office, and she says, 'I don't want to. I changed my mind. What's the point?' The point is that I was trying. Trying is not even in my nature. She owed me something. She says, 'What for? What for?' I said, 'OK, if you don't know what for, I don't know what for. Let's say it's over between us. OK? OK?' I kept saying OK, like I was asking her permission. I told her to pack. I was going to drive her to New York that minute. She didn't want me to. She wanted to take the bus, but I flung her suitcase and purse into the trunk of my car and locked it. We drove to New York."

Again, Dmitri and I walked in silence. We'd often walked this way, sometimes for miles. No girlfriend would have enjoyed the silence, the nothing. Dmitri was thinking this, too. He said, "Girls have no staying power. You always have to do something. Make a plan. Entertain them every minute. You know what I mean? Every damn minute." He meant Nina, I supposed. Big, wild, green eyes, wiry blond hair, narrow hips, gangly white legs. She was a very white bony person; high-strung. She talked fast, bit her nails. She was shy, self-deprecating. She had headaches. She couldn't do this, couldn't do that—a drag on Dmitri's patience—but she did well enough and people loved her. Dmitri would get phone calls at his lab from Nina. She'd say her stomach was upset or there was a funny color in her urine, like blood. He'd say, "Did you eat beets?" She'd groan: "You can't imagine how worried I've been." She worked for her father in a Wall Street brokerage, selling stocks on the telephone. High-stress male society. She thrived in it. She had a mellifluous alto voice, clear, sensible. Clients couldn't see her damaged fingernails.

From Sheridan Square we walked along Grove to Hudson Street, then back to Bleecker and down to Sixth Avenue, then turned toward the park again, passing the same store windows, the same concrete flux of sidewalk mutilated by weather and the weight of people. From below came vibrations and the subway's hollow wailing. Steam lifted through grates.

There was no moon or stars. The air was heavy, dead, fat with water. The black sky rumbled. People seemed to hurry, neurotically agitated, or else to walk with unnatural slowness. Dmitri said, his voice tensely controlled, "Any two people have only so much to say to each other. I mean this in a purely mathematical sense. The quantity of talk in any two people is finite. When they have said it all, they have said it all. There is nothing left for them but repetition. Which is worse than nothing."

Did he mean our friendship was over? No. I supposed he was making a pain referral: He couldn't cry over Nina, so he beat on me.

I said, "Call her up. Say you want her to take you back."

"That's the worst idea I ever heard in my life."

"Well, forget it."

"No."

"You want Nina to take you back, Dmitri."

He yelled, "On my terms."

We continued to walk, approaching Louie's now, a popular bar. I could see the mob inside. You walked down into Louie's, into a basement with a low ceiling. It might be good to be with other people, talk on every side. There was nowhere else to go until Seventh Avenue and the bright white diner, Mother Hubbard's. We could sit at the counter and have hot apple pie, and coffee. I'd pay. It would show affection. Straight ahead was the island on Seventh Avenue, where a kiosk stood blazing with magazines and newspapers. The night would end there for me, buying the *New York Times*, reading it on the subway going home. But not yet.

I said, "Would you like to have coffee, or maybe have a beer?" Dmitri shrugged. We were standing in front of Louie's. "Come on," I said, "Let's have a beer."

I went down into Louie's. He followed, hands still in his pants pockets, as if he meant nobody harm. It was a symbolic gesture, but why was he symbolizing? Did he mean somebody harm? He had a bad temper and was very strong. As a kid, growing up in Manhattan, Dmitri had been in street fights. A small scar, left by a bottle, marked his right temple.

There was no great danger of a fight in Louie's. The crowd was literary, like the crowd at the White Horse on Hudson Street—college students, actors, painters, editors, journalists, and people who wrote copy in advertising agencies. You'd occasionally see important writers, Norman Mailer, Mary McCarthy, Dwight MacDonald. For awhile, Dylan Thomas hung out at the White Horse. Tonight at Louie's I spotted another writer, Francis Bonbon, slender, average height, skin the color of gun metal and hard blue eyes, arrogant glowing eyes.

He was always seen with a woman, always a different one. Each of them, as it is said of lunatics—*certifiably*—beautiful. A writer, but Bonbon was more a figure of life than art. His face couldn't be reconciled with mediocrity. The glowing eyes bespoke a universe of feeling. It was rumored that he was obsessed by sex and liked women to watch him masturbate while he sat in a chair, naked but for high-heeled shoes and sunglasses. He was a Village character, mythical. I'd always been in awe of his shameless operations, his endless women.

It was hot inside, the air was thick. The low ceiling trapped cigarette smoke and odors of rancid beer, perfume, sweat. There was a sharp urinous draft when bathroom doors opened. More people arrived every minute, not discouraged by the crowd. They were anticipating the storm. I saw excitement in the faces, heat in their cheeks, eyes shining. I got the bartender's attention, bought two beers, then shoved through to Dmitri. He'd found a spot against a wall, his back to Bonbon. I slipped between him and Dmitri. Now my back was to Bonbon. I handed Dmitri his beer. He took a quick swallow. I heard Bonbon say, "I've been impotent for a long time, but I think you're the one who is going to change that for me."

Dmitri heard it, too. He grimaced. I wanted to turn and see Bonbon's woman, but restrained myself. I was glad we'd come down into Louie's.

Beyond the voices, I heard thunder building in the sky and the crack of lighting—and then—street lights went out. Louie's went black. The crowd hushed, except for some giggles. Bonbon whispered, "Gimme kiss."

It was like being in the hold of a freighter, in the tropics, at the mercy of a storm. The floor seemed to tip. Screams and crying would begin. People would pray. Bodies leaning and swaying, stood in the fearsome place, between life and death.

Lights went on.

I glanced about, looking for reactions. Bonbon's woman smiled at me, a happy childlike smile. Me?

Even after she registered I felt estranged, seeing her through glass. Nina was the woman with Bonbon.

Not at all a certifiable beauty. How could Bonbon have known she was beautiful? Somebody must have told him. I had these thoughts, then a fiery moral vision: Women needed protection in this bad world—*from themselves*. The Arabs were right. Wrong. I knew only one thing: Nina Winslow, in the public arena, stood with Francis Bonbon. Everybody in the world, man or woman, needs protection from the darkness within. But still, Nina had gone too far, visiting shame on herself and all women, not to mention Dmitri and me. How else could I feel? I was no cynic. There was dreadful pressure in my chest. I really cared. Such feeling must exist or nothing will. Her smile collapsed. She saw what appeared in my face. Doubtless, she'd seen it in other men, too. The tumult, the confusion of jealous blood. Then she saw Dmitri looming behind me, shoving me out of the way, and Nina's big green eyes were shot with distress. I touched the rage in Dmitri's body as I grabbed his arm. "Don't," I said. "Don't say anything. Don't do anything. Come, we're going." I couldn't hold him.

Bonbon, seeing Nina's expression, turned from her, as if to confront Dmitri, but with no sense of what was happening until he saw the huge face of hate and rage falling upon him. Dmitri's hands went to Bonbon's head, seizing it by an ear, and the other hand, still holding the neck of the beer bottle, smeared it against Bonbon's skull as Bonbon's face snapped forward toward Dmitri's. A space opened in the crowd. Grinding his mouth on Bonbon's, as Bonbon flailed in wide arcs at Dmitri's ribs and head, Dmitri kissed him. He kissed Francis Bonbon. They sank slowly toward the floor, Dmitri bending over Bonbon, clutching his head, mouth to mouth.

The crowd wanted to watch, but desire invoked its antithesis when Nina shrieked, "Dmitri, you're disgusting." A few men joined me, tearing at Dmitri, dragging at his shirt and hair. Dmitri let Bonbon go. The mythic head bumped wood. I kneeled beside him, saying, "I'm sorry, I'm sorry. Nothing personal. You'll be all right, Mr. Bonbon," and then I pushed Dmitri toward the street. He didn't resist. Nina came after us, purse and shoes in her hand.

Rain slammed the sidewalk, dazzling blinding rain. I moved Dmitri around the corner, holding an arm. Nina took the other. Dmitri, dopey, clung to his beer bottle. We moved him up some steps into a doorway. Nina smacked the beer bottle. It flashed away into the street and smashed. Dmitri fell back against the door and hung, his face turning as Nina hit at him with her purse, feeble blows, more like pushes. She was crying. He lifted his hands, but didn't defend himself or try to touch her. He was waiting till she finished. I started to intercede; thought better of it. That's how I left them.

At the kiosk, I bought the *New York Times*, and shoved it under my shirt. I hunched over, protecting it from the rain as I ran toward the subway. □

The Fire Raiser

Ivan Klima; translated by Ewald Osers

T he small town was not situated by the sea, but if you climbed the mountain whose slopes began to rise steeply immediately beyond the last house, you could see the sea in the distance. Although accommodation here was only half the price of the seaside resorts, tourists hardly ever visited the place, despite the fact that it was a pretty little town, clean, and with honeyed perfumes wafting up from the gardens. As I walked up one of the steep streets lined with detached houses, a street leading toward the vineyards, I noticed that several of the trees had charred branches.

In the evening I asked my host about this strange phenomenon. He was an elderly man, and although he ran a business he was fond of talking to me about music, literature, and human passions. Like so many people in these parts he was an excellent raconteur, punctuating his speech with the expressive gestures that go with a southern temperament.

He'd had a lifelong friend in the little town, they'd both gone to the local secondary school, but while he himself had not continued his education, his friend had qualified as a pharmacist. As youngsters they had danced in the same ensemble, later they had both sung in the church choir, and eventually they had both got married the same year. Whereas my host had traveled a good deal and had often been away from home for months on end, the pharmacist had remained here; he'd loved the surroundings. He'd soon realized the danger threatening it from the growth of industry and of tourism. So he'd founded a local branch of an organization for the protection of nature, addressed countless meetings, and fought a long and ultimately victorious battle against the construction of a plastics factory in the neighborhood. He soon became one of the best-known and most popular men in the little town. He was not yet forty-five, but he was regarded as the most suitable candidate for the post of mayor. At that point, however, the will of God, or whatever it is that guides our destinies, intervened. First his son died—shot dead accidentally during an army exercise. Soon afterward his wife developed a malignant brain tumor, and although she received all possible treatment she died within a few months. Mourning was not yet over when his daughter's husband, an engineer in an agricultural machinery factory, suffered a fatal accident at work.

Within three years my host's friend, who had lived happily surrounded by his family, found himself as lonely as Job. His daughter and little granddaughter were all that was left to him.

The three of them moved in together for mutual comfort. But his friend withdrew into himself, as if he had lost all interest in what was happening around him. His name and appearance faded from public consciousness. Even at the pharmacy he remained hidden in the prescription cabinet and never showed himself at the counter. He was hardly ever seen about, only now and again would he walk with his little granddaughter. He'd walk up the steep street with her, the street where they

Ivan Klima edited the journal of the Czech Writer's Union during Prague Spring and worked at a variety of jobs (including streetsweeper) between 1969 and 1989. His most recent novels Love and Garbage *and* Judge on Trial *were published in translation by Harper and Row in 1991. It appeared in* Tikkun, *March/April 1991.*

lived, all the way to the vineyards. And they'd return the same way.

The little girl was four when death struck for the last time. It was shortly after Christmas and there had been a rare fall of snow. To please his granddaughter the old man took her out for a walk.

The road climbing up to the vineyards was normally deserted; at that time of year, especially, there wouldn't be anyone about who didn't live there. And yet the fatal car appeared. Maybe the child had taken a sudden step and this had alarmed the driver, but nobody will ever discover why the car went suddenly out of control at that point—maybe some higher authority had decided that the final act of an incomprehensible tragedy should take place there.

The car only struck the child, and then crashed into the stone pillar of a fence. Not many people collected—the street was too empty. The ambulance arrived in no time: it took the injured driver and the child away. But the child was already dead. Oddly enough, no one noticed that the pharmacist had disappeared. No one saw him during the rest of the day, or else whoever saw him remained anonymous. Maybe the unhappy man had wandered blindly about the snow-covered hillside above the vineyards or along one of the paths through the fields that led toward the sea. At some time during the night he must have returned to the town and entered his pharmacy. No one realized how much pure petrol was stocked there: he alone looked after the store and petrol was rarely used. But he took all of it. In the lower part of his street ten cars were parked. He poured petrol over them, one after another. It was a cold windy night and no one observed his actions. What he did could not have taken more than a few minutes.

The cars burst into flame almost instantly. As their tanks exploded the fire flared and spread; its glow was so bright that it was virtually like daylight in the adjacent streets. Apart from the cars, however, the fire almost miraculously caused no damage and injured no one—the arsonist alone died in the flames. Nobody will ever find out if he was too slow getting away or whether he was overcome by despair.

My host added that his friend had been a peaceable man and had obviously acted from shock. His rebellion was pointless, it could not solve anything. The insurance companies paid up and the owners bought themselves new cars. It is unlikely that they, in particular, would run down a child, but others will undoubtedly do so: statistics show that hundreds of children are killed under the wheels of cars every year. And that's not counting those who are fatally affected by their exhaust fumes. But can any fire remove all the cars in the world? There is no force that can deflect man from the road he chooses. Where to? Most probably to hell, my raconteur laughed, to everlasting perdition.

At night, as I was falling asleep with the honeyed perfumes of the gardens and the restful chirping of the cicadas washing over me, that fiery scene appeared before my eyes. For a moment I felt another man's crushing depression. There are desperate or insane actions whose fire illumines the hopelessness, pettiness, or dubiousness of our behavior. Anyone fixing his eyes on them can see what he would not see otherwise—but I don't believe that anyone does this anymore.

In the morning it occurred to me to ask what had become of the driver who'd caused the child's death. Strange that I should have asked, as though I had guessed that the story was not concluded with that horrendous event.

The driver had not been a local. He was a young man and he was devastated by what he had done. He'd been sentenced to prison for some time. When he was released he began to turn up in the little town, or more accurately at the pharmacist's house. Perhaps he felt a need to offer some comfort to its last inhabitant.

It was even being said that there was something between the two of them, and that was why the young man had turned up in the town with his car in the first place. People just couldn't understand how a woman could become involved with a man who'd killed her child and indirectly caused the death of her father. There were some women who'd spit whenever they saw her in the street. As if anyone was entitled to judge God's dispositions. Suppose the child's tragic death was the climax and end of some curse or some trial? And that he who had been its unwitting messenger and instrument was also to announce the advent of a time of conciliation?

In the end the two decided to vanish. One morning he came for her with a horse and cart. They loaded up only a few things and left—no one knew where.

My host saw them with his own eyes as they set out on their way with their horse and cart. One of the horses was totally black, while the other was white, without a single dark patch. It was impossible, he said, not to be reminded of hell and heaven and of their denizens. □

Love Poem

Alan Shapiro

Our first warm morning,
and all over the yard
small insects had hatched
invisibly and were swarming
up from the grass, innumerable,
in a blurred light of wings,
dizzying helix's of rising
through leaf-shadow and sun,
and all so slowly, each one
hovering now or dipping
down before it fanned out
higher and wider, as if
to dawdle in that first
moment of their being
suddenly in air, half-
resisting their own urge
upward so as to feel
the pull of it more keenly.

Imagine at the appointed hour
what it would be like:
earth's old bonds broken,
all the nations of all time
whirling up in a dense haze,
and you and I lost
to each other in that
joyously forgetful going;
our flesh, the juryrigged
and sweat-stained ark
we danced before, danced
hard as we could, in sun
and leaf-shadow, scoured
to mere radiance! Odd,
and not comforting at all,
to think that even to wonder
where you were in that dizzying
multitude, to want to
loiter there a little while
among the shadows would be
too great a gravity
ever to rise against.

Now that you've seen what the first five years looked like ... don't miss the next five!

Subscribe now...

and you can be reading the cutting edge articles, debates, essays, editorials, poetry, and fiction from some of America's most exciting writers and thinkers.

Individuals:

One year:	$31
Three Years:	$88
Five Years:	$140

Institutions & Libraries:

One Year:	$50
Three Years:	$130
Five Years:	$200

Mail check or credit card information (mastercard/visa) to:

TIKKUN 5100 Leona St., Oakland, CA 94619

Foreign Subscribers: Payment must be made in U.S. funds drawn from a U.S. bank or with an international money order in U.S. funds. Additional postage: $12/year for Canada and Mexico, $16 for all other countries. Israeli subscribers: Subscribe in shekelim! Send 75 shekel to TIKKUN, P.O. box 10528 Jerusalem 91103.